Clinical Assessment of Malingering and Deception

Second Edition

© 1997 The Guilford Press
A Division of Guilford Publications, Inc.
72 Spring Street, New York, NY 10012

Printed in the United States of America

This book is printed on acid-free paper.

Last digit is print number: 9   8   7   6   5   4   3

Library of Congress Cataloging-in-Publication Data

Clinical assessment of malingering and deception / edited by
  Richard Rogers.—2nd ed.
     p. cm.
  Includes bibliographical references and index.
  ISBN 1–57230–173–2 (hard)
  1. Malingering—Diagnosis.   2. Deception.   I. Rogers,
Richard, 1950– .
  [DNLM: 1. Malingering—diagnosis. 2. Mental disorders
—diagnosis. W783 C641 1997]
RA1146.C57 1997
616.85'2—dc20
DNLM/DLC
for Library of Congress   96–43033
                                    CIP

Contributors

R. Michael Bagby, Ph.D., is an Associate Professor of Psychology at the University of Toronto. In addition, he is a Senior Research Psychologist and Head of the Section on Personality and Psychopathology at the Clarke Institute of Psychiatry. Dr. Bagby has published numerous articles on dissimulation and coauthored, with Dr. Rogers, the Structured Interview of Reported Symptoms.

Laurence M. Binder, Ph.D., ABPP, is a Diplomate in Clinical Neuropsychology. He is Associate Professor of Behavioral Neurosciences at Oregon Health Sciences University and Director of Postdoctoral Training in Clinical Neuropsychology at the Portland Veterans Administration Medical Center. He also maintains an independent practice.

Jason Brandt, Ph.D., is Professor of Psychiatry and Behavioral Sciences and Director of Medical Psychology at the Johns Hopkins University School of Medicine. Dr. Brandt is also Director of the Cortical Function Laboratory at the Johns Hopkins Hospital.

Steven P. Cercy, Ph.D., obtained his Ph.D. from Southern Illinois University and completed a fellowship in clinical neuropsychology at Beth Israel Medical Center in New York. Dr. Cercy is currently the John P. Boohger Fellow in Memory Disorders in the Department of Psychiatry and Behavioral Sciences at the Johns Hopkins University School of Medicine.

Charles R. Clark, Ph.D., ABPP, obtained his doctorate in clinical psychology from Long Island University and is a diplomate in Forensic Psychology of the American Board of Forensic Psychology. He served as Director of Psychology at the Center for

Forensic Psychiatry in Ann Arbor, Michigan, and is the former Chair of the American Psychological Association Ethics Committee. Dr. Clark is currently in forensic private practice in Ann Arbor.

Alan J. Cunnien, M.D., is a Consultant in Psychiatry at the Mayo Clinic Scottsdale, Scottsdale, Arizona, and Assistant Professor of Psychiatry at the Mayo Medical Center in Rochester, Minnesota. His clinical and theoretical interests revolve around the integration of complex diagnostic, therapeutic, and medicolegal issues into a multispeciality medical and surgical practice.

Roger L. Greene, Ph.D., is Professor of Psychology and Director of Clinical Training at Pacific Graduate School of Psychology in Palo Alto, California. Dr. Greene is one of the foremost authorities on the MMPI-2; the assessment of response styles is an important emphasis of his research.

William G. Iacono, Ph.D., is Professor of Psychology and Neuroscience and Director of the Clinical Psychology Training Program, University of Minnesota. A President of the Society of Psychophysiological Research, he has been a consultant to government agencies on the detection of deception and has carried out both laboratory and field research on polygraphic interrogation. His research interests include psychophysiological and behavioral genetic aspects that give rise to the development of psychopathology.

Kimberly S. Kelly, Ph.D., is an Assistant Professor of Psychology at the University of North Texas. In addition, she is the Coordinator of the Psychoneuroimmunology Research Laboratory where she studies immunological responses of clinical populations.

Robert D. Miller, M.D., Ph.D., is Professor of Psychiatry and Director of the Program for Forensic Psychiatry at the University of Colorado Health Sciences Center. He is also Lecturer in Law at the University of Denver and Director of Research and Education at the Institute for Forensic Psychiatry at the Colorado Mental Health Institute at Pueblo. He has been awarded the Manfred S. Guttmacher Award from the American Psychiatric Association for his outstanding contributions to forensic psychiatry.

Lynn Oldershaw, Ph.D., is an Assistant Professor of Psychiatry at the University of Toronto. In addition, she is a practicing clinical psychologist in the Division of Child and Family Studies, Clarke Institute of Psychiatry. Dr. Oldershaw is also Research Head of the Children at Risk Clinic at the Clarke Institute.

Loren Pankratz, Ph.D., is now an independent consultation psychologist after 25 years at the Portland Veterans Administration Medical Center. He was also Professor of Psychiatry and Medical Psychology at Oregon Health Sciences University. He has a long-standing clinical and research interest in patients who deceive.

Christopher J. Patrick, Ph.D., is an Associate Professor of Psychology at Florida State University in Tallahassee. Dr. Patrick has conducted empirical research on lie detection, focusing on control question test validity, individual differences, and drug effects. His current research, funded by the National Institute of Mental Health, addresses emotion and criminality.

Phillip J. Resnick, M.D., is Professor of Psychiatry and Director of the Division of Forensic Psychiatry at Case Western University School of Medicine. He is Director of the Court Psychiatric Clinic for Cleveland. He has written extensively on malingering and taught workshops on malingering internationally.

Richard Rogers, Ph.D., ABPP, is Professor of Psychology at the University of North Texas. His previous appointments include key positions at the Isaac Ray Center, Rush Medical College; and the Division of Forensic Psychiatry, University of Toronto. His national awards include Distinguished Contributions to Forensic Psychology Award, the Manfred S. Guttmacher Award, and the Amicus Award.

Randall T. Salekin, M.S., researched jury decision making under the direction of James R. P. Ogloff, Ph.D., J.D., at Simon Fraser University. He is currently an advanced doctoral student at the University of North Texas under the direction of Richard Rogers, Ph.D., ABPP. His present research interests include malingering and related response styles.

David J. Schretlen, Ph.D., is Associate Professor in the Department of Psychiatry and Behavioral Sciences at the Johns Hopkins University School of Medicine. Dr. Schretlen also serves as Associate Director for Clinical Services in the Division of Medical Psychology. His research interests include the application of psychometric measures to detect neuropsychiatric symptom distortion.

Kenneth W. Sewell, Ph.D., is Associate Professor of Psychology and Director of Clinical Training at the University of North Texas. Among his research interests is the systematic assessment of response styles among convicted sex offenders.

Glenn P. Smith, Ph.D., is the coordinator of the Posttraumatic Stress Disorder (PTSD) Clinical Team at the James A. Haley Veterans Administration Hospital, Tampa, Florida. His clinical interests include malingering, with a particular emphasis on detection strategies through self-report. Dr. Smith's current research involves the refinement of screening instruments for malingering within the PTSD population.

Lawrence J. Stava, Ph.D., is a unit chief on the Forensic Rehabilitation Services at the Forensic Center, Mendota Mental Health Institute, Madison, Wisconsin. He has used hypnosis extensively in his clinical practice and has taught courses on hypnosis and related methods. Dr. Stava is a member of the Society for Clinical and Experimental Hypnosis.

Robert M. Wettstein, M.D., is an Assistant Professor of Psychiatry and Codirector of the Law and Psychiatry Program at the University of Pittsburgh School of Medicine. He has written and taught extensively in clinical legal matters in mental health care. Dr. Wettstein is editor of *Behavioral Sciences and the Law* and coauthor of *Legal Issues in Mental Health Care*.

Preface

The first edition of *Clinical Assessment of Malingering and Deception* achieved its overriding goal of integrating clinical practice and applied research in its critical examination of malingering and other forms of dissimulation. For the practitioner, the first edition provided a clear description of syndromes associated with dissimulation and a delineation of clinical methods. In addition, the book furnished *threshold models* (i.e., when should the issue be considered?) and *clinical models* (i.e., what are the criteria for reaching a definite conclusion?). For the applied researcher, the first edition reviewed and critiqued available research designs and suggested methodological improvements. The first edition was largely successful at accomplishing its goals. It received the Manfred S. Guttmacher Award from the American Psychiatric Association as an outstanding contribution to forensic psychiatry.

The last 9 years have chronicled an increased growth in the malingering and deception literature with several hundred new research articles. Completely new measures of dissimulation have emerged. Psychological tests have been revised with renewed attention to malingering, defensiveness, and irrelevant responding. Explanatory models of dissimulation have been introduced. Research methods have been refined. Meta-analytic studies have combined data from individual studies. In summary, the need for a second edition of *Clinical Assessment of Malingering and Deception* became very apparent.

Not all second editions are created equal. Our goal was a complete revision of the original edition. With the majority of chapters, the substantive advances are clearly evident. For multiscale inventories, the publication of new measures (e.g., Personality Assessment Inventory [PAI] and Minnesota Multiphasic Personality Inventory—A [MMPI-A]) as well as the revisions of established tests (e.g., MMPI-2 and the Millon

Clincal Multiaxial Inventory—III [MCMI-III]) resulted in major modifications. Heightened clinical interest in syndromes (e.g., false memories and Munchausen by proxy) and methods (e.g., integrity tests and specialized self-report measures) are also reflected in the second edition. In all chapters, systematic attention was paid to the sharpening of conceptual models and lucid description of current findings. No pages and very few paragraphs remain unchanged. For a second edition to be worth its publication, I believe that it must involve a complete reworking of the book. Given the remarkable changes within the field during the last 9 years, we believe that the second edition of *Clinical Assessment of Malingering and Deception* will offer as significant a contribution as the first edition.

Contents

1 Introduction   1
RICHARD ROGERS

Part I
DIAGNOSTIC ISSUES

2 Psychiatric and Medical Syndromes Associated with Deception   23
ALAN J. CUNNIEN

3 Malingered Psychosis   47
PHILLIP J. RESNICK

4 Sociopathy, Malingering, and Defensiveness   68
CHARLES R. CLARK

5 Simulated Amnesia and the Pseudo–Memory Phenomena   85
STEVEN P. CERCY, DAVID J. SCHRETLEN, AND JASON BRANDT

6 Denial and Misreporting of Substance Abuse   108
RICHARD ROGERS AND KIMBERLY S. KELLY

7 Malingering of Posttraumatic Disorders   130
PHILLIP J. RESNICK

8 Children and Deception   153
LYNN OLDERSHAW AND R. MICHAEL BAGBY

Part II
PSYCHOMETRIC ASSESSMENT

9 *Assessment of Malingering and Defensiveness*   169
   by Multiscale Inventories
   ROGER L. GREENE

10 *Dissimulation on the Rorschach and Other Projective Measures*   208
   DAVID J. SCHRETLEN

11 *Malingering on Intellectual and Neuropsychological Measures*   223
   LOREN PANKRATZ AND LAURENCE M. BINDER

Part III
SPECIALIZED METHODS

12 *Drug-Assisted Interviews to Detect Malingering and Deception*   239
   RICHARD ROGERS AND ROBERT M. WETTSTEIN

13 *Polygraphy and Integrity Testing*   252
   WILLIAM G. IACONO AND CHRISTOPHER J. PATRICK

14 *Hypnosis and Dissimulation*   282
   ROBERT D. MILLER AND LAWRENCE J. STAVA

15 *Structured Interviews and Dissimulation*   301
   RICHARD ROGERS

16 *Understanding and Detecting Dissimulation in Sex Offenders*   328
   KENNETH W. SEWELL AND RANDALL T. SALEKIN

17 *Assessment of Malingering with Self-Report Measures*   351
   GLENN P. SMITH

Part IV
SUMMARY

18 *Current Status of Clinical Methods*   373
   RICHARD ROGERS

19 *Researching Dissimulation*   398
   RICHARD ROGERS

References   427

Author Index   493

Subject Index   519

Clinical Assessment of Malingering and Deception

Second Edition

1

Introduction

RICHARD ROGERS, PH.D.

Diagnoses of mental disorders and the evaluation of psychopathology rely heavily on the honesty, accuracy, and completeness of patients' self-reporting. Most symptoms of disorders are not directly observable by others. Therefore, each patient's presentation becomes a critical component of the clinical assessment. Distortions, both intentional and unintentional, complicate greatly the assessment process. This book is devoted to a systematic examination of dissimulation, integrating a distillation of research findings with a discussion of their clinical applications.

Chapter 1 is organized into four major sections: (1) assumptions of honesty and self-disclosure, (2) explanatory models of malingering and defensiveness, (3) basic tools and terminology of dissimulation, and (4) an overview of the book's organization. I examine how changes in the delivery of mental health services may affect patients' honesty and propensity to dissimulate. I consider the often-neglected issue of motivation (e.g., why do malingerers malinger?) and evaluate different explanatory models. I provide a framework for understanding the basic concepts and terms that are necessary for a thorough understanding of malingering and deception. I complete the chapter with an overview of the book's structure and goals.

ASSUMPTIONS OF HONESTY AND SELF-DISCLOSURE

A fundamental but unspoken premise of clinical practice is heartfelt cooperation and good-faith participation by patients in their assessment and treatment. Psychologists and psychiatrists typically assume that shared goals will optimize patients' honesty and self-disclosure. By training, practitioners are deeply imbued in their enduring image as helping professionals. Practitioners may have difficulty accepting that some patients may see them as disinterested bureaucrats, financially motivated businesspeople, agents of social control, or outright adversaries.

tion is needed to assess the truthfulness and completeness of patients' presenting complaints. However, as documented by the recent furor over repressed memories of childhood abuse (e.g., Loftus, 1993b; Wakefield & Underwager, 1992; Williams, 1994), this perspective is shortsighted. The veridicality of content should not be confused with the patient's sincerity and genuine expression of emotions. Content is an important facet of treatment that cannot be summarily dismissed. Therefore, I believe that it is inadvisable for practitioners to ignore issues of dissimulation or deliberate distortion in patients' self-reports during psychotherapy.

A third assumption is that malingering and other forms of dissimulation occur so infrequently that their routine investigation is unwarranted. On this issue, Rogers (1994) observed that infrequency should not be equated with inconsequentiality.[1] However, available data strongly question the rarity of dissimulation among persons receiving mental health services. For example, Rogers, Sewell, and Goldstein (1994) in a survey of 320 forensic psychologists generated estimates of malingering of 15.7% for forensic and 7.4% for nonforensic settings. While the latter estimate (7.4%) might be inflated by forensic experts' involvement in quasi-judicial and administrative proceedings, these percentages are considerable. A subsequent survey of 221 forensic experts (Rogers, Salekin, Sewell, & Goldstein, 1996) yielded comparable results (17.4% and 7.8%, respectively). Rogers, Harrell, and Liff (1993) reviewed the available literature with respect to feigned neuropsychological impairment; very preliminary estimates suggested that as many as half of personal injury evaluatees may be feigning all or part of their cognitive deficits. With respect to insanity evaluations, Rogers (1986) found that 20.8% of defendants engaged in suspected or definite malingering with an additional 5.2% having unintentional distortions in their self-report. Although prevalence data are unavailable, Lorei's (1970) extensive survey of 12,054 staff members from 12 Veterans Administration hospitals underscored the importance of malingering (i.e., second only to dangerousness) in determining a patient's level of adjustment and readiness to be discharged.

Estimates of other response styles are less than adequate. Although the Minnesota Multiphasic Personality Inventory (MMPI) appears to be the most promising measure of general defensiveness, Baer, Wetter, and Berry (1992) reported pervasive problems in establishing consistent cutting scores to determine defensiveness, thus militating against accurate estimates. Extrapolating from MMPI data provided by Greene (1988a, p. 152), some evidence of defensiveness is found in 6–7% of normal individuals. Research by Sabourin and her colleagues (Sabourin, Bourgeois, Gendreau, & Morval, 1989; Sabourin, Lafferriere, et al., 1989) suggests that social desirability is likely to be prevalent in adult psychotherapy patients, seen at a university-based clinic. Moreover, social desirability may have affected reports of treatment outcome and consumer satisfaction, although the data are conflicting (see Gaston & Sabourin, 1992; Hays & Ware, 1986). Inpatients who do not acknowledge their mental disorders and associated impairment appear to underreport their symptomatology in a combination of defensiveness and social desirability (Carsky, Selzer, Terkelson, & Hurt, 1992).

For evidence of inconsistent responding, Greene suggested that 3–5% of normal individuals and 15% of persons with mental disorders manifest some inconsistencies in item endorsements. In a series of four experiments, Berry et al. (1992) found that 3–7% of college and community participants openly acknowledged random responding to many or all MMPI-2 items. In contrast, police recruits with a strong motivation to be hired permanently did not admit to a predominant pattern of random responding.[2]

Several conclusions can be drawn from these prevalence data. First and foremost, prevalence rates for response styles remain virtually uninvestigated. Second, the available data suggest that estimates are highly dependent on settings and referral questions. Third, in spite of variability across settings, the combined prevalence of inconsistent, malingered, and defensive response styles is much too large to ignore, even under the best circumstances.

Practitioners, although possibly swayed by the previous argument, may not change either their assumptions or assessment methods in order to investigate response styles systematically. When conducting workshops, I continue to be dismayed at the number of clinicians that, despite decades of practice, have never observed a single case of dissimulation. The problem is circular. If we never investigate dissimulation, then we may never find it. I believe that our working assumption in clinical practice should be that an appreciable minority of evaluatees engage, at some time, in a dissimulative response style. If we accept this working assumption, then we also accept the responsibility to screen all referrals and actively consider the possibility of malingering and other forms of deception.

What are the day-to-day implications of this discussion for many practitioners, who spend the majority of their professional time in providing treatment? In broad terms, I am suggesting that practitioners can evaluate to what extent treatment is serving the patient's own wants and needs versus others' objectives. Table 1.2 summarizes in the form of four questions the salient issues that can affect honesty and openness in treatment. For purposes of clarity, responses to these salient questions are organized into three categories: "1," autonomous involvement, "2," partially autonomous involvement, and "3," heteronomous involvement. Persons who are self-motivated to seek treatment, self-directed in their treatment goals, self-selecting their mental health professionals, and self-determining access to confidential information can exercise choice and autonomy in meeting their needs and wants. Obversely, when the therapeutic process is largely instigated and controlled by others, dissimulation is one understandable response to perceived coercion.

EXPLANATORY MODELS OF MALINGERING AND DEFENSIVENESS

Rogers (1990a, 1990b; Ustad & Rogers, 1996) outlined the primary motivations implicit in the three explanatory models of malingering; dissimulation occurs because malingerers are (1) mentally disordered (pathogenic), (2) bad (criminological), and (3) attempting to meet their objectives in adversarial circumstances (adaptational). Two prototypical analyses of attributes associated with each model provided empirical support for this conceptualization (Rogers, Duncan, Lynett, & Sewell, 1994; Rogers,

---

TABLE 1.2. Treatment Considerations Regarding the Honesty and Openness of Patients

A. What stimulated the patient to seek treatment at this point?
   1. *Self-initiated*: No one knew or influenced the patient's decision.
   2. *Other-influenced*: The patient was pressured by others to seek treatment.
   3. *Other-initiated*: Others made the decision for the patient to seek treatment.
B. What are the patient's goals?
   1. *Self-directed*: The patient is not answerable to others.
   2. *Congruent*: The patient's goals are compatible with others, including third-party reimbursers.
   3. *Incongruent*: The patient's goals are incompatible with significant others or third-party reimbursers.
C. Who selected the mental health professional?
   1. *Self-selected*: The patient chose.
   2. *Limited self-selection*: The patient chose from a limited pool that was provided by the third-party reimburser.
   3. *Other-selected*: Either a significant other, primary physician, or third-party reimburser chose.
D. Who knows about treatment?
   1. *Self*: No one else has access to patient information.
   2. *Self and reimburser*: Beyond the patient, only the reimburser and their health care professionals have access.
   3. *Others*: Significant others or relevant agencies (e.g., employers and courts) have access.

Note. Knowledge of treatment can be either formal (i.e., written consent) or informal (e.g., pressure from family members or employer access to insurance records).

Salekin, Sewell, & Goldstein, 1996). When items associated with these models were rated for their prototypicality by 320 experts, three strong factors emerged that closely corresponded with the three explanatory models. I briefly summarize the three models and discuss their implications for other response styles.

Pathogenic Model

The pathogenic model postulates that the underlying force behind malingering is a mental disorder. In attempts to gain control over emerging symptoms, the patient creates the symptoms and portrays them as genuine. With the onset of the mental disorder, the patients begins to lose control over the simulated symptoms. The predicted outcome is a worsening of the mental disorder and appearance of true symptoms. The pathogenic model has lost favor, because its predictions have not been borne out and because perceptions of malingering have changed in the last several decades.

The controversy over "accident neurosis" (Miller, 1961) and "compensation neurosis" (Mendelson, 1981, 1985) buttressed anecdotal observations that some persons feigning personal injuries did not continue to deteriorate. Indeed, publicity surrounding persons who appeared to be "cured" following large financial settlements led to such pejorative terms as "compensationitis" and "greenback neurosis." Despite countervailing evidence (see Chapter 7), some clinicians continue to be influenced by Miller's conceptualization and assume that cases without physical injuries are likely to be motivated by secondary gain.

Perceptions of malingering have also evolved. When state hospitals functioned as asylums filled with floridly psychotic persons that were subjected to abysmal living conditions, the assumption, "You would have to be crazy to want to be here," was compelling. This early assumption no longer holds sway with the modernization of inpatient treatment, establishment of adequate living conditions, and concomitant depletion of community resources. A second shift in perception involved increased concerns that criminal defendants might elude justice through feigning. This emphasis of malingering as a malevolent maneuver utilized by antisocial persons foreshadowed the development of the criminological model.

Criminological Model

Promulgation of the criminological model began more than a decade ago with the publication of the third edition of the *Diagnostic and Statistical Manual of Mental Disorders* (DSM-III; American Psychiatric Association, 1980) and continues to be enunciated as part of the diagnostic nomenclature (American Psychiatric Association, 1987; 1994a). Stated obliquely in terms of a "high index of suspicion" (American Psychiatric Association, 1987, p. 360) and "strongly suspected" (American Psychiatric Association, 1994a, p. 683), DSM models presuppose that malingering is likely to occur with (1) persons diagnosed with antisocial personality disorder (APD), (2) evaluations conducted for forensic purposes, (3) persons uncooperative with evaluation and treatment, and (4) persons whose claims are discrepant with objective findings.

The criminological model has faltered on conceptual and empirical grounds. As observed by Rogers (1990b), the only coherent theme for this model is badness, namely, a bad person (APD), in bad circumstances (legal difficulties), who is performing badly (uncooperative). As noted by Rogers (1992), the association between APD and malingering is likely to be illusory.[3] Although persons evaluated in forensic settings are rarely voluntary and may see their own agenda at cross-purposes with the goals of the assessment, we cannot assume that they are likely to malinger. Indeed, many persons faced with the adversarial nature of forensic evaluations may engage in a range of response styles. For example, a sex offender is unlikely to exaggerate paraphiliac behavior. On the contrary, denial and defensiveness are the likely response styles (Rogers & Dickey, 1991).

The selection of "uncooperativeness" as a criterion for malingering is counterintuitive. This criterion better fits involuntary patients who resist efforts at evaluation and intervention. An associated feature of many Axis I disorders is a lack of willing participation in either the assessment or the treatment. Many persons with psychotic disorders are only marginally cooperative with medication. Persons with eating disorders and substance abuse disorders are frequently uncooperative with ongoing assessments of target behaviors. Moreover, malingerers often appear highly cooperative. Many seek out treatment and are willing to discuss and even volunteer symptoms. Although such malingerers are not cooperative in absolute terms (i.e., their participation does not facilitate a true and comprehensive evaluation), they are likely to be cooperative in normative terms (i.e., their participation appears similar to bona fide patients). Therefore, uncooperativeness fails as a criterion, both in identifying malingerers and excluding bona fide patients.

The final criterion, claims discrepant with objective findings, is a notable example of a logical fallacy. It falsely assumes the existence of "objective" data against which inconsistencies can be measured. As observed by Rogers (1990b), if objective findings existed, then malingering would be a nonissue. Although we have objective measures for some medical conditions (e.g., tuberculosis), we do not have analogous measures of mental disorders. Without objective findings, this criterion is untenable. Furthermore, this criterion is likely to misclassify many persons with schizophrenic disorders who are poor historians and misremember crucial personal events (Skodol, 1989). Therefore, if "inconsistencies in self-reporting" were to be substituted for "discrepancies with objective findings," mental health professionals would run a considerable risk of misclassifying genuine patients as malingerers.

Adaptational Model

Rogers (1990a, 1990b) proposed the adaptational model to explain how some persons respond to adversarial circumstances in which they have a substantial personal investment. According to the adaptational model, would-be malingerers engage in a cost–benefit analysis when confronted with an assessment they perceive as indifferent, if not inimical, to their needs. Malingering is more likely to occur when (1) the context of the evaluation is perceived as adversarial, (2) the personal stakes are very high, and (3) no other alternatives appear to be viable. In addition, malingerers' cost–benefit analysis is likely influenced by their estimation of their abilities to succeed, although the available data suggest that simulators grossly overestimate their ability to feign without detection (Kropp, 1992; Linblad, 1994).

Descriptive data are generally supportive of the adaptational model, with higher prevalence rates reported in adversarial settings (e.g., forensic vs. nonforensic) or when the personal stakes are particularly high (e.g., military combat and personal injury suits). Data from group comparisons are also supportive. For example, Walters (1988) found that federal inmates were only likely to feign for a highly desired goal (i.e., single cell) but not under neutral circumstances. Similar data (Braginsky, Braginsky, & Ring, 1969; Wilcox & Krasnoff, 1967) have been reported for highly institutionalized psychiatric patients who exhibited little inclination to feign except when confronted by the threat of discharge.

The adaptational model provides the broadest and least pejorative explanation of malingering. It may assist clinicians in minimizing countertransference (e.g., anger at being duped). The model also suggests a clinical framework from which mental health professionals can explore the evaluatee's perceptions of an adversarial relationship, stated objectives, and alternatives. Often simple inquiries will elicit whether the assessment is perceived as adversarial (e.g., "Was this evaluation your idea?" "Are there ways this evaluation could hurt you?") and the person's stated objectives (e.g., "What do you hope to accomplish by the evaluation?" "Are there any hurdles [potential setbacks] to getting what you need?"). As noted later, the potential motivation to malinger cannot be equated with malingering itself.

Limits of Explanatory Models

Explanatory models are crucial to theory building and provide the necessary framework for attempting to understand why particular response styles are observed. However, explanatory models should not be confused with detection models or assessment methods. In other words, we cannot assume that a person with the *potential* motivation to malinger will actually malinger. For example, just because there are high financial incentives, attorneys attempting to discredit a plaintiff's claim, and an apparent absence of other monetary resources, we cannot conclude in a personal injury case that (1) the reported impairment is not genuine or (2) the plaintiff is exaggerating/fabricating symptoms.

DSM-IV falls victim to this confusion between explanatory and detection models. Although primarily an explanatory model, Rogers (1990a) attempted to test the efficacy of DSM-IV indicators of malingering on a forensic sample. He found that the use of two or more indicators, as specified by DSM-IV, proved ineffective at identifying malingerers. The good news was that two-thirds of the malingerers were correctly classified by this criterion. The bad news was that for every malingerer correctly identified, nearly four times as many bona fide patients were miscategorized as malingerers. In other words, the only available research would suggest that persons exceeding the DSM-IV criterion of two or more indicators have approximately a one-in-five chance (20.1%) of truly being a malingerer. Therefore, the clinical application of this explanatory model is likely to result in gross inaccuracies.

Explanatory Models of Defensiveness

The pathogenic, criminological, and adaptational models could also be applied to defensiveness, although little theoretical work has emerged. From a pathogenic paradigm, denial and repression of psychopathology could be construed as ego defenses over which the patient has little, if any, control (Laughlin, 1970). From this perspective, the underlying mechanism of defensiveness is psychopathological. Unlike the pathogenic model of malingering, however, the defensiveness counterpart does not necessarily predict continued deterioration. For example, use of primitive ego defenses may result in a stable but maladaptive pattern of psychological functioning (Perry & Cooper, 1985). At present, most clinical research does not postulate a pathogenic model of defensiveness but implies greater awareness and control over defensiveness.

A criminological model of defensiveness could be propounded, based on Cleckley's (1976) conceptualization of psychopathy. According to Cleckley, psychopaths are noted

1. *Dissimulation* is a general term to describe an individual who is deliberately distorting or misrepresenting psychological symptoms. Dissimulation may incorporate any of the previous response styles with, of course, the exception of honest responding.

2. *Unreliability* is a nonspecific term used to describe clinically the characteristics of an individual whose response style is not honest and self-disclosing, yet in which no further clarification can be made with respect to his or her intention.

3. *Deception* is an all-encompassing term to describe any and all attempts by an individual to distort or misrepresent his or her self-reporting. This term includes both dissimulation and all other forms of dishonesty. For example, some patients are dishonest about their past and current behavior, attitudes, or perceptions. Such deception may be totally separate from the patient's described psychological functioning (i.e., dissimulation).

4. *Self-disclosure* refers to how much an individual reveals about him- or herself (Jourard, 1971). A person is considered to have high self-disclosure when he or she evidences an honest response style in addition to a high degree of openness. A lack of self-disclosure does not imply dishonesty but simply an unwillingness to share personal information.

5. *Social desirability* (Crowne & Marlowe, 1960) is a construct closely related to defensiveness, but it extends beyond the minimization of psychological impairment. It is composed of two elements: the denial of negative characteristics and the attribution of positive qualities (Carsky et al., 1991). Social desirability clearly plays an instrumental role in perceptions of medical care (Hays & Ware, 1986) and willingness to acknowledge serious mental disorders (Carksy et al., 1992; Mazmanian, Mendonca, Holden, & Dufton, 1987). In clinical practice, I would recommend the use of *defensiveness* to describe persons presenting themselves psychologically in a favorable light, except when scales to assess social desirability are specifically employed.

6. *Impression management* (Tesser & Paulhus, 1983) is a widely researched construct to explain social behaviors by attempting to create a positive image and avoid embarrassment and other negative emotions. Therefore, impression management is often construed as more situationally driven than social desirability, the latter which may reflect a characteristic style of presentation. Again, the term "defensiveness" is generally preferable to "impression management" in clinical settings.

7. *Simulation–malingering paradox* (Rogers & Cavanaugh, 1983) refers to the research problem exemplified by simulation studies of dissimulation in which participants are asked to comply with instructions to fake (e.g., problems or symptoms) in order to study patients who fake symptoms when asked to comply with their psychological or medical assessment.

Gradations of Malingering and Defensiveness

Malingering and defensiveness have traditionally been treated as if they were dichotomous variables. For example, research on the MMPI has attempted to establish "fake-bad" profiles with optimal cutting scores for establishing the presence of malingering.

Although such research is valuable, it does not address the pressing clinical need for established gradations of dissimulation. For diagnostic purposes, it is of critical importance that an individual who is mildly defensive can be differentiated from others who are engaging in gross denial. Similarly, gradations of malingering may be of considerable importance in addressing dispositional issues or making treatment recommendations. The gradations provided in Table 1.3 represent a refinement of previous theoretical work (Rogers, 1984b, 1987) for establishing gradations of dissimulation. In this model, both the terms "malingering" and "defensiveness" are reserved for cases in which there is unequivocal evidence of deliberate dissimulation. In contrast, cases in which intentionality is in doubt would be characterized by the two gradations of unreliability.

These gradations of malingering and defensiveness should be viewed as preliminary, since they have not been tested widely with mentally disordered populations and suspected dissimulators. Research with forensic patients (Rogers, 1984b) suggested that

---

TABLE 1.3. Gradations of Malingering and Defensiveness

Unreliability

1. *Self-report with limited reliability*: The patient answers most inquiries with a fair degree of accuracy, but volunteers little or nothing and may distort or evade on circumscribed topics.
2. *Self-report without reliability*: The patient, through guardedness, exaggeration, or denial of symptoms, convinces the clinician that his or her responses are inaccurate. Such cases may be suspected of malingering or defensiveness, although the patient's intent cannot be unequivocally established.

Malingering

1. *Mild malingering*: There is unequivocal evidence that the patient is attempting to malinger, primarily through exaggeration. The degree of distortion is minimal and plays only a minor role in differential diagnosis.
2. *Moderate malingering*: The patient, either through exaggeration or fabrication, attempts to present him- or herself as considerably more disturbed than is the case. These distortions may be limited to either a few critical symptoms (e.g., the fabrication of command hallucinations) or represent an array of lesser distortions.
3. *Severe malingering*: The patient is extreme in his or her fabrication of symptoms to the point that the presentation is fantastic or preposterous.

Defensiveness

1. *Mild defensiveness*: There is unequivocal evidence that the patient is attempting to minimize the severity but not the presence of his or her psychological problems. These distortions are minimal in degree and of secondary importance in establishing a differential diagnosis.
2. *Moderate defensiveness*: The patient minimizes or denies substantial psychological impairment. This defensiveness may be limited to either a few critical symptoms (e.g., pedophilic interest) or represent lesser distortions across an array of symptomatology.
3. *Severe defensiveness*: The patient denies the existence of any psychological problems or symptoms. This categorical denial includes common foibles and minor emotional difficulties that most healthy individuals have experienced and would acknowledge.

---

dered persons. Without these comparisons, researchers are unable to differentiate whether observed behaviors are evidence of deception, mental disorders, or both.[5] Second, the studies address only falsifications and not specific attempts at the feigning or denial of mental disorders. Third, deception research relies almost exclusively on nonexpert observers, who may differ significantly from mental health professionals in their ability to detect deception.

Polygraph studies of deception frequently utilize a simulation paradigm. Individuals are typically asked to respond dishonestly under specific experimental instructions. Occasionally, the realism of the research is enhanced by asking the participant to engage in a quasi-fraudulent act (e.g., "stealing" from the experimenter).

The primary strength of the simulation design is its well-controlled experimental manipulation of response styles and systematic comparisons among criterion groups. Its main disadvantage is its generalizability to real-world applications. This lack of known generalizability has given rise to the previously described simulation–malingering paradox.

Known-Groups Comparisons

Studies sometimes employ persons in actual clinical or applied settings that have been independently identified by mental health professionals as engaging in dissimulation. These persons are then compared to criterion groups of persons known as (or assumed to be) honest responders. The challenge of this design is the accurate classification of dissimulating persons. Two risks are readily apparent: (1) use of *extreme* groups that are readily identifiable but not representative malingerers or defensive persons, or conversely, (2) use of *spectrum* groups that include persons with features of malingering that are not sufficient to meet the classification. As an example of a spectrum group, Hankins, Barnard, and Robbins (1993) categorized any person with as few as one feigned symptom in the malingering group.

Psychophysiological studies of defensiveness are often an important application of known-group comparisons. For example, penile plethysmography compares phallometric responses of known groups (e.g., persons with pedophilia and persons with sexual sadism) and compares admitters to deniers. Similarly, hair analysis for drug detection examines structural changes in the hair shafts of known users of specific drugs and compares them to nonusers and suspected users (Kelly & Rogers, 1996).

The foremost strength of the known-groups comparison is its generalizability to applied settings. By using actual malingerers and defensive persons faced with real and concrete exigencies, the resulting data are directly applicable to similar persons in comparable settings. Its chief limitation is the establishment of the known groups themselves. Classification of dissimulation is wholly dependent of the accuracy of mental health professionals. Samples of bona fide patients may also include errors, because patients with typical presentations are often assumed to be genuine. Interestingly, simulation and known-groups comparisons complement each other's strengths and compensate for recognized weaknesses.

An extrapolation from the known-groups comparison is the case study approach. In case studies, the comparison to bona fide patients is implicit. In other words, the investigator presents unique and distinctive features that cause the feigner's presentation to be atypical. Less frequently used in the last decade, case studies are primarily employed to introduce a new syndrome (e.g., factitious bereavement or Munchausen by proxy). Given their essentially naturalistic perspective, case studies are ideally suited for such preliminary examinations of novel syndromes and uncommon response styles associated with dissimulation.

Differential Prevalence Design

A relatively recent phenomenon is the differential prevalence design, which is methodologically a poor substitute to the known-groups comparison. With this design, persons with different referral questions or from dissimilar settings are *postulated* to have disparate rates of dissimulation. No attempts, formal or informal, are made to further classify persons within each group as dissimulating or honest. As a typical example, a greater proportion of persons with pending litigation are postulated to be feigning; therefore, comparisons are conducted between litigating and nonlitigating persons. In summary, the differential prevalence design has no way to establish (1) the prevalence rate of dissimulation among different referral groups, (2) the identification of dissimulation in each referral group, or consequently, (3) the divergence, if any, in performance between dissimulating and honest persons. Even if predicted differences are found, the ability to relate these differences to dissimulation is inalterably thwarted by the nature of its design.

AN OVERVIEW OF THE BOOK'S ORGANIZATION

This book has two primary objectives that I consider to be of equal importance. The first is to offer a clear and succinct summary of current research on malingering and deception as it applies to psychological impairment. Inherent in this discussion is the encouragement of more sophisticated research and the careful application of research findings to clinical practice. The second and related objective is the development of an empirically based conceptual model for the evaluation of malingering and deception. The goal of the second objective is to standardize diagnostic evaluations and provide a meaningful framework for clinical decision making.

The scope of this book is determined in part by current status of clinical and applied research. Based on available research, the book focuses predominantly on dissimulation as it relates to psychological and not physical disorders. Thus, although factitious disorders and Munchausen syndrome are discussed, no attempt is made to explore dissimulation of purely physical disorders (e.g., malingered deafness). In addition, several topics are not addressed, since their clinical relevance is limited. For example, a large research literature exists (see, e.g., Burgoon & Buller, 1994; Burgoon, Callister,

& Hunsaker, 1994; Ekman, 1991; Rogers, 1987) on interpersonal variables as they relate to deception. No attempt is made to comprehensively review this vast array of studies because of their limited applicability to patients in psychiatric settings. Such research has questionable usefulness, since it addresses how nonprofessionals detect unspecified deception in nondisordered participants under highly controlled experimental conditions. Therefore, the scope of the book is focused on clinical research and its applications in the assessment of mentally disordered populations.

Format for the Book

This book is organized into four major parts: Diagnostic Issues, Psychometric Assessment, Specialized Methods, and Summary. Part I, Diagnostic Issues, addresses (1) specific syndromes associated with dissimulation; (2) assessment of malingering and deception with special populations, namely, sociopaths, substance abusers, and children; (3) differential diagnosis between genuine and malingered presentations for commonly feigned disorders, such as psychosis and posttraumatic stress disorders; and (4) the evaluation of feigned amnesia and memory impairment.

Part II, Psychometric Assessment, comprises chapters on objective personality measures, projective testing, and intellectual and neuropsychological measures. The purpose of these three chapters is a careful review of current research findings, with the twin goals of improving clinical methods for assessing dissimulation and discarding ineffective traditional techniques.

Part III, Specialized Methods, examines an array of investigative techniques in the assessment of dissimulation. Four such techniques—hypnosis, polygraphy, integrity testing, and drug-assisted interviews—are often employed to assess nonspecific deception. Plethysmography, or phallometric methods of assessing sexual arousal, is reviewed in the light of frequent defensiveness and denial among men who engage in aberrant sexual behavior. The usefulness of structured interviews in the identification of dissimulation is discussed, including a review of the Schedule of Affective Disorders and Schizophrenia (SADS; Spitzer & Endicott, 1978) and the specialized interview referred to as the Structured Interview of Reported Symptoms (SIRS; Rogers, 1992; Rogers, Bagby, & Dickens, 1992). Finally, screens for malingering have received increased recognition; these self-report measures are reviewed comprehensively.

Part IV, Summary, provides a useful integration of clinical methods and research data. These related chapters summarize the important clinical and research issues on the assessment of dissimulation for both practitioners and applied researchers. The first of these chapters discusses how clinical procedures should be employed and proposes a workable model for their clinical applications. The research chapter explores basic research designs, their present status, and future directions in the applied study of dissimulation.

The format for each chapter allows considerable flexibility, given the breadth and diversity of topics. However, each chapter incorporates a distillation of research findings on malingering and deception with a conceptual understanding and heuristic (i.e., empirically untested but clinically accepted) approaches to the assessment of dissimulation. Whenever possible, each chapter offers two research-based paradigms: the threshold model and the clinical decision model. The threshold model addresses the issue of when clinicians should thoroughly evaluate suspected dissimulation. This model employs explicit criteria for establishing at what point sufficient concern is raised (i.e., threshold) to warrant further assessment. The clinical decision model examines how clinicians arrive at their conclusions regarding dissimulation. This model presents explicit criteria for making the clinical determination of malingering and defensiveness. A cursory survey of chapters demonstrates the inherent difficulties of establishing these models when relevant research is limited. As a result, many chapters are missing one or both models, or address less precise issues, such as patients' unreliability.

NOTES

1. An instructive analogy is the FAA inspection of aircraft. Although the FAA rarely detects unsafe planes, very few would argue that its efforts are insignificant.

2. Two possible explanations exist for this finding: (1) Police recruits were highly motivated to complete the MMPI carefully and consistently; and (2) police recruits were highly motivated not to acknowledge their carelessness.

3. The bulk of malingering research, beyond college samples, has occurred in criminal forensic settings. Obviously, common features of these settings are persons with APD who face psycholegal issues. If most research had taken place in geriatric medical settings, would we blithely assume that older age and illness are predictors of malingering?

4. MMPI research (Greene, 1991) suggests that substantial numbers of patients are likely to be defensive, even when an external goal is readily identifiable.

5. In the early development of the SIRS, Rogers, Bagby, and Dickens (1992) found differences on paralinguistic cues between simulators and normal controls. However, these differences disappeared when nondisordered controls were replaced by persons with mental disorders.

vulnerable others, and exaggeration for profit or revenge. Lest we believe that patients have a monopoly on distortion, Novack et al. (1989) found in an anonymous survey of 211 physicians that most would be willing to engage in some form of deception either to secure insurance payment or to prevent patient embarrassment.

Given this diversity in deceptive behavior, the usefulness of the current *Diagnostic and Statistical Manual of Mental Disorders* (DSM-IV; American Psychiatric Association, 1994a) has yet to be fully tested. Are the distinctions between putative disorders (e.g., factitious disorder) and deceptive behaviors that are not granted the status of a mental disorder (e.g., malingering) conceptually meaningful and empirically valid? Factitious disorders and malingering are characterized as mutually exclusive; however, clinical experience demonstrates that various levels of intention can coexist. Thus, the false dichotomy (factitial vs. malingering) in DSM-IV does not correspond to clinical realities.

Inherent in any attempt to classify deceptive behavior are questions of whether and how the clinician is to assess varying degrees of consciousness and voluntariness. This task is complicated further by the fact that these conditions are more likely dimensions rather than discrete entities. Jonas and Pope (1985), for example, demonstrated that somatoform disorders, factitious disorders, and malingering shared startling similarities in age of onset, course, unresponsiveness to treatment, and comorbidity of character pathology. These findings, and the demonstration by Rogers, Bagby, and Vincent (1994) of the response similarities in malingerers and factitious patients, lend strength to suggestions by Jonas and Pope that impossible questions about voluntariness and consciousness be abandoned in favor of phenomenological research into biological, treatment, and outcome parameters in dissimulating patients. Such research would mean less emphasis on individual, patient-based collection of information (which is necessary for case consultations and treatment), with a shift to empirical, data–driven methods to identify deceptive behavior via testing and group comparisons. Emphasis on individual case characteristics calls into question not only the forensic admissibility of information (Ogloff, 1990) but is also counterintuitive—why rely on the report of a deceptive patient?

This chapter defines and differentiates DSM-IV and other syndromes characterized by deception. In addition, it encourages the use of correct terminology, highlights strengths and deficiencies of the DSM-IV diagnostic scheme, and assesses theoretical and clinical utility of current diagnostic labels. Consistent with other chapters, it provides threshold and clinical decision models for major conditions. Other clinical phenomena relevant to deception are also discussed: (1) false claims of abuse or rape; (2) factitious disorders by proxy; (3) dissimulation associated with substance abuse, eating disorders, and personality disorders; (4) compensation neurosis; (5) *pseudologia fantastica*; (6) false memory syndrome; (7) deception associated with chronic fatigue syndrome and other somatic conditions; (8) pain; and (9) denial. Better understanding of the spectrum of deceptive behavior will enhance a more comprehensive and better informed evaluation. At present, factitious disorders and malingering provide sufficient data for diagnostic classification. It is not the intent of this chapter to confer disease status to the other conditions discussed.

FACTITIOUS DISORDERS

DSM-IV diagnostic criteria for factitious disorder (FD) include "A. intentional production or feigning of physical or psychological signs or symptoms. B. the motivation for the behavior is to assume the sick role. C. external incentives for the behavior (such as economic gain, avoiding legal responsibility, or improving physical well-being, as in Malingering) are absent" (American Psychiatric Association, 1994a, p. 474). Subtypes are based upon the relative preponderance of psychological or physical symptoms. DSM-III-R (American Psychiatric Association, 1987) allowed for the presumption of a need to "assume the sick role" based upon absence of external incentives; in contrast, DSM-IV requires evidence of internalized motivation. Although posing difficulties in clinical practice, this requirement is consistent with the notion that factitious disorders are fundamentally a mental disorder (Spiro, 1968), whereas malingering may be viewed from a standpoint of social adaptation (Szasz, 1956).

The determination of voluntariness or intentionality in day-to-day affairs seems intuitive, but diagnostic standards must be more rigorous. Regrettably, none are provided in DSM-IV. Overholser (1990) presented the most thorough review regarding the voluntary control of symptoms. He reported the following criteria: admission of deceit by the patient; presence of physiologically impossible symptoms; observable evidence; symptoms contradicted by objective testing; physical evidence; and non-stereotypical response to treatment. The demonstration of voluntariness carries no implications for consciousness about motivations. In this regard, Eisendrath (1994) made an analogy between factitious disorder and phobias. In both disorders, the patient may act intentionally but may lack awareness of underlying psychological motivations.

How do clinicians assess motivation to assume the sick role? Perhaps the concept of wanting to be a patient is artificial because, as Rogers, Bagby, and Rector (1989) ironically pointed out, wanting to be a patient badly enough bestows the simulator with the diagnosis of FD. Secondary gain cannot be the sole criterion for assumption of the sick role, since external or secondary gains are inherent in all illness (Fenichel, 1945). When patient cooperation permits, the following features may serve to bolster impressions that the predominant motivation for feigned illness is the desire to be a patient: (1) Strong masochistic needs are present; (2) sickness allows inappropriate regression and avoidance of adult (especially sexual) responsibilities; (3) illness symbolizes anger at or conflict with authority figures; (4) psychiatric or medical care fulfills massive dependency needs; or (5) illness symbolizes attempts at mastery of past trauma (repetition compulsion). Clearly, such psychological phenomena are usually unconscious and are difficult to uncover even in cooperative patients. The pitfalls of diagnosing factitious disorders by DSM-IV are emerging: The clinician must determine *conscious* production of symptoms, based upon *unconscious* motives, in an *uncooperative* patient.

In DSM-IV, the presence of external incentives negates diagnosis of FD and suggests the alternative classification of malingering. This criterion runs contrary to knowledge about the multilevel nature of behavior. The mere presence of external gains cannot negate in every case the primacy of psychological motives. The "malingerer" who seems to be avoiding work may actually be motivated by regressive needs and by fear of conflict with authorities. A patient may exaggerate pain to simultaneously obtain narcotics (chemical dependency), avoid conflict with spouse or boss (FD), and avoid a noxious work situation (malingering). Unfortunately, the relative importance of internal and external motivations remains subjective for the examiner and, therefore, prone to theoretical bias. The goal of factitial behavior is not to hoodwink doctors (Asher, 1951), but rather to bolster a fragile sense of self by creating the identity of patient (Spivak, Rodin, & Sutherland, 1994). Incidental secondary gains should not eliminate the diagnosis of FD.

Factitious illness is rare, although many cases presently classified as malingering could be reclassified as factitious if more detailed psychological data were available. Sogi et al. (1989) found no cases of FD among 1,090 patients at two clinic sites. Reich and Gottfried (1983) identified 41 cases of factitious physical illness over a 10-year period at Peter Bent Brigham Hospital. Other data on prevalence found that less than 1% of referrals to the Toronto General Hospital psychiatric consultation service were diagnosed with FD (Sutherland & Rodin, 1990), as were 0.2% of 4,500 visits to Baylor psychiatric emergency services (Carlson, 1985). Screening for FD makes more sense in subspecialty areas. For example, approximately 9% of fever of unknown origin (FUO) cases were factitious (Aduan, Fauci, Dale, Herzberg, & Wolff, 1979), and 9 of 219 (4.1%) psychotic patients admitted to a research ward met criteria for voluntary symptom production (Pope, Jonas, & Jones, 1982). With the conspicuous exception of Munchausen syndrome, most FD patients are female (Taylor & Hyler, 1993). The possibility of gender bias remains, namely, more males diagnosed as malingerers and more females as factitious.

DSM-IV affords no specifiers for severity of factitious disorders, which might correlate with prognosis (as do certain specifiers for mood disorders or hypochondriasis). Severity could be based upon the *level of enactment* of factitious behavior, as suggested by Eisendrath (1984). The isolated production of factitial symptoms or mere falsification of complaints is the lowest level of enactment; this correlates with minor psychopathology and motivation to feign illness under stress. The simulation of disease (e.g., feigned psychosis or factitious hematuria) often indicates more severe pathology of the borderline type (Nadelson, 1979). Moreover, the regular production of verifiable tissue pathology (e.g., injection of pathogens or ingestion of anticoagulants) usually implies severe personality disorder and the pursuit of illness as a way of life. The sole diagnosis of FD is rare; overlap with personality disorders, mood disorders, chemical dependency, adjustment disorders, or eating disorders is the rule (Feldman & Ford, 1994). The occurrence of isolated factitious illness under situational stress raises the possibility that factitious behavior can be adaptive, as Rogers (1990a) suggested for malingering. Characterological or social exigencies may determine how an individual "chooses" between the sick role and external gratification.

Factitious Disorder with Predominantly Psychological Signs and Symptoms

Simulated psychopathology may mimic any genuine syndrome. Symptom presentations are so varied as to defy unitary formulation. The diagnostic legitimacy of psychological FD was questioned by Rogers, Bagby, and Vincent (1994), who found FD patients and malingerers were similar in their patterns of bogus symptoms. Up to 40% of all factitious behavior may be psychological in presentation (Carney & Brown, 1983), but many cases may be missed due to inherent difficulties in objective assessment. For example, detection of feigned alcohol abuse (Caradoc-Davies, 1988) or hypersomnia (Feldman & Russell, 1991) are particularly difficult. Links, Steiner, and Mitton (1989) found a dramatic 13% incidence of factitious psychotic symptoms in hospitalized borderline patients. Clinicians do not know what role social, individual, biological, or practical factors play in the choice of specific syndromes for simulation.

Factitious Psychosis

For almost a century, the term "hysterical psychosis" defined a condition characterized by brief psychotic symptoms with onset during stress, dramatic personality traits, and rapid return to baseline function. Patients with this condition were suggestible and usually hypnotizable (Spiegel & Fink, 1979), raising questions of voluntary control over symptoms. Ritson and Forrest (1970) were the first to evaluate a group of such patients, all presenting clear signs of simulation although several had previous diagnoses of schizophrenia. Absent evidence of voluntary control over symptoms, these patients would be diagnosed today with brief psychotic disorder (American Psychiatric Association, 1994a). Hysterical features and characteristics akin to somatoform disorders were found in 56 cases reviewed by Bishop and Holt (1980). This group seemed to represent a "good prognosis" factitious syndrome with regression under stress.

Another form of factitious psychosis implies a more ominous prognosis. Pope et al. (1982) analyzed phenomenological and outcome data on nine patients with voluntary control over psychotic symptoms. Most patients were females with severe personality disorders and no family history of psychosis. Strikingly, long-term follow-up revealed this group to perform more poorly on measures of global assessment and social function than did patients with manic and schizophrenic disorders. For this characterologically disturbed subgroup, the investigators concluded that "acting crazy may bode more ill than being crazy" (p. 1483). A similar phenomenon was noted by Hay (1983), who found that 5 of 6 patients with feigned psychosis eventually developed schizophrenia. Feigned psychosis apparently entails several possible motivations: a coping strategy for acute stress, a justification of care for incipient "legitimate" psychosis, or a mechanism for permissible regression. Only anecdotal information about treatment of factitious psychosis is available.

Factitious Posttraumatic Stress Disorder

The introduction of posttraumatic stress disorder (PTSD) as a diagnostic entity in DSM-III provided potentially duplicitous veterans and pseudo-veterans with another avenue to psychological care or financial gain, although false claims of other forms of posttraumatic injury have been made for decades (Resnick, 1988). Sparr and Pankratz (1983) described differential diagnostic difficulties in Vietnam veterans with false claims of

(i.e., a function of chronicity, intensity, and morbidity). DSM-III provided separate clinical criteria for chronic and atypical factitious disorders with physical symptoms; such distinction was appropriate because of clear differences in patient demographics and illness severity (Cunnien, 1988). Unfortunately, these subtypes were not retained in DSM-IV.

Chronic Physical Factitious Behavior

Asher (1951) coined the term "Munchausen syndrome" to describe what is now thought to be a rare, archetypical, and untreatable form of physical factitious disorder. Illness induction seems to maintain a lifestyle revolving about hospitalizations, surgeries, and contentious battles with physicians. Asher's tone in his original article was one of anger and befuddlement; these emotions were reflected in anachronistic synonyms for the syndrome: *neurologica diabolica, laparotomophilia migrans,* and *haemorrhagica histrionica.* Asher's typical patient was a male, admitted to the hospital after sudden onset of neurological, abdominal, or hematological symptoms. As objective information failed to corroborate complaints or when falsification of illness was suspected, typical features of belligerence, evasiveness, and demands for drugs or surgery ensued. These patients were uniformly uncooperative, related improbable accounts reminiscent of *pseudologia fantastica,* often had prior admissions with the use of aliases, and frequently discharged themselves angrily. They ingeniously simulated illness by ingesting poisons, inducing blood loss, feigning epilepsy, injecting pathogens, and creating or aggravating wounds.

The psychopathology of factitious patients intrigued Menninger (1934), who opined psychodynamically that addiction to surgery embodied aggression against the self neutralized by its projection onto a perceived sadistic parent represented by the physician. Asher (1951) noted motives, such as desire for attention, a grudge against doctors, desire for drugs, and free lodging; this combination of patient role and external incentives suggests overlap with malingering (Cramer, Gershberg, & Stern, 1971). Spiro (1968) was the first to suggest psychodynamic consistencies in chronic factitial patients. He noted features such as (1) imposture to compensate for ego and superego deficits, (2) choice of the hospital as a stage upon which to enact masochistic conflicts because of the ready availability of suffering and caretaking, (3) masochistic transference reenactment of early parental conflicts, and (4) masochistic identification with the pain-inflicting doctor.

Bursten (1965) hypothesized counterphobic mechanisms. He posited that creation of a hostile, rejecting hospital experience might allow mastery of earlier rejection experiences (a form of repetition compulsion). He suggested that medical care represents both fulfillment and rejection: Many factitious patients are nurses or medical technicians, whereas others have had dependent or romantic relationships with physicians (Cramer et al., 1971). Those conflicts are externalized by the patient, who first demands care and later rejects it by leaving against medical advice. FD patients frequently had serious childhood illnesses and often genuinely or factitially ill parents who served as models of medical deceit (Hyler & Sussman, 1981). Goodwin (1988), noting behavioral similarities between Munchausen syndrome and DID, speculated that behavior usually attributed to voluntariness (*pseudologia,* wandering, disease production) might represent actions of alter personalities. This possibility holds merit for further investigation; amnesia and sudden personality changes could possibly explain sudden departures from the hospital and reentry under an alias. Munchausen syndrome is usually obvious by age 20, but factitious physical behavior has been noted in patients from age 10 (Sneed & Bell, 1976) to 85 (Davis & Small, 1985).

Treatment of Munchausen syndrome is considered impossible due to lack of cooperation, sudden departures, and profound characterological disorder. Selected case reports (e.g., Mayo & Haggerty, 1984) document improvement with treatment based on object relations theory or by behavioral modification combined with suggestion and interpretation (Klonoff, Youngner, Moore, & Hershey, 1983); it remains to be determined whether chronic factitious behavior can enter remission, or whether the associated conflicts are simply channeled into another form of maladaptive behavior such as conversion, substance abuse, or factitious disorder by proxy.

Limited Physical Factitious Behavior

Ninety percent of factitious physical disorders represent mild to moderate forms of illness without the commitment to chronic disease production as seen in Munchausen patients (Eisendrath, 1989). Nadelson (1979) recognized that patients existed with little or no character pathology, who fabricated illness under the influence of situational stress. This group might be detected only via behavioral inconsistencies, excessive comfort in the sick role, or past employment in medicine or allied fields. Unlike chronic factitial patients, this group may not respond with anger at suggestions of factitious etiology and may present simply as passive, helpless patients who do not improve with standard treatment. Intuitively, patients with isolated or episodic factitious behavior should demonstrate better social function and better treatment responsiveness (Eisendrath, 1989) than their chronic counterparts. Eisendrath proposed treatment based on creation of a double bind (i.e., failure to respond to standard treatment would confirm self-induced illness). This scenario capitalizes on suggestibility of factitious patients while allowing them to save face. Cessation of factitious behavior, rather than true insight into psychological causative factors, is probably the best achievable goal. The vicissitudes of confrontation and treatment are thoughtfully described in *Patient or Pretender: Inside the Strange World of Factitious Disorders* (Feldman & Ford, 1994). Although designed primarily for a nonprofessional audience, this text is particularly thorough in its case descriptions and psychological observations.

The variety of feigned illness "selected" to enact the sick role is limitless, but it may bear a relationship to prior medical experience, naive notions about illness, or mere opportunism. Pseudoseizures, for example, occur under stress in up to one-third of patients with known organic seizures (Betts & Boden, 1992). Factitious seizures usually occur in the presence of others, may be initiated or terminated by suggestion, are often bizarre and asynchronous, lack postictal confusion, and respond erratically to anticonvulsant treatment (Guberman, 1982). In such cases, electroencephalogram (EEG) tracings are understandably not characteristic of epileptic attacks. Guberman found two groups of pseudoseizure patients. A Munchausen–like group had recurrent seizures, prior psychiatric hospitalizations, and severe interpersonal problems; a good-prognosis group with limited episodes often acknowledged control over seizures. Pseudoseizure patients need careful assessment because of high reported rates of traumatic experiences including rape and spousal abuse (Bowman, 1993).

Metabolic abnormalities are easily feigned. Self-administration of epinephrine or related compounds mimics pheochromocytoma (Keiser, 1991), and results in elaborate diagnostic tests or surgery. Grunberger, Weiner, Silverman, Taylor, and Gorden (1988) reported long-term follow-up of 10 patients who induced hypoglycemia with surreptitious insulin use. Nine patients were women, six worked in medical settings, five had concurrent diabetes as a symptom model, and only three had favorable psychosocial outcomes. Factitious hypoglycemia is detected via assays for sulfonylurea compounds or by finding physiologically impossible ratios of insulin to C-peptide (Lebowitz & Blumenthal, 1993). Prognosis seems to depend upon the degree of commitment to a factitious lifestyle. Surreptitious use of thyroid hormone is an important differential diagnosis in endocrinological practice (Zellmann, 1979).

A panoply of other forms of factitial behavior have been described. The creation or exacerbation of skin lesions is particularly common (Cotterill, 1992). Up to 2% of FUO patients in a university setting have factitious fever generated by injection of toxins (saliva, stool, chemicals) or by thermometer manipulation (Rumans & Vosti, 1978). Such patients are detected when bacterial cultures reveal unusual organisms, when injection paraphernalia are found, or when urine temperature is normal despite thermometer abnormalities. Demonstrating the potential consequences of these injections, McDaniel, Desoutter, Firestone, and McDonell (1992) reported factitious infection leading to bilateral mastectomy. Long-acting anticoagulants may be ingested both as straightforward suicide attempts and as a means to ensure the patient role (Swigar, Clemow, Saidi, & Kim, 1990). Factitious complaints of cancer are seldom considered on initial presentation, but are later revealed by historical inconsistency and self-destructive behavior (Baile, Kuehn, & Straker, 1992). The emergence of AIDS as a public health problem has been paralleled by its use to adopt the sick role. Factitious AIDS is characterized by insistence on having the illness, contradictory or vague past history, and failure to comply with testing procedures (Frumkin & Victoroff, 1990). Wallach (1994) reviewed diagnostic tools in laboratory detection of factitious disorders.

Factitious Disorder with Combined Psychological and Physical Signs and Symptoms

Eagerness to assume the sick role may lead to seemingly random choices to enact physical, psychological, or mixed symptoms. For example, AIDS and cancer provide ample opportunities for fabrication of both physical complaints and depression. Merrin, VanDyke, Cohen, and Tusel (1986) remarked upon the pitfall of ignoring the possibility of factitious psychological complaints in the face of dramatic physical symptoms and emphasized the need to focus on inconsistencies in both spheres. The psychological need to be a patient does not respect traditional boundaries between physical and mental disorders.

False claims of rape are socially relevant examples of mixed factitious behavior. Kanin (1994) found that 41% of forcible rape complaints over a 9-year period in a small community were fabricated. Over half served an alibi function (malingering to avoid undesirable consequences), but the remainder were interpreted to be false allegations in the service of revenge, sympathy, or attention getting. Kanin parenthetically noted that 50% of forcible rape complaints from two large university campuses were false. Feldman, Ford, and Stone (1994) hypothesized that factitious claims of rape serve multiple psychological functions, such as nurturance, search for rescue from actual current abuse, dissociation from past abuse, or projection of anger (see earlier discussion of masochism and projection in Munchausen syndrome).

MALINGERING

Malingering phenomena traditionally have been viewed in moralistic, simplistic, or strictly behavioral schemes as representative of conscious desires to obtain money or drugs, avoid work or prosecution, or evade undesirable duties. The incidence of malingering cannot be assessed accurately since it overlaps with a host of everyday behaviors (e.g., playing hookey or making excuses to avoid social functions). DSM-IV follows the tradition of previous editions by defining malingering as "the intentional production of false or grossly exaggerated physical or psychological symptoms, motivated by external incentives" (American Psychiatric Association, 1994a, p. 683) and by allowing that malingering may be socially adaptive in isolated circumstances. Malingering is suspected in (1) medicolegal contexts, (2) cases in which objective data fail to corroborate claims of stress or disability, (3) uncooperative patients, and (4) the presence of antisocial personality disorder. Asher (1972) captured the anger of physicians dealing with deceptive behavior by observing that "the pride of a doctor who has caught a malingerer is akin to that of a fisherman who has landed an enormous fish" (p. 145).

Menninger (1935) speculated that clinicians were angered at malingerers because of the naive misperception that such behavior was purely intended to deceive; objectivity is lost as the clinician makes judgments about the morality of deceptive behavior. Similarly, Szasz (1956) believed that any condition with such strong moral overtones represents social condemnation rather than a valid diagnostic entity. Travin and Protter (1984) conceptualized malingering as a social psychological process in which specific goals in a social transaction are pursued in light of individual psychological influences. They believed, as did Gorman and Winograd (1988), that malingering may be comorbid with conversion disorders, personality disorders, and factitial behavior. The classification of disorders along a spectrum from purely unconscious motivation (conversion) to increasingly conscious motivation and voluntariness of action (factitious disorders, malingering) was advocated by Nadelson (1979); clinicians must be alert to underlying psychological factors, even if external incentives are readily apparent.

It is counterintuitive to assume that criminal populations and litigants have a monopoly on malingering. Sierles (1984) found malingering behaviors to be roughly equal in psychiatric, medical, and surgical Veterans Administration (VA) patients, al-

OTHER CLINICAL PHENOMENA
INVOLVING POSSIBLE DECEPTION

Factitious Disorder by Proxy

Meadow (1977) coined the term "Munchausen syndrome by proxy" to describe a peculiar condition in which parents or other caretakers falsified health information or produced factitious disease in dependent children. DSM-IV included research criteria for factitious disorder by proxy (FDBP; American Psychiatric Association, 1994a). Analogous to factitious disorders proper, proxy behavior implies assumption of the vicarious sick role by intentional production or feigning of disease on a second person. The victim is usually a preschool child but could be a disabled adult or even a fetus in utero (Jureidini, 1993). Commonly induced syndromes include bleeding, apnea by suffocation, diarrhea or vomiting, fever (falsified or induced by pathogens), seizures (falsified or induced by insulin overdose), abnormal levels of consciousness, and hypernatremia due to salt poisoning. Children may even learn to feign symptoms under the tutelage of a simulator (Croft & Jervis, 1989).

Rosenberg (1987) reviewed 117 reported cases of FDBP. The perpetrators were biological mothers in 98% of cases, and mortality rates for children approached 9%. Importantly, Munchausen syndrome or related disorders were present in 24% of mothers. Sigal, Gelkopf, and Meadow (1989) described psychodynamic features of FDBP: Mothers appeared to have primitive forms of character pathology; deprived or abusive childhoods; feelings of insecurity; and chronic conflicts with passive, ineffectual husbands (if one was present). Through projective identification, the child becomes a receptacle of mother's conflicts translated into factitious symptoms, and the mother gains security from nurturing hospital personnel. Clinicians may question the statement of Sigal et al. that "the parent usually has no intention of killing or maiming the child" (p. 532). Criminal intent aside, no evidence exists to suggest that this form of child abuse is undertaken with anything other than full understanding about its potential consequences for the child.

Griffith and Slovik (1989) described 11 clinical features common to cases of FDBP. These features include (1) frequent medical evaluations at mother's request, (2) symbiotic mother–child relationship, (3) illness that occurs or worsens in mother's presence, (4) a laissez-faire attitude on mother's part toward the child's illness, (5) history of similar illness in mother or sibling, (6) nursing or medical experience in mother, and (7) maternal history of somatoform or factitious disorder. Feldman and Ford (1994) noted interesting FDBP variants, such as disease induction in pets. More controversially, they also classified overly zealous or naive therapists (e.g., who believe that repressed sexual abuse accounts for everyone's difficulties) as engaging in a form of proxy disease induction. From that perspective, intensively involved therapists may be responsible for the induction of pseudomemories or false abuse allegations (see "False Memory Syndrome," below).

Before further syndromal validity is granted to FDBP in subsequent DSM manuals, concerns about medicalization of illegal behavior (i.e., child abuse) should be addressed: Have sufficient cases been described to justify the formulation of a new diagnostic entity? Do other forms of abuse (e.g., spousal abuse) merit consideration as separate diagnostic syndromes? Should FDBP be listed in DSM as a clinical disorder or as a condition that may be a focus of clinical attention?

Compensation Neurosis

The pejorative term "compensation neurosis" is unfortunately still in clinical usage and generally refers to injured litigants who demonstrate either a disability persisting long after expected recovery or subjective symptoms in excess of clinical findings. Disdain for injured litigants seems based on the simplistic assumption that money or other material compensation would cure the patient (the "green poultice" theory). The observation is true that physical symptoms sometimes improve after monetary settlement for an injury, but this phenomenon should not be equated with malingering. Money is also a powerful psychological motivator, often permitting revenge or punishment in a socially acceptable fashion. It may be victory over an authority figure (e.g., an employer) symbolized by money that the injured litigant seeks, not mere compensation itself. From a psychodynamic perspective, Fenichel (1945) asserted, "The most intense struggles for compensation are fought by patients who are much less in need of money than in need of a sign of parental affection and of assurance against abandonment" (p. 461).

Is there a role for psychological factors in extending or exaggerating disability after an accident (motivation of a neurotic or factitious variety), or is protracted disability primarily a ploy/malingering to obtain further compensation? Miller (1961) believed the latter, coining the term "accident neurosis," and concluding that symptomatic improvement after financial settlement implied freeloading. Martin (1974) observed that the mere presence of compensable injury allowed health care providers a rationalization for poor therapeutic outcome. Clinicians should not forget that behavioral regression is part of any illness (Corradi, 1983), and that compensation issues may contribute to, but not necessarily equate with, broader issues of dependence and disability. Miller's conclusions about the primacy of compensation issues was questioned by Sprehe (1984), who found that 78% of workers' compensation cases did not improve after settlement (see Chapter 6). Mendelson (1982) noted that up to 75% of head, neck, and back injury cases did not return to gainful employment within 2 years after settlement.

Even if symptoms improve after legal proceedings are completed, such improvement is not proof of malingering. As an alternative explanation, protracted litigation lowers patient morale, reduces effectiveness of ongoing treatment, and fosters iatrogenic conditions (Weissman, 1990). In support of this view, better psychological outcome after injury is associated with a longer time period after conclusion of litigation and with a shorter time period between injury and litigation (Binder, Trimble, & McNiel, 1991). The automatic assumption of deceitfulness after compensable injury must be avoided. In assessing work-related injuries, simplistic dichotomous concepts (e.g., genuine disorder vs. compensation neurosis) should be put aside in favor of investigation of complex factors, such as personal and family dynamics, roles of primary and secondary gain, iatrogenic elements, and the symbolic significance of money (Modlin, 1986). The term "compensation neurosis" does not belong in current terminology; it often disguises thinly veiled belligerence and diagnostic uncertainty. Psychogenic factors affecting the perception or manifestation of physical illness should be classified in the appropriate DSM-IV category (e.g., somatoform or factitious disorders, psychological factors affecting medical condition, or malingering).

Pseudologia Fantastica

Compulsive lying, pathological lying, and *pseudologia fantastica* refer to repetitive, quasicompulsive, often patently ridiculous lies with no clear external goal orientation. Everyday lying is so common and nonpathological, moral implications aside, as to be outside the scope of this text. Falsification is by definition a conscious act, although it may serve multiple unconscious motivations (e.g., revenge, mastery, or humiliation).

In her classic paper, Deutsch (1982) noted that normal lies are goal-directed, whereas *pseudologia fantastica* serves as its own gratification. Via psychoanalytic formulation, Deutsch asserted that pathological lies appear to represent daydreams, distortions of past events, or an admixture. Analogous to a verbal conversion reaction, the lie allowed fulfillment of a disguised, otherwise forbidden libidinal wish. In contrast to the profit motive readily discerned in professional liars and the nonsensical quality of organically based confabulation, the perpetration of *pseudologia fantastica* seems designed to bolster self-esteem and promote admiration by others. Unlike the common braggart, however, the pseudologue falsifies a substantial amount of information with bearing upon activities, acquaintances, or personal identity.

King and Ford (1988) reviewed 72 cases of *pseudologia*. They found a strong comorbidity with imposture, disease simulation, and peregrination—suggesting overlap with Munchausen syndrome and APD. King and Ford emphasized the matrix of truth in the pseudologue's tale, the narcissistic gratification inherent in lies, absence of monetary profit, and similar characteristics of the lies (i.e., containing elements of revenge, vanity, and exaggeration). Surprisingly, 40% of their cases demonstrated central nervous system abnormalities. Modell, Mountz, and Ford (1992) found hemithalamic dysfunction in a patient with pseudologia by use of positron emission scanning. Ford et al. (1988) gave a thoughtful analysis of biological, developmental, social, and psychological determinants of *pseudologia fantastica*. They noted complex and sometimes overlapping motivation behind *pseudologia*: assertion of power (oral aggression), wish fulfillment, wishes for autonomy, denial or repression, and regulation of self-esteem.

In summary, lies (fantastic or not) may exist either in isolation or in the presence of another entity, such as factitious disorder or borderline personality. Their presence should prompt a search for underlying psychopathology and for disorders associated with deception rather than imply the existence of a distinct syndrome of compulsive lying. To reemphasize this point, *pseudologia fantastica* is a descriptive term of deceitful behavior that is sometimes associated with a specific syndrome. By itself, this term should not be invoked as an explanatory mechanism for falsehoods or used to imply the absence of volition in the production of such falsehoods.

False Memory Syndrome

The term "false memory syndrome" (FMS; False Memory Syndrome Foundation, 1994) was introduced with formation of the foundation by the same name. Citing a number of respected researchers and practitioners on its advisory board, the FMS Foundation proposed to investigate the widespread phenomena associated with sudden recall of alleged child abuse, to reconcile families, and to establish methods to discriminate between true and false claims of sexual abuse.

Excessive enthusiasm for discovery of childhood abuse as an explanatory factor for adult pathology might lead clinicians to ignore biases induced by avid therapists or by hypnotic regression (Frankel, 1993). Sudden recall of previously "repressed" child abuse has prompted lawsuits against parents or other supposed perpetrators decades after the alleged abuse (Wakefield & Underwager, 1992). Popular books directed to child abuse survivors are often used as bibliotherapy tools, encourage confrontation with alleged abusers, encourage expressions of anger, or give advice on obtaining compensation (e.g., *The Courage to Heal*; Bass & Davis, 1994). At issue in the heated debate on legitimacy of abuse recollections are such factors as the nature and role of repression, accuracy of suddenly recalled memories, and influence of suggestion and hypnosis (see Chapter 5).

Williams (1994) found that 38% of women brought to the emergency room as children for documented sexual abuse did not recall that abuse years later. Pope and Hudson (1995), however, reviewed a number of studies of purported amnesia or repression of abuse experiences and provided alternative explanations (e.g., normal forgetting, underreporting, and simple denial). As they note, psychogenic amnesia tends to be focal rather than to encompass multiple events spanning years. Explicit memory of developmental experiences is intensely personal and usually impossible to verify. Loftus (1993b) opined that (1) memory is malleable and reconstructive, (2) manufactured memories may be indistinguishable from factual ones, and (3) memory could be altered because of transference issues in order to comply with a biased therapist. Other emotionally laden circumstances might also prompt inaccurate recall. For example, Ofshe (1992) directly demonstrated the creation of false memories under conditions of suggestion and interrogation. Moreover, the American Medical Association (AMA) Council on Scientific Affairs (1985) concluded that hypnotic age regression, often used to elicit memories of alleged abuse, is subjective and might lead to pseudomemories and confabulation.

Persinger (1992) documented six cases of sudden recall of prior abuse. The recall occurred under hypnotic suggestion, and all participants had subtle information processing anomalies that might have led to misconstruction of events. In a later study, Persinger (1994) documented the generation of memories in hypnotic-like conditions. He speculated that distortion of events or their temporal order could lead susceptible individuals to misattribute the perpetration of prior abuse or to have apparently "genuine" recall of events that never occurred.

Given the legal ramifications and often unverifiable nature of allegations of abuse against parents or other authority figures, practitioners should avoid targeting abuse as the sole or primary contributor to adult psychopathology (Mullen, Martin, Anderson, Romans, & Herbison, 1993). Sexual abuse is often only part of a broader spectrum of pathogenic behavior and provides patients and therapists a simplistically unitary explanation for adult problems. Undue focus on abuse can be a disservice to the patient by ignoring other clinical issues, encouraging maladaptive expressions of anger, and maintaining primitive notions of causality and blame.

No specific investigations have been conducted on the role of malingering and factitious behavior in the generation of false reports of prior sexual abuse. Since psychological motivations are sometimes responsible for false reports of contemporaneous abuse, however (see "Factitious Claims of Child Abuse," above), practitioners would be naive not to consider that similar mechanisms are responsible for some false reports of prior abuse. Malingered claims should be suspected when substantial financial gain (e.g., lawsuit against a church or government body) is at stake. Factitious claims should be suspected when psychological investigation reveals a substantial likelihood that revenge, displacement of anger, or recent abandonment triggered the abuse allegations.

Chronic Fatigue Syndrome and Related Conditions

Chronic fatigue syndrome (CFS) was granted syndromal validity in 1988 (Holmes et al., 1988). Absence of identifiable medical or psychiatric etiology for fatigue is one criterion, but other criteria overlap with symptoms seen in many psychiatric illnesses (e.g., fatigue, headache, sleep disturbance, neuropsychological complaints, and subjective weakness). CFS probably subsumes a variety of conditions, because no etiological factor has been identified. Assumption of psychogenicity in all cases would be unreasonable, because CFS is probably a heterogeneous condition with an organic substrate in an as-yet-unidentified core group (Krupp, Mendelson, & Friedman, 1991); the same authors suggest an analogy to chronic pain, which has variable organic input with strong modulation by psychological factors.

Given the ease with which CFS symptoms could be feigned, the dearth of reports of malingered or factitious fatigue is surprising. Wessely (1990) and Abbey and Garfinkel (1991) eloquently cited analogies between chronic fatigue and "popular" diagnoses of past years, such as neurasthenia. Not unlike phenomena seen in factitious disorders or malingering, certain vulnerable patients opportunistically may seize upon minor fatigue-producing illnesses to express or avoid current social, occupational, or personal conflicts. McCranie (1980) devised an elegant intrapsychic explanation for the hypochondriacal disease conviction in many CFS patients: (1) Weakness and fatigue are logical consequences of excessive mental and physical work directed at overcoming neurotic fears of failure or dependency; (2) failure of these strivings leads to conscious perceptions of fatigue accompanied by adamant denial of the underlying mechanism; and (3) fatigue comes to symbolize helplessness and to justify withdrawal from an unacceptable situation.

Overt psychiatric illness is common, but not universal, in CFS. Kruesi, Dale, and Strauss (1989) found a 75% lifetime prevalence of mental disorders in 28 patients meeting the criteria set forth by Holmes et al. (1988). Mental disorders usually anteceded the onset of fatigue. In an interesting comparison with patients suffering from documented muscular disease, Wood, Bentall, Gopfert, and Edwards (1991) found CFS patients to have 3.3 times the incidence of psychiatric disorder. Schmaling, DiClementi, Cullum, and Jones (1994) noted similarities between unverifiable cognitive complaints in CFS and those found in depression. Writers (e.g., Imboden, Canter, & Cluff, 1961) have speculated that depression or other psychiatric phenomena can delay recovery from physical illness, as documented for influenza and brucellosis. Some cases of CFS presumably reflect this merger phenomenon, whereas others represent pure somatic illness, and still others signify the opportunistic emergence of false attribution, outright malingering, or factitious disorder.

Similar interactions between psychiatric and organic factors have been proposed in individuals complaining of multiple chemical sensitivities (MCS), diffuse allergic reactions, or other "environmental illnesses" (Simon, Katon, & Sparks, 1990). Self-report checklists suggest that patients with MCS are phenomenologically similar to those with pure somatization; MCS patients also describe high levels of chronic fatigue, chronic pain, and mood disorders (Bell, Peterson, & Schwartz, 1995). Systematic investigation of large populations with environmental syndromes would be helpful in order to understand the role of opportunism and misattribution in the genesis of malingered and factitious complaints. In this regard, Fink (1992) found that 18% of persistent somatizers had been hospitalized at least once for factitious illness.

Pain Disorders

Chronic benign pain is a neurological event tantamount to a "third pathologic emotion" (Swanson, 1984, p. 210). As an affective state, chronic pain is prone to minimization, exaggeration, contamination by other affects or experiences, misattribution, and feigning. Of all presenting medical complaints, fatigue and pain are most subjective and, therefore, the easiest to feign. Fabrication of pain complaints to obtain narcotics, shelter, or medical care is frequently motivated by drug addiction, malingering, and factitious disorders, respectively.

Katon, Egan, and Miller (1985) found that over 51% of patients admitted to a chronic pain treatment program had alcohol abuse or major depression before the onset of pain. They hypothesized that pain served as an expression of psychiatric illness in this subgroup. No data are available on the incidence of factitious disorders in large samples of pain patients; however, Chapman and Brena (1990) described a group of pain patients notable for their verbal or behavioral inconsistencies. This group demonstrated malingering-like behavior (dramatic complaints, few objective findings, and little interest in treatment) and had higher rates of pending litigation than did consistent responders. Phenomena, such as increased pain intensity in the presence of a supportive spouse (Fordyce, Roberts, & Sternbach, 1985) or misperception of functional capacity, could represent malingering, misattribution, or unconsciously motivated sick-role behavior. Undoubtedly, characterological features influence pain perception and response. Pain patients make more use of mechanisms such as catastrophizing, praying, and hoping than do nonpatients with equivalent pain. Notably, the nonpatients are less functionally impaired and less depressed (Zitman, Linssen, & Van, 1992). Although malingering and factitious disorders appear rarely in chronic pain patients presenting for behavioral treatment, emergency room and occupational health personnel are only too familiar with blatant fabrication of pain complaints. Future research must be directed at clarification of potentially deceptive practices, elucidation of characterological features, and predictors of outcome in diverse groups of pain patients.

Denial

In everyday clinical usage, "denial" infers the consciously determined refusal to acknowledge the existence, severity, or implications of phenomena that are apparent to the clinician. Denial in this sense is akin to, but not equivalent to, the unconsciously motivated ego defense of the same name (Fenichel, 1945). Denial may be healthy if it serves an adaptive function to sustain optimism during a fatal illness (Druss & Douglas, 1988) or unhealthy if it prompts failure to comply with needed treatment (Strauss, Spitzer, & Muskin, 1990). Although compliance with treatment may not be a virtue per se, it is clinical common sense that openness (lack of pathological denial) and cooperation (acknowledgment of need for treatment) are helpful. McClure (1978) demonstrated better outcomes in psychiatric patients with less denial.

Denial takes many forms, from refusal to acknowledge facts (e.g., alcoholism), to minimization ("It's not so bad"), to misattribution ("My cough is due to a cold, not to smoking"), to refusal to accept needed treatment based on unrealistic beliefs. Although denial may promote worsening of an illness, it is not equivalent to factitious behavior or malingering, because no desire exists to assume the sick role or to achieve external gains. To the contrary, the denying patient is often affirming the wish to be in good health. Shelp and Perl (1985) reviewed the concept of denial and differentiated among denial of illness, its symptoms, its significance, and its emotional consequences. Other forms of denial are less personalized and more likely to have negative impact upon others. Denial of causation or personal responsibility for illness or injury underlies many episodes of litigation (e.g., blaming a tobacco producer for nicotine addiction). Denial of the randomness of events leads to the search for another to blame, and denial of concurrent illness may lead to inadequate treatment (e.g., refusal of a patient with insomnia to acknowledge alcohol abuse). Awareness of the subtleties of denial takes on an added dimension of importance in criminal and civil litigation, in which motives for behavior affect not only the individual but also those influenced by the individual's distorted perceptions.

CLINICAL APPLICATIONS

DSM–IV criteria for disorders characterized by deception are minimalistic and difficult to apply. Requirements for determining internal versus external motivation create a false dichotomy between factitious disorders and malingering. In clinical practice, overlap often occurs between these conditions, and a given patient may simultaneously demonstrate features of both disorders or shift from one to the other over time. In this regard, DSM-IV criteria do not specify psychological or behavioral parameters that (1) suggest voluntariness of symptom production or (2) assist in differentiating pursuit of the sick role (a psychological conclusion) from pursuit of financial or other external goals (a behavioral conclusion). In the case of malingering, DSM-IV unfairly emphasizes its occurrence with antisocial personalities and in forensic contexts. This chapter has reviewed clinical and research findings that suggest overlap between factitious disorders and malingering; appropriate assessment and management of deceptive behavior requires delineation of conscious and unconscious motivations and goals.

This final section contains models for clinical consideration in the diagnosis of factitious disorders and malingering. Threshold models define minimal clinical information necessary to include a disorder in the differential diagnosis of a medical or psychiatric condition. Clinical decision models describe information necessary, in light of current research and practice, to diagnose FD or malingering. These models are meant to augment DSM-IV criteria and are derived from distillations of diverse behavioral, psychological, and clinical phenomena. The validities of FD and malingering as separate diagnostic entities (see Rogers, Bagby, & Vincent, 1994) remain to be determined. Other clinical conditions described in this chapter (FD by proxy, compensation neurosis, FMS, CFS, pain complaints, and denial) are not provided with distinct threshold or decision models; these conditions may be subsumed under the category of FD or malingering, if appropriate in an individual case, but also overlap considerably with legitimate disorders.

The threshold model for factitious disorder (see Table 2.1) suggests that FD should be considered when evidence of voluntary symptom production, pursuit of the sick role, or other behavior known to be associated with factitious presentations is present. Criteria for voluntariness are similar to those of Pope, Jonas, and Jones (1982). These encompass (1) admission of voluntary control, (2) fantastic or nonstereotypical symptoms, and (3) unconventional symptom response to treatment or environmental occurrences. Bizarre or absurd symptomatology implies deviation even from the normal spectrum of psychotic phenomena. Atypical symptoms may indicate a pathological pursuit of the patient role. The sick role in this context is defined to include pathological degrees of behavioral regression, inordinate comfort in the role of patient (beyond normal secondary gain common to any illness), and active attempts to maintain or promote morbidity. Capacity for significant regression is usually indicative of character pathology, but also can occur under psychological stress in otherwise healthy individuals. Because factitious behavior can occur in the absence of personality disorder (Nadelson, 1979), the presence of character pathology is not necessary to raise the question of FD.

The clinical decision model for establishing FD (see Table 2.2) requires specific findings consistent with voluntariness, implying patient knowledge of disease fabrication but not necessarily his or her motives for simulation. In malingering, the patient is aware of both actions and motivations. Factitious patients commonly admit to disease production when confronted and may acknowledge personal psychological distress or recent conflicts. In other cases, even a patient that maintains denial about self-propagated illness may be judged to have acted voluntarily if disease presentation is incompatible with known mechanisms (e.g., a "seizure" that ends after suggestion, or

TABLE 2.4. Clinical Decision Model for Establishing Malingering

All of the following must be present:

A. Psychological or physical symptoms are clearly under voluntary control as manifested by one or more indicators:
   1. Patient acknowledgment of voluntary control or deceit
   2. Gross symptom production that is inconsistent with physiological or anatomical mechanisms
   3. Direct observation of illness production
   4. Discovery of paraphernalia or substances explaining the production of physical symptoms
   5. Confirmatory laboratory testing (e.g., absence of EEG abnormalities during an observed "seizure")

B. Clinical certainty that illness production occurs in response to:
   1. Pursuit of financial gain, shelter, or drugs, or
   2. Avoidance of work, military duty, prosecution, or legal consequences

C. Another disorder, if present, cannot explain current symptoms.

D. Evidence of desire to assume the sick role, if present, cannot explain the totality of current symptoms.

---

gering is suspected when a strong temporal association between environmental contingencies and illness complaints is established. Whereas factitious symptoms frequently emerge in the context of psychologically meaningful conflicts with family members or occupational roles, malingering is most frequently considered when the sudden onset of inexplicable symptoms is coupled with attainment of external goals (e.g., drugs, shelter, or financial compensation) or with avoidance of subjectively noxious activities (e.g., prosecution or military duty). In contrast to factitious patients who encourage or insist upon physical tests and interventions, malingerers typically abandon their complaints or refuse to cooperate when invasive medical procedures are considered.

The clinical decision model for malingering (see Table 2.4) requires the specific finding of voluntariness in combination with clinical certainty about the pursuit or avoidance of environmental factors. Symptom inconsistency includes phenomena such as (1) bizarre or absurd symptoms not expected even in psychotic disorders, (2) endorsement of improbable symptoms, (3) rapidly fluctuating complaints, or (4) physical complaints without anatomical or neurological basis. Laboratory testing may confirm self-induced illness, for example, when a retrieved "kidney stone" proves to be a grain of sand, or when drug screening reveals anticoagulant after complaints of excessive bleeding. Clinical certainty about intentionality implies patient acknowledgment of external motivations, corroboration by external sources, or strong evidence that symptoms began in conscious response to external events.

Malingering is not to be considered a mental disorder per se, but rather a response style best conceptualized in social psychological terms (Travin & Protter, 1984) or by decision theory (Rogers et al., 1990). In recognition of the nonexclusivity of clinical phenomena and in light of the possibility of multiple levels of intentionality and voluntariness, these models permit factitious disorders and malingering to overlap with each other and with legitimate psychiatric and medical conditions.

3

Malingered Psychosis

PHILLIP J. RESNICK, M.D.

Though this be madness, yet there is method in it.
—SHAKESPEARE, *Hamlet* (Act 2, Scene 2)

The prevalence of feigned psychosis is unknown. In a British study, Hay (1983) found five cases in 12,000 admissions, four of whom subsequently developed schizophrenia. In a series of 320 murderers, three persons feigned psychosis and remained "sane" after a 10-year follow-up (Hay, 1983). Rogers (1986) established a 4.5% prevalence of definite malingering and 20% of moderate deception or suspected malingering in defendants evaluated for insanity but judged sane. The accuracy of such prevalence estimates is highly questionable, since individuals who successfully fake psychosis are never included in the statistics. The apparent low prevalence in nonforensic populations is probably due to a combination of the failure of clinicians to suspect malingering and, before the recent trend toward deinstitutionalization, the apparent lack of motive to malinger psychosis.

Malingered psychosis is likely to increase. Since the deinstitutionalization movement, thousands of chronically mentally ill, who might prefer the stable environment of a psychiatric hospital, are living in marginal circumstances in the community (Travin & Protter, 1984). With drastic curtailments of social programming and the concomitant improvement in hospital conditions, persons with mental disorders may grossly exaggerate their symptoms to seek treatment and shelter (Rogers, 1992).

Schizophrenic patients have shown the ability to present themselves as sick or healthy, depending on their goals (Braginsky & Braginsky, 1967). Society's disenfranchised individuals are starting to shift coping strategies from somatic to psychiatric symptoms. This shift can be attributed to lack of exactitude in psychiatric diagnosis, widespread availability of mental health services, and the decreased stigma associated with mental illness (Bishop & Holt, 1980).

DEFINING THE PROBLEM

Many authors, especially when psychoanalytic influence was at its peak, labeled malingering a form of mental disease. Eissler (1951, p. 252), for example, stated, "It can be rightly claimed that malingering is always a sign of a disease often more severe than a neurotic disorder because it concerns an arrest of development at an early phase." Others have pointed out the irrationality of this view. For example, Wertham (1949, p. 49) noted, "There is a strange, entirely unfounded superstition even among psychiatrists that if a man simulates insanity there must be something mentally wrong with him in the first place. As if a sane man would not grasp at any straw if his life were endangered by the electric chair." In summary, the pathogenic model of malingering (Rogers, 1990a) has been largely supplanted by the *Diagnostic and Statistical Manual of Mental Disorders* (DSM) model.

Malingering is listed in the DSM-IV (American Psychiatric Association, 1994a), as a condition not attributable to a mental disorder. It is defined as the intentional production of false or grossly exaggerated physical or psychological symptoms, motivated by external incentives. Thus, malingering requires a deceitful state of mind. No other syndrome is so easy to define but so difficult to diagnose.

Persons usually malinger psychosis for one of the following five purposes: First, criminals may seek to (1) avoid punishment by feigning incompetency to stand trial, insanity at the time of the crime, or (2) mitigate sentencing. Second, malingerers may seek to avoid conscription into the military, undesirable military assignments, or combat. Third, malingerers may fake psychosis to seek financial gain from social security disability, veterans' benefits, workers' compensation, or damages for alleged psychological injury. Fourth, prisoners may malinger to obtain drugs or to be transferred to a psychiatric hospital with the goals of "easy time" or greater opportunity for escape. Finally, malingerers may seek a psychiatric admission to secure social services, obtain free room and board (known colloquially as "three hots and a cot"), or dodge criminal charges.

Some people malinger to extricate themselves from intolerable situations. One 14-year-old girl feigned hallucinations in order to be hospitalized to escape from sexual harassment by her mother's new boyfriend (Greenfield, 1987). She had previously observed an older cousin's psychotic episode. When her family situation became intolerably chaotic, she was institutionalized on the basis of a feigned psychosis. She volunteered that she had faked her psychotic symptoms only when the hospital staff told her they would be placing her infant with the baby's father.

Several authors (Berney, 1973; Bustamante & Ford, 1977; Folks & Freeman, 1985; Hay, 1983; Pope, Jonas, & Jones, 1982; Schneck, 1970) have suggested that pseudo-malingering should be carefully considered before making a diagnosis of malingering. In Leonid Andreyev's (1902) novel *The Dilemma,* a physician committed murder with a premeditated plan to appear insane (Schneck, 1970). When the physician later began to have true hallucinations, he realized that his psychosis was genuine. The idea of someone becoming mentally ill after malingering insanity in order to escape criminal responsibility has great popular appeal in mystery stories, but is extremely rare in forensic practice. Schneck (1970) suggested that pseudo-malingering is a mechanism to maintain an intact self-image, which would be marred by acknowledging psychological problems that cannot be mastered consciously.

Pope et al. (1982) found nine patients with factitious psychosis out of 219 consecutive admissions to their research unit. Their 7-year follow-up study revealed that all nine patients met DSM-III criteria for either borderline or histrionic personality. None of the patients went on to develop a typical psychotic disorder, but eight of the nine displayed intermittent or continuous factitious symptoms. The researchers concluded that factitious psychotic symptoms were a grave prognostic sign. In this regard, Hay (1983) suggested that the simulation of schizophrenia is usually the prodromal phase of genuine illness. An alternative explanation is that four of Hay's malingerers improved with practice to the point that they were undetectable.

RESEARCH ON MALINGERED PSYCHOSIS

The research literature on detecting malingered psychosis is sparse. No research has examined the ability of clinicians to accurately detect malingered psychosis in their actual practice. Although simulation studies of feigned schizophrenia have demonstrated the effectiveness of standardized measures, such as the Structured Interview of Reported Symptoms (SIRS; Rogers, Bagby, & Dickens, 1992) and the Minnesota Multiphasic Personality Inventory (MMPI; Rogers, Bagby, & Chakraborty, 1993), research has not addressed the effectiveness of clinical assessment alone without the use of these specialized methods. In Rosenhan's (1973) classic study, eight pseudopatients were admitted to psychiatric hospitals, all alleging that they heard very atypical voices. Although they stopped reporting symptoms once they were admitted, all were diagnosed as schizophrenic and remained hospitalized from 9 to 52 days. Although Rosenhan concluded that mental health professionals were unable to distinguish normality from mental illness, the study has been used to illustrate the inability of clinicians to identify feigned psychosis.

Anderson, Trethowan, and Kenna (1959) asked 18 normal participants to simulate mental disease in order to study the phenomenon of *vorbeirden* (the approximate answer), a central symptom in the Ganser syndrome. The simulators were compared with normal controls and two comparison groups: (1) patients with organic dementia and (2) patients with pseudodementia (primary diagnosis of hysteria with conversion symptoms). The simulators most often chose to feign depression or paranoid disorders; their efforts did not closely resemble well-defined mental disorders. Two feigned mental retardation by maintaining an air of obtuseness, vagueness, and poverty of content. The simulators experienced difficulty, however, in suppressing correct answers to questions, because they felt the "pull of reality" throughout the interviews. Fatigue or difficulty sustaining the response style apparently caused simulators to become increasingly normal during prolonged interviews.

Many simulators in the Anderson et al. (1959) study gave approximate answers to questions because they believed they should not give the right answers. To avoid the impression of spuriousness, they gave nearly correct answers in contrast to the more discrepant errors by patients with actual dementia. Moreover, for the patients with organic dementia, perseveration was a striking feature; it was evident when progressing from one question to the next and during serial-seven subtractions. In contrast, no significant perseveration was apparent in malingerers. The authors concluded that the presence of perseveration is a strong indication of true, rather than simulated, organic impairment. The fact that approximate or "near miss" answers were given by simulators lends indirect support to the theory that the Ganser syndrome is a form of malingering.

Sherman, Trief, and Strafkin (1975) instructed a group of Veterans Administration (VA) day-care psychiatric patients to present themselves as (1) severely mentally ill and (2) mentally healthy. Understandably, the more disturbed patients manifested greater differences between the two interviews. In their "malingered" interviews, patients claimed that they had recurrent senseless thoughts, hallucinated noises, and suicidal ideas. The primary differences were in their statements about symptoms, rather than in their interview presentation or behavior.

Cornell and Hawk (1989) studied the characteristics of 39 criminal defendants diagnosed as malingering psychotic symptoms by experienced forensic psychologists at the Michigan Center for Forensic Psychiatry. The prevalence of malingering was 8.0% for 314 consecutive evaluations. They acknowledged that the core problem in developing diagnostic criteria for malingering was the lack of an unequivocal "gold standard." Persons classified with malingering were more likely to endorse bogus symptoms, express suicidal ideation, and report visual hallucinations, absurd replies, and memory problems. Furthermore, their symptoms did not cluster into known diagnostic entities.

Powell (1991) compared 40 mental health facility employees instructed to malinger schizophrenic symptoms with 40 schizophrenic inpatients. The principal measure was the Mini-Mental Status Examination (MMSE; Folstein, Folstein, & McHugh, 1975), a measure of basic cognitive functioning used to screen patients for dementia. Simulators were significantly more likely than schizophrenics to give one or more approximate answers on the MMSE. Simulators also reported a higher occurrence of visual hallucinations, particularly with a dramatic and atypical content (e.g., not ordinary human beings). Simulators often called attention to their delusions.

Hallucinations

Persons alleging atypical hallucinations should be questioned in great detail (see Table 3.1) regarding their content, vividness, and occurrence alone or with others (Seigel & West, 1975). Before discussing the impact of hallucinations on current functioning, patients should be asked to describe past hallucinations and their responses to them. Detailed knowledge about actual hallucinations is the clinician's greatest asset in recognizing simulated hallucinations.

Both psychotic patients (Goodwin, Alderson, & Rosenthal, 1971) and patients with acute schizophrenia (Mott, Small, & Andersen, 1965; Small, Small, & Andersen, 1966) show a high rate of hallucinations (approximately 76%) in at least one sensory modality. These hallucinations are typically associated (88%) with delusions (Lewinsohn,

TABLE 3.1. Topics of Clinical Inquiry for Suspected Auditory Hallucinations

Topic	Representative content
Vocal characteristics	Content, clarity, tone, affect, loudness, duration frequency, continuous–intermittent
Source of the hallucination	Inside/outside head, outside location (e.g., above or behind)
Characteristics of the hallucination	Gender, multiple voices, speaking in second or third person, commands
Relationship to the hallucination	Familiar/unfamiliar voice, known/unknown person
Belief/response to hallucinations	Insight into their unreality, ability to disregard them, belief that others can hear them, affective response to them, converses with them, obeys them
Associated characteristics	Other hallucinations (e.g., visual or tactile), delusions, other psychotic symptoms

1970). The reported prevalence of auditory hallucinations in persons with schizophrenia ranges from 66% (Mott et al., 1965; Small et al., 1966) to 88% (Duncan, 1995). Almost two-thirds (64%) of hallucinating patients described hallucinations in more than one modality (Small et al., 1966). The prevalence of visual hallucinations in psychotics is estimated at 24% (Mott et al., 1965) to 30% (Small et al., 1966). As a comparison, Duncan (1995) found that 54.4% of patients with active schizophrenia had visual hallucinations during the most recent acute episode. Olfactory and tactile hallucinations are less common; Duncan found prevalence rates for the current episode of 22.2% and 12.2%, respectively. Persons with late-onset schizophrenia (i.e., onset after age 45 years) are more likely to have visual, tactile, and olfactory hallucinations (Pearlson et al., 1989).

The Goodwin et al. (1971) study of 116 hallucinating patients provides very helpful data for determining authenticity of reported hallucinations. They found that hallucinations were experienced as generally intermittent, rather than continuous. When patients with schizophrenia were asked if their hallucinations could have been due to their imaginations, 56% responded affirmatively. In contrast, Duncan (1995) examined 90 patients with schizophrenia in the active phase of their disorders. She found that 68.8% were totally convinced of the reality of their hallucinations, while an additional 23.3% were generally convinced of their veridicality.

Auditory Hallucinations

Goodwin et al. (1971) described the following characteristics of auditory hallucinations. Both male and female voices were heard by 75% of the patients. The hallucinatory messages were usually clear; they were vague only 7% of the time. The content of hallucinations was accusatory about one-third of the time. Hallucinations contained both familiar and unfamiliar voices in 88% of the cases.

neurological diseases (Cummings & Miller, 1987). Visual hallucinations in persons over age 60 are most frequently associated with eye pathology, particularly cataracts (Beck & Harris, 1994). In persons denying any drug histories, the presence of colors, shapes, and unformed visual phenomena should arouse the clinician's index of suspicion for eye pathology or malingering.

Dramatic, atypical visual hallucinations should arouse suspicions of malingering (Powell, 1991). One defendant, charged with attempted murder, claimed visual hallucinations of a "green laughing devil, a god with a flowing white beard, a black Doberman pinscher dog, and President Ronald Reagan." When he was asked detailed questions, he frequently replied, "I don't know." He subsequently admitted to malingering.

Hallucinations in Specific Disorders

Alcoholic hallucinosis, following the cessation or reduction of alcohol intake, often involves quite vivid hallucinations. Although the hallucinations are usually voices, the likelihood of noise, music, or unintelligible voices is greater than in schizophrenia. The patient's actions are practically never the result of command hallucinations, but are motivated by the desire to avoid disgrace, injury, or other consequences of the voices' threats (American Psychiatric Association, 1980). Patients discuss alcohol-induced hallucinations more easily than those with schizophrenic hallucinations (Alpert & Silvers, 1970). The disorder may last several weeks or months.

Mott et al. (1965) found that persons hospitalized for alcoholism had an 84% prevalence of hallucinations (75% auditory and 70% visual). Auditory hallucinations, almost invariably perceived as originating from outside the patient's head, may address the individual directly but more commonly discuss him or her in the third person. The major themes in alcoholic hallucinations were spirituality, persecution, and instructions concerning the management of everyday affairs. A majority of alcoholics thought the hallucinations were real at the time but later recognized their unreality; 40% never accepted them as real. Alcoholics are typically frightened by their hallucinations. In contrast, patients with schizophrenia are often frightened in the early stages of their illness but become more comfortable as the illness progresses (Mott et al., 1965).

The modality of hallucinations and nature of delusions can help in the differential diagnosis of psychotic symptoms. Organic hallucinosis can be distinguished from schizophrenia based on an increased prevalence of prominent visual hallucinations and fewer symptoms of thought disorder, bizarre behavior, negative symptoms, and rapid speech (Cornelius et al., 1991). Tactile hallucinations (parasitosis or cocaine bugs) are frequently seen in cocaine psychoses and involve sensations of cutaneous or subcutaneous irritation (Ellinwood, 1972). Unlike paranoid schizophrenics, persons with cocaine psychoses do not report delusions of identity, grandiosity, or beliefs that their families were impostors (i.e., Capgras syndrome; see Mitchell & Vierkant, 1991).

In dissociative identity disorders (DID; formerly multiple personality disorders), auditory hallucinations are perceived more often as originating from within than outside of the head (R. P. Kluft, personal communication, July 10, 1984). The message may be faint or inaudible, due to barriers among the alter personalities. The content is often related to dynamics among the personalities. Although patients usually resist command hallucinations at first, they may give in due to exhaustion or fear of threats made by alter personalities. Somatic hallucinations are common in multiple personality disorders (R. P. Kluft, personal communication, July 10, 1984).

Delusions

In order to recognize a malingered delusion, clinicians must understand the phenomenology of genuine delusions. Delusions are not merely false beliefs that cannot be changed by logic. A delusion is a false statement made in an inappropriate context and most important, with inappropriate justification. Normal people can give reasons, engage in a dialogue, and consider the possibilities of doubt. Persons with true delusions typically cannot provide adequate reasons for their statements.

Delusions vary in content, theme, degree of certainty, degree of systemization and structure, and degree of relevance to the person's life in general. The more intelligent the person, the more elaborate his or her delusional system is likely to be. According to Spitzer (1992), most delusions involve the following general themes: disease (somatic delusions), grandiosity, jealousy, love (erotomania), persecution, religion, being poisoned, and being possessed. Delusions of nihilism, poverty, sin, and guilt are commonly seen in depression. Less frequent delusions include being the descendant of a royal family, having insects under the skin, and a belief that significant others have been replaced by doubles (i.e., Capgras syndrome; Spitzer, 1992). Technical delusions refer to the influence of such items as telephone, telepathy, and hypnosis. By technical means, signals and voices can be transmitted to patients. Delusions of technical content occur seven times more often in men than in women (Kraus, 1994).

Persecutory delusions are more likely to be acted on than any other type of delusion (Wessely et al., 1993). Persons with delusions involving perceived threat or control override may pose a risk to act aggressively. These delusions (see Link & Stueve, 1994; Swanson, Borum, Swartz, & Monahan, 1996) include (1) delusions of control, (2) thought insertion, (3) persecutory delusions, and (4) delusions of being followed. Delusions not associated with increased aggression include (1) being dead, dissolved, or not existing; (2) having one's thoughts broadcasted; and (3) having thoughts that are being taken by external force.

Malingerers may claim the sudden onset of a delusion. In reality, systematized delusions usually take weeks to develop. As true delusions are relinquished, they first become somewhat less relevant to the everyday life of the patient, but the patient still adheres to the delusional belief. A decrease in preoccupation with delusions may be the first change seen with adequate treatment. In a later stage, the patient might admit to the possibility of error, but only as a possibility. Only much later will the patient concede that the ideas were delusions (Sachs, Carpenter, & Strauss, 1974). Thus, malingering should be suspected if someone claims a delusion suddenly appeared or disappeared.

In assessing the genuineness of delusions, clinicians should consider their content and associated behavior. The content of feigned delusions is generally persecutory,

were asked to endorse symptoms for major depression, 97% correctly identified sufficient symptoms to support the diagnosis (Lees–Haley & Dunn, 1994). An individual
feigning depression may go so far as to refuse food for months and even endure tube
feedings. He or she may assume the face of melancholia with some fidelity when in
the presence of observers, concentrating on dysphoric expressions of the mouth, but
the forehead is likely to remain unwrinkled. Genuinely depressed persons often show
a furrowed brow (East, 1927). Although the bodily movements may be purposely
slowed, the malingerer does not usually adopt the forward inclination of the head and
trunk, and flexed hips and knees prominent in major depression with melancholia.
Persons with depression often are more dysphoric in the morning than other times,
but malingerers are unlikely to know this (East, 1927). Persons feigning depression do
not show the physical signs of slowing, such as constipation and slow speech. Suicide
attempts are sometimes made, but as a rule they are clumsy and obviously planned for
their effect on others (Singer & Krohn, 1924).

Feigned mania is difficult to successfully maintain for an extended time, because
it is onerous to feign symptoms of a true disorder: flight of ideas, incoherent speech,
motor excitement, and insomnia (East, 1927). A premature ending of manic symptoms due to fatigue suggests malingering (Davidson, 1952). Moreover, a "therapeutic" response to mood stabilizers or antipsychotics sometimes occurs too quickly in
malingerers to be considered a true response to medication.

An individual suspected of malingering DID should not be approached with a
suspicious or dubious attitude, since skepticism may precipitate frantic efforts to prove
the disorder in genuine cases. Both malingerers and patients with true DID occasionally appear very phony when trying to defend themselves. Extended interviews may
be useful, because unforced dissociation most often occurs between 2.5 and 4 hours.
Malingerers are challenged to appear consistent in the assumed personality's voice,
movement characteristics, and memory (R. P. Kluft, personal communication, 1984).
However, videotaped interviews from the Bianchi case (see Chapter 14) demonstrate
that convincing presentations are possible.

CLINICAL ASSESSMENT OF MALINGERED PSYCHOSES

The clinician should be particularly careful to ask suspected malingerers open-ended
questions and let them tell the complete story with few interruptions. Details can be
clarified later with specific questions. When asking specific questions, care must be
taken to avoid leading or revealing questions. For example, inquiries about hallucinations should be carefully phrased to avoid giving clues about the nature of true hallucinations. The clinician should try to ascertain whether the patient has ever had the
opportunity to observe psychosis (e.g., during prior employment). Clinicians may feel
irritation at being deceived, but any expression of irritation or incredulity is likely to
make the malingerer more defensive (Miller & Cartlidge, 1972).

Clinicians may modify their interview style when patients are suspected of malingered psychosis. The interview may be prolonged, since fatigue diminishes the

malingerer's ability to maintain a counterfeit account (Anderson et al., 1959). Rapid firing of questions increases the likelihood of getting contradictory replies from malingerers but may also create confusion and inconsistencies among mentally disordered persons. The clinician may obtain additional data by asking specific questions. For example, leading questions that emphasize a very different psychosis than the malingerer is trying to portray (Ossipov, 1944) may yield a very incongruous presentation. In addition, questions about improbable symptoms (e.g., upside-down vision) may be asked to test whether the suspected malingerer will endorse them. Another device is to mention, within earshot of the suspected malingerer, some easily imitated symptom that is not present. The sudden appearance of the symptom suggests malingering. With each of these strategies, the clinician must differentiate between acquiescent and malingering response sets. In the case of malingering, the person typically does not assent to issues in general, but only obvious symptoms of psychopathology.

Inpatient assessment should be considered in difficult cases of suspected malingering. Feigned psychotic symptoms are difficult to maintain continuously for 24 hours a day. Ray (1871, p. 455) suggested that suspected malingerers be secretly observed so that "in their moments of forgetfulness or fancied security they may be seen laying aside their false colors and suddenly assuming their natural manners." Sometimes a malingerer will only assume a slumped posture and expression of detachment when clinicians approach, resuming a more natural, laughing appearance on their departure (MacDonald, 1976b). Hospitalized psychiatric patients are quite skillful at detecting a malingerer (Rosenhan, 1973); they have been known to tell malingerers to stop play-acting (Ritson & Forrest, 1970).

After completing a detailed examination, the clinician may decide to confront a patient with his or her suspicions. The suspected malingerer should be given every opportunity to save face. Once feigning is denied, a malingerer may have difficulty admitting it later. Clinicians should opt for more general and less accusatory statements, such as "You haven't told me the whole truth," rather than, "You have been lying to me" (Inbau & Reid, 1967).

CLINICAL INDICATORS OF MALINGERED PSYCHOSES

All malingerers are actors that portray their psychoses as they understand them (Ossipov, 1944). Malingerers often overact their part (Wachspress, Berenberg, & Jacobson, 1953) with the mistaken belief that the more bizarrely they behave, the more psychotic they will appear. As observed by Jones and Llewellyn (1917, p. 80), the malingerer "sees less than the blind, he hears less than the deaf, and he is more lame than the paralyzed. Determined that his insanity shall not lack multiple and obvious signs, he, so to speak, crowds the canvas, piles symptom upon symptom and so outstrips madness itself, attaining to a but clumsy caricature of his assumed role."

Malingerers are eager to call attention to their illnesses in contrast to patients with schizophrenia, who are often reluctant to discuss their symptoms (Ritson & Forest, 1970). Some malingerers limit their symptoms to repeatedly volunteering one or two blatant "delusions" (MacDonald, 1976a). One malingerer stated that he was an "insane lunatic" when he killed his parents at the behest of hallucinations that "told me to kill in my demented state." Malingerers may try to take control of the interview and behave in an intimidating, bizarre manner. The clinician should avoid the temptation to terminate such an interview prematurely. Malingerers sometimes accuse clinicians of regarding them as faking. Although accusations are common among genuinely psychotic persons, they rarely involve matters of feigning.

Malingerers have less success imitating the form than the content of schizophrenic thinking (Sherman et al., 1975). With respect to form, derailment, neologisms, and incoherence are rarely simulated. If the malingerer is asked to repeat an idea, he or she may do it exactly, whereas the genuine patient with schizophrenia will often become tangential. Malingerers rarely perseverate; the presence of perseveration suggests actual organic damage or an extremely well-prepared malingerer. Some malingerers give an incongruous presentation, such as the appearance of profound concentration before they give absurd answers (MacDonald, 1976a). Common errors made by malingerers include the beliefs that (1) nothing must be remembered correctly, and (2) the more inconsistent and absurd the discourse, the better the deception. Malingerers give a greater number of evasive answers than schizophrenic patients (Powell, 1991); they may repeat questions or answer questions slowly to give themselves more time to make up answers.

Malingerers are unlikely to show negative symptoms or the subtle signs of residual schizophrenia, such as impaired relatedness, blunted affect, digressive speech, or peculiar thinking. On the contrary, they find positive symptoms (e.g., hallucinations and delusions) easier to feign because of their obvious association with bizarreness. Malingerers' symptoms may fit no known diagnostic entity but represent symptoms from various psychoses. Malingering should always be considered before invoking a diagnosis of atypical psychosis.

Malingerers are likely to give more approximate answers to questions, such as "53 weeks in the year," than patients with schizophrenia (Bash & Alpert, 1980; Powell, 1991). Malingerers are more likely to answer "I don't know" to questions about psychotic symptoms, such as hallucinations and delusions. This response may simply mean that they do not know what to say when questioned about the details of their purported delusions and hallucinations. When asked whether a purported voice was male or female, one malingerer replied, "It was *probably* a man's voice."

Malingerers are likely to have nonpsychotic alternative motives for their behavior, such as killing to settle a grievance or seeking shelter in a VA hospital. A crime without apparent motive (e.g., random killing of a stranger) may lend credence to the presence of true mental disease. Genuine psychotic explanations for rape, robbery, or check forging are unusual. Malingerers are likely to have contradictions in their accounts of their illness, although some inconsistencies are noted in genuine patients. The contradictions may be evident within the malingerer's account, or between the malingerer's version and other evidence. When malingerers are caught in contradictions, they may either sulk or laugh with embarrassment (MacDonald, 1976a).

Persons who have true schizophrenia may malinger additional symptoms to escape criminal responsibility or seek an increase in disability compensation. These cases are the most difficult to assess accurately. Clinicians have a lower index of suspicion for malingering because of a documented history of psychiatric hospitalizations and the presence of true, albeit, residual schizophrenic symptoms. These malingerers are able to draw upon their prior experience with hallucinations and their observations of other psychotic persons. They know what questions to expect from clinicians. If they spend time in a forensic psychiatric hospital, they are likely to learn how to modify their account to fit closely the criteria for an insanity defense. Clinicians should not think of malingering and psychosis from an "either/or" perspective (Rogers, Sewell, & Goldstein, 1994).

The following case illustrates clinical indicators of feigned psychosis. Mr. B., a 36-year-old man charged with murder, was referred by his attorney for evaluation of an insanity defense. The defendant had his brother killed because he believed that his brother had betrayed the family and violated his honor. Because Mr. B. had no psychiatric history or unusual beliefs about his brother, I informed his attorney that I found no basis for an insanity defense. When the defense attorney referred him for a second psychiatric evaluation, Mr. B. said, "Some people who wanted to see the family business destroyed replaced my brother with a robot." He claimed that he believed "springs and wires would pop out" when his brother was destroyed. A second defense psychiatrist accepted the robot story at face value.

The defendant told the same robot story to a third psychiatrist. Interviews with family members revealed that the defendant had never told them his brother had been replaced by a robot. Upon arrest, the defendant denied any involvement in his brother's killing and made no mention of the robot story. The third psychiatrist concluded that the defendant was malingering. First, no past history of mental illness, unusual beliefs, or hallucinations were found. Second, the "robot belief" was an atypical delusion. Third, anger and greed were rational, alternative motives for the killing. Fourth, during the time the defendant supposedly believed his brother was a robot, the defendant carried out his usual duties. Fifth, the defendant had marked contradictions in his story. Sixth, his symptoms fit no known diagnostic entity. Seventh, his behavior was not consistent with his alleged delusions. Finally, he did not show any residual signs of schizophrenia. Indeed, the defendant's alleged "delusion" was unsupported by any corroborating evidence.

CLINICAL APPLICATIONS

Malingering should be considered in the assessment of all patients. Otherwise, small separate clues of feigning may be overlooked that would lead to a more detailed investigation. In cases of suspected psychosis, the clinician should inquire about the characteristics of hallucinations and delusions, since the typical characteristics of these symptoms have been well researched. Table 3.2 provides a threshold model for the identification of suspicious hallucinations and delusions.

A major focus of this book is the development of clinical decision models for establishment of malingering. Table 3.3 offers such a model for malingered psychosis.

TABLE 3.2. Threshold Model for the Assessment of Hallucinations and Delusions

Malingering should be suspected if any combination of the following are observed:

A. Hallucinations	Continuous rather than intermittent hallucinations
	Vague or inaudible hallucinations
	Hallucinations not associated with delusions
	Stilted language reported in hallucinations
	Inability to state strategies to diminish voices
	Self-report that all command hallucinations were obeyed
	Visual hallucinations in black and white
B. Delusions	Abrupt onset or termination
	Eagerness to call attention to delusions
	Conduct markedly inconsistent with delusions
	Bizarre content without disordered thinking

Before a conclusion is made with respect to malingering, the clinician must first establish that the patient's motivation is both conscious and serves some recognizable goal, other than maintaining a sick role. To make a firm determination of malingered psychosis, the clinician must observe (1) variability in presentation, (2) improbable or incongruous clinical presentation, and (3) corroborative data.

FORENSIC APPLICATIONS

Concern about defendants faking mental illness to avoid criminal responsibility dates back to at least the 10th century (Brittain, 1966; Collinson, 1812; Resnick, 1984). By the 1880s, many Americans considered physicians a generally impious, mercenary, and

TABLE 3.3. Clinical Decision Model for the Assessment of Malingered Psychosis

Meets the following criteria:

A. Understandable motive to malinger

B. Marked variability of presentation as observed in at least one of the following:
   1. Marked discrepancies in interview and noninterview behavior
   2. Gross inconsistencies in reported psychotic symptoms
   3. Blatant contradictions between reported prior episodes and documented psychiatric history

C. Improbable psychiatric symptoms as evidenced by one or more of the following:
   1. Reporting elaborate psychotic symptoms that lack common paranoid, grandiose, or religious themes
   2. Sudden emergence of purported psychotic symptoms to explain antisocial behavior
   3. Atypical hallucinations or delusions (see Table 3.2)

D. Confirmation of malingered psychosis by either:
   1. Admission of malingering following confrontation
   2. Presence of strong corroborative information, such as psychometric data or past history of malingering

cynical lot who might participate in the "insanity dodge" (Rosenberg, 1968). After the Hinckley insanity verdict, columnist Carl Rowan (1982, p. 10B) stated, "It is about time we faced the truth that the 'insanity' defense is mostly last gasp legal maneuvering, often hoaxes, in cases where a person obviously has done something terrible."

Clinical Assessment of Criminal Defendants

Prior to evaluating a defendant, the clinician should be equipped with as much background information as possible, such as police reports, witness statements, autopsy findings, past psychiatric records, statements of the defendant, and observations of correctional staff. Consultations with family members or witnesses are often helpful prior to the clinician's examination.

Clinicians should attempt to learn some relevant information about the defendant or crime that the defendant does not know the clinician knows. One reliable method of assessing veracity is to compare the defendant's self-report with known past information. For example, did the defendant honestly report past criminal activity as recorded on the "rap sheet"? How does the defendant's version of the offense compare to the victim's account (see Hall, 1982)?

Defendants, who may subsequently raise psychiatric issues, should be seen as soon as possible after the crime. If a clinician is employed by a defense attorney, an evaluation of the defendant within a few days of the crime is possible; requests from judges and prosecutors are usually not received until one or more months later. Early evaluation reduces the likelihood that the defendant will have been coached about the legal criteria for insanity by other prisoners or the occasional unethical attorney. The more quickly defendants are seen, the less time they have to plan deception, work out a consistent story, and rehearse their lies. Normal memory distortions are also less likely to occur. Moreover, prompt examination enhances the clinician's credibility in court.

The defendant must be told at the outset about the purpose of the forensic examination and the lack of confidentiality. More complete information will be elicited if the clinician behaves in an empathic, supportive manner. Stone (1984) pointed out the ethical dilemma engendered by having clinicians "seduce" defendants into revealing information that may hurt their cases. Despite proper warnings, the illusions of the "doctor as healer" and "mental health professional as helper" commonly persist. The full exploration of this ethical issue is beyond the scope of the current chapter, but good rapport is helpful in gathering material to detect malingering.

When defendants present with a mixed picture of schizophrenia and antisocial features, countertransference feelings may cause mental health professionals to focus on the antisocial traits and ignore the underlying illness (Travin & Protter, 1984). The clinician must guard against any temptation either to accept a psychotic version at face value or to dismiss it out of hand. Any facile attempt to dichotomize patients into mad (assuming the credibility of the psychotic symptoms) or bad (assuming the fabrication of psychotic symptoms) may undermine the forensic assessment.

The farsighted clinician will record in detail the defendant's early account of the crime, even if he or she is not competent to stand trial. Once defendants are placed in

TABLE 3.5. Threshold Model for the Assessment of Psychosis in Defendants Pleading Insanity

Malingering should be suspected if any of the following are present:

1. A nonpsychotic, alternative, rational motive for the crime
2. Suspicious hallucinations or delusions (see Table 3.2)
3. Current crime fits an established pattern of prior criminal conduct
4. Absence of any active or subtle signs of psychosis during the evaluation
5. Report of a sudden, irresistible impulse
6. Presence of a partner in the crime
7. Double denial of responsibility (e.g., disavowal of the crime plus attributing any criminal behavior to psychosis)
8. Far-fetched story of psychosis to explain the crime
9. Alleged intellectual deficit coupled with alleged psychosis

Michigan Center for Forensic Psychiatry, 98% of successful insanity acquittees acted alone (Thompson et al., 1992). Another indicator is that a malingerer may tell a far-fetched story to fit the facts of a crime into a mental disorder. One male malingerer with prior armed robbery convictions claimed that he robbed only upon the commands of auditory hallucinations and gave away all the stolen money to homeless people.

If a defendant is alleging an irresistible impulse, malingering should carefully be considered. The clinician should be skeptical of an impulse that is not a frequent symptom, associated with a recognized mental disorder. If a defendant denies any previous knowledge of an impulse, lying should be suspected. Experience has shown that it is extremely improbable for an obsessional impulse to be uncontrollable at its first appearance (East, 1927).

Malingering defendants tend to present themselves as blameless within the context of their feigned illness. This tendency was demonstrated by a male defendant who pled insanity to a charge of stabbing an 1-year-old boy 60 times with an ice pick. He reported that for 1 week prior to the homicide, he was constantly pursued by an "indistinct, human-like, black blob." He stated that he was sexually excited and intended to force homosexual acts on the victim but abandoned his plan when the boy began to cry. When he started to leave, 10 faces in the bushes began chanting, "Kill him, kill him, kill him." He yelled, "No," and repeatedly struck out at the faces with an ice pick. The next thing he knew, "the victim was covered with blood." The autopsy showed a cluster of stab wounds in the victim's head and neck—inconsistent with the defendant's claim that he struck out randomly at multiple faces in the bushes. His version showed a double avoidance of responsibility: (1) The faces told him to kill, and (2) he claimed to have attacked the faces, not the victim. After his conviction, he confessed to six unsolved, sadistic homosexual killings.

Defensiveness after Psychotic Crimes

Injustice may also result from the simulation of sanity (see Table 3.6). Denial of psychiatric symptoms is not uncommon in persons who have committed crimes (Dia-

TABLE 3.6. Variations of Defensiveness regarding Psychosis during the Crime

A. Faking wellness during the act itself (e.g., extremely rare)
B. Retrospective falsification to appear "well during the crime" in the evaluation
   1. Still psychotic at the evaluation
   2. No longer psychotic at the evaluation

mond, 1956). Defendants often find the stigma and consequences of mental illness far worse than those of criminality (Halleck, 1975). In addition, persons who are genuinely mentally ill may feel more in control of their illness by alleging that earlier symptoms were malingered. Defendants may retrospectively distort accounts of their acts due to amnesia, an acute confusional state, or a current desire simply to have past behavior make sense. Collateral information from witnesses is therefore invaluable in assessing defendants that deny any mental disorders.

Since the burden of raising the issue of insanity lies with the defendant, a grave miscarriage of justice may occur if the defendant chooses not to reveal his or her mental disorder. This denial places a heavy responsibility on clinicians to uncover any evidence of psychological impairment. Diamond (1986) elicited relevant psychopathology through the use of hypnosis in the trial of Sirhan Sirhan for the assassination of Robert Kennedy. Even after listening to the tape recording of the hypnotic interviews, Sirhan alleged that the tapes were faked and denied any significant psychological impairment. Sirhan may have been mentally disordered, but he was convicted of first-degree murder with the recommendation of the death penalty.

CONCLUSION

The detection of malingered psychosis is often a challenging task. The decision that an individual is malingering is ascertained by assembling all of the clues from a thorough evaluation of a patient's past and current functioning with corroboration from clinical records and other persons. Although the identification of a person with malingered psychosis may be viewed by some clinicians as a distasteful chore, the accurate assessment of response styles is essential in treating patients and critical in conducting forensic assessments. Indeed, clinicians bear considerable responsibility in differentiating true from feigned psychosis.

4

Sociopathy, Malingering, and Defensiveness

CHARLES R. CLARK, Ph.D.

The relationship between sociopathy and malingering is an issue about which much frequently is assumed and little is understood. Certainly, the recommendation of the fourth edition of the *Diagnostic and Statistical Manual of Mental Disorders* (DSM-IV; American Psychiatric Association, 1994, p. 683) that malingering should be strongly suspected in the presence of an antisocial personality disorder is intuitively appealing. Sociopaths, designated as individuals with antisocial personality disorder (APD) in the formal nosology of DSM-IV, are widely understood to be prone to present with "false or grossly exaggerated physical or psychological symptoms" that constitute malingering (American Psychiatric Association, 1994, p. 683).

An older view of malingering, designated as the "pathogenic model" (Rogers, 1990a, 1990b), treats malingering as a symptom of genuine mental illness acting as a defense against the disintegration of the very condition that is feigned (e.g., Eissler, 1951). This view finds little current support among forensic psychologists (see Rogers, Sewell, & Goldstein, 1994). For purposes of comparison, Meloy's (1988) psychodynamic view of psychopathy identified an "endogenous" need for deception by the psychopath; this compulsive deception serves to stave off disorganizing symptoms and thus protect the narcissistically grandiose self. But although Meloy posits deceptions as an essential project/need of the psychopath, he considers malingering to be different. Meloy views malingering as exogenous in the sense that it is attuned to the situation and aimed as securing a clear advantage for the person (e.g., avoidance of punishment for criminal acts). Similarly, Travin and Protter (1984) assert that deception occurs on a continuum of conscious awareness and motivation; nonetheless, they view malingering as a "fully conscious sociopathic adaptation" (p. 191).

The perception of malingering as pathognomonic of sociopathy or some other disorder is questioned by research presented in this chapter. First, although the actual prevalence of malingering among sociopaths is difficult to determine with certainty, most sociopaths are not malingerers. When sociopaths do malinger, their feigning is likely to be controlled by exigencies and opportunities rather than simply reflect the sociopath's character traits. Second, a view of malingering as quintessentially socio-pathic suggests that sociopaths are better feigners than others. Contrary to expecta-tions, research does not support the belief that sociopathy conveys any advantage to undetected malingering; rather, it suggests that some sociopaths may be more obvious and easily detectable in their attempts to feign mental disorder than are nonsociopaths. Third, as exemplified by the "adaptational model" (Rogers, 1990a, 1990b), malinger-ing may be expected in a wide variety of individuals in different situations and is not behavior limited to sociopaths.

The groundless assumption that there is any necessary connection between malin-gering and sociopathy is likely to derail the clinical identification of feigned presenta-tions. If the absence of demonstrable sociopathy is permitted to weigh against a judg-ment that a person is malingering, false negatives (i.e., missed cases of malingering) will be an inevitable result. Conversely, the assumption that sociopaths are likely to be ma-lingerers may lead to false positives (i.e., bona fide patients misclassified as malingerers). Even in cases in which sociopaths are likely to malinger, the establishment of conduct disorder and psychopathy rely heavily on history and self-report (e.g., undetected crimes). Since both sociopathy and malingering are socially undesirable, concealment is typically bidirectional: Sociopaths attempt to conceal their malingering, and malingerers strive to conceal their sociopathy. In summary, use of clinical intuition and the DSM-IV recom-mendation (American Psychiatric Association, 1994) to suspect that an individual with APD may be malingering will lead to unwarranted suspicion in many cases, and even to the dismissal of genuine presentations as merely feigned.

SOCIOPATHY AND DECEPTION

The terminology used to describe sociopathy has undergone considerable change, as has the conceptualization of the condition itself (Guttmacher & Weihofen, 1952; Hare, 1970; Mednick & Christiansen, 1977; Meloy, 1988; Salekin, Rogers, & Sewell, in press). Malingering per se has not played a central role in the conceptualization of sociopathy, although deception more broadly considered is logically related to this disorder, a condition marked by an absence of moral constraints. In common with its predecessors DSM-III and DSM-III-R (American Psychiatric Association, 1980, 1987), the current DSM-IV (American Psychiatric Association, 1994) presents the view that lying or untruthfulness is an important component of APD, even though it need not always be present. Commonsensically, dishonesty and deception would appear to be necessary features of antisocial behavior (e.g., the possession of stolen property needs to be "explained"). In clinical assessment, however, mental health professionals may not be able to catch the sociopath in demonstrable lies.

Comprehensive discussions of sociopathy have always included lying as an essen-tial component of this disorder. Cleckley (1976) and Doren (1987) have emphasized the sociopath's propensity for untruthfulness and insincerity; they viewed such decep-tion as one of the defining characteristics of the disorder. Yochelson and Samenow (1976), in their extensive examination of the "criminal personality," similarly viewed this tendency to lie as central to the condition. Yochelson and Samenow pointed out that lying is a fundamental pattern of life for sociopathic individuals and an essential precondition of their criminality; to choose a criminal lifestyle necessitates lying for purposes of self-preservation. When apprehended, sociopaths understandably may create any deception that will reduce their own personal accountability. Their "stories" are crafted to conform to whatever the sociopaths deem will fit society's view of what constitutes a good excuse or an understandable motive. Meloy (1988) also considers deception to be "ubiquitous within the psychopathic process." Leaving aside denial, which he views as an unconscious maneuver, Meloy contends that the psychopath's characteristic deception may not only be "exogenous," marked by an intent to obtain some advantage or improvement in circumstances, but may also be "endogenous," involving compulsive deception that is not situationally determined or aimed at any discernible external gain (pp. 120–121).

Research on the prevalence of deception in antisocial and conduct-disordered youth provides empirical support to the less rigorous clinical reports on adults (e.g., Cleckley, 1976; Yochelson & Samenow, 1976, 1977). Stouthamer-Loeber (1986), in her review of seven studies, found that conduct-disordered youth displayed chronic or problem lying at a prevalence rate of 49%, or 2.5 times greater than normal samples. This finding of frequent deception in this population is consistent across sources of clinical data, including parental observations (e.g., Patterson, 1982), teacher ratings (e.g., Behar, 1977; Ferguson, Partyka, & Lester, 1974), and for inpatient and outpa-tient settings (e.g., Rutter, Tizard, & Whitmore, 1970; Stewart & DeBlois, 1984).

The perceived link between sociopathy and deception was further supported by an investigation of the clinical features of sociopaths by Rogers, Dion, and Lynett (1992), who assessed the degree to which various symptoms or attributes of sociopathy are viewed as prototypical of APD. Community participants ($n = 250$) rated attributes drawn from DSM-II, DSM-III, and DSM-III-R APD symptoms (American Psychiatric Association, 1968, 1980, 1987) and from Hare's Psychopathy Checklist (PCL; Hare, 1991) for the extent to which they were prototypical of APD. A principal components analysis iden-tified four factors accounting for 46.6% of the variance. The largest factor (15.1% of the variance) involved 14 features denoting impaired relationships and deception; these behavioral criteria included characteristics such as "no regard for the truth," "pathologi-cal lying," and "conning, lack of sincerity." High prototypicality ratings (i.e., > 5 on a 7-point scale) included "no regard for the truth" ($M = 5.40$) and "pathological lying" ($M = 5.37$), two attributes from the DSM-III and DSM-III-R criteria for APD.

Rogers, Duncan, Lynett, and Sewell (1994) pursued this strategy of prototypical analysis with an expanded list of attributes; additional items were drawn from the then-forthcoming DSM-IV. In this investigation, prototypicality ratings were assigned by 331 forensic psychiatrists, again using a 7-point scale of perceived importance of at-tributes to the concept of APD. In contrast to Rogers, Dion, et al. (1992), they found the factor "tapping deception" along with "callousness and lack of personal empathy" (manipulation and lack of guilt) was the second largest factor and accounted for 11.1% of the variance. Consistent with the previous study, high prototypicality ratings were found for "no regard for the truth" ($M = 6.33$) and "pathological lying" ($M = 5.66$), together with "deceitful and manipulative" ($M = 5.72$). Initial prototypical data (Rogers, Salekin, Sewell, & Zaparnik, 1996) suggested that even inmates accept dishonesty and deception as a hallmark of APD.

Deception, both broadly considered and more narrowly delineated, is an important and necessary component of sociopathy. To date, however, no investigations have explored the relationship of malingering as a specific form of deception to the concept of sociopathy. Despite this lack of demonstrated relationship, the DSM has continued to assert that APD signals an increased likelihood of malingering. The actual prevalence of malingering among sociopaths is an empirical question, still in search of large-scale studies.

MALINGERING BY SOCIOPATHS

Lees-Haley (1991) pointed out that no generally acknowledged epidemiological data exist on the base rate or prevalence of malingering. Information on the approximate incidence of malingering among various diagnostic groups is not available, nor is basic demographic data regarding the occurrence of malingering, beyond the observations of Yudofsky (1985), that malingering seems to occur more often in men from young adulthood to middle age. From the author's observations, relatively few individuals who warrant the diagnosis of APD attempt to malinger, despite a potential adversarial setting and a pending trial. Malingering appears to be a relatively unpopular option among sociopaths, even though the obverse may be true (i.e., a disproportionate number of malingerers may also be sociopaths).

Research data on the incidence of malingering among sociopaths is scattered at best. Cornell and Hawk (1989) reviewed examination records of 314 consecutive pretrial forensic evaluations for competency and/or criminal responsibility in Michigan. Defendants were rated as diagnosable as psychotic, malingered psychosis, or nonpsychotic. Although cases were not classified by sociopathy, all were criminal defendants and charged mostly with felonies. Of the 314 participants, only 25 or 8% were rated as very likely to be malingering or definitely malingering. The typical malingerer in this study had a 10th-grade education, was charged with a crime against person, and had been charged several times in the past, most often with crimes against persons. Cornell and Hawk did not discuss sociopathy but suggested that the relative seriousness of the malingerers' charges was what had motivated them to feign psychosis.

Rogers, Gillis, Dickens, and Bagby (1991) evaluated the discriminant and concurrent validity of the Structured Interview of Reported Symptoms (SIRS; Rogers, 1992) using samples in their second study that included forensic evaluation patients of the Metropolitan Forensic Service, Toronto's Clarke Institute of Psychiatry. A group of 25 individuals were identified as probable or definite malingerers from a group of approximately 700 patients, yielding a prevalence rate of 3.5%.

Another, more general estimate for the prevalence of malingering was derived from a larger study by Rogers, Sewell, and Goldstein (1994). With 320 very experienced forensic clinicians (> 95% psychologists), Rogers and his colleagues asked for estimates of malingering from past forensic and nonforensic evaluations. The respondents indicated that on average 15.7% of forensic and 7.4% of nonforensic patients had malingered during their evaluations. No other broadly based estimates are available on large samples of clinicians.

A number of studies provide malingering prevalence estimates based not on overall clinician judgment or classification, but on psychometric indices of malingering, symptom overreporting, or exaggeration. As such, these studies cannot be considered to provide base rates of malingering but rather suggest estimates for signs of malingering and overreporting.

Grossman and Wasyliw (1988) examined what they perceived to be a stereotype, namely, that the majority of criminal defendants pleading insanity fabricate or exaggerate symptoms. They employed MMPI (Hathaway & McKinley, 1967) measures of exaggeration, including the Obvious–Subtle subscales (Wiener, 1948), F-K (Gough, 1950), and the Dissimulation Scale (Ds; Gough, 1957). Pretrial defendants (n = 49) being evaluated for fitness or competency to stand trial and/or sanity or criminal responsibility were compared to individuals in outpatient or inpatient treatment (n = 52). Grossman and Wasyliw hypothesized that pretrial participants, for whom a feigned mental illness might be advantageous, would produce the greater evidence of exaggeration than patients in treatment. Although this was found, only a minority of either group evidenced any exaggeration. The majority of pretrial participants (55.1%) showed no evidence of feigning/exaggeration on any of the three indices.

Wasyliw, Grossman, Haywood, and Cavanaugh (1988) augmented the Grossman and Wasyliw study with additional competency and insanity evaluations. Not surprisingly, the results corresponded with the companion study. A comparison of White and minority participants found no significant differences on the malingering indices.

Heilbrun, Bennett, White, and Kelly (1990) examined an MMPI-based model of malingering and deception, which incorporated 11 criteria operationalized as either MMPI or psychiatric evaluation data. The criteria were applied to 159 Florida forensic patients who had been adjudicated incompetent to stand trial or legally insane. Classification of patients yielded the following estimates of response styles: malingering (9%), defensiveness (21%), or irrelevant responding (16%). Interestingly, some of the incompetent patients might be motivated to malinger, but the incentive for patients already adjudicated as insane would likely be toward defensiveness (i.e., release from a maximum security hospital) rather than malingering.

The apparent infrequency of malingering by sociopaths is further supported by Hinojosa's (1993) investigation of two MMPI-2 indices of malingering on different criterion groups, including simulators instructed to malinger, patients with mental disorders, criminal defendants diagnosed as sociopathic, and insanity acquitees. The MMPI-2 validity indices did not discriminate simulators from those with genuine disorders. Moreover, and contrary to expectations, the sociopathic group did not produce malingered profiles but instead appeared to minimize and deny psychopathology.

An important caveat regarding the assumption of malingering by individuals scoring high on psychological testing is afforded by studies that reveal the frequency with which suspicious-looking test results reflect no clear deception. Wetzler and Marlowe (1990) examined the prevalence of "faking bad" by psychiatric inpatients on three measures: the MMPI, the MMPI-2, and the Millon Clinical Multiaxial Inventory–II (MCMI-II; Millon, 1987). Fake-bad profiles were produced by 9% of the MMPI records and 17% of the MCMI-II profiles. However, the authors pointed out that the most likely explanation for these findings was that the indices reflected not intentional dissimulation, but severity of psychopathology and distress. The forensic utility of the MMPI/MMPI-2 in the assessment of malingering and psychopathy was reviewed by Rogers and McKee (1995). They concluded that many forensic evaluations produced deviant MMPI-2 records, including elevations on Scales F and 4, regardless of whether the evaluation was pretrial, presentence, or postconviction. Rogers and McKee also examined MMPI-2 data on a large South Carolina sample of defendants evaluated for insanity (i.e., based on clinical judgment: 149 defendants sane and not mentally ill, 50 sane and mentally ill, 25 meeting the guilty but mentally ill standard, and 21 meeting the insanity standard). All groups, including those with genuine disorders, had moderate to marked elevations on Scale F (i.e., M's from 74 to 89) and three of the four groups on Scale 4 (i.e., M's from 62 to 72). However, few of the defendants were deemed to be malingering based on a comprehensive psychological evaluation. Rogers and McKee recommended caution with respect to the use of MMPI-2 measures of faking, keeping in mind the frequency with which criminal defendants, in general, often have elevated scores, whether or not they have been feigning a mental disorder (p. 120).

Specific measures have been devised to assess response styles, particularly malingering (see Chapter 17). Employing the SIRS, Gothard, Viglione, Meloy, and Sherman (1995) examined feigned incompetency to stand trial with 115 male defendants and correctional inmates. Of the 60 competency evaluations, evidence of feigning was found in 7 cases (prevalence rate of 11.7%). Overall, the SIRS proved highly effective at distinguishing suspected malingerers and simulators from genuine patients. Both defendants and inmates in this study were correctly classified, with one exception, in regard to feigning. Previous research (Rogers, Gillis, Dickens, & Bagby, 1989; Rogers, Gillis, & Bagby, 1990) has demonstrated that correctional participants under standard instructions do not appear to produce feigned SIRS results. Although these studies do not address the prevalence of malingering among sociopaths as such, the correctional status of an individual (i.e., indirect evidence of sociopathy) does not lead to any greater likelihood of malingering, at least as assessed by the SIRS.

In summary, the prevalence of malingering by sociopathic individuals or incarcerated offenders is relatively low, perhaps occurring at a rate of as little as 3–8% (Rogers, 1990a). This conclusion is in stark contrast to what might be expected from the view of sociopaths as characteristically deceptive in general. Research has not addressed in any clear fashion another important question, whether sociopaths malinger at a greater frequency than other diagnostic groups. On a commonsensical basis, sociopaths would have more occasions to dissimulate, especially when apprehended for criminal offenses.

This dissimulation might take the form of either malingering (e.g., insanity plea) or defensiveness (e.g., denial of paraphilias) in order to escape the consequences of their criminal actions. Sociopaths may frequently dissimulate within the context of criminal prosecution or incarceration; however, their incentives are similar to those of other individuals facing criminal charges. Indeed, this is the point made by Rogers (1990a, 1990b) in delineating his adaptational model of malingering, which would not posit a greater frequency of malingering by sociopaths once situational variables are controlled.

DIFFERENCES IN MALINGERED PRESENTATIONS ASSOCIATED WITH SOCIOPATHY

Plausibly, a portion of socialized sociopaths may be more adept than others at lying and dissimulation. Particularly within the forensic context, the successful assessment of malingering requires considerable understanding of sociopathy. A naive clinician might be convinced that a sociopath's outpouring of tears and sobbing are necessarily evidence of genuine distress. Although dysphoria is common among sociopaths (Reid, 1978), a dramatic presentation of remorse or depression should raise the index of suspicion regarding the validity of a sociopath's self-report. It should be borne in mind, however, that not all colorful and extravagant presentations of malingering are made by sociopathic individuals, and that many sociopaths may provide lackluster performances.

Research is not available on the question of whether true stylistic differences exist in how sociopaths and others malinger. Resnick (1984) has held that criminal defendants most often feign auditory hallucinations. In addition, he has observed that criminal defendants often fabricate symptoms that appear superficially organic but are incongruous in their presentation. As observed in cases presented later in this chapter, criminal defendants who malinger often present with gross confusion, disorientation, and attention–concentration deficits of such extremes as to strain credibility.

Since deception is the *métier* of the sociopath, an important question is whether sociopaths are more convincing when they malinger. Meloy and Gacano (1995) asserted that psychopathic malingerers (1) often perform worse than true patients with organic impairment on neuropsychological assessment, and (2) manifest impairment on psychological measures that are not commensurate with behavioral observations. Their position supports a view that sociopaths may be inferior malingerers and more easily detectable than are nonsociopaths. Validity data regarding the SIRS at least support a conclusion that individuals with correctional backgrounds can be routinely detected in their malingering, because sociopaths may be more obvious in their feigning. For instance, Rogers et al. (1990), in a discriminant analysis of SIRS data, found that 17.5% of community participants foiled the detection strategy, but no correctional simulators were able to remain undetected on the SIRS when feigning mental illness.

Rogers, Kropp, Bagby, and Dickens (1992) examined the ability of correctional inmates to feign specific disorders, including posttraumatic stress disorder, schizophrenia, and mood disorders. The SIRS was effective in identifying malingering for these disorders. Based on DSM–III–R criteria, 16 of the 45 inmates (35.6%) were categorized as antisocial. An examination of SIRS scale scores for APD and non-APD subgroups failed to indicate any significant differences; this finding lends indirect support to Rogers's assertion (Rogers, 1990a, 1990b) that APD is a questionable indicator of malingering (p. 646) and demonstrates the lack of any special ability among sociopaths for malingering.

Kropp (1994; see also Rogers, 1995, p. 250) focused directly on the ability of sociopaths to malinger mental illness. A correctional sample was assessed by the SIRS with 50 inmates randomly assigned to an experimental condition (i.e., fake mental illness) and 50 to a control condition (i.e., respond honestly). Participants were rated for psychopathy with the Psychopathy Checklist—Clinical Version (PCL-CV; Hare, Cox, & Hart, 1989), permitting their classification as high or low in psychopathy. Kropp expected that the more psychopathic individuals would be more effective malingerers on SIRS, and that they would report more symptoms in the honest condition. Although slight trends were found consistent with these hypotheses, psychopaths as a group were not significantly better effective than nonpsychopaths at simulating mental illness.

In retrospect, the failure to identify any advantage enjoyed by psychopathic malingerers is not surprising, given the mastery of specific pathological presentations that is required to evade detection on a structured interview method, such as SIRS. But a study by Lindblad (1994) demonstrated that even persons involved in the criminal justice system who also had a history of treatment for major mental illness were no more effective than others at feigning mental disorders. The failure of persons despite antisocial backgrounds or prior episodes of mental disorders is a further argument in favor of an adaptational rather than pathognomonic explanation of malingering.

Cogburn (1993) failed to support the more general hypothesis that sociopaths are more effective liars. She used DSM-III-R APD criteria (American Psychiatric Association, 1987), the PCL-R (Hare, 1991), and the Socialization (*So*) Scale for the California Psychological Inventory (CPI; Gough, 1987b) to rate psychopathy in both undergraduate and criminal participants. Participants then took part in videotaped structured interviews in which they tried to persuade an interviewer about their participation in two socially desirable and two socially undesirable acts. In reality, only one of each condition (i.e., socially desirable and socially undesirable) had occurred. Naive judges viewed the videotapes and rated the participants' believability. Higher PCL-R ratings were associated with lower ratings of perceived truthfulness, regardless of whether the participants were being deceptive. The Cogburn study raises the tantalizing notion that sociopaths may appear more dishonest, thus obscuring the relationship between lying with APD.

In summary, empirical differences between the malingering by sociopaths and by others have yet to be demonstrated. In the final analysis, the form of malingering, its frequency, and its duration may have far more to do with the context of the malingering than with personality variables. Diagnostic differences among malingerers may be relevant to malingering only to the extent that they indirectly give rise to a perceived need to malinger. For example, sociopaths may be at greater risk of committing and being apprehended for criminal offenses; some sociopaths may elect to malinger following arrest, although perhaps not in any greater proportion than nonsociopaths in the same adversarial circumstances. A systematic exploration of how malingering by sociopaths varies according to context would further our clinical applications to this diagnostic group.

SOCIOPATHY IN MALINGERERS

The previous section addressed whether sociopaths have a greater tendency than others to malinger, and whether their malingering differed in effectiveness or presentation. A different perspective on the same issue is the prevalence of sociopathy among those who do malinger. Sierles (1984) reported an attempt to assess, among other diagnostic variables, the frequency of sociopathy among malingerers. Although his research sample (i.e., Veterans Administration inpatients and medical student controls) and design (i.e., data based only on a self-report survey) permit little generalizability, Sierles found a significant correlation between self-report indices of malingering and sociopathy. Similarly, Guttmacher and Weihofen (1952) reported research conducted during World War II that revealed that a large percentage of servicemen assessed as malingerers were also diagnosed as psychopaths. In the absence of any methodological description, it is unknown whether the diagnosis of psychopathy was not often invoked simply as an explanation for the observed malingering. In a review of the malingering literature, Yudofsky (1985) noted that the most commonly associated feature of malingering in the adult population is APD.

Gacano, Meloy, Sheppard, Speth, and Roske (1995) reported a strong association between psychopathy and malingering in hospitalized insanity acquitees. A malingering group was composed of 18 insanity acquitees who met the following criteria: an absence of Axis I diagnoses or symptoms, no prescription for psychotropic medication, and a documented history of self-reported exaggeration or malingering of mental disorder in order to gain access to hospitalization. They were compared to a group of 18 successive admissions to the forensic hospital on the basis of DSM-III-R diagnoses of APD and psychopathy ratings from the PCL-R (Hare, 1991). In terms of diagnosis, none of the malingerers were seen as psychotic, and 100% of the malingering group received the APD diagnosis.[1] The malingering group had average PCL-R total scores of 34.9, exceeding the cutoff of 30 for psychopathy, and considerably higher than the comparison group ($M = 19.4$). It is difficult to interpret these findings because of the small number of participants and the inclusion criteria that biased the sampling, and, most important, because the malingering participants appear to have been handpicked by psychologists that were asked to recall insanity acquittees who met the inclusion criteria. It is possible, if not likely, that the cases identified by this nonsystematic method were unusually vivid and not representative of malingerers in this setting. With the exclusion of psychotic cases, sociopathy and its associated features may well add to the vividness of particular cases.

In the final analysis, some degree of association between malingering and sociopathy is likely, although the research literature does not afford an accurate estimation.

However, deception clearly does occur beyond sociopathy. Ford, King, and Hollender (1988) related lying to developmental issues, cognitive dysfunction (e.g., Korsakoff's psychosis), factors in the social environment, and emotional trauma. In terms of pathology, they described deception as common to several Axis II conditions, including histrionic, narcissistic, and borderline personality disorders, as well as APD.

A correlational analysis of test results produced by personal injury plaintiffs reported by Grillo, Brown, Hilsabeck, Price, and Lees-Haley (1994) suggests that although malingering or exaggeration of symptomatic complaints may be expected among those with antisocial personality features, it is not confined to that group. Correlations of personality disorder scale scores on MCMI-II (Millon, 1987) were performed on validity and response-set indicators on the MMPI-2 (Butcher, Dahlstrom, Graham, Tellegen, & Kaemmer, 1989). Unfortunately, MCMI-II modifier and correction indices (e.g., Disclosure, Desirability, and Debasement), which assess response styles and distortion, were not included in the data analysis. Without taking into account the degree to which the MCMI-IIs were affected by response sets, we cannot evaluate the authors' conclusion, consistent with the view of Ford et al. (1988), that elevations on MMPI-2 validity scales may reflect both Axis II (i.e., borderline, antisocial, avoidant, passive–aggressive, and schizotypal personality disorders) and Axis I disorders. According to the authors, their results indicate the need for caution in interpreting MMPI-2 validity scale elevations as indicating malingering; they also present alternative explanations, including genuine psychopathology or unconscious exaggeration.[2] In taking this position, they appear to suggest a pathogenic model of malingering with evidence of exaggeration or feigning serving as a possible indicator of some underlying and genuine psychopathology.

The degree of sociopathy associated with malingering has been difficult to address, partly due to the difficulties with accurately identifying actual malingerers. An equal, if not greater, problem in this regard is the diffuse and ambiguous nature of sociopathy, psychopathy, and APD as related constructs. This lack of clarity is observed clearly in relatively poor interrater reliabilities (Rogers, Dion, & Lynett, 1992; Rogers, Duncan, Lynett, & Sewell, 1994). In particular, clinicians appear unable to ascertain reliably APD variables associated with deception, even with the use of structured interviews. Pfohl, Coryell, Zimmerman, and Stangl (1986), despite moderate agreement on the APD diagnosis, found poor reliability for the item "disregard for the truth" (kappa = .35). Hasin and Grant (1987) found generally poor agreement between two diagnostic measures of APD (i.e., Schedule of Affective Disorders and Schizophrenia, Lifetime version; Endicott & Spitzer, 1978; and the Diagnostic Interview Schedule; Robins, Helzer, Croughan, & Ratcliff, 1981). For the item, persistent lying, the kappa of .04 approximated chance agreement.

Responding to evidence of its apparently low predictive value, Cunnien (1988) advised that the presence of APD not be considered grounds to suspect malingering (p. 33). Given the absence of any strong demonstrable connection between sociopathy and malingering, Rogers (1990a, 1990b) criticized its use in DSM diagnosis. In an archival study of forensic evaluations, he reviewed the records of 24 malingerers, and 113 randomly selected, nonmalingering forensic patients, based on the DSM-III-R indices for malingering. The use of two or more indices (suggested by DSM-III-R and DSM-IV) produced an unacceptably high false-positive rate of 79.9%. Rogers concluded, "At least within a forensic sample, the presence of APD (antisocial personality disorder) does not appear to signal a greater likelihood of malingering" (1990a, p. 326).

Rogers stressed the importance of disentangling (1) explanatory models of malingering that address the question of *why* people malinger, from (2) detection models that address the question of *who* is malingering. In terms of an explanatory model, Rogers (1990a, 1990b) proposed an adaptational paradigm. An adaptational model assumes no link between sociopathy and malingering, nor, like the older pathogenic model, does it assume that malingered symptoms mask or emerge from genuine psychopathology. Instead, the adaptational model postulates that (1) malingerers perceive the assessment or treatment as adversarial, and (2) using a cost–benefit analysis, they consider malingering the best means of achieving their goals. Such an approach, Rogers pointed out (1990b), would not entail any criminological assumptions regarding either the antisocial pasts or medicolegal contexts in the evaluation of malingerers.

To investigate the importance of the criminological and other explanatory models of malingering, Rogers, Sewell, and Goldstein (1994) conducted a prototypical analysis of malingering with 320 forensic experts. An extensive list of attributes for malingering was compiled, representing the criminological, pathogenic, and adaptational models. A principal components analysis with varimax rotation yielded a three-factor solution, accounting for 41.2% of the variance, that corresponded closely to the three explanatory models. Of particular interest to this chapter, criminological attributes that stress lack of accountability, superficiality, and adult criminal behavior were seen as being at least moderately important to malingering. In comparing models, Rogers and his colleagues concluded that the adaptational model was the highest in prototypicality followed by criminological model. A nonsignificant trend was observed among those experts who endorsed criminological attributes to report a higher proportion of malingerers as having APD than did other respondents.

In summary, the scant evidence from far-flung sources does not support either the assumption that malingering is particularly common among sociopaths, or that malingering is an extension of sociopathic behavior. Certainly within forensic and other legal contexts, clinicians are likely to scrutinize the validity of reported symptomatology, thereby leading to an increased detection rate.[3] In addition, sociopaths are more likely than others to be arrested and be faced with highly adversarial circumstances in which some form of dissimulation might be anticipated; however, this heuristic observation is *irrelevant* to clinical assessment. The *relevant* issue is whether sociopaths feign more than others who face the same highly adversarial circumstances. Although many defendants are diagnosed with APD, the diagnostic issue is whether the proportion of malingering is significantly larger for APD versus non-APD referrals. This crucial issue has not been adequately addressed, although the preliminary data Rogers (1990a) would suggest that APD is not a useful discriminator.

The connection between sociopaths and malingering has yet to be demonstrated. Despite this, I believe that antisocial persons presenting for forensic evaluations may shape their malingering to meet their specific needs and objectives within this context. To exemplify this point, I include four case vignettes that demonstrate how the legal context may influence the style of presentation.

CASE VIGNETTES

Available research indicates that the clinical characteristics of malingering sociopaths are variable at best. In line with Rogers's (1990a, 1990b) conceptualization of malingering as behavior that is not necessarily reflective of personality, I expect that the form of malingering and its associated features will reflect the exigencies of the malingerer's situation rather than the malingerer's sociopathy or other traits. Although the following vignettes involve sociopathic individuals, their forensic context is likely to influence the nature of their malingering.

A Safe-Sex Serial Killer

Defendant T.D. admitted to a series of 11 murder–rape offenses after he was identified by a woman he had raped but who subsequently escaped. A male prostitute himself, T.D. lured female prostitutes into abandoned buildings, often on the pretext of giving them money or crack cocaine in exchange for sex. After they undressed, he would overpower them physically and strangle them during the rape; as they died, he came to climax. T.D. would use condoms, some of which were later found with the badly decomposed corpses, which he had hidden beneath debris in the buildings where the rapes and killings occurred.

According to T.D.'s account at the time of the first interview, the offenses would occur after he had sex with a man, when a "being" named Tony (also his own street name) would appear and begin to ridicule him, degrading him for his homosexual conduct and telling him that he was not a real man. Feeling "guilty," and urged by Tony, T.D. said that he would seek sexual relations with a woman to prove his manhood. While he was engaged in sex, Tony reportedly would tell him that women were no good, and that he should kill the women to prove his manhood. In response to these apparent hallucinations, he reported killing. Only as the women were struggling, he said, would he be able to achieve an erection and climax. After each woman had died, Tony directed him to hide the body, and he would comply. Two female beings also appeared to him. One being, whose name he recalled only with difficulty ("Omeya, Ozala, Ollola—Mayolla, that's it!"), was a mother-type figure in a flower-patterned dress with gray hair and a featureless face, who would comfort him and allow him to rest his head on her leg. A second being, identified as "Mary," was colorless except for completely black eyes without irises. T.D. claimed that Mary would also comfort him and had encouraged him to confess to the murders and rapes once he was arrested. When I asked for the last names of the "beings" he had described, he responded that Tony's name was Smith, Mayolla's name was Brown, and Mary's name was Jane. While in jail, he stated, he was also visited in his cell by a man he recalled as a caseworker from a juvenile facility, who had sexually abused him. T.D. also reported an "imaginary friend," a dog named Pete.

T.D. told me that he had related his involvement with Tony, Mayolla, and Mary, and the roles they played in the offenses, to the police at the time of his arrest and to a psychiatrist in a previous examination. A review of the records found no such report to the police, and Tony, although mentioned in his discussion with the psychiatrist, was presented in a very different role. Interestingly, he did report an imaginary dog to the psychiatrist, but this dog's name was Ralph, rather than Pete. Moreover, in a second interview some weeks after my first, the defendant was unable to replicate his description of the hallucinatory figures who had supposedly abetted his offenses. He reported, for instance, that Mary had brown eyes and indicated that neither Mayolla nor Mary had last names. When asked about the apparent discrepancies, T.D. blamed them on the police and the psychiatrist.

A Man with Lots of Out-of-Body Experiences

E.T. acknowledged that he killed his supervisor with a shotgun in a busy urban intersection on a Saturday afternoon. E.T. had just learned from his supervisor that he was terminated. After E.T. had put his belongings in the trunk of his car, he pulled out a loaded shotgun, pursued his supervisor, and fatally shot him four times. E.T. described a dissociative experience of watching himself remove the shotgun, stating that shotgun "went off" once. Describing dissociative amnesia in addition to this out-of-body experience, he claimed that he could remember nothing else until he was ordered by a police officer to drop the gun. In an earlier report to another examiner, the defendant had recalled a second shot before he lost conscious awareness.

E.T. also reported "hallucinations" in jail, including visions of men coming into his cell at night and beating him, as well as demons and gargoyles threatening him. He readily endorsed unlikely symptoms asked by the clinician. He agreed that he experienced burning and tingling sensations in his head as he was hearing voices ("like my body would go numb sometimes"). When asked if he saw objects change color, he responded, "When you asked me that, it was as if things started to shake, and colors were coming in front of my face." Asked about unusual smell and taste sensations, he responded that he did have "cotton mouth," adding, "My stomach just got upset—I want to give you the right answers, but I don't know in my mind what is the right answer." He also indicated that he saw a haze over the city buildings outside the windows of the examination room, "like they're radioactive," and when I commented that I did not see what he was referring to, he stated, "When you turned around, it went away." E.T. also reported that he was having "out-of-body" experiences in the jail, as he had also had at the time of the slaying, and he told me that his ex-wife would be able to verify that he had many such experiences. He helpfully provided her telephone number and encouraged me to call her. His wife told me that E.T. had advised that I would be calling, and had coached her about out-of-body experiences. However, she disclosed no knowledge of E.T. having these experiences.

An Air Pirate with Amnesia

Z.K. had been arrested for a series of armed robberies when he escaped from police custody. While being transported to another jail by police helicopter in leg irons and other restraints, he seized an officer's gun and hijacked the aircraft. He directed the pilot to land the helicopter in a part of the city not far from where his family lived. Upon landing, he escaped into the neighborhood. Subsequent witness accounts indicated that he had visited the home of friends, met with his mother, changed clothes, and left in a taxi. Z.K. was finally arrested several months later in a city about 700 miles away. He had apparently been apprehended for assault, and had secured admission to a psychiatric hospital. While in the hospital, his original case was featured on a nationally broadcast television show concerning wanted criminals, which led to his extradition.

At the time of the first interview, Z.K. indicated that he had no memory of the helicopter hijacking and escape, or of his travels in the intervening months prior to his arrest. He incorrectly named the season during which he had escaped. Z.K. apparently could not provide any details of his extradition. He appeared very poorly oriented for present time and circumstances. His speech was primitive and almost childlike, and he tended to respond to questions in a telegraphic manner, using as few words as possible and avoiding complete sentences. In stark contrast to this presentation, he spoke in a spontaneous and detailed manner about having been struck in the head by a corrections officer prior to the hijacking, suggesting that his memory, as well as his behavior in general, had been affected by a head injury. Objective medical evidence of a head trauma was not present. Z.K. was also able to provide a detailed description of hallucinations he said he had been experiencing since childhood. These hallucinations included the benign voice of his dead father, as well as the voice of "Lucifer," which urged him to hurt himself. He also detailed his complaint of a conspiracy against him by the legal authorities and reported that poison was being introduced into his salads in the jail. He stated that he had advised a corrections counselor about the hallucinations, although the counselor denied that the defendant had made any such report.

An Unbelievably Sick Man

K.O. was charged in an armed robbery of a gas station and evaluated for competency to stand trial. On examination he appeared to be disoriented for time and place ("I don't know. I can't remember. . . . I'm so forgetful, it's unbelievable!"). K.O. related that he knew nothing about his legal situation and could not understand any aspect of court procedure. Marked discrepancies were observed. He criticized the psychologist for not following the specifics of a court order. In addition, he explained a fine point of law that was altered recently by statute and favorably affected his sentencing.

K.O. complained strenuously of various hallucinations and, without being challenged, insisted on his honesty in reporting them: "I ain't bullshitting, man." He pointed out repeatedly that he was so sick that "it's unbelievable." K.O. complained of voices that tormented him constantly, although he indicated subsequently that he was fine during the examination, and that the voices only bothered him at "around midnight to 2:00 A.M." He similarly complained of "visions": "Just shadows in my room, at nighttime. I think the devil's in my room." He insisted, "I get so sick it's unbeliev-able! I may look okay, but I'm really bad!" He elaborated on his visions of the devil: "I feel like I'm having sex with the devil, laying there sleeping, feel like I'm being raped. . . . It's terrible! And I get this blurry vision stuff, and I feel real hot. I'm so sick, every single day! . . . It's unbelievable! Nobody knows it. . . . I ain't kidding you." He acknowledged that he was not hallucinating during the examination, but he indicated that the voices and visions would start again "as soon as you leave." He offered that he felt the need for "a change," and suggested: "The best thing for me is to put me in a place where they can take care of me, give me medication every day."

These case vignettes are quite representative of the symptom presentations com-monly seen among sociopathic individuals with criminal charges undergoing pretrial evaluations focused on their mental state at the present time and at the time of the offense. Although two of these individuals have had some success in their criminal activity— T.D. succeeded in killing 11 women and evading apprehension until a chance identifi-cation by his only surviving victim, and Z.K. managed a daring escape from police custody and months of eluding arrest—it is apparent from these vignettes that their presentations of mental disorder are neither clever or sophisticated. Sociopaths appear to be no more effective than others in presenting plausible symptoms, and as suggested by Cogburn's (1993) research and the case of K.O., they even may be unsuccessful at portraying them-selves as truthful. Lack of expert knowledge of genuine mental disorders, coupled with the poor judgment that so often characterizes sociopaths, may make the falseness of their claims transparent. In all of these cases, the types of errors incorporated in the SIRS scales (Rogers, 1992) are quite apparent, such as E.T.'s extremely unlikely claim of two simul-taneous dissociative reactions (i.e., depersonalization and amnesia) and the unlikely speci-ficity of K.O.'s hallucinations between midnight and 2:00 A.M.

The feigned disorders of these defendants appear to be modeled on a lay concep-tion of psychosis that is often at variance with the features of actual disorders. A pseudo-organic presentation of disorientation and confusion, as illustrated by Z.K., is not uncommon in malingerers, although such symptoms, particularly in association with psychotic features, are not ordinarily to be found among genuine patients. Hallucina-tions involving devils or demons seem to have an especially enduring appeal to malin-gerers, along with visits from dead relatives, but these complaints are not commonly encountered among persons with genuine psychoses. Similarly, the not-infrequent invisible dog may signal an especially poor attempt at malingering. Amnesia of one sort or another, as in the cases of E.T. and Z.K., is not a common accompaniment to psychotic symptoms but may have real utility for some sociopaths who cannot easily explain their criminal behavior by means of other mental disorders. Some sociopaths appear to believe that amnesia constitutes exculpation.

A striking observation from these vignettes is not the malingerers' sociopathy so much as their pressing and even desperate needs to escape from an adversarial situa-tion. In each case, the feigned presentation was crafted to address the facts of the case that were not in serious dispute. In each case, the malingerer evidently calculated that greater benefits would be found in deception rather than honesty. In each case, the realistic alternative to successful malingering involved extensive prison sentences. Although informed by the context (pretrial evaluations), the presentations appeared aligned with the adaptational model.

CLINICAL APPLICATIONS

Table 4.1 outlines a threshold model for assessing malingering among sociopaths. The threshold model does not in any way suggest that most sociopaths are malingerers, or conversely, that most malingerers are sociopaths. Rather, it emphasizes contextual and motivational factors that are not specific to sociopathy and warns against the unwarranted assumptions that individuals with criminal or antisocial background are likely to be feigning presentations of mental disorder. Conversely, the threshold model warns

---

TABLE 4.1. A Threshold Model for Malingering in the Presence of APD or Sociopathy

A. *Presence of sociopathy*: In the presence of clinical indications of sociopathy, malingering should be suspected if both B and C apply, but should not be assumed otherwise. An absence of demonstrable sociopathy should not be considered as evidence weighing against the identification of malingering, if B and C are applicable. Clinical indicators of sociopathy may be either of the following:

1. The individual presenting mental disorder is diagnosed with an antisocial personality disorder, or is rated high in psychopathy by means of standardized assessment techniques.
2. In the absence of a known history of sociopathy, the individual presenting a mental disorder is being charged with an offense that, if true, would itself suggest sociopathy. Elements of such an offense might include deception, cruelty, or other indications of a lack of empathic concern; lack of any indication of remorse or moral compunction; and the apparent presence of such common "criminal" motivations as financial gain, nonconsensual sexual gratification, anger, and revenge.

B. *Adversarial context*: The individual presenting symptomatic complaints is seen in a context in which a highly adversarial potential exists, such as an evaluation focusing on mental state at the time of an alleged offense, assessment of competency to stand trial, or evaluations for work-related benefits, compensation for injury, or a civil-damage award.

C. *Understandable motivation*: The presentation of a mental disorder occurs when a plausible advantage is potentially present for being evaluated as disturbed. Such motivations may be observed in cases involving criminal charges, particularly felony charges, and compensation cases. In both contexts, the potential motivation is understandable.

D. *Objective indications of malingering or exaggeration*: In order to guard against "negative halo" assumptions that a combination of sociopathy and atypical presentation is malingering, obtaining objective evidence of malingering is crucial, including structured interview data (e.g., the SIRS), and objective test data (e.g., the MMPI-2).

Note. For the purposes of simplicity, threshold criteria list only sociopathy. However, these criteria should also be considered for APD or psychopathy as measured by the Psychopathy Checklist.

against the simplistic assumption that the absence of sociopathy offers any assurance regarding the genuineness of presented symptoms.

Further research is needed to determine the extent to which the criminological model has merit in assessing the probability of malingering. At the present time, clinicians have no defensible basis on which to conclude that sociopathy, ipso facto, increases the likelihood of feigning. Although sociopaths are frequently found in highly adversarial forensic contexts, this frequency does not suggest that sociopaths exceed nonsociopaths in attempts to feign. Simply put, malingering should not be viewed, as once generally assumed, to be an extension of sociopathic behavior.

Empirical data, although sparse, suggest that the malingering attempts by sociopaths are no more effective than those of nonsociopaths. The use of standardized clinical indicators, including the MMPI-2 and the SIRS, are strongly recommended to improve the accuracy of assessments with both sociopathic and nonsociopathic populations. Finally, the clinician may be well justified when performing complicated assessments for the court in describing the suspected dissimulation but leaving unanswered the referral question when the dissimulation sufficiently obscures the psycholegal issues (Rogers, 1986).

NOTES

1. The finding that none of the malingerers were psychotic is a methodological artifact, since psychotic persons were excluded from the malingering group. This exclusion is likely to exaggerate greatly the association between psychopathy and malingering.

2. The authors appear to make the tenuous assumption that participants feigned on the MMPI-2 but responded honestly to the MCMI-II. A more plausible set of assumptions is that (1) feigning occurred on both measures, (2) these correlations are indicative of exaggeration, and (3) MCMI-II elevations should not be interpreted. Also, the authors appear to assume that malingerers are mentally disordered, since the MCMI-II is only validated for clinical populations. If this is the case, the study is fatally flawed, since their hypothesis could not possibly be disproved.

3. Note, however, that an increased detection rate does not imply an increased accuracy. Not infrequently, forensic reports have been reviewed in which the clinician summarily concluded that an uncooperative defendant with a prior criminal history met three of the four DSM indices and, therefore, was malingering.

5

Simulated Amnesia and the Pseudo-Memory Phenomena

STEVEN P. CERCY, Ph.D.
DAVID J. SCHRETLEN, Ph.D.
JASON BRANDT, Ph.D.

Memory complaints are very common symptoms in most clinical practices. Not infrequently, a patient presents with memory symptoms that are out of the ordinary and so atypical as to be suspected of fabrication or, at least, marked exaggeration. The symptoms may consist of the inability to recall specific, highly salient facts or incidents from the past (i.e., retrograde amnesia), the sudden remembrance of traumatic episodes from the past (i.e., "recovered" memories), or the severely impaired ability to learn and establish permanent new memories (i.e., anterograde amnesia). These memory symptoms are often accompanied by other cognitive complaints and signs of psychopathology (Rubinsky & Brandt, 1986). Typically, the pattern and/or severity of such memory symptoms is not easily understood by reference to established facts in cognitive science or clinical neurology. In these cases, the clinician's task is to differentiate, based on scientific knowledge and known pathophysiological mechanisms, between genuine, neurologically based memory phenomena and their simulated counterparts.

This chapter reviews some of the nonneurological aberrations of memory and suggests a conceptual framework for appreciating these presentations. In addition, we describe some methods that may be useful in the identification of pseudo-amnesia and pseudo-remembering. We begin with a brief overview of the phenomenology of "organic" memory disorders. Under the rubric of "nonneurological" amnesia, we examine (1) the traditional yet controversial diagnosis of dissociative amnesia and (2) the clinical presentation of feigned amnesia. Next, we review and critically evaluate the empirical literature on the differentiation of organic memory disorders from dissociative amnesia and feigned amnesia. Finally, we will turn our attention from false forgetting to false remembering. The characteristics of individuals and situations that promote confabulation and the creation of false memories are reviewed.

AMNESIA AND MEMORY IMPAIRMENT DUE TO BRAIN DAMAGE

The "amnestic disorder" (DSM-IV 294.0) is a syndrome characterized by severe impairment in the ability to remember new information (anterograde amnesia) or recall previously learned information (retrograde amnesia) in the absence of pervasive cognitive impairment, as would be seen in dementia or delirium. In addition, this memory impairment must be a direct physiological consequence of a "general medical condition," and the impairment must interfere with social functioning (American Psychiatric Association, 1994a; Caine, 1993).

Perhaps the most studied form of amnestic disorder is "chronic global amnesia," in which anterograde amnesia is severe and permanent. Etiologies of chronic global amnesia include alcoholic Korsakoff's syndrome, infectious processes (e.g., viral encephalitis), strokes, cerebral hypoxia, and other neurological conditions that affect the limbic system, basal forebrain nuclei, and/or diencephalon. The critical lesion in most of these cases appears to be in the mesial aspect of the temporal lobes (i.e., hippocampus, entorhinal cortex), or in midline diencephalic structures (i.e., medial thalamus, mammillary bodies of hypothalamus; see Gade & Mortensen, 1990; Speedie & Heilman, 1982; Squire & Moore, 1979).

Several more limited forms of the amnestic syndrome exist. "Material-specific amnesia" refers to chronic anterograde amnesia limited to verbal or nonverbal (spatial) information. This form of amnestic syndrome is seen most often following lateralized lesions associated with temporal lobectomy, stroke, trauma, and tumors. For example, among patients undergoing surgery for intractable epilepsy, excision of the left anterior temporal lobe usually leads to impaired memory for verbal, but not for nonverbal, information; the converse has been observed following excision of the right anterior temporal lobe (Milner, 1968; Smith, 1989). "Transient global amnesia" is a rare condition characterized by the acute onset of severe anterograde amnesia and limited, temporally graded retrograde amnesia (greater impairment of recent than remote memory) that typically resolves within a day (Kritchevsky, 1989). This syndrome is typically seen during transient ischemic attacks (TIAs) that temporarily reduce blood flow to the mesial temporal lobe (Evans, Wilson, Wraight, & Hodges, 1993). Even rarer is a condition called "focal retrograde amnesia" (Kapur, 1993). Here, the patient experiences a relatively isolated, permanent loss of memory for autobiographical and public events of the past, usually combined with mild anterograde memory loss (Goldberg, Hughes, Mattis, & Antin, 1982; Kapur, Young, Bateman, & Kennedy, 1989; O'Connor, Butters, Miliotis, Eslinger, & Cermak, 1992). As will be discussed later, most patients who present with isolated amnesia for the past actually are feigning amnesia or have dissociative amnesia, which is defined in part by the absence of an observed neurological abnormality. In the few reported cases of genuine focal retrograde amnesia, however, brain imaging studies have revealed structural or functional brain abnormalities (Kapur Ellison, Smith, McLellan, & Burrows, 1992; Yoneda, Yamadori, Mori, & Yamashita, 1992). Electrophysiological abnormalities in one or both temporal lobes also have been reported in focal retrograde amnesia (Damasio, Graff-Radford, & Damasio, 1983).

Memory impairment that is less severe or less circumscribed than in the amnestic syndrome is seen in a wide variety of neurological disorders. In these conditions, the memory deficit is best regarded as a symptom rather than a syndrome. For example, memory impairment is a requisite feature of dementia, regardless of the underlying disease entity (e.g., stroke, Alzheimer's disease, brain injury, normal pressure hydrocephalus). Although not always present, memory deficits are observed frequently in schizophrenia, major depression, epilepsy, Parkinson's disease, and anoxic and metabolic encephalopathies, to name just a few of the more prevalent conditions. In addition, memory impairment is often an unfortunate side effect of some neuropsychiatric treatments, such as electroconvulsive therapy (ECT) for major depression. The quality and severity of the memory disorder in these clinical conditions vary considerably. Unfortunately, this variability complicates the development of methods to distinguish between feigned and genuine memory impairment. For example, evaluating a claim of acquired memory impairment secondary to ECT requires knowledge of research not only on feigned memory impairment, but also on the range of observed effects of ECT. Likewise, deciding whether a victim of mild head trauma is exaggerating complaints of forgetfulness requires an appreciation of the full spectrum of neuropsychological consequences of brain injury.

DISSOCIATIVE AMNESIA

What had been called "psychogenic" amnesia in the third revised edition of the *Diagnostic and Statistical Manual of Mental Disorders* (DSM-III-R) was designated as dissociative amnesia in DSM-IV. This condition is defined by episodes, typically following emotional trauma or severe stress, during which important personal information is not recalled. The exclusion criteria include dissociative identity disorder, dissociative fugue, posttraumatic stress disorder, acute stress disorder, direct effects of substance abuse, and amnestic disorders. Dissociative phenomena have a long, rich history in psychodynamic theory and case studies. However, the validation of dissociative amnesia as categorically distinct from conscious and deliberate simulation (faking) has been problematic.

Most published cases of dissociative amnesia are characterized by the sudden onset of memory impairments for autobiographical events and knowledge, often including the patient's own identity (Kanzer, 1939; Schacter, Wang, Tulving, & Freedman, 1982; Wong, 1990). However, fragments or "islands" of intact memory may occur within the amnestic period (Kanzer, 1939; Schacter et al., 1982). The recall of generic factual information (i.e., semantic memory) may or may not be preserved (Schacter et al., 1982). The selective impairment of remote memory typically occurs in the absence of anterograde amnesia (Abeles & Schilder, 1935; Wong, 1990), but impaired new learning has been reported in some cases (Gudjonsson & Taylor, 1985; Schacter et al., 1982). The duration of dissociative amnesia varies from a few days (Schacter et al., 1982) to more than 1 year (Kopelman, Christensen, Puffett, & Stanhope, 1994). Similar to its onset, dissociative amnesia often resolves abruptly with full return of memories from the amnestic period (Lyon, 1985; Schacter et al., 1982; Wong, 1990).

Some investigators have postulated that dissociative amnesia develops in some individuals following actual traumatic events accompanied by extreme emotional arousal (Kopelman, 1987). In fact, significant antecedent stress has been associated with most reported cases of psychogenic amnesia. Of 1,000 consecutive admissions to an inpatient neurology ward during World War II, 14% were identified as having dissociative amnesia (Sargant & Slater, 1941). In the same series, comorbid psychopathology was common, with anxiety, depression, and somatization being most frequent. Preexisting psychopathology has also been described in more recent case reports (Kopelman et al., 1994; Wong, 1990). Psychological and pharmacological treatments of psychogenic amnesia have yielded mixed results, ranging from partial improvement to complete resolution of the retrograde amnesia (Gerson & Victoroff, 1948; Kopelman et al., 1994; Lyon, 1985; Russell & Nathan, 1946; Stuss & Guzman, 1988; Wong, 1990).

In most cases, the characteristics that distinguish dissociative amnesia from the amnestic syndrome are reasonably clear; they include the presence of a significant psychological stressor, the loss of one's personal identity, concurrent or preexisting major psychopathology, and the absence of structural cerebral lesions or functional cortical abnormalities. In addition, legal involvement (either criminal charges or civil suits) has been reported in many cases of dissociative amnesia.

Dissociative amnesia may bear a striking resemblance to focal retrograde amnesia and, therefore, requires great care in clinical decision making (Kopelman, 1987). In one case reported by Stuss and Guzman (1988), a 46-year-old man developed severe, selective retrograde amnesia following the onset of a seizure disorder. His amnesia included failure to recognize family members and familiar places, but his personal identity remained intact. He also had a mild impairment in factual knowledge. An electroencephalogram (EEG) revealed bilateral temporal abnormalities, and positron emission tomography (PET) scan showed hypometabolism in the left temporal lobe. The working hypothesis was that this represented a case of focal retrograde amnesia (i.e., "organic"). However, while a sodium amytal (amobarbitol) interview was conducted, the patient's memory for his past improved dramatically. In brain-disordered amnesic patients, sodium amytal typically produces increased drowsiness and less responsiveness, whereas in patients with dissociative disorders, it more often results in mild intoxication, a decrease of inhibitions and defenses, and freer report of distressing material. This result suggested to Stuss and Guzman that the patient's memory for autobiographical information was intact but inaccessible during his amnestic episode. Although this was interpreted as indicating that the patient's amnesia was at least partially dissociative, it is certainly conceivable that the drug reversed a pathological inhibition produced by the patient's brain disorder. In other words, a pharmacological reversal of amnesia is equally compatible with a genuine amnestic syndrome and a dissociative amnesia.

Historically, dissociative amnesia has been interpreted within a psychoanalytic framework. More recently, however, cognitive-psychological formulations have appeared. One such hypothesis is that dissociative amnesia represents an extreme manifestation of "directed forgetting." In experiments on directed forgetting, individuals study some material and are then instructed to forget that material. On an unanticipated recall test, they remember less of the material than participants that were not directed to forget (Bjork, 1989). Other cognitive formulations of dissociative amnesia focus on the distinction between the presence of material in memory and its accessibility. Kopelman et al. (1994) described the treatment of a patient with psychogenic amnesia, who was found wandering on the London subway. She was unable to recall her own name, home town, or names of family members. Following the administration of sodium amytal, however, she recalled "a considerable amount" of autobiographical information for which she previously had been amnesic.

DETECTION OF FEIGNED AMNESIA

In the past decade, considerable progress has been made in the development of techniques to detect feigned memory impairment. However, the reliable differentiation of simulated and genuine memory impairment remains elusive, and some problems (e.g., determination of conscious vs. unconscious motivation) may remain intractable. In the sections that follow, the paradigms used to detect feigned memory impairment will be described, and the problems associated with each are discussed. With these considerations in mind, the empirical findings on feigned memory impairment are reviewed.

Problems in Measuring Feigned Memory Impairment

A fundamental constraint on the study of malingering involves the problem of criterion validity. Simply stated, no "gold standard" exists to determine with certainty whether a patient is feigning symptoms independent of the clinical tests or experimental procedures being investigated. Patients who are being deceptive rarely admit it. One experimental method to address the lack of independent verification is the use of simulation designs. In these studies, persons with normal memory are instructed to simulate the performance of memory-disordered patients. The performance of simulators can then be compared to that of normal persons or patients with impaired memory instructed to perform at their best. Although simulation studies maximize internal validity (i.e., the confidence with which a causal relationship can be inferred between manipulation of feigning and memory test scores; see Cook & Campbell, 1979), their external validity (i.e., generalizability to actual malingerers) remains open to question. Moreover, since independent verification of malingering is exceedingly rare, the extent to which simulators' test results resemble those of actual malingerers cannot be determined with certainty.

Another consideration in simulation studies is the specific instructions given to simulators. Only recently has this issue been given attention in the research literature. A few studies, for example, have examined the influence of providing simulators with information regarding the clinical characteristics of individuals with genuine memory disorders (Baker, Hanley, Jackson, Kimmance, & Slade, 1993; Rose, Hall, & Szalda-Petree, 1995). However, not only do these studies vary in the amount and type of coaching, but they also differ in a more subtle way. Some studies instruct participants to perform "like someone with a [real] memory impairment," whereas others instruct subjects to perform "like someone trying to fake a memory impairment." These instructions are qualitatively distinct and might result in systematic performance differences.

Electrophysiological Approaches

Relatively few studies have examined the effectiveness of electrophysiological measures in detecting feigned memory impairment. Because electrophysiological methods for detecting deceptive response sets are reviewed in Chapter 13, we present only a brief overview of these methods.

Wiggins, Lombard, Brennan, and Heckel (1964) examined skin conductance responses in a patient with psychogenic amnesia. They found no differences between responses to neutral questions and emotional questions concerning events occurring during the period of retrograde amnesia. Lynch and Bradford (1980) found that criminal defendants who claimed mild or circumscribed retrograde memory deficits produced equivocal polygraph findings, whereas those who claimed more severe amnesia produced polygraph results that more definitively indicated autonomic arousal.

Event-related potentials (ERPs) have also been used to detect deceptive response sets. Several researchers have shown that the P300 wave is greater in amplitude in normal participants denying knowledge of minor transgressions than in participants admitting to such knowledge (Farwell & Donchin, 1991; Johnson & Rosenfeld, 1992; Rosenfeld, Angell, Johnson, & Qian, 1991; Rosenfeld, Nasman, Whalen, Cantwell, & Mazzeri, 1987). Similar results have been obtained for recognition of digit strings (Rosenfeld, Sweet, Chuang, Ellwanger, & Song, in press) and knowledge of word lists, stories, and personal information (autobiographical events, telephone numbers; see Rosenfeld et al., 1991; Rosenfeld, Ellwanger, & Sweet, 1995; Rosenfeld et al., 1987).

Specific Measures of Malingered Amnesia

Neuropsychologists have attempted to develop cognitive tests that are sensitive to feigned brain dysfunction. One general strategy has been to develop tests that are so simple that even moderately brain-damaged patients perform well, but that appear to be difficult. The "floor effect" strategy (Rogers, Harrell, & Liff, 1993) assumes that the naive faker will "overplay" the role and fail on very simple tasks. In practice, however, two problems exist with this strategy. First, many would-be malingerers discern the underlying strategy and avoid performing poorly on the tasks. Second, despite the apparent simplicity of the tasks, some patients with documented brain damage or neuropsychiatric disorders have difficulty succeeding on them.

These problems are exemplified by the Rey 15-Item Memory Test (Rey-15; Rey, 1964). In this very popular test of feigned memory impairment, an array of 15 letters, numbers, and shapes (five rows of three items each) is shown to the patient for 10 seconds, whereupon the patient attempts to reproduce the array. The fact that *15 separate items* will be shown, and *only 10 seconds* will be allowed for memorization are emphasized. In actuality, however, the stimuli are repetitive and conform to an obvious pattern, making the task relatively simple. Based on her clinical observations, Lezak (1983) originally recommended that a score of fewer than 9 correct out of 15 correctly recalled items suggests feigned memory impairment. However, subsequent studies of patients with mental retardation (Goldberg & Miller, 1986), neurological disorders (Lee, Loring, & Martin, 1992), and psychiatric disorders (Guilmette, Hart, Giuliano, Leininger, 1994; Hays, Emmons, & Lawson, 1993; Schretlen, Brandt, Krafft, & Van Gorp, 1991) have demonstrated that the Rey-15 generally lacks specificity (correct identification of nonfeigners) at a variety of cut scores. Furthermore, in some contexts, the Rey-15 has been shown to have low sensitivity (correct identification of feigners) as well (Bernard & Fowler, 1990; Davidson, Suffield, Orenczuk, Nantau, & Mandel, 1991; Schretlen et al., 1991). Thus, the utility of the Rey-15 for detecting feigned memory impairment, particularly in the absence of corroborating evidence, appears to be limited.

Symptom validity testing (SVT; Pankratz, 1983; Pankratz, Fausti, & Peed, 1975) is a commonly used paradigm for assessing malingering, and it has been applied in the development of a number of tests of feigned amnesia (Binder & Willis, 1991; Brandt, Rubinsky, & Lassen, 1985; Hiscock & Hiscock, 1989). The fundamental element of all SVT procedures is the presentation of a set of stimuli, followed by a forced-choice recognition test (see Chapter 11). Typically, 25 to 100 stimuli are presented individually followed by two-alternative forced-choice recognition. With any number of recognition foils, chance performance (pure guessing) can be determined statistically. With two alternatives, purely random responding will result in 50% correct, with the binomial distribution specifying the probability of various deviations from 50% correct. Individuals who deviate statistically below chance are presumed to be feigning memory impairment, because systematic responding (whether correct or incorrect) requires intact memory. Research related to SVT is reviewed extensively in Chapter 11 under the rubric of "forced choice testing."

One SVT-type technique, originally described by Lezak (1983), served as the basis of the Recall–Recognition Test devised by Brandt et al. (1985). These investigators presented a 20-word list to 42 participants: 12 normal adults, 14 patients with Huntington's disease (a neuropsychiatric disorder whose victims have considerable memory impairment), 5 patients with traumatic brain injury, 10 simulators (college students instructed to role play amnesia), and 1 criminal defendant claiming memory impairment as a mitigating circumstance in his trial. Participants read each word as it was presented and immediately thereafter attempted free recall. Once the recall phase was complete, a two-alternative recognition test was administered. Each of the 20 target words was typed on a card along with a distractor word; the person's task was simply to identify the word read a few minutes earlier. Brandt et al. (1985) found that free-recall scores of simulators and the suspected malingerer were comparable to those of the brain-disordered patients. However, on recognition testing, the normal adults and both patient groups demonstrated above-chance performance, whereas the simulators performed within chance range (6 to 14 items correct). The suspected male malingerer recognized only 3 of 20 target words, worse than his free-recall performance and clearly below chance. The conclusion was that the criminal defendant had withheld information on this task.

A slightly different version of this task, which rarely yields below-chance performance, was administered to 25 patients with memory impairment (15 of whom had traumatic brain injury), 48 simulators, and 27 normal control participants (Wiggins & Brandt, 1988). The simulators tended to underestimate the free-recall impairments but overestimate the recognition impairments of memory-disordered patients. In a follow-up study (Brandt, 1992), 11 patients with chronic global amnesia and 4 suspected malingerers performed comparably on free recall. However, the suspected malingerers recognized significantly fewer words than the amnesics. Relative to free recall, recognition improved by at least 9 words in 9 of 11 amnesics, whereas no suspected malingerers showed a recognition advantage of this magnitude. In another study (Iverson, Franzen, & McCracken, 1991), patients with memory impairment, normal adults, and experimental simulators were read a list of 21 words, followed by free recall and then a two-alternative forced-choice recognition test. As in the Brandt (1992) study, patients with memory impairment and the simulators performed comparably on free recall, but the simulators performed significantly worse than the patients on recognition. A cut score of 12 or fewer words correctly recognized yielded 100% sensitivity (correct classification of simulators) and 95% specificity (correct classification of patients).

All of these SVT tasks examine the effects of feigned impairments of *anterograde* memory or the acquisition of new information. A novel SVT approach involves creating a set of questions to test *retrograde* memory based on information gathered (1) from police reports regarding a crime, or (2) from family members regarding the patient's autobiography. A set of plausible alternatives is then generated, and the questions are presented either in a yes–no or forced-choice format. Presumably, if the individual attempts to feign ignorance of pertinent facts or events, performance might fall below chance. Several case studies have recently been reported in which suspected (Denney, in press; Frederick & Carter, 1993; Frederick, Carter, & Powel, 1995) or confirmed (Denney & Wynkoop, 1995) malingerers showed this response pattern. The main problem associated with this procedure is that the a priori probability of selecting each member of a stimulus pair may not be equal, due to social desirability or other factors. Denney (in press) attempted to address this limitation by administering the same sets of questions to 60 normal adults who were ignorant of the pertinent events. He showed that the mean probability for responding correctly to all questions was .54, and the range of probabilities approximated the normal distribution, as would be expected in a sample of naive participants. In the clinical or forensic setting, this method of control, although clearly worthwhile, might prove unwieldy and extremely time consuming. Nevertheless, further investigation of this procedure appears warranted.

Another malingering-specific measure is the Personal History Interview (PHI), developed by Wiggins and Brandt (1988). This autobiographical questionnaire consists of 14 questions, most of which can be answered reasonably, even by severely amnesic patients. Responses to each question are scored as Correct/Plausible or Incorrect/Implausible/Don't Know. When the PHI was administered to 27 normal adults, 13 patients with genuine amnesia, and 48 simulators, the simulators gave more Incorrect/Implausible/Don't Know responses than the genuine patients overall, particularly to those questions involving personal identity (Brandt, 1992). The genuine patients gave more Incorrect/Implausible/Don't Know responses only to questions tapping delayed recall and delayed recognition, precisely the items expected to be most difficult for genuinely memory-disordered patients.

Another malingering-specific technique involves the investigation of serial position effects on tests of word-list learning. When memorizing word lists, normal individuals generally recall more words from the beginning (primacy effect) and end (recency effect) of the list than from the middle region, resulting in the classic U-shaped serial position curve. Wiggins and Brandt (1988) first examined serial position effects as an indicator of feigned memory impairment using a 20-word list that was presented only once. They found that patients with amnesia showed suppression of the primacy effect, which is consistent with previous research (Baddeley & Warrington, 1970; Milner, 1978), whereas simulators generated a normal U-shaped serial position curve. Thus, the simulators' performance was *quantitatively* like that of amnesics, but was *qualitatively* different (i.e., same pattern as unimpaired persons).

Bernard (1991) used the Rey Auditory Verbal Learning Test (AVLT; Rey, 1964) to distinguish traumatically brain-injured patients with memory impairment from normal individuals simulating memory impairment. Averaging across trials, he found that both simulators and patients with traumatic brain injury demonstrated a U-shaped serial position curve. However, the simulators recalled proportionately *fewer* words from the primacy region than did patients with traumatic brain injury, who showed poorer recall overall. These findings are consistent with previous studies examining serial position effects in traumatic brain injury (Goldstein, Levin, & Boake, 1989). However, Cercy, Radtke, and Chittum (1995) found no differences in serial position effects between traumatically brain-injured patients with chronic memory impairment and simulators. Instead of a single list, they used a series of five word lists designed to produce interference effects. This change in procedure altered serial position effects substantially. Overall, studies of serial position effects to detect feigned memory impairment have yielded mixed results, probably due to methodological differences among studies. The data suggest that a normal or near-normal primacy effect might distinguish both suspected malingerers and patients with more widespread cognitive impairments from patients with dense, circumscribed amnestic syndromes.

Traditional Psychometric Approaches

One of the most common techniques for detecting feigned memory (and other cognitive) impairments involves the identification of aberrant response patterns on standard clinical neuropsychological tests. Unlike malingering-specific measures, clinical tests of memory were not designed specifically to detect feigning, and therefore may lack construct validity for this purpose. The cognitive processes involved in feigned memory impairment probably are quite different from those that underlie genuine memory impairment. Nonetheless, some of these tests have been used to predict feigned memory impairment with varying degrees of success.

Several investigators have found that the Logical Memory and Visual Reproduction subtests from the Wechsler Memory Scale—Revised (WMS-R; Wechsler, 1987) do not consistently differentiate between memory impairments due to traumatic brain injury and feigned memory impairment (Bernard, 1990; Bernard, Houston, & Natoli, 1993; cf. Greiffenstein, Baker, & Gola, 1994). However, in a study that compared the WMS-R profiles of simulators and patients with traumatic brain injury (TBI) matched for age and overall memory test performance (Mittenberg, Azrin, Millsaps, & Heilbronner, 1993), simulators produced lower scores on the WMS-R Attention/Concentration Index ($M = 70.9$, $SD = 18.2$) than did the patients with traumatic brain injury ($M = 95.9$, $SD = 14.5$). Furthermore, a discriminant analysis of subtest scores correctly classified 83% of simulators and 91% of TBI patients. Thus, simulators appear to overestimate the degree of attentional impairment that is characteristic of individuals with genuine memory impairment due to moderate TBI. However, Mittenberg et al. (1993) did not cross-validate their discriminant function on independent samples of patients and simulators. Perhaps more important, their discriminant function analysis assumed the base rate of malingering to be 50%. This estimate is undoubtedly higher than the true base rate in most clinical settings, leading to a significant bias in the predictive value of the discriminant function.

In another simulation study that did attempt to cross-validate a discriminant function based on WMS-R subtests, Bernard, McGrath, and Houston (1993) found the sensitivity was comparable to that obtained by Mittenberg et al. (1993) with 79% of simulators correctly classified. However, the specificity was somewhat lower with 80% of patients correctly classified. Low specificity is especially problematic in the clinical determination of malingering, because false-positive errors result in the labeling of an honest person as a "feigner." Furthermore, like Mittenburg et al. (1993), Bernard et al. (1993) assumed the base rate of feigned memory impairment to be 50%.

Binder, Villanueva, Howieson, and Moore (1993) examined the influence of motivation to feign on AVLT performance in patients with mild TBI. They divided patients seeking financial compensation for their injuries (assumed by the authors to have a higher probability of malingering than patients not seeking monetary awards) into two groups: those who scored below or above a previously established cutoff on an SVT-type task, namely the Portland Digit Recognition Test (PDRT; Binder & Willis, 1991). After equating the groups for overall learning across trials, delayed recognition memory for the low-PDRT scorers was worse than for high-PDRT scorers and TBI patients not seeking compensation. A fundamental limitation of this study, like many others, involves the assumption that patients seeking monetary damages in lawsuits or making disability claims after a mild TBI are malingering (i.e., differential prevalence design; see Chapter 1). It is certainly possible that the reason why these patients are claiming damages for neuropsychological impairment is because they have been affected more adversely by their head injuries than the "typical" patient with the same objective degree of trauma.

Bernard (1991) found that simulators displayed *better* immediate recall, delayed recall, and recognition memory on the AVLT than did patients with TBI. In contrast, Greiffenstein et al. (1994) found that *worse* AVLT recognition performance distinguished suspected malingerers from individuals with mild or severe TBI. Trueblood and Schmidt (1993) conducted a study in which consecutively referred patients with minor TBI were screened for feigning/exaggeration with SVT. On the California Verbal Learning Test (Delis, Kramer, Kaplan, & Ober, 1987), suspected malingerers recalled *more* words overall but recognized *fewer* words than age- and education-matched patients with TBI. These findings are consistent with those obtained in several studies by Brandt and his associates (Brandt, 1992; Brandt et al., 1985; Wiggins & Brandt, 1988).

The Recognition Memory Test (RMT; Warrington, 1984) appears, by virtue of its format, to be well-suited to the task of detecting feigned memory impairment. The RMT is composed of two subtests: word and face recognition. Following the presentation of each set of 50 stimuli for the patient to encode (by making pleasantness judgments), a two-alternative, forced-choice recognition test is administered. Thus, even if a respondent has no memory at all for the target stimuli, the binomial distribution of equal probability responses suggests that a score of 17 or fewer correct is highly unlikely ($p = .03$) and constitutes significantly below-chance performance. Using this procedure, Millis (1992) found that compensation-seeking, mild TBI subjects performed significantly worse than moderate and severe TBI patients on both word recognition (*M*'s of 29.1 versus 38.8) and face recognition (*M*'s of 28.4 vs. 34.4) but were not below chance as a group. A discriminant function using both subtests yielded a 76% correct classification rate overall, certainly not sufficient for clinical decision making. Millis and Putnam (1994) subsequently obtained an overall correct classification rate of 83% in a cross-validation sample. When a non-compensation-seeking, employed group with mild TBI was added, the RMT achieved an overall correct classification rate of 93% (Millis, 1994). However, the same criticism of the differential prevalence design, promulgated by Binder and associates (1993), applies to these studies.

Investigational Techniques

As psychological research develops new paradigms into normal and abnormal memory functioning, these methods are incorporated into studies of feigned memory impairment and dissociative amnesia. For example, analysis of the buildup and release of proactive interference (PI) has been studied as a method of detecting feigned memory impairment. PI occurs when previously learned information interferes with the acquisition or recall of subsequently presented information. In a word-list learning paradigm, PI is manifested as a decline in recall across different word lists. PI is maximal when recall is required for items that are highly similar, such as words drawn from the same semantic category (e.g., vegetables). Release from PI is demonstrated when a list of words from a different semantic category (e.g., animals) is presented and memory performance rebounds to near its original level (Wickens, 1970). TBI patients with memory impairment typically show a normal buildup and release from PI (Cercy et al., 1995; Goldstein et al., 1989). If a patient feigning memory impairment withholds words in free recall, he or she may do so without considering the influence of PI or its reduction with a shift in category; that is, the naive malingerer is presumed not to appreciate the learning principles that apply even to brain-damaged amnesics. In fact, however, no differences in degree of PI or release from PI have been found between simulators and patients with TBI (Baker et al., 1993; Cercy et al., 1995). This nonsignificant finding may suggest that PI is an automatic cognitive process (Hasher & Zacks, 1979) that is outside conscious control.

Baker et al. (1993) investigated the influence of distraction during the interval between stimulus presentation and recall. They found that simulators and memory-impaired patients performed comparably when recalling list items following a 20-second interval of backward counting. However, the simulators performed consistently more poorly when distraction occurred during the interval. Thus, similar to the findings on recall and recognition discussed earlier, simulators appear to overestimate the severity of impairment on some simpler tasks.

A few studies have attempted to differentiate simulators from genuine amnesics based on implicit memory tasks. Amnesic patients generally show nearly normal performance on tests of priming and related tasks that do not require explicit recollection of the learning episode (i.e., implicit memory; Graf, Squire, & Mandler, 1984; Moscovitch, 1984; Schacter, 1987). For example, when amnesic patients read or otherwise process words (e.g., FARE) without being asked to remember them, and are then shown word stems (e.g., FA__) or word fragments (e.g., F__R__), the probability that they respond with the previously shown word is greater than the probability of responding with a higher frequency alternative (e.g., FAIR or FIRE). Such priming is thought by many to be mediated by a relatively independent neurocognitive system (Squire, 1994).

Wiggins and Brandt (1988) hypothesized that simulators would not know that amnesic patients perform near normally on tests of implicit memory and would perform poorly on these tasks. They tested this hypothesis with three groups: patients with the amnestic syndrome, normal persons performing their best, and normal simulators feigning amnesia. First, a list of 20 words was presented for free recall. Immediately thereafter, a word-stem completion task was administered. The word-stem completion task was readministered 24 hours later. The free recall of the simulators fell between that of the normal adults and amnesic patients. On word stem completion, the amnesic patients generated as many target words as the normal adults on both days. The simulators completed fewer word stems with target words, both immediately and 24 hours after presentation, than either the amnesic patients or normal adults, but neither of those differences reached statistical significance. According to Brandt et al. (1985), researchers cannot reject the possibility that the average person has a tacit knowledge, namely, that word-stem completion assesses a different kind of memory than the deficits found with an amnestic syndrome. In other words, simulators would have no reason to dissimulate on a measure they suspect (correctly) to be unrelated to the purported impairment.

Horton, Smith, Barghout, and Connolly (1992) reported a series of five experiments on the effects of instructions on implicit memory. In each study, participants were randomly assigned to one of three groups. Normal control (NC) participants received no specific instructions, whereas uncoached simulators (US) were asked to feign amnesia and given detailed descriptions of the upcoming memory tests. Coached simulators (CS) received the same information as the US group plus specific details regarding the performance of amnesics on implicit memory tests. Horton et al. found that the US group performed more poorly than either the NC or CS group on measures of word-stem and word-associate priming. Horton et al. (1992, experiment 2) also replicated the findings of Wiggins and Brandt (1988), in which simulators showed normal priming on word-stem completion and word-association tasks. Horton et al. attributed the discrepancy in priming between the two studies to differences in the nature of the instructions provided. Unfortunately, these investigators did not include a group of patients with genuine memory impairments. They argued that since amnesic patients generally show normal implicit memory, the normal control participants could serve as the comparison group. However, some of these phenomena appear to be task-specific, and therefore an amnesic comparison group would have been appropriate.

Kopelman et al. (1994) constructed a word-completion task to examine priming effects in a patient with dissociative amnesia. They found that completion of surnames of people known prior to the onset of the amnestic period was much lower than completion of names of people whom the patient met after onset. More important, completion of preonset names (13% correct) was lower than completion of names of totally unfamiliar people (20% correct), suggesting the suppression of intact remote memories. These data are consistent with studies of deliberate remote memory suppression in suspected or confirmed malingerers (Denney, in press; Denney & Wynkoop, 1995; Frederick & Carter, 1993; Frederick et al., 1995). Direct comparison between suspected malingerers and patients diagnosed with dissociative amnesia on priming-type measures of implicit memory may help determine whether it is meaningful at all to continue to distinguish between these two groups on this particular dimension.

The "feeling-of-knowing," (i.e., an individual's confidence that he or she actually has a memory or partial memory), has been applied in attempts to detect feigned memory impairment. One limitation in the application of this phenomenon is that amnesic patients vary in the accuracy of their feeling-of-knowing. As a group, patients with alcoholic Korsakoff's syndrome are impaired in making these metamemory judgments, but other amnesics of other etiologies are not (Shimamura & Squire, 1986). Schacter (1986) found that normal adults and simulators did not differ on the accuracy of free recall for details of a written passage or videotape. However, simulators performed below chance on a forced-choice recognition test, and they gave lower feeling-of-knowing ratings than adults performing at their best. However, a subsequent study of feeling-of-knowing (Bradley, MacDonald, & Fleming, 1989) failed to find differences between simulators and normal participants. Unfortunately, neither of these studies included memory-disordered patients, precluding any determination of whether self-rated feeling-of-knowing has utility for discriminating between genuine and feigned memory impairment. Kopelman and colleagues (1994) obtained feeling-of-knowing ratings from a female patient with dissociative amnesia. Her feeling-of-knowing for the names of people known prior to the onset of her condition was no better than that for unfamiliar people, but it improved after administration of sodium amytal. This pattern is consistent with Schacter's (1986) findings of lower feeling-of-knowing ratings in simulators relative to normals adults. Overall, the feeling-of-knowing phenomenon appears to have potential for the detection of feigned amnesia, but further development is necessary.

Finally, chronometric paradigms represent another interesting but largely unexplored approach to the detection of feigned memory impairment. These paradigms focus on the timing of particular aspects of test performance, such as the latency of individual responses and the effects of manipulation of task parameters on latency. The underlying premises of this approach are that (1) malingerers do not consider or appreciate the role of response latency or speed in memory test performance, and (2) malingerers may take longer to respond overall, because they presumably have to suppress first the correct response and then concoct an incorrect (but, hopefully, plausible) alternative. Rose and colleagues (1995) recently adapted the PDRT to include a measure of response latency. Simulators, regardless of coaching, produced significantly longer response latencies than normal control participants, but shorter than TBI patients. On cross-validation, a discriminant function, based PDRT number correct and response latency, resulted in 74% sensitivity and 100% specificity to faking.

Directions for Future Research

In order to maximize the predictive value of simulation studies for the detection of feigned amnesia in the clinic, future studies should include (1) meaningful incentives to simulate the specified condition, (2) at least minimal coaching for feigning memory impairment (e.g., "Don't be obvious in your attempt to appear memory-disordered"), and (3) meaningful clinical comparison groups (e.g., patients with genuine memory impairment, preferably of the etiology in question, and patients with other forms of cognitive impairment). For studies comparing patients with and without known brain damage, additional work is needed on developing methods for the independent assessment of feigning. For example, the method used by Greiffenstein and colleagues (1994) and possibly an analogue of the Structured Interview of Reported Symptoms (SIRS; Rogers, Bagby, & Dickens, 1992) may be helpful. The use of "at-risk" patient samples (e.g., injured disability claimants) in a differential prevalence design is problematic, because their test results are difficult to interpret even if they perform more poorly than non-compensation-seeking patients with comparable injuries.

Although not designed to assess feigning, several standard clinical tests of learning and memory hold promise for differentiating between feigned and genuine memory deficits (Bernard, 1991; Millis, 1994; Mittenberg et al., 1993; Trueblood & Schmidt, 1993). Development of additional indices and scoring methods for standard clinical instruments, as well as the cross-validation of previously derived decision rules with different study designs and populations, would be extremely valuable. Such studies have immediate clinical utility, as they have the potential to expand the clinical use-fulness of existing memory tests. The use of malingering-specific tests has produced promising results as well. One consistent finding across tasks and studies is that individuals feigning memory impairment tend to underestimate the free-recall impairment of genuinely memory-disordered patients, but overestimate their recognition impairment (Brandt, 1992; Brandt et al., 1985; Iverson et al., 1991; Trueblood & Schmidt, 1993; Wiggins & Brandt, 1988). Thus, the refinement of tests such as the Recall–Recognition Test (Brandt et al., 1985) and others that use the basic SVT paradigm is recommended. Further study of serial position effects, response latency, implicit memory, feeling-of-knowing, and perhaps even memory for the source or temporal order of newly learned information may ultimately prove useful for the determination of malingering. Finally, consideration of base rates in studies of feigned memory impairment is critical. The prevalence of faking affects the predictive value of methods used for detecting feigned memory impairment; failing to account for base rates will result in inaccurate predictions. We acknowledge, however, that determining the true prevalence of malingering in any clinical population is practically impossible.

CLINICAL APPLICATIONS

At the time the first edition of this volume was published, Brandt (1988) concluded that no reliable instruments existed for the valid detection of feigned memory impairment across all cases. Since then, substantial research has addressed this issue, but still, no single instrument or method has been shown on cross-validation to possess greater than 90% sensitivity and specificity for the detection of feigned memory impairment. Nevertheless, across studies that compared either simulators or suspected malingerers with various clinical samples, two methods have been shown to differentiate between feigned and genuine memory impairment with reasonably good (75–90%) sensitivity and specificity. These methods allow for the comparison of recall versus recognition memory and the comparison of learning/memory versus attention. In general, studies that permit such comparisons have found that simulators and suspected malingerers tend to overestimate the impairments that actual memory-disordered patients display on tests of recognition memory and on tests of attention or immediate memory (e.g., digit span).

Although below-chance performance on recognition memory testing constitutes compelling evidence of feigning, relatively few suspected malingerers (or even simulators) feign this blatantly. In other words, clinicians may have a high level of confidence that below-chance performance signifies feigning, even though few malingerers will be so extreme in their responses. Consequently, as an indicator of feigning, below-chance performance has much greater specificity than sensitivity.

An interesting application of SVT technique to evaluate complaints of circumscribed retrograde amnesia involves the post hoc construction of forced-choice memory tests based on autobiographical events for which the suspected malingerer claims no knowledge (Denney & Wynkoop, 1995; Frederick & Carter, 1993; Frederick et al., 1995; Kopelman et al., 1994). Examination of free-recall serial position effects has greater promise as an indicator of feigned amnestic syndrome (Wiggins & Brandt, 1988) than it has as an indicator of feigned memory impairment secondary to traumatic brain injury (Bernard, 1991; Cercy et al., 1995). Other aspects of memory functioning, such as the buildup and release of PI, implicit memory, response latency, and feeling-of-knowing have not received sufficient study, or have yielded such mixed results that conclusions about their potential usefulness for the detection of malingering are infeasible.

Because many neuropsychiatric and medical conditions involve memory impairments, and the nature and severity of these impairments vary to such a great degree, context of the evaluation plays a crucial role in making a determination of malingering. The motivation for malingering is presumed to be different in dissimilar settings, which consequently affects the base rates. Thus, we might speculate that an otherwise healthy elderly person, with no prior history of mental disorders, who develops severe memory problems following a stroke is much less likely to malinger than a young adult who suffered a mild concussion in an automobile accident after a high-speed police chase. The same test score might lead to opposite conclusions for two persons, based on the nature of the injuries and the clinical context. For example, chance performance on a forced-choice memory test easily could represent genuine memory impairment in a hemiplegic patient who is recovering from a recent, severe, traumatic brain injury, whereas the same performance could represent convincing evidence of malingering in an otherwise healthy person of average intelligence who never lost consciousness or demonstrated any other evidence of brain injury following a minor automobile accident 3 years earlier.

Despite the difficulties inherent in clinical reasoning about malingering, certain patterns of memory test results in the context of an appropriate clinical picture can be interpreted with relative confidence as indicative of feigning. Consider, for example, a recent patient we examined. A 41-year-old man sustained a work-related electrical injury with first- and second-degree burns to his right hand. The absence of entry or exit wounds suggested that he sustained a flash-type burn, and that the electricity did not pass through his body. His coworkers reported that the patient did not lose consciousness, and he was released from the hospital emergency room after burn treatment. Several weeks later, the patient began complaining of depressed mood, severe memory problems, difficulty concentrating, and a variety of physical symptoms. He continued working, albeit in a slightly reduced capacity. Repeated neurological examinations invariably were normal (except for cognitive complaints), as were computed tomography, EEG, and auditory evoked potential studies. The patient later sued the regional utility company for $2.7 million in damages, claiming that he had developed depression and a postconcussive syndrome as a result of his accident. Testing revealed a WMS-R General Memory Index of 84 and an Attention/Concentration Index of 65. On the AVLT, he showed no discernible improvement in recall over the five learning trials, and he recognized only 6 of the 15 target words after a 20-minute delay. He correctly reproduced 12 stimuli from the Rey-15. His performance on a modified version of the PDRT revealed flawless discrimination of target and distractor digit strings following 5-second delays, but chance discrimination following 15-second delays. On the Recall–Recognition Test, he showed normal free recall (8 of 20 words) but grossly abnormal recognition (13 of 20 words; chance performance). He produced a Wechsler Adult Intelligence Scale—Revised Full-Scale IQ of 85 and earned average scores on the Trail Making and Wisconsin Card Sorting Tests. However, he displayed severe psychomotor slowing bilaterally on the Grooved Pegboard Test. His cognitive complaints were judged to be disproportionate to and inconsistent with the injuries he sustained, and his test results were thought to reflect symptom exaggeration.

Conversely, certain patterns of memory test results, given an appropriate context, can be interpreted with confidence as indicative of genuine amnesia, even in the absence of corroborating neurodiagnostic evidence. For example, a 79-year-old woman was referred for neuropsychological evaluation because of a history of progressive memory decline. She had attended a prestigious women's college and worked as an art editor for a newspaper. Her medical history was unremarkable. Two years before the evaluation, her husband began noticing that she was forgetting appointments, misplacing personal items, getting lost while driving, and repeating questions, all of which seemed to worsen over time. On her initial neuropsychological evaluation, she had a Full-Scale IQ of 132; her performance on tests of attention and concentration, cognitive processing speed, language, visuospatial ability, and concept formation were generally above average to superior. In sharp contrast, her delayed recall of verbal material (0% retention on WMS-R Logical Memory) and visual material (29% retention on WMS-R Visual Reproductions) was impaired. The results of her neuropsychological evaluation suggested the diagnosis of amnestic disorder. Follow-up neuropsychological testing conducted 1 year later and subsequent testing revealed no further decline in any cognitive domain, including memory, thereby ruling out a dementia syndrome. Currently, this patient remains unambiguously amnesic. However, there is no evidence of brain abnormality on neuroimaging studies or any other diagnostic tests.

Several factors that bear on the determination of malingering involve clinical observations and judgments that are difficult to state in operational terms. As a result, these factors are better construed as representing the "art" of clinical neuropsychological assessment. One example is the finding of gross inconsistencies between test performance and everyday functioning. In the first case, described earlier, despite a WMS-R Attention/Concentration Index of 65 and other findings suggestive of severe cognitive dysfunction, the malingerer continued to function normally at work, where he made competitive bids on construction projects. A related factor involves grossly inconsistent performance across tests or testing occasions. During the evaluation described earlier, this man's ability to match angled line segments on the Judgment of Line Orientation Test was severely abnormal, although his reproduction of the Rey–Osterrieth complex figure was accurate, complete, and well-proportioned. A third factor involves test findings that do not "make sense" neurologically, as when a patient whose mood disorder is effectively treated with six applications of unilateral ECT, and who shows no evidence of adverse neurological effects, later develops severe, persistent deficits on serial neuropsychological assessment. Finally, suspicion of feigning is aroused in the examiner by patients who display unusual behaviors during testing. Of course, psychologists must allow considerable latitude for the variety of responses to testing shown by different patients. Still, the clinician occasionally is struck by an individual's evasiveness, discomfort, or unconcern that is qualitatively distinct from the distress, embarrassment, suspiciousness, apathy, and irritability that are more common responses of neuropsychiatric patients to testing.

Based on these considerations, Table 5.1 summarizes a threshold model for feigned amnesia. In any context in which the motivation to feign amnesia is likely, these indicators should be considered. As a threshold model, any highly anomalous findings (indicators 1 through 5 in Table 5.1) that are not typically found with amnesic patients warrant further investigation. In addition, grossly inconsistent behavior (i.e., between testing or between testing and usual functioning) justifies further evaluation. Finally, evasive and markedly uncooperative behavior during testing, but not observed in other contexts, deserves further assessment.

Despite important advances during the last decade, only a circumscribed clinical decision model can be proposed. Based on the SVT, performances below chance signify a high probability of feigned amnesia. In addition, highly anomalous performance (multiple indicators among 1 through 5 in Table 5.2), which are confirmed independently, also have a high probability of identifying feigned amnesia.

PSEUDO-REMEMBERING

"Pseudo-remembering" is a general term that we use to refer to a class of phenomena wherein individuals report mental experiences as if they were recollections of actual, historical events. Included under this rubric are confabulations, certain delusions, dis-

---

TABLE 5.1. Threshold Model for Feigned Amnesia

In an appropriate context, feigning should be fully investigated in cases of memory impairment in which any of the following indicators are present:

1. Impairment of attention or immediate memory that is much worse than impairment of overall learning and memory
2. Standardized scores on tests of recognition memory that are lower than standardized scores on tests of free recall
3. Reports of dense retrograde amnesia in the absence of other neurological abnormality
4. Reports of dense retrograde amnesia together with intact new learning and memory
5. Gross inconsistency between test performance and everyday functioning
6. Gross inconsistency across tests or testing occasions
7. Evasive, uncooperative, or other unusual test-taking behavior

---

TABLE 5.2. Clinical Decision Model for the Determination of Feigned Amnesia

In an appropriate context, feigned amnesia can be determined by either of the following:

1. Forced-choice recognition memory test performance that is worse than chance (e.g., fewer than 6 correct choices on a 20-item, two-alternative recognition memory test)
2. Multiple indicators from Table 5.1 and strong corroborative evidence of feigned amnesia, including (a) admission of feigning when given feedback on indicators in Table 5.1 or (b) unequivocal independent evidence (e.g., the accident never occurred, or documentation of the person's unimpaired functioning outside the evaluation)

torted memories of actual events, "recovered memories"/"false memories," and outright lying.

Recent media reports notwithstanding, interest in pseudo-memories is not new. Kraepelin (1887) and Korsakoff (1891) wrote about false memories produced by patients with brain disease. These "delusions of remembrance" (Kraepelin, 1887) or "pseudoreminiscences" (Korsakoff, 1891) are often quite fantastic and may be produced spontaneously. Other times, they are provoked by questioning from the clinician. This latter variety is often referred to as the "confabulation of embarrassment" under the assumption that the telling untrue stories was a way to disguise one's severe memory deficits. Thus, not only do patients with amnesia show abnormal forgetting, they also may demonstrate aberrant remembering.

During the past 5 years, substantial controversy has developed over the validity of so-called "recovered memories." Vivid memories of emotionally traumatic events (often sexual abuse in childhood) are reported to emerge after many years of repression or amnesia. Although the characteristics of "recovered memory syndrome" as a clinical entity have been described (e.g., Ofshe & Singer, 1994), the construct has yet to be defined clearly. Indeed, some critics have argued that "false memory syndrome" is a more accurate term, as a substantial proportion of "recovered" memories involved events that could be proven objectively never to have occurred. The same critics argue that many persons giving reports of horribly traumatic experiences are highly suggestible individuals, who were engaged in "recovered-memory" psychotherapy at the time they began making their claims (Loftus, 1993b; McHugh, 1992; Ofshe & Singer, 1994). Given the limited scientific data that relate directly to the veracity of "recovered" memories, we review studies that bear on this issue indirectly by examining (1) the durability of memories formed in childhood, and (2) the susceptibility of memory to the distorting influences of events that occur after memory formation, in children and adults.

Susceptibility of Memory to Distorting Influences

In a series of classic studies, Bartlett (1932) demonstrated that when individuals repeatedly attempt to recall a story, their accounts become increasingly distorted. Elements that are deemed noncritical are omitted, and the narrative undergoes a process of "normalization" or "rationalization." Bartlett concluded that normal long-term memory is *reconstructive* rather than *reproductive,* or what he termed "an effort after meaning." Since Bartlett's study, a considerable body of scientific evidence has amassed indicating that, far from being a "snapshot" of reality, normal memory for events is subject to distorting influences. Erroneous memory can be demonstrated even for emotionally neutral and motivationally insignificant information, such as word lists. Furthermore, participants' confidence in the accuracy of their falsely "recalled" lists is often high (Hintzman, 1988; Roediger & McDermott, 1995; Underwood, 1965). Numerous studies, mostly by Loftus and her colleagues, have demonstrated that providing incorrect or misleading information after a memory is established can lead individuals to later report the memory incorrectly (Loftus, Donders, Hoffman, & Schooler, 1989; Loftus & Hoffman, 1989; Loftus & Ketcham, 1991; Loftus, Miller, & Burns, 1978; Loftus & Palmer, 1974; Loftus & Zanni, 1975). Moreover, these suggested events may be described in considerable detail (Schooler, Clark, & Loftus, 1988; Schooler, Gerhard, & Loftus, 1986), and confidence in the accuracy of these altered memories is often high. Research has established firmly that confidence in a memory correlates only very weakly with its fidelity (Greene, Flynn, & Loftus, 1982).

Several interpretations have been offered for the effect of biasing language and misleading information on memory. Belli (1989) used the term "misinformation acceptance," in which the reporting of a memory is biased by the presentation of subsequent information, but the memory trace itself is not altered in any way (McCloskey & Zaragosa, 1985). An alternative hypotheses is that misleading information interferes with *access* to the memory trace for an event (Loftus & Palmer, 1974; Loftus et al., 1989), rather than merely biasing the individual's response. Other studies suggest that misleading information interferes with the integrity of memory trace itself (Belli, 1989; Weingardt, Loftus, & Lindsay, 1995). Loftus and colleagues maintain that misleading information is incorporated into the individual's memory, resulting in a *reconstruction* of previous events consistent with all available information (Loftus & Hoffman, 1989).

Many patients with pseudo-memories are particularly inaccurate about when and where critical events transpired. Thus, their encoding of *context* is affected to a greater extent than their encoding of *content.* This phenomenon, referred to as "source forgetting" (Schacter, Harbluk, & McLachlan, 1984) in the experimental psychology literature, also can be seen in normal elderly persons, genuine amnesic patients, and brain-impaired patients without amnesia. Elderly adults with a relative weakness on tasks assessing executive functions dependent on the frontal lobes make more incorrect source attributions than those with other deficits (Glisky, Polster, & Routhieaux, 1995). The more severe form of this phenomenon, "source amnesia," has been demonstrated in patients with confirmed frontal lobe lesions (Janowsky, Shimamura, & Squire, 1989), and amnesics with alcoholic Korsakoff's syndrome (Shimamura & Squire, 1987). Thus, forgetting or mistaking the context in which an event occurred is not uncommon and may contribute to distortions and misattributions of those events, especially in some vulnerable persons. One speculation is that patients with unambiguously false memories would perform more poorly of experimental source memory tasks and, perhaps, on aspects of difficult clinical tasks of executive functioning.

Accuracy of Early Childhood Memories

The susceptibility of recall accuracy to the effects of misleading postevent information has clear implications for the reliability of eyewitness testimony (Lindsay & Johnson, 1987; Loftus, 1979). Less clear are the implications of this phenomenon for "recovered" childhood memories. Some writers (Darton, 1991; Herman & Harvey, 1993) have argued that laboratory studies of misinformation interference effects lack external validity because (1) such findings are based mostly on adult participants rather than children, and (2) the memories experimentally distorted by postevent information are much less salient and emotionally charged than those associated with traumatic experiences, such as sexual abuse.

In response to these criticisms, several studies have shown that recall of events by children also is subject to distortion by postevent information (Ceci & Bruck, 1993; Dale, Loftus, & Rathbun, 1978; Lipscomb, Bregman, & McCallister, 1984). Ceci, Loftus, Leichtman, and Bruck (1994) found that children "remembered" events that were merely discussed or suggested by others as having actually occurred, and that "source misattribution" was more pronounced in younger children. Lindsay and Johnson (1987) suggested that such misattributions may account for children's false beliefs about fictitious events. Perhaps most crucial for the recovered-memory/false-memory debate is the evidence that durable, permanent memories of childhood events are not formed before the age of 3 or 4 years (Kihlstrom & Harackiewicz, 1982; Nadel & Zola-Morgan, 1984; Pillemer & White, 1989), when the development of the hippocampus, a structure that mediates the consolidation and storage of memories is complete (Eckenhoff & Rakic, 1991; Scoville & Milner, 1957; Squire & Zola-Morgan, 1991).

Of course, not all studies of children have found that misleading postevent information is associated with the production of false memories. In one study, 5- and 7-year-old girls received a medical checkup that included either a genital and anal examination or a scoliosis examination. None of the girls who received scoliosis examinations reported genital contact, despite the use of misleading, directed questions (Saywitz, Goodman, Nicholas, & Moan, 1991). In another study, 3- to 7-year-olds accurately recalled 88% of the components of a stressful urogenital examination immediately, and their recall remained high 6 weeks later (i.e., 83%; Merritt, Ornstein, & Spicker, 1994). Thus, at least in some circumstances, children accurately recall events that are presumably unpleasant and subject to interference from postevent information.

Clear facts regarding children's memories of actual traumatic experiences are meager. Malmquist (1986) studied the effects of witnessing the murder of one or both parents, or of later viewing the murder scene, in 16 children between 5 and 10 years old. All the children reported experiencing intrusive thoughts about the event, most developed affective symptoms and nightmares, some developed somatization disorders, and two developed specific situational phobias. Although none of the children failed to recall the event, most engaged in active behavioral avoidance ("I stayed away from situations that remind me of it") and/or cognitive avoidance ("I didn't let myself have thoughts about it"). Thus, even in the face of severe emotional stress, these chil-

dren readily remembered traumatic events. However, the interval between the parental murder and the time the study was conducted was not reported. In addition, longitudinal follow-up was not conducted to determine how the passage of time affected
these memories.

   In contrast to Malmquist (1986), Williams (1994) reported that 38% of 129 women
did not acknowledge specific incidents of sexual abuse when interviewed 17 years later.
As children, these women had been examined in a hospital emergency room following a sexual assault (ages 10 months to 12 years). However, 68% of the women reported remembering at least one other episode of childhood sexual abuse, making the
repression argument less convincing. Not surprisingly, women sexually assaulted before the age of 7 were significantly less likely to report any memory of the event than
women assaulted at an older age. Loftus, Garry, and Feldman (1994) have argued that
episodes of sexual abuse that occurred after the "index" event in Williams's (1994)
study might have decreased the salience of, or have become confused with, the earlier
event, thereby decreasing the likelihood of reporting the index event. Moreover, not
reporting an episode of sexual abuse, even in response to specific inquiries, is not the
same as not remembering it. Some women in this study may have deliberately opted
to deny the index event for any of a number of reasons, including the protection of
the perpetrator.

   Research clearly demonstrates that it is not unusual for adults to forget such salient events as automobile accidents (Cash & Moss, 1972), deaths of family members
(Usher & Neisser, 1993), and hospitalizations (Means & Loftus, 1991) only months
after their occurrence. Furthermore, a variety of factors can induce distorted recall of
events by individuals who have no evidence of "organic" amnesia. Critics of laboratory research argue that many such studies lack external validity and do not generalize
to such "real-life" circumstances as "recovering" memories of childhood sexual abuse.
Conversely, a few studies have shown that both adults and children are able to recall
singular traumatic events reliably. However, the literature does not clearly distinguish
whether children who experience trauma before the age of 3–4, when neural memory
systems are not fully developed, show less reliable memory of the event than children
whose traumatic experiences occur later. We do not know whether children who can
recall traumatic events weeks or months afterward are likely to later "forget" the event
or become unable to access the memories at some future time. The effects of repeated
versus isolated instances of sexual abuse on recall of those episodes also have not been
investigated. Additional empirical research is needed to determine how intrapersonal
(e.g., premorbid personality and psychopathology), interpersonal (e.g., relationship
between victim and perpetrator, family interactions, and social support), and environmental (e.g., nature, duration, frequency, and intensity of the traumatic experience)
variables mediate the development of "repressed" memories or forgetting, and how
the same classes of variables influence the "recovery" or fabrication of memories in
adulthood. Finally, the role of source forgetting and source misattribution warrants
further investigation as a potential explanation for errors in the recall of traumatic events
that have little basis in reality.

CONCLUSIONS

Remembering is a fundamentally personal experience. In fact, our memories of our own pasts largely define us as individuals. Furthermore, remembering is a highly private event; any effort to discover whether someone is recollecting an event accurately is, at best, an educated guess.

The amnestic syndrome is a well-recognized consequence of some forms of cerebral damage, although the nexus between an injury (e.g., motor vehicle accident) and its sequelae (e.g., memory impairment) is not invariable and is certainly vulnerable to deliberate distortions. In addition, dissociative amnesia and other nonneurological memory impairments lack any known pathophysiology. They are particularly difficult to distinguish from role playing or feigning. Despite these differences, researchers and clinicians are cautioned that a facile dichotomization of memory disorders into "true" and "pseudo" amnesia does not take into account that (1) the range of behavioral expressions of brain damage is not fully known, (2) even brain-disordered patients may be motivated to exaggerate impairments, and (3) there is undoubtedly a neurobiology of dissociative amnesia. Finally, the absence of a demonstrated neurological substrate does not disprove the existence of dissociative amnesia.

Less well developed are our conceptualizations of pseudo-remembering. Confabulation in memory-disordered, brain-damaged patients has been recognized for over a century, and the "recovery" of "repressed" memories through psychoanalysis was a widely accepted phenomenon early in the 20th century. Today, the explosion of patently false memories, especially of early sexual trauma, are often prompted by well-meaning, but misguided therapists. We may be able to understand these pseudo-memories by reference to well-established principles that govern the establishment, elaboration, and reconstruction of all memories. The creation of memories, even false memories, is governed by rules. By systematically investigating those rules, the process of scientific inquiry will disengage the recovered-memory/false-memory debate from the tabloids and work toward a better understanding of these complex memory phenomena.

ACKNOWLEDGMENT

Preparation of this chapter was supported, in part, by the John P. Boogher Fund Memory Disorders Research.

6

Denial and Misreporting of Substance Abuse

RICHARD ROGERS, Ph.D.
KIMBERLY S. KELLY, Ph.D.

Social sanctions and stigmatization associated with substance abuse have proliferated during the last several decades. Recent initiatives include greater penalties for drunken driving and the adoption of random drug tests and other detection procedures in employment settings (Gibson & Manley, 1991; Rosen, 1987). Even the prior use of marijuana became an issue in the 1992 presidential election; the self-serving protestation, "I did not inhale," was viewed by many with incredulity and by some as damning evidence of dissimulation. The continued war on drugs, with broad public support, symbolizes our outward intolerance of chemical dependency and its putative link with crime, irresponsibility, and erosion of mainstream values.

The schism between publicly professed attitudes and private behaviors is illustrated by widespread, nonmedical use of drugs. National surveys have suggested that substantial proportions of adults have experimented with illicit drugs (National Institute on Drug Abuse, 1991). Moreover, Epidemiologic Catchment Area (ECA) studies from the early 1980s indicated that the lifetime prevalence of diagnosable drug abuse/dependence is more than 10% in adults in the 18- to 44-year-old range (Rounsaville, 1985). Among adolescents, more than one-half of high school students have experimented with illicit drugs (Mills & Noyes, 1984; Newcomb & Bentler, 1989). Since very few substance abusers openly acknowledge their practices, the maintenance of public attitudes does not correspond with private behaviors. As a result, individuals have learned to deny and minimize substance abuse in the service of twin objectives: (1) avoidance of prosecution and (2) social desirability.

Anonymous survey data of adolescents suggest that a substantial minority are likely to minimize their substance abuse, despite assurances of confidentiality. For example,

Bailey, Flewelling, and Rachal (1992) surveyed students from grades 6 to 9 twice within a 1-year interval. They found that more than 10% (16.1% for alcohol and 10.3% for marijuana) of acknowledged users reported a history of use at T_1 but denied *any* history at T_2. They also found errors in estimated use (i.e., greater at T_1 than T_2) and that only one-third were consistent in reporting age of first use. Bachman and O'Malley (1981), extrapolating from their data on 16,654 high school seniors, concluded that these participants were likely to underestimate their substance abuse over the last year. They speculated that reports for the last year are likely to capture only one-third of actual substance abuse. Neither study was designed to identify persons who consistently deny or minimize drug involvement. Consequently, these results, even under conditions of anonymity, suggest substantial underestimates in reported substance abuse.

Criminalization of substance abuse confounds estimates of its ingestion. Persons are unlikely to be entirely forthcoming when faced with potential consequences of criminal sanctions as well as judicial hearings on such issues as parenting (e.g., child negligence, fitness to parent, and child custody) and employability (e.g., revocation of professional licensure and torts arising from drug-related work injuries). With even the possession of certain drugs constituting a felony, we should not be surprised if research participants routinely deny or underestimate their drug usage. On the opposite end of the spectrum, offenders arrested for very serious crimes may be motivated to report, overreport, or fabricate drug use as a mitigating factor in sentencing (Rogers & Mitchell, 1991).

OVERVIEW

Specific Terminology

An expanded list of terms is used to characterize response styles for substance abusers: disacknowledgment, misappraisal, denial, and exaggeration (see Table 6.1). The first two response styles tend to be specific to cases of misreported substance abuse. For "disacknowledgment," the person disclaims knowledge (e.g., "I don't know" and "I don't remember") of either the drug usage or its behavioral consequences. Whether this disacknowledgment is sincere is often open to question. As a more general response style, "misappraisal" refers to the misreporting of substance abuse in which there is no question about the person's sincerity. In other words, there is no observable effort to dissimulate; distortions are based on misinformation rather than a deliberate attempt to deceive.

The two other response styles parallel the more general terms of "defensiveness" and "malingering." In the substance abuse literature, "denial" is the accepted term for defensiveness. Although much less common, cases are observed that involve a magnification of substance usage or its effects. These cases are referred to as "exaggeration." An important distinction must be made between exaggeration and malingering. Only when a putative substance abuser fabricates or grossly overstates symptoms (psychological or physical) is this response style designated as malingering. Other forms of magnification are termed "exaggeration."

TABLE 6.1. Response Styles Specific to Substance Abuse

Response style	Dimensions of distortion (amount/usage and behavioral consequences)
Disacknowledgment	The person reports "not knowing" important elements of drug ingestion or its effects on behavior; blackouts and other memory impairment are frequently implicated. The person's sincerity is very difficult to establish.[a]
Misappraisal	The person reports inaccurately usage or consequences of usage. For example, most persons are unaware of the potency, purity, or even types of illegal drugs consumed. Persons with alcoholic disorders have trouble recalling correctly the number of drinks. Because of memory impairment, a person may rely on others' account of the behavioral consequences.[b] Designation of this response style questions only the person's accuracy and not sincerity.
Denial[c]	The person deliberately minimizes or disavows drug use or its consequences. Motivation may include social desirability, attempts to avoid treatment, and unwillingness to accept responsibility for concomitant behavior (e.g., driving while intoxicated).
Exaggeration[d]	The person deliberately exaggerates or fabricates drug use or its consequences. The motivation for exaggeration may include boasting about drug consumption and mitigation of other unacceptable behavior (e.g., unwanted sexual advances).

[a]One phenomenon occasionally observed in forensic settings is the double disclaimer: "I know I didn't do it [the criminal act]. But if I did, I was so impaired on drugs, I don't remember doing it."
[b]We suspect, based on the malleability of memories, that some persons are not aware that their "memories" are recreations of others' observations.
[c]Although commonly referred to as denial in the substance abuse literature, this response style is also described as defensiveness (see Chapter 1).
[d]This response style should not be referred to as malingering except under circumstances in which the person is grossly exaggerating or fabricating psychological or physical symptoms toward the achievement of an external goal.

Prevalence of Dissimulation

The prevalence of defensiveness and denial among drug users has not been well established. Guthmann and Brenna (1990) employed the Client Substance Index (CSI) in conjunction with the California Psychological Inventory (CPI) and concluded that approximately 50% of juvenile delinquents were faking good on the CSI. A great concern was that the lack of convergence between the CSI and clinician assessments ($r = .04$) on which delinquents were feigning good. Winters, Stinchfield, Henly, and Schwartz (1991) examined general defensiveness among large samples of adolescent drug users and controls. For defensiveness, they found moderate levels in 44.5% of drug users and 61.6% on controls, and marked levels in 3.6% and 8.5%, respectively. As a general measure of defensiveness derived from the Marlowe–Crowne, these estimates do not directly address denied or minimized substance abuse.

Fabricated drug use, observed in the endorsement of fictitious drugs, appears to be relatively rare in nonclinical adolescent populations (Petzel, Johnson, & McKillip,

1973). Among clinical populations, Winters et al. (1991) reported low percentages of adolescents in treatment (5.1% and 6.3%) that exaggerated their drug use. No attempt was made to address inconsistent or random responding; therefore, these percentages may be inflated by adolescents responding erratically on the surveys.

Several observations temper our use of these prevalence data. First, the studies are limited only to adolescent populations. Second, the crucial difference between "drug" defensiveness and "general" defensiveness is typically not made (see also Smart & Jarvis, 1981). Third, the sole study (Guthmann & Brenna, 1990) that compared clinical judgment to test results found virtually no correlation. In summary, we suspect that denial of substance abuse is widespread but lack accurate prevalence estimates for both adult and adolescent populations.

Types of Distortion

Distortions may occur on three dimensions: (1) amount and type of substance abuse, (2) immediate behavioral and psychological effects of substance abuse, and (3) consequent impairment and psychological sequelae from cumulative substance abuse. Laboratory procedures focus principally on the amount and type of substance abuse for varying intervals: immediate (e.g., Breathalyzer), short-term (e.g., urinalysis), and long-term (e.g., hair analysis). In contrast, psychometric methods tend to focus on long-term effects and sequelae of substance abuse. Examples arising from chronic substance abuse include syndromes/disorders (e.g., alcohol dependence), cognitive deficits (e.g., patterns of memory impairment on neuropsychological tests), and clinical correlates (e.g., personality characteristics, such as delinquency, commonly associated with substance abusers). For instance, the Substance Abuse Subtle Screening Inventory (SASSI; Miller, 1985, 1994) is employed to evaluate unacknowledged chemical dependence based on clinical correlates; this psychometric method offers no data on the amount and usage of alcohol and drugs.

Distortions in the immediate behavioral and psychological effects of substance abuse have not been systematically investigated. The most closely related research, although not ideal, involves the Comprehensive Drinker Profile (CDP; Miller & Marlatt, 1984, 1987) which examines characteristic patterns of alcohol abuse with reasons and effects of drinking and certain situational variables. In conclusion, we have no standardized measures for assessing the behavioral consequences of drinking. In other words, although a patient may be accurate and forthcoming about both the amount of drug abuse and its long-term effects, we have no data about the accuracy of self-reporting as related to specific incidents. This gap is particularly germane to forensic evaluations in which issues of impaired judgment and erratic behavior are often more relevant to the assessment than usage (e.g., blood alcohol concentrations [BACs]) or diagnosis.

The relationship of blood alcohol to intoxicated behavior is highly variable. Even the same individual can respond differently to identical BACs, depending on mood state and other situational factors (de Wit, Uhlenhuth, Pierri, & Johanson, 1987). Mikkelsen (1985) observed that clinical intoxication generally occurs between levels from 100 to 200, although concentrations as low as 30 may result in intoxication. MacDonald (1976a) reported cases of chronic alcoholics whose BAC level ranged between 350 and 450 and yet appeared to be relatively sober. As observed by Rogers and Mitchell (1991), investigators are highly divergent in their views of BAC and its relationship to clinical intoxication.

An important caution is that *unreported* substance abuse cannot be equated with *denied* substance abuse. Research by Moore et al. (1989) on alcoholism in hospitalized patients is particularly instructive. A sample of 2,002 medical and psychiatric patients were administered one of two face-valid screens; results of these screens were compared to physician interviews. On medical units, the great majority of patients with alcohol abuse or dependence were missed by their attending physicians (range of missed diagnosis was 65–93%). Even on the psychiatric service, roughly one-third (35%) of these diagnoses were overlooked. Because the criterion measure consisted primarily of face-valid questionnaires, we must assume that many of the missed diagnoses resulted from diagnostic neglect rather than patient distortion. This conclusion is bolstered by correlates of socioeconomic status (SES); physicians were more likely to miss diagnoses of alcohol abuse or dependence among patients with private insurance, more years of education, and higher incomes. Finally, it is important to note that these findings were not from a community hospital but a world-renowned teaching and research facility.

Chapter Organization

The following sections organize the assessment of substance abuse into two major components: clinical and laboratory methods. In clinical methods, brief screens, such as Michigan Alcohol Screening Test (MAST; Selzer, 1971) and Drug Abuse Screening Test (DAST; Skinner, 1982), offer rapid and relatively effective means of evaluating self-acknowledged substance abuse. Given the simplicity of these screens, we believe they should be used as a basis of comparison. In other words, do more elaborate procedures possess greater discriminant validity than brief self-report screens, particularly in cases of denied or exaggerated drug use? Other clinical methods include structured interviews and multiscale inventories; these methods adopt a broad-spectrum approach toward psychological impairment and incorporate syndromes and scales for substance abuse. Finally, specialized methods have been developed specifically for the comprehensive assessment of substance abuse.

CLINICAL METHODS

The validation of substance abuse measures is predicated on the accurate measurement of the external criterion, namely the use/misuse of alcohol and drugs (see Table 6.2). However, many studies are satisfied simply to use uncorroborated self-reporting as an external criterion measure. Practitioners can quickly recognize the nonindependence

TABLE 6.2. Types of Test Validation for Substance Abuse Measures and Their Relevance to Honesty and Dissimulation

1. *Self-report by self-report.* Acknowledged use/nonuse is employed as the criterion. The paradox is that honesty is assumed for the self-described use/nonuse to assess forthrightness on the substance abuse measure.

2. *Self-report by informant report.* Often a family member is used as an informant to satisfy this criterion. This approach assumes the user will be more honest with family members than with clinicians.

3. *Self-report by treatment history.* Documented history of treatment provides an excellent criterion for a longitudinal perspective of substance abuse. Substance abusers are likely to know that denial of use will be detected; therefore, they are likely to be more forthcoming than the target group (i.e., individuals for whom substance abuse has not been established).

4. *Self-report by laboratory methods.* Laboratory methods can accurately establish current (urinalysis) and long-term (hair analysis) drug use. This approach is an effective means of verifying drug use, although not its behavioral effects. This method has not been used in the validation of substance abuse measures.

5. *Self-report by convergent indicators.* The degree of association between two or more substance abuse measures is evaluated. Since the external validity of most measures is based on either 1 or 2, the convergence of measures also remains vulnerable to response styles.

6. *Self-report by simulation design.* Users and nonusers are asked simulate on substance abuse measures. Although rarely used, the simulation design provides direct information on the vulnerability of substance abuse measures to distortion.

and paradoxical nature of this approach. Other research has relied upon informants and convergent indicators from other measures. Although a modest improvement over the "self-report by self-report" validity, such studies are still largely dependent on secondary sources of self-report. Two types of external validity are generally effective: (1) treatment history for establishing drug-related disorders and (2) laboratory methods for confirming the use or nonuse of alcohol and drugs. As noted in subsequent sections, research can easily be conducted on the vulnerability of substance abuse measures to denial and exaggeration. Optimally, studies should combine treatment history and laboratory methods as external criteria with simulation studies of denial and exaggeration. Babor, Stephens, and Marlatt (1987) provide a thoughtful review of criterion measures and the relevant literature.

Screens for Substance Abuse

MAST

The MAST (Selzer, 1971) is one of the earliest and most widely used screens for alcohol abuse. It consists of 25 descriptive statements that are asked by the clinician as a screening for alcohol abuse and concomitant impairment. Although apparently effective in classifying alcohol abuse and dependence among inpatients seeking treatment for self-acknowledged problems (e.g., Moore, 1972; Ross, Gavin, & Skinner, 1990), its usefulness among patients denying substance abuse is brought into question. Because of its high face validity, data (Otto & Hall, 1988; Otto, Lang, Megargee, & Rosenblatt, 1988) suggested that patients can easily fake the MAST by denying alcohol abuse.

SAAST

Swenson and Morse (1975) modified the MAST to produce a self-report version that is referred to as the Self-Administered Alcoholism Screening Test (SAAST). The SAAST is composed of 34 items that are presented in a yes–no format. Employing the SAAST, Swenson and Morse discovered 9 of 100 controls with elevated scores; 6 of these were later revealed to have significant histories of alcohol abuse. In addition, 16 of 100 alcoholics, in spite of their current involvement in inpatient alcohol treatment, were characterized as defensive, based on their low SAAST scores. Like the MAST, these data would suggest that the SAAST is fakable.

DAST

The DAST (Skinner, 1982) parallels the MAST with questions regarding nonprescribed drug use. It is composed of 28 self-report items as a quantitative index of problems associated with substance abuse. The content of the items reflects frequency of drug use, and interpersonal, legal, and medical problems associated with drug use. Results of 223 referred individuals were examined in light of validity scales on the Basic Personality Inventory (BPI; Jackson, 1976). They found correlations with denial (−.28) and social desirability (−.38), suggesting that scores may have been influenced by these response styles. Skinner suggested that the DAST is only "minimally influenced by response style biases of denial and social desirability" (p. 369). This interpretation must be tempered by two observations: (1) The study was composed of persons voluntarily seeking treatment and may not generalize to other populations; and (2) the BPI scales reflect general denial and social desirability, and were not intended to evaluate undisclosed drug use and attendant problems. Although the correlation for social desirability (−.38) is not large, it is similar to those correlations found for the primary criterion measure, namely the frequency of drug use (r's range from .19 to .55; median = .35). In summary, we believe that the DAST is as vulnerable to denial and exaggeration as the MAST and other face-valid screens.

RAPI

White and Labouvie (1989) developed the Rutgers Alcohol Problem Index (RAPI) for the rapid screening of alcoholism among adolescents. The RAPI entails 23 face-valid items, presented in a questionnaire, regarding the potential negative effects of problem alcohol use. The authors have experimented with different time frames (e.g., last 3 years or "ever") and different response categories. In addition, the authors acknowledge the potential for denial or exaggeration, both of which have not been researched with the RAPI.

AAIS

The Adolescent Alcohol Involvement Scale (AAIS; Mayer & Filstead, 1979) is a 14-item multiple-choice scale for the assessment of alcohol use and resulting problems. Although severity of scores appeared to associated with criterion groups, the authors supply no data on response styles. Rather, they assume that adolescents minimizing alcohol problems might still be detected, based on an entirely unrelated study of adult drunken drivers.

ADI

Harrell and Wirtz (1989) constructed the Adolescent Drinking Index (ADI) as a 24-item self-report for the assessment of problem drinking. Items are rated on their accuracy of self-description (e.g., "like me a lot") or their frequency (i.e., "never" to "4 or more times"). Although the ADI appears to discriminate effectively among criterion groups (e.g., Maag, Irvin, Reid, & Vasa, 1994), no research has investigated its usefulness with adolescents that are minimizing or exaggerating their alcohol use and resulting impairment.

CAGE

Mayfield, McLeod, and Hall (1974) developed the CAGE questionnaire as a measure of covert problem drinking. To decrease the face validity of the CAGE, they embedded six alcohol-content questions in a screening interview of 16 inquiries. Four of the six alcohol-content questions addressed pathological alcohol use. Of 142 alcoholic inpatients, they found that 19 (13.4%) denied alcohol-related problems (i.e., a score of 0 or 1). As with other screening measures, the generalizability of the CAGE to nondisclosing individuals has not been tested.

PESQ

Winters (1992), an author of the Personal Experience Inventory (PEI), developed a screening version that was named the Personal Experience Screening Questionnaire (PESQ). The PESQ is composed of 18 face-valid items that are scored on a 4-point scale of frequency. Although data suggested that approximately 15% of the PESQ protocols were invalid because of compromised self-reporting, no indicators are available for denial or exaggeration.

DUSI

Tarter and Hegedus (1991; see also Tarter, Laird, Kabene, Bukstein, & Kaminer, 1990) developed the Drug Use Screening Inventory (DUSI) for use with both adolescents and adults reporting alcohol or other drug abuse. As the longest of the screens (152 items on 10 domains), the items extend beyond substance abuser per se to address general functioning (behavior patterns, physical and mental health, social and family functioning, and adjustment at school/work). No data are provided on response styles.

Structured Interviews

Rogers (1995) articulated the methodological advantages of structured interviews for differential diagnosis. One particular advantage is the standardization of clinical inquiries and responses so that direct comparisons can be accomplished between the patient and significant others. Generally speaking, the level of patient–informant agreement tends to be relatively modest, even when no evidence of dissimulation is found. Therefore, a lack of agreement does not signify deception. In this section, we will briefly review (1) Axis I interviews that contain substance abuse components and (2) targeted substance abuse interviews.

Each of the primary Axis I interviews (i.e., Schedule of Affective Disorders and Schizophrenia [SADS], Diagnostic Interview Schedule [DIS], and Structured Clinical Interview for DSM-III-R Disorders [SCID]; see Chapter 15) include sections on substance abuse. The SADS (Spitzer & Endicott, 1978), for example, exhibits very good interrater reliability but only modest test–retest reliability when used with substance abusing patients (e.g., Hasin & Grant, 1987; Rounsaville, Cacciola, Weissman, & Kleber, 1981). The DIS-III-A (Robins et al., 1985) focuses extensively on substance abuse and dependence (i.e., alcohol, barbiturates, opioids, cocaine, amphetamines, hallucinogens, cannabis, and tobacco). The DIS substance abuse sections have considerable evidence of concurrent and convergent validity (e.g., Gavin, Ross, & Skinner, 1989; Griffin, Weiss, Mirin, Wilson, & Bouchard-Voelk, 1987; Ross, Gavin, & Skinner, 1990). The most extensive coverage of substance abuse in found on the SCID (Spitzer, Williams, Gibbon, & First, 1990) on which eight drug classes are rated on as many as 15 symptoms and associated features. Williams et al. (1992) found that the interrater reliability of the SCID for drug and alcohol abuse fluctuated widely across clinical settings. No studies have examined the vulnerability of Axis I interviews to the denial or exaggeration of substance abuse. Although these measures have varying degrees of face validity for other sections, items that address substance abuse are very direct and easily identified. Therefore, we would suspect that clinical and nonclinical populations would have no difficulties in modifying their reported substance abuse, either through exaggeration or denial.

Increased interest in substance abuse disorders has led to the development of targeted interviews. In the following paragraphs, we describe two targeted interviews that focus on substance abuse.

Comprehensive Drinker Profile

Miller and Marlatt (1984) developed the Comprehensive Drinker Profile (CDP) as a structured interview for the assessment of alcoholism and treatment potential. Because alcoholics are frequently inaccurate in their accounts of current drinking, an elaborate schedule is constructed for the last week, and consumption is related to estimates of BAC across days and episodes. Although fakable, the elaborate structure discourages blatant denial of alcohol use. As an additional precaution against misreporting, a corroborative form of the CDP is available. Surprisingly, research by Miller, Crawford, and Taylor (1979) concluded that informants were as likely to overestimate as underestimate alcohol consumption. As expected, patients who were mandated to treatment were less likely to be forthcoming about alcohol use as self-referred patients.

Rogers (1995) wondered whether the knowledge that informants would be employed might affect the honesty and completeness of alcoholics' self-reporting. Initial research by Graber and Miller (1988) found no significant differences. Depending on the clinical setting, however, practitioners may wish to inform patients that collateral interviews are an important component of the assessment process. Of course, such a warning may encourage certain patients to become more circumspect in their defensiveness or denial.

ASI and T-ASI

McLellan, Luborsky, Woody, and O'Brien (1980) developed the Addiction Severity Index (ASI) for the assessment of substance abuse and its impact on overall functioning. The ASI, chiefly validated male Veterans Administration patients, emphasizes the treatment needs of individual patients. McLellan et al. reported that only 11 of 750 (1.5%) interviews produced invalid information; the basis of this estimate was not reported. We suspect that these investigators did not systematically screen patients for response styles but reported only very blatant cases of dissimulation. Kaminer, Bukstein, and Tarter (1991) developed the Teen-Addiction Severity Index (T-ASI) as a parallel measure to the ASI. This modified interview has been tested on small samples of adolescent inpatients (see also Kaminer, Wagner, Plummer, & Seifer, 1993), but no data are provided on response styles, either exaggeration or denial.

Scales on Multiscale Inventories

Many multiscale inventories include scales for the assessment of substance abuse and its behavioral correlates. Within the scope of this chapter, we focus on the two inventories on which considerable substance abuse research has been conducted: the Minnesota Multiphasic Personality Inventory (MMPI/MMPI-2) and the Millon Clinical Multiaxial Inventory (MCMI).

MMPI Scales

Clopton (1978) has documented the extensive efforts of utilizing the MMPI to distinguish alcoholics on the basis of profiles or specialized scales. Of these early efforts, the MacAndrew scale (*MAC*; MacAndrew, 1965) has emerged as an extensively tested measure of suspected substance abuse. The *MAC* scale is composed of 49 items that originally differentiated alcoholic outpatients from nonalcoholic outpatients with a cutting score of ≥ 24. Its use has been subsequently expanded to include both alcohol and drug abuse. Despite its early promise, however, the MAC has come under increasing attack. Gottesman and Prescott (1989) reviewed 74 MAC studies and concluded that it was not suitable for clinical practice. More specifically, they were concerned with its insufficient positive predictive power of 15% (i.e., only 1 in 7 alcoholics was correctly identified). Other problems with the MAC include its potential confound with antisocial features and modest discriminability among criterion groups. Wolf, Schubert, Patterson, Grande, and Pendleton (1990) found that individuals with antisocial personality disorder (APD) received higher MAC scores than did substance abusers (see also Rathus, Fox, & Ortins, 1980). Other research (e.g., Levinson et al., 1990; Moore, 1984) had demonstrated only modest group differences among criterion groups with nonusers often achieving elevations beyond the cutting score (e.g., Miller & Streiner, 1990), particularly for minorities (Greene, 1991). For adolescents, Ganter, Graham, and Archer (1992) demonstrated that different cutting scores from ≥ 25 to ≥ 28 were optimal, depending on the criterion groups, to establish even a moderate sensitivity (≥ 55%). In contrast, Gripshover and Dacey (1994) found that the MAC scale had excellent sensitivity with substance abusers (≥ 90% across conditions) but very poor specificity (≤ 20%). Likewise, Otto, Lang, Megargee, and Rosenblatt (1988) established a very high sensitivity (.98) but modest specificity (.30). Even with these latter results, the clinical utility of the MAC as a screen is called into question, unless the base rate of suspected substance abuse is very high.

The MAC scale was modified in the MMPI-2 with the substitution of four items (i.e., the MAC-R). This substitution appears to have little effect on the performance of the MAC-R (see Greene, Arredondo, & Davis, 1990). More recent studies (Greene, Weed, Butcher, Arredondo, & Davis, 1992; Weed, Butcher, McKenna, & Ben-Porath, 1992) have found mean elevations slightly above the cutting score for most male substance abusers and slightly below the cutting score for most female substance abusers.

Otto et al. (1988) examined the usefulness of the MAC scale to detect White males denying their alcohol dependence. They found that 47.5% eluded detection on the MAC. They also found that the MMPI Mp (Positive Malingering Scale; Cofer, Chance, & Judson, 1949) identified 75% of the defensive profiles. Although not directly tested, this finding provides a tantalizing hypothesis that the combined use of a specialized scale of substance abuse (e.g., the MAC) and a general measure of defensiveness (e.g., Mp) may produce effective classification rules.

MacAndrew (1986) also constructed a 36-item Substance Abuse Proclivity (SAP) for differentiating young males (age range from 16 to 22) with substance abuse problems from normal and clinical samples. As noted by Greene (1991), the SAP produced very similar results to the MAC, thus questioning its incremental validity. In its application to the MMPI-2, Greene et al. (1992) found negligible differences between substance abusers and others on the SAP.

Weed et al. (1992) developed two new scales for the assessment of substance abuse on the MMPI-2: (1) the Addiction Acknowledgment Scale (AAS), a 13-item face-valid measure of which 9 items address the misuse of alcohol or drugs; and (2) the Addiction Potential Scale (*APS*), a 39-item scale with a varied content, unrelated to substance abuse. They found similar elevations on the *APS* (*M*'s from 28.4 to 30.7) across both gender and type of abuse (alcohol, drug, or both) that were somewhat higher than nonabusing criterion groups (*M*'s from 23.3 to 23.9). Greene et al. (1992) found more modest differences between abusers (*M*'s from 26.8 to 27.6) and nonabusers (*M*'s from 23.6 to 23.8). Interestingly, Fantoni-Salvador and Rogers (1995) found the *AAS* to be superior to the *MAC* and *APS* in identifying Hispanic patients with alcohol dependence. In summary, the *APS* and the *AAS* evidence modest improvements over the *MAC* but have not been tested in simulation research in which known substance abusers are instructed to deny or minimize their drug use.

MCMI Scales

The Millon Clinical Multiaxial Inventory (MCMI; Millon, 1983) has two scales for the assessment of substance abuse: the Alcohol Abuse Scale, designated as Scale *B*, is composed of 31 items (7 face-valid items address alcohol abuse). The Substance Abuse Scale, designated as Scale *T*, is composed of 46 items, 5 of which are face-valid. As noted by Bryer, Martines, and Dignan (1990), research has found that the scales are highly intercorrelated (.65 by Jaffe & Archer, 1987, and .76 for the MCMI-II by Millon, 1987). These correlations are not surprising, given the item overlap (16 items) between the two scales, as well as their concordance in clinical practice.

The discriminability of the Scales *B* and *T*, even with acknowledged substance abusers, has been called into question. Although Millon (1983) was able to establish moderate sensitivities (.71 and .76) for these scales, other investigators have not been so successful. Craig and Weinberg (1992) reviewed 16 MCMI studies of substance abuse. Of these, three studies reported classification rates; none of the sensitivity rates exceeded 50%. Miller and Streiner (1990) found that the sensitivity of Scale *B* was low when compared to DIS current (.36) and lifetime (.33) diagnosis in a sample of 175 inpatients and outpatients. If the MCMI scales are unsuccessful with acknowledged substance abusers, many of whom were actively involved in treatment, how can they be expected to detect unacknowledged or misreported substance abuse?

The MCMI scales appear to be vulnerable to faking. Millon (1983) instructed participants to appear psychologically disturbed. Both scales *B* and *T* were markedly elevated (base rate [BR] > 85). Craig, Kuncel, and Olson (1994) investigated the effectiveness of the MCMI substance abuse scales in detecting denied drug use. They found that 52% of drug abusers were able to successfully deny drug or alcohol abuse. On a more hopeful note, those unable to elude detection tended to be persons with more severe addictions.

In summary, the MCMI appears to have very modest discriminant validity for the detection of substance abusers. At best, its results should be viewed as a screening measure. In other words, if high scores are recorded, then further investigation is warranted. Moreover, the sole study by Craig et al. (1994) suggests that the MCMI

may have incremental validity over the MAST and DAST in detecting abusers denying severe addiction. On the other hand, the presence of low scores does not signify
the absence of substance abuse.

Specialized Measures

Because of constraints on chapter lengths, we emphasize the two specialized measures:
the Personal Experience Inventory (PEI; Winters & Henly, 1989) and the Substance
Abuse Subtle Screening Inventory (SASSI; Miller, 1985). Both measures have substantial research on test validation that includes investigation of response styles. In
addition, a brief summary of the Alcohol Use Inventory (AUI; Wanberg, Horn, &
Foster, 1977) is provided.

PEI

The PEI is composed of 33 scales and 300 items that are organized into two broad
dimensions that address the severity of drug use and associated psychosocial problems.
The PEI is intended for use with adolescents, aged 12–18, who have a minimum reading
level of grade 6 and are cooperative with the assessment (Dahmus, Bernardin, &
Bernardin, 1992). Research has demonstrated good reliability (see Winters & Henly,
1989; Winters et al., 1991) and consistent evidence of diagnostic validity (e.g., Henly
& Winters, 1988; Kennedy & Minami, 1993; Winters, Stinchfield, & Henly, 1993).
The validity data are limited to general constructs (e.g., severity of abuse) rather than
specific drugs or patterns of drug use. Importantly, most research has used treatment
history as the external criterion for establishing substance abuse.

Two PEI scales specifically address response styles. The Infrequency Scale (7 items)
is intended to measure faked drug use by the endorsement of fictitious drugs and
improbable statements related to drug use and procurement. The Defensiveness Scale
(11 items) was derived from Marlowe–Crowne and designed to measure general
defensiveness. Winters et al. (1991) imposed a categorization on these two scales that
was rational (i.e., inspection of frequency distributions) rather than empirically based.
Participants with scores ≥ 3 were judged to be "faking bad" on the Infrequency Scale.
On the Defensiveness Scale, scores of ≥ 4 and ≤ 8 were deemed to be moderate defensiveness and >8 as high defensiveness. For 886 delinquents receiving treatment for drug
abuse, approximately 5.7% were placed into the faking-bad category in contrast to
2.6% on high school controls. As previously noted, the Defensiveness Scale is not specific to drug use. Therefore, the percentages of moderate defensiveness (44.5% of drug
users and 61.6% of controls) are not surprising.

Winters et al. (1993) adopted a different standard for ruling PEI protocols to be
invalid. Participants who scored in the 90th percentile on either the Infrequency or
Defensiveness scales of the normative sample for drug users were classified as invalid.
Based on this standard, 21 of 111 delinquents (18.9%) were declared invalid. Again,
the rationale for this decision rule was not made explicit.

Guthmann and Brenna (1990) compared PEI results with clinicians' judgments on 95 delinquent residents. The authors do not provide sufficient data on the frequency of dissimulation or sources of disagreement. However, the available data suggest little concordance of clinical opinion with faking bad ($r = .14$) or defensiveness ($r = .28$).

In summary, the authors of the PEI should be commended on their attention to response styles, including exaggeration and defensiveness. However, much research is left to be accomplished, particularly on the discriminant validity of the PEI with dissimulation. To date, we have no systematic comparisons of criterion groups (defensive, exaggerating, and control). Without such comparisons, we cannot establish optimum cutting scores. For the present, marked elevations on the Infrequency Scale should trigger a more complete evaluation of exaggeration. Marked elevations on the Defensiveness Scale should not be interpreted as denial or minimization of drug use, since these elevations are more common among nonusers than users.

SASSI

Miller (1985) developed the SASSI as a measure that would be effective with both acknowledged and unacknowledged substance abuse. From this perspective, the SASSI offered several advantages over other substance abuse measures: (1) The SASSI has two scales for the assessment of denied or minimized use; (2) the SASSI covers both alcohol and drug use; and (3) a separate adolescent version is available. The greatest shortcoming of the SASSI is the lack of sustained research, particularly with respect to denial and defensiveness.

The original SASSI study of denial asked 50 polydrug abusers and 36 alcoholics to conceal all chemical use and to make the best impression possible. Their results were compared to the same sample and other criterion groups under honest instructions. Provisional subscales and decision rules were generated that likely represented an overfitting of the data. These provisional decision rules appeared to be highly successful with defensive male alcoholics (92%) and moderately successful with defensive substance abusers (73–82%). Although correctly described as "provisional," further research on their accuracy has not been forthcoming, despite the recent publication of a revised version (SASSI-2; Miller, 1994). As acknowledged by the author, no attempt has been made to identify exaggerated substance abuse.

Svanum and McGrew (1995) examined the usefulness of the SASSI in screening 495 students, 57 of whom met DSM-III-R criteria for substance abuse. They found that the SASSI rules were ineffective at detecting most substance abusers, with a sensitivity of .33. When the SASSI did classify a person as a substance abuser, the positive predictive power was very modest (PPP = .25), which meant only 1 in 4 persons classified as a substance abuser by the DSM-III-R criteria was identified on the SASSI. Interestingly, the MAST outperformed the SASSI as a screening measure.

The SASSI-A (Miller, 1990) is a parallel version that was developed for adolescents (age range 12–18). Its decision rules appeared to be moderately successful at identifying chemically dependent adolescents (83%) and marginally successful at classifying adolescents without substance abuse (72%) or denying substance abuse (69%). An unreported number manifested an unexpected response pattern that resembled either exaggerated or random profiles; these participants were removed from the classifications reported earlier.

Rogers, Cashel, Johansen, Sewell, & Gonzalez (in press) attempted to replicate these results with 319 adolescent offenders in residential treatment on a dual diagnosis unit. For substance abusers openly acknowledging their alcohol and drug problems, the SASSI-A, as expected, was highly accurate. For the 82 adolescents that minimized their abuse, the hierarchical decision rules identified 75.6%. The greatest concern was the misclassification of nonusers as abusers. Of the 19 nonusers in the study, the decision rules incorrectly classified more than two-thirds (68.4%) as abusers. Rogers et al. also reported initial data that questioned the SASSI-A's generalizability with Hispanic populations. When controlling for the level of substance abuse, significant differences were found on several SASSI scales.

Many of the SASSI and SASSI-A items appear to have an antisocial or delinquent content. Given the concordance between antisocial behavior and substance abuse, this strategy of capitalizing on antisocial attitudes and behavior to identify substance abusers is likely to be effective in some settings. We would caution, however, that the use of the SASSI and SASSI-A in court-referred populations may actually be stymied by this strategy. In these cases, the diagnostic task is to differentiate abusing and nonabusing offenders. The danger is that the SASSI and SASSI-A, as found by Rogers et al. (1995), may misclassify nonabusing offenders, based on this underlying strategy.

AUI

The Alcohol Use Inventory (AUI; Wanberg, Horn, & Foster, 1977; Horn, Wanberg, & Foster, 1990) is a well-designed measure of 147 items that address three domains: styles of alcohol use, unfavorable consequences of drinking, and perceived beneficial consequences of drinking. The 16 scales evidence little overlap, appear conceptually related to treatment status (outpatient, acute inpatient, and chronic inpatient), are relatively stable across ethnic groups, and have excellent reliability (see Horn et al., 1990; Rohsenow, 1982; Wanberg et al., 1977; Wanberg, Lewis, & Foster, 1978). The AUI has two scales designed to measure deterioration and disruption as a result of chronic alcohol use. The second scale is designed as a cross-check on the first; individuals who differ more than three sten scores are considered to be invalid. However, the effectiveness of this index has not been empirically demonstrated. In a cluster-analytic approach, Kline and Snyder (1985) identified one subtype of alcoholics with clinical elevations on the MMPI F scale but found remarkably little differences between this and other groups on the AUI scales. The actual meaning of this finding is obscure; perhaps F elevation was more associated with confusion and psychopathology than exaggerated alcoholic use. In summary, the AUI is a well-validated measure that may serve as a useful adjunct to the assessment of suspected substance abuse.

LABORATORY METHODS

Breathalyzer

Psychologists and other mental health professionals rarely employ Breathalyzer data in their evaluation and treatment of substance abusing patients. Sobell, Sobell, and VanderSpek (1979) demonstrated its potential usefulness in multiple samples of alcoholic patients. They administered the Breathalyzer under one of two conditions, either routinely to patients involved in treatment or selectively to patients in treatment suspected of drinking. The results were very similar; approximately half the patients who had been drinking denied their ongoing alcohol use. Certainly, the treatment potential for selective Breathalyzer use has not been fully tested.

Most mental health professionals have access to Breathalyzer data following the arrest of a person on charges of drinking while intoxicated (DWI; Jalazo, Steer, & Fine, 1978), although its use is gradually growing for employment screenings (Cohen, 1984). Because different BACs are employed to define intoxication, clinicians must be careful to distinguish *legal* intoxication (BACs ranging in levels from 80 to 100) from *clinical* intoxication (behavioral disturbance likely to include one or more of the following: slurred speech, incoordination, unsteady gait, nystagmus, attention and memory problems, and stupor/coma; see American Psychiatric Association, 1994a). Chronic alcoholics with increased tolerance may show no evidence of intoxication with BAC levels ≥ 100 (American Psychiatric Association, 1994a). As observed by Mikkelsen (1985), marked variations in BAC have been associated with clinical intoxication, with the majority becoming visibly intoxicated at levels between 100 and 200.

The standard for most Breathalyzers, according to Kapur (1994) is the 2,100:1 alveolar breath:blood conversion; this ratio is conservative and tends to underestimate the actual BAC. Although Simpson (1987) concurred that most BAC are underestimates, he asserted that a substantial minority (19–23%) of those tested may have overestimates of their BAC.

Potential errors in Breathalyzer results are possible if the test is administered directly after drinking. Because of residual alcohol vapor in the mouth, artificially high readings are possible if readings are taken within 20 minutes of alcohol consumption. Few technical problems occur in Breathalyzer administration, particularly with the widely adopted computer-based models. Although concerns have been raised regarding the effective maintenance of Breathalyzers (Trichter, McKinney, & Pena, 1995), these concerns can easily be addressed through documentation and service records.

The relationship of alcohol consumption to BAC is highly variable. In testing BAC with 64 male participants, who had fasted for 4 hours, O'Neill, Williams, and Dubowski (1983) found that low dose (0.5 g/kg, or approximately 27 ounces of beer for a 150-pound male) had dramatic effects on BAC levels (range from 32 to 109). High doses (1.0 g/kg) also had marked ranges (99 to 180). On average, low dosages peaked 31 minutes after drinking, whereas high dosages peaked 51 minutes following alcohol consumption.

Urinalysis

Urine screens for illicit drugs and misuse of prescribed medications have become commonplace with random as well as selected drug testing. For employment, workers may be asked to participate in drug screens in both civilian (MacDonald & Roman, 1994) and military (Morgan, 1984) settings. Drug treatment programs (Harford & Kleber, 1978) and police arrest (Graham & Wish, 1994) may also incorporate urinalysis into their procedures.

Urinalysis may be used to screen for a number of drugs including amphetamine, barbiturates, benzodiazepines, cocaine metabolites, methadone, phencyclidine (PCP), morphine, ethanol, and cannabinoids (Morgan, 1984). Urinalysis is a generally effective measure within a rather narrow window of detection, typically ranging from 1 to 3 days. The notable exception is cannabis, which is sometimes detected after an 8-week period.

Three types of urinalysis are readily available for the assessment of suspected substance abuse: immunoassay, chromatography, or gas chromatography–mass spectrometry (GC-MS) methods (Kapur, 1994). Immunoassay procedures are comparatively less expensive and therefore widely used, despite their potential for misclassification. Immunoassay techniques (Mieczkowski, Landress, Newel, & Coletti, 1993) are based on antigen–antibody reactions with the antibody being radioisotope-, fluorescence-, or enzyme-labeled. In the first two procedures, the labeled antibody is introduced to a urine sample; if a sample is drug-positive, binding with the labeled antibody will occur, and the amount of radioactivity or fluorescence will be measured. If the antibody is enzyme labeled, it will bind with a drug-positive sample, and the enzyme will cause some measurable reaction. Immunoassay methods are the first step in evaluating suspected urine samples.

Chromatography or chromatography–mass spectrometry should be used to verify any positive findings on immunoassay methods. These methods involve the separating, typically with gas or fluid, and in the case of mass spectrometry, the "fingerprinting" of a drug or its metabolites (Kapur, 1994). The technical expertise required for sample preparation is fairly sophisticated, but a positive result via GC-MS is considered to be extremely accurate.

The accuracy of urinalysis can be affected by several environmental factors that extend beyond the laboratory procedures that may result in either false positives or false negatives:

1. Common over-the-counter medications may test positive for illicit drugs (e.g., Alka-Seltzer Plus and Sudafed; Potter & Orfali, 1990).
2. Ingestion of poppy seeds may result in false positives for cocaine use (Baer, Baumgartner, Hill, & Blahd, 1991).
3. Ingestion of large amounts of water prior to testing (i.e., flushing) may result in false negatives (Baumgartner, Hill, & Blahd, 1989).
4. Contamination of urine (e.g., mixing with toilet water) can result in false negatives (Kapur, 1994); direct observation of the urine collection, although intrusive, can minimize this risk.

Urinalysis may play a useful adjunctive role in the treatment of substance abusers. Treatment Alternatives to Street Crime (TASC; Hirschel & McCarthy, 1983), a comprehensive treatment program for persons arrested on drug charges, employs urine testing as an essential component of the treatment. Its purpose is the verification of patient reports of drug abstinence. Clinicians likely differ in their views of whether urinalysis is an intervention or an outcome measure. We prefer to conceptualize urinalysis as an intervention, with the threat of detection serving as a temporary, albeit externally imposed, treatment. In this light, the goal of treatment would be the replacement of this external threat with more internalized motivations. Moreover, the disavowal of drug use in the presence of a drug-positive screen provides useful data on denial and defensiveness.

Hair Analysis

Kelly and Rogers (1996) reviewed the current literature on hair analysis as it applies to misreported drug use. The procedure involves radioimmunoassay of hair (RIAH) to determine current (within last 4 weeks) and past drug use. Because metabolites of illicit drugs are embedded in the hair shaft, the shaft becomes a chronology of drug use–nonuse. Depending on the hair length, laboratories are able estimated patterns of drug use based on (1) the relative position of positive results, and (2) the relatively stable growth of scalp hair (approximately 0.5 inches per month). Concentrations of these metabolites are proportional to drug use, which allows laboratories to estimate not only their presence but the extent of their use.

The efficacy of hair analysis has been investigated through animal models that have demonstrated a nearly perfect linear relationship between amount of ingestion and residue in hair samples. Ethical and legal constraints have limited its testing in humans to experimental designs. Although several investigators have administered compounds chemically associated with illegal drugs (e.g., Baumgartner, Hill, & Blahd, 1989; Nakahara, Shimamine, & Takahashi, 1992) and measured residue in scalp hair, most researchers have employed indirect and less precise methods with self-reporting of drug use as the external criterion. A further validation is performed by confirming RIAH results with the more sensitive GC-MS. Employing GC-MS as a criterion, RIAH has proven more than twice as effective as urinalysis in detecting in testing for commonly abused drugs (e.g., cocaine, PCP, and opiates; Feucht, Stephens, & Walker, 1994; Mieczkowski, Barzelay, Gropper, & Wish, 1991). The difficulty in reviewing this literature (see Kelly & Rogers, 1996) is that classificatory accuracy is expressed in the form of percentages rather than more interpretable estimates, such as specificity and sensitivity. Of crucial importance, investigators have not found cases of false positives; in the published literature, positive results on the RIAH have always been confirmed by GC-MS. As a precaution, we recommend that positive RIAH findings in clinical practice be confirmed, either by acknowledgment of the suspected user or through GC-MS.

The RIAH has several important limitations. First, RIAH is not useful for suspected alcohol abuse. Second, different laboratories use different extraction procedures (e.g., solvent-based, acid-based, or antibody extraction) that preclude precise comparisons across laboratories. Third, external contamination (e.g., marijuana or crack cocaine smoke) may possibly alter drug estimates, although many researchers believe the proper washing of hair samples prior to extraction obviates this potential problem.

From a treatment perspective, RIAH offers an unequaled opportunity to assess types and patterns of substance abuse. Whether a patient is decreasing/increasing drug use is critical to measuring treatment success. For validation of psychometric measures, RIAH can provide a close approximation to "ground truth" in establishing clear criteria between abusers and nonabusers. The chief limitation of RIAH, as with all laboratory procedures, is that is provides little data on behavioral responses. Its primary use by clinicians is likely to be for the confirmation or questioning of reported ingestion rather than the effects of drug use.

In summary, we believe that RIAH with appropriate confirmation is the assessment method of choice for the following clinical and research issues:

1. *Retrospective.* At a specified period in the past, was the patient ingesting specific drugs?
2. *Longitudinal.* What pattern of drug use can be documented in the past year?
3. *Behavioral correlates to drug use.* In both clinical and research realms, what pattern of symptoms and associated features are related to specific drug use?
4. *Criterion-related validity.* For establishing criterion groups of specific users and nonusers, what are the consistent differences on designated scales?

CLINICAL APPLICATIONS

Many, if not most, diagnoses of substance abuse disorders are missed simply because patients are not asked about these disorders (see Moore et al., 1989). This oversight is unforgivable, given the panoply of substance abuse measures. The excuse occasionally heard, "Well, they didn't say they had a problem," disavows the distorted self-perceptions and attributions of substance abusers as well as the effects of pervasive social stigmatization. In both medical and psychiatric populations, substance abuse and associated problems must be addressed systematically.

Psychologists and other mental health professionals may simply assume that they will be able to detect intoxicated patients among those in treatment, thereby obviating the need for a more systematic investigation. In a classic study of 705 alcoholic patients, Sobell et al. (1979) found that clinicians were not particularly effective at detecting those who were under the influence of alcohol. Of those patients denying intoxication, clinicians correctly identified between 50% and 67% as verified by breath analysis of blood alcohol level (i.e., > .10%). False positives ranged across samples from 0% to 17%. Clearly, clinical observation alone is insufficient for the detection of ongoing substance abuse.

A relevant but virtually unexplored issue is the misuse of prescribed medications in clinical populations. An early study by Ballinger, Simpson, and Stewart (1974) suggested that substantial numbers (11.9%) of psychiatric inpatients ingested nonprescribed medications in a cross-sectional study. Another 6.4% had undetectable levels of the prescribed medication, suggesting treatment noncompliance. Although nursing staff medication errors may account for a few inaccuracies, these variations among inpatients raise considerable concern.

Screens and many specialized measures assume forthrightness and complete self-disclosure, not only about the type and frequency of substance abuse, but also its short- and long-term sequelae. Such assumptions, in light of our current knowledge of widespread denial, are likely to be naive. Still, the systematic use of screens is likely to be helpful in discovering undiagnosed cases of substance abuse. Toward this objective, we recommend the systematic use of screens, such as the MAST and the DAST.

We propose in Table 6.3 a threshold model for denied or minimized substance abuse. Because inconsistencies in reported drug use may have many determinants (e.g., confusion secondary to drug use, unawareness of consumed drugs, and contradictory accounts by co-users), we should not assume that discrepancies per se are evidence of dissimulation. Certain patterns of inconsistencies (e.g., peers vs. parents) signal the need for a full investigation of suspected substance abuse. As summarized in Table 6.3, two psychometric measures, the SASSI with nonminorities only and the CDP, can provide quasi-objective data, indicating a risk of denied or minimized substance abuse.

Exaggerated substance abuse does not appear to be a common response style (see Table 6.4). However, in certain settings, persons may be motivated to fabricate drug use as an explanation or excuse for misconduct. For example, many sex offenders imply that alcohol or drugs clouded their judgment, distorted their sexual interests, or impeded their "normal" self-control. Use of fictitious drugs or improbable statements (see PEI Infrequency Scale) is likely to detect very blatant attempts at feigning. Much more problematic are cases of "idiosyncratic" reactions. For example, some offenders will report a "blackout" after ingesting some "bad" or laced marijuana. Careful inquiry into atypical effects may be helpful in distinguishing purely self-serving explanations from more believable descriptions. For instance, use of hallucinogens is unlikely

---

TABLE 6.3. Threshold Model for Denied or Minimized Substance Abuse

Marked discrepancies in reported substance abuse, as evidenced by one or more of the following:

1. Acknowledgment of substance abuse with friends/peers but denial with persons in authority (e.g., police, health care providers, or parents)
2. Denial or gross minimization of past substance abuse in contradiction of past treatment or arrest records
3. Denial of any substance use in substantial disparity with performance on face-valid measures of substance abuse (i.e., screening measures or structured interviews)
4. For nonminorities, substantial elevations on SASSI's defensiveness scales
5. Computation of BAC levels for the CDP based on informants' report that are strikingly higher than self-report and partially verifiable from other sources

Note. SASSI, Substance Abuse Subtle Screening Inventory; CDP, Comprehensive Drinker Profile; BAC, Blood alcohol concentration.

TABLE 6.4. Threshold Model for Exaggerated Substance Abuse

Marked discrepancies in reported substance abuse, as evidenced by one or more of the following:

1. Denial of substance abuse with friends/peers but exaggeration with persons in authority (e.g., police, health care providers, or parents)
2. Gross exaggeration of past substance abuse in contradiction of past treatment or arrest records
3. Elevation of the PEI Infrequency Scale
4. Endorsement of fictitious drugs or ascribing very atypical behavioral effects from known drug use (e.g., prolonged hallucinatory experiences from the use of marijuana)

Note. PEI, Personal Experience Inventory.

to produce command hallucinations focused solely on execution of a well-planned bank robbery.

We caution against drawing any immediate conclusions about the endorsement of fictitious drugs and deliberate exaggerations. Drug users may be motivated to appear knowledgeable or be simply confused by the myriad of street and scientific terms. Clinicians can easily test the limits of credibility by associating uncommon effects (e.g., accelerated hair growth) to different fictitious drugs.

Clinical decision models provide the basis for determining whether patients reporting substance abuse are engaging in some form of dissimulation. Unfortunately, our ability to make accurate classifications is substantially curtailed. For denied or minimized drug use, laboratory measures (see Table 6.5) provide an accurate measure for specific time periods. Of these, hair analysis is likely to have the broadest applications to both evaluations and subsequent treatment. Only in rare cases in which disinterested witness are able to provide disconfirming evidence of denied substance abuse should these determinations be warranted in the absence of laboratory data.

The limitation of this model is that it does not address the immediate or long-term behavioral effects of drug use. Large-scale normative research is urgently needed on what symptoms and correlates should be expected with specific drug use, verified through laboratory procedures. At present, highly skilled clinicians with extensive

TABLE 6.5. Clinical Decision Model for Denied or Minimized Substance Abuse

1. For a specific event, independent witnesses that disconfirm patient's denial of substance abuse
2. For a very limited time period (2–12 hours, depending on level of intoxication and metabolism rates), positive evidence of alcohol use as indicated by Breathalyzer results
3. For a circumscribed period of time (36–72 hours), positive evidence of substance use as indicated by urinalysis results; however, chronic use of cannaboid substances can be detected for a more extended period from 2 weeks up to 8 weeks
4. For an extended period of time (minimum time is 4 weeks; maximum is dependent on hair length but could extend to several years), positive evidence of drug use as indicated by hair analysis results

experiences with drug users are likely to have some knowledge base on associated features with particular drug patterns. Their ability to distinguished bogus from genuine drug effects has not been empirically tested.

We have intentionally not included psychometric data in the clinical decision model. More specifically, the PEI Defensiveness Scale is a measure of social desirability and does not appear to have discriminant validity with respect to denied drug use. In the same vein, the SASSI scales capitalize on their delinquency content (limiting their usefulness in forensic, court, or correctional settings) and lack demonstrated validity with minority populations. These measures should not be used in the determination of denied drug use.

We have not proposed a clinical decision model for exaggerated drug use, because of the paucity of research on accurate classification. Of course, the absence of laboratory data may provide a convincing argument of exaggerated drug use. For example, Moeller, Fey, and Sachs (1993) reported that forensic cases may include fabricated substance abuse as a mitigating or exculpatory factor. In this regard, hair analysis may be useful in certain retrospective evaluations.

7

Malingering of Posttraumatic Disorders

PHILLIP J. RESNICK, M.D.

Mental disorders that occur after trauma include posttraumatic stress disorder (PTSD), acute stress disorder, adjustment disorders, depressive disorders, anxiety disorders, conversion disorders, postconcussion syndromes, and occasionally psychoses. The feigning of PTSD and acute stress disorder deserves special consideration. Unlike other diagnoses, these disorders establish a causal link between a traumatic event and a potentially compensable disorder. In addition to this focus, the chapter addresses the potential for feigning as it relates to concussion, conversion disorders, and the "compensation neurosis" controversy. Because of its frequency in certain clinical settings, special emphasis is given to malingered PTSD in the combat veteran.

The concept of traumatic neuroses first arose from the belief that an accidental concussion to the spine caused abnormalities of the sympathetic nervous system (Clevenger, 1889). According to Hamilton (1906), the disorder was seized upon by dishonest litigants seeking compensation after accidents. Prior to the concept of traumatic neuroses, personal injury cases were based on obvious injuries (e.g., loss of a limb) with objective and incontrovertible evidence that the injury had occurred (Trimble, 1981).

Posttraumatic disorders have been described by various terms, many of which are pejorative and suggestive of feigning (see Table 7.1). Diagnostically, PTSD was classified as gross stress reaction in the first edition of the *Diagnostic and Statistical Manual of Mental Disorders* (DSM-I; American Psychiatric Association, 1952) and subsequently was subsumed within the diagnostic category of "adjustment reaction to adult life" in DSM-II (American Psychiatric Association, 1968). The introduction of PTSD as an official diagnosis in DSM-III (American Psychiatric Association, 1980) caused a sharp increase in clinicians' sensitivity to this disorder and heightened concern about potential malin-

TABLE 7.1. The PTSD Controversy: Terms of Historical or Clinical Significance for Its Description

Accident neurosis	Postaccident anxiety syndrome	Accident victim syndrome
Postaccident syndrome	Aftermath neurosis	Posttraumatic syndrome
American disease	Profit neurosis	Attitudinal pathosis
Railway spine	Compensation hysteria	Rape trauma syndrome
Compensationitis	Secondary gain neurosis	Compensation neurosis
Traumatic hysteria	Fright neurosis	Traumatic neurasthenia
Greek disease	Traumatic neurosis	Greenback neurosis
Triggered neurosis	Justice neurosis	Unconscious malingering
Litigation neurosis	Vertebral neurosis	Mediterranean back
Wharfie's back	Mediterranean disease	Whiplash neurosis

Note. Terms in this table were modified from Mendelson (1984).

gering. The diagnostic criteria for PTSD were again modified in DSM-IV (American Psychiatric Association, 1994a); the most recent criteria are listed in Table 7.2.

DSM-IV also introduced a new diagnosis, namely, acute stress disorder. This disorder emphasizes dissociative symptoms as a result of the trauma. Beyond that, the symptoms generally parallel PTSD (see Table 7.3). The duration of acute stress disorder is explicitly demarcated (i.e., minimum of 2 days and maximum of 4 weeks). DSM-IV (American Psychiatric Association, 1994a, p. 431) stated that acute stress disorder may persist and warrant the diagnosis of PTSD. Because of its time-limited nature, it is unlikely that individuals will feign acute stress disorder alone. Therefore, subsequent discussions will focus on PTSD and draw attention to acute stress disorder only when needed.

TERMINOLOGY FOR DESCRIBING RESPONSE STYLES

"Malingering" is listed in DSM-IV (American Psychiatric Association, 1994a) as a condition not attributable to a mental disorder. It is defined as the intentional production of false or grossly exaggerated physical or psychological symptoms motivated by external incentives, such as financial compensation. In contrast, "factitious disorders" involve the intentional production of symptoms in order to assume a patient role. Both disorders require a deceitful state of mind and a deliberate production or gross exaggeration of symptoms.

Several other terms are useful in the description of malingering phenomena. "Pure malingering" is the feigning of a disorder that does not exist at all in a particular patient. "Partial malingering" is the conscious exaggeration of existing symptoms or the fraudulent allegation that prior genuine symptoms are still present. In addition, the term "false imputation" refers to the ascribing of actual symptoms to a cause consciously recognized by the patient to have no relationship to the symptoms. For example, authentic psychiatric symptoms due to clearly defined stresses at home may be falsely attributed to a traumatic event at work in order to gain compensation. In addition to conscious deception, some individuals mistakenly believe that there is a relationship between an accident and

TABLE 7.2. A Distillation of DSM-IV Criteria for PTSD

A. Exposed to a traumatic event with both:
   1. Actual or threatened death or serious injury, or a threat to the physical integrity
   2. A response with intense fear, helplessness, or horror
B. The traumatic event is persistently reexperienced by:
   1. Recurrent and intrusive distressing recollections (e.g., images, thoughts, or perceptions)
   2. Recurrent distressing dreams
   3. Acting or feeling as if the traumatic event was recurring (e.g., reliving the experience, illusions, hallucinations, and dissociative flashback episodes)
   4. Intense psychological distress at exposure to internal or external cues that symbolize or resemble an aspect of the traumatic event
   5. Physiological reactivity upon exposure to internal or external cues that symbolize or resemble an aspect of the traumatic event
C. Persistent avoidance of stimuli associated with the trauma and numbing of general responsiveness (not present before the trauma), as indicated by at least three of the following:
   1. Efforts to avoid thoughts, feelings, or conversations associated with the trauma
   2. Efforts to avoid activities, places, or people that arouse recollections of the trauma
   3. Inability to recall an important aspect of the trauma
   4. Markedly diminished interest or participation in significant activities
   5. Feeling of detachment or estrangement from others
   6. Restricted range of affect (e.g., unable to have loving feelings)
   7. Sense of foreshortened future (e.g., does not expect to have a career, marriage, children, or a normal life span)
D. Persistent symptoms of increased arousal (not present before the trauma), as indicated by at least two of the following:
   1. Difficult falling or staying asleep
   2. Irritability or outbursts of anger
   3. Difficulty concentrating
   4. Hypervigilance
   5. Exaggerated startle response
E. Duration of the disturbance (symptoms in B, C, and D) is more than 1 month.
F. The disturbance causes clinically significant distress or impairment in social, occupational, or other important areas of functioning.

Note. Several criteria for children are different; please refer to American Psychiatric Association (1994a).

their psychological or physical disability. These patients may fail to realize that consecutive events do not necessarily have a causal relationship (Collie, 1917). Such genuine misperceptions should be differentiated from conscious attempts at deception.

RELUCTANCE TO DIAGNOSE MALINGERING

The authenticity of mental illness, identified largely on the basis of observed behavior and subjective history, can be challenged less readily than physical illness, which is often verified on the basis of physical and biological evidence of disease. Mental health pro-

TABLE 7.3. Distillation of DSM–IV Criteria for Acute Stress Disorder

A. Exposed to a traumatic event with both:
1. Actual or threatened death or serious injury, or a threat to the physical integrity
2. A response with intense fear, helplessness, or horror

B. Either while experiencing, or immediately after experiencing, the distressing event, the individual has at least three of the following dissociative symptoms:
1. Subjective sense of numbing, detachment, or absence of emotional responsiveness
2. A reduction in awareness of one's surroundings (e.g., "being in a daze")
3. Derealization
4. Depersonalization
5. Dissociative amnesia (i.e., inability to recall an important aspect of the trauma)

C. The traumatic event is persistently reexperienced in at least one of the following ways: Recurrent images, thoughts, dreams, illusions, flashback episodes, or a sense of reliving the experience; or distress upon exposure to reminders of the traumatic event.

D. Marked avoidance of stimuli that arouse recollections of the trauma (e.g., thoughts, feelings, conversations, activities, places, or people).

E. Marked symptoms of anxiety or increased arousal (e.g., difficulty sleeping, irritability, poor concentration, hypervigilance, exaggerated startle response, and motor restlessness).

F. The disturbance causes clinically significant distress or impairment in social, occupational, or other important areas of functioning, or the individual is prevented from pursuing some necessary task, such as obtaining necessary medical or legal assistance, or mobilizing personal resources by telling family members about the traumatic experience.

G. Duration is 2 days to 4 weeks; onset within 4 weeks of the traumatic event.

H. Not due to the direct effects of a substance (e.g., drugs of abuse, medication) or a general medical condition and is not merely an exacerbation of a preexisting Axis I or Axis II disorder.

fessionals have a low index of suspicion for malingering, given the wide range of conditions that must be considered before making the diagnosis (Pollack, 1982). For example, 11 psychiatric reports failed to mention the possibility of malingering in a man who was "mute" for 2 years after a head injury. However, a skeptical neurologist observed the man speaking normally after an office visit (Miller & Cartlidge, 1972).

Concern over legal liability is a major reason for clinicians' hesitancy to label someone a malingerer, even though court testimony about malingering is protected by immunity (Restatement, Torts Sec. 588 [1938]). Historically, authors (e.g., Davidson, 1952) conservatively suggested that the clinician should only state in cases of feigning that there is no objective evidence to support the patient's subjective complaints. The possibility of provoking a physical assault by calling a person a malingerer is another source of concern (Hofling, 1965). For instance, one Australian man committed suicide after killing two orthopedic surgeons and wounding a third who had diagnosed him as malingering a back injury (Parker, 1979). An autopsy demonstrated no back injury, thereby proving the doctors were "dead right."

The increased sophistication of detection methods has lessened the likelihood of misclassifying malingerers. I recommend, however, that the classification be made only when very strong evidence is available. In less clear-cut cases, the report may be described as unreliable (see Chapter 1). Clinicians must bear in mind the far-ranging effect of misclassification; to miscategorize a person as malingering may have devastating health care, financial, and legal consequences.

INCIDENCE

The incidence of malingered psychological symptoms after injury is unknown. Estimates vary from 1% (Keiser, 1968) to over 50% (Miller & Cartlidge, 1972; Henderson, personal communication, October 13, 1986), depending upon whether the source works for plaintiffs' attorneys or insurance companies. The incidence of malingering varies with economic conditions; for example, it increases when layoffs are imminent (Downing, 1942). Atypical performance on psychological testing has frequently been observed among persons seeking compensation, with preliminary estimates as high as 64% of personal injury cases (Heaton, Smith, Lehman, & Vogt, 1978) and 47% for workers' compensation cases (Youngjohn, 1991). However, not all persons with atypical performances are necessarily malingering (see Rogers, Harrell, & Liff, 1993). In this respect, pure malingering is considered infrequent in post-traumatic cases, but exaggeration of symptoms is quite common (Jones & Llewellyn, 1917; Trimble, 1981). Some malingered claims of psychic damages originate after claims for physical injury are unsuccessful (Henderson, personal communication, October 13, 1986).

The incidence of diagnosed malingering varies with the astuteness and skepticism of the clinician. Braverman (1978) found only seven "true" malingerers out of 2,500 industrially injured persons; each malingerer immediately terminated his or her case when confronted with the clinician's suspicion of malingering. A U.S. General Accounting Office follow-up study on persons considered 100% disabled was more alarming. Approximately 40% of those studied showed *no* disability whatsoever one year after their disability determinations (Maloney, Glasser, & Ward, 1980).

MOTIVATION AND LEGAL CONTEXT

North American society has become so litigious that the hypothetical response of an injured male worker who has just regained consciousness after a brick has fallen on his head is not "Where am I?" but "Whose brick was it?" (Trimble, 1981). When litigants claim personal injury, especially psychological symptoms, the public often suspects that they are malingering. Opinions expressed in the media contribute to this skepticism. For example, Berman (1987, p. 10A) wrote, "In most civil liability cases before the bar, you can count on more chicanery, lying, and misrepresentation than a household with a cheating husband, a spendthrift wife, and a teenage delinquent. Another co-conspirator is the malingerer, with his lawyer-fostered dreams of living high on the hog ever after. Tort was its name, but now fraud is its game." Few personal injury cases reach the courts without an allegation of malingering expressed or at least implied (Lipman, 1962).

Public hostility toward the suspected malingerer is understandable, especially in view of the fact that the malingerer's undeserved financial gain is necessarily associated with another's undeserved loss (Braverman, 1978). Suspicions of malingering help to explain why damages awarded for posttraumatic psychological symptoms are substantially less than those for physical injury, in spite of the fact that limitations on the patient's life actually may be greater (Trimble, 1981).

The primary motivation to malinger PTSD is financial gain. Once an individual becomes a litigant in a personal injury suit or files a worker's compensation claim, the efforts of attorneys for both the plaintiff and defendant may alter both the patient's attitudes and the course of the illness. The plaintiff's lawyer may overdramatize the client's impairment to the point of being "a salesman of pain, sorrow, agony and suffering" (Averbach, 1963, p. 195). In contrast, defense attorneys often assume an attitude of disbelief and imply that the individual is not suffering from *any* genuine psychiatric symptoms. Such litigants may understandably become angry, based on the belief that they are going to be cheated (Enelow, 1971). This polarization of views is likely to be extended, at least from the patients' perspective, to the evaluating clinicians and affect their participation and presentation to each side in the assessment process.

It is the rare individual who is not influenced to some degree by the possibility that an injury may lead to financial gain (Keiser, 1968). Schafer (1986) believed that having a compensable injury promotes a "little larceny" in most litigants. Financial compensation has different meanings to different people: (1) economic security, (2) revenge against a hated employer or the person responsible for the accident, and (3) symbol of love. In addition to financial compensation, sympathy and social support may be consciously sought by malingerers (Keiser, 1968).

In cases in which exaggeration or partial malingering is combined with real injury, compensation should be made relative to the extent of the actual injury (Keiser, 1968). Legally, malingering constitutes fraud; if it can be proved, the claimant is not entitled to any payment for the alleged condition. To actually convict an individual of perjury, however, the jury must be convinced beyond a reasonable doubt of intentional faking. Such convictions are rare and require a separate legal proceeding. More commonly, civil juries simply make no award in cases in which they believe that the plaintiff is malingering.

PSYCHIATRIC SYMPTOMS FOLLOWING TRAUMA

Psychoses are infrequently malingered after personal injury. Although fraudulent plaintiffs are willing to go to a great deal of trouble to get substantial awards, they are rarely willing to undergo inpatient hospitalization (Davidson, 1952). Moreover, psychotic symptoms are often less plausible after many forms of psychological trauma. Claimants are likely to malinger PTSD, and less often depression (please refer to Chapter 3 for feigned depression and psychosis). In cases of PTSD that follow accidents, the clinical picture may be complicated by physical symptoms, pain, and the sequelae of concussion.

Concussion

Approximately 2,000,000 closed head injuries occur each year in the United States (Department of Health and Human Services, 1989). PTSD is commonly seen after vehicular accidents that cause head injury and concussion. *Postconcussive syndrome* (PCS) is manifested by headaches, dizziness, increased anxiety, emotional lability, blurred vision, concentration deficits, and memory problems (Binder, 1986; Lishman, 1978). Even without loss of consciousness, head injuries may cause symptoms that can be easily confused with PTSD (Trimble, 1981).

Epidemiological studies indicate that a considerable number of minor head trauma patients report memory impairment, difficulty concentrating, a low threshold for fatigue, and abnormal levels of irritability (Gorman, 1993; Wrightston & Gronwall, 1980). Barth et al. (1983) found that neuropsychological assessment 3 months after minor head injury (i.e., unconsciousness less than 20 minutes) showed reduced cognitive efficiency in patients who were not involved in litigation. Mild dysphoria, general psychological discomfort, and problems returning to previous employment were associated with this cognitive dysfunction. In assessing cognitive changes, Wechsler intelligence scores are not particularly sensitive to subtle changes in information processing (Rutherford, Merrett, & McDonald, 1977; Wrightston & Gronwall, 1980). Neuropsychological assessment, with its focus on attention–concentration skills, visuomotor functioning, memory abilities, and emotional status is more useful in the differential diagnosis of head injury and PTSD.

Trimble (1981) observed that available techniques are not sufficient to detect the subtle organic changes that may result from head injury. For example, brain injury due to axonal shearing may not be evident on computed tomography (CT) or magnetic resonance imaging (MRI) scans (Moulton, 1987). In addition, the regions of the brain primarily affected by closed head injuries are the midbrain, temporal and frontal cortex, and areas close to the limbic system. Lesions in these sites may lead to changes in behavior, mood, and feeling without significant cognitive disability.

Kelly (1975) suggested that posttraumatic syndrome is originally the result of minor cerebral damage. From this perspective, impairment is perpetuated mainly by the negative attitudes of the medical profession, which are evidenced by (1) failure to explain the cause of the symptoms in the first place, (2) denial of the symptoms' existence or the unsympathetic declaration that they are related to the question of compensation, (3) refusal to provide proper treatment, and (4) statements that the symptoms will not disappear until the case is settled.

PCS must also be distinguished from PTSD and acute stress disorder. All three disorders involve an antecedent traumatic experience and overlap in their symptoms. Criterion C of PTSD (see Table 7.2) shares several features with PCS: (1) Both disorders can include amnesia for some element of the traumatic event; and (2) depressive symptoms (e.g., anhedonia, feelings of detachment, restricted range of affect, and pessimism regarding the future) are common to both. Furthermore, most of the elements of Criterion D in PTSD are common to PCS. They include sleep disturbance, irritability or anger outbursts, difficulty concentrating, and intolerance of loud noises (Binder, 1986; American Psychiatric Association, 1994a).

A trauma victim can develop both PTSD (or acute stress disorder) and PCS in response to the same injury (McAllister, 1994). Price (1994) has erroneously argued that the two entities are logically incompatible, because an individual who suffered a head injury with loss of consciousness cannot have reexperiencing phenomena referable to that event. Price suggested that the patient's diagnosis should be PCS or malingering, but not PTSD. However, the moment of impact does not constitute the only portion of the traumatic event that can meet Criterion A of PTSD (American Psychiatric Association, 1994a). With partial or complete clearing of the short retrograde amnesia associated with a head injury, trauma victims may develop reexperiencing symptoms due to the frightening, helpless experience of a car speeding toward them, or an assailant chasing them with a club.

Considerable research has been conducted on faked memory loss (see Chapter 5). Although actual retrograde amnesia is characteristically brief in mild head injury, malingerers tend to overplay their memory loss. They may give implausible answers to questions regarding overlearned autobiographic data (e.g., their own name, age, gender, and social security number; Brandt, 1992; Levin et al., 1992).

Several clues may be helpful in distinguishing faked from genuine memory problems. Brain injury typically does not impair procedural memory, such as driving a car or riding a bicycle. If memory is impaired for new learning, recollection of the head injury itself suggests faking, although some individuals have difficulty separating their memories from accounts provided by others. Malingering is also suggested if the person scores more poorly on questions labeled "memory testing" than on other questions. Persons with faked anterograde amnesia sometimes score worse than chance on symptom validity testing (see Chapters 5 and 11).

Among the three components of PCS—emotional, cognitive, and physical—emotional symptoms are the most subjective and easiest to malinger. Unless asked specific questions or coached by others, malingerers typically do not volunteer certain complaints, such as intolerance to loud noises or bright lights. These symptoms often occur in individuals with demonstrable impairment in information processing on neuropsychological testing (Bohnen, Twijnstra, Wijnen, & Jolles, 1991). This association allows the examiner to couple the assessment of a subjective emotional complaint to a testable neuropsychological parameter.

Aubrey, Dobbs, and Rule (1989) tested college students' knowledge of minor head injury symptoms. True head trauma patients frequently complained that they experienced memory problems, decreased concentration, difficulties with emotional control, anxiety, and depression that had a profound effect on their social relationships. Although over 80% of the college students thought that the common physical symptoms were a likely outcome, less than 50% had similar beliefs about cognitive symptoms. In contrast, Mittenberg and his colleagues (Mittenberg, D'Attilio, Gage, & Bass, 1990; Mittenberg, DiGiulio, Perrin, & Bass, 1989) found that simulators may have an accurate understanding of the psychological sequelae of PCS. Thus, knowledge of these symptoms cannot be used as evidence that the presentation is genuine.

Conversion Disorder

Patients may have persistent pain or loss of motor or sensory functioning after an injury that cannot be explained by organic pathology. The differential diagnosis includes malingering, conversion disorder, and pain disorder. The distinction between conversion disorder and malingering can be extremely difficult (see Chapter 2). In both conditions, clinicians are confronted with similar discrepancies between laboratory findings and self-report, objective signs, and subjective symptoms. Tests for malingering that are valid with reference to organic diseases are invalid in conversion disorders (Lipman, 1962; Smith, 1967). The differential diagnosis is further complicated by the fact that individuals with conversion disorders may also malinger.

Both malingerers and patients with conversion disorder may desire to avoid unpleasant activities (e.g., disliked work) and seek support (e.g., financial) from the environment. The critical element that distinguishes conversion disorder from malingering is that conversion symptoms are not under voluntary control. Patients with conversion disorders deceive themselves as well as others; obversely, malingerers consciously deceive others, but not themselves (see Table 7.4). Disability due to conversion disorder may serve a wide range of psychological needs. It may legitimize latent dependency needs, allow punitive retaliation against an employer or a spouse, provide escape from an intolerable situation, accomplish temporary resolution of preexisting life conflicts, allay anxiety and insecurity, or indulge a masochistic need to experience pain (Martin, 1970).

In contrast to the malingerer, the person with conversion disorder is ill. If the illness can be shown to be caused by a particular injury, it is compensable (Cole, 1970). For example, if a man developed hysterical paralysis of the legs (conversion disorder) after a frightening auto accident in which he was not physically injured, the disability would be a direct result of the accident. The paralysis would not be voluntary or a conscious choice for the injured victim. Clinicians' ability to distinguish conversion disorder from malingering depends on their ability to measure consciousness, an extremely difficult task. With respect to consciousness, Rosanoff (1920, p. 310) wrote, "It is strange that so futile a consideration, one so obviously belonging to the domain of metaphysics and not science, as the question of degree of consciousness of a mental process should . . . be chosen as a criterion of clinical diagnosis!"

TABLE 7.4. Differences in Motivation for Malingering and Conversion Disorder

Diagnosis	Symptoms for gain	Awareness of purpose
Malingering	Yes	Yes
Conversion disorder	Yes	No

Note. Modified from Trimble (1981).

Jonas and Pope (1985) suggested that a gender bias may exist in the diagnostic classification. Clinicians tend to diagnose somatization disorder and conversion disorder primarily in women—as if clinicians believe that women are the preferred victims of unconscious conflicts and lack voluntary control. In contrast, men are more often assigned the classification of malingering, implying that men tend to be consciously aware of their motivations and in command of their actions.

The following clinical characteristics may assist in the differential diagnosis between malingering and conversion disorder:

1. The malingerer often presents as sullen, ill-at-ease, suspicious, uncooperative, resentful (Huddleston, 1932), aloof, secretive, and unfriendly (Engel, 1970). Patients with conversion disorder are more likely to be cooperative (Trimble, 1981), appealing, clinging, and dependent (Engel, 1970).

2. The malingerer may try to avoid examination, unless it is required as a condition for receiving some financial benefit (Soniat, 1960; Engel, 1970). The patient with conversion disorder welcomes examinations (Rosanoff, 1920; Hofling, 1965). Whereas the malingerer may decline to cooperate with recommended diagnostic or therapeutic procedures, patients with conversion disorder are typically eager for an organic explanation for their symptoms (Trimble, 1981) and are anxious to be cured (Rosanoff, 1920; Hofling, 1965).

3. The malingerer is more likely than the patient with conversion disorder to refuse employment that could be handled in spite of some disability (Davidson, 1952).

4. The malingerer is likely to give every detail of the accident and its sequelae; the patient with conversion disorder is more likely to give an account that contains gaps, inaccuracies (Huddleston, 1932), and vague, generalized complaints (Chaney, Cohn, Williams, & Vincent, 1984).

Table 7.5 presents a distillation of key differences between malingering and conversion disorders. This synopsis should assist clinicians by providing a framework for rendering this important differential diagnosis.

THE COMPENSATION NEUROSIS CONTROVERSY

The term "compensation neurosis" was introduced by Rigler (1879), in reference to the increase in reported disability following railway accidents after compensation laws were introduced in Germany in 1871 (Trimble, 1981). Kennedy (1946, p. 19) described compensation neurosis as a "state of mind, born out of fear, kept alive by avarice, stimulated by lawyers, and cured by a verdict." In a less emotional vein, Rickarby (1979, p. 333) defined compensation neurosis as "that behavior complex associated specifically with the prospect of recompense and is in contradistinction to traumatic neurosis and psychiatric illness . . . precipitated by the stress of illness, accident, or injury." Patients who are perceived to have disability that is out of proportion to the tissue damage after injury are often labeled as exhibiting compensation neurosis (Modlin, 1960).

TABLE 7.5. Differential Diagnosis between Malingering and Conversion Disorder Following Trauma

Malingering	Conversion disorder
Uncooperative, suspicious, aloof	Cooperative, appealing, dependent
Avoids examinations	Welcomes examination
Refuses employment with partial disability	Accepts employment with partial disability
Describes accident in full detail	Describes accident with gaps and inaccuracies

Miller (1961) contributed to the controversy about compensation neurosis with his paper on "accident neurosis" following head injury. Clinical features of this syndrome included evaluated persons' unshakable conviction in their unfitness for work, an inverse relationship between the degree of disability and the severity of the injury, and absolute failure to respond to therapy until the compensation issue was settled. Miller reported nearly all the patients (48 out of 50) recovered completely without treatment within 2 years after the claim was settled. Miller has often been quoted in both the literature and the courtroom as evidence that patients are likely to improve with cessation of litigation.

Many authors have subsequently disputed this claim (Kelly, 1975; Kelly & Smith, 1981; Mendelson, 1982, 1984; Trimble, 1981; Weighill, 1983). One reason for the lack of agreement between Miller and subsequent authors regarding the effect of compensation on posttraumatic disorders is that Miller employed a rather encompassing definition of malingering. Indeed, Miller (1961, p. 993) suggested that the distinction between conscious and unconscious motives is of little consequence. "Their only purpose is to make the observer believe that the disability is greater than it really is."

Many studies failed to support Miller's (1961) original findings (Balla & Moraitis, 1970; Dworkin, Handlin, Richlin, Brand, & Vannucci, 1985; Tarsh & Royston, 1985). For instance, psychological reactions associated with physical illness in Spain, where there is no provision for compensation, differ very little from those associated with compensable accidents in Australia (Parker, 1977). Thompson (1965) found that only 15% of 190 patients with "posttraumatic psychoneurosis" whose claims had been finalized reported that their symptoms were "better" after litigation had concluded. Similarly, Kelly and Smith (1981) found that few patients with posttraumatic syndrome who had not returned to work by the settlement date went on to return after settlement.

Thompson (1965) reported that financial settlement had a negligible benefit on the course of the illness in 500 patients with posttraumatic psychoneurosis. Mendelson (1981) conducted psychiatric evaluations on 101 patients who were referred after auto or industrial accidents. Sixty-seven percent of the patients failed to return to work nearly 16 months after their compensation claim had ended. In a study with important implications, Kelly (1975) found that when treatment was applied early and efficiently in posttraumatic syndromes, compensation and noncompensation cases did not differ in recovery time. In the same vein, Peck, Fordyce, and Black (1978) found that neither litigation nor representation by attorneys had a significant effect upon the pain behavior of persons with workers' compensation claims.

Some attorneys and clinicians use the term "compensation neurosis" as a pejorative epithet. Although "neurotic" is often used as a disparaging term, the further designation of "compensation" is doubly demeaning (Modlin, 1960). Moreover, the diagnosis of "compensation neurosis" is invalid, because it is not supported by any of the criteria customarily applied to the validation of disease entities (Mendelson, 1985). The literature does not support the proposed outcome criteria (i.e., the view that such patients invariably become symptom free and resume work within months of the finalization of their claims). On the contrary, up to 75% of those injured in compensable accidents may fail to return to gainful employment 2 years after legal settlement (Mendelson, 1982).

CLINICAL ASSESSMENT OF MALINGERED PTSD

The diagnosis of PTSD requires an assessment of the traumatic event and reported symptoms. DSM-IV changed the criteria for the traumatic event from objective (event markedly distressing to almost anyone) to subjective (personal response of intense fear, helplessness, or horror). Whether this modification broadens the application of PTSD to a greater number of trauma victims remains to be investigated. Davidson (1993) identified 11 pretrauma vulnerability factors for PTSD: (1) female gender, (2) early sexual or other childhood trauma, (3) parental poverty, (4) behavior disorder in childhood or adolescence, (5) early separation or divorce of parents before age 10, (6) introversion, (7) poor self-confidence before age 15, (8) prior psychiatric disorder, (9) a history of psychiatric illness among first-degree relatives, (10) life stress before and after the trauma, and (11) high neuroticism. Within a broader context, Earls, Smith Reich, and Jung (1988) investigated mental disorders following a natural disaster (i.e., a devastating flood); children's flood-related symptoms did not appear to be associated the intensity of their flood experiences but were closely related to preexisting disorders.

The diagnosis of malingered PTSD requires a meticulously detailed history of symptoms, treatment efforts, and careful corroboration of information. While taking the history, the clinician must be careful not to communicate any bias or give any clues about how PTSD manifests itself. If the clinician begins the evaluation in a challenging manner, the adversarial nature of the assessment may affect response style and possibly encourage the evaluated person to attempt to justify impairment with more extreme symptoms.

The diagnosis of PTSD is based almost entirely on the patient's self-report of subjective symptoms. The accessibility of specific DSM-IV criteria permits the resourceful malingerer to report the "correct" symptoms. However, careful investigation can provide partial corroboration of these symptoms. For example, the assertion that individuals dream or think about a traumatic event should be verified by others who are not related to the litigation. In addition, the clinician must obtain a detailed history of living patterns preceding the stressor. For instance, symptoms (e.g., difficulty concentrating or insomnia) may have been present before the traumatic event. Baseline activity in a typical week before the stressor should be compared with reported impairment at the time of the evaluation. The clinician must carefully examine the reasonableness of the relationship between the symptoms and the stressor, the time elapsed between the stressor and symptom development, and the relationship between any prior psychiatric symptoms and current impairment. As a caution, however, some traumatized persons have a significantly delayed onset (American Psychiatric Association, 1994a).

The clinician should insist on detailed illustration of PTSD symptoms. Coached claimants may know which PTSD symptoms to report, but may not be able to elaborate on them with convincing personal-life details. Invented symptoms are more likely to have a vague or stilted quality (Pitman, Sparr, Saunders, & McFarlane 1996). The examiner should see if claimants minimize other causes of their symptoms or exaggerate the severity of the compensable accident. Clinicians should also look for behavioral observations in the mental status examination of such overt symptoms as irritability, difficulty concentrating, and exaggerated startle response.

Third parties should be excluded from the actual evaluation of the person for two important reasons. First, the presence of relatives or close friends precludes using them as semi-independent sources to verify the accuracy of symptoms. Second, should the clinician wish to gently confront the person being evaluated with the possibility of malingering, the absence of a third party will reduce loss of face. A sympathetic understanding about the temptation to exaggerate symptoms of PTSD increases the likelihood that a person will acknowledge it; conversely, trying to shame the person into admission, especially with witnesses, is likely to increase anger and denial.

The clinician who suspects malingering may use certain stratagems based on the belief that use of subterfuge in assessing deceit is justified. Insurance companies routinely make surreptitious videotapes of suspected malingerers (Schafer, 1986). When inquiring about the symptoms of PTSD, the clinician may ask about symptoms that are not typically seen in this disorder. For example, inquiry could be made about symptoms, such as increased talkativeness, inflated self-esteem, or decreased need for sleep. Within earshot of the patient, mention could also be made of a very atypical symptom, implying that it is usually present; the clinician can then see if the patient complains of this symptom. Of course, the clinician must rule out an acquiescent response set, usually via questions unrelated to the reported symptoms. In particularly difficult assessments, inpatient observation may be helpful in monitoring alleged symptoms, such as social withdrawal, sleep disturbance, and exaggerated startle reactions.

Psychological Testing

Psychological tests typically are designed to evaluate response styles more generally with comparatively little attention to specific disorders, such as PTSD. The MMPI-2 has two scales designed to assess combat-related PTSD: *PK* (Keane, Malloy, & Fairbank, 1984) and *PS* (Schlenger & Kulka, 1987) scales. Both scales have substantial overlap with each other and general clinical scales (Scales 2, 3, 4, 7, and 8). According to Greene (1991), the two scales appear to measure general maladjustment and emotional distress. Thus, their ability to assess PTSD, genuine or feigned, is brought into question.

Keane, Caddell, and Taylor (1988) developed the Mississippi Scale for Combat-Related PTSD (MS-PTSD). The MS-PTSD is a 35-item, 5-point Likert-type scale for assessing DSM-III-R criteria and associated features. Although the MS-PTSD appears to be useful in assessing PTSD in Vietnam veterans, recent studies have clearly demonstrated its vulnerability to feigning. More specifically, three studies (Dalton, Tom, Rosenblum, Garte, & Aubuchon, 1989; Frueh & Kinder, 1994; Lyons, Caddell, Pittman, Rawls, & Perrin, 1994) found that non-PTSD and noncombat veterans could easily feign on the MS-PTSD.

The vulnerability of psychological tests to detect specifically feigned conditions associated with trauma requires further attention. Chapters 9, 15, and 17 may be especially useful, since they include studies that are relevant to PTSD.

Sodium Amytal Interviews

The term "truth serum" is a misnomer for sodium amytal and other drug-assisted interviews. Although amytal is sometimes useful in recovering genuinely repressed memories, it is not accurate in the classification of malingering (see Chapter 12). Both Baro (1950) and Hofling (1965) found that persons simulating traumatic neurosis retained or further exaggerated their malingered symptoms upon receiving sodium amytal. One-half of the participants in the Redlich, Ravitz, and Dession (1951) study were able to refrain from disclosing an important personal issue while under the influence of sodium amytal. Kalman (1977) described a case vignette in which simulation was maintained during the amytal interview. One hospitalized soldier, noted for loud outbursts, continued shouting during his sodium amytal interview. At one point, however, in the middle of his violent shouting, he said in a quiet voice, "Doctor, give me a cigarette"; he then resumed shouting.

Psychophysiological Testing for PTSD

Currently the most specific diagnostic test for PTSD is psychophysiological measurement. It addresses the DSM-IV PTSD diagnostic criterion, "physiological reactivity on exposure to cues that symbolize or resemble an aspect of the traumatic event" (Pitman, Saunders, & Orr, 1994). Blanchard, Kolb, Pallmeyer, and Gerardi (1982) reported that they could discriminate with 95.5% accuracy between veterans suffering from genuine PTSD and a control group by playing an audiotape of combat sounds. They measured veterans' heart rates, systolic blood pressure, and muscle tension with a forehead electromyelogram. Measure of the heart rate alone allowed correct classification of 90.9%.

A limitation of early standard stimuli (e.g., machine-gun fire) was that they did not effectively reproduce what was uniquely stressful about a particular traumatic experience. For example, sounds of ground combat may have little meaning for a pilot whose stress involved being shot down. However, Lang (1985) devised a procedure that circumvented this difficulty by substituting script-driven imagery of personal events for standard auditory stimuli. A person's traumatic and other personal scripts are played back in a psychophysiology laboratory. Measurements are made of heart rate, skin conductance, and tension in a muscle of the face.

Research participants using this technique have included combat veterans as well as victims of road accidents, assaults, and other noncombat traumas (Orr, Pitman, Lasko, & Herz, 1993; Pitman et al., 1994; Shalev, Orr, & Pitman, 1993). The proportion of PTSD participants correctly identified ranged from 61% to 88%, and the proportion of non-PTSD subjects correctly identified ranged from 79% to 100%. In addition, 16 non-PTSD participants from the first study returned to the laboratory for a retest. They were instructed to simulate the physiological responses of PTSD participants. Only 25% were able to do so successfully (Pitman et al., 1994). The Veterans Health Administration is pursuing a large-scale investigation at 15 VA medical centers regarding the application of psychophysiological laboratory assessment in the evaluation of PTSD in Vietnam veterans (Keane, Kolb, & Thomas, 1991).

As with the result of any medical test, psychophysiological test results should not be expected to stand on their own. They must be interpreted within the context of other available information. Moreover, the purpose of such testing is to assess PTSD-related symptoms, not truthfulness (Pitman et al., 1994). Meeting the criterion of physiological reactivity to stimuli that resemble a traumatic event is neither necessary nor sufficient for the diagnosis of PTSD in DSM-IV. Thus, the psychophysiological data must be used in conjunction with other aspects of a complete forensic evaluation (Pitman & Orr, 1993).

CLINICAL APPLICATIONS

A threshold model of eight criteria is proposed for determining when clinicians should thoroughly investigate the possibility that an individual is malingering psychological symptoms after a traumatic incident (see Table 7.6). Any combination of these criteria in the assessment of PTSD is considered sufficient to meet the threshold model.

TABLE 7.6. Threshold Model for the Evaluation of Malingering in Posttraumatic Disorders

Any combination of the following criteria:

1. Poor work record
2. Prior "incapacitating" injuries
3. Markedly discrepant capacity for work and recreation
4. Unvarying, repetitive civilian dreams
5. Antisocial personality traits
6. Overly idealized functioning before the trauma
7. Evasiveness
8. Inconsistency in symptom presentation

A person who has always been a responsible and honest member of society is not likely to malinger PTSD (Davidson, 1952). According to Braverman (1978), malingerers are more likely to be marginal members of society with few binding ties or long-standing financial responsibilities, such as home ownership. The malingerer may have a history of sporadic employment, previous incapacitating injuries, and extensive absences from work. Malingerers frequently depict themselves and their prior functioning in exclusively complimentary terms (Layden, 1966). The malingerer may assert incongruously an inability to work, but retain the capacity for recreation (e.g., enjoyment of theater, television, or athletic activities). In contrast, the patient with genuine PTSD is more likely to withdraw from recreational activities as well as work.

The malingerer may pursue a legal claim tenaciously, while alleging depression or incapacitation due to symptoms of PTSD (Davidson, 1952). Malingerers are unlikely to volunteer information about sexual dysfunction (Sadoff, 1978; Chaney, Cohn, Williams, & Vincent, 1984), although they are apt to emphasize their physical complaints.

Malingerers are also unlikely to volunteer information about nightmares unless they have read the diagnostic criteria for PTSD. Genuine nightmares in PTSD show variations on the theme of the traumatic event (Garfield, 1987). For example, a woman who was raped may have dreams in which she feels helpless and is tortured without being raped. The malingerer who does not know the expected dream patterns may claim repetitive dreams that *always* reenact the traumatic event in exactly the same way.

Except for combat veterans and survivors of sexual assault, posttraumatic nightmares usually begin to fade rapidly after several weeks. After a traumatic event, the event may be dreamed almost literally a few times, and then, gradually, other elements are included as the event becomes woven into the rest of the person's dream life. Posttraumatic nightmares, as contrasted with lifetime nightmares unrelated to trauma, are almost always accompanied by considerable body movement (van der Kolk, Blitz, Burr, Sherry, & Hartmann, 1984). Body movement may be confirmed by the sleeping partner or disarray of sheets and covers.

In veterans' posttraumatic nightmares, by contrast, the encapsulated traumatic combat scene may become isolated. When activated, the nightmare occurs in an almost identical fashion for many years. After the fading of the initial posttraumatic nightmares, a male veteran may begin to wake up terrified and report that he has dreamed of the horrible event exactly or almost exactly as it happened (van der Kolk et al., 1984). Veterans with PTSD generally report awakening from a dream that involves reliving the trauma, experiencing strong emotions that would have been appropriate reactions to the original traumatic event—usually rage, intense fear, or grief. Less often, they describe awakening in terror without recalling any of the actual dream (Ross, Ball, Sullivan, & Caroff, 1989).

Malingerers may seem evasive during the interview and be unwilling to make definite statements about returning to work or financial gain (Powell, 1991). One method of evading questions is to say that an explanation is too complicated, or that it would take too long to explain. When such persons are told that there is no limit on time, they may attempt further evasions, suggesting, for example, that the clinician would not be able to understand the situation, even if it were explained (East, 1927).

Contradictions between the first and subsequent versions of events were viewed by Schwartz (1946) as evidence of malingering. However, depending upon inconsistencies of memory as proof of malingering is hazardous. Buckhout (1974) found inaccuracies in memories of observed events in nonmalingerers. In a series of studies, Loftus (1979) established that memory distortion increases over time, while people become more certain about the accuracy of their memories. In establishing the presence of malingering, the clinician must differentiate between suspicious memory impairment and expected memory distortions (Rogers & Cavanaugh, 1983).

A clinical decision model for establishing the diagnosis of malingered PTSD is presented in Table 7.7. This model must be viewed as tentative, based on the current status of empirical research. The clinical decision model requires the clinician to establish (1) the individual's motivation for faking, (2) the presence of at least two associated characteristics, and (3) strong confirmatory evidence of malingering.

MALINGERED PTSD IN THE COMBAT VETERAN

In 1979, the United States government initiated Operation Outreach to handle readjustment and psychiatric problems for Vietnam veterans (Lynn & Belza, 1984). Malingering of PTSD became easier after lists of PTSD symptoms were widely distributed by national service organizations (Atkinson, Henderson, Sparr, & Deale, 1982). In addition, veterans with true PTSD at Vet Centers and VA hospitals provided other veterans with firsthand opportunities to observe these symptoms (Lynn & Belza, 1984).

Estimates of the prevalence of PTSD among Vietnam veterans have ranged from 20% to 70% (Ashlock, Walker, Starkey, Harmand, & Michel, 1987; Friedman, 1981; Wilson & Zigelbaum, 1983). According to Lynn and Belza (1984), the incidence of malingered or factitious PTSD in the Reno VA Hospital was 7 out of 125 patients

---

TABLE 7.7. Clinical Decision Model for Establishing Malingered PTSD

A. Understandable motive to malinger PTSD
B. At least two of the following criteria:
    1. Irregular employment or job dissatisfaction
    2. Prior claims for injuries
    3. Capacity for recreation, but not work
    4. No nightmares or, if nightmares, exact repetitions of the civilian trauma
    5. Antisocial personality traits
    6. Evasiveness or contradictions
    7. Noncooperation in the evaluation
C. Confirmation of malingering by one of the following criteria:
    1. Admission of malingering
    2. Unambiguous psychometric evidence of malingering or strong corroborative evidence of malingering

---

hospitalized for PTSD in a 5-month period. This estimate of 5.6% may be conservative, since only "severe" PTSD cases are hospitalized.

Motives to Malinger Combat PTSD

Veterans may be motivated to malinger PTSD for four primary reasons: (1) to obtain compensation, (2) to be admitted to a VA hospital, (3) to gain the retrospective glamour of combat, and (4) to reduce punishment for criminal conduct. Obtaining compensation has been the primary motive for veterans to malinger PTSD since the VA has accepted the delayed type of PTSD as a potentially compensable disorder since 1980 (Bitzer, 1980). When PTSD is malingered for the purpose of gaining hospital admission, it must be distinguished from factitious PTSD. Factitious PTSD allows a veteran to assume the patient role, whereas malingered PTSD may serve other goals, such as providing shelter or documentary support to seek compensation.

Soldiers have sporadically fabricated stories about their combat experiences to attain praise, sympathy, or to exaggerate masculine prowess (Pankratz, 1985). Individuals not in combat may also be motivated to fabricate military experiences to gain admiration (Lynn & Belza, 1984). Ashlock et al. (1987) suggested that claiming to be a Vietnam veteran in a psychiatric ward may seem like an easy way to gain status by appearing braver and more masculine to staff members and other patients.

In the criminal justice system, the diagnosis of PTSD may serve as a basis for an insanity defense, a reduction of charges, or mitigation of penalty. Veterans charged with serious crimes may consequently be highly motivated to malinger PTSD, or falsely to impute a causal link between a crime and genuine PTSD. Wilson (1981) reported three types of clinical presentations that have led to successful insanity defenses: (1) A veteran may enter into a dissociative state due to a flashback and resort to survivor skills learned in Vietnam; (2) a veteran with severe survivor guilt may commit acts to have himself killed in order to be reunited with comrades killed in action; (3) a veteran may engage in sensation-seeking behavior (e.g., drug trafficking) to relive combat excitement. In assessing the validity of the relationship between PTSD and a crime, the clinician should consider whether the crime scene recreates the combat trauma, and whether dissociation or bewilderment are evidenced at the time of the criminal conduct.

Approaches to Detection

Clinicians evaluating PTSD in Vietnam veterans must exercise special care to maintain their objectivity. Countertransference may occur because of strong feelings for or against the Vietnam war. As noted by Atkinson et al. (1982), recounting of gruesome events in Vietnam, expressions of painful affect, and outbursts of anger can be stressful for both veterans and clinicians. Some clinicians feel moved to diagnose PTSD on the basis of fragmentary symptoms because they feel a sense of moral responsibility for the Vietnam veteran as a victim (Atkinson, Henderson, Sparr, & Deale, 1982; Pankratz, 1985).

The clinical interview is the single most important component in assessing PTSD (Fairbank, McCaffrey, & Keane, 1986). However, cooperation with the interview may be complicated by several factors. First, the antipathy many Vietnam veterans feel toward the federal government may interfere with the evaluation process (Atkinson et al., 1982). Second, some veterans find it very difficult to discuss their traumatic, painful memories with even a sympathetic clinician. Third, some veterans try to minimize their difficulty; other veterans exaggerate actual symptoms of PTSD for fear of failing to receive necessary treatment or deserved compensation (Fairbank et al., 1986).

The clinician should gather a detailed military history. To receive VA compensation, the severity of the stressor must be rated as "catastrophic" (Atkinson et al., 1982). Military records and eyewitness accounts are critical, because they provide the only independent substantiation of the stressor and, hence, the disorder (Sparr & Atkinson, 1986). As described by Breslau and Davis (1987), the events most highly correlated with PTSD in Vietnam veterans are participation in atrocities and high numbers of combat stressors. The relationship between the alleged stressors and the symptoms that are being reexperienced should be carefully elucidated.

Some veterans claiming PTSD underwent no combat or stressful military experience at all. Sparr and Pankratz (1983) reported five alleged Vietnam veterans who presented with symptoms of PTSD; three asserted that they were former prisoners of war. In fact, none had been prisoners of war, four had never been in Vietnam, and two had not been in the military. In the same vein, Lynn and Belza (1984) reported seven veterans that presented with PTSD symptoms to a VA hospital despite no exposure to Vietnam or combat. One veteran's fabrications were so convincing that an Outreach Program hired him as a Vet Center counselor.

Collateral sources of information should include data from a variety of sources. The veteran's spouse and relatives should be interviewed to validate current PTSD symptoms and assess premilitary behavioral adjustment. Records documenting exposure to combat or other stresses during service in Vietnam are often difficult to obtain. Personnel files are often not revealing, although unit logs and data from other members of the same unit are better resources. One simple procedure is to see whether the veteran's discharge papers (Form DD 214) indicate overseas service. The discharge papers should also include campaign and service articles (Lynn & Belza, 1984), but the record of awards is not always complete (Early, 1984). Since the veteran's discharge papers may be falsified, Sparr and Atkinson (1986) recommend acquiring a copy directly from the U.S. Department of Defense. In addition, VA medical centers have a national Register, which can supply information about prisoners of war through a single phone call. Finally, before concluding that a veteran is lying about Vietnam experiences, the clinician must consider the remote possibility that all parties to an event may be sworn to secrecy in a guerilla war (Early, 1984).

Graphic stories of battle are not conclusive proof of PTSD. The accounts presented by veterans malingering PTSD can be just as vivid and detailed as genuine PTSD patients (Hamilton, 1985). Vet Center consultation with actual combat veterans can help pinpoint lack of knowledge of the geography and culture of Vietnam (Lynn & Belza,

1984). Ashlock et al. (1987) noted that some veterans with malingered PTSD were able to pass multiple screening interviews by both Vietnam veterans and staff. Several, however, were discovered by group members within the first 2 days of the program.

Psychological Testing in Combat PTSD

Some psychological tests may be helpful in assessing the genuineness of PTSD in veterans. The *PK* of the MMPI scale has been cross-validated on Vietnam veterans for the determination of PTSD. Fairbank, McCaffrey, and Keane (1985) compared MMPI scores of Vietnam veterans with PTSD with those of a group of veterans instructed to malinger PTSD. In their initial study, the authors were able to accurately classify over 90% of the participants. As previously noted, the problem with the *PK* scale is that subsequent studies produced variable results on its ability to identify combat-related PTSD.

Hyer, Fallon, Harrison, and Boudewyns (1987) compared three groups of Vietnam inpatients: PTSD combat, non-PTSD combat, and noncombat. Their study applied fake-bad indicators based on the MMPI obvious/subtle differences and the *F* scale to these groups. Results showed that (1) a carefully distinguished PTSD group responded differently to obvious and subtle items than other inpatient Vietnam groups, and (2) the *F* scale was elevated in the PTSD group. This latter finding is open to interpretation. Either a proportion of the PTSD persons were overreporting their symptomatology or combat PTSD experiences are sufficiently atypical to account for *F*-scale elevations.

Perconte and Goreczny (1990) attempted to replicate previous studies that used the *F* scale and a PTSD subscale of the MMPI to discriminate Vietnam veterans with PTSD from well-adjusted veterans who feigned symptoms of PTSD. Discriminant analysis of *F* and PTSD subscale scores correctly identified only 43.6% of the participants; thus, it failed to support the use of the MMPI in detection of fabricated PTSD symptoms in a veteran population.

The MS-PTSD is a 35-item inventory for the diagnosis of combat-related PTSD; its high face validity makes this scale vulnerable to faking. Dalton et al. (1989) found that 77% of their participants were able successfully to fake PTSD. Likewise, Lyons et al. (1994) found that the scores of individuals instructed to respond "as if" they had PTSD did not differ from the scores of veterans with PTSD. Finally, Frueh and Kinder (1994) confirmed the ease of faking the MS-PTSD by using undergraduates. The MS-PTSD does not provide useful data when feigning is suspected.

The use of the Rorschach to investigate feigned symptoms of combat-related PTSD was investigated by Frueh and Kinder (1994; see also Chapter 10). Participants included a control group, a role-informed malingering group, and Vietnam veterans with PTSD. Results indicated that malingerers were able to achieve scores similar to the PTSD patients on most Rorschach variables. Malingerers typically gave responses that were overly dramatic and less complicated, less emotionally restrained, and indicated a greater sense of impaired reality testing as compared to PTSD patients.

Differential Diagnosis

The differential diagnosis of Vietnam PTSD includes malingering, factitious disorder, antisocial personality disorder (APD), and genuine PTSD due to a nonmilitary stressor. New life stressors, such as divorce, unemployment, or legal problems may occur after military discharge. In some circumstances, the clinician must discern whether a patient's PTSD is the result of a combat experience or a nonmilitary stressor. A coexisting mental disorder, such as psychosis or depression, may further complicate the assessment of PTSD (Atkinson et al., 1982).

The differential diagnosis between APD and PTSD may be difficult. Although the presence of APD does not rule out PTSD, it should increase the clinician's index of suspicion for malingering. Unfortunately, many individuals with PTSD have antisocial symptoms, such as an inconsistent work pattern, poor parenting, repeated legal difficulties, inability to maintain an enduring attachment with a sexual partner, episodes of irritability, reckless behavior, failure to honor financial obligations, and a history of impulsive behavior (Walker, 1981). Veterans with PTSD may also show substance abuse, rage, and suspiciousness. Identification of developmental symptoms of APD (conduct disorder) prior to age of 15 is critical. However, an uninvestigated issue is whether the sensation-seeking component of APD increases the likelihood for exposure to PTSD-evoking events. In summary, the presence of APD may signal the need for a more detailed evaluation but provides no proof of feigned PTSD.

Clinical Indicators of Malingered Vietnam PTSD

A common chief complaint in veterans with malingered PTSD is fear that they might lose control and harm others (Pankratz, 1985); the expression of this fear is likely to gain them admission to psychiatric hospitals. Malingerers tend to overplay their Vietnam experience. They might say, "I've got PTSD. I've got flashbacks and nightmares. I'm really stressed out" (Merback, 1984). Veterans with true PTSD are more likely to downplay their combat experience (e.g., by saying "Lots of guys had it worse than me").

Melton (1984) suggested several factors that help to differentiate the veteran with true PTSD from malingered PTSD. Whether veterans attribute blame to themselves or others is one good discriminator. On one hand, individuals with true PTSD are likely to feel intense levels of guilt and perceive themselves as the cause of their problems. On the other hand, malingerers are more likely to present themselves as victims of circumstance. They often begin the session with statements that imply that their life predicaments are a direct result of Vietnam; they condemn authority and the war. In the first visit, veterans with true PTSD are often resistant to openly admitting that their problems may be related to their experience in Vietnam. They are likely to come in because of family members' insistence or due to recurrent loss of employment, depression, outbursts of anger, or substance abuse.

Melton (1984) reported that the themes of intrusive recollections and dreams are often different between true and malingered PTSD. Veterans with PTSD often report themes of helplessness, guilt, or rage. Dreams in true PTSD generally convey a theme of helplessness with regard to the particular traumatic events that occurred during combat. In malingered PTSD, the themes of intrusive recollections are more often anger toward generalized authority; dreams emphasize themes of grandiosity and power. The reportedly reexperienced "trauma" in malingerers is often not consistent with their self-reports of the original trauma (J. R. Smith, personal communication, June 10, 1987).

Differences have been observed between veterans with true and malingered PTSD in their expression and acknowledgment of feelings (Melton, 1984). In true PTSD, the veterans often deny or have been numbed to the emotional impact of combat. In malingered PTSD, veterans often make efforts to convince the clinician how emotionally traumatizing Vietnam was by "acting out" their alleged feelings. The true PTSD veteran generally *downplays* symptoms, whereas the malingerer *overplays* them. For instance, veterans with true PTSD try not to bring attention to their hyperalertness and suspicious eye movements. In contrast, PTSD malingerers may present their suspiciousness with a dramatic quality. As an example, a male PTSD malingerer may volunteer that he thinks of nothing but Vietnam and "relishes" telling his combat memories.

An important characteristic of PTSD is the avoidance of environmental conditions associated with the trauma. For example, PTSD veterans may stay home on hot rainy days because of the resemblance to Vietnam weather. Camping may be avoided because of reexperienced expectations of trip wires in the bush. In addition, crowds may be avoided because combat usually occurred "in a crowd." In malingered PTSD, the veteran is unlikely to report such postcombat reactions to environmental stimuli (Melton, 1984).

Other characteristics have been noted that differentiate between actual and malingered PTSD in Vietnam veterans. These characteristics, summarized in Table 7.8, include how guilt and anger are experienced. The clinical indicators for malingered

TABLE 7.8. Clinical Indicators of Malingered Vietnam PTSD

Salient features	Genuine PTSD	Malingered PTSD
Relationship of symptoms to Vietnam	Minimize	Emphasize
Target of blame	Self	Others
Characteristic dreams	Helplessness and guilt	Grandiosity or power
Emotions associated with combat	Deny impact	"Acts out" on apparent feelings
Combat stories	Reluctant to tell	"Relishes" telling
Combat-related guilt	Survivor guilt[a]	Generalized guilt over surviving
Avoidance of environments reminiscent of Vietnam or combat	Yes	No
Focus of anger	Own helplessness	Persons in authority

[a]Survivor guilt in genuine PTSD patients is typically centered on specific combat situations and not generalized to surviving the war itself.

Vietnam PTSD are based primarily on case reports and must therefore be considered tentative.

CONCLUSION

The assessment of malingered psychiatric symptoms after traumatic events is complex, because self-reports of subjective symptoms are difficult to verify. The differential diagnosis between malingering and conversion disorder rests entirely on the clinician's ability to discern what is conscious and under voluntary control. The clinician may approach the matter of detecting malingered posttraumatic disorders from "the viewpoints of an investigator searching to unearth a crime, a moralist trying to undo a suspected offense against social principle . . . or a contestant locked in game-play with an antagonist" (Braverman, 1978, p. 43). No matter how they perceive their role, clinicians must be thoroughly grounded in the phenomenology of PTSD and aware of common differences between genuine and malingered PTSD.

8

Children and Deception

LYNN OLDERSHAW, Ph.D.
R. MICHAEL BAGBY, Ph.D.

A fundamental facet of clinical assessment is a consideration of whether the informant, irrespective of age, is responding in an honest and forthright manner. This concern becomes even more relevant when assessing children who historically have been depicted as less than credible informants of their own thoughts, feelings, and behaviors. The present chapter addresses problems of dissimulation in the clinical assessment of children. We exclude from this discussion the very general issues regarding children's accuracy and veridicality outside the clinical realm.

The present chapter begins with a brief overview of children and deception. This introduction is followed by two major sections: The first section explores general issues related to dissimulation among children in a clinical context with the goal of comparing children's dissimulation with adults. Specifically, the first section examines (1) children's motivation to deceive during clinical assessment, (2) their perception of the assessment process and its influence on their deceptive tendencies, (3) parental issues related to dissimulation among children, (4) the relevance of developmental factors, and (5) the types of dissimulation most commonly observed among children. The second section applies clinical knowledge toward an understanding of dissimulation tendencies in children, including their detection and prevention. It also reviews and evaluates current measures designed to identify malingering and deception among children during clinical assessment.

We adhere to the definition of dissimulation presented in Chapter 1, "a general term to describe an individual who is deliberately distorting or misrepresenting his or her psychological symptoms." As such, this chapter is limited to a discussion of *intentional* acts of deception and excludes those types of deception believed to be unintentional in nature. Examples of unintentional distortions include self-deception (see Silver, Sabini, & Miceli, 1989) and a repressive defense style (see Fritz, Spirito, & Yeung, 1994).

OVERVIEW

Various forms of deception constitute an important dimension of human actions and interactions. Deceptive communication (Miller & Stiff, 1993), with its manifold goals, social sanctions, and manifestations, is clearly beyond the scope of this chapter. For readers interested in the nature of lying among children, Stouthamer-Loeber (1986) provides a masterful review. She explored children's lies in natural settings, typically as told to parents. When telling falsehoods to significant others, especially parents, some children experience what Quinn (1988) termed "detection apprehension," that is, the fear that parents will detect their lies and punish them. Allied with detection apprehension is a closely related phenomenon, namely "deception guilt." According to Quinn, a number of children that do deceive their parents may be motivated to confess by remorse and anxiety.

Research suggests that the family dimension may also affect the discernment of dishonesty, perhaps because of the strong emotions associated with lying to parents. Indeed, children's fear that parents are more adept than strangers at detecting their lies is supported by research findings showing that parents can successfully detect their children's attempts at deception (Morency & Krauss, 1982), whereas adult strangers are more readily foiled by children's deceptive efforts (Allen & Atkinson, 1978).

Deception by children sometimes serves to protect parents and other family members. Children are often called upon during investigations to provide information about significant others, most notably their parents. Although such accounts are deemed important for such purposes as custody and access assessments, and child welfare investigations, children's veracity is often called into question. When reporting negative information on a parent, considerable potential exists for children to either intentionally withhold information (out of fear or a desire to protect), or in some cases to report deliberately more negative behavior than actually exists (possibly to protect or please the other parent). Children's veracity is of particular concern in sexual assaults and related crimes in which the child victim is often the only witness; the credibility of his or her statement about the perpetrator is critical in reaching a just verdict. The credibility of children's testimonies in such cases has been a subject of considerable research and debate (e.g., Ceci, Ross, & Toglia, 1987; Goodman, 1984; Goodman & Clarke-Stewart, 1991).

Little is known about the accuracy of children's accounts of their own psychological symptoms and the extent to which dissimulative tendencies are operative in their clinical assessments. Self-appraisal of social, emotional, and personality characteristics is complex and prone to distortion. Indeed, many aspects of an individual's psychological state are subjective and constitute a domain for which self-report is the primary modality (Quay & La Greca, 1986; Reynolds, 1993). Thus, the assessment of such qualities as personality, attitudes, values, temperament, emotions, cognitive style, behavior, and other psychological and personological aspects of children are vulnerable to dissimulation. Because of the inherent subjectivity, little concordance is found between parents' and their children's report of psychological symptoms. Rogers (1995, Chapter 6) found, even with the use of structured interviews, that levels of parent–

child agreement were disappointing. Before children are assumed to be less than forth-coming about their symptoms and problems, we need to review the Achenbach, McConaughy, and Howell (1987) meta-analysis of 119 studies of children from clini-cal and nonclinical settings. They consistently found poor agreement across sources (e.g., teachers, parents, and children). However, children typically report fewer symp-toms of depression than do their parents and treating clinicians (Kazdin, Colbus, & Rodgers, 1986; Kazdin, French, Unis, & Esveldt-Dawson, 1983; Tisher & Lang, 1983). Possible reasons for this disparity include (1) children do not experience these symp-toms as noteworthy, (2) parents overpathologize, and (3) children are defensive and deliberately minimize their psychopathology. If nothing else, marked discrepancies between parent and child reports of children's psychopathology underscore the need to assess response styles on a familywide basis. In addition, children may report inac-curate accounts of their own emotions and behavior because of their limited compre-hension of clinical inquiries. Even when questions are posed in simple words and sen-tence structure, they are vulnerable to misunderstandings (see Breslau, 1987).

Children are frequently assessed to determine their intellectual functioning and to evaluate possible learning disabilities. Although children in these instances are un-able to "fake good" (e.g., appear more intelligent), the opportunity is presented for feigned cognitive deficits. McCaffrey and Lynch (1992) explored neuropsychological practitioners' ability to detect malingering in children and adolescents. In their study, malingered profiles were produced by instructing children not to do their best on neuropsychological tests. In reviewing the case materials, mental health professionals categorized the feigned profiles as abnormal, but none attributed these abnormalities to malingering. Likewise, Faust, Hart, Guilmette, and Arkes (1988) demonstrated the inability of neuropsychologists to detect malingering in children who were asked to "fake bad" on a battery of neuropsychological measures. The question remains whether clinicians' inaccuracies reflect (1) their good-faith assumptions that children put for-ward their best performances or (2) the inadequacies of assessment methods.

DIFFERENCES BETWEEN CHILDREN AND ADULTS

Developmental Considerations

Unlike adults, developmental factors play a critical role in understanding children's deception during clinical assessment. A primary consideration is whether very young children are developmentally capable of intentional deception. In order for children to provide intentionally false statements about themselves or a situation, they must first master the concept of false belief (Bussey, 1992). To intentionally deceive, chil-dren must recognize that their false statements can actually mislead others. Once children acquire the concept of false belief, they realize that in order to successfully lie they must convince another of the veracity of a false statement. Although some researchers (e.g., Chandler, Fritz, & Hala, 1989) have shown that children as young as 2½ years of age are capable of employing deceptive strategies, the general consensus is that before the age of 3, children's understanding of the concept of false belief is limited (Bussey, 1992; Wimmer, Gruber, & Perner, 1984), thus compromising their ability to deceive.

Developmental studies designed to assess children's ability to deceive have been conducted primarily in contexts outside of clinical assessment. Based on these studies, some commentators (see Quinn, 1988) have concluded that (1) first graders cannot successfully tell a lie, but their deceptive ability increases with age; and (2) children are able to successfully fool their peers, adult strangers, and their parents by the fourth grade. Methodologically, these researchers typically have asked children to try to deceive someone by presenting false information about a particular stimulus. As examples, Feldman and White (1980) asked children to convince peers that a good drink tasted bad and a bad drink tasted good, whereas Morency and Krauss (1982) had children observe pleasant and unpleasant slides, and asked them to convey a false impression about the slides to others through facial cues while viewing the slides. In one sense, these scenarios are similar to deception in clinical assessment in that the children are presenting a false impression to others. However, the critical difference is that children in research studies were presenting information that was external to themselves (e.g., drinks and slides). Children may have greater difficulty in deception when falsifying information about themselves in matters that are important to them.

Lewis and his colleagues (see Lewis, 1993) conducted a series of studies using the following paradigm: A child participant is brought into a room and instructed not to look at a toy. The child is then left alone for 5 minutes, and his or her behavior is covertly videotaped. If the child looks at the toy, the experimenter immediately returns, and after a moment says to the child, "Did you peek?" The child's verbal and nonverbal response is recorded. This paradigm is similar to clinical assessment situations because (1) children are put in a position to deceive an adult stranger, rather than a peer or a familiar adult; (2) children are reporting on their own behavior, rather than stimuli external to them; and (3) punishment is not implied by the adult stranger.

Using this paradigm with children from ages 2½ to 6, Lewis (1993) was unsuccessful in differentiating those children who lied from those who truthfully admitted to peeking. An examination of their verbal and nonverbal (e.g., facial expressions and body movements) behavior revealed no differences between truth tellers, liars, and controls (i.e., nonpeekers) at any age. Moreover, adults were not able to detect liars at any age, beyond chance levels. In this simple act of deception, even very young children could successfully deceive adult strangers.

Lewis's (1993) research suggests that children's ability to deceive is a skill learned very early, and these deceptive skills increase over the first 6 years of life. This increase in deceptive ability is revealed in research indicating that the lies told by very young children typically take the form of simple denial ("No") or misleading confirmation ("Yes"), whereas the lies of older children and adolescents are more sophisticated elaborations (Bussey, 1992). This developmental shift has important implications for assessment. Given that many of the self-report measures and interviews allow for simple "yes–no" responses, even very young children appear to be quite capable of lying successfully with little likelihood of being detected. To the extent that elaborations are required and children are requested to provide more unstructured information about themselves, deceptive tendencies will either be less frequent in children under the age of six or more readily detected.

Another developmental consideration with preschool-aged children is their tendency to exaggerate their attributes and abilities. Indeed, young children have been called "developmental optimists," perceiving their competencies much more positively than they actually are (Stipek, 1981). To the extent that these children believe what they are saying, regardless of how unrealistic such beliefs are, it is a serious mistake to misconstrue their overly inflated estimates as intentional deception. However, an evaluator lacking knowledge of this particular developmental stage may interpret such blatant exaggerations of one's competencies as an active attempt at defensiveness.

Preschool-aged children often do not understand complex emotions and can rarely describe feelings beyond such simple emotions as mad, sad, scared, or happy (Harter, 1983). If the clinical assessment is designed to explore emotions, such as guilt, frustration, or confusion, young children are not likely to provide an accurate description of their own feelings. Because of this developmental limitation, children may choose to make up answers rather than admit that they do not understand.

Types of Deception

Considerable attention has been paid to the identification and detection of malingered psychopathology among adults, with less focus on other forms of dissimulation (see Kropp & Rogers, 1993, for a review). The reverse appears to be true with children, where accounts of malingering in the clinical literature are quite rare. One explanation for the relatively low frequency of malingering among children is suggested by Quinn (1988), who notes that considerable skill is required to malinger, including skills in role playing, impression management, and deception. Not until children reach latency age and adolescence do they acquire these complex skills, and, in turn, display an increased ability to malinger. This hypothesized developmental shift is reflected in the deception literature, with the advent of studies and clinical accounts of successful malingering among latency-age children and adolescents (Faust et al., 1988; Greenfield, 1987; Stein, Graham, & Williams, 1995). Studies of malingering among younger children do not exist in the published literature.

Motivation to Deceive

In understanding dissimulation, especially malingering, clinicians must identify clearly the objectives underlying the choice to misrepresent the truth. Motives for dissimulation among adults include unwarranted compensation, avoidance of prosecution, and attainment of a desirable position (Pope, Butcher, & Seelen, 1993). For children, such tangible motivators are not as readily apparent; the challenge for clinicians and researchers alike is to identify less overt motivations (e.g., attention and approval) that may be involved in children's deception during clinical assessment.

The Child's Perception of the Assessment

With adults, both clinicians and their clients typically operate with comparable knowledge regarding the general purpose of the assessment. More specifically, both understand the purpose of the assessment, its likely conclusions (e.g., psychological impairment), and the probable outcome of these conclusions (e.g., financial settlement). When clinicians assess children, the child often does not have an accurate understanding of the assessment procedures and its purpose. Commonly, children are assessed with little knowledge or even false knowledge of its purpose (Evans & Nelson, 1977; Mash & Terdal, 1988). Greater effort must be expended when assessing children to understand their perceptions of the evaluation and its purposes.

The appraisal of children's perceptions, both at the outset and throughout the assessment, enables clinicians to better grasp potential motives to deceive or malinger. For instance, if a female child is under the false impression that she will be sent to a foster home if she reports depressive symptoms, her motivation may be influenced by the desired outcome. She may either intentionally over- or underreport such symptoms, depending on her desire to live in a foster home. Similarly, performance on intelligence testing can be strongly influenced by the child's perception of the purpose of the testing. Children labeled as gifted often express a desire to "fit in" with the other children (MacLeish, 1984). If a gifted child holds the belief that superior performance on an intelligence test will lead to further alienation from peers, he or she may be motivated to intentionally underperform, a possibility that may apply to those children labeled as "gifted underachievers" (Rim & Lowe, 1988). In summary, greater knowledge of the child's often unique understanding of the assessment assists clinicians in remedying misperceptions and understanding the motives for dissimulation.

The Child's Perception of the Clinician

An obvious difference between children and adults is that children typically assume a subordinate role relative to adults and, therefore, are more easily influenced by them than are other adults. In the assessment context, the role of the clinician is considerably more influential in directing the child's responses than with adult clients. An important determinant of whether a child will report a specific event to an adult depends on the anticipated outcome for reporting that information (Bandura, 1991); children are generally apt to tell the truth to an adult out of fear of being caught. As previously noted, however, this fear may not be as strongly activated when the adult is a stranger, as is the case in clinical assessment.

Some children may express whatever they believe adults will respond to positively, regardless of its truthfulness. In one study, Fuchs and Thelen (1988) revealed a strong correlation between outcome expectancy and the likelihood of emotional expression among children. Specifically, the more children believed their parents would react negatively to their expression of negative emotion, the less likely they were to express such emotion during assessment. Indeed, children as young as 3 and 4 years old have been shown to inhibit negative emotional displays when in the presence of the examiner (Cole, 1986). Conversely, if a child believed that an adult examiner actually wanted negative symptoms, he or she might malinger to satisfy the perceived adult expectation.

A striking example of malingering to meet clinician's expectations was observed in the psychological assessment of a 9-year-old boy by a female clinician. The client presented as very anxious, continually fidgeting with his hands throughout the assessment. Despite assurances by the clinician, the boy often looked tentatively at her after responding and often asked if he had answered correctly. The clinician tended to give positive cues (e.g., nod and smile) and generally become more animated when the boy endorsed psychological symptoms. An examination of the child's test results revealed a clear pattern of increased endorsement of symptoms as the evaluation progressed. In other words, this child was probably sensitive to the cues from the clinician and changed his response pattern to conform to her expectations. This response style is an interesting combination of acquiescence and dissimulation, and appears to be largely iatrogenic.

The fact that the child in this case vignette appeared anxious during the evaluation speaks to another issue that must be considered. Research (Duffy & Martin, 1973; Zimmerman, 1970) has shown that highly anxious children are more sensitive to social reinforcement, because they have a strong fear of negative evaluations by others. Such children may be affected strongly by cues from the clinician because they fear criticism and failure. Logically, highly anxious children are more likely to present false information to clinicians if presented with positive reinforcement. Similarly, anxious children would be less likely to deceive in assessment in which these reinforcements are not present. Indeed, children diagnosed with anxiety symptoms have been found to display a lower than average rate of lying in natural settings, likely because they recognize that falsehoods are not socially acceptable. In contrast, children diagnosed with conduct disorders reveal a higher than average rate of lying (Stouthamer-Loeber, 1986). In other words, the personality and/or diagnostic status of a given child will interact with his or her tendency to deceive during assessments, and specifically, his or her tendency to prevaricate in order to please the clinician.

The Role of the Family

The family context typically plays an important role in assessing children, whereas it is less often considered in the clinical assessment of adults (La Greca, 1983, 1990). This observation illustrates two main differences between children and adults. First, because children are under the social control of others in their environment (Mash & Terdal, 1988), their actions are highly influenced by parents and others in authority. With respect to dissimulation, certain family variables appear to be related to children's defensiveness in psychological assessments. Specifically, children tend to be more defensive during assessments when they (1) are raised in highly religious families (Francis, Lankshear, & Pearson, 1989); (2) have mothers who work outside the home; or (3) grow up in environments characterized by parental rejection, inconsistent discipline, parental dishonesty, and parental pressure to perform (Makaremi, 1992). In other words, children are strongly affected by their family environment, and an understanding of any observed deceptions during assessment must take into account the family context. Moreover, the degree of manipulativeness in parents correlates with their children's ability to deceive others (Kraut & Price, 1976).

Parents' psychopathology can also influence children's forthrightness. Cole, Barrett, and Zahn-Waxler (1992) found that children of depressed and anxious parents tend to suppress their own negative emotions of tension and frustration. One possible explanation for this suppression is children's attempts to reduce conflict when a parent is emotionally unstable (Coyne, 1976). Therefore, children with a psychologically disordered parent may exhibit a tendency to underreport their own symptoms. Clinicians must take this tendency into account in understanding an important antecedent to defensiveness.

A second implication associated with the family context is that children's functioning, as measured during assessment, is intricately tied to how they are perceived within the family. Most conclusions about a child's adjustment are based on multiple sources of information, including parents who are knowledgeable about children's behavior across time and situation (Achenbach & Edelbrock, 1983). Clinicians must recognize that issues of dissimulation in the assessment of children include not only a child's self-report but also parental reports about the child, which may also be distorted (Goodnow, 1988). Parental distortions are not always intentional (e.g., parental depression often results in more negatively biased reports of children). Instances do occur in which parental reports of their children are distorted deliberately. For example, a parent involved in a child–custody assessment may distort a child's symptoms to reveal the poor parenting by his or her former spouse. Alternatively, a parent with temporary custody may intentionally minimize the child's psychological problems to portray falsely an ideal custody placement. Use of parents as informants in the assessment of children adds an additional level of complexity to the assessment of dissimulation. Clinicians should not immediately assume that any marked disparity reflects children's deceptions. Other viable alternatives include (1) honest differences between parents and their children and (2) parental prevarications about their children.

CLINICAL ASSESSMENT OF DISSIMULATION

Clinical Interviews

Accurate comprehension is fundamental to clinical interviews. Clinicians must ascertain whether the child understands the questions. What may appear to be an unmistakable instance of lying could simply be the result of the child's misunderstanding of the questions. As previously indicated, young children typically have limited understanding of the words and phrases that adults use to describe the many nuances of human emotions. Asking a young child to describe his or her behavior or the behavior of others in specific situations sometimes yields more accurate information than asking a child to label his or her moods. Many children also fail to describe accurately or completely events in their environment, due to a relatively limited verbal repertoire.

Children's self-monitoring is likely to be more variable than adults during clinical interviews. Some young children describe events the way they see them, without censoring their statements. In contrast, many children may have been taught very specific rules of communication, especially to adults, to which they may comply rigidly. For example, some children are taught not to openly disagree with persons in authority. Others have been taught to meet adult expectations. In both cases, distortions may serve the perceived needs of the situation. As previously noted, children are vulnerable to the subtle messages from the interviewer and/or another adult. During the interview, clinicians should be alert to subtle messages and conduct the questioning in a manner that minimizes these influences. For example, when interviewing a child, the effect of acknowledgment must be carefully monitored. Acknowledgment enhances rapport and is typically viewed as neutral; however, it may also influence the child to continue talking, increasing the chance of inadvertent reinforcement of specific content that may bias or even alter the child's presentation.

Open-ended questions greatly minimize the possibility that the interviewer will lead the child to state conclusions that are suggested by the question itself. In contrast, closed-ended questions, especially leading questions, may encourage acquiescence. For example, leading questions, such as "Do you think you need to work harder in school?" almost invariably will elicit a "yes" response. In general, open-ended questioning not only maintains rapport but minimizes potential distortion of information provided by the child (e.g., defensiveness). When closed-ended questions are necessary, one useful technique is to offer neutral alternatives.

Another type of question, generally counterproductive, is the "why" question. A "why" question is often perceived by children as requiring them to account for or justify behavior rather than to describe what led to the behavior. These questions typically result in feelings of defensiveness and possibly hostility toward the interviewer. For example, the question, "Why is it that you don't take your pills?" would be better rephrased as "What things don't you like about taking pills?" (La Greca, 1990).

One method to foster rapport and possibly reduce the motivation to deceive would be to inform the child, in a manner in which he or she clearly could understand, the reasons and implications of the assessment. If children do not understand why the assessment is being conducted, they may assume the worst and modify their response style accordingly. Of course, children also may engage in some form of dissimulation when they realize that the true objectives of the evaluation differ from their own goals.

Detection of Dissimulation on Psychological Tests

Multiscale inventories and other psychological measures for children have paid comparatively little attention to response styles. Unlike adult measures, test developers appear to have made an implicit assumption that children and adolescents will be forthcoming and forthright regarding their psychological functioning. In this section, we organize the current data on children's response styles by individual measures.

The Personality Inventory for Children

The Personality Inventory for Children (PIC; Wirt, Lachar, Klinedinst, & Seat, 1984) is a 600-item, true–false parent-report inventory.[1] The PIC was designed to be used for children and adolescents from the ages of 3 through 16. It was validated with methodology similar to the MMPI; the primary difference, of course, is that the questions regarding the child are answered by adult respondents, usually the child's parents. Although this section focuses primarily on children's capacity to dissimulate, we include the PIC because adult reporting may greatly influence children evaluations (La Greca, 1990).

The PIC includes five scales to assess informant response style. Three scales are standard: the Lie (*L*) scale, the Frequency (*F*) scale, and the Defensiveness (*DEF*) scale. In addition, the evaluation of response styles is supplemented by two experimental scales: the K (*K*) scale and the Social Desirability (*SD*) scale.

The *L* scale is composed of 15 rationally derived items. It is designed to identify a defensive response set manifested by a tendency to ascribe the most virtuous of behaviors and to deny minor, commonly occurring behavior problems in the child described (Wirt et al., 1984). Conceptually, the *L* scale is similar to the *L* scale on the MMPI and MMPI-2. Very few studies have been conducted to assess the effectiveness of the *L* scale to detect defensiveness. As evidence of convergent validity, Wirt et al. reported that the *L* scale correlates positively with other scales on the PIC designed to assess defensiveness (i.e., *DEF, K, SD*). In an earlier study, Lachar and Gdowski (1979) found that only 8% of the respondents derived from a large heterogeneous child and adolescent sample produced *T* scores on the *L* scale that were greater than 59. Employing this cut score, McVaugh and Grow (1983) found that 82% of honest parents and 86% of parents instructed to be defensive were correctly classified. In a repeated measures design, Daldin (1984, cited in Wirt et al., 1984) asked 25 mothers of children being evaluated at a guidance center to complete the PIC under honest and defensive instructions. Only 4% of the PIC protocols in the honest condition had *T* scores on *L* > 59, whereas 92% of those in the defensive condition exceeded this cut score.

The DEF scale consists of 23 empirically derived items designed to assess the tendency for parents to be defensive about their child's behavior (Myers, 1974, cited in Wirt et al., 1984). The items for this scale were selected by obtaining PIC protocols of those mothers independently assessed as "high defensive" or "low defensive." In a differential prevalence design, Myers found that the *DEF* scale was more elevated in mothers of delinquent than mothers of mentally disordered boys. In the same study, Myers also found that a cutting score of *T* > 59 correctly identified 93% of the low-defensive protocols and 88% of the high-defensive protocols. On a normative basis, Lachar and Gdowski (1979) found that only 4% of the children and adolescents had DEF *T* scores ≥ 70, whereas 14% obtained DEF *T* scores > 59 ≤ 70.

The two experimental scales for the assessment of defensiveness are not well validated. The *K* scale consists of 28 items that distinguished 600 normative from 200 mentally disordered boys. All *K*-scale items are keyed in the false direction. The *K* scale correlates positively with other measures of defensiveness on the PIC (*L, DEF, SD*) and negatively with scales measuring psychopathology. Based on ratings by 10 judges, the *SD* scale consists of 25 items with the highest, and 25 with the lowest social desirability ratings. Although the *SD* scale correlates significantly with other PIC scales of defensiveness, no other validity data are available.

The only scale on the PIC designed to assess malingering is the *F* scale. The *F* scale can also be used to detect other response distortions, such as unintentional exaggeration and random responding. The *F* scale is composed of 42 items, which were seldom endorsed (≤ 5%) in both the normative and clinical samples. In the construction of the *F* scale, an effort was made to distribute the items across the various clinical scales so that no single pattern of severe disturbance would "artificially" elevate the *F* scale. In the initial normative study, 20% of the profiles from mentally disordered youth had *T* scores ≥ 110 on the *F* scale. In contrast, McVaugh and Grow (1983) found that a cut score of ≥ 110 correctly identified 93% of malingered and 100% of honest protocols.

The Behavior Assessment System for Children

The Behavior Assessment System for Children (BASC; Reynolds & Kamphaus, 1992) is another measure for the psychological assessment of children, with specific scales designed to assess response styles. The BASC is a multimethod, multidimensional instrument for the evaluation of behavior and self-perceptions in children aged 4–18 years. The BASC is comprised of the Self-Report of Personality (*SRP*) and two rating scales: the Teacher Rating scale (*TRS*) and the Parent Rating scale (*PRS*). All three scales have an *F* index to assess malingering; only the *SRP* has the *L* index as a measure of defensiveness.

The *F* index on both the *TRS* and the *PRS* consists of separate scales for children (ages 6–12 years) and adolescents (12–18 years). The use of separate scales for different ages presumably represents developmental differences in the capacity to malinger. No description of scale development for these various *F* indexes are provided in the manual, and no data are provided with respect to the recommended cut scores: 70 (Caution) and 90 (Extreme Caution). The *L* index exists only for the adolescent version of the *SRP*, as the authors of the BASC believe that younger children invariably score high on such indexes. The *L* index is comprised of 13 items; no description of scale development or validation is provided.

The Adolescent Version of the Minnesota Multiphasic Personality Inventory

The Adolescent Version of the Minnesota Multiphasic Personality Inventory (MMPI-A; Butcher et al., 1992) is a 478-item instrument designed to provide psychological assessment of adolescents between the ages of 14 to 18. Like the MMPI-2, it contains scales designed to detect malingering and defensiveness. Conceptually, these scales operate much the same way as the validity scales on the MMPI-2. Given the recent publication of the MMPI-A, very little data are available on the effectiveness of these validity scales.

Like the MMPI and MMPI-2, the MMPI-A consists of three standard validity scales designed to assess fake-bad and fake-good responding: L, F, and K scales. The L and K scales assess defensiveness, whereas the F scale can be used to evaluate malingering. The F scale on the MMPI-A consists of two subscales: $F1$ (33 items from the first 350 items) and $F2$ (33 items, of which 16 occur after item 350). The F-K index is bidirectional and can be used to assess both defensiveness and malingering.

Stein et al. (1995) examined the extent to which the validity scales on the MMPI-A could differentiate nonclinical adolescents instructed to fake bad from both clinical and nonclinical adolescents who completed the test under standard instructions. The results indicate that F, $F1$, $F2$, and F-K successfully differentiated simulators from honest responders. In the most clinically relevant comparison (i.e., the simulation sample vs. the clinical comparison sample), a F scale $\geq$ 23 correctly classified 98% of the girls and 100% of the boys in the clinical sample, and 80% of the girls and 72% of the boys in the simulation sample. In addition, the new validity scales ($F1$ and $F2$) were also quite effective at detecting fake-bad responding. For example, optimum cut scores for $F1$ were $\geq$ 14 for girls (100% of honest patient and 76% of malingered profiles) and $\geq$ 11 for boys (98% of honest patient and 74% of malingered profiles). On the F-K index, a cut score $\geq$ 19 correctly classified 99% of honest patients and 74% of simulators. Overall, these results indicate that the validity scales and F-K index are effective distinguishing accurately fake-bad MMPI-A profiles from those profiles produced by bona fide, honestly responding students.

Rogers, Hinds, and Sewell (1995) evaluated the effectiveness of the MMPI-A validity indicators and two other measures (i.e., Structured Interview of Reported Symptoms [SIRS] and the Structured Inventory of Malingered Symptomatology [SIMS]) for the evaluation of feigned profiles. The sample consisted of 53 dually diagnosed adolescent offenders residing in a residential treatment facility. In addition to using the standard validity scales employed by Stein et al. (1995), Rogers et al. (1995) extracted items from the MMPI-A that corresponded to a number of additional validity indices used on the MMPI and MMPI-2, including the $Dsr2$, the newly developed Fp scale, the O-S index, and the Lachar–Wrobel critical items. Using a repeated measures, within-group design, Rogers et al. (1995) found that the F, $F1$, $F2$, and Fp scale were not particularly effective at distinguishing honest from feigned protocols. Although all these scales produced more than adequate negative predictive power (NPP), ranging from .91 to .93, none produced acceptable levels of positive predictive power (PPP), ranging from .45 to .74. A similar pattern emerged for $Dsr2$, the O-S index, and the Lachar–Wrobel critical items, with the NPP ranging from .89 to .91 and the PPP ranging from .57 to .64. Only the F-K index produced adequate levels of both PPP (.83) and NPP (.91).

Specialized Measures of Malingering: The SIRS and the SIMS

Rogers et al. (1995) also examined the effectiveness of the SIRS and the SIMS for the assessment of feigning among adolescents. The measures are described elsewhere in detail for the SIRS (Chapter 15) and the SIMS (Chapter 17); however, both were validated on adult populations. The Rogers et al. study was the first to examine the usefulness of these measures with an adolescent population.

For the SIRS, the Rogers et al. (1995) study found that the adult decision rules produced an excellent NPP of .98 and an acceptable PPP (.79). Attempts to optimize the classification yielded a slightly lower NPP (.94) and a better PPP (.89). The SIMS was not as effective as either the MMPI-A or the SIRS, with composite indexes producing levels of NPP ranging from .85 to .94 and PPP ranging from .49 to .83.

Combined Measures in the Assessment of Feigning

Rogers et al. (1995) also performed a two-stage discriminant function analysis in order to determine if the combination of the SIRS and the MMPI-A validity scales could enhance predictive capacity. For the SIRS, the NPP was .98 and the PPP was .78, with an overall classification rate of 87.8%. As a group, the MMPI-A validity scales and indicators alone produced a NPP of .85 and a PPP of .87, with an overall classification rate of 85.8%.[2] In combination, the scales produced a NPP of .94 and a PPP of .91, for an overall classification rate of 93%.

Overall, data from the Rogers et al. (1995) study appears to suggest that the use of both the SIRS and the MMPI-A in the assessment of malingering among adolescents enhances the predictive capacity. Use of the MMPI-A alone may produce an unacceptable number of false positives (i.e., bona fide patients miscategorized as malingerers). In the Rogers et al. data, the true positives only slightly exceeded the false positives when estimates were corrected for base rates. On the other hand, the SIRS requires an investment of clinical time that may not be justified in cases where no indicators of malingering have been observed.

THRESHOLD AND CLINICAL DECISION MODELS

Clinicians must be concerned about the general dearth of systematic research on response styles with child and adolescent populations. Of the response styles, very little is known about defensiveness and its assessment. For defensiveness, we cannot offer either a threshold or clinical decision model. Despite scales on the BASC and the MMPI-A to assess defensiveness, we were alarmed at the lack of empirical validation. At present, clinicians should avoid drawing any firm conclusions regarding defensiveness from these measures.

More research is available for malingering with adolescents. As a result, we have proposed a threshold model in Table 8.1 for when malingering should be fully evaluated. Although the classification rates appear promising, particularly for the SIRS and the MMPI-A, the lack of systematic cross-validation militates against the establishment of a clinical decision model.

With reference to Table 8.1, we have adopted the adult decision rules for the SIRS, because these rules are well validated and have a superb NPP (.98) with adolescents. For the MMPI-A, the two studies by Stein et al. (1995) and Rogers et al. (1995)

TABLE 8.1. Threshold Model for Malingering among Adolescents

Malingering should be fully evaluated if any of the following are present:

1. On the SIRS, any primary scale in the definite range or any two primary scales in the probable range
2. On the MMPI-A, an *F-K* index > 20
3. On the SIMS, a total score > 40
4. On clinical interviews, overendorsement of rare or improbable symptoms

demonstrate the potential problems with variable cut scores that overfit the data. We are encouraged, however, by the *F-K* index (> 20) that appears to be effective across the two studies. Although the SIMS is less effective than the SIRS or MMPI-A, its ease of administration and low reading level (approximately 5th grade) are reasons for its consideration. Finally, clinicians should be alert for extremely atypical presentations, especially when rare or improbable symptoms are presented. To reemphasize a crucial point, the purpose of this threshold model is to signal the need for a comprehensive evaluation of malingering, not the determination of malingering itself.

NOTES

1. The most recent revision allows the clinician to administer abbreviated versions of the PIC.

2. Although these classification rates appear comparable, the base rates for malingering in clinical settings are likely to be much lower than the 50% rate used in this within-subjects design. As calculated by Rogers, Hinds, and Sewell (1995), at the estimated prevalence of malingering among adult forensic populations (i.e., 15.7%), the MMPI-A has an overall classification accuracy of 85.3% compared to the SIRS at 94.9%.

II

PSYCHOMETRIC ASSESSMENT

9

Assessment of Malingering and Defensiveness by Multiscale Personality Inventories

ROGER L. GREENE, PH.D.

This chapter reviews the use of multiscale personality inventories to assess whether malingering or defensiveness may have been involved in a person's responses. After summarizing the development of validity scales on the Minnesota Multiphasic Personality Inventory (MMPI), the steps in assessing the validity of the MMPI-2 are reviewed with specific attention paid to malingering or defensiveness. Each section also includes a discussion of other multiscale personality inventories.

The primary focus of this chapter is the Minnesota Multiphasic Personality Inventory–2 (MMPI-2; Butcher, Dahlstrom, Graham, Tellegen, & Kaemmer, 1989), because the MMPI-2 is the most widely used and researched multiscale measure of psychopathology. Frequent references are made to the original MMPI (Dahlstrom, Welsh, & Dahlstrom, 1972, 1975) because much research on malingering and defensiveness was conducted on the MMPI and extended directly to the MMPI-2, often without any further validation. I assume that the reader is familiar with the clinical interpretation of the MMPI-2; interpretive information on the MMPI-2 can be found in Butcher and Williams (1992), Graham (1993), and Greene (1991). In addition, the reader is urged to consult the classic references on the original MMPI (Dahlstrom et al., 1972, 1975). Additional data on the use of the MMPI-2 and the Millon Clinical Multiaxial Inventory (MCMI) in substance abusers, and the use of the MMPI-A with adolescents are provided in Chapters 7 and 8, respectively.

An important facet of this chapter is the inclusion of normative data on the MMPI-2. I integrated these data from 3,475 patients with mental disorders in inpatient and outpatient treatment settings. An effort was made to ensure that a broad range

of diagnoses were represented. For malingering and defensiveness, all inconsistent profiles (Variable Response Inconsistency scale [VRIN] > 14) were removed prior to the
development of the normative tables.

Several other multiscale personality inventories also are discussed: the California
Psychological Inventory—Revised (CPI-R; Gough, 1987b, 1989; McAllister, 1986;
Meyer & Davis, 1992); the Millon Multiaxial Clinical Inventory–III (MCMI-III;
Choca, Shanley, & Van Denburg, 1992; Millon, 1987, 1994); the Personality Assessment Inventory (PAI; Morey, 1991); and the Sixteen Personality Factor Questionnaire (16 PF; Karson & O'Dell, 1976). Discussion of these latter inventories also will
include, where appropriate, references to relevant interpretive data.

DEVELOPMENT OF VALIDITY SCALES

In the development of the MMPI, Meehl and Hathaway (1946) were convinced of
the necessity of assessing two dichotomous categories of test-taking attitudes: plus getting
("faking bad") and defensiveness ("faking good"). Consistent with other chapters in
this text, these two categories will be designated respectively as malingering and
defensiveness. Meehl and Hathaway considered three possible strategies to assess
malingering and defensiveness: inconsistent responses to similarly-worded items,
extremely desirable but infrequently endorsed items, and empirically identified items.

As a first strategy, the clinician could provide the person with an opportunity to
distort the responses in a specific way and observe the inconsistency of the person's
responses to items phrased either identically or in the negative rather than the affirmative. A large number of inconsistent responses suggests that the person was either
incapable or unwilling to respond consistently. Although Meehl and Hathaway rejected this solution, the MMPI group booklet form included 16 identically repeated
items (Test–Retest [TR] Index; Dahlstrom et al., 1972), and Greene (1978) developed the Carelessness (*CLS*) scale that can be used to detect inconsistent responding
on the MMPI. Because there are no repeated items on the MMPI-2, the *TR* Index
cannot be utilized. However, two new MMPI-2 scales were developed that are variations on the *CLS* scale: the Variable Response Inconsistency scale (*VRIN*) and the
True Response Inconsistency scale (*TRIN*). These two scales are discussed later in
this chapter.

As a second strategy, Meehl and Hathaway (1946) considered providing an opportunity for the person to answer favorably when a favorable response would almost
certainly be untrue. This strategy involves the development of items with extremely
desirable but very rare human qualities. If a person endorsed a large number of these
items, the probability is very high that the responses would be dishonest. The Lie (*L*)
scale was developed specifically for this purpose. Items for the *L* scale, based on the
work of Hartshorne and May (1928), reflect behaviors that, although socially desirable, are rarely true of a given individual. A large number of endorsements on the *L*
scale indicates defensiveness.

An infrequency (F) scale was developed according to a variant of this second strategy for assessing test-taking attitudes. Items for the F scale were selected primarily because they were answered with a relatively low frequency by a majority of the original MMPI normative group. In other words, if a person endorsed a large number of the F-scale items, that person would be responding in a manner that was atypical of most people in the original normative group. In addition, the content of these items is varied so that any specific set of experiences or interests of a particular individual is unlikely to result in many of the items being endorsed in the deviant direction. This strategy was extended on the MMPI-2 with the creation of the F_B scale, which consists of items that were endorsed infrequently in the last 300 items.

As a third strategy, Meehl and Hathaway (1946) considered using an empirical procedure to identify items that elicit different responses from persons taking the test in an appropriate fashion and those who have been instructed to malinger. Gough's Dissimulation scale (Ds; Gough, 1954), based on this procedure, is described later. Meehl and Hathaway adopted a variant of this third strategy with the K scale that was developed to differentiate inpatients with normal profiles from putatively normal individuals with abnormal profiles.

Meehl and Hathaway (1946) also empirically determined the proportions of K that when added to a clinical scale would maximize the discrimination between the criterion group and the normative group. Since Meehl and Hathaway determined the optimal weights of K to be added to each clinical scale in an inpatient population, they warned that other weights of K might serve to maximize the identification of individuals in other clinical settings. This issue of the optimal weights for different populations has received little attention (see Greene, 1980; Wooten, 1984). Moreover, several investigators have questioned the usefulness of the K correction procedure (Colby, 1989; McCrae et al., 1989). Despite these warnings and almost nonexistent research, the K correction procedure was continued on the MMPI-2 without further validation.

Assessing the validity of an individual MMPI-2 profile or any other multiscale personality inventory is a multistep process that must be carried out in a sequential manner. An overview of these steps is provided in Figure 9.1. This process for the assessment of response styles involves three main steps: completeness (i.e., item omissions), consistency, and accuracy (e.g., malingering and defensiveness). Although the primary focus is on the MMPI-2, each of these sections also provides an overview of how this particular step is evaluated by other multiscale personality inventories.

ITEM OMISSIONS

The first step in assessing the validity of an MMPI-2 profile is to evaluate the number of items omitted (see Figure 9.1). The term "item omissions" is a misnomer, because it includes not only unendorsed items, but also items endorsed as both true and false, and items endorsed on the answer sheet other than in the allotted spaces.

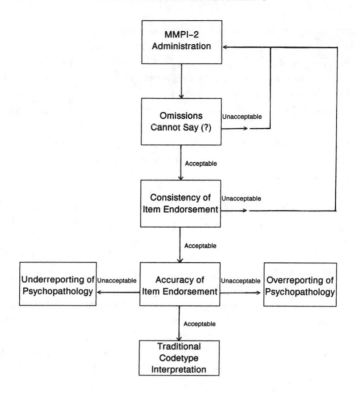

FIGURE 9.1. Steps in assessing MMPI-2 validity.

Persons completing the MMPI-2 occasionally make comments about the items on the answer sheet that the clinician may miss unless it is checked carefully. Consequently, clinicians need to check the answer sheet meticulously and tabulate the number of item "omissions."

Table 9.1 presents the number of items omitted in normal individuals and patients with mental disorders. As noted in Table 9.1, over 75% of normal individuals and persons with mental disorders omitted no items, 90% omitted 2 or fewer items, and more than 20 items were omitted by 1% or less. The most frequently omitted items[1] in the MMPI-2 normative sample were item 211 ("I have been inspired to a program of life based on duty which I have since carefully followed") in women and items 132 ("I believe in a life hereafter") and 217 ("My relatives are nearly all in sympathy with me") in men. The most frequently omitted items in the clinical sample were 215 ("I brood a great deal") in men and 559 ("The people I work with are not sympathetic with my problems") in women.

Clearly the changes in the item pool, which occurred in the restandardization of the MMPI-2, have removed most of the objectionable content and outdated terminology that were a serious problem on the original MMPI (Butcher & Tellegen, 1967) and frequently resulted in omitted items. Clinicians no longer have to explain "drop-

TABLE 9.1. Number of Omitted MMPI-2 Items in Normal and Mentally Disordered Samples

Percentile	*T* score	Normal individuals	Patients with mental disorders
99	79	15	20
98	75	10	12
95	68	5	4
90	63	2	2
85	60	1	1
80	58	1	0

Note. Normal individuals (*n* = 2,600) are from Butcher et al. (1989); patients with mental disorders (*n* = 3,475) are from Greene (1995).

the-handkerchief," whether Lincoln is more important than Washington, or reading *Alice in Wonderland*.

Clinical Applications to the MMPI-2

Omission of a large number of items on an multiscale personality inventory is an infrequent problem in most clinical assessments. When a large number of items is omitted, it is detected easily by a careful check of the answer sheet. Occasionally a very defensive or possibly paranoid person will be encountered who refuses to endorse most of the items. These personality characteristics are readily apparent in a clinical interview and, consequently, easily identified by the clinician. Omission of items is not typically an issue when malingering is involved, since the person must endorse the items in order to malinger. In some instances, however, persons may omit a large number of items because they claim they are too impaired to complete the MMPI-2.

Other Multiscale Inventories

Item omissions are not addressed specifically in most multiscale personality inventories besides the MMPI-2 and the PAI. A general statement may be made that an omission of a large number of items may affect the validity of any profile. However, neither the CPI-R, MCMI-III, or 16 PF states explicitly that item omissions should be checked or provide any criteria to indicate how many items may be omitted before the validity of the inventory is affected adversely. According to Morey (1991), the PAI profile should not be interpreted if more than 17 items were omitted. Clearly, the clinician should review the answer sheet for any personality inventory used and ascertain whether the person has omitted a large number of items. In most instances, simply asking the person to review these items and provide his or her best response is sufficient to eliminate this potential problem. Research is needed to address how many items can be omitted on these various personality inventories before their validity is compromised.

CONSISTENCY OF ITEM ENDORSEMENT

The next step in assessing the validity of the person's responses, after item omissions have been checked and found to be in the acceptable range, is to assess the consistency of item endorsement (see Figure 9.1). Consistency of item endorsement verifies that the person has endorsed the items in a reliable manner. This procedure is necessary to ensure that the person has endorsed the items consistently before any assessment of their accuracy is made. To highlight these differences, *consistency* of item endorsement may be conceptualized as being independent of item content, whereas *accuracy* of item endorsement is dependent upon item content. Thus, measures of the consistency assess whether the individual has provided a reliable pattern of responding to the items throughout the inventory regardless of their content, whereas measures of the accuracy of item endorsement assess whether the individual has attempted to distort his or her responses to the items in some specific manner.

Random Sorts

One method of trying to simulate inconsistent patterns of item endorsement has utilized groups of random sort MMPI-2s ("true" and "false" are assigned randomly to each item). Even a cursory inspection of these profiles (see Graham, 1993, pp. 40–41; Greene, 1991, p. 127) arouses the clinician's suspicions of a random response style. Subsequent examination of several validity indices confirms the high probability of such a response pattern. In general, the larger the number of items on the validity scale/index being used, the better the detection of a random sort will be. Since the F scale consists of 60 infrequently endorsed items, random sorts should "endorse" approximately 30 items (i.e., a T score > 120). Thus, the F scale tends to be one of the most reliable indicators of a random sort (Carlin & Hewitt, 1990; Dahlstrom et al., 1972; Rogers, Dolmetsch, & Cavanaugh, 1983; Sewell & Rogers, 1994). Similarly, the F_B scale consists of 40 infrequently endorsed items, and a random sort should produce a raw score around 20 and a T score > 120.

A second method of simulating inconsistent responses involves generating groups of profiles based on patterns of item endorsements such as TFTF, TTFTTF, FFTFFT, and so on. These profiles are identified almost as easily as random sorts, and again, the larger the number of items on the validity scale/index, the better these profiles are detected (Dahlstrom et al., 1972; Nichols, Greene, & Schmolck, 1989). Huba (1986) has developed a statistical test to assess whether the individual switches between "true" and "false" responses more or less often than would be expected by chance. The test requires computer scoring of the inventory to look for all specific sequences of stereotyped responses. Table 9.2 provides these data for the MMPI-2 normative group and a sample of patients with mental disorders. Only 4.4% of the normal men and 5% of the normal women had revised Z scores greater than +1.96 or less than −1.96 (i.e., more than plus or minus two standard deviations), whereas 7.8% of the male patients and 10.4% of the female patients exceed these same revised Z scores. The revised Z statistic appears to reflect more accurately the typical pattern of endorsing the MMPI-2

TABLE 9.2. Distribution of Z Scores for Runs Test in Assessing Inconsistency of Item Endorsement

	Normal individuals				Patients with mental disorders			
	Z		Revised Z		Z		Revised Z	
Range	*n*	%	*n*	%	*n*	%	*n*	%
				Men				
−2.50 to	35	0.031	7	0.006	93	0.039	36	0.015
−2.24 to −2.49	18	0.016	4	0.004	35	0.015	16	0.007
−1.96 to −2.23	28	0.025	9	0.008	62	0.026	24	0.010
−1.64 to −1.95	51	0.045	25	0.022	91	0.038	42	0.017
−1.15 to −1.63	146	0.128	69	0.061	241	0.100	130	0.054
1.14 to −1.14	771	0.678	917	0.806	1,603	0.666	1827	0.759
1.15 to 1.63	39	0.034	56	0.049	113	0.047	160	0.066
1.64 to 1.95	21	0.018	22	0.019	57	0.024	61	0.025
1.96 to 2.23	3	0.003	6	0.005	30	0.012	36	0.015
2.24 to 2.49	5	0.004	4	0.004	14	0.006	15	0.006
2.50 to	21	0.018	19	0.017	68	0.028	60	0.025
				Women				
−2.50 to	55	0.038	0	0.000	38	0.036	13	0.012
−2.24 to −2.49	48	0.033	8	0.005	12	0.011	5	0.005
−1.96 to −2.23	53	0.036	21	0.014	27	0.025	9	0.008
−1.64 to −1.95	89	0.061	35	0.024	40	0.038	14	0.013
−1.15 to −1.63	228	0.156	102	0.070	88	0.083	39	0.037
1.14 to −1.14	889	0.608	1,118	0.765	715	0.671	783	0.735
1.15 to 1.63	54	0.037	96	0.066	63	0.059	82	0.077
1.64 to 1.95	18	0.012	36	0.025	33	0.031	37	0.035
1.96 to 2.23	9	0.006	18	0.012	7	0.007	34	0.032
2.24 to 2.49	5	0.003	9	0.006	4	0.004	7	0.007
2.50 to	14	0.010	19	0.013	39	0.037	43	0.040

items because of their nonrandom order. This test is particularly promising since it correlates nearly 0 with both *VRIN* and *TRIN*, and therefore provides another independent measure of the consistency of item endorsement.

Inconsistency Scales

Patients may endorse the items inconsistently by a variety of methods. Rather than focusing on how persons generate inconsistent responses, the focus here is on how to assess consistency of item endorsement. Two scales for assessing the consistency of item endorsement on the MMPI-2 are *VRIN* and *TRIN*. *VRIN* consists of 67 pairs of items that have similar or opposite item content. These pairs of items are scored if the patient is inconsistent in his or her responses. *VRIN* actually consists of 49 pairs of unique items, since two separate response patterns are scored for 18 of these 67 item pairs.

The last column of Table 9.3 illustrates the distribution of scores on *VRIN* if the person randomly "endorsed" the MMPI-2 items. Since only one of the four possible combinations of "true" and "false" response patterns are scored on each of the 67 pairs of items on *VRIN*, the average score in such random sorts is 16.75 (i.e., 67 item pairs/ 4 alternatives). Some 15.6% of these random sorts are at or below the Butcher et al. (1989) recommended cutting score of 13 (*T* score of 80). However, patients in clini-

TABLE 9.3. Frequency of Scores on the Variable Response Inconsistency Scale (*VRIN*) for the MMPI-2 Normative Group, Patients with Mental Disorders, and Random MMPI-2s

VRIN	MMPI-2 normative %	cum %	Mentally disordered %	cum %	Random profiles %	cum %
0	1.4	1.4	0.6	0.6	0.0	0.0
1	4.9	6.3	3.7	4.2	0.0	0.0
2	9.1	15.4	6.7	10.9	0.0	0.0
3	14.4	29.8	9.4	20.3	0.0	0.0
4	15.1	44.8	11.9	32.2	0.0	0.0
5	15.4	60.3	13.6	45.8	0.0	0.0
6	13.7	74.0	12.7	58.5	0.0	0.0
7	9.7	83.7	10.6	69.1	0.1	0.2
8	6.7	90.4	9.6	78.7	0.1	0.3
9	3.7	94.2	7.4	86.2	0.6	0.9
10	2.5	96.7	4.5	90.7	1.5	2.4
11	1.8	98.5	3.1	93.8	2.6	5.0
12	1.0	99.5	1.6	95.4	4.5	9.6
13	0.4	99.8	1.6	97.0	6.1	15.6
14	0.0	99.9	0.5	97.6	8.0	23.7
15	0.0	99.9	0.7	98.3	9.6	33.2
16	0.1	100.0	0.8	99.1	14.2	47.4
17			0.3	99.3	11.3	58.8
18			0.3	99.6	12.0	70.7
19			0.1	99.7	9.5	80.2
20			0.2	99.9	7.0	87.2
21			0.0	99.9	5.4	92.6
22			0.0	99.9	3.5	96.1
23			0.1	100.0	1.9	98.0
24					1.0	99.0
25					0.5	99.5
26					0.2	99.7
27					0.2	99.9
28					0.1	100.0
Raw scores						
M	5.05		6.23		16.80	
SD	2.56		3.29		3.24	

Note. Normal individuals (*n* = 2,600) are from Butcher et al. (1989); patients with mental disorders (*n* = 3,475) and random profiles (*n* = 2,500) are from Greene (1995).

cal settings with scores on *VRIN* as high as 13 or 14 appear to have endorsed the items consistently. As summarized in Table 9.3, 23.7% of random sorts are ≤ 14.

Research is needed to determine empirically the optimal cutting score on *VRIN* to indicate an inconsistent pattern of item endorsement since cutting scores of 10 (Greene, 1991), 13 (Butcher et al., 1989), and 14 (Berry, Baer, & Harris, 1991) have been suggested. Given this variation in optimal cutting scores, the following general guidelines can be followed for ranges of scores on *VRIN*:

1. A score of 7 or lower, there is a high probability that the patient has endorsed the items consistently.
2. A score of 8–15, it is not clear whether the patient has endorsed the items consistently or inconsistently. In this latter case, the clinician is encouraged to examine the indexes described in the next section. These indexes may be useful even in cases where *VRIN* is 7 or lower to ensure that the items have been endorsed consistently, particularly during the later portions of the MMPI-2.
3. A score of 16 or higher, there is a high probability that the patient has endorsed the items inconsistently.

Infrequency Scales

Several infrequency scales are available for the MMPI-2 that also can be used to assess the consistency of item endorsement. The *F* scale and the Back *F* (*F_B*) scale are composed of items that were endorsed less than 10% of the time by the normative sample on the MMPI and MMPI-2, respectively. Three additional infrequency scales have been developed recently for the MMPI-2: Fake Bad (*FBS*; Lees-Haley, English, & Glenn, 1991), Psychiatric *F* (*Fp*; Arbisi & Ben-Porath, 1995), and Inconsistent Response (*IR*; Sewell & Rogers, 1994). *FBS* consists of 43 items endorsed infrequently by personal-injury malingerers; *Fp* consists of 27 items endorsed infrequently in patient samples; and *IR* consists of 16 items, eight of which are scored on *Fp*, endorsed infrequently in patient samples. The intercorrelations among these infrequency scales except for *FBS* average .75 (see Table 9.4). The correlations of the inconsistency scales with the infrequency scales tend to be fairly low (< .30) which suggests that they are measuring different aspects of the consistency of item endorsement.

One advantage of *VRIN* over infrequency scales in the assessment of the consistency of item endorsement is that *VRIN* is not affected by the presence of psychopathology. Elevations on infrequency scales can represent either (1) an inconsistent pattern of item endorsement; *or* (2) less frequently, the person's acknowledgment of the presence of psychopathology; *or* (3) the person's malingering of psychopathology (see Accuracy of Item Endorsement section). In contrast, *VRIN* is relatively unaffected by the type and severity of psychopathology, as can be seen in the similar means and standard deviations in the MMPI-2 normative group and the patients with mental disorders (see Table 9.3). *VRIN* also is not affected by malingering or defensiveness, since the person has to endorse the items consistently to alter their responses. In fact, a potential indicator of a malingered or defensive MMPI-2 profile is one in which the person

TABLE 9.4. Intercorrelations among Inconsistency and Infrequency Scales

Normal individuals

Inconsistency scales				Infrequency scales			
	TRIN	Z'		FBS	F_B	Fp	IR
VRIN	.04	.08	F	.14	.59	.57	.41
TRIN		.02	FBS		.26	.08	.01
			F_B			.53	.49
			Fp				.58

Inconsistency scales with infrequency scales

	F	FBS	F_B	Fp	IR
VRIN	.37	.16	.39	.25	.22
TRIN	.14	−.02	.23	.11	.13
Z'	.16	.04	.16	.05	.06

Patients with mental disorders

Inconsistency scales				Infrequency scales			
	TRIN	Z'		FBS	F_B	Fp	IR
VRIN	.11	−.03	F	.52	.87	.79	.74
TRIN		−.01	FBS		.52	.31	.27
			F_B			.72	.74
			Fp				.79

Inconsistency scales with infrequency scales

	F	FBS	F_B	Fp	IR
VRIN	.20	.09	.20	.31	.29
TRIN	.30	.14	.33	.28	.31
Z'	.02	.00	.03	.01	.01

Note. F, Infrequency scale; F_B, Back Infrequency scale; FBS, Fake-Bad scale; Fp, Psychiatric Infrequency scale; IR, Inconsistent Response scale; TRIN, True Response Inconsistency scale; VRIN, Variable Response Inconsistency scale; Z', Revised Z score for runs test.

has been *more* consistent than would be expected. Consequently, VRIN can provide an independent estimate of the consistency of item endorsement. VRIN will detect some profiles with inconsistent responses that would be considered consistent by infrequency scales and also can demonstrate that the person has been endorsing the items consistently despite elevated scores on the F and F_B scales (see Evans & Dinning, 1983; Gallucci, 1985; Maloney, Duvall, & Friesen, 1980; Wetter, Baer, Berry, Smith, & Larsen, 1992). These findings indicate that VRIN and infrequency scales are *not* measuring identical processes in test-taking attitudes (Fekken & Holden, 1987) and consequently cannot be simply substituted for one another.

Since the items on the F and F_B scales are endorsed infrequently, persons would be expected to endorse approximately the same number of items on each scale. Consequently, the *absolute* value of the difference between the number of items that the person has endorsed on each scale can be used as a measure of the consistency of item endorsement.

Table 9.5 provides the distribution of this measure of the consistency of item endorsement for the MMPI-2 normative group, a large sample of patients with mental disorders, and randomly endorsed MMPI-2s. Exactly 70% of random profiles have a score of 7 or higher on this index, with a mean of 10. Less than 26% of these random sorts with *VRIN* scores in the intermediate range (8–15) had scores of 6 or lower on this index. Thus, the clinician can be fairly confident that the person has endorsed the items consistently if this index is 6 or lower when *VRIN* is in the intermediate range

TABLE 9.5. Frequency of Scores on $|F-F_B|$ for the MMPI-2 Normative Group, Patients with Mental Disorders, and Random MMPI-2s

$F-F_B$	MMPI-2 normative %	cum %	Mentally disordered %	cum %	Random profiles %	cum %
0	10.4	10.4	8.8	8.8	1.0	1.0
1	24.4	34.8	16.9	25.7	2.5	3.6
2	21.0	55.8	16.8	42.4	3.0	6.5
3	17.0	72.8	13.2	55.6	3.2	9.7
4	11.8	84.7	11.5	67.1	3.7	13.4
5	6.2	90.8	8.5	75.6	4.3	17.7
6	4.0	94.8	6.0	81.6	5.6	23.3
7	2.2	97.0	4.6	86.2	6.7	30.0
8	1.5	98.4	3.5	89.6	7.2	37.2
9	0.7	99.1	2.7	92.4	8.0	45.3
10	0.4	99.5	2.2	94.6	8.2	53.5
11	0.3	99.8	1.4	96.0	8.7	62.2
12	0.1	99.8	1.0	96.9	7.5	69.7
13	0.0	99.9	0.8	97.8	7.1	76.8
14	0.0	99.9	0.5	98.3	5.6	82.4
15	0.1	100.0	0.6	98.8	4.0	86.5
16			0.2	99.0	4.3	90.8
17			0.2	99.3	2.7	93.5
18			0.3	99.5	2.1	95.6
19			0.2	99.7	1.5	97.0
20			0.2	99.9	1.0	98.0
21			0.0	99.9	1.0	99.0
22			0.0	99.9	0.4	99.3
23			0.1	100.0	0.3	99.6
24					0.2	99.8
25					0.2	99.9
26					0.0	99.9
27					0.0	100.0
Raw scores						
M	2.63		3.95		10.00	
SD	2.07		3.48		4.99	

of 8–15. Similar relationships between the scores on the other infrequency scales (*FBS*, *Fp*, and *IR*) could be developed.

Clinicians typically assume that the patient has followed the same pattern of item endorsement for all 567 items. This assumption may not always be appropriate, since patients' motivation and ability to concentrate may change as they complete the test. For example, a patient could endorse the first 400 items consistently and then endorse the remainder of the items inconsistently. Berry and his colleagues (Berry et al., 1991; Berry, Wetter, Baer, Larsen, Clark, & Monroe, 1992) have examined the ability of measures of consistency of item endorsement to detect persons who were instructed to respond randomly after completing 100, 200, 300, 400, or 500 items appropriately. They found that *F*, *F_B*, and *VRIN* were effective at detecting persons who endorsed the items randomly, and that these measures were more accurate as the number of items endorsed randomly increased.

Clinicians should realize that *VRIN* may be insensitive to cases in which the person begins to endorse the items inconsistently part way through the MMPI-2 (see Berry et al., 1991). Since only one of the four possible combinations of "true" and "false" response patterns are scored on each of the 67 pairs of items on *VRIN* (i.e., scoring is not symmetrical), the probability of endorsing any single pair of items is .25, not .50. Consequently, an individual still may have a low score on *VRIN*, since the first item in a pair has been *endorsed appropriately*.

All items for the MMPI-2 standard validity and clinical scales occur in the first 370 items. If inconsistent responding is observed after item 370, clinicians could still score and interpret the standard scales. If blocks or groups of items could be assessed for inconsistency rather than for the entire 567 items, those items up to the point where the patient started responding randomly could be scored. One advantage of hand-scoring *VRIN* is that the clinician can evaluate whether inconsistent responses tend to be distributed evenly throughout the MMPI-2 or begin to occur after some specific point.

As shown in Table 9.6, *VRIN*, *F*, and *F_B* items are distributed throughout the MMPI-2 so clinicians could determine when individuals start to make inconsistent responses. This approach might be particularly appropriate for intermediate scores on *VRIN* where it is more difficult to make an assessment of the consistency of item endorsement.

TABLE 9.6. Distribution of Validity Scale Items by Blocks of 100

Blocks	Number of items		
	F	*F_B*	*VRIN*
1–100	16	0	4
101–200	17	0	6
201–300	17	2	9
301–400	10	13	9
401–500	0	11	10
501–567	0	14	11

TRIN consists of 23 pairs of items. *TRIN* is very similar to *VRIN* except that the scored response is either "true" or "false" to both items in each pair. Unlike *VRIN, TRIN* has virtually no published research and negligible information on its use clinically other than the fact that very high ($\geq$ 13; i.e., true biased) or very low ($\leq$ 5; i.e., false biased) scores (Butcher et al., 1989) may reflect inconsistent item endorsement.

Although *VRIN* is useful in identifying inconsistent patterns of item endorsement, the clinician should keep in mind that an acceptable score indicates only that the person has endorsed the items consistently and not necessarily accurately, since the person can consistently malinger or be defensive. Moreover, since *VRIN* assesses only the consistency of the person's responses, it will not detect "all true" (*VRIN* = 5) or "all false" (*VRIN* = 5) response sets, which are consistent but nonveridical test-taking sets. These response sets are detected easily by *TRIN* (scores of 23 and 0, respectively).

Reaction Time

The advent of computer-administered MMPI-2s enables clinicians to examine the reaction time for each item response. Very rapid reaction times would suggest that the person has not taken sufficient time to read the items carefully and should be suggestive of inconsistent item endorsement. Research that evaluates such a hypothesis and provides guidelines for interpreting the obtained reaction times is needed. In addition, any changes in the person's reaction time across the 567 items could be measured easily by blocks of items. Research to test other response styles also is feasible. For example, persons who have very slow reaction times may be trying to malinger or be defensive, since they are trying to make sure that they are providing the "correct" response to each item (see Holden & Kroner, 1992).

Clinical Applications to the MMPI-2

The importance of assessing consistency of item endorsement *before* trying to assess accuracy of item endorsement cannot be overstressed. Otherwise, inconsistent patterns of item endorsement may be labeled inappropriately as malingering (e.g., Rogers et al., 1983; Wetter et al., 1992).

A variety of reasons exist to explain why a person may endorse the items inconsistently on any multiscale personality inventory. These potential reasons, as well as strategies for how each of them may be resolved, are summarized in Table 9.7.

Other Objective Personality Inventories

Consistency of item endorsement is generally assessed by a single scale on most other multiscale personality inventories. These scales are usually similar to the infrequency scales on the MMPI-2 in that they are composed of items with low frequency of endorsements.

An infrequency scale for the CPI was developed by selecting items that were endorsed by no more than 5% of the normative samples. Since high scores on the CPI

TABLE 9.7. Potential Causes of and Solutions for Inconsistent Item Endorsement

Cause	Solution
1. Patient has not been told why the MMPI-2 is being administered.	1. Explain why the MMPI-2 is being administered and how the data are to be used.
2. Inadequate reading ability or comprehension.	2. Present the MMPI-2 orally by tape administration (see Greene, 1991, Chap. 2).
3. Limited intellectual ability.	3. Present the MMPI-2 orally by tape administration (see Greene, 1991, Chap. 2). Dahlstrom et al. (1972) reported that tape administrations are effective with IQs as low as 65.
4. Too confused psychiatrically neuropsychologically.	4. Readminister the MMPI-2 once the person is less confused.
5. Still toxic from substance abuse.	5. Readminister the MMPI-2 once the person is detoxified.
6. Noncompliant or uncooperative.	6. Be sure person understands the importance of the MMPI-2 for treatment/intervention and readminister the MMPI-2. If the person is still noncompliant that issue becomes the focus of treatment.

were designed to measure positive traits, the deviant response was reversed for each item and the scale was renamed as the Communality (*Cm*) scale. *T* scores of ≤ 29 (men) and ≤ 24 (women) on the *Cm* scale usually are seen in random responses, but may also be observed in malingering (Gough, 1987b; McAllister, 1986; Megargee, 1972).

The Validity Index on the MCMI-III (Millon, 1987, 1994) is designed to identify random or confused responding. The Validity Index consists of three nonbizarre items that were endorsed by less then 0.01% of the persons from clinical populations. An Index score of 2 or more renders the profile invalid and terminates the automated interpretive system. A score of 1 is labeled unreliable, and the clinician is advised to be cautious.

The Infrequency (*INF*) scale of the PAI consists of 8 items that are endorsed rarely and are unrelated to psychopathology, whereas the Inconsistency (*ICN*) scale consists of 10 pairs of highly correlated items (Morey, 1991). Scores of 68T to 74T on *INF* and 64T to 72T on *ICN* should be viewed with caution, and scores of 75T or higher on *INF* and 73T or higher on *ICN* should be considered invalid.

The Random scale on the 16 PF is composed of 31 items, with a cutting score of 5 or greater used to identify random responses (Karson & O'Dell, 1976, pp. 153–154). This scale only can be scored on Form A of the 16 PF. Scoring the Random scale is somewhat complicated because 23 items are scored if endorsed, and 8 items if they are *not* endorsed (i.e., these latter 8 items are endorsed by most people taking the 16 PF, similar to the *Cm* scale on the CPI).

All of these multiscale personality inventories provide some means of assessing consistency of item endorsement and at least preliminary data on these scales. All inventories except for the 16 PF provide for routine scoring of these scales by the clinician. More research is needed with each of these inventories to determine how well these scales assess consistency of item endorsement in various clinical settings with different samples.

ACCURACY OF ITEM ENDORSEMENT

The next step in the process of assessing the validity of a multiscale personality inventory, after item omissions and consistency of item endorsement have been checked, is to verify the accuracy of item endorsement (see Figure 9.2). Accuracy of item endorsement verifies whether the person has adopted a response set either to malinger or be defensive. Since the person's inventory data only reveal that the items have been endorsed inaccurately, clinicians must determine the person's motivation for inaccurate item endorsement from an interview that includes a review of the person's reasons for agreeing to complete the personality inventory.

Although the point should be self-evident, any measure of malingering or defensiveness is likely to be confounded with measures of psychopathology, since the person is being evaluated on those dimensions (Schretlen, 1990). The critical issue is the probability that the extent and severity of psychopathology reported by the person is an accurate reflection of his or her history and background. Consequently, clinicians and researchers should not be surprised that measures of malingering are related positively to measures of psychopathology, whereas measures of defensiveness are related inversely to measures of psychopathology. In evaluating the probability that the person is malingering or being defensive, the clinician must evaluate the base rate with which malingering or defensiveness occurs in his or her specific setting in order to have an appropriate estimate of positive predictive power[3] (i.e., the probability that a person said to be malingering or defensive is classified accurately).

Several basic issues about malingering and defensiveness must be made explicit before the scales and indexes for assessing accuracy of item endorsement are discussed. First, researchers assume that malingering and defensiveness represent a unitary continuum that is characterized by the malingering at one end and defensiveness at the other (see Figure 9.2). Consequently, accurate patterns of item endorsement gradually will shade into malingering or defensiveness as one moves across this continuum; no

| Underreporting of Psychopathology | Accurate Item Endorsement | Overreporting of Psychopathology |

FIGURE 9.2. Accuracy of item endorsement conceptualized as a single dimension.

exact point exists at which the person's performance suddenly reflects either malingering or defensiveness. Instead, a probability statement can be made that this person's performance reflects either malingering or defensiveness. Second, given that malingering and defensiveness exist on a continuum, numerous scales can be used to assess both response sets, with high scores reflecting malingering and low scores reflecting defensiveness. Scales with dual purposes will be reviewed first, followed by scales limited to a single purpose (malingering or defensiveness). Third, many persons, when they decide to malinger, attempt to do so by "faking bad" in a global and extreme manner that is easily detected in most circumstances. The issues of persons malingering specific disorders and the effects of coaching (e.g., being given information about validity indicators used to detect malingering and defensiveness) will be explored following examination of global dissimulation. Fourth, the presence of malingering or defensiveness does not rule out actual psychopathology. A person who actually has a specific mental disorder also can malinger or be defensive about the presence of psychopathology. The scales and indexes to assess accuracy of item endorsement *cannot* determine whether the person actually has psychopathology, only whether the person has provided an accurate self-description.

MALINGERING AND DEFENSIVENESS: ENDPOINTS ON A CONTINUUM

A number of scales and indexes are used to assess malingering and defensiveness, with high scores reflecting malingering and low scores reflecting defensiveness. These scales and indexes tend to be biased toward "true" responses when reflecting malingering, since items that are endorsed "true" on the MMPI-2 have a high probability of reflecting significant psychopathology (see Table 9.8). Thus, clinicians and researchers should be alert to the possibility that a malingered profile actually reflects a bias to endorse the items "true." The exception to this generalization is those MMPI-2 items assessing somatic functioning, in which "false" is typically the deviant response. As can be seen in Table 9.9, the intercorrelations among these measures are high and in some cases are virtually interchangeable. The reader should realize that it is *not* necessary to score all of these scales for assessing malingering or defensiveness for every person. A number of different scales will be illustrated that are sensitive to malingering and defensiveness. The reader will need to determine the scale(s) most appropriate for his or her specific treatment setting and patients.

Several reviews of the MMPI assessment of malingering and defensiveness are available to the interested reader (Franzen, Iverson, & McCracken, 1990; Greene, 1988a; Schretlen, 1988). In addition, two separate meta-analyses of malingering were conducted on the MMPI (Berry, Baer, & Harris, 1991) and MMPI-2 (Rogers, Sewell, & Salekin, 1994). Berry et al. found that the F scale, Ds scale, and the Gough Dissimulation index (F-K) had the largest effect sizes on the MMPI, whereas Rogers et al. found that the F scale, F-K, and the total T score difference on the obvious and subtle subscales (Wiener, 1948) had the largest effect sizes on the MMPI-2. In both studies, the effect sizes exceeded 2.00 and were substantial in magnitude.

TABLE 9.8. Percentage of Items Endorsed "True" for Malingering Scales and Defensiveness Scales

Scale/index	% true
Infrequency	
Infrequency (*F*)	68.3
Back Infrequency (*F$_B$*)	92.5
Psychiatric Infrequency (*Fp*)	66.7
Inconsistent Response (*IR*)	81.3
Critical items	
Koss & Butcher (1977)	84.7
Lachar & Wrobel (1979)	72.9
Obvious subscales	
Depression (*D-O*)	43.6
Hysteria (*Hy-O*)	37.5
Psychopathic Deviate (*PD-O*)	71.4
Paranoia (*Pa-O*)	87.0
Hypomania (*Ma-O*)	87.0
Subtle subscales	
Depression (*D-S*)	16.7
Hysteria (*Hy-S*)	3.6
Psychopathic Deviate (*Pd-S*)	18.2
Paranoia (*Pa-S*)	29.4
Hypomania (*Ma-S*)	65.2
Malingering scale	
Gough Dissimulation (*Ds*)	82.8
Defensiveness scales	
Lie (*L*)	0.0
Correction (*K*)	3.3
Other Deception (*ODecp*)	54.5
Superlative (*S*)	12.0
Wiggins Social Desirability (*Wsd*)	72.7

The initial studies of dissimulation provided the participants with general or global instructions to either malinger or be defensive with a variety of normal populations: students (Austin, 1992; Bagby, Rogers, & Buis, 1994; Graham, Watts, & Timbrook, 1991; Wetter et al., 1992; Worthington & Schlottmann, 1986; Woychyshyn, McElheran, & Romney, 1992); professionals (Gough, 1954; Lachar & Wrobel, 1979); and community samples (Wetter, Baer, Berry, Robinson, & Sumpter, 1993); as well as in clinical samples: patients with mental disorders (Bagby, Rogers, Buis, & Kalemba, 1994; Graham et al., 1991; Rogers, Sewell, & Ustad, 1995); and correctional/forensic patients (Bagby, Rogers, & Buis, 1994; Iverson, Franzen, & Hammond, 1995; Walters, 1988; Walters, White, & Greene, 1988).[4] These studies typically reported that the malingering or defensive group could be successfully distinguished from the group taking the test honestly, although the specific scale or index employed and the optimal cutting score tended to vary widely from study to study. As expected, research has demonstrated greater difficulty in distinguishing between the group instructed to malinger (i.e., simulators) and actual patients than between simulators and normal individuals.

TABLE 9.9. Intercorrelations among Scales Measuring Malingering and Defensiveness in Normal Individuals and Patients with Mental Disorders

Scale/index	KBSum	LWSum	F-K	O-S	% true
Normal individuals (Butcher et al., 1989)					
F	.66	.67	.75	.58	45
KBSum		.92	.79	.82	73
LWSum			.79	.82	72
F-K				.84	80
Total O-S					78
Patients with mental disorders (Greene, 1995)					
F	.85	.86	.94	.82	71
KBSum		.96	.91	.93	83
LWSum			.91	.94	81
F-K				.91	85
Total O-S					84

Note. F, Infrequency; KBSum, total number of Koss and Butcher (1973) critical endorsed; LWSum, total number of Lachar and Wrobel (1979) critical endorsed; F-K, Gough (1950) Dissimulation index; Total O-S, total T score difference between the Obvious and Subtle subscales (Wiener, 1948); % true, percentage of scale items endorsed "true."

This line of research has been critiqued because such global instructions have little external validity (Rogers, 1988a; Sivec, Lynn, & Garske, 1994; Wetter, Baer, Berry, & Reynolds, 1994). To parallel real-world circumstances, researchers have suggested that participants must have or be given specific knowledge of the psychopathology to be simulated.

The next series of studies made disorder-specific criteria available to the participants who were then instructed to malinger: borderline personality disorder (Sivec, Hilsenroth, & Lynn, 1995; Wetter et al., 1993; Wetter et al., 1994); closed head injury (Lamb, Berry, Wetter, & Baer, 1994); paranoia (Sivec et al., 1994); posttraumatic stress disorder (Fairbank, McCaffrey, & Keane, 1985; Wetter et al., 1993); schizophrenia (Rogers, Bagby, & Chakraborty, 1993; Wetter et al., 1993); and somatoform disorders (Sivec et al., 1994). Two generalizations can be formulated from this series of studies. First, validity scales usually have good success at detecting those disorders, such as schizophrenia (Rogers, Bagby, & Chakraborty, 1993) and borderline personality disorder (Sivec et al., 1995; Wetter et al., 1994) that are characterized by extensive and severe psychopathology. Again, the specific scale or index that is most successful varies by study, as does the optimal cutting score. Second, persons who are instructed to malinger a specific disorder that is characterized by circumscribed and less severe psychopathology are able to do so quite readily and are fairly difficult to detect (Lamb et al., 1994; Wetter et al., 1993).

The final series of studies investigated the effects of providing the participants with information about the validity scales that would be used to detect malingering or defensiveness (Lamb et al., 1994; Rogers, Bagby, & Chakraborty, 1993), sometimes in combination with information about diagnostic-specific criteria. The more information provided to the participants about the validity scales, the better they are able to malinger without being detected (Baer, Wetter, & Berry, 1995; Rogers, Bagby, & Chakraborty, 1993). Information about validity scales is more valuable in avoiding detection as malingering than is diagnostic-specific criteria (Rogers, Bagby, & Chakraborty, 1993).

The ethics of providing participants with specific information about the disorders to be assessed as well as the role of validity scales in assessing malingering or defensiveness have been debated (Ben-Porath, 1994; Berry, Lamb, Wetter, Baer, & Widiger, 1994). These ethical issues are quite complex, and anyone who is contemplating research on coached dissimulation should consult these articles.

Infrequency Scales

The F scale is the traditional index of malingering on the MMPI-2, since its items were selected to detect unusual or atypical ways of endorsing (Dahlstrom et al., 1972). As noted earlier, four other infrequency scales on the MMPI-2 can be scored: F_B, FBS, Fp, and IR. The intercorrelations (see Table 9.4) clearly demonstrate that all of these scales, except FBS, are essentially equivalent to one another. Consequently, this discussion will be limited to the traditional F scale. High scores on the F scale can occur for three reasons: (1) inconsistent patterns of item endorsement, (2) the presence of actual psychopathology, or (3) malingering. Low scores can occur for two reasons: (1) the absence of actual psychopathology or (2) defensiveness. Thus, the reason(s) for a high or low score on the F scale are very difficult to ascertain without considering the other indicators of the consistency and accuracy of item endorsement. Clinicians are probably safe to conclude that a raw score greater than 26 (T score > 110) on the F scale does not reflect actual psychopathology, but it could reflect either an inconsistent pattern of item endorsement or malingering. Similarly, a raw score of 0 (T score < 40) could reflect the absence of psychopathology or defensiveness. Since different clinical decisions will be made depending upon the reason for the specific score on the F scale, clinicians should use the other validity indicators described in this chapter to make this discrimination. Thus, the best use of the F scale, and other infrequency scales, is in conjunction with other validity indicators.

Tables 9.10 and 9.11 provide normative data on a variety of validity indicators including the F scale for normal individuals and patients. As expected, patients with mental disorders endorse approximately three times as many F-scale items as normal individuals. Interestingly, 50% of patients with mental disorders endorse 8 or fewer F-scale items. This relatively small number of F-scale endorsements could reflect that these items actually are infrequent in certain clinical settings and/or that a sizeable percentage of psychiatric patients are defensive.

TABLE 9.10. Percentiles for Measures of Malingering and Defensiveness in Normal Individuals (Butcher et al., 1989)

%ile	T score	F	KBSum	LWSum	F-K	O-S	Ds	% true
99	79	14	38	49	6	161	26	57
98	75	12	36	46	4	138	24	54
95	68	10	30	37	0	105	20	50
90	63	8	23	31	−3	78	17	47
85		6	21	27	−5	60	16	45
80	58	6	18	25	−6	44	14	43
75		5	16	23	−8	34	13	42
50	49	3	10	15	−12	−6	9	37
25		1	5	10	−16	−41	6	33
20	42	1	4	8	−17	−49	5	32
15		0	3	7	−18	−57	4	31
10	38	0	2	6	−20	−66	4	30
5	36	0	1	4	−21	−80	3	28
2	33	0	0	3	−23	−93	2	27
1	32	0	0	2	−24	−99	1	25

Note. High scores are suggestive of malingering, whereas low scores are suggestive of defensiveness. *F*, Infrequency; KBSum, total number of Koss and Butcher (1973) critical endorsed; LWSum, total number of Lachar and Wrobel (1979) critical endorsed; *F-K*, Gough Dissimulation index (1950); Total *O-S*, total *T* score difference between the Obvious and Subtle subscales (Wiener, 1948); *Ds*, Gough Dissimulation scale (Gough, 1954); % true, percentage of scale items endorsed "true."

The optimal cutting score on the *F* scale to identify persons who are malingering within clinical samples has ranged from 17 (Bagby, Rogers, Buis, & Kalemba, 1994) to 23 (Graham et al., 1991) and 28 (Rogers, Bagby, & Chakraborty, 1993).[5] A cutting score of 17 would classify nearly 20% of the patients in Table 9.11 as malingering, whereas a cutting score of 28 would classify a little over 5% as malingering.

Critical Items

Despite the inherent difficulties in understanding responses to individual MMPI items (providing the original impetus for the empirical selection of items on the MMPI), clinicians have been unwilling to ignore the information that might be contained in those responses. The original set of "critical" items (i.e., problems that require careful scrutiny if answered in the deviant direction) was rationally selected by Grayson (1951). Grayson's early work on critical items has since been followed by the development of other sets of critical items (Caldwell, 1969; Koss & Butcher, 1973; Lachar & Wrobel, 1979).[6] Because critical items have obvious or face-valid content, they provide another means of assessing the accuracy of item endorsement. Large numbers of critical items are endorsed by persons who are malingering or experiencing extensive, severe psychopathology; obversely, very few critical items are endorsed by persons who are defensive or experiencing no psychopathology. The Lachar and Wrobel (1979) critical items will be used to illustrate this procedure, although any critical–item set could be used to assess accuracy of item endorsement.

Lachar and Wrobel (1979) developed their critical items to be face-valid (obvious) descriptors of psychological concerns. They first identified 14 categories of symptoms that (1) motivate people to seek psychological treatment and (2) assist the clinician to make diagnostic decisions. A group of 14 clinical psychologists reviewed each MMPI item and nominated items as face-valid indicators of psychopathology in 1 of these 14 categories. These items were validated empirically by contrasting item response frequencies for normals and clinical samples matched for gender and race. Lachar and Wrobel were able to validate 130 of the 177 items nominated. After eliminating 19 items that were highly duplicative of item content, they arrived at a final list of 111 (20.2%) critical items. In the restandardization of the MMPI, 4 of these items were deleted so that there are 107 Lachar and Wrobel critical items on the MMPI-2.

The total number of critical items that are endorsed by the person can become another index of the accuracy of item endorsement based on large (malingering) or small (defensiveness) numbers. Tables 9.10 and 9.11 summarize the total number of Koss and Butcher (1973) and Lachar and Wrobel (1979) critical items that are endorsed by normal individuals and patients, respectively. Patients with mental disorders endorse almost three times as many critical items than normal individuals. The fact that the typical individual (50th percentile) endorses 10 of the Koss and Butcher critical items and 15 of the Lachar and Wrobel critical items may suggest that at least some of these items are *not* as "critical" as originally thought. Surprisingly, almost 15% of patients endorse fewer total critical items than the average normal individual.

TABLE 9.11. Percentiles for Measures of Malingering and Defensiveness in Patients with Mental Disorders (Greene, 1995)

%ile	T score	F	KBSum	LWSum	F-K	O-S	Ds	% true
99	79	39	69	90	33	316	43	69
98	75	35	66	87	28	304	41	66
95	68	30	62	79	22	273	38	62
90	63	24	56	71	16	238	34	58
85		21	51	65	12	211	30	56
80	58	18	47	60	9	190	28	54
75		15	44	55	6	172	26	52
50	49	8	28	38	−4	93	17	44
25		4	15	22	−12	15	10	36
20	42	3	13	20	−13	1	9	35
15		3	11	17	−15	−15	7	33
10	38	2	8	13	−17	−36	6	31
5	36	1	5	9	−20	−62	4	28
2	33	0	2	5	−22	−83	2	25
1	32	0	1	4	−24	−93	2	23

Note. High scores are suggestive of malingering, whereas low scores are suggestive of defensiveness. *F*, Infrequency; KBSum, total number of Koss and Butcher (1973) critical endorsed; LWSum, total number of Lachar and Wrobel (1979) critical endorsed; *F-K*, Gough (1950) Dissimulation index; Total *O-S*, total *T* score difference between the Obvious and Subtle subscales (Wiener, 1948); *Ds*, Gough (1954) Dissimulation scale; % true, percentage of scale items endorsed "true."

F-K Index: Gough Dissimulation Index

Another validity indicator, the F-K index (Gough, 1950), was developed by combining two of the three traditional MMPI validity scales. The reader is cautioned *not* to confuse the F-K index (Gough Dissimulation index) with the Gough Dissimulation scale (Ds) that will be described below. Ds is a set of empirically derived items designed to assess malingering only, while the F-K index utilizes the relationship between the standard validity scales of F and K to assess both malingering and defensiveness. Gough (1947, 1950) suggested that the *raw* score of the F scale minus the *raw* score of the K scale would be useful in screening MMPI profiles for accuracy of item endorsement. If the F-K index was greater than +9, the profile was designated as malingering. If the F-K index was less than 0, the profile was classified as being defensive. Intermediate scores on the F-K index (0–9) indicated accurate item endorsement (i.e., valid profiles). Gough (1950) reported that the F-K index readily detected malingering; in one sample, it accurately classified 97% of the authentic profiles and 75% of those malingered.

Most MMPI and MMPI-2 studies of the F-K index have utilized normal persons instructed to feign psychopathology. Numerous investigators (Austin, 1992; Graham et al., 1991; Woychyshyn et al., 1992) have confirmed the ability of the F-K index to identify students instructed to malinger. Several of these investigators (Graham et al., 1991; Woychyshyn et al., 1992) also noted that the F scale alone identified malingering as or even more efficiently than the F-K index. The optimal cutoff scores in these studies has ranged from 6 (Sivec et al., 1994) to 17 (Graham et al., 1991).

Higher cutting scores on the F-K index are required to distinguish between normal individuals who are trying to malinger and patients. Optimal cutting scores have ranged from 12 (Iverson et al., 1995) to 27 (Graham et al., 1991). Rothke et al. (1994) have provided extensive tables of the distribution of the F-K index in samples of patients with mental disorders, head–injured patients, disability claimants, job applicants for police and priest positions, and substance abusers, as well as the MMPI-2 normative group. Substantial differences were observed in the F-K index for these various samples. They suggested that clinicians using the F-K index consider the specific diagnostic group being studied as well as the person's gender.

Tables 9.10 and 9.11 summarize the distribution of scores for the F-K index in normal individuals and patients, respectively. Normal individuals achieve mean scores of nearly −12 on this index, while the psychiatric patients achieve mean scores of −4. If F-K scores greater than +9 are labeled as malingering, 20% of the patients would be so classified. Since the F scale also may reflect the presence of actual psychopathology, use of this cutting score would yield an unacceptably high false–positive rate (persons who are said to be malingering who are actually experiencing significant psychopathology). A cutting score much higher than +9 would be needed on the F-K index to decrease the number of false positives; available studies are not clear whether a more appropriate cutting score can be identified for this index, partially because the F scale also is elevated by actual psychopathology.

Obvious and Subtle Items

Comparison of subtle versus obvious items has shown some promise in detecting malingering and defensiveness. In the early research, Wiener and Harmon (Wiener, 1948) performed a rational inspection of MMPI items, identifying obvious items as those that were easy to detect as indicating emotional disturbance, and subtle items as those that were relatively difficult to detect as reflecting emotional disturbance. This procedure resulted in the identification of 110 subtle and 146 obvious items. Although Wiener and Harmon had intended to develop subtle and obvious subscales for each clinical scale, they succeeded for only five scales: Scales 2 (D), 3 (Hy), 4 (Pd), 6 (Pa), and 9 (Ma). Thus, these five scales can be divided into subtle scores and obvious scores. The other clinical scales were composed primarily of obvious items, so it was not possible to develop subtle and obvious subscales for them. These clinical scales also include the scales that require the most K correction (Scales 1 [Hs], 7 [Pt], and 8 [Sc]).

The available research on the Wiener and Harmon subtle and obvious subscales does not suggest explicit criteria for defining malingering or defensiveness. Clinicians are probably safe to assume that a person who achieves T scores of ≥ 90 on all five obvious subscales and T scores near 50 on all five subtle subscales is trying to malinger. The converse relationship between scores on the obvious and subtle subscales should arouse the suspicion of defensiveness. If we assume that malingering and defensiveness are global response styles, one method for creating a criterion to assess malingering and defensiveness would be to sum the differences between the obvious and subtle subscales. The T scores for each of the obvious and subtle subscales are calculated, their differences are determined on each clinical scale, and these differences have been summed into a single overall total (see Table 9.12). Raw scores on the obvious and subtle scales must be converted to T scores *before* computing this difference score, since the obvious and subtle subscales do not have the same number of items. For example, the Scale 2 (D) obvious subscale consists of 39 items, whereas the subtle subscale has only 18 items. Employing this methodology, a person with an extreme difference score of +250 strongly indicates malingering. In contrast, a person with a difference score of −100 strongly suggests defensiveness.

Three issues must be addressed before the use of this difference score to assess accuracy of item endorsement is explored. First, other obvious and subtle scales could be used to assess accuracy of item endorsement (Greene, 1991, pp. 128–132). The Wiener and Harmon (Wiener, 1948) obvious and subtle subscales were selected because they have the longest history of usage in the MMPI field. Indeed, the high degree of item overlap among the various obvious and subtle scales and their high correlations suggest that any of these obvious and subtle scales would work equally well (Dubinsky, Gamble, & Rogers, 1985). However, the definition of item subtlety varies in different sets (Ward, 1986). Second, the question of whether large differences on the individual clinical scales have any significance has not been explored (e.g., it is not clear whether a difference of +30 points on Scale 2 has the same meaning as +30 points on Scale 9). Third, these obvious and subtle subscales are *not* being used to pre-

TABLE 9.12. Case Example for Assessing Accuracy of Item Endorsement by the Difference between Obvious and Subtle Subscales

Scale	Patient 1		Patient 2	
	T score	Difference	T score	Difference
2 (D)				
Obvious	98			50
Subtle	28	+70	74	−24
3 (Hy)				
Obvious	95		41	
Subtle	45	+50	64	−23
4 (Pd)				
Obvious	98		45	
Subtle	55	+43	66	−21
6 (Pa)				
Obvious	83		48	
Subtle	52	+31	67	−19
9 (Ma)				
Obvious	82		37	
Subtle	69	+13	49	−12
Total of difference scores		+207		−99

Note. Wiener and Harmon's (Wiener, 1948) Obvious and Subtle subscales were used in these examples.

dict specific clinical criteria, since research has reasonably well established that obvious scales are better predictors of most criteria than subtle scales (Jackson, 1971). Instead the difference between the obvious and scale subscales is being used as an index of the accuracy of item endorsement.

A renewed debate has emerged during the last decade over the usefulness of obvious and subtle scales. One issue, beyond the scope of this chapter, is whether obvious or subtle items are better predictors of external criteria (cf. Dahlstrom, 1991; Jackson, 1971; Weed, Ben-Porath, & Butcher, 1990; Wrobel & Lachar, 1982). The second issue, relevant to this discussion, is the usefulness of the obvious and subtle scales as a measure of malingering and defensiveness with advocates both pro (Brems & Johnson, 1991; Dannenbaum & Lanyon, 1993; Dush, Simons, Platt, Nation, & Ayres, 1994; Greene, 1988b; Lees-Haley & Fox, 1990) and con (Schretlen, 1990; Timbrook, Graham, Keiller, & Watts, 1993; Weed et al., 1990). Hollrah, Schlottmann, Scott, and Brunetti (1995) have provided an overview of the methodological issues that arise in determining the convergent and divergent validity of the obvious and subtle subscales that should be consulted by anyone interested in this topic. Timbrook et al. (1993) concluded that the total T-score difference between the obvious and subtle subscales provided no additional information beyond that provided by the traditional validity scales. The correlations between the total T-score difference on the obvious and subtle subscales and the other measures of malingering reported in Table 9.9 would suggest that all of these measures of malingering are essentially interchangeable. What remains to be established is whether any particular scale or index works more effectively in a given setting or with a specific population. The work of Dush et al. (1994) might suggest, however, that the total *T*-score difference on the obvious and subtle subscales could provide additional information in pain patients in which the keyed direction ("true") of the obvious items is opposite from the deviant response ("false") for most somatic items on the MMPI-2.

The optimal cutting scores on the total *T*-score difference between the obvious and subtle subscales has been extremely variable. Cutting scores have ranged from +106 (Rogers, Bagby, & Chakraborty, 1993), +160 (Sivec et al., 1994), +169 (Bagby, Rogers, & Buis, 1994), +179 (Bagby, Rogers, Buis, & Kalemba, 1994) to +200 (Fox, Gerson, & Lees-Haley, 1995).

Tables 9.10 and 9.11 present the distribution of the total *T*-score difference between the Wiener and Harmon (Wiener, 1948) obvious and subtle subscales for normal individuals and patient with mental disorders, respectively. The 50th percentile of this difference score in normal samples is −6, while in patient samples it is +93. Patients score higher on this index than normals, since they should be acknowledging the presence of some form of psychopathology that will increase their score on the obvious subscales.

Based on the data presented in Tables 9.10 and 9.11, the clinician can decide what percentage of persons should be labeled as malingering. Clearly, difference scores in the range of +250 to +300 are strongly suggestive of malingering. However, the clinician must decide what is the lower limit for classifying a person's responses as reflecting malingering. For example, if difference scores of +190 or higher are deemed to be suggestive of malingering, 20% of the patients would be so classified. The optimal cutting scores on this index reported above that ranged from +106 to +200 suggest that a lower cutting score would be appropriate in most clinical settings.

A difference score above whatever cutting score is used to identify malingering must be used as a threshold rather than as a clinical decision. Clinicians always must verify that the person is malingering rather than actually experiencing severe psychopathology. When the difference score exceeds +250 to +300, an interview and other collateral sources should easily confirm whether the person is malingering or experiencing pervasive and severe psychopathology. Occasionally in an inpatient setting, difference scores above 200 will be seen in a nonmalingering person. In an outpatient setting, it is extremely unlikely for difference scores in this range to reflect actual psychopathology, since the person should be so impaired that he or she would be unable to function.

MALINGERING-ONLY SCALES

Gough Dissimulation Scale

The Gough Dissimulation scale (*Ds*; Gough, 1954) consists of 74 items that significantly differentiated a group of neurotic persons from groups of college students and professional psychologists instructed to simulate neuroses on the MMPI. The items pertain not to neuroticism but to the prevailing stereotypes about neuroticism. The psychologists and students scored three to four times higher than neurotic persons on the Ds scale. The professional psychologists were only slightly better at simulating neurosis than the students, and both groups were easily identified by the Ds scale.

Research with Ds on the MMPI-2 has been limited by the fact that it is not recognized as one of the standard scales to be scored routinely. No consensus has been observed whether original or revised version of Ds should be used. Given these limitations, the few existing studies of Ds have found it to be effective (Bagby, Rogers, & Buis, 1994; Bagby, Rogers, Buis, & Kalemba, 1994; Rogers, Bagby, & Chakraborty, 1993; Wetter et al., 1993, 1994). Because Berry, Baer, and Harris (1991) in their metaanalysis of the MMPI found that Ds had one of the largest effect sizes, this scale needs to be used in malingering research.

Tables 9.10 and 9.11 summarize the range of scores that are seen on Ds for normal individuals and patients with mental disorders, respectively. Raw scores ≥ 26 occur in 1% of the normal individuals and 25% of the psychiatric patients. If a raw score of 38 or higher on the Ds scale were used to indicate malingering, 5% of the patients would be classified as endorsing the items inaccurately, whereas none of the normal adults would be so classified.

Clinical Applications to the MMPI-2

Five different classifications of scales/indexes to assess malingering have been described. The reader will need to select the scale/index that is most appropriate for specific populations and treatment settings. In instances where a global response style to malinger or be defensive is present, clinicians will *not* find it necessary to use several scales/indexes simultaneously, since they are correlated highly and consequently are redundant (see Table 9.9). However, when a specific form of psychopathology is being simulated, a scale such as Ds may be more appropriate (Petersen & Viglione, 1991).

A point worthy of emphasis is that once a profile has been defined as malingered, it *cannot* be interpreted as a valid profile. The person's specific reasons for malingering should be ascertained by a clinical interview, and the profile can be described as reflecting such a process; however, neither the MMPI-2 codetype (the highest clinical scale or the high-point pair) nor the individual scales can be interpreted.

The reader also should note once an MMPI-2 is characterized as malingered, the interpretive process stops. The person could have the MMPI-2 readministered, although such a procedure may not result in a valid profile. Once a person is motivated, for whatever reason, to malinger, he or she may have difficulty responding to the items accurately in subsequent administrations. Researchers have not established whether malingering is likely to persist across treatment settings for a particular person, although Audubon and Kirwin (1982) found at least some situational influences on response style.

Although the codetype from a malingering profile *cannot* be interpreted, several empirical correlates of such profiles have been identified in a manner similar to Marks, Seeman, and Haller's (1974) description of a K+ profile. Both Greene (1988b) and Hale, Zimostrad, Duckworth, and Nicholas (1986) found that persons who malingered were very likely to terminate treatment within the first few sessions; frequently, they did not return after the initial session. This finding that these persons terminate treatment quickly is almost exactly the opposite of what might be anticipated, since these persons were historically described as "pleading for help" and would be expected to remain in treatment longer than most persons. Additional research is needed to determine whether other empirical correlates of malingering can be validated.

Other Multiscale Personality Inventories

Most multiscale personality inventories provide some means of assessing malingering. The CPI-R uses the Well-Being scale (*Wb*) to assess malingering. The *Wb* is virtually identical to the Gough Dissimulation Scale—Revised (*Ds-r*; Gough, 1957). The deviant response for the items was reversed so that low scores now reflect malingering, whereas high scores reflect a self-portrayal of well-being. Little research exists on the validity of the *Wb* as an index of malingering (Megargee, 1972).

The Debasement scale (Scale *Z*) of the MCMI-III (Millon, 1987, 1994) is designed to assess malingering and is essentially unchanged from the MCMI-II. Bagby, Gillis, Toner, and Goldberg (1991) reported that the Debasement scale was effective in identifying students who were instructed to malinger on the MCMI-II. Wierzbicki and his colleagues (1993; Wierzbicki & Daleiden, 1993; Wierzbicki & Howard, 1992) have examined the effectiveness of the obvious and subtle scales of the MCMI to assess malingering in college students and male prisoners. They found a differential index of responding to obvious and subtle items to be useful to identify malingering. Even here, critics are found on the interpretive use of the subtle items (Peterson, Clark, & Bennet, 1989).

The Negative Impression scale of the PAI (*NIM*; Morey, 1991) is used to assess malingering. The *NIM*, an infrequency scale, consists of 9 items with highly atypical psychotic, dysphoric, and organic content. A moderate elevation on *NIM* (73 *T* through 91 *T*) suggests some degree of exaggeration of complaints and problems, whereas a score greater than 91 *T* on *NIM* suggests that the person is malingering, and the test results should be assumed to be invalid. Morey (1993) also has developed a series of indexes that can be used to identify malingering on the PAI. Rogers, Ornduff, and Sewell (1993) found that *NIM* could identify students who were malingering schizophrenia, but had more difficulty identifying students malingering depression and generalized anxiety. Rogers, Sewell, Morey, and Ustad (1995) conducted a substantial study of the PAI, utilizing 182 naive and coached simulators that feigned specific disorders; these simulators were compared to 221 genuine patients with the same disorders. They found that *NIM* was moderately effective with naive simulators but that a discriminant model was generally more effective.

Only available on Form A of the 16 PF, the Faking-Bad Scale is composed of 15 items that were endorsed by participants instructed to give as bad an impression as possible. A cutting score of 6 is used to identify malingering. More research is needed on this scale.

In summary, each of these multiscale personality inventories provide some means for the assessment of malingering. These scales are scored routinely on the CPI-R,

MCMI-III, and PAI, which should encourage the clinician to be aware of them, whereas malingering can be assessed on Form A of the 16 PF by the use of additional scales. Limited research exists on the validities of these scales and, more important, on the usefulness of the specific cutting scores that have been suggested.

DEFENSIVENESS

The use of infrequency scales, critical items, the F-K index, and the Wiener and Harmon (Wiener, 1948) obvious and subtle subscales to assess malingering was described earlier. Low scores on these same scales and indexes can be used to assess defensiveness. The only information that will be covered in this section is the research on optimal cutting scores and the data presented in Tables 9.10 and 9.11.

Baer, Wetter, and Berry (1992) reported the results of a meta-analysis of MMPI measures of defensiveness. The largest effect sizes were found for scales not scored routinely on the MMPI: Wiggins's (1959) Social Desirability scale (Wsd), the Wiener (1948) obvious subscales, and the Positive Malingering (Mp; Cofer, Chance, & Judson, 1949) scale. The effect sizes for these three scales averaged nearly 1.50; in contrast, effect sizes for the L and K scales averaged 1.00, whereas the effect size for F-K averaged .71.

Infrequency Scales

Little research on infrequency scales addresses their effectiveness in isolation as measures of defensiveness, other than simply to note that low scores will be encountered. Typically the F scale is considered in conjunction with the K scale (i.e., the F-K index) to assess defensiveness. Since the typical normal individual (50th percentile) endorses three F-scale items (Table 9.10), clinicians could assume that patients who endorse three or fewer items are being defensive. Using this criterion, 20% of psychiatric patients would be classified as being defensive (Table 9.11).

Critical Items

The total number of the Koss and Butcher (1973) or Lachar and Wrobel (1979) critical items that are endorsed can be used as another index of defensiveness. A person who is trying to be defensive would be expected to endorse few of these items, since their item content is obvious (face valid) and unambiguously reflective of psychopathology. Tables 9.10 and 9.11 summarized the total number of critical items that were endorsed by normal individuals and patients with mental disorders, respectively. Using a typical normal individual (50th percentile) who endorses 10 of the Koss and Butcher critical items and 15 of the Lachar and Wrobel critical items as a criterion, about 15% of the psychiatric patients endorsed fewer total critical items than the normal individuals. Again, the reader should note that about 20% of patients are identified as being defensive by this index, similar to what is found with other scales/indexes.

F-K Index: Gough Dissimulation Index

Gough's initial reservations about the efficiency of the *F-K* index in detecting defensiveness have been corroborated by numerous investigators. Most studies have found extensive overlap in the distributions of the *F-K* index in students who took the MMPI-2 normally and then retook the MMPI-2 under defensive instructions. Consequently, clinicians have problems in establishing a consistent cutting score on the *F-K* index that reliably distinguishes normal student profiles from their defensive profiles. The optimal cutting scores on the *F-K* index in college students instructed to be defensive have ranged from −11 (Bagby, Rogers, Buis, & Kalemba, 1994), −12 (Baer et al., 1995), −13 (Austin, 1992), to −15 (Bagby, Rogers, & Buis, 1994).

One problem with the *F-K* index in identifying defensiveness is that anyone who is (1) acknowledging the capability to handle his or her own problems, (2) well-adjusted (high raw score on *K*), and (3) not experiencing stress or conflict (low raw score on *F*) will most likely be defined as being defensive rather than normal by this index. Thus, normal persons taking the MMPI-2 often will be inappropriately classified as being defensive on the *F-K* index.

If scores of ≤ −12 on the *F-K* index are used a criterion of defensiveness (50th percentile in normal individuals; see Table 9.10), then 25% of patients would be so classified (see Table 9.11). Again, a sizable percentage of patients evaluated in a clinical setting are being defensive. Since normal individuals routinely achieve negative scores on this index (see Table 9.10), the *F-K* index will *not* distinguish between normal individuals scoring in this range and defensive patients. However, if clinicians know that this person should be reporting psychopathology because of his or her presence in a treatment setting, then the *F-K* index can alert them to the possibility of defensiveness.

Obvious and Subtle Scales

Low scores, usually negative scores, on the total *T* score difference between the Wiener and Harmon (Wiener, 1948) obvious and subtle subscales can be used as a measure of defensiveness. Few studies have reported optimal cutting scores for this measure; the results have been variable and ranged from +17 (Bagby, Rogers, Buis, & Kalemba, 1994) and −24 (Bagby, Rogers, & Buis, 1994), to −79 (Austin, 1992).

Since a normal individual's typical score on this index is −6 (see Table 9.10), a clinician could decide that any person in a treatment setting who scores less than −6 is being defensive. By this criterion, nearly 20% of the patients would be classified as being defensive. As with the other indexes and scales to assess defensiveness, a similar percentage of persons are identified as being defensive.

DEFENSIVENESS-ONLY SCALES

Five scales have been developed to assess defensiveness: Lie (*L*); Correction (*K*); Positive Malingering (*Mp*); Superlative (*S*; Butcher & Han, 1995); and Wiggins's (1959) Social Desirability (*Wsd*). The deviant response for most of these scales is "false" (see

Table 8.8); in fact, *L, K,* and *S* are virtually totally false-endorsement scales. The intercorrelations among these measures are much more variable (see Table 9.13) than was seen in the measures of malingering (see Table 9.9).

Lie Scale

The Lie (*L*) scale consists of 15 items that were selected to identify persons who are deliberately trying to be defensive. Although denial and defensiveness are characteristic of most high scorers on the *L* scale (Butcher & Williams, 1992; Graham, 1993; Greene, 1991), persons with any degree of psychological sophistication will not be detected. Because low scores on the *L* scale can occur with defensive individuals, the usefulness of the *L* scale for detecting defensiveness is constrained. The distributions for the *L* scale in normal individuals (Table 9.14) and patients with mental disorders (Table 9.15) are very similar, which confirms its limitations as a measure of defensiveness.

Correction Scale

The Correction (*K*) scale is a traditional measure of defensiveness on the MMPI-2 with high scores (*T* scores > 59) in patients with mental disorders indicating defensiveness and the unwillingness to acknowledge any type of psychological distress. These persons typically lack insight into their own functioning, which makes prognosis for any type of psychological intervention very poor. The actual behaviors and symptoms

TABLE 9.13. Intercorrelations among Scales Measuring Defensiveness in Normal Individuals and Patients with Mental Disorders

Scale/index	K	S	ODecp	Wsd	% false
Normal individuals (Butcher et al., 1989)					
L	.32	.40	.55	.46	.34
K		.82	.32	.03	.81
S			.40	.11	.83
ODecp				.80	.19
Wsd					−.14
Patients with mental disorders (Greene, 1995)					
L	.46	.52	.59	.46	.45
K		.88	.48	.23	.83
S			.55	.29	.85
ODecp				.85	.37
Wsd					.09

Note. L, Lie; K, Correction; S, Superlative (Butcher & Han, 1995); ODecp, Other Deception (Nichols & Greene, 1991); Wsd, Wiggins (1959) Social Desirability; % false, percentage of all 567 items endorsed "false."

TABLE 9.14. Percentiles for Measures of Defensiveness in Normal Individuals (Butcher et al., 1989)

%ile	T score	L	K	ODecp	S	Wsd	% false
99	79	10	25	23	44	21	73
98	75	9	24	21	42	20	72
95	68	7	22	19	39	17	70
90	63	6	21	17	36	16	68
85		5	20	16	34	15	67
80	58	5	19	15	32	15	66
75		4	18	14	31	14	65
50	49	3	15	11	25	12	61
25		2	11	9	19	9	56
20	42	1	11	8	17	9	55
15		1	10	7	16	8	53
10	38	1	9	6	13	8	51
5	36	0	7	5	11	7	48
2	33	0	5	4	8	6	43
1	32	0	4	3	7	5	41

Note. High scores are indicative of defensiveness. *L*, Lie; *K*, Correction; *ODecp*, Other Deception (Nichols & Greene, 1991); *S*, Superlative (Butcher & Han, 1995); *Wsd*, Wiggins (1959) Social Desirability; % false, percentage of all 567 items endorsed "false."

about which the person is being defensive probably will not be discernible from the clinical scales, because they are likely to be within the normal range.

The distributions for the *K* scale in normal individuals (Table 9.14) and patients with mental disorders (Table 9.15) also are very strikingly similar despite the different qualities tapped by this scale in normal individuals and patients (Butcher & Williams, 1992; Graham, 1993; Greene, 1991).

Positive Malingering Scale

The Positive Malingering (*Mp*) scale was developed to identify defensiveness. Cofer et al. (1949) asked groups of college students to endorse the MMPI items like an emotionally disturbed person (malingering) or so as to make the best possible impression (defensiveness). They then identified 34 items that were insensitive to malingering and yet susceptible to defensiveness ("positive malingering"). They found that a cutting score of ≥ 20 correctly identified 96% of the accurate and 86% of the defensive MMPIs. They also noted that scores on the *Mp* scale tended to be correlated positively to scores on the Wiener (1948) subtle scales.

Baer et al. (1992) found in their meta-analysis that *Mp* had one of the largest effect sizes in students instructed to be defensive. The optimal cutting score for *Mp* for student samples have ranged from +9 (Bagby, Rogers, Buis, & Kalemba, 1994) to +13 (Baer et al., 1995) and +14 (Bagby, Rogers, & Buis, 1994). Nichols and Greene (1991) have updated the *Mp* scale for the MMPI-2 and renamed the scale Other Deception (*ODecp*).

TABLE 9.15. Percentiles for Measures of Defensiveness in Patients with Mental Disorders (Greene, 1995)

%ile	T score	L	K	ODecp	S	Wsd	% false
99	79	11	25	24	44	22	74
98	75	10	24	22	42	21	72
95	68	8	22	20	38	20	70
90	63	7	20	18	34	18	67
85		6	18	17	30	17	65
80	58	6	17	16	28	16	63
75		5	16	15	26	15	62
50	49	4	12	11	18	12	54
25		2	8	8	12	10	46
20	42	2	7	7	10	9	44
15		1	6	6	9	8	42
10	38	1	6	5	8	7	39
5	36	0	4	4	6	6	36
2	33	0	3	3	4	5	31
1	32	0	3	2	3	4	29

Note. High scores are indicative of defensiveness. L, Lie; K, Correction; S, Superlative (Butcher & Han, 1995); ODecp, Other Deception (Nichols & Greene, 1991); Wsd, Wiggins (1959) Social Desirability; % false, percentage of all 567 items endorsed "false."

Tables 9.14 and 9.15 summarize the range of scores that were found on the ODecp scale in normal individuals and patients, respectively. Raw scores of 19 or higher were found in about 5% of the normal individuals and the patients, and the distributions of scores tend to be similar in the two groups.

Superlative Scale

Butcher and Han (1995) developed the Superlative (S) scale to assess persons who present themselves in a superlative manner, which is encountered frequently in individuals screened in personnel settings. As noted earlier, most of the items on the S scale are false, and it correlates significantly (.82 to .88) with the K scale (Table 9.13). As would be expected, normal individuals (Table 9.14) achieve higher scores on the S scale than patients with mental disorders (Table 9.15), but the distributions become fairly similar at marked elevations (raw scores > 38).

Wiggins's Social Desirability Scale

Wiggins (1959) developed his Social Desirability (Wsd) scale to discriminate college students who took the MMPI in a socially desirable manner from those who took the test honestly. As noted earlier, Wsd has one of the largest effect sizes in identifying students directed to be defensive (Baer et al., 1992). The distribution of scores of the normal individuals (Table 9.14) and patients with mental disorders (Table 9.15) are very similar throughout the entire range.

Clinical Applications to the MMPI-2

Five different scales/indexes for assessing defensiveness have been described. The reader should select the scale/index that is most appropriate for specific populations and treatment settings. The selection of one of these scales/indexes of defensiveness is more difficult than for malingering, because they appear to be measuring different aspects of defensiveness, as indicated by their relatively low intercorrelations (see Table 9.13). Research is needed that examines which of these scales/indexes of defensiveness is most appropriate in a particular clinical setting by validating these scales/indexes with independent measures of defensiveness.

When a person's responses have been identified as being endorsed inaccurately because of extreme defensiveness, the standard profile is no longer interpretable since it reflects an invalid response set. The clinician will have little reason to try to interpret such a profile, however, since defensiveness usually results in no clinical scales being elevated to a T score of 65 or higher on the MMPI-2, and frequently no clinical scales are at or above a T score of 60. The clinician should describe the person's style of defensiveness, determine the potential causes for this response set, and assess the implications for treatment/intervention.

Once defensiveness is identified in a clinical setting, the empirical correlates of such a response set can be studied. Persons who are defensive are likely to see their problems as less troubling to themselves, and hence they are less motivated to change. Their problems also may be more chronic in nature, and consequently they may be more difficult to treat if they remain in treatment. Duckworth and Barley (1987) have provided a valuable summary of the correlates of persons who produce such MMPI profiles.

Other Multiscale Inventories

Most multiscale personality inventories also provide some means of assessing defensiveness. This section describes the use of specific scales to assess defensiveness on other multiscale personality inventories. Limited research exists on these scales to validate their usefulness and the appropriateness of the cutting scores that are suggested.

The CPI-R uses the Good Impression (*Gi*) scale to assess defensiveness. *Gi* consists of 40 items that identified high school students instructed to endorse the items as if they were applying for an important job or trying to make an especially favorable impression. T scores ≥ 65 are thought to raise the issue that the person may be defensive.

The Social Desirability scale (Scale *Y*) on the MCMI-III (Millon, 1994), measuring the tendency to be defensive, was developed by asking students to be defensive. Bagby et al. (1991) found that *Y* identified 72% of students who were instructed to be defensive. However, Retzlaff, Sheehan, and Fiel (1991) found that *Y* identified only 52% of their participants, and Fals-Stewart (1995) found that it was ineffective at classifying substance-abusing patients that were instructed to be defensive.

The Positive Impression scale of the PAI (*PIM*; Morey, 1991) is a 9-item scale designed to assess defensiveness. A moderate elevation (57*T* through 67*T*) suggests that the person reported him- or herself as relatively free of minor shortcomings, whereas scores greater than $67T$ reflect extreme denial of common shortcomings readily admitted by most individuals. As cross-validation, Cashel, Rogers, and Sewell (1995) found that PIM was only modestly successful at identifying defensive persons, but that a discriminant function was relatively effective. Morey (1993) also has developed a series of indexes that can be used to identify defensiveness on the PAI.

The Motivational Distortion scale of the 16 PF is used to assess defensiveness. It is composed of 15 items that distinguished individuals who were instructed to endorse the items so as to provide the most favorable picture of themselves. A cutting score of 6 or higher is used to identify defensiveness.

CONCLUSIONS

Tables 9.16 and 9.17 summarize the scales/indexes that can be used to assess item omissions, consistency of item endorsement, and accuracy of item endorsement on the MMPI-2, and the possible cutting scores that might be used in with normal individuals and individuals in a clinical setting, respectively. Clinicians should proceed through each step in order: (1) Item omissions should be checked before examining consistency of item endorsement; and (2) consistency of item endorsement should be checked before considering accuracy of item endorsement. Clinicians need to determine which scale/index of malingering and defensiveness is the most appropriate for their particular settings and whether raising or lowering the cutting scores would facilitate the identification of malingering or defensiveness. The establishment of the base rates with which malingering and defensiveness are encountered in a specific clinical setting and the consequences of misidentifying (false positives) or not identifying (false negatives) malingering or defensiveness are mandatory in deciding what cutting scores should be used and whether a cutting score should be modified. Clinicians also need to establish the empirical correlates of malingering and defensiveness so that better assessments, treatments, and interventions can be made when these response sets are encountered in clinical settings. Finally, clinicians should understand that although this chapter has emphasized the MMPI-2, the same rationale for assessing consistency and accuracy of item endorsement, and the need for extensive validation are applicable to all multiscale personality inventories.

TABLE 9.16. Cutting Scores for Assessing MMPI-2 Validity in Normal Individuals (Butcher et al., 1989)

I. Item omissions

					Percentile					
	1	2	5	10	25	50	75	90	95	98	99
?	0	0	0	0	0	0	0	2	5	10	15

II. Consistency of item endorsement

					Percentile					
	Consistent									Inconsistent	
	1	2	5	10	25	50	75	90	95	98	99
VRIN	0	0	1	1	3	4	6	8	9	11	12
$|F\text{-}F_B|$	0	0	0	0	1	2	3	5	6	8	9

III. Accuracy of item endorsement

					Percentile					
	Defensiveness									Malingering	
	1	2	5	10	25	50	75	90	95	98	99
F	0	0	0	0	1	3	5	8	10	12	14
KBSum	0	0	1	2	5	10	16	23	30	36	38
LWSum	2	3	4	6	10	15	23	31	37	46	49
F-K	−24	−23	−21	−20	−16	−12	−8	−3	0	4	6
Total *O-S*	−99	−93	−80	−66	−41	−6	34	78	105	138	161
Ds	1	2	3	4	6	9	13	17	20	24	26
% true	25	27	28	30	33	37	42	47	50	54	57
L	10	9	7	6	4	3	2	1	0	0	0
K	25	24	22	21	18	15	11	9	7	5	4
ODecp	23	21	19	17	14	11	8	6	5	4	3
S	44	42	39	36	31	25	19	13	11	8	7
Wsd	21	20	18	17	14	12	9	8	7	6	5
% false	73	72	70	68	65	61	56	51	48	43	41

Note. ? = Cannot Say; *VRIN*, Variable Response Inconsistency; $|F\text{-}F_B|$, absolute value of *F* (raw)-F_B (raw); *F*, Infrequency; KBSum, Total number of Koss and Butcher (1973) critical items endorsed; LWSum, Total number of Lachar and Wrobel (1979) critical items endorsed; *F-K*, Gough (1950) Dissimulation Index; Total *O-S*, Total *T* score difference on the Wiener and Harmon Obvious and Subtle subscales; *Ds*, Gough (1954) Dissimulation scale; % true, percentage of items endorsed "true"; *L*, Lie; *K*, Correction; *ODecp*, Other Deception (Nichols & Greene, 1991); *S*, Superlative (Butcher & Han, 1995); *Wsd*, Wiggins (1959) Social Desirability; % false, percentage of items endorsed "false." Scores on *L, K, ODecp, S, Wsd,* and % false are inverted since higher scores indicate defensiveness.

TABLE 9.17. Cutting Scores for Assessing MMPI-2 Validity in Clinical Settings (Greene, 1995)

I. Item omissions

	Percentile										
	1	2	5	10	25	50	75	90	95	98	99
?	0	0	0	0	0	0	0	1	4	12	20

II. Consistency of item endorsement

	Percentile										
	Consistent									Inconsistent	
	1	2	5	10	25	50	75	90	95	98	99
$VRIN$	0	0	1	2	3	5	8	10	12	15	16
$|F\text{-}F_B|$	0	0	0	0	1	3	5	8	10	13	16

III. Accuracy of item endorsement

	Percentile										
	Defensiveness									Malingering	
	1	2	5	10	25	50	75	90	95	98	99
F	0	0	1	2	4	8	15	24	30	35	39
KBSum	1	2	5	8	15	28	44	56	62	66	69
LWSum	4	5	9	13	22	38	55	71	79	87	90
$F\text{-}K$	−24	−22	−20	−17	−12	−4	6	16	22	28	33
Total $O\text{-}S$	−93	−83	−62	−36	15	93	172	238	273	304	316
Ds	1	2	4	6	10	17	26	34	38	41	43
% true	23	25	28	31	36	44	52	58	62	66	69
L	11	10	8	7	5	4	2	1	0	0	0
K	25	24	22	20	16	12	8	6	4	3	3
$ODecp$	24	22	20	18	15	11	8	5	4	3	2
S	44	42	38	34	26	18	12	8	6	4	3
Wsd	22	21	20	18	15	12	10	7	6	5	4
% false	74	72	70	67	62	54	46	39	36	31	29

Note. ?, Cannot Say; *VRIN*, Variable Response Inconsistency; $|F\text{-}F_B|$, absolute value of F (raw)-F_B (raw); *F*, Infrequency; KBSum, Total number of Koss and Butcher (1973) critical items endorsed; LWSum, Total number of Lachar and Wrobel (1979) critical items endorsed; *F-K*, Gough (1950) Dissimulation Index; Total *O-S*, Total *T* score difference on the Wiener and Harmon obvious and subtle subscales; *Ds*, Gough (1954) Dissimulation scale; % true, percentage of items endorsed "true"; *L*, Lie; *K*, Correction; *ODecp*, Other Deception (Nichols & Greene, 1991); *S*, Superlative (Butcher & Han, 1995); *Wsd*, Wiggins (1959) Social Desirability; % false, percentage of items endorsed "false." Scores on *L, K, ODecp, S, Wsd*, and % false are inverted since higher scores indicate defensiveness.

APPENDIX. ITEM COMPOSITION FOR MMPI-2 SPECIAL VALIDITY SCALES

All means and standard deviations are based on the MMPI-2 normative group (Butcher et al., 1989).

Arbisi and Ben-Porath (1995) Psychiatric F: Fp (Total: 27 items)
Males: $M = 1.16$, $SD = 1.38$; females: $M = 1.03$, $SD = 1.26$

True						False				
66	114	162	193	216		51	77	90	93	102
228	252	270	282	291		126	192	276	501	
294	322	323	336	371						
387	478	555								

Butcher and Han (1995) Superlative: S (Total: 50 items)
Males: $M = 25.02$, $SD = 8.69$; females: $M = 25.48$, $SD = 8.29$

True						False				
121	148	184	194	534		15	50	58	76	81
560						87	89	104	110	120
						123	154	196	205	213
						225	264	279	284	290
						302	337	341	346	352
						373	374	403	420	423
						428	430	433	442	445
						449	461	486	487	523
						538	542	545	547	

Gough (1954) Dissimulation: Ds (Total: 58 items)
Males: $M = 10.08$, $SD = 5.32$; females: $M = 10.57$, $SD = 5.64$

True						False				
11	17	18	19	22		57	75	83	108	125
28	30	31	40	42		188	278	318	404	429
44	54	61	72	81						
85	92	111	166	190						
195	205	221	252	258						
268	274	287	292	294						
300	307	310	320	329						
362	395	412	419	421						
425	431	433	435	436						
451	458	463								

Gough (1957) Dissimulation—Revised: Ds-r (Total: 32 items)
Males: $M = 5.89$, $SD = 3.50$; females: $M = 6.63$; $SD = 3.86$

True						False				
11	18	22	28	30		57	75	83	108	278
31	40	44	81	85		318				
92	111	205	221	274						
292	300	320	329	362						
395	419	433	451	458						
463										

Lees-Haley, English, and Glenn (1991) Fake Bad: FBS (Total: 43 items)
Males: $M = 11.67$, $SD = 3.81$; females: $M = 13.76$, $SD = 4.14$

True						False				
11	18	28	30	31		12	41	57	58	81
39	40	44	59	111		110	117	152	164	176
252	274	325	339	464		224	227	248	249	250
469	505	506				255	264	284	362	373
						374	419	433	496	561

Nichols and Greene (1991) Other Deception: ODecp (Total: 33 items)
Males: $M = 13.38$, $SD = 4.46$; females: $M = 11.47$, $SD = 4.07$

True						False				
49	100	133	184	194		21	29	41	77	89
201	206	207	211	220		93	183	196	203	232
239	257	261	345	350		290	326	341	428	442
356	416	439								

Sewell et al. (1994) Inconsistent Response: IR (Total: 16 items)
Males: $M = 0.95$, $SD = 1.10$; females: $M = 0.63$, $SD = 0.93$

True						False		
114	182	228	234	322		51	77	93
332	336	355	407	478				
511	527	530						

Wiggins (1959) Social Desirability: *Wsd* (Total: 33 items)
Males: $M = 12.72$, $SD = 3.68$; females: $M = 12.14$, $SD = 3.27$

True						False				
25	49	80	100	131		29	41	77	93	183
133	184	194	201	206		203	232	326	341	
207	211	220	249	257						
263	345	351	354	356						
366	402	416	439							

NOTES

1. Reproduced from the MMPI-2 by permission. Copyright © 1943 (renewed 1970), 1989 by the University of Minnesota Press. Published by the University of Minnesota Press. All rights reserved.

2. The reader who needs more information on the effects of base rates on positive and negative predictive power should consult Baldesserini, Finkelstein, and Arona (1983).

3. Research in this area is very prolific; in the interest of conserving space, there has been no attempt to be exhaustive in citing references. Several citations have been provided for all major issues so that the interested reader will have easy access to the literature. In addition, emphasis has been placed on MMPI-2 research even though most of these issues arose with the MMPI.

4. Although clinicians would find it comforting if more similarity existed in optimal cutting scores, given the heterogeneity of patient samples, settings, and the base rates with which malingering and defensiveness occur, there is little reason to expect a high degree of convergence. Regardless of the differences reported in optimal cutting scores on the same measure across studies, the discrimination between malingering and actual psychopathology should be easier as higher cutting scores are utilized, since the clinician will have access to the person's background and reasons for being evaluated.

5. For a thorough discussion of critical items, the interested reader should see pages 130–131 in Graham (1993) or pages 220–226 in Greene (1991).

10

Dissimulation on the Rorschach and Other Projective Measures

DAVID J. SCHRETLEN, Ph.D.

Some of the earliest studies of malingering and response distortion involved the Rorschach Inkblot Test. Moreover, the Rorschach and other projective instruments remain among the most widely used measures in clinical psychological assessment. Although the investigation of dissimulation on projectives has not kept pace with the recent expansion of dissimulation research using multiscale inventories and neuropsychological tests, several interesting and informative studies have been reported. This chapter primarily reviews studies of dissimulation on the Rorschach Inkblot Test, beginning with a series of studies (Fosberg, 1938, 1941, 1943) that fostered the belief that the Rorschach was impervious to response distortion. Although several studies during the 1950s and 1960s reported evidence of its susceptibility to faking, some proponents still contend that the Rorschach and other projective measures cannot be faked. Recent findings render this contention nearly impossible to defend. What remains unclear is not whether individuals can distort their Rorschach results, but whether such distortion can be detected.

Relatively few studies have been reported since Schretlen (1988), Stermac (1988), and Perry and Kinder (1990) reviewed this literature. Nevertheless, these recent studies include several whose methodological advantages can be appreciated only in the context of earlier research. Thus, both early and recent studies of dissimulation on the Rorschach are reviewed in historical fashion to (1) outline the hazards that have plagued this research, and (2) describe strategies that have been developed to avoid these hazards. This presentation will be followed by a review of the effects of defensiveness on the Rorschach. Finally, the relatively limited research involving dissimulation on other projective measures is reviewed, including the Holtzman Inkblot Technique, Thematic Apperception Test (TAT), Sentence Completion Test (SCT), and Group Personality Projective Test (GPPT).

EARLY STUDIES AND CASE REPORTS

In a series of early reliability studies, Fosberg (1938, 1941, 1943) introduced the concept of "fakability" in connection with the Rorschach. His objective was to determine whether persons could alter their test responses in a manner that would change the configuration or interpretation of their score profiles. Using chi-square analyses in his first study, Fosberg (1938) found no significant association between score frequencies and four different instructional sets in two normal adults. Consequently, he accepted the null hypothesis that, "all four records do not vary significantly from each other" (p. 12). Based on the finding of high test–retest correlations among 129 participants who were given varied instructions in his second study, Fosberg (1941) concluded that "the Rorschach withstood all attempts at manipulation by participants in the two directions of making better and worse impressions" (p. 83). This conclusion was consistent with Frank's (1939) widely accepted "projective hypothesis" that the Rorschach measures processes and traits that are largely unconscious and essentially beyond volitional control. In any case, Fosberg assumed that if participants who were told to make a "bad" impression did not produce quantitative differences in their score profiles, then there was no need to verify whether their faked protocols were indistinguishable from honest records.

Even as Fosberg argued that the Rorschach was not "fakable," however, contrary findings were being reported. Rosenberg and Feldberg (1944) described 15 characteristics that frequently appeared in the Rorschach protocols of 93 soldiers who were identified as "known" or suspected malingerers based on psychiatric examinations. Examples of putative signs of malingering included few responses, percepts with vague form, recognizing difficult forms while failing to report easy forms, and asking repeated questions about test directions. Although Rosenberg and Feldberg did not include a control group, 87% of the protocols produced by their suspected malingerers contained at least four of these characteristics.

Early observers described the clinical characteristics of suspected malingerers. For example, Benton (1945) noted characteristic features of Rorschach protocols given by military men who were strongly suspected of malingering physical complaints in order to avoid active duty. Salient features included few responses, slow reaction times, frequent card rejections, failure to give the most common Popular responses, and a general attitude of perplexity and pained compliance with testing. Also based on clinical observations, Hunt (1946) similarly concluded that the Rorschach protocols of malingerers typically contain, "a general paucity of responses, the rejection of numerous cards, an unduly large number of Popular responses, and some perseveration or repetition of previous responses" (p. 253). Wachspress, Berenberg, and Jacobson (1953) illustrated their clinical experience of malingering with a report of 3 men suspected of feigning psychotic symptoms. In contrast to the dramatic and deviant responses these men produced on other tests, examination with the Rorschach yielded "evasive but less distorted records" (p. 472).

Cronbach (1949) later criticized Fosberg's (1938) use of chi-square analysis to test the hypothesis that Rorschach variable frequencies produced by individual participants would vary significantly with instructional set. The problem was that any effect of instructional set would be dwarfed by the extreme frequency differences that characterize various Rorschach variables (e.g., common location responses vs. rare pure color responses). Cronbach (1949) also contended that Fosberg's (1941) second correlational study was no more sound than his first because "pairs of values such as W_1-W_2, D_1-D_2, etc. were entered in the same correlation [matrix]," so that "high correlations would have been obtained even if the scores correlated had been produced by two different subjects" (p. 424). Moreover, Carp and Shavzin (1950) demonstrated that some experimental simulators instructed to make "good" and "bad" impressions on successive administrations of the Rorschach could deliberately alter their Rorschach results. Although Carp and Shavzin incorrectly used chi-square methods to compare each participant's two protocols, their study was the first experimental demonstration that the Rorschach was susceptible to faking.

Feldman and Graley (1954) reported the first experiment to investigate both aspects of fakability. Using a within-subject design, they asked whether the Rorschach results of 72 students instructed to respond as if they were "very emotionally disturbed" would differ from the results of 30 students (a subgroup of the 72) who took the test earlier under standard instructions. Following Cronbach's (1949) guidelines for chi-square analyses, Feldman and Graley found substantial group differences on several Rorschach scores. Compared to protocols obtained under standard instructions, the faked protocols contained significantly more m (inanimate movement), $CF + C$ (non-form-dominant color responses), FC (form-dominant color responses), and sexual anatomy responses. Faked responses frequently were characterized by dramatic contents such as fire, blood, and explosion/smoke. Consistent with Benton's (1945) observations, faked protocols contained fewer responses overall and fewer Popular responses than honest protocols. Interestingly, no group difference in $F+\%$ (good form responses) was found. Each of four judges correctly classified 65–83% of the protocols according to instructional set. Finally, when Feldman and Graley asked participants to describe how they approached the faking task, the participants reported (1) avoiding the normal response, (2) emphasizing sex, (3) mentioning symptoms, (4) using a specific or unspecified mental disorder as a guide, and (5) reporting aggressive or gory percepts.

Apparently unaware of the Feldman and Graley study, Easton and Feigenbaum (1967) employed a similar within-subject design to investigate whether students instructed to make an "unfavorable" impression in order to "stay out of the army" would produce Rorschach protocols that differed from their own records taken under standard instructions. These investigators found that the faked protocols contained fewer responses overall and fewer Popular responses than honest records. Form quality and the presence of dramatic contents were not examined.

RECENT STUDIES

The overall increase in psychometric research on response distortion and malingering is shown by the fact that more controlled studies have been reported during the past

15 years than during the preceding 40 years. Recent studies also reflect a growing awareness not only of potential pitfalls specific to research with the Rorschach, but of methodological problems associated with malingering research in general.

Seamons, Howell, Carlisle, and Roe (1981) reported a within-subject study of four groups, each with 12 participants: nonschizophrenic prison inmates, patients with latent schizophrenia, patients with residual schizophrenia, and patients in the active phase of schizophrenia. Participants took the Rorschach under two instructional sets: (1) to "appear as if you are a normal, well-adjusted individual," and (2) to "appear as if you are mentally ill, as if you are psychotic." Summed across all four groups, when participants were instructed to appear mentally ill, they produced significantly higher scores on 4 of 48 variables examined, including the number of dramatic and blood responses, *ep* (experience potential), and inappropriate (incongruous and fabulized) combinations, but they gave fewer Popular responses. These findings are consistent with the inference that symptom exaggeration on the Rorschach may present in the form of dramatic, morbid, and bizarre responses. However, instructing patients with schizophrenia to "appear as if you are mentally ill" could be construed as an instruction to answer honestly. Conversely, instructing patients to "appear normal and well-adjusted" could be construed as a defensive response set. This confound in the instructional sets used by Seamons et al. makes it impossible to draw any direct conclusions about malingering from their study. Nevertheless, they did demonstrate that psychiatric patients can deliberately alter their Rorschach protocols.

Bash and Alpert (1980) reported the results of a well-designed study in which Bash administered a comprehensive battery of standard clinical tests and experimental measures to 120 male inpatients on a prison ward of a psychiatric hospital. The sample included four groups of 30 adults who were diagnosed before testing as malingering, schizophrenic (with or without hallucinations), or mentally ill but not psychotic. Tests were scored by a rater who was blind to group membership. For all protocols, a score of 1 (present) or 0 (absent) was assigned for each of 13 putative "signs" of malingering; scores for each sign were summed to yield a "malingering index." The suspected malingerers produced significantly higher scores on this index than the other three groups. However, 3 of the 13 signs accounted for most of the group effect: malingerers rejected more cards, gave fewer Popular responses, and gave a lower proportion of pure form (*F%*) responses. Contrary to expectations, the suspected malingerers did *not* give significantly more responses with poor form (*F−%*) or aggressive contents than other patient groups. As noted in Stermac's (1988) earlier review, Bash and Alpert included the Rorschach in a larger battery of tests and did not report the accuracy of participant classification based solely on Rorschach malingering scores. Still, Bash and Alpert (1980) reported the first "known-groups" comparison to demonstrate that the Rorschach protocols of individuals clinically identified as malingering could be distinguished from those of well-matched comparison group participants.

Pettigrew, Tuma, Pickering, and Whelton (1983) devised a study to test the observation (e.g., Exner, 1978) that malingerers often use bizarre and/or dramatic wording in responses that otherwise reflect little or no perceptual distortion. Pettigrew et al. administered a multiple-choice, group version of the Rorschach test to three groups:

(1) 62 undergraduate student simulators instructed to respond as they thought a "psychotic or insane person would," (2) 75 students given standard instructions, and (3) 55 hospitalized patients with psychotic diagnoses. All 10 standard Rorschach inkblots first were reproduced in miniature on a single page. Then participants were presented five sets of response alternatives for each blot and asked to pick the response "that most resembles what the blot looks like to you." Four alternative response types were provided for each set: Type-1 responses involved good form and bizarre/elaborate wording; Type-2 responses involved good form and nonbizarre wording; Type-3 responses involved poor form and nonbizarre wording of roughly equal length as Type-1 responses; Type-4 responses involved poor form and neither bizarre nor elaborate wording. As predicted, the simulators produced more ($M = 31.5$, $SD = 10.4$) responses with good form but bizarre wording (Type 1) than either inpatients with psychotic diagnoses ($M = 13.3$, $SD = 6.7$) or the students given standard instructions ($M = 15.0$, $SD = 6.0$). Using 29 or more Type-1 responses as a cutting score, 39 (62.9%) simulators, no inpatients, and one (1.3%) student control were classified as simulators. Collapsed across all response types, the simulator and normal control groups chose the highest percentage of responses with good form (64.5% and 74.7%, respectively), whereas only 56.4% of the responses selected by inpatients involved percepts with good form. In summary, this study cleverly avoided the statistical problems that result from group differences in the length of Rorschach protocols and provided clear operational definitions of the response characteristics that have been attributed to malingerers. However, the study has methodological limitations: The simulators were given no coaching about psychotic mental disorders, and no incentive was provided for successfully eluding detection. Regrettably, cross-validation of these findings with independent samples has not been reported.

Albert, Fox, and Kahn (1980) reported one of the first studies to compare coached and uncoached simulators. In this study, Albert administered the Rorschach to four groups of six participants. Six college students and six inpatients with paranoid schizophrenia were given standard instructions. Another six students were instructed to malinger paranoid schizophrenia after coaching (i.e., reviewing a 25-minute audiotaped description of schizophrenia). The remaining six students were instructed to malinger paranoid schizophrenia without coaching (i.e., not reviewing an audiotaped description). Subsequently, 261 Fellows of the Society for Personality Assessment were sent one protocol from each group. These expert judges were asked to provide a psychiatric diagnosis, indicate their certainty of the diagnosis, rate protocols on eight dimensions of psychopathology, and indicate how likely it was that each protocol was malingered. Forty-six Fellows, who had been members of the Society for an average of 20.6 years, returned complete data. Based on their judgments, the uncoached simulators were diagnosed with psychosis as frequently as the inpatients with schizophrenia. Interestingly, the coached simulators were diagnosed as suffering from psychoses *more frequently* than the genuine patients. Regardless of their accuracy, the judges expressed equal confidence in their diagnostic judgments across participant groups. Their judgments of malingering did not differentiate between feigned and genuine protocols.

Exner (1978, 1991) criticized the Albert et al. (1980) study on three grounds: (1) The examiner was not masked to the participant condition (thereby posing the risk of experimenter bias); (2) records were not scored before sending them to the Fellows; and (3) no information regarding the judges' experience or their approach to interpretation was reported. The latter two limitations were addressed by the subsequent reanalysis of 3 protocols randomly selected from each group (Kahn, Fox, & Rhode, 1988). These 12 protocols were rescored using Exner's (1974) Comprehensive Scoring System, and the resulting scores were subjected to computer interpretation using a program developed by Exner (1985). Although the program was not designed to detect malingering, it does identify protocols as "questionably valid" or "invalid" based on the total number of responses. Only one protocol (by an inpatient with schizophrenia) was rejected by the computer program as invalid. Another three (one from each of the other groups) were identified as questionably valid. The program generated a total of 196 statements (74 different ones) for the 12 protocols. Five statements are designated as "psychotic quality descriptors." These statements include, for example, "possible schizophrenia," "marked deficit in perceptual accuracy," and "clear cognitive slippage." Analyzed in this fashion, no psychotic descriptors were generated by the normal protocols, and only one such descriptor was generated for the two valid schizophrenic protocols. In contrast, eight psychotic descriptors were found in the protocols of uncoached simulators, and 13 psychotic descriptors emerged from the protocols of the coached simulators. Thus, compared to the Fellows used in their 1980 study, the computer program misidentified fewer normal control participants as psychotic. However, the same program generated more psychotic quality descriptors for both groups of simulators than it did for the inpatients with schizophrenia. Although Cohen (1990) criticized Kahn et al. (1988) for equating protocol invalidity with malingering, neither he nor Exner (1978, 1991) discussed any other possible explanations of these negative results. One possibility is that even though participants faked paranoid schizophrenia while taking the Rorschach, the judges were unable to diagnose *malingering* based on the obtained protocols. Malingering can be identified only in the context of an obvious external incentive to produce or exaggerate symptoms. Thus, even if the judges suspected some symptom exaggeration, they would have been wrong to identify these protocols as malingered. The follow-up study by Kahn et al. (1988) showed that an actuarial method outperformed clinicians in the differentiation of normal adults and psychiatric inpatients, but their reanalysis could not remedy the failure to provide clinicians with the contextual information necessary to determine their sensitivity to malingering.

In contrast to earlier studies of feigned psychosis and general maladjustment, Meisner (1988) investigated whether participants could simulate depression on selected Rorschach variables. Nine of 67 undergraduate students were excluded because their MMPI Depression *T* scores exceeded 69, or they did not comply with the instructions. Of the remaining participants, 29 were given a written description of depression, instructed to appear severely depressed, and offered a $50 cash reward for the most convincing display of depression on the Rorschach and Beck Depression Inventory. Another 29 students served as controls and took the same tests under standard instructions. Comparison of their results revealed that the two groups differed significantly on 3 of 14 Rorschach scores examined, although the largest group difference was noted on the Beck Depression Inventory (i.e., an M of 24 for simulators compared to an M of 3.4 for nonclinical controls). On the Rorschach, fakers gave fewer responses overall, but more responses with Bl (blood) and Mor (morbid contents) than students who answered honestly. Because Meisner compared only those Rorschach scores with putative relevance to the diagnosis of depression, no indication of whether the two groups gave different numbers of Popular or poor form responses was given. In addition, no data were presented regarding whether experts would have perceived these simulators as mentally disordered, even if not depressed. Moreover, the study did not include a clinical criterion group, thus precluding the most relevant comparison of simulators to genuinely depressed patients.

Exner (1991) described the reanalysis of a dissertation study by Mittman (1983), in which 90 expert judges originally examined sets of six scored Rorschach protocols that were randomly selected from 30 protocols obtained from normal adults, inpatients with schizophrenia, inpatients with depression, and coached or uncoached simulators feigning schizophrenia. For the 91 judgments rendered on the protocols of uncoached simulators, Mittman found only 1 classified a simulator as malingering; 18 classified feigned protocols as normal, and the remaining 72 judgments diagnosed a mental disorder. The results for coached fakers were even worse: Of 90 judgments rendered, only one classified a simulator as malingering; four classified feigned protocols as normal, and the remaining 85 judgments diagnosed a mental disorder. Moreover, only 51 (57%) of 89 judgments rendered concerning the protocols of six patients with schizophrenia correctly diagnosed the presence of that condition. For the purposes of reanalysis, Exner (1991) reported that all 30 Rorschach protocols were rescored to include the revised Schizophrenia ($SCZI$), Depression ($DEPI$), and Coping Deficit (CDI) Indices. Although only 1 of the 12 simulators produced a revised $SCZI$ score of 6, suggesting a "strong" likelihood of schizophrenia, 6 of the 12 simulators produced critical scores on either the $DEPI$ or CDI or both. In short, Exner (1991) opined, "This partial reanalysis of Mittman's data yielded nothing that would alter the conclusion that, under some circumstances, nonpatient subjects may be able to approximate serious disturbance if set to do so" (p. 435).

Perry and Kinder (1992) were particularly concerned with how differences in the number of responses to the test stimuli affect statistical analyses of group differences on Rorschach scores. They administered the Rorschach to two groups of undergraduate students. Students in the experimental group were given a description of schizophrenia and then told to respond as if they suffered from this disorder. Students in the control condition received standard instructions. Group comparisons were based on only the first or second response to each card, depending on differences in response productivity between the two groups. After controlling for the number of responses, simulators produced higher scores on the $SCZI$, $WSum6$ (weighted sum of special scores), $X-\%$ (responses with poor form), and $M-\%$ (human percepts with poor form) than honest controls. The simulators also reported significantly fewer Popular responses and a lower

X+% (good form responses). Unfortunately, these investigators did not include a group of patients with schizophrenia, thereby precluding determination of whether the simulated protocols could be distinguished from those of genuine patients.

Frueh and Kinder (1994) used a criterion group of 20 Vietnam veterans diagnosed with posttraumatic stress disorder (PTSD) for comparison with an experimental group of 20 undergraduate students, who were given a brief description of PTSD and then instructed to "malinger the disorder" on all subsequent tests (i.e., Rorschach, Mississippi Scale for Combat-Related PTSD, and scales *L, F,* and *K* of the MMPI-2). In addition, a control group of 20 students, randomly selected from the undergraduate pool, was administered the same tests under standard instructions. No adjustment for group differences in total responses given was needed, as the groups were roughly equivalent in response productivity. The students instructed to fake PTSD produced significantly higher scores than genuine patients and student controls on several Rorschach measures, including *X*−%, *Lambda* (pure form responses), *SumC* (sum of color-determined responses), and the number of responses with *Dramatic* contents. The simulators produced fewer responses with good form (*X*+%) than the patients and normal participants. Group differences did not emerge on any of 17 other Rorschach measures, including *Mor* (morbid responses), *SCZI,* or *WSum6.*

Netter and Viglione (1994) recently reported a study in which 40 nonpatient adults were randomly assigned to a simulation or control group and administered a number of tests, including the Rorschach. After reading a description of schizophrenia, the simulators completed a questionnaire to assess their understanding of the illness. Then they were instructed to "convince the Rorschach examiner that they were indeed schizophrenic." The results of both groups were compared with those of 20 patients with schizophrenia. These three groups were compared on eight standard Rorschach measures, as well as reaction times, and two special scores developed by Viglione (1990): *derepressed contents* (responses that involve aggressive or morbid special scores), and *modified responses* (responses that the participant spoils or modifies by adding features with poor form quality, "rambling" about, or making comments that reflect personal distress). Although more simulators than patients with schizophrenia gave modified responses, this difference failed to reach statistical significance. Normal adults gave slightly (but not significantly) more responses involving derepressed contents than did simulators and actual patients. The most disappointing result was that 9 simulators (compared to 14 patients and 3 normal participants) scored 4 or more on the *SCZI.*[1] This finding suggests that 45% of the simulators would be classified, with a moderately high likelihood, as warranting the diagnosis of schizophrenia. Moreover, only 14 of the 20 patients with schizophrenia scored 4 or more on the *SCZI,* and this proportion was not significantly higher than the proportion of simulators who achieved this score. When *modified responses* were removed from the analysis, the modified *SCZI* yielded significant differences between all three groups. The simulators also displayed significantly longer reaction times than did those in the other two groups. Interestingly, larger group differences were noted on the Eckblad and Chapman (1983) Scale of Magical Thinking than on any Rorschach measure.

Ganellen, Wasyliw, Haywood, and Grossman (1996) classified a sample of 48 criminal defendants referred for pretrial competency evaluations as either suspected malingerers ($n = 13$) or honest responders ($n = 35$), based exclusively on whether their MMPI *F* scale *T* scores exceeded 90. Later examination of their Rorschach protocols revealed nonsignificant group differences in the number of responses, proportion of responses with good form (*X+*), poor form (*X–*), or unusual form (*Xu*), or the number or responses involving Special Scores (*Sum 6*), Level 2 special scores, and Deviant Responses (*DR*). Neither were group differences found for the proportion of defendants who produced critical scores on the *SCZI*. However, suspected malingerers did report more Dramatic Contents (i.e., Blood, Sex, Fire, Explosions, Morbidity, and Aggression) than the presumed honest defendants. As noted by Ganellen et al., the principal limitation of this archival study was its exclusive reliance of the MMPI *F* scale to determine whether defendants were malingering. Not only has the classification accuracy of this scale been shown to range markedly from 54% to 100%, but 8 of 18 studies found that higher *F*-scale cutting scores than used by Ganellen et al. are required for optimal classification (Berry, Baer, & Harris, 1991). Given this limitation of criterion validity, the findings reported by Ganellen et al. (1996) are difficult to interpret.

DEFENSIVENESS ON THE RORSCHACH

Few studies have examined the effects of defensive response sets, such as attempts to simulate good adjustment on the Rorschach. When Fosberg (1941) administered the Rorschach to 129 participants with instructions to make good and bad impressions, he found that basic structural features of the results were not altered, and that many test–retest correlations exceeded .80. Carp and Shavzin (1950) found that 20 participants similarly instructed to make good versus bad impressions on successive administrations of the Rorschach did produce group differences on some variables. In contrast, Seamons et al. (1981) found that prison inmates and patients instructed to appear normal and well adjusted gave more Popular responses and fewer responses containing *ep*-related variables, dramatic contents, and inappropriate combinations than when the same groups were instructed to appear mentally ill or psychotic. Unfortunately, the Carp and Shavzin (1950) and Seamons et al. (1981) studies share a common limitation: One cannot determine *which* response set ("good" vs. "bad" impression) was responsible for the observed effects. In an unpublished study, Exner and Sherman (1977) readministered the Rorschach to 10 patients with schizophrenia on the same day, after suggesting to the patients on an individual basis, that they probably could "improve" their test performance. Although the second records obtained from each patient generally differed from the first in terms of location scores, contents, and length, all 10 of the second records were judged as schizophrenic by three judges who were naïve to the purpose of the study. More recently, Exner (1991) described the protocols of 50 men and women who were administered the Rorschach during child-custody evaluations. Exner assumed that, "subjects involved in custody disputes would be prone to attempt simulation of very good adjustment" (1991, p. 429). Reportedly, over 50% of these individuals produced significant scores on the Intellectualization Index, 52% gave more than two PER (Personalized) responses, and 36% gave more than seven Popular responses. As an example of a differential prevalence design, Exner assumed that parents in child–custody cases would present themselves in the best possible light, which would be evidenced by obvious answers and efforts to represent themselves as unusually mature or sophisticated on testing. Because of the prevalence rate for social desirability in child–custody evaluations has not been established, the basis of this assumption remains untested.

Ganellen (1994) administered the Rorschach to 16 White commercial airline pilots, who were referred for psychological evaluation following inpatient treatment for an alcohol or substance abuse disorder. The pilots were assumed to have considerable incentive to respond defensively, as they were seeking reinstatements of their licenses.[2] Furthermore, every pilot had an elevation on at least one of four MMPI "indicators" of defensiveness. Unfortunately, Ganellen did not employ the most effective MMPI indicators of general defensiveness (see the meta-analysis by Baer, Wetter, & Berry, 1992) or any indicators of denied substance abuse (see Chapter 7). Ganellen hypothesized that the pilots would demonstrate defensiveness on the Rorschach in the form of fewer responses, a constricted response style (*Lambda* > 1), an increased number of conventional (Popular) responses, decreased effort (few Blend responses), reduced integration (*Zf*), and numerous Personalized responses (PER). Although Ganellen did not administer the Rorschach to a control group, these hypothesized differences were not observed in relation to normal adults, except on the number of PER responses (i.e., pilots, $M = 3.12$; normals, $M = 1.05$. Moreover, when Ganellen compared the MMPI profiles of his 16 "defensive" pilots to pilot applicants, the two groups produced "nearly identical" results (p. 429) on most MMPI validity and clinical scales. Two conclusions are evidenced from these findings: (1) Empirical support was provided for only one of six hypotheses, and (2) the categorization of defensiveness is open to question. At best, the number of PER responses as indicative of defensiveness requires fuller investigation.

In summary, no well-controlled Rorschach studies of defensiveness were found. However, the available data suggest that Rorschach test results are susceptible to distortion as a result of deliberate attempts by subjects to conceal psychopathology or present themselves in the best possible light. Without validated Rorschach indicators of defensiveness, psychologists may wish to consider alternative methods of assessment in cases in which defensiveness or social desirability appears to be at issue.

OTHER PROJECTIVE MEASURES

One widely used projective method of personality assessment involves asking patients to complete sentence stems using their own words. Despite the popularity of sentence completion tasks (SCT), their susceptibility to aberrant response sets has received little attention. Timmons, Lanyon, Almer, and Curran (1993) recently examined the responses of 51 psychiatric disability claimants to a 136-item SCT that was developed for use in psychiatric disability evaluations. The authors devised a rating scheme wherein every response is scored for each of 12 putative malingering characteristics. Examples of such characteristics include denigration of doctors, persecution/neglect, work focus, problem focus, claims of personal honesty, and lack of compliance with the disability determination system. Based on principal components analysis, three factors presumed to represent malingering strategies were identified: (1) angry negativity/no fair deal, (2) disability exaggeration/overinvestment, and (3) excessive virtue/honesty. Unfortunately, correlations between these SCT factor scores and various MMPI validity and clinical scale scores ranged from only .26 to .44. In a second study, 39 undergraduate students completed a shortened version of this SCT under each of four instructional sets. First they were instructed to simulate successful recovery from an accident. Then, before each of the next three administrations, students read a paragraph describing one of the three "malingering strategies" and were instructed to simulate persisting symptoms following a minor accident using that strategy. Although the students were able to alter their SCT factor scores in a manner that reflected the coaching they received, this study did not include a normal control group, a meaningful clinical comparison group, or a group of uncoached simulators. Consequently, whether this SCT and its available scoring strategy have any utility for the detection of feigning remains to be demonstrated.

Another common projective assessment technique is the Thematic Apperception Test (TAT), wherein examined persons compose stories in response to drawings shown to them. Kaplan and Eron (1965) administered 20 TAT cards to 72 naive (undergraduate) or sophisticated (graduate) students in psychology with instructions to respond honestly ($n = 36$) or as "aggressive, very hostile persons" ($n = 36$). Six measures with acceptable interrater reliability were examined. The results showed that the simulators modified their affect scores relative to honest respondents, and that the sophisticated students were able to feign more effectively than naive students. In two other studies, Young (1972) found that participants altered their TAT scores in response to the perceived expectations of examiners, whereas Hamsher and Farina (1967) found systematic differences in response to two instructional sets: (1) Be as open and revealing as possible; and (2) be as closed and guarded as possible. In summary, these studies clearly demonstrate the fakability of the TAT.

Holmes (1974) conducted two simulation studies of the TAT and different aspects of defensiveness. In the first study, 60 undergraduate students were instructed to either (1) simulate high achievement and motivation or (2) respond honestly. The results showed that students clearly modified their responses. In the second experiment, Holmes examined whether students could conceal overall personality traits, as opposed to only achievement and motivation. Again, the results revealed significant group differences in response to the two instructional sets, indicating an ability to conceal traits. Importantly, in both experiments, an independent clinician was unable to classify protocols as honest or defensive at a rate better than chance.

Another projective test that is similar to the Rorschach is the Holtzman Inkblot Technique. Kreiger and Levin (1976) administered an abbreviated form of this test to 23 patients with schizophrenia. The study was designed to investigate the effects of role expectations. Patients were administered the Holtzman twice: first, with the instructional set to respond as if they were hospital employees, and second, with the instructional set to respond as psychiatric patients. When the patients responded as if they were hospital employees, they produced scores that reflected less psychopathology than when they responded honestly as patients. Kreiger and Levin concluded that psychotic verbalizations and perceptual distortions on the Holtzman varied in response to role expectations.

Finally, Brozovich (1970) investigated whether normal adults could feign emotional disturbance on the Group Personality Projective Test (GPPT). The GPPT is a 90-item, multiple-choice task in which respondents view a scene and select the alternative that best describes what they believe is taking place. Brozovich administered the GPPT twice to 38 students, once with instructions to appear emotionally disturbed, and again 1 week later with instructions to appear well adjusted (i.e., respond defensively). The results showed that students did alter responses in accordance with the instructional sets. However, because this study did not include a normal control group or a clinical comparison group, one cannot determine *which* instructional set produced changes in the GPPT results, or whether any pattern of responses would distinguish between feigned and genuine protocols.

SUMMARY

Four Rorschach reports reviewed earlier involved relatively systematic clinical observations of suspected or "known" malingerers in military settings (Benton, 1945; Hunt, 1946; Rosenberg & Feldberg, 1944; Wachspress et al., 1953). These case reports describe the test-taking behaviors and results more thoroughly than they describe the illnesses or symptoms that were malingered. Despite the apparent heterogeneity of feigned illnesses and symptoms observed, some consistencies emerged on testing with the Rorschach. Suspected malingerers frequently gave few responses, showed prolonged reaction times, rejected more cards, failed to give the most Popular responses, asked repeated questions (or made comments) about the test, and showed an attitude of perplexity or pained compliance.

Case reports may be more informative about malingering than simulation studies that lack appropriate clinical comparison groups. The reason for this conclusion is that even if the latter studies are analyzed correctly, they cannot yield valid inferences about how well feigned and real psychopathology can be differentiated by using the Rorschach. Easton and Feigenbaum (1967), Feldman and Graley (1954), Seamons et al. (1981), Meisner (1988), and Perry and Kinder (1992) all demonstrated that nonpatient adults can deliberately alter their Rorschach test results. These investigators also reported provocative leads in the search for signs of malingering on the Rorschach. But their failure to include a clinical comparison group precludes drawing inferences about whether any signs of feigning that emerged from these studies would generalize to comparisons with bona fide patients. Moreover, unlike the case reports described earlier, none of these studies included suspected malingerers but relied instead on experimental simulators.

Other common methodological limitations include giving simulators global instructions to make their "worst impression," "fake bad," or "malinger" a mental disorder. With the possible exception of Meisner (1988), the participants who served in these studies also were not given any meaningful incentives to conceal their deception, further undermining the generalizability of the obtained findings. Despite their limitations, these studies disprove earlier claims that the Rorschach cannot be faked, as they present compelling evidence that individuals can deliberately alter their test results. These studies also provide some support for anecdotal reports that malingerers tend to give few responses overall, report few Popular responses, and provide an inordinate number of responses with morbid, aggressive, or dramatic contents.

Some of the best controlled studies reviewed earlier further suggest that individuals can produce Rorschach results that resemble those of patients who suffer from schizophrenia (Albert et al., 1980; Exner, 1991; Kahn et al., 1988; Netter & Viglione, 1994). The one study (i.e., Frueh & Kinder, 1994) to examine whether normal adults could simulate PTSD found that they generally were successful. In short, these findings converge on the conclusion that the Rorschach is susceptible to faking.

Whether simulators produce an identifiable pattern or "signature" that differentiates their protocols from those of patients who actually suffer from the relevant symptoms or disorder is another question. On this point, the data also are reasonably clear. No sign or constellation of signs reliably distinguishes the Rorschach protocols of persons faking schizophrenia from genuine patients. Some investigators have found that suspected malingerers or simulators feigning schizophrenia (or psychosis) reject more cards, give fewer Popular responses, and report more percepts that involve blood, morbidity, and bizarre contents, or that merit special scores (Bash & Alpert, 1980; Netter & Viglione, 1994; Seamons et al., 1981). In one particularly well-designed study that employed a multiple-choice version of the Rorschach, Pettigrew et al. (1983) found that adults simulating psychosis selected more responses involving bizarrely worded percepts with otherwise good form than either genuine patients or normal students answering honestly. Others (e.g., Exner, 1991; Netter & Viglione, 1994; Perry & Kinder, 1992), however, have found that simulators can produce abnormal findings on several Rorschach indices of psychotic thought disorder (*SCZI, WSum6*) and perceptual distortion (*X–%, M–%*).

Surprisingly few empirical studies examine how defensiveness affects Rorschach performance. The few published studies suggest that the Rorschach may be quite susceptible to deliberate distortion due to defensiveness and social desirability, at least among nonpsychotic individuals. Possible signs of defensiveness include many Popular responses, few (or no) responses with bizarre or dramatic contents, positive scores on the Intellectualization Index, and Personalized responses (Carp & Shavzin, 1950; Exner, 1991; Seamons et al., 1981).

Even more so than is the case with the Rorschach, the available data are insufficient to determine whether the SCT, TAT, Holtzman Inkblot Test, GPPT, or any other projective measure has promise as a means to assess malingering or defensiveness. Like the Rorschach, however, these other projective tests certainly appear to be susceptible to aberrant response sets and, in this sense, appear to be "fakable."

DIRECTIONS FOR FUTURE RESEARCH

Reviewers of this literature repeatedly have observed that investigators who use the Rorschach to study group differences must be cognizant of the fact that between-group differences in response productivity (R) can influence many other scores and indices derived from this test. This lack of independence among scores requires some form of experimenter control. Cronbach (1949) suggested three alternative strategies to control for this potential confound: (1) Rescore a fixed number of responses for each protocol; (2) construct subgroups that are equated on number of responses; and (3) analyze normalized scores. Others (Exner, Viglione, & Gillespie, 1984; Perry & Kinder, 1990) have suggested that statistical control can be obtained through partialing or residualizing scores. Of course, if experimental groups do not differ in response productivity (e.g., Frueh & Kinder, 1994), or if the experimental design calls for participant classification based on the idiographic review of protocols by experts (e.g., Albert et al., 1980; Bash & Alpert, 1980), the need for such experimenter control is obviated.

Dissimulation studies of projective methods are often imprecise in the presentation of instructional sets. Mentally disordered participants in within-subjects design should be given an honest condition (i.e., standard instructions), so that meaningful comparisons can be made. Moreover, simulation research should carefully adhere to established methods (see Chapter 19) for ensuring compliance and motivation.

THRESHOLD AND CLINICAL DECISION MODELS

Despite the recent publication of several excellent investigations of dissimulation on the Rorschach, Stermac's (1988) conclusion that the available findings preclude development of a clinical decision model to conclusively detect malingering is still valid. In fact, given the absence of a "signature" that reliably distinguishes faked or malingered protocols from those of patients who actually suffer from the targeted condition, any inference that a given Rorschach protocol contains findings that are indicative of malingering probably requires both an appropriate context (e.g., the presence of an external incentive to malinger) and independent factors that increase the likelihood of malingering (e.g., extreme elevations on fake-bad indicators of the MMPI-2; see Chapter 9). Thus, for individuals with external incentives to exaggerate psychiatric symptoms, and who show signs of symptom exaggeration on interview or other psychological tests, certain Rorschach findings probably can be interpreted as consistent with the *suspicion* of malingering.[3] Such findings at least signal the need for further investigation of possible malingering. At present, the available research findings do not allow for specific definitions or quantification of Rorschach malingering indicators, other than those shown in the Table 10.1. More precise specification of these indicators, and the development of heretofore unrecognized signs, must await future research.

TABLE 10.1. A Threshold Model for the Suspicion of Malingering on the Rorschach

Assuming the presence of an appropriate context and other factors that increase the likelihood of malingering, the following Rorschach signs are consistent with the inference of feigning:

1. Very few responses and/or frequent card rejections
2. A *marked* paucity of Popular responses (e.g., less than three)
3. Numerous responses with dramatic, morbid, or bizarre contents, particularly when they involve ordinary form quality
4. Repeated questions about the purpose of testing or an attitude of pained compliance

NOTES

1. The Schizophrenia Index was revised in 1989, thereby precluding direct comparisons with earlier studies.

2. This assumption is tenuous for those pilots who were successfully treated and had nothing to hide.

3. However, if the MMPI-2 (see Chapter 9) or a screening measure for feigning (see Chapter 17) is employed, an unresolved issue is whether the Rorschach adds incremental validity.

11

Malingering on Intellectual and Neuropsychological Measures

LOREN PANKRATZ, Ph.D.
LAURENCE M. BINDER, Ph.D.

When the first edition of this chapter was written in 1988, few professionals were concerned about the assessment of malingering on neuropsychological assessment. Malingering was then considered mostly a circumscribed problem in criminal forensic settings. More recently, psychologists and psychiatrists have become increasingly aware that feigning is observed in a wide range of settings with a spectrum of presentations, which include feigned cognitive and neuropsychological impairment. The current chapter documents these changes and summarizes the up-to-date literature on the assessment of feigned cognitive deficits.

The chapter is organized into five major components. First, we review the history of professional opinion about closed head injury, which has led to widely different conclusions about the veracity of patients' claims. Second, we address methodological concerns regarding the assessment of feigned cognitive deficits. Third, we examine key research findings on neuropsychological assessments and feigning. Fourth, we describe current assessment strategies for dissimulation in neuropsychological assessment. Fifth and finally, we suggest a threshold model for when malingering should be considered and a clinical decision model for confirming the classification.

HISTORICAL PERSPECTIVE

Influential English neurologist Henry Miller popularized the idea of accident or compensation neurosis. He based his conclusions on his observation of 4,000 patients that were examined for medical–legal assessment after accidents (Miller, 1961, 1966; Miller

& Cartlidge, 1972). Miller concluded that compensation neurosis and postconcussive symptoms existed in an inverse relationship to the severity of injury. Furthermore, he believed that symptoms were resolved only after court settlement, and that patients maintained their symptoms as long as the possibility of further compensation remained viable. Subsequently, many clinicians responded to brain-injured patients as if rehabilitation or intervention was useless until after legal settlement. Neurosurgeons were divided on the issue of whether the symptoms following head injury were chiefly related to organic, emotional, or compensation issues (Auerbach, Schefflen, & Scholz, 1967).

Some of Miller's clinical observations remain valid today for the detection of fraud. He appropriately focused the attention on the possibility of illness behavior, neurosis, and malingering; nevertheless, some of his assumptions about head injury are now known to be inaccurate. For example, his assumption that professionals engage in less compensation neurosis can be disputed by differences between professionals and nonprofessionals in personal control over their work demands and time schedules.

Binder's (1986) review questioned the basic premise of Miller regarding mild head injury and symptom presentation. Symptoms have been found consistently in head-injured persons not involved in compensation, and these symptoms are not necessarily resolved by settlement (Denker & Perry, 1954; Jacobson, 1969; Kelly, 1975; Merskey & Woodforde, 1972; Oddy, Humphrey, & Uttley, 1978; Wrightson & Gronwall, 1981).

By the 1980s, many neuropsychologists (see McMordie, 1988) held for the most part that damage secondary to mild head trauma had been vastly underrated. The sensitive instruments of neuropsychology were believed to demonstrate an array of deficits reflecting the underlying minor neuronal damage. The assumption that mild head trauma could cause significant cognitive problems was often bolstered by findings of cognitive deficits. The use of neuropsychology in the courts increased, because neuropsychologists could easily find abnormalities when no other evidence suggested their presence (Larrabee, 1992).

More recently, some experts believe that a small minority of mild head trauma patients may have mild organic problems with persistent symptoms (Alexander, 1995). However, both clinicians and researchers have difficulty in accurately identifying these patients because of their low base rates. Furthermore, a meta-analytic review showed that financial incentives play a significant role in disability after mild head trauma (Binder & Rohling, 1996).

METHODOLOGICAL CONCERNS IN THE ESTABLISHMENT OF FEIGNED AND GENUINE COGNITIVE DEFICITS

Normal Variation in Nonclinical Samples

In his American Psychological Association presidential address, Matarazzo (1990) noted that psychologists were hasty to offer opinions in court about brain injury without the continued professional patient–client responsibility common to standard practice. Matarazzo acknowledged that vigorous cross-examination in court had forced him to reconsider the scientific soundness of his opinions about brain injury. His analysis of the Wechsler Adult Intelligence Scale—Revised (WAIS-R) normative data revealed some sobering conclusions.

When Matarazzo (1990) analyzed the raw data from normal persons on which the WAIS-R was standardized, he found that differences between Performance IQ and Verbal IQ, although normally distributed around a mean difference of zero, actually showed a remarkably large standard deviation (11 points) and a range from −43 to +49 points. Two other differences were remarkable: (1) Normal individuals showed substantial scatter in subtest scores; and (2) test–retest differences were surprisingly variable. Thus, diagnoses of brain damage could not be based on intraindividual variability that was similarly found in normal persons. His conclusions were clear: First, clinicians too often rendered diagnosis of brain dysfunction; second, neuropsychological assessment was not a task for the uninformed or the inexperienced clinician.

Clinical studies showed that most patients with mild head injury had few severe sequelae (Levin, 1989, 1990). Some patients, however, seemed to display profound disability, especially in the context of seeking compensation. Were these patients malingering or were they displaying the normal variations of minor injury? In the face of this enigma, the question arises as to how malingerers can be identified by neuropsychologists. Research on the question has not been easy because of two methodological problems: the selection of participants, and the selection of measures.

Selection of Research Participants

Research on malingering is hampered by the same problem that plagues research on lie detection. The clinical researcher never knows whether a participant obtained from a clinical sample is suitable, because the participant may not be truthful. Researchers must rely either on a simulation design or known-groups comparison (Rogers, Harrell, & Liff, 1993; see Chapter 19). Both research designs have drawbacks.

Pankratz (1988) criticized research with simulators as problematic, because it is based on two common but incorrect assumptions: (1) that malingerers are normal people who cheat, and (2) that more intelligent persons are better cheaters. As an additional consideration, studies have shown that 10–20% of participants are unable or unwilling to simulate even when given incentives (Goebel, 1983; Heaton, Smith, Lehman, & Vogt, 1978; Rogers, 1988b). Some noncomplying participants report that they are too honest to fake or too motivated to do less than their best. Simulation research must exclude both noncompliant feigners and dissimulating patients/controls.

One successful simulator in Goebel's study reported that her strategy was to "lie a lot . . . play dumb, try to appear frustrated, keep getting fidgety" (p. 70). Her strategy, which successfully eluded detection, did not rely on her having an intellectual understanding of brain–behavior relationships. She was simply able to play the role of malingerer better than others; no evidence exists that this skill is dependent upon IQ (Iverson, 1995).

Given the proper circumstances, ordinary people can be convincing liars (DePaulo, Stone, & Lassiter, 1985; Ekman, 1985). However, some dishonest persons have practiced certain skills sufficiently to make them highly successful (Ekman, Freisen, & O'Sullivan, 1988; Exline, Thibaut, Hickey, & Gumpert, 1970). We believe that many malingerers are practiced deceivers who happen upon an opportunity. For this reason, college students are probably not the best participants for simulation studies, because they have less experience in interacting with (and deceiving) health care professionals.

On the other hand, selecting a "known group" for the study of malingering also presents methodological problems. Known malingerers are hard to identify because of low diagnostic sensitivity and interclinician agreement (Rogers, 1990a). As previously noted, confusion about how much behavior change may be created by minor head injury has compounded problems in the classification of feigned cognitive deficits. The crucial issue remains on how to identify known malingerers. One alternative proposed by Greiffenstein, Baker, and Gola (1994) was to operationalize malingering of cognitive deficits as meeting two or more of the following criteria: (1) two or more severe impairment ratings on neuropsychological tests, (2) an improbable history of symptoms, (3) total disability in work or social role, or (4) claims of remote memory loss. Although reasonable, the danger of misclassification is apparent in their circularity of definition. Further work is needed to augment our understanding of normal sequelae of mild brain injury, allowing better definitions and identification of groups in which malingerers might be found (Levin, 1989, 1990).

KEY RESEARCH FINDINGS

Accuracy of Neuropsychologists

Early studies attempted to separate malingerers from brain-injured patients on the basis of standard neuropsychological tests and batteries. Given only raw data, neuropsychologists were unable to make impressive predictions. For example, the hit rate in the classic study by Heaton et al. (1978) ranged from chance to 20% above chance. Even worse, Faust, Hart, and Guilmette (1988) found that not one of 42 neuropsychologists identified malingering after examining the test profiles of children who were instructed to fake brain injury. In fact, about three-fourths of the neuropsychologists indicated moderate or greater confidence in their wrong conclusions. One explanation for these disappointing results is that the neuropsychologists did not find malingering because they did not consider it in their differential diagnosis. More recently, Trueblood and Binder (1995) forewarned neuropsychologists in a study that involved feigned cognitive deficits; clinicians were highly accurate in distinguishing malingering from traumatic brain injury.

Assessment of Motivation to Malinger

Binder (1990) described a small series of patients who showed evidence of malingering on forced-choice testing as well as other neuropsychological measures. Binder and Willis (1991) found that mild head trauma patients with financial incentive performed worse on a forced-choice test than patients who had well-documented brain dysfunction. Binder (1993) extended this finding to a larger series of patients and found that one-third of the mild head trauma patients seeking benefits evidenced very poor performance.

Millis (1992) found that participants with claims of mild head injury, as a basis for seeking financial compensation, obtained significantly lower scores on both subtests of the Recognition Memory Test than did rehabilitation inpatients with documented moderate and severe traumatic brain injuries. A replication study (Millis & Putnam, 1994) tested 20 additional participants, all of whom sought compensation for alleged vocational disability. All participants had either brief loss or no loss of consciousness, normal radiographic findings, and no focal neurological deficits. These patients scored significantly lower than a brain-injured group ($n = 66$) who were not seeking compensation. A cross-validation discriminant function yielded an overall correct classification rate of 83%.

Several additional studies have confirmed these findings that some persons with external incentives produce very poor performances on neuropsychological measures. For example, Youngjohn, Burrows, and Erdal (1995) evaluated 55 consecutive patients with persisting postconcussion syndrome that were pursuing or receiving financial compensation. Almost half evidenced very poor performance on the Portland Digit Recognition Test (PDRT), with only 28% performing as well as noncompensated brain-injured patients. Guilmette, Whelihan, Sparadeo, and Buongiorno (1994) evaluated 50 consecutive outpatients referred for Social Security evaluations that had either complaints or neuropathological conditions that suggested cognitive deficits. Using a forced-choice digit-recognition test developed by Hiscock and Hiscock (1989), they concluded that one-fifth of the claimants produced invalid and uninterpretable neuropsychological test protocols, and an additional one-fifth produced protocols that were questionable because of poor effort.

Greiffenstein et al. (1994) studied 73 postconcussive patients with chronic complaints and identified 43 individuals (58.9%) with overt signs of malingering. Examination of their test results showed no differences in the scores of probable malingerers and patients with serious traumatic brain injury on such measures of recall as the Wechsler scales and the Rey Auditory Verbal Learning Test. In contrast, four of five apparent malingering measures appeared to differentiate probable malingerers from other patients with either chronic postconcussive complaints or serious traumatic brain injury. Importantly, this study showed that on standard tests of mental functioning, malingerers can produce scores similar to those of patients with serious brain injury.

In summary, strong external incentives appear to be linked with poor performances in a substantial number of cases. In this brief review, approximate range was 20–60% of the patients with mild head injury and financial incentives had improbably poor performances. In the next section, we examine strategies to identify persons feigning cognitive deficits.

ASSESSMENT OF FEIGNED COGNITIVE DEFICITS

Standard neuropsychological assessment involves review of medical records, psychological interview, and testing. Test results are then compared with the patient's symptoms and history. When questions of malingering arise, assessment should focus on the issue of cooperation as soon as possible. As we have already indicated, forced-choice testing assesses the patient's effort and provides a measure of cooperation within the assessment. Extremely poor performances are indicative of malingering. Because of their efficacy, we begin with a discussion of forced-choice strategies.

Forced-Choice Testing

In a series of case studies, Pankratz and his colleagues demonstrated that forced-choice techniques were an effective means of assessing questionable sensory deficits, such as deafness, blindness, color blindness, tunnel vision, blurry vision, deafness, tactile anesthesias, and paresthesias (Pankratz, 1979; Pankratz, Binder, & Wilcox, 1987; Pankratz, Fausti, & Peed, 1975). In 1983, Pankratz suggested that forced-choice strategies could clarify neuropsychological issues, such as questions of feigned memory complaints. Binder and Pankratz (1987) further documented the ability of forced-choice testing to assess feigned memory impairment in a case study. Originally these techniques were called "symptom validity assessment" (SVT; Pankratz, 1988), but we now prefer the more generic term "forced-choice testing."

Forced-choice testing is composed of two elements: (1) A specific ability is assessed by a large number of items presented in a multiple-choice format; and (2) a person's performance is compared to the likelihood of success based on chance alone (i.e., no ability). All widely used forced-choice tests have two multiple-choice alternatives; therefore, the probability of purely guessing (i.e., analogous to no ability whatsoever) the correct response is 50%. Scores significantly lower than chance performance suggest that sensory cues must have been perceived, but the patient chose not to report the correct answer; other viable explanations are not apparent (Rogers, Harrell, & Liff, 1993). The compelling conclusion is that the patient who scores below probabilities is deliberately motivated to perform poorly. The conclusion of malingering, however, must be derived from the total clinical context (Frederick, Sarfaty, Johnston, & Powel, 1994).

Development of Standardized Forced-Choice Tests

Hiscock and Hiscock (1989) proposed an important modification of forced-choice testing by increasing levels of apparent difficulty on a digit-recognition task. In turn, the Hiscock procedure was modified into the Portland Digit Recognition Test (PDRT; Binder, 1990; Binder & Willis, 1991). The PDRT augmented the Hiscock procedure by the addition of a distracting mental activity between the presentation of the stimulus to be remembered and the recognition probe. As with the Hiscock test, the patient is led to believe that the task increases in difficulty; this supposed gradation in difficulty presents patients who want to demonstrate a disability with an obvious opportunity to exaggerate or fabricate their deficit.

Binder and Willis (1991) provided validation of the PDRT by testing six groups of adults. Three of the groups had no financial incentives, and one nonpatient group was instructed to simulate brain injury. Two additional groups had real-life incentives to appear damaged, one with minor head trauma and one with documented brain dysfunction. The most relevant group for comparison was the one whose members had brain dysfunction but were not seeking compensation and, thus, had no financial incentive for impairment. Most members of this group had suffered moderate or severe traumatic brain injury or EEG-verified medically intractable epilepsy.

The group with brain dysfunction and no financial incentives performed similarly to the group of patients with mood disorders, and both of these groups performed in a manner significantly superior to that of the two compensation-seeking groups as well as a group of nonclinical simulators. Patients with minor head trauma who were seeking compensation were, on the other hand, significantly worse than the groups that were either not seeking compensation or responding under simulation instructions.

This study provided cutting scores that enabled examiners to assess more accurately the motivation to perform poorly. Because it was no longer necessary to rely solely on scores significantly below a chance performance, less extreme scores could be used with greater sensitivity to identify potential malingerers. The cutting scores representing the lower limit of brain-dysfunction performance were replicated in another, larger sample (Binder & Kelly, 1996). Some of these patients were from an acute traumatic brain-injury rehabilitation unit at Montebello Rehabilitation Hospital in Baltimore. Thus, the cutting scores used to identify patients without financial incentive and diagnosed with mild to severe brain dysfunction have been cross-validated in multiple sites. The worst performance based on 120 brain-dysfunction participants was 39 of 72 items correct (i.e., 54.2%); the second worst performance was 42 of 72 items correct (i.e., 58.3%).

Studies of the Hiscock forced-choice procedure (Guilmette, Hart, & Giulianao, 1993; Prigatano & Amin, 1993) have suggested that, of the two, the PDRT is more difficult for genuine patients, although no direct comparisons have been conducted. Brain-dysfunction patients average about 95% correct responses on the Hiscock compared with approximately 80% correct on the PDRT. The distraction task on the PDRT probably accounts for the difference in difficulty.

The difference in difficulty between the Hiscock and the PDRT may have clinical implications. The PDRT may yield more frequently performances that are significantly statistically worse than chance; such performances provide the most persuasive psychometric evidence of malingering to clinicians (Trueblood & Binder, 1995). Although no clearly defined cutting scores are yet available for the Hiscock, they are likely to be established. We anticipate that these cutting scores may be so high that a person attempting to malinger will have a very narrow window through which to avoid detection on the Hiscock.

Although the PDRT has reliable cutting scores, it takes longer to administer than the Hiscock test. To shorten the administration time of these tests, an abbreviated version of the PDRT has been developed (Binder, 1993). In addition, a computerized version of the PDRT has been developed, which has the additional advantage of being able to measure response latency (Rose, Hall, & Szalda-Petree, 1995); however, it is not commercially available. A computerized version of the Hiscock Forced-Choice Procedure called the Multi Digit Memory Test is available.

The Recognition Memory Test, a standard neuropsychological test, has also been utilized as a forced-choice test (Millis, 1992; Millis & Putnam, 1994). It has the advantage of validly measuring verbal and visual recognition memory in the patient who is well motivated. Cutting scores have been tentatively established below which patients with a history of traumatic brain injury typically do not fall (Iverson & Franzen, 1994). Its length of 50 visual items and 50 verbal items is sufficient for establishing binomial probabilities with patients who perform worse than chance.

The 21-Item Test (Iverson, Franzen, & McCracken, 1994) is a shorter forced-choice task. On this test, the recognition section is more effective than the recall task for the discrimination of malingering. However, the test's brevity decreases the probability of obtaining statistical significance in patients performing worse than chance.

Rogers, Harrell, and Liff (1993) noted that the main limitation of forced-choice testing is the relatively small proportion of simulators that score below binomial probabilities (see also Binder & Kelly, 1996; Iverson & Franzen, 1994; Slick, Hopp, Strauss, Hunter, & Pinch, 1994). However, below-chance performances provide the most convincing data of feigned cognitive deficits. The establishment of cutting scores and discriminant functions has now greatly enhanced the sensitivity of forced-choice tests in which scores exceed chance but are below scores found in clinical populations (Binder, 1993; Millis & Putman, 1994).

Other Tests for Malingering

Several authors have reviewed the strategies (Rogers, Harrell, & Liff, 1993) and tests used in the assessment of malingering (Binder, 1992; Franzen, Iverson, & McCracken, 1990; Haines & Norris, 1995; Lezak, 1995; Zielinski, 1994). Tests that appear difficult but are actually easy to perform are probably the best measures of motivation (Bernard, Huston, & Natoli, 1993). For example, Rey's 15-Item Test (Rey-15) presumes that 15 items represent a difficult memory task, although the grouping of items simplifies this task. Cutting scores have been suggested at seven or fewer correct (Guilmette, Whelihan, et al., 1994; Lee, Loring, & Martin, 1992) or less than two rows (Arnett, Hammeke, & Schwartz, 1995). A normal performance, therefore, does not rule out malingering, but the test frequently results in false positives (i.e., classifying genuine patients as malingerers). Because of its ease of administration, the Rey-15 may be used as a simple screen, although its modest sensitivity and specificity argues against relying solely on this method.

Recognition versus Recall

Because performance on recognition tasks is easier than recall, the Rey Auditory Verbal Learning Test recognition task is useful for the assessment of malingering. Scores of less than six correct occur much more frequently in patients with mild head injuries and financial incentives than in patients without financial incentives and significant brain dysfunction (Binder, Villanueva, Howieson, & Moore, 1993). Similarly, low scores on the recognition task of the California Verbal Learning Test (Millis, Putnam,

Adams, & Ricker, 1995) and the Memory Assessment Scales (Beetar & Williams, 1995) also appear useful.

Performance Curve

Some malingerers have problems achieving the expected proportion of correct responses as the item difficulty increases. They often fail a more-than-expected proportion of easy items, given their performance on difficult items (Frederick & Foster, 1991). Gronwall and Wrightson (1974) suggested that the Paced Auditory Serial-Addition Test might be helpful for detecting poor motivation if performance was better on harder trials than on easier trials. However, Strauss, Spellacy, Hunter, and Berry (1994) found that the test weakly discriminated simulators from brain-injured patients. More promising results were found on the Raven's matrices, comparing performance on Sets A and B with Sets D and E (Gudjonsson & Shackleton, 1986). Although no longer commercially available, Frederick and Foster (1991) adapted the Test of Nonverbal Intelligence (TONI) as a forced-choice test of feigned intellectual abilities; they found that the performance curve, in conjunction participants' consistency, proved to be highly effective in distinguishing simulators from genuine patients.

Qualitative Differences

Qualitative aspects of performance are also an important part of the assessment process. Using the Bender–Gestalt, Bruhn and Reed (1975) found that college student participants could not successfully produce the deficits of patients with brain injury. Their guidelines for detection included the following propositions: (1) brain-injured patients simplify drawings; (2) distortions recur in similar designs; (3) brain-injured patients will be consistent in their performance at similar difficulty levels; and (4) brain-injured individuals make specific rotations and responses (e.g., difficulty with the intersection on card 6). Qualitative distortions on the Bender–Gestalt were also identified by Schretlen, Wilkins, Van Gorp, and Bobholz (1992).

Rawling and Brooks (1990) identified errors specific to patients with head injury (duration of posttraumatic amnesia for at least 2 weeks) and presumed simulators (patients pursuing claims, whose posttraumatic amnesia lasted 24 hours or less). When tested on the WAIS-R and the Wechsler Memory Scale (WMS), the simulation group tended to perform worse on most variables, but none approximated statistical significance. However, Rawling and Brooks identified 15 signs specific to the simulators and 5 associated with the head-injured patients. Based on errors specific to each group, the authors developed a Simulation Index. In a subsequent validation study, the specificity of the Simulation Index was insufficient for clinical use (Milanovich, Axelrod, & Millis, 1996).

Atypical Performance

Mittenberg, Azrin, Millsaps, and Heilbronner (1993) addressed feigned problems with attention and concentration on the Wechsler Memory Scale—Revised (WMS-R).

Simulators averaged two standard deviations below normal on an attention/concentration index score but were only one standard deviation below normal on a general memory index score. If the general memory index exceeded the concentration/attention index by 25 points or more, the probability of simulation was .85. Individuals with a severely impaired attention span usually should not demonstrate a less impaired overall memory.

Some malingerers fake deficits on certain subtests while maintaining few decrements in estimates of overall functioning. For example, malingerers may demonstrate severe deficits on simple measures of manual dexterity and tactile sensation (Binder & Willis, 1991; Heaton et al., 1978). Compared with head trauma patients, simulators have greater deficits on measure such as the Speech-Sounds Perception Test, finger tapping, finger localization, grip strength, and sensory extinctions. Consequently, atypical performances may signal the possibility of feigning.

Marked Inconsistencies

Gross discrepancies between what is expected after an injury and what is reported or observed on testing require explanation. Within broad parameters, the severity of neuropsychological deficits can be predicted from knowledge of the acute brain injury. Mild head injury, one of the most common forms of compensable injury seen by neuropsychologists, has a predictable outcome. Within several weeks of mild head injury, the subjective complaints normally outweigh the objective cognitive deficits (Dikmen, Machamer, Winn, & Temkin, 1995; Dikmen, Ross, Machamer, & Temkin, 1995; Levin & Grossman, 1978). Brain damage in the form of contusions and diffuse axonal injury can clearly be present acutely. Mild or even moderate neuropsychological deficits might be observed within a few weeks of seemingly mild head injury, but substantial improvement likely will occur in the first 3 months. Indeed, controlled studies show little evidence of cognitive deficits persisting beyond the first few weeks. The deficits of mildly injured patients will, at their worst, be comparable to the more fully recovered moderate to severe head-injured patient. Expertise and experience with brain-injured patients increases the knowledge of the expected course of recovery for specific patients.

The neuropsychologist can identify inconsistent response patterns that are suggestive of malingering. For example, severe slowing on finger tapping (scores less than 50% of the mean for most age groups) is probably inconsistent with normal performance on Digit Symbol, a measure of graphomotor speed. In addition, missing easy items on tests that measure previously acquired verbal or visual skills would be inconsistent with most forms of brain damage and cases of mental retardation (Schretlen, 1988). Bizarre responses are noteworthy but lack sensitivity, because they occur with low frequency (Trueblood, 1994).

In summary, the clinician should attend to the possibility of malingering anytime financial issues or other external incentives are present. Sometimes untruthfulness and exaggeration can be detected within the diagnostic interview; however, more likely sources of suspicion will arise from the medical records, tests of motivation, and other discrepancies between the injury and test results. Knowledge of neuropsychological syndromes enables the clinician to make predictions about deficits from information about the acute injury. However, the presence of an organic disorder does not rule out malingering. Similarly, the diagnosis of factitious disorder is not dependent on the medical findings but on evidence that the patient unnecessarily maintains him- or herself in the sick role.

Malingering on testing does not preclude the possibility of genuine neuropsychological deficits. However, it may be impossible to assess the extent of real neuropsychological deficits in a patient who is poorly motivated. Just as the MMPI clinical scales should not be interpreted with an invalid profile (Greene, 1988a), the interpretation of neuropsychological deficits should stop once the diagnosis of malingering has been made. Instead, an estimate of the patient's functioning can be attempted from knowledge of the severity of the brain injury as assessed by neurological and neuroradiological findings. Neuropsychological assessment describes patient functioning only when the patient has cooperated completely on tests administered in a standard protocol.

THRESHOLD AND CLINICAL DECISION MODELS

Threshold Model

The threshold criteria for suspecting dissimulation should be set relatively low so that cases of possible malingering are fully evaluated. Obviously, the setting or context for neuropsychological evaluation should be considered as well. A survey of psychologists and neurosurgeons revealed that most believe financial incentives play some role in the postconcussive syndrome (McMordie, 1988). Yet, many clinicians fail to appreciate the energy that some patients expend in an attempt to obtain disability pensions so they will no longer have to work. In this vein, a sampling of reports in civil forensic cases (see Lees-Haley, Smith, Williams, & Dunn, 1996) suggested that most neuropsychologists do not administer specialized measures for the possible identification of malingered cognitive deficits.

Table 11.1 presents some specific threshold issues for considering the possibility of malingering in neuropsychological assessment. Lying and other forms of deception clearly suggests the possibility of malingering. The patient who is untruthful about autobiographical details may be untruthful about symptoms as well. Information should

TABLE 11.1. Threshold Model of Malingered Neuropsychological Impairment

Any of the following factors suggest the possibility of malingering:

1. Lying to health care providers
2. Marked inconsistency between present diagnosis and neuropsychological findings
3. Marked inconsistency between reported and observed symptoms
4. Resistance, avoidance, or bizarre responses on standard tests
5. Failure on any specific measure of neuropsychological faking
6. Functional findings on orthopedic or neurological exams
7. Late onset of cognitive complaints following an accident

be checked for accuracy, including military history, school achievement, athletic accomplishments, employment, and significant losses.

Marked inconsistencies and discrepancies also signal the need for a full investigation of possible malingering. Likewise, atypical presentations are a cause for concern. For example, delayed onset of neuropsychological symptoms following an accident suggests the possibility of malingering. Bizarre responses or a lack of cooperation must also be considered. In addition, reports of the patient's neurological and orthopedic examinations should be scrutinized for mention of functional findings, marked pain behavior, and varying presentations of the past medical history.

Unusual or unexpected findings, on the other hand, do not necessarily represent malingering. However, once any threshold criterion has been met, the clinician must evaluate the meaning of unexpected findings. Neuropsychological assessment depends on highly specific, normative information, collected in precise ways that elicits the patient's best effort. Once questions of malingering arise, less experienced clinicians should probably discontinue neuropsychological assessment and describe the results as invalid or possibly invalid. Patients can be needlessly overexposed to test material, compromising future assessment. Some experienced clinicians may prefer to give a lengthy test battery to assess more thoroughly the possibility of malingering or other nonorganic diagnoses. When tests have been repeated over time, unexpected findings, such as deteriorating performance in the absence of complicating conditions, will suggest malingering.

Clinical Decision Model

The purpose of a clinical decision model is the establishment of empirically validated cutting scores for effectively classifying malingerers of cognitive impairment. Given the current status of research, a formal clinical decision model is not feasible. Instead, we discuss broad dimensions that must be considered in making this determination.

In neuropsychological assessment, as with other assessments, a full range of medical, cognitive, and psychiatric possibilities must be evaluated. Because neuropsychological measurements require the patient's cooperation, the clinician should focus on motivation throughout the assessment process. Malingering (e.g., deliberate attempts to feign cognitive deficits) must be differentiated from other examples of suboptimal motivation (e.g., decreased interest due to depression). The following issues must be considered.

- Are the scores influenced by a medical condition?
- Are the scores consistent with a mental disorder?
- Are there other contextual issues to rule out malingering?

Medical Conditions

Norms of neuropsychological tests are usually established on patients without complicating medical problems. By necessity, we must often test patients when they are sick and taking prescribed medications that affect the central nervous system. Unusual or unlikely scores may be artifacts of individuals having been tested while sick or on psychoactive medications. Although a vast number of medical conditions may cause cognitive problems, they are usually easy to distinguish from malingering. Nonacute medical conditions cause nonspecific problems with memory, thinking speed, and attention; they do not cause problems with motivational measures.

Mental Disorders

To diagnose a mental disorder, it is necessary to show that the fourth edition of the *Diagnostic and Statistical Manual of Mental Disorders* (DSM-IV) inclusion criteria are met and that no other explanation provides a better understanding of the symptoms. The classification of malingering is determined when symptoms occur in a context of obtaining external incentives, and the symptoms are not otherwise understandable. Thus, the important task is to rule out alternative explanations, including factitious disorders and genuine disorders.

Malingering implies that the symptoms do not arise from a mental disorder. However, mental disorders may affect the ability to follow directions and give optimal performance. For example, depression may decrease scores on timed tests, although other tests may be unaffected (e.g., word association measures of verbal fluency; Hawkins et al., 1995). Naturally, clinicians will need to evaluate the genuineness of psychological symptoms in persons for whom feigned cognitive deficits are suspected.

Malingering is sometimes confused with other disorders associated with deception, namely drug seeking (Pankratz, Hickam, & Toth, 1989), factitious disorders (Reich & Gottfried, 1983), hospital wanderers (Pankratz & Jackson, 1994), and difficult patients with characterological problems (Emerson, Pankratz, Joos, & Smith, 1994). A history of head injury may also be associated with psychological disorders; common disorders are PTSD and depression (Ruff, Wylie, & Tennant, 1993). Again, a thorough differential diagnosis is essential (see Chapter 2 for an overview).

Other Contextual Issues

The patient's performance on tests can be greatly influenced by social factors, belief systems, and emotional states. Instances of mass hysteria illustrate how symptoms can be produced in the context of an emotionally charged social context (Olkinuora, 1984). Although symptoms can seize quite ordinary persons, psychological and social stress can predispose certain individuals (Small & Nicholi, 1982).

Patients sometimes try to convince the examiner that they have significant problems that warrant treatment and fear these problems might be overlooked (Iverson, 1995). Such fears can lead to exaggerations that border on the hypochondriacal (Gottfried & Reich, 1983). "Sick building syndromes" and toxic chemical exposures can lead to wildly variant neurological-type symptoms. Clinicians must gather information carefully and discourage spurious self-victimization (Brewin, Andrews, & Gotlib, 1993; Lees-Haley & Brown, 1992; Rothman & Weintraub, 1995).

The role of diagnostician includes responsibilities to the patient and the broader society. Some patients will lose respect and personal freedoms from the diagnosis of brain dysfunction; for others, the classification of malingering has serious consequences as well. Although some have debated the usefulness of the malingering classification (see Pankratz & Erickson, 1990), we believe that clinicians must strive for accuracy. Sensitive clinical skills are necessary to provide feedback about diagnostic conclusions, and sometimes it will be in the best interest of the patient to provide mental health support (Binder & Thompson, 1995).

III

SPECIALIZED METHODS

12

Drug-Assisted Interviews to Detect Malingering and Deception

RICHARD ROGERS, Ph.D.
ROBERT M. WETTSTEIN, M.D.

The use of barbiturate-facilitated interviews as an avenue to truth has had a long and colorful history. Beginning in the 1930s, case studies began to appear that advocated the use of sodium amytal (amobarbital) in the treatment of highly agitated patients and the elicitation of suppressed and repressed material (Bohn, 1932; Horsley, 1936; Lindemann, 1932). Contemporaneous with these early investigations, Lorenz (1932) advocated the use of barbiturate-assisted interviews to uncover the truth in criminal investigations. Since that time, drug-assisted interviews have been employed for such diverse purposes as abreactions in dissociative or posttraumatic mental disorders, diagnosis of organic and functional psychoses, treatment of war neuroses and conversion reactions, investigation of amnesia, and examination of possible deception (Kwentus, 1981; Naples & Hackett, 1978; Perry & Jacobs, 1982). This chapter briefly reviews empirical studies of drug-assisted interviews and relates their findings to the clinical literature on drug interviews and deception.

Dysken, Chang, Casper, and Davis (1979) conducted a comprehensive review of case studies and empirical research from 1930 to 1974. Across 55 studies, the authors found that most research lacked the methodological rigor of more recent research. For example, studies were rarely double-blind with random assignment of research participants. In addition, the dosage levels varied remarkably across studies from 100 to 1,500 mg per interview. Interestingly, the review found that each of the 55 investigations had reported some value for drug-assisted interviews in diagnosis and treatment of psychiatric patients. Because of the lack of experimental rigor, Dysken and his colleagues recommended that the use of barbiturates be limited to (1) mobilizing catatonic patients, (2) the diagnosis of intellectual impairment, and (3) lessening negative affect associated with trauma.

More rigorous research has examined the use of barbiturates and other psychoactive substances in facilitating diagnostic inquiry. It is important to emphasize that these studies have made no attempt to investigate systematically the therapeutic value of drug-assisted interviews or their efficacy in the assessment of deception. Hain and his colleagues from the University of Virginia (Hain, Smith, & Stevenson, 1966) conducted the first controlled studies of amobarbital, comparing its results to hydroxydione (an anesthetic), methamphetamine, and a saline placebo. A sample of 49 nonpsychotic psychiatric patients, previously known to the investigators, were administered one of these four substances in a double-blind procedure. Based on a 60-minute drug-assisted interview, patients did not differ in their rate or amount of speech, desuppression, or derepression across drug conditions. Patients with hydroxydione had more difficulty with speech, less anxiety, and decreased attentionality in comparison with the other conditions. Patients with methamphetamine experienced the most anxiety and the highest degree of attentiveness. Patients in the amobarbital condition tended to fall in the intermediate range on these variables. Results of a 24-hour postinterview survey suggested that more changes in perception resulted from the methamphetamine than other conditions, although such changes appear relatively balanced between positive and negative effects. The investigators further acknowledged that the use of conservative dosages of medications may have minimized drug effects across conditions. Despite further analysis of these results (Smith, Hain, & Stevenson, 1970; Stevenson, Buckman, Smith, & Hain, 1974), the usefulness of these techniques in eliciting suppressed or repressed materials failed to be demonstrated.

Buckman, Hain, Smith, and Stevenson (1973), in an attempt to explain the disappointing results in previous research, decided to modify their earlier research design. Succinctly put, they decided to sacrifice some methodological rigor for increased clinical relevance (see Chapter 19). In order to parallel more closely clinical practice, they removed the double-blind safeguard and the standardized dosage. However, patients and observers responsible for the ratings remained masked to experimental condition. Despite these modifications, the results suggested few changes because of either amytal or an amytal–amphetamine combination. Surprisingly, the dosages of amytal remained relatively stable, despite the general lack of observed changes.[1] The very modest group size ($n = 8$) may also explain nonsignificant results.

Dysken and his associates (Dysken, Kooser, Haraszti, & Davis, 1979) conducted a double-blind study in which 20 nonmedicated, newly admitted inpatients were administered amobarbital and placebo interviews in a counterbalanced, within-subjects design. A statistically nonsignificant trend was observed for the drug condition in eliciting additional information. The authors concluded that amobarbital interviews were no more effective than placebo interviews in eliciting symptoms of schizophrenia and depression. Interestingly, they noted its diagnostic usefulness with a catatonic schizophrenic patient who responded specifically to the amobarbital interview.

Amytal may also be useful in the assessment of catatonic conditions. McCall, Shelp, and McDonald (1992) conducted a randomized double-blind trial of amobarbital in 20 inpatients with catatonic mutism, the only trial of its kind. Six of the 10 patients who initially received a 10-minute infusion of amobarbital were judged as having definitely responded to it. No patients who were infused with saline responded to that intervention, but four of these saline nonresponders subsequently responded to amobarbital when crossed over to that condition. In all, 50% of the patients responded to amobarbital and none to saline.

In contrast to these experimental designs, Marcos, Goldberg, Feazell, and Wilner (1977), in an uncontrolled study of 31 uncommunicative and negativistic inpatients, found high-positive results in establishing rapport and eliciting previously unreported symptomatology. Such marked discrepancies between positive outcomes of uncontrolled studies and the relatively negative results of a few experimental studies has yet to be adequately explained. One likely explanation is that the uncontrolled studies, although lacking in methodological rigor, are addressing more relevant cases. Logically, it is unreasonable to expect that any technique might elicit much new information in patients who do not have substantial repression and suppression.

DRUG-ASSISTED INTERVIEWS AND DISSIMULATION

Research on the effectiveness of drug-assisted interviews in the assessment of malingering generally has been limited to a handful of case studies. The emphasis of the following discussion will, therefore, be primarily on the clinical literature as it relates more generally to dissimulation. Issues addressed under the rubric of dissimulation and drug-assisted interviews are (1) fakability of sedation, (2) suggestibility under sedation, (3) degree of control over self-report under sedation, and (4) confabulation and the emergence of new symptoms.

No research has been undertaken to examine the fakability of sedation in drug-assisted interviews. Since dosages of amobarbital are clinically titrated to ensure a deep state of relaxation, it is conceivable that a patient may attempt to look more sedated than he or she actually is. Much reliance is placed on the clinician to observe the pharmacological effects of amobarbital carefully. As noted by MacDonald (1976a) and Herman (1985), patients may show an initial euphoria and talkativeness, yet with higher dosages manifest a thickening and slurring of speech, skipping numbers in counting backwards from 100, and nystagmus. Given the specificity of these physiological signs, potential simulators would be challenged in (1) their knowledge of these indices and (2) their ability to reproduce them. With respect to the latter, slurred speech and eye-movement disturbances may be more difficult to feign convincingly, especially when the barbiturates are exerting a disinhibiting influence.

On possible strategy to reduce the likelihood of a feigned drug state is the use of shorter acting barbiturates, such as sodium brevital. Clinicians may be reluctant with sodium amytal to increase dosages out of concern that the patient may fall asleep for several hours, resulting in a costly but useless procedure. With shorter acting barbiturates, this concern is lessened, because dosages can be more closely titrated and pronounced drowsiness averted.

Physiological studies are not readily available on changes in pulse, respiration, or cerebral–cortical electrical activity associated with drug-assisted interviews.[2] However, we have not searched the medical literature with respect to dose-related changes in these indices. The application of such research findings would provide a more objective basis for ruling out the possibility of simulated sedation. In addition, the combination of drug-assisted interviews and polygraph methods deserves empirical investigation.

A concern raised by the literature on hypnosis is whether patients in drug-assisted interviews are hypersuggestible. Research by Orne (1979), for example, suggests that hypnotized participants may respond to the demand characteristics of the hypnotic situation and be encouraged to have more memories, whether accurate or not. A further concern is that patients' distortions under amobarbital might become pseudo-memories, indistinguishable from other memories. Piper (1993) summarized the literature as it relates to suggestibility and pseudo-memories, and concluded that both are likely to occur in drug-assisted interviews. We are more restrained in our interpretation of this research for two reasons: (1) The cited studies represent early uncontrolled studies; and (2) clinical descriptions typically emphasize salient features and not their absence. Thus, we are unclear how to interpret the fact that only a small minority of early studies describe increased suggestibility.

The most prudent course of action is to assume that suggestibility is a potential problem in drug-assisted interviews. In this regard, clinicians must attempt to avoid at all costs implicit or explicit messages that either the patient (1) is not telling the whole story, or (2) is deliberately distorting his or her self-report. Such demand characteristics may unduly influence the patient to either embellish or change his or her recall. Furthermore, based on the analogue with clinical hypnosis (e.g., Putnam, 1979; Zelig & Beidleman, 1981), clinicians should assiduously avoid leading questions. Given the possible vulnerability for pseudo-memories, clinicians should ask open-ended, nondirective questions to the maximum extent feasible when conducting drug-assisted interviews (Herman, 1985; MacDonald, 1976a; Rogers, 1986a).

The most critical dimension of drug-assisted interviews is the degree of control patients have over their self-report. The primary mechanism of such interviews is the disinhibitory function of the barbiturate on a patient's attempt to withhold or distort his or her self-report. Despite early and unsupported claims of amobarbital as a "truth serum," it is generally accepted that the degree of control exerted by an individual is highly variable (Rogers, 1986). Early case studies have noted that patients may deliberately misrepresent events or information during a drug-assisted interview (Lambert & Rees, 1944; Ripley & Wolf, 1947). Adatto (1949), in interviews with 50 forensic patients, found 3 persons who had fabricated new accounts of their behavior while under drug-assisted interviews. This finding would seem to suggest that at least some patients may not only maintain prior fabrications, but also create de novo deceptions during their drug-assisted interviews. Pertinent to the earlier discussion of hypersuggestibility and pseudo-memories, the 3 patients had (1) engaged in dissimulation prior to the drug-assisted interview and (2) admitted to fabricating the stories during follow-up interviews.

Much controversy has occurred about the use of amobarbital interviews to "recover" memories of past sexual abuse. Evolving from, or related to, a psychotherapeutic technique involving recovery of traumatic memories in dissociative-disordered patients for abreactive purposes described by Kolb (1985), amobarbital interviews have been used to recover memories in amnestic states (Slaby, 1994), and to recover memories of past sexual abuse (Terr, 1994). Many authors have explicitly rejected the use of amobarbital interviews to recover memories of past sexual abuse (Pendergrast, 1995; Piper, 1993), citing their ineffectiveness in the first place, as well as the risk of inducing pseudo-memories.

The risk of medications producing pseudo-memories, which are completely believed by the involved patients, has been documented. In England and Canada, more than 40 patients sedated with benzodiazepines by dentists and physicians for oral surgery, intubation, and endoscopy have alleged that they had been sexually assaulted. In many of these cases, assaults were very unlikely to have occurred, due to the presence of other professionals throughout the procedure. Rather, the drug was thought to have induced or released the sexual fantasy. In some cases, criminal or licensure complaints were brought against the professional involved (Brahams, 1989, 1990a, 1990b, 1991).

Redlich, Ravitz, and Dession (1951) conducted a study of nine normal participants who were asked by the first examiner to reveal one or several shame- or guilt-producing incidents in their lives. Participants were then instructed to create a "cover story" that would be maintained throughout a drug-assisted interview with an independent clinician. Two participants provided rather trivial guilt-producing incidents (i.e., lying about age and stealing two library books while a teenager) and were able to maintain the deception without difficulty. Of the remaining seven who admitted to substantial guilt-producing behavior, two made complete admissions, and two made partial admissions during the amobarbital interviews. Although limited in sample size, the findings suggest considerable variability in normal persons' degree of control over self-reporting.

No research is available on what types of patients under which circumstances will attempt to maintain dissimulation during drug-assisted interviews. Empirical study is necessary to establish whether dissimulating patients are identifiable by their presentation. Interestingly, Shoichet (1978) conducted amobarbital interviews with 75 pain patients, of whom 7 (9.3%) were determined to be feigning (1) pain and associated symptoms, and (2) resulting disability. Although an uncontrolled study, it provided several engaging observations. First, patients with feigned pain, unlike other pain patients, claimed spontaneously that their symptoms worsened during the amobarbital interviews. Second, patients with feigned pain described an exacerbation of their symptoms following the interview that required further medical interventions. Third, purported disabilities occasionally disappear during the amobarbital interview. This final observation must be tempered by the fact that patients with conversion disorders may also evidence remarkable improvements in physical symptoms during drug-assisted interviews (e.g., Hurwitz, 1989; Stevens, 1986; Stiebel & Kirby, 1994).

Only one study has investigated coached simulation. Dysken, Steinberg, and Davis (1979) instructed nine mental health staff members on how to feign catatonic stupor. They found that these participants were uniformly successful at refusing psychomotor commands and maintaining a fixed arm position. Although the combination of general mental health training and specific instructions were successful, the generalizability of these results to less sophisticated simulators is unknown. We suspect that patients rarely feign catatonia, and that responsiveness to amobarbital is not determinative of either malingering or a genuine condition (see McCall et al., 1992).

Clinical observations of patients during drug-assisted interviews may provide some clues with respect to their openness and level of cooperation. In such cases, intra-individual differences are notable; some persons become guarded and uncooperative only in addressing specific topics. However, we cannot infer from a lack of cooperation that the individual is dissimulating. An alternative explanation is that an individual characteristically and almost instinctively avoids emotionally upsetting topics. Despite this caution, clinicians can utilize marked changes in demeanor and speech for further exploration of specific issues. Clearly, research is needed on paralinguistic and nonverbal cues of dissimulating patients who are struggling to keep their stories consistent.

A final consideration is the emergence of new or different symptoms during drug-assisted interviews. Research would suggest that most psychiatric patients do not significantly alter their clinical presentation during drug-assisted interviews (Dysken, Chang, Casper, & Davis, 1979; Dysken, Kooser, Haraszti, & Davis, 1979; Kwentus, 1981). Research by Woodruff (1966) on schizophrenics, depressed patients, and control groups revealed that schizophrenic patients occasionally disclosed previously unreported delusions and hallucinations but not affective symptoms during drug-assisted interviews. Depressed patients and control groups manifested no differences in symptoms. Interestingly, Marcum, Wright, and Bissell (1986) reported a case in which a multiple personality disorder was diagnosed during an amobarbital interview of a depressed young male. Furthermore, patients suspected of organic brain syndrome may demonstrate previously absent disorientation, confabulation, and denial of illness (Weinstein, Kahn, Sugarman, & Linn, 1953; Weinstein, Kahn, Sugarman, & Malitz, 1954). The clinician must therefore be alert that changes, as noted earlier, may be found in nondissimulating, mentally disordered patients. Nevertheless, indiscriminant changes in symptomatology, including the emergence of contradictory symptoms, greatly increase the likelihood of dissimulation.

Dissimulation of Neurological and Somatic Disorders

Malingering of a variety of neurological symptoms, syndromes, and diseases is encountered with an undetermined prevalence in a variety of clinical, industrial, and legal settings. This dissimulation has included malingered pain, anesthesia, hyperesthesia, dizziness, visual changes, blindness, deafness, gait disorder, tremor, contracture, stuttering, dysarthria, aphasia, mutism, seizures, amnesia, fugue states, delirium, dementia, and coma (Boffeli & Guze, 1992; Gorman, 1984; McDonald, Kline, & Billings, 1979; Miller & Cartlidge, 1974; Plum & Posner, 1980; Shoichet, 1978; Stevens, 1986). Such symptoms may be maintained for long periods of time, often prompting invasive diagnostic procedures or elaborate physical therapies. In clinical reports, amobarbital interviews have been reported as useful in the differential determination of conversion reactions versus malingering or organic disease. Amobarbital prompts a usually transient remission of functional disorders in general, and conversion reactions in particular (e.g., aphonia, amnesia, confusion, gait impairment, paralysis, dystonia), but an exacerbation or precipitation of neurological dysfunction (e.g., disorientation, pathological reflexes, paresis); exceptions are cases of intoxication-induced cognitive impairment or ictal psychosis in which improvement occurs (Perry & Jacobs, 1982; Plum & Posner, 1980; Ward, Rowlett, & Burke, 1978; Weinstein et al., 1953). The malingerer of organic symptoms may refuse the amobarbital interview, and his or her symptoms will usually fail to respond to its use (Lambert & Rees, 1944; Stevens, 1986). Furthermore, patients with organic pain continued to experience their pain and physical complaints while under amobarbital; those with functional pain syndromes improved during amobarbital, and those who malingered either guarded against the relaxation produced by amobarbital, or became agitated, histrionic, and later hostile when confronted with the diagnosis (Shoichet, 1978).

Some cases of neurological feigning apparently resolve rapidly, following amobarbital interviews. Maurice-Williams and Marsh (1985) examined 14 cases of simulated illness, including 7 cases motivated by external incentives (i.e., malingering), and 3 by maintenance of a sick role (i.e., factitious disorder). They employed amobarbital interviews as a component of treatment and were able to establish full recovery in less than 1 month for 9 of 14 cases (64.3%). We are left to speculate whether this rapid resolution was not partially determined by the inherent difficulty in feigning paraplegia or tetraplegia for extended periods.

For the identification of neurological malingering, clinicians must have sufficient consultations to provide comprehensive physical and neurological examinations of the suspected patient in order to detect signs and symptoms of any diagnosable organic disorder. Differential diagnoses may require extensive neuropsychological testing (see Kopelman, Christensen, Puffett, & Stanhope, 1994; also Chapter 11) or specialized neurological testing, including skull X rays, lumbar puncture, electroencephalogram, CT (computed tomography) scans, nuclear magnetic resonance scans, and auditory and visually evoked potentials to exclude neuropathology. As in the case of functional psychiatric disorders, the amobarbital interview is generally considered an adjunctive, rather than definitive, procedure in assessing suspected neurological malingering.

USE OF DRUG-ASSISTED INTERVIEWS IN THRESHOLD AND CLINICAL DECISION MODELS

Practical considerations in the use of drug-assisted interviews involve threshold and clinical decision models. These two models attempt to capture essential issues of *when* drug-assisted interviews should be conducted (i.e., threshold model) and *how* dissimulation is determined (i.e., clinical decision model). The following sections will briefly delineate these two models.

Threshold Model

The paucity of validity studies on the usefulness of drug-assisted interviews would argue for its selective use and conservative interpretation. From this perspective, the authors recommend its use only in circumstances in which other, better validated methods are unsuccessful and the diagnostic issue is considered essential. Based on this reasoning, Table 12.1 provides a summary of diagnostic issues for which drug-assisted interviews may be considered.

One application of the threshold model is relevant to patients with factitious disorders and others that deny or withhold information about their background and past treatment. Patients with factitious disorders are often defensive about their past and grossly minimize or categorically deny prior involvement with mental health professionals (McDonald, Kline, & Billings, 1979). As observed by Marriage, Govorchin, George, and Dilworth (1988), amobarbital data may provide invaluable sources of names and facilities for independently confirming or disconfirming a patient's self-report.

Drug-assisted interviews might best be conceptualized as a challenge test (Rogers, 1987) that may, in certain cases, assist in establishing of dissimulation. The term "challenge test" is applied, since its finding may assist in *ruling in* but not *ruling out* dissimulation. Given the limited studies reported earlier, the absence of any observable dissimulation is not necessarily indicative of honesty and self-disclosure. Therefore, drug-assisted interviews may be selectively employed to assess dissimulation but have no utility in determining truthfulness.

A criminal forensic case presented by Atkins (1991) illustrates several potential problems regarding the overinterpretation of amobarbital interviews. A former boyfriend observed an "exotic" dancer with her current boyfriend and shot her immediately following her performance on stage. After several suicide attempts, he was remanded to a forensic hospital for assessment and treatment. According to the case summary, he warranted the diagnosis of major depression, but no psychotic symptoms were observed during 15 months of treatment. Because of reported amnesia regarding the time of the offense, an amobarbital interview was administered. In brief excerpts (all quotes are from Atkins, 1991, p. 44), the defendant related, "She turned into the devil . . . the devil with pitchforks and everything and fire and everything." Report-

TABLE 12.1. Threshold Model for the Use of Drug-Assisted Interviews in the Assessment of Dissimulation

Clinical presentation	Criteria
Elective mutism	Any current presentation
Suspected amnesia	Inconsistent with dissociative or organic amnesia
Circumscribed episode	Only when corroborative data are absent and retrospective assessment of a major mental illness is essential
Denial of suspected psychosis	Rare circumstances in which inpatient observation and corroborative interviews are inconclusive
Improbable self-report	Only when self-report is critical to a dispositional or forensic issue
Unexplained neurological symptoms such as seizures, stuttering, and aphasia	Only when neuropsychological and neurological procedures are inconclusive and other clinical data are suggestive of dissimulation

edly firing out of fear, he described the male devil as a *her* ("She wiggled her bottom, she wiggled her breasts"). The defendant also characterized her as a "breathing dragon with a pick." Expert testimony was proffered that the defendant was psychotic and legally insane at the time of the offense. Such testimony appears to be based on the tenuous assumption that the defendant's report is veridical; however, amobarbital interviews cannot establish the veracity of any defendant's account. Additional causes for concern are threefold: (1) the interview data are markedly inconsistent with inpatient observations; (2) the defendant's depiction of the devil is highly atypical (e.g., wiggling breasts as sufficiently threatening to justify his shooting); and (3) inconsistencies in describing the devil's gender (male and female) and weapon (pitchfork and pick). An atypical presentation and gross inconsistencies in the clinical data should alert clinicians to the possibility of feigned psychosis (see Chapter 3).[3]

Clinical Decision Model

The clinical literature (e.g., Herman, 1985; MacDonald, 1976a) has focused primarily on the role of drug-assisted interviews in the determination of malingering. Drug-assisted interviews appear, however, to have a greater application in the establishment of deception and defensiveness regarding functional psychiatric syndromes than in the determination of malingering. As previously noted, participants can withhold information or deceive during amobarbital interviews (Adatto, 1949; Gerson & Victoroff, 1948; Lambert & Rees, 1944; Ripley & Wolf, 1947). The criteria for establishing dissimulation in drug-assisted interviews have not been clearly articulated. Discussions in the clinical literature often center on marked inconsistencies in self-report as the sole indicator of dissimulation (e.g., Rogers, 1986). Such an approach is unnecessarily limited since other indicators may be potentially more useful (see Table 12.2).

Clinicians should be observant of inconsistencies in self-report in the drug-assisted interview itself and as the interview data compare with prior clinical presentations. In addition, nonverbal attempts to withhold information, such as clenching jaws or refusing to respond, may provide useful evidence of patients' attempts to withhold and possibly distort their self-report. In contrast, indicators of autonomic arousal, paralinguistic cues, and inconsistencies in affect, although representing avenues of future research, are inappropriate for clinical assessment since they lack any validation in this context. In particular, inconsistencies in affect are likely to be the result of the drug interview itself (see, e.g., Smith, Hain, & Stevenson, 1970) and have no direct bearing in determining the interviewee's veracity.

Admissions of dishonesty, either given spontaneously during the drug-assisted interview or in a subsequent follow-up interview, are potentially the most useful in establishing dissimulation. If different or contradictory material is elicited during the drug-assisted interview, the clinician should employ a follow-up inquiry. During the subsequent interview, the clinician should offer the patient an opportunity to clarify these apparent discrepancies. Admissions of dissimulation with exploration of the patient's motivation in a follow-up interview are invaluable in establishing dissimulation.

TABLE 12.2. Indicators of Deception in Drug-Assisted Interviews

Indicators	Comments
Spontaneous admission of dishonesty	Not reported in clinical literature; would require careful follow-up
Inconsistencies in self-report between prior clinical presentation and the drug interview itself	Most common indicator in clinical literature; not valid with leading questions
Nonverbal indicators of withholding information	Potentially useful, although not discussed in clinical literature; examples would be clenching jaws or selective mutism
Autonomic arousal	Analogous to polygraphy; not studied in the experimental or clinical literature
Paralinguistic cues	Social psychological studies are not generalizable to drug-assisted interviews
Inconsistencies in affect	Unlikely to be useful, given affective changes occurring with drug interviews
Admission of dishonesty in follow-up interview is either spontaneous or comes when confronted with inconsistencies	Potentially most useful; negated by leading questions or confrontation during the drug-assisted interview

The use of drug-assisted interviews as the sole measure for establishing malingering or defensiveness is discouraged. For specific styles of dissimulation (i.e., malingering and defensiveness), drug-assisted interviews are best conceptualized as an adjunct measure that provides ancillary data in those cases where such investigations are necessary. As noted earlier, findings from drug-assisted interviews must be interpreted conservatively, given the limited validation research. Table 12.3 provides a model for establishing the unreliability or probable dissimulation of a particular patient. It should be observed, with regard to the latter category, that an admission of dissimulation and an understanding of the motivation for such dissimulation are necessary for making this determination.

TABLE 12.3. Clinical Decision Model for Establishing Dissimulation in Drug-Assisted Interviews

Description	Criteria
Unreliable	Markedly inconsistent self-report *or* nonverbal indicators of withholding
Probable dissimulation	All of the following: Markedly inconsistent self-report Admission of dishonesty in the follow-up interview Motivation for deception is understandable in light of the patient's goals

Nonbarbiturate Interviews

This chapter is mainly devoted to the discussion of barbiturate interviews and their potential role in the assessment of dissimulation. Investigators have also examined the use of amphetamines and subclinical dosages of an anesthetic (e.g., hydroxydione) in the evaluation of dissimulation. In addition, an argument could be made for the use of placebo drug interviews (see, e.g., Dysken, Kooser, Haraszti, & Davis, 1979) as a potential method of eliciting new information. These alternatives to barbiturate interviews will only be briefly discussed, since there is essentially no research on their usefulness in assessing dissimulation.

Amphetamines, either alone or in combination with barbiturates, have been used to facilitate recall and depression in treatment cases (Kwentus, 1981). Their effect in comparison to phenobarbital, hydroxydione, and a placebo have been described (Smith et al., 1970). Use of methamphetamine produced the most anxiety, greatest ease of speech, and highest degree of attention in comparison with the other conditions (Hain et al., 1966).

Hydroxydione has also been investigated in drug-assisted interviews. In research reported by Hain and associates (1966), 500 mg of hydroxydione resulted in more incoherent and inconsistent speech, less anxiety, and less attentiveness than the amobarbital, amphetamine, and placebo conditions. Hydroxydione has been employed in one case study to assist with a highly defensive patient who had denied a suicide attempt (Peck, 1960). According to Kwentus (1981), hydroxydione is not currently available.

Jauch, Loch, Earl, and Bauer (1993) advocated the use of intravenous droperidol in drug assisted interviews. Droperidol is a neuroleptic drug that has antipsychotic and anesthetic properties (Kaplan & Sadock, 1988). In an uncontrolled trial with 10 adolescent delinquents, they reported considerable success in addressing denied antisocial behavior and underlying conflicts. Interestingly, they taped the drug-assisted interviews and used them as a vehicle for subsequent therapy.

Golechha, Sethi, Misra, and Jayaprakash (1986) advocated the use of ketamine, a nonbarbituate anaesthetic agent, as an alternative to amobarbital in drug-assisted interviews. The description of the study is unclear with respect to whether the procedures were masked for either the patients or one of the raters.[4] With higher dosages of ketamine, 8 of 20 patients evidenced significant revelations of psychological conflicts and guilt feelings. Although encouraging, these results should be interpreted as preliminary, based on their small sample size, methodological limitations, and transcultural considerations.

Ethical and Forensic Considerations

The process of obtaining informed consent for drug-assisted interviews is problematic when the purpose of such interviews is the detection of malingering and deception. Fully informed consent, whether oral or written, would require that the person be informed that the examination is being conducted for the sole purpose of assessing malingering and deception, as well as the likely consequences of such an evaluation. Additional consent disclosures include the nature of the procedure, its physiological risks, its alternatives, and the right of the person to terminate the procedure at any time (Fabian & Billick, 1986). Some examiners, however, might conclude that such extensive disclosures would interfere with the accuracy of the interview data, and decide to withhold them, arguably without ethical justification, on the basis of the "therapeutic privilege" as an exception to informed consent.

Several legal evidentiary problems are presented by the use of drug-assisted interviews in forensic assessments (Annotation, 1986). The interview results are usually admissible at trial when the interviewer testifies that all or part of his or her conclusions are based on the test. Inculpatory or exculpatory statements made during the drug-assisted interview, as in any forensic interview, however, are generally not admissible at trial to prove the truth of an issue; drug-assisted interviews will not be admissible as "truth serum" (Adelman & Howard, 1984; Curran, 1983). Given the litigation against mental health professionals regarding the appropriateness and conduct of amobarbital interviews, it is advisable that such interviews be videotaped in their entirety. Consideration should also be given to the use of an additional mental health professional to witness, but not participate, in the procedures.

CONCLUSION

As a general rule, drug effects on human participants are determined by the interaction among a variety of specific and nonspecific factors. These factors include the setting, personality of the patient, expectancies of the patient and physician, the type and quality of the relationship between the patient and physician, preparation of the drug, its route and schedule of administration, as well as the pharmacological properties of the drug (Buckalew & Coffield, 1982). This multiplicity of factors is even more critical to keep in mind in the context of drug-assisted interviews used to detect malingering and deception, undoubtedly a complex interpersonal and investigational procedure. Here, an injected substance is used purportedly to reveal memory, affect, or cognition not ostensibly available to the participant or others, or to assess authenticity of the patient's presentation.

Despite the paucity of research data concerning the use and misuse of drug-assisted interviews to detect dissimulation, clinicians continue to find such interviews, particularly using short-acting barbiturates such as amobarbital, useful in the diagnosis and treatment of mental disorders. For functional mental disorders, clinical reports indicate that drug-assisted interviews are more useful in detecting defensiveness than malingering. Amobarbital interviews may also prove to be useful in detecting malingering of neurological syndromes, although controlled research is not available. In both cases, however, drug-assisted interviews should only be employed as adjunctive procedures, conducted after other evaluations and investigations have proved to be inconclusive.

NOTES

1. In clinical practice, psychiatrists and other physicians might increase the dosage if desired results were not forthcoming.

2. Matthews (1992) reported that EEG data are available on amytal with presurgery epileptic patients.

3. Our use of this case report is for illustrative purposes only; we do not have access to any primary data and have no opinion about the expert's testimony in the case.

4. Although participants gave informed consent for narcoanalysis, no details are provided on whether this included the type of drug or the dosage. Of the two raters used, a medical consultant administered the procedures and, therefore, was aware of the drugs and dosages. The second rater was most likely aware of when ketamine was used, because its route of administration (intramuscular) differed from the control groups (intravenous drip), but not necessarily the dosage levels.

13

Polygraphy and Integrity Testing

WILLIAM G. IACONO, Ph.D.
CHRISTOPHER J. PATRICK, Ph.D.

Outside of clinical settings, the most widely used methods for assessing honesty rely on polygraph techniques and questionnaires designed to assess integrity. With the possible exception of IQ testing, perhaps no aspect of psychological measurement has generated more controversy than the use of these psychological procedures. The basis of this controversy is twofold: (1) civil liberty considerations focused on the intrusiveness and infringement of personal rights associated with such evaluations, and (2) concerns regarding their psychometric properties, especially their validity. We organize this chapter into two sections, addressing polygraphy and integrity testing. We describe these assessment techniques and their uses. We also discuss the underlying theory and evaluate the empirical evidence for their reliability and validity.

POLYGRAPHY

Anytime a serious allegation is made against an individual and the pertinent incriminating and exculpatory evidence is equivocal, someone likely will suggest using polygraphy to resolve the issue. Polygraphy is widely used in North America, especially by government agencies, with tens of thousands of tests carried out annually. Law enforcement agencies use the polygraph to examine suspects, complainants, and witnesses, and the U.S. government uses it for national security screening. In the private sector, polygraph tests are utilized in insurance investigations, for civil suits, to resolve family disputes, and to screen prospective and current employees. Because the U.S. Supreme Court recently rewrote the rules for the admissibility of scientific evidence (*Daubert v. Merrell Dow Pharmaceuticals,* 1993), many lawyers, especially defense attorneys whose clients have passed a polygraph, are having courts reevaluate the admissibility of polygraph results as evidence in criminal trials (see Iacono & Lykken, 1997, for an analysis of polygraphy in light of the *Daubert* decision).

Preemployment polygraph examinations provided for many years a popular method of screening employees regarding their honesty. Because of their quick and inexpensive administration and "results" (i.e., incriminating admissions in a substantial proportion of cases), preemployment polygraph testing became widespread, with upwards of two million tests conducted annually by the late 1980s (O'Bannon, Goldinger, & Appleby, 1989). However, federal legislation, enacted in 1988, prohibits private employers from requiring or even requesting applicants to undergo polygraph tests as a condition of employment. The Employee Polygraph Protection Act covers not only the polygraph but also any "mechanical or electrical device" used to render an opinion as to honesty or dishonesty. It also prohibits random testing of current employees and limits the use of the polygraph in specific investigations of job-related wrongdoing. All governmental agencies and some types of jobs and industries (i.e., security guards and pharmaceutical manufacturers) are exempt from the Act. According to Libbin, Mendelsohn, and Duffy (1988), this law banned 85% of all polygraph examinations conducted in the United States.

The Polygraph Instrument

A polygraph is a multichannel electronic device that records physiological signals on moving chart paper. Typically, recordings include (1) palmar sweating (galvanic skin response, or GSR) from electrodes applied to the fingertips, (2) respiratory rhythm (rate and amplitude) from pneumatic tubes placed around the chest and abdomen, and (3) cardiovascular activity (blood pressure changes and pulse) from a partially inflated blood pressure cuff placed around the arm. Modern field polygraphs are designed to fit in an attaché case and can be attached to portable computers that digitize and interpret the physiological readings. Although field polygraph technology has changed little during the last 45 years, the quality of the physiological recordings has been improved and matches that of sophisticated laboratory equipment (Patrick & Iacono, 1991a). Little controversy arises over the recording methods used in polygraphy. What makes polygraphy controversial is its weak psychological foundation and psychometric properties.

Detecting Liars: An Overview of Polygraph Techniques

Early in the history of polygraphy, examiners erroneously believed there was a characteristic physiological response associated with lying. We now know that no such identifiable response exists. Hence, to identify liars, examiners employ techniques that require the comparison of responses to different questions, one of which is relevant to the issue under investigation.

The two types of polygraph procedure that are used in field applications are referred to as the relevant/irrelevant technique (RIT), typically used for employee screening, and the control question technique (CQT), usually used in criminal cases. Both procedures can more accurately be considered "polygraph–assisted interviews" than psychological tests, and both have as their major objective the eliciting of self-inculpatory admissions from examinees. A third procedure, the Guilty Knowledge Test (GKT), seldom used in actual investigations, provides an objective method to determine the probability that a criminal suspect possesses crime-relevant knowledge that only the police and the perpetrator of the crime could be expected to know.

The Relevant/Irrelevant Test

The RIT compares responses to relevant questions (e.g., "On March 12, did you shoot Scott Fisbee?") to irrelevant questions (e.g., "Are you now seated?" or "Is today Friday?"). If the relevant question elicits a larger physiological response than the irrelevant question, the subject is judged deceptive. Equivalent responses to the two types of question indicate truthfulness. Because the irrelevant question does not provide an adequate control for the emotional impact of being asked an accusatory question, the RIT is strongly biased against the innocent and, consequently, largely has been abandoned as a tool in criminal investigations.

Today, the RIT is used primarily as an employee screening tool to investigate the possible misbehavior and character flaws of current or prospective employees. In this context, the irrelevant questions are intended to give the respondent a break in what otherwise would be a long series of potentially embarrassing, relevant questions dealing with topics such as drug and alcohol use, marital infidelity, or protecting the security of classified information. Any relevant question that elicits a comparatively strong reaction is apt to be probed further, usually by asking the subject to explain why certain questions elicit strong reactions, and through further examination using more specific, relevant questions pertinent to the issue of concern (e.g., types of drugs used, last time they were used, whether their use was habitual). The physiological reactions, rather than being formally scored and evaluated, generally provide the examiner an excuse for interrogation. The outcome of the procedure is determined largely by how satisfied the examiner is with the explanations and demeanor of the examinee during this stressful interrogation.

The theory on which the employee screening RIT is based is poorly developed, and no published studies appear in scientific journals addressing its validity. Although civil libertarians object to these tests (Pyle, 1985), there is little argument about the effectiveness of employee screening. Under the stress of this procedure, many employees admit to misdeeds that otherwise would go undetected, and the threat of a polygraph is widely perceived to have some deterrent value. However, the extent to which unfit employees pass these tests is unknown. It is this type of polygraph test that Aldrich Ames, the convicted spy, passed repeatedly while turning over CIA secrets to the Soviet Union.

The Guilty Knowledge Test

The most theoretically sound polygraph technique is the GKT (Ben-Shakar & Furedy, 1990; Iacono & Lykken, 1997; Lykken, 1981). The GKT is a type of multiple-choice detection procedure in which subjects are asked factual questions about an incident (e.g., "If you stole the attaché case, you'll know what unusual item was in it.") while their physiological responses are recorded to alternative answers (e.g., "Was it the Book of Mormon . . . a squirt gun . . . a boat in a bottle . . . a pornographic magazine . . . a kite?"). The questions are chosen so only the police and the guilty person know which alternative is correct. An innocent person could only fail a GKT by being unlucky enough to give a strong reaction to the correct alternative on many such questions (a typical GKT might have 10 questions, each with 5 multiple-choice alternatives). By choosing questions thoughtfully, however, examiners can create multiple-choice questions that deal with material easily identifiable by the guilty.

Laboratory studies of the GKT indicate high accuracy, with hit rates often of 100% for innocent and about 90% for guilty persons (Ben-Shakar & Furedy, 1990; Iacono & Patrick, 1988). The only field investigations (i.e., studies of actual cases) of GKT validity have been carried out in Israel (Elaad, 1990; Elaad, Ginton, & Jungman, 1992). These studies demonstrated accuracy close to 100% for innocent subjects, but the hit rates were disappointing for guilty suspects. However, the GKT was constrained by the number of items, averaging fewer than two per subject. Because the sensitivity of the GKT increases dramatically with the number of items, tests as abbreviated as those used by these Israeli polygraphers cannot be expected to work well with guilty subjects.

Ironically, given its inherent soundness, the polygraph profession shuns the GKT because (1) not all crimes can be investigated using this technique, and (2) it takes more effort (e.g., a visit to the crime scene—polygraphers seldom do this) to generate a carefully constructed GKT than it does to create the questions for a standard CQT. However, the chief reason polygraphers do not use the GKT is that they believe strongly in the high accuracy of the CQT, a belief that, as we shall see, is based on the misleading and unrepresentative type of feedback they receive when administering CQTs.

The Control Question Test

Psychologists are likely to encounter the CQT in practice, because it is the only method widely used in forensic settings. Hence, the CQT will serve as the focus of the remainder of this review.

Description. The CQT is actually a collection of related procedures, all of which involve comparing the physiological responses to relevant questions, such as those used with the RIT, to the reactions elicited by "control" questions. The control questions are assumed to represent the responses to "known lies" or at least to be disturbing to the accused, because they involve minor transgressions that are fairly common. Although they do not deal specifically with the crime, they generally focus on a related theme and are introduced to the subject in such a manner as to indicate that the test could be failed if the subject appears dishonest to these questions (Raskin, 1989). For instance, in the case of a shooting or a sex crime, control questions respectively might take the form "Have you ever tried to hurt someone to get revenge?" or "Have you ever committed an unusual sex act?" The assumption is that everyone would be dis-

turbed by such questions, which are intended to provide "an estimate of how innocent subjects would react if their answers to relevant questions were actually deceptive" (Raskin, Honts, & Kircher, 1996, p. 9).

The CQT is based on the assumption that innocent persons, because they are
only concerned about their responses to control questions, will respond more to these
questions than the relevant questions. By contrast, the guilty person is expected to
produce a larger response to relevant than control questions because the answers to
the relevant questions evoke greater concern.

Because the blood pressure cuff produces ischemic pain if inflated for more than
about 3 minutes, the length of the CQT is determined by the number of questions
that can be asked before discomfort sets in. The typical CQT consists of about 10
questions, 3 of which are relevant questions that are paired with 3 control questions;
the other questions are essentially filler items that are not used in chart interpretation.
The set of 10 questions is typically repeated at least twice, and usually three times,
with the order of questions altered from one repetition or "chart" to the next.

To determine the outcome of a CQT, some examiners adopt a "global" approach,
integrating their evaluation of the physiological reactions to control and relevant questions with other information. They go beyond the physiological record by appraising
the quality of the evidence against the subject and the subject's conduct during the
polygraph interrogation, which includes an interview during which the subject is asked
to give an account of his or her involvement in the crime. In contrast, most modern
examiners attempt to disregard information not contained in the polygraph charts and
base their decision entirely on the physiological recordings that they "numerically"
score. For each of the three physiological channels and for each pair of questions, a
score of −3 is assigned if the response to the relevant question is much larger than the
response to the control question, a score of +3 if the response to the control question
is much larger, and values intermediate to these are given depending on how much
larger the response to one question is compared to the other. These scores are summed
over questions, channels, and charts to yield a sum, usually falling between −27 and
+27. Typically, a total score between +5 and −5 is interpreted as inconclusive (requiring the test to be redone at another time), more negative scores indicate deception,
and more positive totals are indicative of truthfulness. Despite claims by polygraphers
who use numerical scoring that they do not rely on extraphysiological data in their
evaluation of truthfulness, Patrick and Iacono (1991b) demonstrated that they nevertheless take it into account when rendering their opinions about subjects' truthfulness.

Recently, a variant of the CQT called the "directed lie test" (DLT) has been
growing in popularity (Raskin et al., 1996). With this variant, the control questions
are replaced by questions that the subject is told to lie to, such as "Before 1996, did
you ever even make one mistake?" The subject is told to answer this question "no"
while deliberately thinking of instances when he or she had, in fact, done what was
being denied. The DLT is intended to circumvent the problems inherent to the use of
conventional control questions and simplify the administration of the polygraph
examination.

Utility. The CQT is typically applied in cases in which alternative methods of investigating the crime have been exhausted and the evidence remains inconclusive. If an examiner concludes that a subject has failed a CQT, a posttest interrogation takes place in which the subject is pressured to confess. Subjects often do confess, thereby resolving a crime that otherwise most likely would be left indeterminate. This confession-inducing aspect of CQT polygraphy attests to the practical utility of the CQT, rather than its scientific merit or validity. Government agencies justify its continued use based on this utility (Iacono & Lykken, 1997).

If the subject fails and does not confess, the case is nevertheless apt to be considered resolved with the conclusion that the guilty person has been identified by the failed test. Because this suspect most likely cannot be prosecuted using as evidence the failed test, and because the other evidence against the suspect is ambiguous despite exhaustive efforts, the investigation is closed. A passed test leads to the conclusion that an appropriate suspect has not been identified, and the investigative file is left open in case further evidence comes to light at some future time. In this way, many law enforcement agencies combine investigative work with polygraph testing to manage a significant fraction of their case load (Iacono, 1995; Patrick & Iacono, 1991b).

Reliability. The reliability of the CQT has received little attention. Study after study has shown that blind examiners scoring the same charts tend to produce highly correlated results, indicating high interjudge reliability ($r \geq .85$), especially for charts that are numerically scored (Iacono & Lykken, 1997). Test–retest reliability, or the likelihood that two different examiners testing the same suspect would reach the same verdict, has not been systematically studied.

An Evaluation of CQT Theory. As Iacono and Patrick (1987, 1988) and others (Ben-Shakar & Furedy, 1990; Iacono & Lykken, in press; Lykken, 1981) have noted, the CQT's theoretical assumptions are so psychologically naive that great skepticism should greet claims of its accuracy. Particularly troubling is the assumption that the control question, whether of the conventional or directed lie variety, provides an adequate psychological control for the emotional impact of the relevant question. The problem with this assumption is that the control question deals with something that is relatively unimportant, whereas the relevant question has obvious pertinence even to innocent persons. Think for a moment about the last time you were falsely accused; you may have blushed and noticed an increased heart rate or your hands becoming sweaty. Such subtle physiological changes can be detected easily with a polygraph. However, the polygraph cannot differentiate between an honest denial and outright lying to such an emotionally charged question. In other words, to the extent that the control and relevant questions are not matched for their psychological significance, even the innocent can be expected to respond more strongly to the accusatory relevant questions.

It is also doubtful that examinees will necessarily be lying or unduly concerned when they respond to conventional control questions. The subject may be responding honestly or unable to recall an incident that would make answering the control question "no" a lie. In addition, the ambiguous wording of these questions affords the opportunity for subjects to rationalize that they are being truthful when they answer them. Again, all of these deficiencies of the control question indicate that the CQT is biased against the innocent.

The notion that the guilty will necessarily be more disturbed by the relevant than the control questions, although seemingly on a firmer footing, is also debatable. Poorly worded and misinterpreted relevant questions may not elicit an appropriately strong response. Occasionally, the control question may be more threatening than the relevant question because, for example, it covers an undetected crime that could greatly worsen the subject's predicament. Also, the accusation contained in the relevant question is likely to be one that the subject has been repeatedly confronted with and repeatedly denied. By contrast, the material contained in the control question likely occurs for the first time in the context of the polygraph examination. Research has established that repeated presentation of similar stimuli leads to habituated autonomic nervous system responding (e.g., Iacono & Lykken, 1983), even within a lie detection context (Iacono, Boisvenu, & Fleming, 1984). Habituation is thus more likely to affect relevant questions, diminishing the response to these questions and increasing the likelihood that the guilty will pass.

The most serious threat to the believability of passed CQTs comes from research documenting that up to 80% of guilty subjects can learn to appear truthful by augmenting their physiological response to control questions. Honts and colleagues (Honts, Hodes, & Raskin, 1985; Honts, Raskin, & Kircher, 1987, 1994) conducted several laboratory studies demonstrating that through the use of countermeasures (e.g., biting the tongue, pressing toes on the floor, or performing mental arithmetic in response to control questions), guilty subjects cannot be detected by experienced examiners. These results were obtained with less than 30 minutes of instruction on the theory of the CQT and the use of countermeasures, suggesting that the CQT can be thwarted with little training. Countermeasures may be more problematic for the DLT because the directed lie question is introduced to the subject as providing an example of a response to a known lie (Raskin, 1989). By making the purpose of the question so transparent, subjects are likely to understand its significance and the value of augmenting their response to it.

Passed CQTs can be called into question when they are the results of "friendly" tests. These CQTs are arranged by a defendant's attorney, and their results are protected by attorney–client privilege. If the client fails the test, the results are never publicized because to do so would serve only to undermine the client's case. However, if the client passes the test, the attorney attempts to get the result admitted into evidence before the court. Proponents of polygraphy argue that the CQT works because the subject fears detection. However, subjects have little to fear with friendly tests, because a failed test will not affect the prosecution of the case. Moreover, under these circumstances, the polygrapher knows that a truthful verdict is hoped for, a factor that is likely to subtly influence the procedure in favor of the desired result. Last, the base rate of guilt among criminal defendants awaiting trial is likely to be high and probably higher than 50%. As Meehl and Rosen (1955) have noted, the proportion of classifi-cation errors likely to be false negatives increases substantially as the base rate of a char-acteristic exceeds 50%. Hence, the percentage of friendly tests passed by deceptive individuals can be expected to be disproportionately high (see Iacono & Patrick, 1988). To date, no studies have addressed the validity of friendly tests.

Methodological Limitations of CQT Validity Studies. Evaluating the accuracy of the CQT is fraught with major methodological problems. In laboratory studies, naive subjects composing the "guilty" group are instructed to enact a mock crime and "in-nocent" subjects, given no such instruction, are told they are "suspects" for such a crime. These volunteers are subsequently given a CQT, and the hit rates for the two groups are determined. Like all analogue studies, the external validity of these inves-tigations is suspect, so much so that we do not believe they can be used to estimate the accuracy of the CQT in actual settings. Laboratory investigations place noncriminal subjects in situations in which the motivational and emotional concerns are quite un-like those found in real-life polygraph examinations in that (1) no reason exists for experimental subjects to fear detection, (2) the guilty have little incentive to try to beat the test, (3) the innocent are unlikely to be concerned about the relatively mean-ingless relevant questions, and (4) the innocent are more likely to be concerned about the privacy-invading control questions. Another major difference is that in analogue studies, unlike real life, the procedure is standardized. Consequently, the results of well-conducted laboratory studies can be expected to overestimate the validity of field applications.

The alternative to analogue investigations is field studies that examine how well the CQT performs in actual criminal investigations. Although the appeal of working with such cases is readily apparent, these studies are severely compromised by the dif-ficult problem of how to establish ground truth. The commonly employed method is to rely on confessions to identify the culpable and establish as innocent cosuspects in the same case. As noted earlier, pursuing a confession following a failed test is a stan-dard aspect of CQT interrogation, so it is relatively easy to obtain cases that include confessions. However, relying on confessions obtained this way creates a biased sample. The only subjects included in such a study are those whose charts were scored cor-rectly by the original examiner; that is, all obtained confessions will necessarily follow a CQT that was scored deceptive. Because the criterion is not independent of the outcome of the CQT, use of the confession as the criterion will necessarily lead to the conclusion that the polygraph test was accurate. Omitted from the results are all of the polygraph errors arising from those occasions when an innocent person failed a test because, absent a confession, all such cases would be excluded. In addition, all the errors in which a guilty subject passed a test would be excluded, because no effort would be made to obtain a confession under these circumstances. Hence, confession studies grossly overestimate CQT accuracy for guilty subjects, because only those who failed the CQT are included.

Confession studies overestimate the accuracy for innocent subjects, because their innocence is also not independent of polygraph test outcome. In a typical case involving multiple suspects, individuals are tested until one is judged deceptive. This common practice means that those polygraphed suspects established as innocent when a cosuspect fails and confesses will have been judged truthful on their CQTs. Hence, because the only subjects included in field studies will tend to be those correctly diagnosed by the original examiner, these studies provide an overly optimistic estimate of CQT validity. Iacono (1991) demonstrated that even under circumstances in which the CQT has no better than chance accuracy, studies relying on confessions to establish ground truth will erroneously lead to the conclusion that the CQT has nearly 100% accuracy.

Importantly, the fact that many subjects fail a CQT and subsequently confess their guilt to the polygrapher naturally reinforces the polygrapher's conviction that the CQT is nearly infallible; however, this reinforcing feedback is selective. The practice of polygraphy affords examiners little opportunity ever to learn of their errors, because the examiner has no means to detect those who are erroneously deemed deceptive or truthful.

In summary, the methodological problems with analogue and field studies make it impossible to accurately estimate CQT validity. Nevertheless, the field studies provide some insight concerning the upper limit of CQT accuracy.

Field Studies of CQT Validity. Reviews of field validity studies yield very different conclusions depending on which studies are accepted as methodologically adequate. Most field studies of CQT accuracy are either unpublished or published in nonscientific journals, such as those promoted by the American Polygraph Association or the International Association of Chiefs of Police. Limitations of these investigations include (1) use of individuals trained as polygraph practitioners who have little or no research training; (2) serious methodological shortcomings, in addition to the confession-bias problem noted earlier; and (3) the absence of scientific peer review (see Iacono & Lykken, 1997; Iacono & Patrick, 1988; Raskin, 1986; Raskin et al., 1996). Not surprisingly, these studies conclude that the CQT has high accuracy, typically exceeding 90%, and support the exaggerated accuracy claims promulgated by the polygraph profession.

All field studies relying on confession-verified cases published in scientific journals are summarized in Table 13.1. These studies indicate, as our analysis of CQT theory suggested, that the CQT is strongly biased against innocent persons. Despite the fact that these studies are also affected by the confession-bias problem and thus provide an overly optimistic index of accuracy, the average hit rate across studies is considerably less than the 90% claimed by polygraph proponents.

These studies reflect primarily the results of "adversarial" CQTs, such as those administered by the police. For all, the polygraph charts were rescored blindly by examiners with no knowledge of the case facts. Had blind scoring not been used, their hit rates would be expected to approach 100%, given the confession-bias problem that leads to the inclusion of only cases that the original examiner judged correctly. In fact, for the Horvath (1977) study, the original examiners agreed with the confession criterion in 100% of the cases, and for the Patrick and Iacono (1991b) investigation, the agreement was over 96%.[1] Although polygraph proponents have cited the success of the original examiners in these reports as evidence for the CQT's high accuracy (e.g.,

TABLE 13.1. Summary of Studies of CQT Validity That Were Published in Scientific Journals and That Used Confessions to Establish Ground Truth

	Horvath (1977)	Kleinmuntz & Szucko (1984)	Patrick & Iacono (1991b)	Mean
Percent guilty correctly classified	77	76	98	84
Percent innocent correctly classified	51	63	55	56
Mean percent	64	70	77	70

Abrams, 1989; Raskin et al., 1996), these numbers are purely an artifact of the method used to select cases.

The Patrick and Iacono (1991b) study differs from the other two studies in several important respects. First, we endeavored to overcome the CQT outcome/confession contamination problem in this study by searching police files for confessions that were obtained outside of and subsequent to the polygraph examination. Because the police tend to close files when an individual fails a CQT, almost all of the confessions we uncovered came from cases in which subjects passed their tests. When these confessions, which were not dependent on anyone having failed a test, were used as the ground-truth criterion, the accuracy of the CQT for blindly rescored charts was only 57% for innocent subjects. This study thus provides the strongest evidence to date that the CQT is strongly biased against innocent people. Moreover, because the original examiners were much more likely to judge these subjects innocent than the blind examiners who rescored the charts, these data indicate that the original examiners probably based their decisions partially on extraphysiological information, information that they correctly evaluated as supportive of their subjects' truthfulness, despite the fact that the physiological data in the polygraph charts did not support such a conclusion.

Second, the Patrick and Iacono (1991b) research differs from the other two studies in how charts were scored. Patrick and Iacono's examiners used numerical scoring, whereas the other two investigations relied on the global method. Because the global approach encourages the examiners to use case facts and their subjective impressions to determine CQT outcome, a subsequent confession for the global method is somewhat independent of the physiological data. Thus, the blind rescoring of the polygraph charts in these studies provides a fairer estimate of how well the physiological data can be used to determine guilt and innocence than one would expect had the original examiners used numerical scoring to evaluate the charts. In fact, to the extent that the original examiner strictly follows numerical scoring rules and ignores case information, the blind numerical rescoring of the charts provides an index of reliability, not validity.

Computer-Assisted Polygraphy

Vendors of field polygraphs are now packaging their instruments with portable computers that digitize the analogue signals, score the charts, and issue an interpretation of the results in the form of a statement indicating the probability that the subject is truthful (e.g., "The probability that the subject was truthful in response to the relevant questions is .9930"). Computer scoring will necessarily be reliable. However, there is little evidence that computer scoring is any more valid than manual scoring of CQT charts (Iacono & Lykken, 1997). In the first place, computerized polygraphy does nothing to reduce the dependence on the complex interaction that takes place between examiner and examinee, which leads to the choice and formulation of relevant and control questions. This unstandardized, subjective aspect of the CQT remains intact with computer scoring. In the second place, the algorithms used to score and interpret polygraph data and the assumptions on which they are based are considered proprietary and are, therefore, not in the public domain. Consequently, they cannot be independently evaluated. Last, all of the problems inherent to the evaluation of the CQT also apply to computer interpretations.

Scientific Opinion about Polygraph Testing

We doubt that any studies of polygraph validity will ever be executed that either improve substantially on the methodology of the published studies or will definitively address the validity issue. In the absence of adequate validity studies, decisions about how and when to use these techniques must be based on the scientific plausibility of their assumptions. For this reason, Iacono and Lykken (1997) have conducted surveys of psychologists to assess their opinions regarding claims about polygraphy. The results of such surveys have special value because the rules governing the admissibility of scientific evidence that many state and all federal courts follow take into account the degree to which the technique is endorsed as legitimate by the "relevant scientific community."

Members of two organizations, the Society for Psychophysiological Research (SPR) and the American Psychological Association (APA), were surveyed regarding their views about the CQT and the GKT. For the APA survey, the Fellows in the Division of General Psychology were surveyed (n = 226). The SPR survey was targeted at half of its nonstudent membership who had U.S. addresses (n = 214). For each group, over 160 responded, yielding survey return rates of about 74% and 91%, respectively, for APA and SPR members.

The key results for questions that overlapped the two surveys are summarized in Table 13.2. These results, very similar for members of both organizations, indicate that (1) scientists have little confidence in the accuracy of the CQT, (2) they are opposed to the admission of polygraph evidence in court, and (3) they hold a favorable impression of the GKT. Further analysis indicated that even scientists highly informed about polygraphy were skeptical about the CQT and positive about the GKT.

The Future of Polygraphy

In the last decade, the question of polygraph accuracy has taken a backseat to the question of its utility. Unquestionably, government and law enforcement agencies will continue to value their ability to use the polygraph to collect information about employ-

TABLE 13.2. **Opinions of Members of the Society for Psychophysiological Research and the American Psychological Association about CQT and GKT Polygraphy**

Questionnaire item	Percent in agreement	
	SPR members	APA fellows
CQT is scientifically sound.	36	30
Would advocate admitting failed CQTs as evidence in court.	24	20
Would advocate admitting passed CQTs as evidence in court.	27	24
CQT can be beaten by augmenting responses to control questions.	99	92
GKT is scientifically sound.	77	72
Reasonable to conclude that an individual who fails 8 of 10 GKT items has guilty knowledge.	72	75

ees and criminal suspects. It is possible that the GKT will begin to be used in criminal investigations, where it could be employed to advantage. It is also possible that sophisticated new recording procedures, such as those that rely on the measurement of cerebral evoked potentials (e.g., see Allen, Iacono, & Danielson, 1992; Farwell & Donchin, 1991; Rosenfeld, Angell, Johnson, & Qian, 1991), will be introduced to field applications. However, because the practitioners of polygraphy are satisfied with their current techniques, they have little motivation to alter their practices or introduce new ones. Consequently, polygraphy likely will continue in its current form indefinitely.

Clinical Applications

Psychologists should be wary of polygraph testing. As Iacono and Patrick (1988) noted, many problems associated with reliance on polygraph techniques in clinical or forensic settings include (1) inadequate research addressing their validity, (2) the lack of polygraphy training forcing psychologists to rely on the opinions of polygraphers who are inadequately trained in psychophysiology and psychometrics, and (3) the dearth of information available on the use of these procedures with clinical populations.

The outcome of a RIT should be given no weight whatsoever. When given in the context of a criminal investigation, this procedure can be expected to have a very high false-positive rate. Because the RIT is so psychologically unsophisticated, it would be easy for a subject to figure out how to defeat it using countermeasures, thus casting doubt on the validity of a passed test. When used for employee screening, the RIT constitutes little more than an opportunity for a polygrapher to pressure the examinee to make admissions. Whether the test is passed or failed depends more on how open and believable the examinee appears to the polygrapher than on the physiological data.

Although the CQT has a somewhat stronger theoretical foundation than the RIT, it is vulnerable to the same criticisms. The best studies, summarized in Table 13.1, indicate that the CQT is strongly biased against innocent subjects. In addition, any guilty subject who bothered to research the CQT well enough to understand the underlying rationale should be able to generate a false-negative outcome using countermeasures.

Even though the GKT has been studied minimally in actual criminal settings, because its theoretical foundation is so sound, the results of a competently administered GKT may have probative value. This is especially true for a failed GKT. Because of its format, it is possible to calculate the probability that one could fail the test by chance, and this figure is obviously informative. A good GKT should have a minimum of 5 questions with 5 alternative answers and ideally have 10 questions. It would not be necessary for all items to be failed for the subject to be considered guilty. For example, the likelihood of an innocent person failing 6 items on a 10-item GKT is less than .01. Of course, it is possible that an innocent individual could produce such GKT outcomes because the test was poorly administered (e.g., the examiner gave the test in a manner that communicated which alternatives dealt with guilty knowledge), or because the guilty alternatives could be expected to have special relevance even to innocent individuals. To reduce these possibilities, the test could be administered by someone who did not know which alternatives reflected guilty knowledge. In addition, one or more nonsuspects could be administered the test to determine the probability that a innocent person would appear guilty on this particular GKT (see Iacono et al., 1984).

A passed GKT could not be interpreted with similar confidence, because it would always be possible to generate items that even the guilty person would not recognize due, for example, to poor memory about the crime or the failure to attend to certain details. To have confidence in a passed GKT, a psychologist would want to determine the probability of the outcome (given the number of questions and multiple-choice alternatives for each) and the likelihood that the GKT items were adequate given knowledge of the case facts and the suspect. The GKT may also be susceptible to countermeasures, but recent research has demonstrated that cerebral evoked potentials can be used to identify who possesses guilty knowledge (Allen et al., 1992; Farwell & Donchin, 1991). Because these potentials have latencies on the order of milliseconds, it is unlikely that subjects will be able to adopt countermeasure strategies that could be used to defeat an evoked potential–based GKT.

INTEGRITY TESTING

Dishonesty is a serious problem in the American workplace. Recent estimates of business losses attributable to employee theft run as high as $25 billion annually (U.S. Congressional Office of Technology Assessment, 1990). Among other relevant statistics, Murphy (1993) cited the following: (1) More than 40% of retail and 36% of manufacturing employees admit to some form of theft on the job; (2) employee pilferage plays a primary role in 30% of small-business failures; and (3) the incidence of job-related theft is increasing at a rate of 15% per year. Other forms of employee malfeasance exact a high cost as well, whether they involve clear-cut crimes (e.g., fraud, bribery, vandalism) or more broadly defined "counterproductive" behaviors (e.g., tardiness or absence, misuse of sick leave, on-the-job alcohol or drug use).

Personnel selection strategies designed to identify and screen out job applicants who are likely to engage in dishonest or counterproductive behaviors provide one solution to this problem. Three main screening techniques have been utilized in recent years: polygraph examinations, background checks, and paper-and-pencil integrity tests. As we have noted, the Employee Polygraph Protection Act passed by Congress in 1988 has almost totally eliminated the use of polygraph screening tests in the private sector. In the traditional background investigation, information is obtained from prior employers or other relevant sources (e.g., credit reports, criminal records) concerning the applicant's past performance and credibility. However, because of the potential for libel action, corporations are becoming increasingly reluctant to provide information about former employees. Other sources of information may be costly and time consuming to check, or legally inaccessible to businesses.

The third major employment screening strategy, integrity testing, involves paper-and-pencil instruments designed to measure traits or behaviors associated with job dishonesty or counterproductivity. The use of honesty testing for personnel selection originated, along with many other forms of psychological assessment, during the Second World War. Betts (1947) developed the Biographical Case History (BCH) scale as the first face-valid honesty test. The BCH was used at first to screen out undesirable military recruits and subsequently for personnel selection. The first honesty test to gain widespread use was the Reid Report, developed in the late 1940s by police polygraph examiner John Reid. This questionnaire was originally validated against polygraph results. In the early 1950s, the first "veiled purpose" honesty test was developed: the Personnel Reaction Blank (PRB), which included more subtle questions about attitudes and self-perceptions designed to assess resistance to "wayward impulse" (Gough, 1971).

However, the use of integrity testing for personnel selection has developed into a truly significant social phenomenon in the wake of the 1988 federal polygraph legislation. With several million tests currently administered annually in the United States (Sackett, 1994), the prevalence of integrity testing now rivals or exceeds the usage of polygraph screening at its peak. Reflecting its importance, the U.S. Congressional Office of Technology Assessment (1990) and the American Psychological Association (1985; Goldberg, Grenier, Guion, Sechrest, & Wing, 1991) have released significant position papers on integrity testing.

This section reviews the major categories and types of integrity tests, the evidence concerning their reliability and criterion-related validity, and recent research on the construct validity of integrity tests. The chapter concludes with a discussion of controversies and legal issues surrounding their use and future trends in the field.

An Overview of Integrity Tests

Integrity tests are most frequently used as a preemployment assessment tool to screen out applicants who are likely to be dishonest or irresponsible on the job. In a smaller proportion of cases, integrity tests are administered to current employees to (1) guide decisions about promotion, (2) assist in specific-incident investigations (e.g., theft or loss), or (3) "encourage" continuing awareness of company standards for honesty and productivity. Tests devised specifically for use with current employees (see O'Bannon et al., 1989) include the Employee Attitude Inventory, the Phase II Profile/Current Employee Version, the Reid Survey III, the Stanton Inventory, and the Wilkerson Employee Input Survey.

The term "integrity test" was adopted during the past decade.[2] Before this, these instruments were commonly known as "honesty tests." This shift in terminology, embraced by publishers and other proponents of these tests, probably reflects two factors. First, honesty is a controversial concept from the standpoint of psychological measurement (Kleinmuntz, 1995). Early work by Hartshorne and May (1928) discouraged the notion that honesty is a stable trait that can be reliably measured, a conclusion that currently persists (U.S. Congressional Office of Technology Assessment, 1990). Second, honesty is a uniquely cherished attribute in our society, and techniques that label individuals as "dishonest" are likely to provoke criticism. The preference for the term "integrity test" also reflects a broadening of the notion of what these tests measure. In an influential review paper, Sackett, Burris, and Callahan (1989) suggested that preemployment integrity tests can be separated into two classes. *Overt integrity tests* (or "clear purpose" tests) contain questions that ask directly about attitudes toward dishonesty and the applicant's own past involvement in illegal activities. This type of test includes instruments such as the Personnel Selection Inventory (see Craig, 1986; Sauser, 1985), Phase II Profile (see Kleinmuntz, 1989; Moreland, 1989), Reid Report (see Brodsky, 1978; Willis, 1986a), and Stanton Survey (see Ganguli, 1985; Wheeler, 1985; Willis, 1986b). These measures are aimed at assessing a job applicant's potential for theft and other wrongdoing. Examples of overt integrity test questions (cited in U.S. Congressional Office of Technology Assessment, 1990, pp. 31–32) include "How often do you tell the truth?"; "Do you feel guilty when you do something you should not do?"; and "In any of your other jobs, was it possible for a dishonest person to take merchandise if a dishonest person had your job?"

Personality-oriented tests (or "veiled purpose" tests) have appeared mostly within the past 10 years and comprise the other class of integrity tests. In contrast to overt tests, personality-based questionnaires consist of items not directly or obviously related to theft or dishonesty but rather to personality characteristics, such as dependability, conventionality, impulsiveness, and emotional stability. Personality-oriented integrity tests are more concerned with the prediction of broadly defined counterproductivity and occupational adjustment than theft or dishonesty per se. Tests of this type include Gough's Personnel Reaction Blank (PRB; 1971; see Hough, 1986), the Employment Productivity Index, the Inwald Personality Inventory (see Bolton, 1985; Fekken, 1986; Juni, 1992; Swartz, 1985; Waller, 1992), the Personnel Decisions, Inc. (PDI) Employment Inventory (see Johnson, 1986), and the Reliability Scale of the Prospective Employee Potential Inventory, formerly known as the Hogan Personnel Selection Series (see Leung, 1992; Lifton & Nannis, 1986; Sundberg, 1992). Representative test items include the following true–false formatted questions: "You like to take chances" and "You are usually confident in yourself" (cited in U.S. Congressional Office of Technology Assessment, 1990); "You work steady and hard at whatever you undertake" and "You never would talk back to a boss or a teacher" (cited in Sackett et al., 1989).

Reliability

The available literature indicates that integrity tests generally demonstrate acceptable reliability according to most standard psychometric criteria (see Goldberg et al., 1991). O'Bannon et al. (1989) reviewed test–retest reliability data for the principal "honesty" scales of several integrity tests. Reliability coefficients ranged from .56 to .97, with most coefficients exceeding .80. The lowest figure, .56 for the PRB (Gough, 1972), was for a lengthy test–retest interval and may reflect changes in the sample over time (O'Bannon et al., 1989). Sackett et al. (1989) hypothesized that restrictions in the range of scores within different samples may also contribute to variations in reported reliabilities across studies.

Sackett et al. (1989) cited internal consistency estimates of .85 or higher for several overt integrity tests, including the Personnel Selection Inventory, Phase II Profile, Reid Report, and Stanton Survey. These authors conjectured that indices of homogeneity would generally be lower for personality-based tests, given their broader scope. In this regard, Sackett et al. cited coefficients of .73 and .65 for the PRB in college male and female samples, and .63 overall for the Hogan Reliability Scale.

Validity

In evaluating the validity of integrity tests, the most crucial questions pertain to criterion-related validity and construct validity. Criterion-related validity is concerned with whether integrity tests are effective for their intended purposes (i.e., to identify employees who are likely to engage in theft or other counterproductive behaviors). Construct validity deals with whether these tests actually measure what they purport to measure (i.e., integrity, honesty, or trustworthiness; see Goldberg et al., 1991).[3]

Until quite recently, most validation research on integrity testing was focused on criterion-related validity. Test publishers have been preoccupied with demonstrating that these tests can benefit businesses by screening out "dishonest" employees and reducing inventory shrinkage; they have devoted little effort to determining how these tests relate to established psychological constructs. Increased attention to construct validation of integrity inventories was identified as an important priority by the American Psychological Association Task Force on the Prediction of Dishonesty and Theft in Employment Settings (Goldberg et al., 1991), and this call has begun to be answered in recent research (e.g., Barrick & Mount, 1991; Lilienfeld, Andrews, & Stone-Romero, 1994; Ones, Schmidt, & Viswesvaran, 1994b; Tett, Jackson, & Rothstein, 1991; Woolley & Hakstian, 1992).

Criterion-Related Validity

Research Strategies. Different criterion-oriented research strategies have been used to assess how effective integrity tests are as a means of identifying undesirable job applicants or employees (Guastello & Rieke, 1991; Murphy, 1993; O'Bannon et al., 1989; Sackett & Harris, 1984; U.S. Congressional Office of Technology Assessment, 1990). As noted earlier, some of the earliest integrity tests (e.g., the Reid Report) were validated against preemployment polygraph test outcomes. An obvious problem with this approach is that the validity of the criterion itself is highly suspect: The traditional polygraph screening examination was based on dubious assumptions, and little evidence has accrued for its validity as anything other than a "bloodless" third degree for extracting confessions (Iacono & Patrick, 1987). Furthermore, the relationship between polygraph and integrity test outcomes could be attributable to shared, systematic error: Those who fail polygraph tests due to excessive anxiety and guilt may also be prone to confess to temptations and transgressions on integrity tests.

A second approach used to validate integrity tests has been the *contrasted groups* approach, in which test scores from the general population are compared with select groups who are expected to differ on some specific dimension. Most of these studies have used juvenile delinquents or adult prisoners as comparison groups. Gough (1971), for example, reported substantial differences between delinquent and nondelinquent individuals in average PRB scores. Using optimal cutoff scores, he was able to correctly classify 80% membership of the two criterion groups. The principal limitation of this approach is that it can provide only indirect support for the validity of integrity testing as a personnel screening tool, since these comparison samples consist of nonapplicants with potentially unique test-taking attitudes and motivations and are assessed in a nonemployment context.

A third approach has been to conduct *time series* (otherwise termed "shrinkage reduction") studies in which indices of company performance, such as inventory shrinkage or employee termination rates, are computed before and after initiation of an integrity screening program. The focus of these studies is thus on the organization as a whole rather than on the performance of individual employees. Studies of this kind have been conducted with a variety of integrity inventories, and many report substantial decreases in unaccountable business losses or employee turnover following the introduction of preemployment integrity testing (O'Bannon et al., 1989; Sackett & Harris, 1984). The principal weakness of this approach is that changes in company performance may be explained by factors other than integrity testing. A significant confound occurs when integrity screening is introduced concurrently with other interventions designed to combat counterproductivity. In other cases, coincidental shifts in corporate leadership, economic conditions within the community, or available employment alternatives may contribute to the observed changes in inventory shrinkage and turnover.

Recent reviews have focused on counterproductive behaviors and overall job performance as indices of employee behavior for assessing the criterion-related validity of integrity tests. Two main indices of employee counterproductivity have been examined: self-report and external criteria. *Self-report* criteria include admissions of theft, past dishonest or illegal activities, and counterproductive behaviors on the job, such as absenteeism or drunkenness (see Ones, Viswesvaran, & Schmidt, 1993). A problem with this index of counterproductivity is that the criterion (self-reported wrongdoing) may not be independent of the predictor (integrity testing). Relationships between admissions and integrity test scores may simply reflect a general propensity to disclose or not to disclose indiscretions. This propensity would be expected to inflate validity coefficients in studies of overt integrity tests that include questions about past indiscretions. Some self-report criterion studies have collected integrity test data and admissions data concurrently within the same protocol. A more subtle but related form of contamination may operate in studies of personality-based tests; individual differences in social desirability similarly may influence test responses and admissions of misconduct. Indeed, considerable evidence is available on the relationship between integrity test scores and measures of social desirability (Sackett & Harris, 1984; Sackett et al., 1989).[4]

External criteria have also been used to assess employee counterproductivity. These criteria include recorded incidents of rule breaking on the job, disciplinary actions, and terminations for theft or other forms of dishonesty. A limitation of this approach is criterion sensitivity: Not all dishonest or disruptive behaviors are detected or recorded. However, research is needed to determine the direction of influence of this variable on validity estimates. Criterion insensitivity could suppress validity correlations to the extent that low-integrity scorers commit transgressions for which they are not caught. On the other hand, validity coefficients would be inflated if test scorers were systematically more adept at avoiding detection for their misdeeds.

In keeping with the recent trend toward broadening of the integrity concept (Sackett et al., 1989), validation studies have increasingly focused on overall job performance as an outcome criterion. Job performance is most often assessed using supervisory ratings of employees, and, in some cases, production records for individual employees. The more common measure, supervisory ratings, could be problematic to the extent that integrity test scores and supervisory ratings are mutually influenced by tendencies toward impression management and socially desirable responding. Individuals skilled at conveying a false image may score well on integrity tests and also impress job supervisors for reasons that have nothing to do with integrity or productivity.

Reviews of Validation Research. Several reviews regarding the criterion-related validity of integrity tests have been published within the past decade. Traditional evaluative summaries of the existing validity data have appeared in reviews by Guastello and Rieke (1991), O'Bannon et al. (1989), Sackett and Harris (1984), Sackett et al. (1989), and U.S. Congressional Office of Technology Assessment (1990). The American Psychological Association Task Force on integrity testing undertook an independent paper-by-paper review of the validation literature, but did not include a description of this review in its final report (Goldberg et al., 1991).

The conclusions arising from these different reviews have been decidedly mixed. Sackett and Harris (1984) noted that most of the studies up to that time were methodologically flawed and subject to alternative interpretations. More recently, Sackett et al. (1989) concluded that advances had been made toward establishing the predictive validity of integrity tests, although some important caveats to this conclusion were identified. O'Bannon et al. (1989) concluded that some encouraging evidence for integrity test validity had emerged but that more research was needed, an assessment with which the American Psychological Association Task Force agreed (Goldberg et al., 1991). The U.S. Congressional Office of Technology Assessment (1990) report, on the other hand, was noncommittal in its evaluation: "The research on integrity tests has not yet produced data that clearly supports or dismisses the assertion that these tests can predict dishonest behavior" (p. 8). In contrast, Guastello and Rieke's (1991) review of validation studies of honesty scales from the three most prominent overt integrity tests (Personnel Selection Inventory, Reid Report, and Stanton Survey) was sharply negative: "The honesty tests reviewed are of such marginal validity (less than 1% of the criterion variance accounted for) that their continued use in pre-employment settings is seriously questioned" (p. 501).

In addition to these qualitative reviews of the literature, four quantitative meta-analyses of validation research on integrity testing have appeared. Meta-analysis (see Hunter & Schmidt, 1990) is a psychometric procedure in which statistical effects are aggregated across independent studies to yield an estimate of the "true" relationship under investigation, and of the variance between studies that is attributable to artifacts (e.g., sampling error, unreliability of measurement, and range restriction) and systematic moderating influences (e.g., nature of the study sample, and methods of measurement). Three meta-analyses focused on specific integrity tests: the Employee Attitude Inventory (McDaniel & Jones, 1986), the Personnel Selection Inventory (McDaniel & Jones, 1988), and the Stanton Survey (Harris, undated). Each of these studies reached positive conclusions concerning the criterion-related validity of integrity testing. However, a potential weakness of these meta-analyses (see Sackett et al., 1989) is their focus on overt integrity tests and reliance either predominantly or solely on self-report (admissions) criteria, which would be expected to inflate validity estimates.

The fourth meta-analysis of integrity test validity by Ones et al. (1993) was much more extensive. This meta-analysis included all available criterion-related validity studies of integrity testing. The authors concluded that integrity tests as a whole have substantial validity for predicting employee performance and counterproductive behaviors in the workplace, and they reported an estimated "true validity coefficient" of .41 for integrity tests as predictors of supervisory ratings of job performance. Because of its scope and potential impact, this report merits detailed discussion.

Their meta-analysis incorporated data from 183 separate sources, including (1) empirical studies of integrity testing cited or published in scholarly or trade journals, (2) relevant published or unpublished technical reports available from testing corporations, and (3) raw data and correlational analyses from corporate-sponsored validation studies that had not yet been compiled into technical reports. Twenty-five different integrity tests were represented in the meta-analysis, including two of the five current employee inventories listed earlier (Employee Attitude Inventory and Reid Survey) and all of the preemployment inventories.

Ones, Viswesvaran, and Schmidt used interactive meta-analysis procedures (Hunter & Schmidt, 1990) to examine 665 criterion-related validity coefficients obtained from the aforementioned sources. These coefficients included 389 for overt integrity tests and 276 for personality-based inventories. Approximately two-thirds of the validity coefficients (n = 443) employed counterproductive behaviors (i.e., self-report or external measures of theft, violence, drug abuse, absenteeism, etc.) as the criterion, whereas the rest (n = 222) employed indices of job performance (i.e., supervisory ratings or production records).

Two major meta-analyses were performed. The first evaluated the validity of integrity tests as a whole for predicting the criterion of overall job performance. The mean observed (i.e., raw) validity coefficient across samples (n = 222) was .21; the estimated mean true validity (after correcting for statistical artifacts including sampling error, criterion and predictor unreliability, range restriction, and dichotomization of scores) was .34. The second major meta-analysis assessed the validity of integrity tests as a whole for predicting the criterion of counterproductive behaviors, as indexed by admissions-based and external indices. The mean observed validity coefficient across samples (n = 443) was .33; the estimated mean true validity (after correcting for statistical artifacts in the data) was .47.

They also assessed the moderating effects of different variables on validity estimates. For estimates based on the criterion of job performance, the variable that most clearly affected validity coefficients was job status, with a mean estimated true validity of .40 for job applicants and .29 for current employees. In addition, there was some evidence that concurrent validities overestimated predictive validities for employees, but not job applicants. None of the other variables examined—type of integrity test (overt vs. personality-based), criterion measurement method (supervisory ratings vs. production records), or complexity of job position (high, medium, or low)—was found to systematically affect estimates of test validity based on job performance criteria.

For validity estimates based on the criterion of counterproductive behaviors, several moderating factors were identified. Overt integrity tests were found to be more strongly predictive than personality-based tests (estimated true validity = .55 and .32, respectively), although comparative data were available only from studies using a broad definition of counterproductivity (i.e., general disruptiveness). Estimated validity was generally higher when based on self-report criteria (.58) than when based on external criteria (.32). Employee samples yielded higher validity estimates (M = .54) than applicant samples (M = .44) for overt tests, but not personality-based tests. Coefficients derived using concurrent validation strategies systematically exceeded predictive validities (M's = .56 vs. .36), particularly in the case of overt tests.

To summarize, the results for validity coefficients based on job performance criteria were quite straightforward. Ones, Viswesvaran, and Schmidt concluded from these data that (1) the best estimate of integrity test validity for the criterion of job performance in personnel selection settings (derived from predictive studies of job applicants) is .41, and (2) overt and personality-based tests are similarly valid as predictors of supervisory ratings of job performance. On the basis of this latter finding, the authors hypothesized that both types of test may assess a broad construct of conscientiousness linked to "generally disruptive tendencies."

For the criterion of counterproductive behaviors, the authors concluded that integrity test validity is "quite substantial," but moderated by various factors. Most notably, validity coefficients were higher for self-report as compared to external criteria, and for concurrent as compared to predictive measurement strategies. As noted earlier, these findings may reflect an interdependence between predictor and criterion in studies that assess counterproductivity on the basis of admissions, especially when criterion data are obtained concurrently with the integrity test. They further concluded that theft behavior is less well predicted from integrity test scores than broad counterproductivity, at least in the case of overt tests (no validity estimates specific to theft were available for personality-based inventories). Nonetheless, the authors advanced the general conclusion that "the validity of integrity tests is positive and in useful ranges for both overall job-performance criteria and counterproductive-behaviors criteria" (1993, p. 694).

Their meta-analysis is unique in its scope and sophistication. However, as is true of any empirical work, this report suffered from significant weaknesses that limit the confidence one can place in its conclusions. Foremost among these is the credibility of the body of data included in the meta-analysis (see U.S. Congressional Office of Technology Assessment, 1990). Only a fraction of the research surveyed by Ones et al. consists of published articles in scholarly journals, and an even smaller proportion derives from top-quality, peer-reviewed sources. This observation raises questions about the presence of biases (e.g., experimenter expectancy and selective reporting of results) in the database as a whole (cf. Sackett et al., 1989).

The conclusions of Ones et al. (1993) can be questioned on other grounds as well. The authors fail to consider systematic biases that might act to inflate validity estimates for the most common outcome criteria, for example: (1) the lack of predictor/criterion independence for admissions-based criteria and (2) parallel effects of impression management on integrity measures and supervisory ratings of job performance. In addition, the authors endorse the use of integrity testing on the basis of their findings, without adequately considering how these results may translate into practice. For one thing, "true validities" computed via meta-analysis greatly overestimate the validity for practical purposes associated with any specific test (e.g., mean observed validities in the Ones et al. (1993) study were substantially smaller than "true validity" estimates). Moreover, in practice, integrity tests are usually evaluated dichotomously using "pass–fail" cutoff scores (Goldberg et al., 1991). Ones, Viswesvaran, and Schmidt presented relationships between integrity test scores and criterion variables in terms of correlation coefficients, and "in cases where no correlations were reported, using the information supplied, [we calculated] the phi correlation and then corrected it for dichotomization" (p. 683). It is not clear what the "true validity" coefficients they computed say about the predictive validity of decisions based on cutoff scores for specific integrity tests.

In summary, the Ones et al. (1993) meta-analysis is the most complete summary to date on the criterion-related validity of integrity testing. However, the validity estimates reported by these authors remain suspect because the database from which they were derived is of questionable credibility. Firm conclusions regarding the accuracy of integrity testing as a personnel selection tool must await the accumulation of a truly independent database that has undergone rigorous scientific scrutiny enroute to publication.

Construct Validity

Recent studies have directly compared overt and personality-based integrity inventories and found, notwithstanding differences in their content and intended scope, that the two types of tests measure something in common. Wooley and Hakstian (1992) examined relationships between three personality-based instruments (i.e., PRB, Hogan Reliability Scale, and the PDI Employment Inventory) and one overt integrity test (i.e., Reid Report). As expected, the personality-based tests showed moderate to high intercorrelations. In addition, the Honesty scale of the Reid test evidenced moderate correlations with the three personality-based inventories (mean $r = .30$). Not surprisingly, Reid's Punitive scale, designed to assess attitudes toward punishing others, was uncorrelated with these other tests.

Similarly, Ones, Schmidt, and Viswesvaran (1994b) administered a variety of overt (i.e., Personnel Selection Inventory, Reid Report, and Stanton Survey) and personality-based integrity tests (i.e., Hogan Reliability scale, Inwald Personality Inventory, PDI Employment Inventory, PRB) to a sample of 1,365 college students. Raw correlations between the two types of tests ranged from .20 to .55; the average "true score" correlation (i.e., correcting for unreliability of the measures) was .52. These authors conjectured that "both types of integrity tests derive their validity from the general factor they share" (p. 13).

Ones et al. (1993) hypothesized that the two types of tests assessed a general factor of "conscientiousness" in predicting job performance. In its report, the American Psychological Association Task Force (Goldberg et al., 1991) speculated that these tests tap a set of related constructs that can all be subsumed under a broad construct of "trustworthiness," but acknowledged that research on the construct validity of integrity tests was scarce. Certainly, the case for the validity of integrity testing would be strengthened by a more conclusive demonstration that these tests actually measure some specifiable construct or constructs of interest with conceptual links to the realm of behavioral deviance.

Relationship to Personality Constructs. Several studies have provided useful data regarding these measures and personality constructs. Woolley and Hakstian (1992) examined relationships between a battery of integrity tests (one overt and three personality-based tests) and selected scales from three personality inventories (California Psychological Inventory [CPI; Gough, 1957], Sixteen Personality Factor Questionnaire [Cattell, 1949], NEO Personality Inventory [Costa & McCrae, 1985]) in a sample of 289 university undergraduate students. A joint factor analysis of the integrity tests and general personality scales revealed that the personality-based integrity tests all loaded on a large common factor, which the authors termed "Socialized Control." This factor was defined principally by the Class II scales of the CPI (especially Socialization), which comprises items dealing with behavioral deviance (e.g., past rule breaking, nonconformity, alcohol abuse, and trouble with the law) and excitement seeking or impulsivity. The one overt integrity test (the Reid Report) loaded most highly on a separate factor ("Intolerance of Dishonesty"), but this factor was correlated moderately (.35) with the "Socialized Control" dimension. Woolley and Hakstian concluded that the three personality-based integrity tests all assess a common higher-order dimension of self-discipline or behavioral inhibition, and that the one overt test included in their study measures a distinct, but related construct.

Lilienfeld et al. (1994) studied personality correlates of the Reid Report, the same overt integrity test examined by Woolley and Hakstian (1992). These researchers found that total scores on the Reid Report were positively correlated with indices of behavioral inhibition, socialization, and harm avoidance, and negatively related to measures of anxiousness and hostility. These findings are consistent with the hypothesis that overt integrity tests, such as the Reid Report, tap into broad personality constructs.

Barrick and Mount (1991) conducted a meta-analysis of 117 published and unpublished criterion-related validity studies of personality testing for the purpose of personnel selection. Personality scales from various inventories were classified according to the Five-Factor model of personality by a panel of trained raters. The Five-Factor ("Big Five") model incorporates the following dimensions: *Extraversion* (e.g., sociability, assertiveness, and activity), *Emotional Stability/Neuroticism* (e.g., presence vs. absence of anxiousness, hostility, and insecurity), *Agreeableness* (e.g., soft-heartedness, cooperativeness), *Conscientiousness* (e.g., dependability, planfulness, and responsibility), and *Openness to Experience* (e.g., originality and broad-mindedness).

Although Barrick and Mount (1991) did not specifically investigate integrity tests, they did explore relationships between the Big Five personality dimensions and various job-related indices, including performance ratings, a criterion that Ones et al. (1993) found to be predicted successfully by integrity tests. Barrick and Mount found that Conscientiousness, as defined by a range of personality scales, was consistently the best predictor of all job-related criteria, including supervisory ratings of job performance, across all occupational groups. Extraversion was also a significant predictor of job performance, but only for two occupational categories (i.e., management and sales). Openness to Experience predicted employee responsiveness to training, but not general job performance. Emotional Stability and Agreeableness did not significantly predict either job performance or training proficiency in this study. Barrick and Mount concluded that traits of dependability and trustworthiness are most highly predictive of job success. However, noting that validity coefficients for subjective measures of job performance (e.g., supervisory ratings) substantially exceeded those for objective measures (e.g., employee productivity records), these authors acknowledged that ratings of job performance could have been biased by employees' social reputations.

Tett et al. (1991) also conducted a meta-analysis to investigate the relationship between personality measures and job performance criteria. This study included data from 86 separate studies and evaluated the validity of eight dimensions of personality, including the Big Five, as predictors of job performance. These authors restricted their analysis of the Big Five personality dimensions to studies that used a confirmatory strategy (i.e., those in which an a priori rationale was given for assessing particular traits as predictors of performance in specific jobs). In contrast with Barrick and Mount (1991), Agreeableness was found to be the best overall predictor (estimated true validity = .33), followed by Openness to Experience (.27), Emotional Stability (−.22), Conscientiousness (.18), and Extraversion (.16).

Ones, Mount, Barrick, and Hunter (1994a) challenged the findings of Tett et al. (1991) on several grounds. In the first place, the Tett et al. meta-analysis included far fewer studies and markedly smaller sample sizes than Barrick and Mount's analysis. Furthermore, Tett et al. did not specify the procedures they used to assign scales from different personality inventories to the Big Five categories. According to Ones et al., differences in findings between the two studies could stem from differences in how personality scales were classified. Ones et al. also suggested that Tett et al. did not adequately consider the potential influence of moderator variables on the relationships they examined. Ones et al. concluded that "because of the technical errors and inadequate Big Five analyses, the [Tett et al.] study does not accomplish its intended purpose" (p. 156).

Ones, Schmidt, and Viswesvaran (1994c) specifically examined the degree to which the Big Five personality factors contribute to the relationship between integrity tests and supervisory ratings of job performance. These investigators used the following sources of information to construct the matrix of estimated "true-score correlations" between integrity, the Big Five dimensions, and performance ratings: (1) correlations between the Big Five and job performance (from Barrick & Mount, 1991), (2) correlations between integrity tests and job performance (from Ones et al., 1993), (3) correlations among the Big Five personality dimensions (from the published literature in the field of personality), and (4) correlations between integrity tests and the Big Five dimensions (from the integrity-testing literature).

From the meta-analytically derived matrix of intercorrelations, Ones et al. (1994c) concluded that both overt and personality-based integrity tests were most strongly related to Conscientiousness (mean estimated true-score correlation = .42), followed by Agreeableness (.40), and Emotional Stability (.33). Correlations with the Extraversion and Openness to Experience dimensions were negligible (–.08 and .12, respectively). These investigators also found that the combination of Conscientiousness, Agreeableness, and Emotional Stability predicted integrity test scores better than any of the factors alone. The results of Ones et al. thus converged with those of Barrick and Mount in suggesting that Conscientiousness is a prominent element of integrity tests, and also with the findings of Tett et al. (1991), which suggested that Agreeableness and Emotional Stability also mediate relationships between integrity scores and job performance. Ones et al. (1994c) concluded that "these three constructs permeate all types of integrity tests in varying degrees. Even though overt tests on the surface tap into 'attitudes,' it is clear from [our results] that they tap into personality constructs, and with a pattern similar to personality-based integrity tests" (p. 17).

Integrity versus Antisociality. These results concerning the personality correlates of integrity tests suggest links to a clinical domain that has been the subject of considerable research. Traits associated with a lack of integrity or "broad conscientiousness" (e.g., dishonesty, nonconformity, irresponsibility, aggressiveness, and impulsivity) are also central to the concept of antisocial personality disorder (APD; American Psychiatric Association, 1994a). An intriguing hypothesis is that integrity tests measure something in common with APD.

In this regard, it is noteworthy that the first personality-based integrity test (PRB; Gough, 1971) was a variant of the CPI Socialization (So) scale, which originally was devised to discriminate between delinquent and nondelinquent youth. Furthermore, Woolley and Hakstian (1992) found that other personality-based integrity inventories were substantially related to scores on the Class II scales of the CPI, and the So scale in particular.

Substantial evidence exists on the relationship between the So scale and psychopathy, a construct related to antisocial personality. The most widely recognized inventory for the assessment of psychopathy in criminal offenders is Hare's (1991) Revised Psychopathy Checklist (PCL), which is rated on the basis of a diagnostic interview and information contained in archival records. Harpur, Hakstian, and Hare (1988) demonstrated through factor analysis of its constituent items that the PCL comprises two distinct but correlated factors. The first represents the "core personality features of psychopathy" and includes items dealing with affective and interpersonal traits (e.g., talkativeness, deceit, manipulativeness, and deficient capacities for emotional responsiveness, remorse, and empathy). The second factor ("antisocial lifestyle") is defined by items dealing with early behavioral deviance, stimulation seeking, aggressiveness, impulsiveness, and irresponsibility.

Of interest to the present discussion are findings (Harpur, Hare, & Hakstian, 1989; Smith & Newman, 1990) indicating that the PCL antisocial factor, but not the core personality factor, is substantially related to the CPI So scale and to other phenomena, including sensation seeking, alcohol and drug abuse, and APD. On the basis of these findings, a strong relationship would be predicted between the construct underlying integrity tests and the PCL antisocial factor.

One of us (Patrick) examined correlations between the abbreviated NEO Personality Inventory (Costa & McCrae, 1985), a widely used measure of the "Big Five" dimensions of personality, and the two factors of the PCL in a male inmate sample ($n = 80$). The antisocial factor was significantly related to all three of the dimensions (Conscientiousness, Agreeableness, and Neuroticism/Emotional Stability) that appear to lie at the heart of integrity tests (Ones et al., 1994c). Of these "integrity-related" dimensions, the personality factor of psychopathy was related only to Agreeableness, and then only as a function of variance shared with the antisocial factor (i.e., controlling for scores on the antisocial factor, the relationship was not significant).

These results are consistent with the hypothesis that integrity tests measure constructs related to antisociality. In view of the documented relationship between indices of antisocial personality and criminal recidivism, it is not surprising that integrity tests predict some of the variance in counterproductivity and job performance. However, these data also suggest that integrity tests are poor indicators of the core personality features of psychopathy, and that, as critics have argued, these tests may fail to detect unprincipled liars who are skilled in impression management.

Controversial Aspects of Integrity Testing

Integrity testing is by its nature a controversial enterprise. Tests that serve as arbiters of who is deemed hirable are apt to be the target of debate in a democratic society (see, e.g., Camara & Schneider, 1994, 1995; Kleinmuntz, 1995; Lilienfeld, Alliger, &

Mitchell, 1995; Ones, Viswesvaran, & Schmidt, 1995; Rieke & Guastello, 1995). The historical link between integrity testing and another highly controversial enterprise—polygraph testing—has helped to fuel this debate. Critics of integrity testing have raised several major concerns with the practice.

False-Positive Misclassification and Labeling

The issue is the extent to which people, who would have been honest and dependable workers, are denied employment because their integrity test scores fall below the established cut score for hiring. The criterion-related validity of integrity testing is at best moderate (Ones et al., 1993), and according to Sackett et al. (1989), 30–60% of all individuals who take integrity tests "fail" them. Critics (e.g., Kleinmuntz, 1995) argue that the rate of false-positive errors (i.e., misclassification of honest people as dishonest based on integrity test results) is unacceptably high.

Furthermore, the frequency of false-positive misclassifications will vary with the base rate of dishonesty in an employment setting (i.e., the proportion of persons who actually engage in theft or other serious deviance after being hired). Even a test with high validity will misclassify a substantial number of individuals as untrustworthy if the existing base rate of dishonesty is low. The counterargument is that personnel selection of some kind is always necessary in the employment setting, and any selection technique with proven validity will result in fewer errors of classification than a strictly random selection procedure (Goldberg et al., 1991; Ones et al., 1993; Sackett, 1994). From this viewpoint, the essential issue is the incremental validity of integrity testing, not its absolute validity.

A further concern with integrity testing is that the consequences of failing such tests may be more serious and far-ranging than is true for other personnel screening methods. The labeling of a person as dishonest, untrustworthy, or lacking in integrity is likely to carry a greater stigma than an unfavorable hiring decision rendered on grounds of insufficient experience, ability, or skill (Goldberg et al., 1991; U.S. Congressional Office of Technology Assessment, 1990). There is no evidence that integrity test results are routinely released from one employer to another. However, nondiscrimination laws make it necessary for employers to maintain records of information used in hiring decisions, and there are no official standards governing the use or dissemination of such information. Recently, the Association for Personnel Test Publishers (APTP, 1990) formulated the Model Guidelines for Preemployment Integrity Testing Programs (for a review, see Jones, Arnold, & Harris, 1990), but currently no mechanism exists for enforcing these recommendations.

Fakability

The obverse of the false-positive issue is the concern that integrity tests are vulnerable to deliberate distortion by individuals who are motivated to appear trustworthy. This problem may be more of a concern with overt tests, which inquire transparently about attitudes toward and past episodes of wrongdoing (Ryan & Sackett, 1987). Alliger,

Lilienfeld, and Mitchell (1996) examined the degree to which scores on overt and personality-based integrity tests are affected by instructions to deliberately dissimulate. Relative to noninstructed controls, participants who were told to "fake good" achieved somewhat higher scores on an overt integrity test, and those who received explicit coaching on how to appear trustworthy achieved substantially higher scores. However, scores on a personality-based test were not affected by faking instructions or coaching.

Although "faking good" may be easy to accomplish with an overt integrity test, the available data suggest that this does not occur routinely (Murphy, 1993). Goldberg et al. (1991) suggested some reasons why this may be true, including the possibility that prospective employees tend not to perceive integrity tests as crucial to hiring, and a "false-consensus effect," whereby applicants assume that their own peculiarities and indiscretions are "normal" and hence reportable. Another possibility is that the transparency of overt integrity questions leads respondents to infer that candidness will be interpreted favorably (Alliger et al., 1996). Presumably, these factors will become less influential as public awareness of the purposes and methods of integrity testing increases.

Overreliance on Integrity Testing in Personnel Selection

Another concern is that integrity tests, because of their scientific aura and ease of administration, may come to be used in many settings as the sole criterion for hiring. Test publishers have in some cases promoted this inclination by making exaggerated claims about the merits of integrity testing without mention of collateral selection strategies (Kleinmuntz, 1995; U.S. Congressional Office of Technology Assessment, 1990). A related concern is that integrity testing will tend to supplant approaches that focus on encouraging honesty and productivity in the workplace (e.g., communication of company standards, fair management practices, and employee incentive programs).

Adverse Impact

A crucial issue in the use of integrity tests is the extent to which these tests discriminate against legally protected groups. Fairness in hiring is mandated by many federal, state, and local statutes. The Equal Employment Opportunity Act of 1972, for example, explicitly prohibits discrimination in the preemployment screening context. A common criterion for determining whether a selection strategy has "adverse impact" is the "four-fifths" rule contained in the Uniform Guidelines on Employee Selection Procedures adopted by the federal government in 1978: A personnel selection procedure is considered nondiscriminatory if the proportion of persons in any protected group deemed hirable by its criteria equals or exceeds four-fifths of nonprotected persons deemed hirable.

The weight of available evidence indicates that integrity test are not, as a whole, biased against protected groups (Goldberg et al., 1991; O'Bannon et al., 1989; Sackett & Harris, 1984; Sackett et al., 1989). To the extent that consistent differences in rates of selection have been obtained, they have tended to favor protected groups. In particular, integrity tests are more likely to be passed by females than males, and by older individuals than younger ones. This finding is in keeping with a considerable body of research indicating a lower incidence of criminal deviance among females than males, and older than younger persons. We found no evidence that integrity tests systematically discriminate against racial minorities.

Adherents of integrity testing maintain that the lack of adverse impact is one compelling argument for the use of these tests. Scores on the other major class of personnel selection inventories (i.e., ability tests) do differ systematically as a function of race. Ones et al. (1993) argued convincingly that, because scores on ability tests and integrity tests are uncorrelated, the combined use of integrity testing and ability testing would lead to a substantial increase in predictive validity while reducing adverse impact.

However, the same essential caveat applies here as with the literature on the criterion-related validity of integrity testing, namely, the quality and credibility of the research base, much of which has been sponsored or conducted by test publishers. Both the American Psychological Association Task Force report and the U.S. Congressional Office of Technology Assessment report acknowledged the need for additional research.

Privacy and Informed Consent

The issue is whether the types of questions asked on an integrity test comprise an unjustified intrusion into the respondent's private life. This concern has been raised particularly in regard to overt integrity tests, which include blunt questions about personal wrongdoing. Questions of privacy have also arisen because of the historical association between integrity testing and polygraph testing.

The issue of privacy is a complex one, because although privacy is a basic value in American society, it eludes simple definition and is not broadly protected by law (U.S. Congressional Office of Technology Assessment, 1990). Although an implicit recognition of the right to privacy exists according to various amendments to the U.S. Constitution, this protection applies primarily to intrusions by the government and not to the actions of private employers (Bergmann, Mundt, & Illgen, 1990). In some states, tort (common) laws exist to protect individuals from wrongful acts that have been interpreted to cover invasions of privacy (O'Bannon et al., 1989). Whether these laws would extend to intrusive questions on integrity tests, however, is not clear, because in such instances courts are inclined to weigh the interests of the employee against the needs of the employer (Bergmann et al., 1990). Indeed, the one privacy case to have arisen to date from the use of an integrity test (Heins v. Commonwealth of Pennsylvania, Unemployment Compensation Board of Review, 1987) was resolved in favor of the employer.

A related issue concerns informed consent. The *Standards for Educational and Psychological Testing* published by the American Psychological Association (1985) specify that informed consent can be considered implied when job applicants are tested, but the American Psychological Association Task Force (Goldberg et al., 1991) expressed the viewpoint that "[t]he pressure on applicants to submit to testing must be balanced by an obligation on the part of examiners to explain fully the application procedures," an opinion also stated in the U.S. Congressional Office of Technology Assessment (1990) report on integrity testing. A similar recommendation was made in the *Model Guidelines for Preemployment Integrity Testing Programs* (Association for Personnel Test Publishers, 1990).

Legal Status of Integrity Testing

At present, only two state legislatures have introduced laws prohibiting or restricting the use of integrity tests. Massachusetts prohibits the practice entirely; this restriction was accomplished by an amendment to the state Polygraph Act, which extended the meaning of the term "lie detector" to include not just polygraph machines but "any other device, mechanism, instrument, or written examination" used for the purpose of rendering a decision as to truthfulness or honesty. The state of Rhode Island added a less restrictive clause to its Polygraph Act that prohibits the use of written integrity testing as the *primary* basis for an employment decision. Legal precedent suggests that antipolygraph laws in other states will require specific rewording in order to be extended to integrity tests (Arnold, 1991; O'Bannon et al., 1989).

The Future of Integrity Testing

O'Bannon et al. (1989) identified several emerging developments within the field of integrity testing. These included (1) a broadening of the content domain of integrity tests to include characteristics such as drug abuse potential, emotional stability, hostility, productivity, and likely tenure of employment; (2) increased use of automated test administration and scoring; (3) increased openness on the part of integrity test publishers and facilitation of research by independent investigators; (4) growth of advocacy groups in the business sector; and (5) continuing criticism of the practice and ongoing efforts to enact regulatory legislation.

Some additional trends can be anticipated as well. Recent meta-analytic findings regarding the construct validity of integrity testing should inspire the development of new inventories that optimally measure the broad personality dimensions underlying the spectrum of integrity tests (cf. Ones et al., 1994c). In this regard, further efforts will hopefully be made to establish links between the domain of integrity testing and other extant literatures (e.g., personality factors underlying criminality and psychopathy). As the focus of the field shifts away from theft and honesty toward job performance and adjustment, it is likely that personality-based tests will increasingly supersede overt tests, and "integrity" tests may come to be known by other names (e.g., "employment adaptability tests," or "productivity predictors"). Finally, considering the independence between integrity and ability tests and the unique merits of each (Ones et al., 1993), it is likely that applicant screening tests will be devised that assess both domains.

Clinical Applications

Although, on balance, overt integrity tests appear to have some validity, these tests account for considerably less than 20% of the variance in criterion measures. However, even tests with relatively low validity can have utility from the vantage point of personnel screening, in which the focus is on the aggregate of persons screened for employment purposes. In this context, the important question is whether the test improves on chance classification. In many hiring decisions, most qualified applicants will not be hired. Rather than use a selection procedure with no validity, it is argued that a honesty test with even modest validity has utility.

The low validity and many problems inherent to these tests makes it difficult to use them in a clinical setting where the assessment of a single person is important. Unfortunately, little information is available concerning the effects of different cut scores on classification accuracy, so it is not even possible to have confidence in the significance of extreme scores on these tests. The inability to interpret integrity test scores is exacerbated by the fact that most of the tests and their scoring keys are proprietary. In addition, most of the existing literature is unpublished. These factors combine to make it difficult to determine how these tests could be used to advantage in a clinical decision-making context. Hence, it would be imprudent for clinicians to place much stock in individual scores from these inventories.

ACKNOWLEDGMENTS

The authors wish to acknowledge Scott Lillienfeld for helpful comments on a draft of this paper and the support of grants MH48657 and MH52384 from the National Institute of Mental Health.

NOTES

1. This information was not available for the remaining study.

2. It should be noted that most integrity tests are keyed such that *low scores* are indicative of the characteristic of interest (i.e., a lack of integrity).

3. This definition of "construct validity" is Anastasi's (1988). The term has also been defined more broadly as a superordinate concept subsuming other forms of validity (Cronbach & Meehl, 1955).

4. However, the positive relationship between social desirability and integrity test scores does not submit to easy interpretation. Modern personality theory acknowledges that social desirability scales reflect not just response sets, but also meaningful personality traits (see Anastasi, 1988). Thus, it is not clear whether people who present well on integrity tests do so because they are motivated to appear socially acceptable, or because they really are less disposed to think and do bad things.

14

Hypnosis and Dissimulation

ROBERT D. MILLER, M.D., Ph.D.
LAWRENCE J. STAVA, Ph.D.

Hypnosis evokes in public and even some professional circles the concept of direct access to forgotten memories and withheld thoughts of psychological or forensic significance. Within this framework, hypnosis has been viewed by some adherents as an avenue to the truth that minimizes attempts at deliberate distortion. This chapter begins with an overview of hypnosis that underscores the controversy surrounding this phenomenon. Next, the clinical applications of hypnosis are discussed, including its ability to assist in memory recall and methods to demonstrate that hypnotic state has occurred. Finally, the relevance of hypnosis to legal issues is examined.

OVERVIEW

The Nature of Hypnosis

A significant controversy continues within the scientific community as to the nature of hypnosis (Frankel, 1976). From a historical perspective, hypnosis has been conceptualized through different explanatory models. These models are important to the current chapter because they imply different levels of conscious control over the material that is revealed during the hypnotic state. Table 14.1 summarizes the early descriptions of hypnosis that impose various physiological and psychological explanations for this phenomenon.

Critics of the traditional view of hypnosis have considered "the trance state" with reference to the demand characteristics of the hypnotic situation. Interpersonal dimensions are propounded by Sarbin and Coe (1972) and Barber, Spanos, and Chaves (1974). As presented in Table 14.1, the theoretical underpinnings for hypnosis range from social psychology to psychoanalytic thinking.

282

TABLE 14.1. Varying Descriptions of Hypnosis: Historical and Current

Investigator	Description
Mesmer (1779/1948)	"Animal magnetism" as a process by which the unequal distribution of magnetic fluids in the human body could be rectified, thus curing disease
De Puysegur (1784/1943)	Compared hypnotism to somnambulism
Charcot (1886)	A clinical state similar to hysteria, with neurophysiological features
Janet (1907)	Similar to hysteria and including dissociative phenomena
Bernheim (1884/1964)	A state of heightened suggestibility
Sarbin & Coe (1972)	From a social psychology viewpoint, defined hypnosis as role playing by the participant
Barber et al. (1974)	Analyzed hypnosis in terms of the imagination and expectations of the participant
Gill & Brenman (1959)	An archaic transference in which passive–dependent longings and magical expectations are directed toward the hypnotist
White (1941)	Two intertwined processes: goal–directed striving in the context of an altered state of consciousness
Shor (1959, 1962)	Altered state, with the trance representing a fading of the generalized reality orientation; he also combined role playing (Sarbin & Coe, 1972) with archaic transference (Gill & Brenman, 1959)
Hilgard (1973)	Neodissociation theory posited a hierarchy of control systems, with a dominant system typically identified by the person as the *self*; he hypothesized that hypnosis occurs when the nondominant system is dissociated from the dominant system

In summary, we believe that hypnosis represents a very complex phenomenon that is not adequately explained by any single existing theory. However, we see most promise in the three-factor theory of Shor (1959, 1962) and Hilgard's (1973, 1977) neodissociation approach. Other theories, which do not conceptualize hypnosis as involving an altered state of consciousness, do not provide adequate explanations for much of the behavior characterized as hypnotic. The concept of an altered state also seems particularly relevant for understanding certain types of psychopathology, such as dissociative identity disorder (DID) and other dissociative phenomena.

Measurement of Hypnotizability: Hypnotic Susceptibility Scales

Considerable controversy remains on how to measure operationally the hypnotic state. One major effort has been to use sophisticated psychological scales to measure hypnotic susceptibility. Early efforts to measure susceptibility by White (1930), Barry, MacKinnon and Murray (1931), Davis and Husband (1931) and Friedlander and Sarbin (1938) were largely descriptive and unstandardized. Weitzenhoffer and Hilgard (1959) standardized the original Friedlander and Sarbin scale by developing the well-validated Stanford Hypnotic Susceptibility Scale, Forms A and B.

With the Stanford Scales, participants are given a standardized hypnotic induction and subsequently asked to perform various motor tasks (e.g., eye closure, arm rigidity, and eye catalepsy) that are rated by the investigator. The scales have excellent interrater reliability of .83 to .90 (Hilgard, 1965), and stability for Form A (i.e., test–retest correlations of .60 over a 10-year period; Morgan, Johnson, & Hilgard, 1974). The Stanford Scales also correlated with participants' self-reports with several external measures: (1) reported pain reduction through hypnotic suggestion at .50 (Hilgard, 1967), and (2) clinical estimates of hypnotic responsiveness at .78 (Hilgard, 1979).

Newer versions of the Stanford Scale include Scale C, which was developed to measure cognitive distortions associated with hypnosis (Weitzenhoffer & Hilgard, 1962). Its psychometric properties appear similar to Scales A and B. To differentiate among participants with a high level of hypnotic susceptibility, the Stanford Profile Scales I and II were developed that utilized more difficult tasks, such as analgesia and deafness (Weitzenhoffer & Hilgard, 1963).

Shor and Orne (1962) developed the Harvard Hypnotic Susceptibility Scale as an adaptation of Form A of the Stanford Scales for group administration with the use of self-ratings. Concurrent validity has been assessed between the Harvard Scale and Form C of the Stanford Scale with correlations ranging from .53 to .83 (Bongartz, 1985; Coe, 1964; Evans & Schmeidler, 1966; Sheehan & McConkey, 1979).

Barber and his coworkers developed two scales to assess participants' ability to become imaginatively involved with hypnotic suggestions based on his cognitive-behavioral model of hypnosis (Barber, 1972; Barber & Wilson, 1977; Spanos & Barber, 1974). The Barber Suggestibility Scale (Barber & Glass, 1962), with eight hypnotic suggestions, is highly reliable (Barber, 1965; Barber & Glass, 1962; Barber & Calverly, 1963, 1964) and moderately correlated with the Stanford Hypnotic Susceptibility Scale, Form A (Ruch, Morgan, & Hilgard, 1974). The Creative Imagination Scale was developed for more direct clinical use and is reliable. In general, Barber's scales correlate poorly with the Harvard Scales (McConkey, Sheehan, & White 1979) and have been criticized for ignoring significant components of hypnosis (Hilgard, 1982; Monteiro, MacDonald, & Hilgard, 1980).

The Hypnotic Induction Profile (HIP; Spiegel & Bridger, 1970) was based primarily on the apparent relationship between the ability of participants to roll their eyes up on command and hypnotic susceptibility. The HIP is the only widely used test of hypnotic susceptibility that is not significantly correlated with the Stanford Scales (Orne et al., 1979).

Extensive research has been conducted on each of these scales. They correlate reliably with clinical observations, and moderately predict responses to other hypnotic experiences. A limitation to their use in the authentication of trance states is that they have been validated on similar clinical observations with no external criterion of trance validity. In addition, the experimental designs assumed genuine responses on the part of participants; however, data are not available on the ability of the scales to detect dissimulation. Thus, the scales may be useful for threshold estimation of a participant's potential to experience the hypnotic state, but should not be considered as guarantees either of actual susceptibility or of the authenticity of subsequent trance behavior. In summary, the scales are face valid and thus can be simulated by participants.

THE USE OF HYPNOSIS IN CLINICAL PRACTICE

Clinical hypnosis is used in mental health practice for several treatment objectives. For example, hypnosis has been employed as a method for uncovering unconscious material, and, more recently, as an adjunct to behavioral techniques for pain reduction, weight loss, and smoking cessation. In such applications, clinicians have usually been concerned more with the results of the procedure than with the validity of the methods; however, hypnosis may also be used in circumstances in which the accuracy of the information elicited is important.

When hypnosis is used as a general method for overcoming unconscious resistance, the accuracy of the material produced is usually less significant than the emotional content. Screen (i.e., emotionally laden but factually inaccurate) memories may be as useful therapeutically as accurate memories of actual events; such screen memories constitute "narrative truth." Forensic clinicians are generally forced, however, by the prospect of court testimony and cross-examination to be more concerned than are their nonforensic colleagues with the validity of the hypnotic state itself and the material produced under trance (known as "historical truth"). Given the increasing demands to present evidence on the authenticity of trances and trance-derived material, nonforensic clinicians must also become cognizant of hypnosis's vulnerability to simulation and dissimulation.

Even within clinical practice, the validity of the hypnotic state and the historical truth produced in trance are sometimes significant. Clinicians may be concerned with patients' resistance and utilize hypnosis in an attempt to circumvent defensiveness as part of the treatment process. In addition, hypnosis and other purportedly memory-enhancing techniques, such as drug-assisted interviews (see Chapter 12), are used most frequently in cases of amnesia and related dissociative states. Here, the accuracy of material elicited may be crucial to establishing patients' identities and returning them to their former lives.

Simulation of Hypnosis

Early clinical literature (e.g., Breuer & Freud, 1895/1955; Prince, 1906; Schreiber, 1973) contains anecdotal case reports of the use of hypnosis to reestablish lost memories in cases of dissociation. These cases are presented at face value without any systematic attempt to investigate whether the patient was actually in trance or the material produced was accurate. More recently, researchers have attempted to address these issues more directly under laboratory conditions.

Researchers have explored the differences in hypnotized and nonhypnotized behavior in within-subject designs. Differences have been observed for tests of color blindness (Erickson, 1939; Rock, 1961, cited in Barber, 1962) and "anesthetized" limbs (Scars, 1932). Use of hypnotized participants as their own controls has been criticized (e.g., Barber, 1962; Sutcliffe, 1958) because of practice effects and participants' desire to please the investigators.

Studies (e.g., Orne, 1959, 1972; Sheehan, 1971; Sheehan & Tilden, 1985; Spanos, Radke, Bertrand, Addie, & Drummond, 1982; Weitzenhoffer & Sjoberg, 1961) have also used between-subjects designs. These studies employed two groups: (1) a highly hypnotizable and (2) a control group that were not hypnotizable. Participants were exposed to the same hypnotic induction by an investigator masked to their group membership. These studies have methodological limitations, because they did not sufficiently control for the motivational differences between groups (Barber, 1962) or differences in personality types (Sheehan, 1971). To address this first concern, Barber (1962) compared hypnotized subjects with several groups of nonhypnotized controls, including a group that had been given strong incentives to experience the states to be suggested, but were not given formal hypnotic inductions. The hypnotized participants could not be distinguished by the standard test measures from high-incentive controls, although they could be differentiated from low-incentive controls. This study suggested that participants exposed to situations involving strong demand characteristics and/or who have high motivation to experience (or at least to appear to experience) the effects of trance, may be difficult to distinguish from those persons actually in trances.

Several prominent authors (Coe, 1989; deGroot & Gwynn, 1989; Spanos, 1986; Spanos, deGroot, & Gwynn, 1987) have concluded that participants in genuine trance cannot be distinguished from participants instructed to simulate a trance. Other investigators have examined techniques to distinguish real from simulated hypnotic amnesia. For example, Kennedy and Coe (1994) found no differences between simulators and hypnotized persons on nonverbal signs of deception. In contrast, Spanos, James, and deGroot (1990) reported that simulators recognized "forgotten" words at lower levels than expected by chance (i.e., symptom validity testing, or SVT) significantly more often than did nonsimulators. As an interesting possibility, Kinnunen, Zamansky and Block (1994) reported that electrodermal skin conductance response provided an effective method for detecting deception in the laboratory for both hypnotized and nonhypnotized participants.

The laboratories utilized in these research studies are significantly different from clinical settings. Therapists usually have far more knowledge about their patients than researchers do of their participants. Because of this greater familiarity, clinicians might be more successful than researchers at detecting simulated hypnotic states. In the absence of hypnosis research on hypnosis by therapists, these controlled studies underscore the vulnerability of hypnosis to undetected simulations.

HYPNOSIS IN THE EVALUATION AND TREATMENT OF MEMORY LOSS

A substantial literature exists on hypnosis and the genuineness of memory impairment. For example, Power (1977) contended that genuine amnesia is likely to have a gradual onset, whereas simulated amnesia tends to display an abrupt onset. Bradford and Smith

(1979) found that genuine amnesias tend to be patchy, whereas complete amnesia tends to be simulated. Many authors (Gorman, 1984; Keschner, 1960; Power, 1977; Price & Terhune, 1919; Sadoff, 1974) have suggested that inconsistencies in recall over time tend to indicate simulation. Several commentators (Bradford & Smith, 1979; Kanzer, 1939; Lennox, 1943; Power, 1977; Sadoff, 1974) have suggested that the psychiatric history of the patient and the circumstances of the memory loss, particularly the potential secondary gain, may assist in determining the validity of the claimed amnesia. For an extended discussion of feigned amnesia and memory loss, the reader is referred to Chapter 5.

Recall without Hypnosis

Before discussing the role of hypnosis in the detection of simulated amnesia, a general overview of memory recall is helpful. Early investigators have underscored how unintentional distortions of memory are commonplace. For instance, Binet (1905) was one of the first researchers to describe the suggestibility of memory recall. Similarly, Bartlett (1932) told short stories to various persons and asked them to repeat the stories at several-year intervals; he found systematic distortions of the memories with time. Whipple (1918) reviewed the psychological literature on eyewitness reports and again demonstrated significant distortions in memory recall.

A major research effort has examined the influence of questions' form on witnesses' recollections. Investigators usually have presented scenarios (e.g., films or staged activities) to participants and subsequently questioned them about their recollections. Historically, Muscio (1916) demonstrated that the form of questions strongly influenced participants' responses, and that free recall produced less detail but also significantly fewer mistakes than did structured inquiries. These findings have subsequently been replicated in many studies (Hilgard & Loftus, 1979; Lipton, 1977; Loftus & Palmer, 1974; Loftus & Zanni, 1975; Marquis, Marshall, & Oskamp, 1972; Wells, 1978). For example, Lipton (1977) demonstrated that participants who had viewed a film recalled only 21% of 150 possible details but with 91% accuracy in unstructured narrative recall. With structured questions, participants recalled 75% of the details but with only 56% accuracy.

Analogue studies have also demonstrated that simple changes in language can produce significant results. For example, Loftus and Zanni (1975) found that participants who were asked questions in the form "Did you see *the* . . . ?" as opposed to "Did you see *a* . . . ?" were two to three times more likely to respond positively, even when the correct answer was "no." Loftus and Palmer (1974) found that participants who were asked questions about filmed automobile accidents using words, such as "bumped" or "smashed," estimated the speeds of the vehicles as significantly higher than participants questioned with words such as "contacted" or "hit."

Hypnosis and Recall

Some authors (e.g., Schafer & Rubio, 1978) believe that memory is comparable to a videotape recording that cannot be changed but only recalled in greater or lesser detail.

It is claimed that hypnotically enhanced recall produces increased information without any additional distortion. Arons (1967) asked witnesses to recall information first without hypnosis and then in trance; he reported greater detail with no more distortion after hypnosis. Putnam (1979) criticized this conclusion by pointing out that the greater detail could have resulted from repeated efforts at recall, not from the hypnosis per se.

Reiser (1986) claimed in a review of 700 police-investigative cases that hypnosis enhanced witnesses' recall, and that 80% of the information, which could be independently verified, proved to be accurate. Further investigation of these findings with more rigorous procedures is certainly warranted. Kroger and Douce (1979), although recognizing the potential distortions inherent in the use of hypnosis, still argued for its use in recall. Schafer and Rubio (1978) argued that hypnosis should be useful for enhancing recall of traumatic events by removing witnesses' anxiety and, thus, permitting them to recall more fully.

Bryan (1962) asserted that witnesses cannot lie while under hypnosis. According to him, the questions are directed at the subconscious rather than conscious mind when the subject is in a deep hypnotic trance. Hence, the answers also come from the subconscious mind. Especially if the questions are rapidly fired in quick succession, Bryan declared, "The patient does not have time to 'think' on a conscious level; and because his thinking process is disrupted by hypnosis, he can only release information from the subconscious mind. He therefore invariably responds with the correct answer" (p. 245). Bryan also maintained that this conclusion was supported by polygraph and drug-assisted interviews.

The consensus of research is that hypnosis (1) amplifies the distortions found in eyewitness recall, and (2) participants are capable of lying while in a trance. Studies (e.g., Hilgard & Loftus, 1979; Orne, 1961; Ripley & Wolf, 1947; Stalnaker & Riddle, 1932) revealed that hypnotized participants recalled events in greater detail than unhypnotized participants, but that the degree of distortion also increased. Putnam (1979) failed to find that hypnotized participants recalled greater detail than those not hypnotized, but did corroborate that hypnotized participants gave significantly more incorrect responses. He also found that hypnotized participants were significantly more confident in the accuracy of their answers, whether correct or not, than were those who were not hypnotized.

The hypnotic simulation studies (Green et al., 1990; Kennedy & Coe, 1994; Kinnunen et al., 1994; Lynn, Rhue, Myers, & Weekes, 1994; Spanos & Bures, 1993; Spanos et al., 1990) have demonstrated clearly that participants are capable of lying while apparently under a trance. The empirical evidence is consistent: Hypnosis is not a "truth serum." Hypnosis appears, at least in controlled studies, to exaggerate the suggestibility of witnesses (1) because of the demand characteristics of the hypnotic situation, and (2) because hypnotizable participants are more suggestible than non-hypnotizable persons, even without formal trance induction. Considerable caution should be exercised in determining the veridicality of material produced under hypnosis.

Patients in clinical practice are less likely than persons evaluated for courts to have conscious motives to simulate trance or distort their answers under hypnosis. Nevertheless, patients are likely to have strong reasons to please their therapists; therefore, the demand characteristics of the hypnotic state are increased. Even a simple encouraging statement that the patient will be able to remember lost material presents a powerful incentive for the patient to remember *something*, regardless of its accuracy.

Clinicians, using hypnosis to recover forgotten material or to overcome unconscious resistance, should frame their trance inductions and subsequent questions carefully in order to minimize the suggestibility of the situation. Open-ended questions (e.g., "Tell me what you remember") are to be preferred to leading questions (e.g., "Do you remember your father punishing you?"). If the accuracy of hypnotic recall is important, efforts should be made to confirm reported details through independent sources. Clinicians should also be aware of the increased confidence patients have in memories recovered in trance and not confuse conviction with accuracy. In a report issued by the National Institute of Justice, Orne, Soskis, Dinges, Orne, and Tonry (1989) stated, "Hypnosis can either increase the inaccuracy of recollections without diminishing confidence in the 'memories,' or it can increase confidence without increasing accuracy, or both" (p. 9).

CLINICAL APPLICATIONS

The use of hypnosis to verify the accuracy of patients' responses has limited applicability in clinical practice. Limitations include (1) lack of independent verification that a patient actually is hypnotized; (2) the ability of certain patients to dissimulate while appearing to satisfy all the criteria for being in trance; and (3) the increased likelihood of inaccurate memories being produced under hypnosis. These limitations are summarized in Table 14.2.

A review of Table 14.2 highlights the difficulties inherent in the employment of clinical hypnosis for the detection of deception. Perhaps the most effective use of hypnosis is in the evaluation of the ambivalent patient who appears to be denying significant psychopathology or trauma. Under these circumstances, the clinician should weigh the risks (e.g., the reporting of additional psychopathology in highly suggestible patients) and benefits (e.g., the elucidation of the patient's dynamics). Anecdotal case reports yield mixed results on the efficacy of this use (Erickson & Kubie, 1941; Schneck, 1967; Spiegel, Detrick, & Frischholz, 1982). Other applications of hypnosis to the assessment of dissimulation, such as the detection of malingering or of simulated trance states, are not justified by current research data.

A relevant question is whether clinicians should *ever* employ hypnotic techniques in the investigation of dissimulation, given the availability of other more reliable methods, such as structured interviews and psychometric assessments (see Chapters 9, 11, 15, and 17). Hypnosis may well be most valuable when used in conjunction with other assessment procedures, such as a "challenge test" for divulging previously unreported psychopathology or the examination of highly inconsistent data. It is considered a challenge test because hypnosis may assist in *ruling in* probable dissimulation; but if no discrepancies are perceived, hypnosis cannot *rule out* the possibility of dissimulation, since clinicians can never determine the veracity or completeness of patients' self-reports on the basis of hypnosis alone.

TABLE 14.2. Clinical Application of Hypnosis to the Assessment of Dissimulation

Response style/memory loss	Clinical issues	Research findings
Defensiveness	Can hypnosis assist in uncovering denied psychopathology?	Mixed results
Malingering	Can hypnosis assist in verifying questioned psychopathology in cases of suspected malingering?	Untested
Deception	Can hypnosis assist in the detection of untruthfulness?	No
Deception	Can participants lie under hypnosis?	Yes
Genuine amnesia	Can hypnosis assist in recovery of forgotten memories?	Tentatively yes
Feigned amnesia	Can hypnosis distinguish between actual and feigned amnesia?	No
Recovered memories	Can more information be recalled?	Yes, but with more inaccuracies
Recovered memories	Can memories of long-past events be accurately recovered?	Very controversial; no research support
Simulated trances	Can clinicians distinguish between actual and simulated hypnotic trances?	No

Clinicians may also wish to consider the use of hypnosis when they are stymied in the evaluation of nonforensic psychiatric patients. Table 14.3 presents possible indications for the consideration of when hypnosis may be useful. For example, hypnosis might be utilized for understanding the motivation underlying patients' presentation, particularly regarding the denial or minimization of psychopathology. In such situations, hypnotizable patients' resistance may be sufficiently lowered through hypnosis to permit therapists to circumvent the anxiety and/or to confront denial or dissimulation in a context safer to the patient.

Clinicians must weigh the potential benefits of increased understanding against the possibility that the patient's actual memories will be distorted further by hypnosis. The indications presented in Table 14.3 specifically exclude the use of hypnosis with patients involved in the civil or criminal courts, except when apparent amnesia is central to the case. As will be discussed, hypnosis with forensic patients is particularly controversial and involves specific motivations to dissimulate, which are not usually found in nonforensic patients.

A primary focus of this text is to establish clinical decision-making models with explicit criteria for the determination of dissimulation. Given the inherent difficulties in the use of hypnosis, explicit threshold and clinical decision models are not warranted. Clinicians are urged, however, to evaluate carefully any marked contradictions or discrepancies between hypnotic and nonhypnotic interviews. As noted by Orne (1979), much of the assessment in forensic cases, including unstructured and structured interviews, should already be completed prior to the use of hypnosis. The same *caveats* apply to nonforensic cases. Results from hypnotic interviews should be considered "true" only if they can be independently verified and are psychologically consistent for the patient in question. In these circumstances, hypnosis is directed more toward the investigation of a patient's motivation and response style than to the discovery of factual inaccuracies.

Recovered Memories of Childhood Sexual Abuse

A major controversy has arisen in both the clinical and legal worlds concerning the recovery of memories by adult patients of being sexually abused as children. Recover-

---

TABLE 14.3. Possible Indications for Hypnotic Investigation of Dissimulation

1. Highly anxious nonforensic patients who appear unable or unwilling to discuss psychopathology
2. The assessment of suspected organic amnesia (e.g., blackouts) in nonforensic patients
3. As a "challenge test" to nonforensic patients whose clinical presentation is improbable or preposterous (the use in forensic patients is complicated by bars to admissibility of their testimony in many jurisdictions)
4. Criminal defendants or civil plaintiffs whose apparent amnesia prevents them from presenting their cases (hypnotically enhanced testimony is always admissible for criminal defendants, and in most cases of civil plaintiffs)
5. As an attempt to understand the motivation of patients independently assessed as malingering or as suffering from a factitious disorder

ing "repressed memories" differs from recognizing physical child abuse because the revelations come not from health care professionals observing abused victims, but from the victims themselves, who claim to have recovered repressed memories of sexual abuse from years earlier. These memories rarely return spontaneously; rather, their recovery usually occurs during the course of psychotherapy. Many therapists use hypnosis as one method to facilitate the "de-repression" of such memories (Lindsay & Poole, 1995; Udolf, 1983). Legally, some states have extended statutes of limitations on tort cases stemming from such abuse, thus facilitating action taken by patients against their alleged abusers (Kanovitz, 1992).

The problems with the validity of hypnotically enhanced memories are particularly relevant to these cases. In other circumstances, the "historical truth" is less important clinically than the "narrative truth" (Diamond, 1980; Kanovitz, 1992; Udolf, 1983). However, the clinical and legal effects of patients remembering they were sexually abused as children are so powerful that the validity of such memories is crucial. Some ardent advocates of recovered memories assume that they are always true (e.g., Bass & Davis, 1988), whereas extreme critics describe the recovered memories as the "false memory syndrome" and argue that no proof supports the existence of repression (Merskey, 1994). Such critics argue that recall is irrelevant without demonstrable repression.

More moderate critics (Bloom, 1994; Erdelyt, 1994; Kihlstrom, 1994) do not deny that memories can be repressed; they argue that techniques (e.g., hypnosis) are too suggestive to result in valid memories, particularly in the hands of overly zealous therapists. Research on the deliberate production of false memories (called "pseudo-memories") yield somewhat conflicting results, but generally concur that pseudo-memories can be induced more easily in hypnotized than nonhypnotized participants.

Kanovitz (1992) countered this conclusion on several grounds. First, she argued that the research literature should not be applied to childhood memories recovered during hypnotherapy, because clinicians and researchers are looking at two dissimilar populations and observing different phenomena. Research participants lack any emotional involvement in the events they are asked to recall; these events are brief and have no personal meaning for participants. By contrast, Kanovitz argued, patients who were sexually abused as children have strong personal memories that have been indelibly imprinted on their memories over extended periods. According to Kanovitz, these strong personal memories are unlikely to be modified through hypnosis. She cited Loftus and Doyle (1987), who stated, "In a highly stressful state people concentrate more on just a few features from their environment, and they consequently pay less attention to others. This selectivity of attention can be seen when people experience crimes involving weapons" (pp. 50–51). Experiences associated with fear make much stronger memories (Loftus, 1979; Terr, 1991). As indirect support for the salience of recovered memories, Ofshe and Singer (1994) reported cases in which their recovery in therapy was crucial to treatment.

The American Medical Association Council on Scientific Affairs (1986) reported on recollection with hypnosis and found that "the current literature does not support the use of hypnosis on casual or moderately involved witnesses" (p. 6). But the American Medical Association further stated that existing laboratory research findings do not provide definitive answers about the workings of hypnosis in clinical situations.

Kanovitz claimed that, even in the laboratory, conscious attempts to implant detailed memories have generally been ineffective. For instance, Laurence, Nadon, Nogrady, and Perry (1986) concluded that only highly hypnotizable participants (perhaps 10–15% of persons in the general population) are capable of sufficiently deep trances to set aside reality. In their study, only 22% of even highly hypnotizable participants accepted the false memory of being awakened by a bang at night. Of the remainder, 27% became confused about whether they had slept through the night, and 51% rejected the attempted implant. Furthermore, their attempts to plant hypnotic pseudo-memories failed with all participants that scored in the lower range of hypnotizability. Hilgard (1977) reported a study in which a hypnotized participant was asked to visualize a person after that person had moved. Even when highly hypnotizable participants were able to carry on conversations with absent persons, they may well have had no difficulty in distinguishing between the real and hallucinated persons.

Other data support the possible implantation of pseudo-memories. Weekes, Lynn, Green, and Brentar (1992) reported that hypnotized participants not only accepted more false memories suggested by investigators but also reported more pseudo-memories in total than did nonhypnotized participants. Several authors reported that highly hypnotizable participants reported more pseudo-memories than did low-hypnotizable participants (Barnier & McConkey, 1992; Labelle, Laurence, Nadon, & Perry, 1990; McConkey, Labelle, Bibb, & Bryant, 1990; Spanos & Bures, 1993). Sheehan, Statham, and Jamieson (1991) reported that delayed recall of pseudo-memories was significantly higher after hypnosis. Of particular relevance, Sheehan, Green, and Truesdale (1992) reported a positive association between increased rapport with the hypnotist and more pseudo-memories in cued recall.

Under legal-style examination, highly hypnotizable participants were more likely than low-hypnotizable participants to present pseudo-memories on direct examination, but also to disavow them under cross-examination (Spanos, Gwynn, Comer, Baltruweit, & de Groh, 1989). McCann and Sheehan (1989) also reported that hypnotized participants had increased confidence in pseudo-memories during free recall, but that the confidence fell appreciably during testing that required the recognition of forced choices.

Pseudo-memories are not limited to hypnosis. Garry and Loftus (1994) reported that pseudo-memories can be easily induced in unhypnotized participants. Lynn et al. (1994) gave pseudo-memory suggestions to low-hypnotizable participants asked to simulate being hypnotized and to highly hypnotizable participants under hypnosis. Researchers masked to the condition could not distinguish between feigned and actual pseudo-memories.

Spanos and McLean (1986) challenged pseudo-memories using a "hidden observer" technique (i.e., participants were told that they could distinguish reality and fantasy in a state of deep concentration); many participants disavowed the pseudo-memories. However, research by Weekes et al. (1992) did not find that the hidden observer technique resulted in rejection of pseudo-memories. Interestingly, more pseudo-memories were reported when verification for a reported event was not possible (Lynn, Milano, & Weekes, 1991; McCann & Sheehan, 1988); fewer were reported when participants were offered an incentive to distinguish between false suggestions and actual occurrences (Murrey, Cross, & Whipple, 1992).

Yapko (1994) surveyed 869 psychotherapists in clinical practice regarding their views on memory, hypnosis, and the possibility of creating false memories of sexual abuse. Survey data indicate that although psychotherapists largely viewed hypnosis favorably, they often did so on the basis of misinformation. A significant number indicated that they erroneously believed, for example, that memories obtained through hypnosis were more likely to be accurate than those simply recalled, and that hypnosis can be used to recover accurate memories, even from as far back as birth.

More recently, Loftus (1994, 1995) has responded to criticisms regarding the artificiality of laboratory research. She and colleagues have used adult participants' family members to suggest childhood memories to the participants. Without using hypnosis, certain traumatic, but false, childhood memories (e.g., having a finger caught in a car door, or being lost at night in a closed department store) were investigated. Her team was able to successfully induce such pseudo-memories in 25–33% of participants with increasing confidence at repeated inquiries. When the team used imaging techniques similar to those used by therapists to recover their patients' repressed memories, they were even more successful. They also discovered that once such memories were experimentally implanted, patients began to have dreams about the memories.

More dramatic but much less frequent are recovered memories of ritual childhood abuse by satanic cults. As with child sexual abuse, such memories have their clinical supporters (Rockwell, 1994) and critics (Coons, 1994; Mulhern, 1994; Spanos, Burgess, & Burgess 1994), who argue that hypnosis and other suggestive techniques have created, rather than uncovered, such memories.

Wakefield and Underwager (1992) discussed the growing backlash by parents accused of past child sexual abuse based on memories recovered in therapy, often through hypnosis. Preliminary results of a survey of 133 families accused by an adult child of abuse indicated some unexpected characteristics. The families appeared to be functional, intact, and successful. The feature common to the sample appeared to be the therapy received by the adult children. The authors discussed criteria for assessing the probability–improbability of an allegation of recent remembered abuse.

FORENSIC APPLICATIONS

The most frequent use of hypnosis in the forensic context is for the validation and attempted resolution of apparent memory loss. Two frequent situations occur in which these techniques are employed: (1) enhancement of memories by potential eyewitnesses to legally relevant events, and (2) evaluation of claimed amnesia in a defendant in a criminal or civil proceeding. Unlike clinical practice, hypnosis in legal situations is usually performed by consultants retained explicitly for that purpose.

Hypnosis and Eyewitness Testimony in the Legal Context

Hypnosis has been used for years in an attempt to enhance the memories of witnesses to legally relevant situations, such as crimes and events leading to injury or property damage. Until relatively recently, most courts had held that testimony affected by hypnosis was inadmissible because it had not been generally accepted by the scientific community for all the reasons previously presented (*People v. Ebanks*, 1897; *People v. Harper*, 1969). As hypnosis began to be studied and practiced more scientifically, some exponents argued that it had achieved sufficient reliability to be admissible. A number of courts found that hypnosis affects the credibility but not the admissibility of testimony and thus permitted its introduction (*Harding v. State*, 1968; *United States v. Miller*, 1969; *State v. McQueen*, 1978; *Clarke v. State*, 1979; *Key v. State*, 1983; *People v. Boudin*, 1983).

As the use of hypnosis to enhance or recover memory became more widespread, so did the controversy over its use in the courtroom. In the legal context, in which the validity of testimony is in question, the distortions inherent in hypnotically enhanced testimony assume greater importance (Diamond, 1980; Orne, 1985). Critics (e.g., Diamond, 1980; Orne, 1979; Worthington, 1979) argued that the increased certainty displayed by witnesses who have been hypnotized often makes their testimony completely resistant to cross-examination. This apparent certainty, in conjunction with the popular belief that hypnosis is a form of psychological "truth serum," lends an unwarranted credibility to such witnesses, when, in fact, their testimony should properly be viewed as *less* credible than that of unhypnotized witnesses (Dilloff, 1977; Spector & Foster, 1977; Wilson, Greene, & Loftus, 1985).

Steblay and Bothwell (1994) examined the accuracy of hypnotic recall through a meta-analysis of 24 studies. Hypnotized participants were found to be minimally less reliable than controls in recall accuracy; when leading questions were used, a slight recall deficit was found for hypnotized participants. The performance of hypnotized participants showed wide variability, indicating the influence of moderator variables. Hypnotized participants showed greater recall accuracy for nonleading questions after intervals ranging from 24 hours to 1 week. With longer intervals, hypnotized participants had both more recall errors and more pseudo-memories than their nonhypnotized counterparts.

In an affidavit submitted to the U.S. Supreme Court (*Quaglino v. California*, 1978), Orne (1979) recommended five criteria to be followed before admitting hypnotically enhanced testimony: (1) that only a specially trained psychiatrist or psychologist be employed, who is otherwise not involved the case; (2) that only minimal details be presented in writing to the clinician to document the information base; (3) that the participant be asked for free recall before hypnosis is attempted; (4) that a videotape of

the entire session(s) be made; and (5) that no persons except the clinician and participant be present during the session(s). These criteria, in part or as a whole, have subsequently found favor with other courts (*People v. Hurd*, 1980; *State v. Hurd*, 1981; *State
v. Armstrong*, 1983). Several courts have adopted similar guidelines (*Biskup v. McCaughtry*,
1994; *House v. State*, 1984). However, difficulties in implementing these protections
have convinced Orne (1985) to call for absolute rejection of such testimony.

At the other end of the spectrum, Dr. Martin Reiser, who established the training
seminars in hypnosis for the Los Angeles Police Department, has completely rejected the
contention that hypnosis can distort memories. He has argued, both in court and in the
literature, using anecdotal case reports as well as statements based on over 700 cases, that
legally relevant new information was uncovered during hypnosis in 75% of cases, and
that the verifiable information was found to be accurate in 80% of the cases.

An intermediate position was taken by Spiegel and Spiegel (1984). They recognized the potential for distortion inherent in the use of hypnosis to enhance memory
but argued that it is sufficiently valuable, when properly used, to warrant its retention.
They pointed out that witnesses are seldom tested for hypnotic susceptibility before
attempts are made to hypnotize them. If witnesses are, in fact, not susceptible, then
attempts at hypnosis per se should not be expected to introduce any distortions in their
recollections; nevertheless, tests of susceptibility are still relevant, in order to establish
their lack of hypnotizability. On the other hand, if potential witnesses have high susceptibility, then even routine questioning, without formal trance induction, might be
expected to induce significant distortion because of the participants' suggestibility.

During the 1970s and early 1980s, courts generally restricted the admission of
hypnotically enhanced eyewitness testimony. In addition to the courts that accepted
Orne's restrictions, others have held that witnesses who have been hypnotized may
not testify concerning anything discussed under hypnosis, although they may testify
about matters covered prior to hypnosis (*United States v. Adams*, 1978). Still other courts
went further and excluded *all* testimony from witnesses who have previously been
hypnotized (*Greenfield v. Commonwealth*, 1974; *United States v. Andrews*, 1976; *State v.
Mack*, 1980; *People v. Shirley*, 1982; *State ex rel. Collins v. Superior Court*, 1982).

More recently, some jurisdictions have adopted an intermediate position that hypnotically enhanced eyewitness testimony is not excluded per se, but affects the credibility, rather than the admissibility, of the testimony (*Alderman v. Zant*, 1994; *Beachum v.
Tansy*, 1990; *Biskup v. McCaughtry*, 1994; *House v. State*, 1984; *Orndoff v. Lockhart*, 1990;
Stafford v. Maynard, 1994; *State v. Armstrong*, 1983; *United States v. Gatto*, 1991; *White v.
Leyoub*, 1994). Some courts have held that the witnesses' prehypnosis statements should
be compared with their posthypnosis statements, and their testimony admitted unless
there are significant differences (*Beachum v. Tansy*, 1990; *Orduff v. Lockhart*, 1990; *Stafford
v. Maynard*, 1994; *United States v. Gatto*, 1991). Other courts have held that the testimony may be admitted, but the party introducing the testimony may not reveal that it
was obtained under hypnosis, because such revelations might unduly suggest that the
testimony is reliable (*Alderman v. Zant*, 1994; *House v. State*, 1984).

The U.S. Supreme Court addressed the issue of testimony by criminal defendants who have been hypnotized. In *Rock v. Arkansas* (1987), the Court reaffirmed

Washington v. Texas (1967), which previously held that the Sixth Amendment was designed "to make the testimony of a defendant's witnesses admissible on his behalf in court" (p. 23). The Court concluded that a per se exclusionary rule barring testimony from criminal defendants who have been hypnotized is unconstitutional because of its violation of the Sixth Amendment.

The Tennessee Supreme Court had an occasion to interpret *Rock* in *State v. Alley* (1989). Sedley Alley had sexually assaulted and murdered a young woman and subsequently confessed to the crimes. He claimed to suffer from DID and was evaluated by clinicians. One clinician hypnotized Mr. Alley, videotaped the session, and reported that Mr. Alley had changed personalities during the session. Other clinicians reviewed the tape and concluded that Mr. Alley was malingering. After a pretrial hearing, the trial judge ruled that the tape was inadmissible because it was too sensational and because the use of hypnosis would mislead the jury. On appeal, the Tennessee Supreme Court held that the trial court had not violated *Rock*; Mr. Alley could still testify, and the experts who had conducted the hypnotic session and viewed the tape could testify as to their conclusions. The California Supreme Court reached a similar conclusion in *People v. Milner* (1988).

Kuplicki (1988) has extended the Court's analysis to argue that the test for admissibility of hypnotically enhanced testimony should be constitutional. He concluded that testimony of defense witnesses should generally be admitted, whereas testimony from prosecution witnesses should be excluded. Because of the presumption of innocence, defendants' witnesses should be permitted to testify, despite the potential limits on their testimony. However, state witnesses should not be allowed, because the use of hypnotically enhanced prosecution testimony may infringe on the defendant's right to confront accusers.

Hypnosis in the Legal Evaluation of Amnesia

Reports in the forensic literature indicate that a significant number of defendants referred for psychiatric evaluation claim to be amnesic for the details of their alleged crimes. The reported percentage of criminal defendants who claim amnesia has ranged from 23% (Parwatikar, Holcolmb, & Menninger, 1985) and 31% (Leitch, 1948) to 65% of defendants referred for psychiatric evaluation (Bradford & Smith, 1979). In criminal cases, the admissibility of hypnotically enhanced testimony is most frequently considered with competency to stand trial regarding the ability of an amnesic defendant to assist counsel. Most courts have held that amnesia per se does not bar prosecution (*Bradley v. Preston*, 1968; *Commonwealth ex rel. Cummins v. Price*, 1966; *Davis v. State*, 1978; *People v. Thompson*, 1983; *State v. McClendon*, 1948; *United States ex rel. Parson v. Anderson*, 1973; *United States v. Borum*, 1972; *United States v. Stevens*, 1972). One exception is the decision in *Wilson v. United States* (1968). The District of Columbia Circuit Court of Appeals held that "loss of memory should bar prosecution only when its presence would, in fact, be crucial to the construction and presentation of a defense and hence essential to the fairness and accuracy of the proceedings" (391 F.2d at p. 462). Other courts have held that treatable amnesia might justify an initial finding of incompetency in order to permit attempts at resolution of the amnesia (*People v. McBroom*, 1968), or a continuance to permit treatment to occur prior to trial (*Cornell v. Sup. Ct.*, 1959). Courts have been reluctant to equate amnesia with incompetency because of the facility with which amnesia can be simulated (Koson & Robey, 1973).

Because of the popular reputation of hypnosis as a guarantor of truth, defense attorneys have attempted to present the results of hypnotic sessions in which their clients have "recovered" memories that appear to exonerate them. Courts usually have rejected attempts to present the results of hypnotic or amytal sessions as evidence, holding them to be self-serving or hearsay (*People v. McNichol*, 1950; *People v. Ritchie*, 1977; *State v. Papp*, 1979). However, hypnosis of defendants to assist defense counsel has been permitted (*People v. Cornell*, 1959; *State ex rel. Sheppard v. Koblentz*, 1962). Prosecutors have also attempted to utilize hypnosis with defendants in order to obtain the "truth," which in these cases generally means a confession. Cases in which confessions obtained under such circumstances may be inadmissible include *Leyra v. Denno* (1954) and *People v. Hughes* (1983).

Defendants have also claimed that their criminal acts were committed under the influence of hypnosis, and thus they should not be held responsible (Note, 1952). Courts generally have rejected these arguments as well, either refusing to believe that the defendant was in fact hypnotized (*Earhart v. State*, 1991; *People v. Marsh*, 1959) or holding that hypnosis cannot be considered sufficiently powerful to induce an otherwise guiltless person to commit a crime (*People v. Worthington*, 1894).

Hypnosis in Civil Cases

Attorneys in civil cases have also attempted to utilize hypnosis to enhance the memories of witnesses and principals. For example, in *Crockett v. Haithwaite et al.* (1978), the plaintiff was the driver of a car in which her friend was killed. Her insurance would pay for the damages, if she had been forced off the road, not if the accident were due to her own negligence. Before hypnosis, she had no recollection of any other vehicle. Since remembering another vehicle under hypnosis would not only assuage her guilt, but also result in recovery of significant damages from the insurance company, the court ruled that her testimony of remembering under hypnosis that a van had forced her off the road was inadmissible.

Civil courts have allowed hypnotically enhanced testimony. For example, the appeals court in *Landry v. Bill Garrett Chevrolet, Inc.* (1983) ruled that a plaintiff who had undergone clinical hypnosis to deal with traumatic amnesia after an automobile accident, and recovered details of the accident, was competent to testify. But in *Tardi v. Henry* (1991), the Illinois Court of Appeals struck down a verdict for a plaintiff diagnosed as suffering from borderline personality disorder, who recovered memories of being abused by a neurosurgeon during treatment. The Court held that the plaintiff's testimony was riddled with inconsistencies, and the plaintiff was incompetent to testify because of the hypnosis. In *United States v. Todd* (1992), the defendant argued that a school counselor had hypnotized students and produced false claims of sexual molestation. Questioning of the school counselor on these grounds was not permitted.

Hypnosis in the Recovery of Memories of Childhood Sexual Abuse

The cases cited earlier involve the use of hypnosis to recover recent memories of trauma or abuse. Far more controversial is the use of hypnosis, as well as other forms of direct suggestion, to encourage patients to recover allegedly repressed memories of childhood abuse in adult patients. Kanovitz (1992) provided numerous reasons why hypnotized patients should be allowed to testify regarding repressed memories of childhood abuse. First, she asserted that research on eyewitness testimony is not applicable, given the length and trauma of the abuse. Second, most participants lack the imagination to fabricate and retain complex false memories. Third, although hypnosis probably cannot enhance memories for participants with normal recall ability, clinical cases abound in which it is successful with patient memories. Fourth, lack of success in laboratory research may be due to a failure of the information provided to participants to be registered in the first place. Fifth, powerful memories associated with childhood trauma are resistant to hypnotic influences. Sixth, the legal system can provide adequate protection against confabulated sexual abuse claims without excluding hypnotically enhanced memories.

Lawsuits against therapists who allegedly create false memories are becoming more common. Although few cases have reached the appellate level, courts have shown that they are willing to recognize a cause of action in such suits. In *State v. Cheshier* (1994), on a motion for summary judgment by a psychologist alleged to have implanted false memories of childhood sexual abuse, the court held that a cause of action and material issues of fact existed, and therefore denied the motion.

Simulation of Hypnosis

Appellate courts have had occasion to rule on whether witnesses had been hypnotized. In *State v. Joly* (1991), the Connecticut Supreme Court ruled that a trial court has the discretion to determine whether a witness in a criminal trial had been hypnotized, even without expert testimony. The court noted that even experts cannot consistently distinguish between actual and pretended hypnosis, since no reliable criteria are known for detecting the state of hypnosis. Decisions about whether the witness was in a hypnotic state appear to be highly variable, sometimes relying on statements by lay witnesses and sometimes employing expert testimony. Zitter (1994) argued that courts, in their attempts to determine whether a witness has been hypnotized, should focus on various characteristics the witness exhibited in language (e.g., use of the present tense during age regression), or observable signs (e.g., eyelid fluttering or deep breathing). Zitter also argued that hypnotic susceptibility scales may assist the expert to form an opinion as to the credibility of trance. As previously noted, the vulnerability of hypnotic susceptibility scales to dissimulation has not been researched.

The Bianchi Case

Many issues of forensic hypnosis arose in the notorious case of the "Hillside Strangler." The case involved questions of the validity of trance, simulation of amnesia, and simulation of multiple personality. Kenneth Bianchi was arrested and charged in a series of stranglings in Washington and California. During the pretrial period, Bianchi claimed amnesia for the periods surrounding all the crimes. During evaluations using hypnosis, another personality appeared to emerge that admitted to having committed the crimes. Prosecution expert Martin Orne concluded, after conducting his own attempts at hypnosis, that Bianchi was simulating both the hypnotic state and a multiple personality (i.e., DID).

An independent police investigation produced strong evidence that suggested Bianchi had been planning his defense for years. Bianchi was ultimately convicted of the murders in Washington (*State v. Bianchi*, 1979). In the subsequent trial for the California murders (*People v. Buono*, 1983), Bianchi's cousin Buono was the principal defendant. The prosecution's case was based substantially on the statements of Bianchi, who had agreed to testify to avoid the death penalty. Because of the California prohibition against testimony by previously hypnotized witnesses, the prosecution had to establish that Bianchi had, in fact, simulated the hypnotic state in his series of interviews with clinicians in Washington. Dr. Orne's testimony was instrumental in assisting the trial judge in ruling that Bianchi had not been hypnotized and could therefore testify. The issues involved have been discussed in great detail by the chief expert witnesses (Allison, 1984; Orne, Dinges, & Orne, 1984; Watkins, 1984).

CONCLUSIONS

A wealth of research has examined the issues of simulated amnesia and simulated hypnosis. Despite this effort, no definitive tests exist to determine whether a person exposed to a hypnotic induction is truly hypnotized. In addition, the validity ("narrative truth") of material produced under hypnosis is questionable; the truthfulness of hypnotic statements are particularly vulnerable when obvious motives exist to dissimulate (e.g., criminal prosecutions), and when the recalled events are brief and unexpected. Therapists must particularly exercise considerable restraint in controversial areas, such as recovering memories of childhood abuse, and should not attempt to impose their preconceptions on their patients.

Clinicians should exercise great care in the determination of claimed amnesia (see Chapter 5). Features associated with genuine amnesia are sometimes clinically helpful to these assessments. When hypnosis is used to recover memories, hypnotic susceptibility should be tested first. Clinicians should be conversant with the empirical literature and have a solid foundation for their position on recovered memories. Any resulting testimony must be based on a thorough knowledge of the relevant state and federal case laws. This chapter's brief review of selected cases is no substitute for a comprehensive understanding of relevant statutes and case law that is provided by involved attorneys. We recommend, where allowed by law, that Orne's (1979) criteria be followed throughout the evaluation process. These criteria include a specially trained independent consultant that (1) is supplied with a written, preestablished database; (2) obtains the participant's free recall prior to the videotaped hypnotic session(s); and (3) conducts the evaluation without the presence of observers.

15

Structured Interviews
and Dissimulation

RICHARD ROGERS, Ph.D.

Clinical interviews compose the essential core of current diagnostic and assessment methods. Historically, their role in the assessment of dissimulation has been more nebulous since much of the interview literature, especially on malingering, was based on a handful of nonsystematic case studies (Rogers, 1987). Traditional unstructured interviews are often haphazard in their evaluation of malingering and defensiveness with an overreliance on unvalidated hunches. However, clinical advances have been realized both in the identification of useful detection strategies and the development of standardized interviews (Rogers, 1995).

The goals of this chapter are twofold. For application to traditional interviews, I review empirically based strategies that have demonstrable merit in the assessment of malingering and related response styles. For more systematic evaluations, I examine applications of structured interviews to dissimulation. Among structured interviews, the Structured Interview of Reported Symptoms (SIRS; Rogers, Bagby, & Dickens, 1992) is featured as a specific measure to investigate feigning.

DETECTION STRATEGIES FOR
TRADITIONAL INTERVIEWS

Clinicians rely heavily on unstructured clinical and diagnostic interviews in their evaluation of psychiatric patients. Such traditional interviews form the basis of history taking, psychodynamic formulations, and diagnoses of most mental disorders. The greatest asset of clinical interviewing is its versatility and adaptability to diverse patient populations and settings. On scientific grounds, this asset is also its greatest liability.

The diversity and individuality of interviews and interviewing styles render impractical the standardization necessary for empirical study. Therefore, the usefulness of traditional interviews in the evaluation of dissimulation is difficult to test empirically.

The sparse research literature on interviews would suggest that motivated patients can both malinger (Rosenhan, 1973) and respond defensively (Sherman, Trief, & Strafkin, 1975). I suspect that most persons engaging in dissimulation, outside of forensic contexts, remain undetected on the basis of traditional interviews. At our university training clinic, I have consulted on four cases of malingering or suspected malingering in the last 12 months. In each case, the issue of feigning was raised by standardized data (e.g., MMPI-2) but never by traditional interviews. In review of these cases and my consultation with colleagues from other settings, I surmise that a common theme is partially responsible for missed cases of malingering. Most individuals feigning mental disorders are experiencing *genuine distress* regarding their current life circumstances. Understandably, clinicians equate the genuineness of this distress with the genuineness of symptom presentation.

My hypothesis is that most clinicians do not possess an adequate threshold model in conducting their unstructured interviews for when dissimulation should be suspected. If we were to assume that this hypothesis is true, then several alternatives might be considered:

- Augment traditional interviews with standardized measures of dissimulation, such as multiscale inventories (e.g., MMPI-2) or screening instruments (see Chapter 17).
- Incorporate clinical inquiries (e.g., bogus symptoms) into traditional interviews to provide an additional source of data.
- Attempt to ascertain the likelihood of dissimulation on the basis of motivation and external incentives.

As a first alternative, psychologists and other mental health professionals would likely be on the safest ground in augmenting their unstructured interviews in combination with standardized measures. If evidence of dissimulation is obtained, then clinical interviews may provide additional data with respect to response styles. A second alternative is the development of certain subsets of questions designed to assess response styles. This alternative differs from the first, in that the set of questions have not been empirically validated but exemplify specific detection strategies. Although lacking standardization, these inquiries can be more closely tailored to common referral questions. For example, no standardized psychological measures evaluate systematically dissimulation related to eating disorders or purported headaches. Clinicians in specialized settings may wish to devise questions related to specific syndromes.

The third alternative, likelihood of dissimulation, should not be ignored, although it rarely can be assessed with much accuracy. In other words, the presence of a potent external incentive should not be disregarded. However, prevalence data would suggest that even the strongest external incentive does not increase the likelihood of dissimulation to even a 50% probability. For example, Rogers (1986), in a multicenter study of insanity evaluations, found that despite strong external incentives (i.e., lengthy incarceration or even the death penalty), only 4.5% of sane defendants engaged in definite malingering, with an additional 19.7% involved in moderate deception or suspected malingering.

Interview-Based Strategies for Malingering

Rogers (1990a) proposed a classificatory model of malingering that incorporated four well-established strategies, which are conducive to clinical interviews. Detection strategies were only included in the model if they met the following criteria: (1) validated by both simulation design and known-groups comparisons, (2) established by multiple assessment methods (i.e., interview-based and psychometric), and (3) replicated in multiple studies. These detection strategies are described individually.

Rare Symptoms

This strategy involves the overendorsement of symptoms and associated features that occur only occasionally in patients with mental disorders. This strategy has been validated with the *F*, *Fb*, and *Fp* scales of the MMPI-2 and the *RS* scale of the SIRS. Rare symptoms is one of the most robust strategies for the detection of feigned mental disorders.

Indiscriminant Symptom Endorsement

Rogers (1984b) observed that some malingerers evidently adopted the strategy that "more is better," as observed in the sheer number of endorsed symptoms. When presented with a large array of psychological symptoms and associated features, mental health professional should suspect feigning when more than two-thirds are endorsed. Based on research with the MMPI/MMPI-2 Lachar and Wrobel critical items list (see Greene, 1988b; Rogers, Sewell, & Salekin, 1994; Chapter 9) and the *SEL* scale of the SIRS, two-thirds endorsement of symptoms signals the need for further evaluation for the possibility of feigning.

Blatant Symptoms

Malingerers are more likely to endorse a high proportion of symptoms that are obvious indicators of severe psychopathology. For individuals feigning depression, an example of a blatant symptom would be suicidal ideation. In contrast, an example of a subtle symptom is early morning awakening. An important distinction must be observed: Malingerers generally do not produce more blatant than subtle symptoms. Rather, they present a greater number of blatant symptoms than expected in clinical populations.[1] Because of their face validity, blatant symptoms are likely to be modified on the *O-S* indicator of the MMPI-2 and the *BL* scale of the SIRS.

Improbable Symptoms

A substantial minority of malingerers report fantastic or preposterous symptoms. Research on the M Test (see Chapter 17), the Validity Index of the Millon Clinical Multi-axial Inventory (MCMI), and the *IA* scale of the SIRS indicates that some malingerers endorse or create symptoms that are ludicrous. In clinical interviews, absurd details are occasionally supplied in response to inquiries. In one case, neon-green blood spurted from a gigantic Satan who was successfully vanquished in the patient's living room with a handy chain saw; a 60-foot Christ waited outside his small cottage to congratulate him on his accomplishment. Often questions must be inserted in the clinical interviews for the specific purpose of eliciting improbable symptoms.

Cornell and Hawk (1989) performed a systematic assessment of differences in clinical presentation between 39 malingerers and 25 genuinely psychotic patients. Differences were observed in speech, with malingerers giving more absurd responses (28.2% vs. 12%), less incoherence (5.1% vs. 36%), and fewer neologisms (2.6% vs. 36%) than psychotic patients. With respect to symptom presentation, exaggerated behavior (61.5% vs. 24%), bogus symptoms (20.5% vs. 0%), and visual hallucinations (46.2% vs. 4%) were found more often with malingerers.[2] The Cornell and Hawk study is noteworthy as a rare study that investigated the usefulness of certain presentations as indicative of malingering. The study underscores the point that traditional interviews, even when performed by highly experienced forensic psychologists, are unlikely to yield consistent findings that accurately discriminate between malingerers and psychotic patients. Nevertheless, certain criteria (e.g., absurd responses, bogus symptoms, and visual hallucinations) may signal the need for a more comprehensive investigation.

Clinicians, particularly in specialized settings, may structure questions that become a part of each assessment. In a posttraumatic stress disorder (PTSD) setting (see Chapter 6), a subset of rare and improbable symptoms could be generated that would be asked of each patient. A possible example might be "Are flashbacks sometimes in black and white, almost like a documentary film?" In this way, specific questions can be asked systematically that (1) exemplify a well-validated detection strategy (i.e., rare symptom), and (2) have highly relevant content. With experience, highly anomalous presentations can signal the need for a comprehensive investigation.

Confirmation and Clarification of Malingering

The preceding section concluded that traditional interviews may be useful in establishing informal threshold criteria to indicate when a more thorough evaluation is required. A second use of traditional interviews is to provide ancillary data when standardized measures have established malingering. For example, if data from the MMPI-2 and SIRS indicate a high probability of feigning, clinicians may wish to conduct an additional clinical interview. The goals of further interviews are twofold: (1) to provide specific examples of feigning, and (2) to establish the most plausible motivation for feigning.

Many psychologists and other mental health professionals choose to "test the limits" of those feigning mental disorders. In other words, the more extreme the effort at feigning, the less likely that any "honest mistake" would explain the highly incongruous results. For example, one malingerer reported that items did not remain constant in size. With further questioning, it was found that he had a shrinking dog whose limbs became telescoped and the body contracted, until the dog "popped" out of existence. With this and many other detailed examples, the classification of malingering found on standardized measures was clarified and convincing examples were provided.

As discussed in Chapter 18, clinicians need to examine the motivation for dissimulation. Simply put, what does the dissimulating individual expect/hope to accomplish? This assessment of motivation must take into account the individual's statements about his or her objectives. As observed in Chapter 2, motivation is an important element in the differential diagnosis between factitious disorders and malingering.

Detection of Defensiveness

Few guidelines exist for the clinical assessment of defensiveness employing traditional interview methods. The most striking observation is the disparity between clinical data regarding a patient (i.e., psychiatric history or observations of others) and the patient's presentation. Importantly, experimental studies have generally held that even inpatients may modulate their psychopathology and appear to function better, at least for brief periods, than has been characteristic of them in the past (Braginsky & Braginsky, 1967; Fontana, Klein, Lewis, & Levine, 1968; Sherman et al., 1975). The external criteria for these studies were hospital records and extended clinical observations of the patients. Likewise, studies of outpatients (Sabourin, Laferriere, et al., 1989; Sabourin, Bourgeois, Gendreau, & Morval, 1989) suggested that social desirability and defensiveness are likely to be common response styles.

Minimization of psychological difficulties may differ both in degree and motivation. For example, patients may wish to appear to be functioning at a higher level to meet an external need (e.g., regain employment or be psychologically fit as a parent) or an internal one (e.g., pride or unwillingness to acknowledge a patient status). Degrees of defensiveness may range from a "glossing over" minor difficulties to an outright denial of severe psychological impairment. A critical issue in establishing defensiveness is the patient's awareness of his or her response style (Dicken, 1960). A viable alternative is that the patient is simply incorrect in his or her appraisal of psychological distress and impairment. Such misperceptions are sometimes noted in chronically mentally ill individuals who have normalized their psychiatric difficulties. Moreover, persons with narcissistic personality disorders often magnify their accomplishments and minify their psychological impairment.

Defensive patients, who deny symptoms, are often identified on the basis of the aforementioned disparity between observed and reported symptoms (studied under "anonymous" and "real-life" conditions; Baker, 1967; Kirchner, 1961). In addition, severe forms of defensiveness are typically characterized by an overly positive presentation and endorsement of "idealistic attributes" (Liberty, Lunneborg, & Atkinson, 1964). More problematic are cases in which the patient minimizes but does not deny his or her symptomatology. Such cases, similar to malingering, require careful investigation employing corroborative data. Use of the MMPI-2 (see Chapter 9) is strongly encouraged in any cases in which (1) the patient's presentation is consistently more positive than other clinical data, or (2) the patient presents him- or herself in a highly favorable light.

Mental health professionals may augment their traditional interviews by the addition of detection strategies based on minimization of common symptoms or the endorsement of overly positive attributes. Common symptoms (see subsequent section on the Schedule of Affective Disorders and Schizophrenia [SADS] and defensiveness) can be identified that nearly all persons have experienced at some point in their past history. Common symptoms include worries, anxiety, feelings of inadequacy, concerns about the future, and feelings of dysphoria. Clinicians may wish to establish for their own practices a subset of common symptoms to ask patients routinely. A second approach is to ask specific questions about positive attributes. Persons reporting only favorable descriptions of themselves are likely to be defensive. As with other response styles, the informal use of specific items should signal the need for a more thorough evaluation.

Paralinguistic Cues and Dissimulation

Rogers (1987) summarized paralinguistic cues that have been associated with malingering and other forms of dissimulation. Although nonverbal cues are readily apparent in traditional interviews, I question the clinical applicability of these indicators (e.g., latency of response and increased hesitations) to malingering in particular. Although studies demonstrated that unimpaired persons asked to dissemble exhibited more of these indicators, no comparisons were made either with (1) clinical populations or (2) persons simulating mental disorders. In preliminary research on the development of the SIRS, we found that mentally disordered persons displayed similar nonverbal cues to persons attempting to feign. I do not recommend the use of nonverbal cues to deception, especially in cases of suspected feigning.

THE SADS AND OTHER STRUCTURED INTERVIEWS

Structured interviews offer a systematic method of evaluating symptoms and associated features of mental disorders. Structured interviews standardize (1) the form and sequencing of clinical inquiries and (2) the quantification of endorsed symptoms. For comparison purposes, semistructured interviews provide required questions that may be supplemented by the clinician's own questions in cases of ambiguity. Because of their standardization, uniform comparisons are possible between genuine patients and persons with various response styles.

Marked inconsistencies in *traditional* interviews may occur for reasons beyond response style (i.e., irrelevant responding, defensiveness, and malingering). Such inconsistencies may result from (1) differences in the wording of clinical inquiries; (2)

contextual differences, based on the sequencing of questions; and (3) variations in how responses are recorded. Although some clinicians doubt that changes in wording may produce different results, studies of standardized questions from different semistructured interviews for specific symptoms (both Axis I and Axis II) amply demonstrate this point (Rogers, 1995).

Structured interviews, in comparison to traditional interviews, provide systematic comparisons with the form and sequencing of questions held constant. As described later, the patient's self-reporting can be examined for consistency on three parameters: (1) across time (identical questions at different times), (2) with informants (collateral interviews with identical questions), and (3) with unstructured narrative (patient's free-flowing account with structured questions).

The Schedule of Affective Disorders and Schizophrenia (SADS; Spitzer & Endicott, 1978) is featured in this section for two distinct reasons. First, its reliability tends to be superior to other Axis I disorders. Therefore, variations of response patterns are unlikely to be simply the result of measurement error. Second, descriptive data on expected symptom patterns of the SADS with genuine patients are available. Accordingly, clinicians have a basis of comparison for establishing anomalous response patterns that may suggest a specific response style.

Description of the SADS

The SADS was designed as the centerpiece measure of the National Institute of Mental Health collaborative study on depression. Because a primary issue was the differential diagnosis of mood disorders from other commonly occurring diagnoses, the SADS sought to measure in great detail the intensity, duration, and other manifest characteristics of patients' symptomatology (Endicott & Spitzer, 1978). The SADS was constructed for the standardization of diagnostic interviewing in four separate ways: First, it specifies the structure of the interview and the systematic progression of questions regarding possible symptoms and associated features; second, the SADS employs standardized clinical inquires in the form of general nondirectional questions that are followed by specific probes; third, the SADS offers a reliable scoring method of quantifying symptom severity and degree of impairment; fourth, it was designed to be utilized with the empirically based Research Diagnostic Criteria (RDC; Spitzer, Endicott, & Robbins, 1978).

The SADS was constructed to collect clinical data at discrete periods. For example, Part I of the SADS was designed to examine closely the patient's symptoms during the severest part of the last episode and at the present time. In contrast, Part II offers a more longitudinal approach to mental disorders, with the goal of specifying their onset and the duration of prior episodes.

SADS: Nonempirical Approaches
to Malingering and Deception

The SADS allows clinicians an in-depth examination of the patient's consistency of self-report. As previously noted, variability in the patient's self-report on unstructured interviews may be due to (1) changes in the style or emphasis of clinical questions, (2) the idiosyncratic reporting of clinical information, or (3) changes in the patient's account. Because of the standardization of SADS, clinicians are able to control other sources of variability and, therefore, isolate discrepancies in the patient's self-report.

Psychological assessments typically progress from unstructured accounts to more structured methods. This format allows the patient to describe his or her presenting problems and past history, relatively uninfluenced by directed questions. This arrangement also provides a natural point of comparison. More specifically, are there marked discrepancies between unstructured and structured reports? Such discrepancies, per se, do not indicate dissimulation. Severely impaired patients are sometimes highly variable in their accounts. Rather, the lack of inconsistencies speaks more to patients' reliability.

For extensive evaluations spanning multiple interview times, systematic comparisons can be made by readministering portions of the SADS. Although minor variations in self-reporting are to be expected, marked changes (unexplainable by treatment interventions) are a cause of concern. A patient should be further evaluated that suddenly "resolves" significant and long-standing symptoms. Similarly, the abrupt emergence of many symptoms requires further investigation.

Rogers and Cunnien (1986) recommended in cases of suspected dissimulation that relevant portions of the SADS be used in corroborative interviews to offer direct comparisons between the patient's self-reporting and others' observations. Clinicians are cautioned not to accept an informant's view as necessarily more accurate than the patient's. Informants vary in contact with the patient and the accuracy of their observations. In addition, some informants have their own agenda (e.g., "protecting" the patient's interests). Again, the lack of inconsistencies is likely to be more instructive than their presence.

The SADS requires more skill and sophistication for patients attempting to malinger than traditional interview methods. Although not an impenetrable shield against fabrication, malingerers must convincingly present detailed self-reports organized into discrete episodes with plausible description of its onset, distinguishing and prominent symptoms, severity, and duration. As noted by Rogers (1986; Rogers & Cavanaugh, 1983), such dissimulation requires considerable sophistication, since potential malingerers often become confused regarding the emergence of symptoms across specific time periods. The task for malingering patients is made more difficult by their need to consistently differentiate potentially irrelevant and contradictory symptoms from those that are plausible in the simulation of a mental disorder. Faced with this formidable task, the author has observed that some patients simply overendorse a wide array of diverse symptomatology.

Defensiveness is more difficult to assess on the SADS than malingering. Patients' ready denial of any mild experiences of distress would raise, of course, the index of suspicion regarding defensiveness. Most patients presenting for a clinical examination (voluntary or otherwise) are experiencing some subjective distress and at least several mild symptoms. The task for the clinician is to assess whether (1) the total denial of symptoms is consistent with other clinical data, (2) the presented symptoms are plausible with the patient's current circumstances, and (3) the patient's self-report is consistent with clinical observations. A further consideration is the deliberateness of any apparent denial, since some patients have such a distorted and inflated self-image as to be unaware of problems patently obvious to others. Such distortions should be evident, however, on nonclinical topics, in contradistinction to more selected defensiveness.

Defensiveness may be easier to assess in patients with chronic mental disorders than those with brief episodes. Patients with chronic mental disorders are often forthcoming about their objectives. Patients, unhappy with the continued side affects of their medication, may grossly minimize their depression. Patients seeking a less restrictive environment may deny any distress in an effort to qualify for community placement. Chronicity provides a relatively stable benchmark from which to judge unexpected improvements. Extensive file data may prove invaluable for comparisons with patients' SADS data.

The same patient may utilize both malingering and defensiveness (i.e., hybrid responding). Perhaps the most dramatic example occurs occasionally in personal injury cases when patients categorically deny any symptoms or impairment in their premorbid functioning while asserting catastrophic changes following their injuries. Some distortions result from an uncontrived polarization of perspectives (i.e., the wonderful past vs. the wretched present) and others from deliberate distortions.

SADS: Empirical Approaches

An inherent difficulty in any study of dissimulation is the absence of a verifiable independent criterion for malingering or defensiveness. One possible alternative, at least in the construction of a threshold model, is to examine normative response patterns. Individuals who manifest highly unusual self-reports, whether they maximize or minimize psychological impairment, reflect an increased likelihood of dissimulation. As with all clinical investigations of dissimulation, clinicians must avoid overreliance on any single indicator of the SADS.

The primary focus of this section is normative SADS data from three separate sources. Samples that substantially exceed these cutting scores deserve fuller evaluation for possible dissimulation. In addition, the Ustad (1996) study included a small number of suspected malingerers. The three samples were composed of the following:

• *Forensic patients.* Rogers (1988b) combined data from two forensic sites: the Isaac Ray Center, Rush Medical School, Chicago (see also Rogers, Thatcher, & Cavanaugh, 1984) and the Metropolitan Forensic Service (METFORS), Clarke Institute of Psychiatry, Toronto. Both sites are university-based clinics evaluating a broad range of forensic patients. The combined sample was 104 evaluatees.

• *Patients with schizophrenia.* Duncan's (1995) data focused on 90 patients in the active phase of schizophrenia. These patients were involved in a partial hospitalization program following inpatient stays and participated in a study of medication compliance. Because patients with schizophrenia sometimes respond atypically to structured interviews, this sample provides a useful comparison.

• *Jail referrals.* Ustad (1996) conducted a study in a large metropolitan jail of referrals for psychiatric treatment. Many of these referrals were considered emergencies, based on the severity of the presenting problems and expected psychopathology. With the use of the SIRS and M Test for classification purposes, two subsamples were identified: (1) genuine patients with no indications of feigning (*n* = 50), and (2) suspected malingerers, exceeding the cut scores on the SIRS *(n* = 22).

Detection of Feigning on the SADS

Following the paradigm of Rogers (1988b), five potential strategies for the detection of feigning were examined: rare symptoms, contradictory symptoms, symptom combinations, symptom severity, and indiscriminant symptom endorsement. Each strategy is described here.

Rare Symptoms. As previously defined, "rare symptoms" are genuine symptoms that are seen only infrequently in clinical populations. For the purposes of this classification, rare symptoms were demarcated as those which were observed in ≤ 5% of patients in the forensic sample (see Table 15.1). These symptoms were also designated as "rare" among the honest jail referrals (range from 0% to 3.7%). However, the symptoms with psychotic content were endorse by substantial percentages of schizophrenic patients (1.4–56.7%) with the exception of neologisms. The remaining three items relate to manic symptoms during the last week.

Attempts to establish an accurate cutting score[3] proved unsuccessful. The optimum classification for feigning (one or more rare symptoms) correctly indentified 63.6% of suspected malingerers and misidentified only 4% of jail referrals. However, an unacceptable percentage of patients in the active phase of schizophrenia were misclassified (78.8%). Accordingly, rare symptoms on the SADS are not recommended for the detection of possible feigning.

Contradictory Symptoms. Seven item pairs of opposite content (e.g., psychomotor agitation and psychomotor retardation) were identified rationally as a measure of consistency and an indirect measure of possible feigning. Because of the nature of the strategy, these symptoms tend to be related to mood (see Table 15.2). Among forensic and schizophrenic samples, very small percentages of contradictory symptoms were observed. In contrast, two of the seven contradictory symptoms (i.e., 272–314 and 334–342) were found more frequently in jail referrals.

An optimum cutting score of one or more contradictory symptoms enabled us to rule out 123/140 (87.9%) of genuine clinical cases. Moreover, this cutting score identified for further evaluation 68.2% of suspected malingerers.

Symptom Combinations. This strategy, also used with the SIRS, involves symptoms that are common by themselves but rarely occur together. For the identification of SADS symptom combinations, the following selection process was implemented: (1) each symptom of a pair was endorsed by ≥ 30% of the forensic sample, and (2) both

TABLE 15.1. Rare Symptoms in SADS Evaluations

	Clinical samples			
			Jail referrals	
Numbers and descriptors	Forensic	Schizophrenic	Honest	Malingerers
354 Elevated mood (past week)	4.0	0.0	1.9	18.2
356 Less sleep (past week)	2.0	2.2	1.9	13.6
360 Increased activity (past week)	3.1	0.0	1.9	9.1
427 Thought withdrawal	2.0	30.0	1.9	36.4
430 Delusions of guilt	2.0	17.8	0.0	13.6
432 Somatic delusions	5.0	16.6	0.0	27.3
475 Loosening of associations	4.1	56.7	3.7	4.5
476 Incoherence (past week)	2.9	14.4	0.0	13.6
514 Poverty of content of speech	4.2	31.1	3.7	0.0
515 Neologisms	2.0	0.0	0.0	0.0

Note. For the clinical samples, Forensic = Rogers's (1988b) report on 104 forensic patients (suspected malingerers were removed); Schizophrenic = Duncan's (1995) study of 90 actively psychotic patients from partial hospitalization programs with extensive histories of schizophrenia; Jail referrals = Ustad's (1996) study of 122 inmates referred for psychological assessment with sample is divided into 22 suspected malingerers and 50 nonfeigning referrals based on the SIRS (referrals that were placed in the indeterminate category or had missing data were excluded).

symptoms rarely occurred together (i.e., ≤ 10%). Unlike contradictory symptoms with their manifestly opposite content, symptom combinations are based entirely on an actuarial procedure that is not necessarily rational or obvious. Even with knowledge of this strategy, persons attempting to feign are unlikely to have any effective means to elude detection on symptom combinations because of their inability to recognize uncommon symptom pairs.

TABLE 15.2. Contradictory Symptoms in SADS Evaluations

	Clinical samples			
			Jail referrals	
Numbers and descriptors	Forensic	Schizophrenic	Honest	Malingerers
234–353 Depressed and elevated mood	4.8	2.2	0.0	0.0
242–361 Worthlessness and grandiosity	1.9	0.0	1.9	4.5
272–314 Insomnia and hypersomnia	5.1	3.3	14.8	27.3
315–357 Decreased and increased energy	1.0	0.0	3.7	13.6
317–320 Decreased and increased appetite	2.9	1.1	3.7	4.5
326–359 Decreased and increased interests	1.0	1.1	3.7	9.1
334–342 Psychomotor retardation and agitation	1.0	1.1	25.9	54.5

Note. For the clinical samples, Forensic = Rogers's (1988b) report on 104 forensic patients (suspected malingerers were removed); Schizophrenic = Duncan's (1995) study of 90 actively psychotic patients from partial hospitalization programs with extensive histories of schizophrenia; Jail referrals = Ustad's (1996) study of 122 inmates referred for psychological assessment with sample is divided into 22 suspected malingerers and 50 nonfeigning referrals based on the SIRS (referrals that were placed in the indeterminate category or had missing data were excluded).

A few symptom combinations are expected with genuine patients, based simply on their actuarial selection; however, an increased pattern of endorsement would be very atypical. Altogether, 12 pairs were identified by this procedure; this number was augmented by 3 additional pairs that met the same criteria on both schizophrenic and honest jail referral samples.[4] For 5 of the 12 original pairs, instances were found in which the 10% criterion was exceeded in either the schizophrenic or honest jail referral samples. We decided to retain these items, based on the following observations: (1) The criterion was exceeded in only one of the three samples, (2) the overall percentage of honest patients does not exceed 10%, and (3) the percentage in the sample that exceeds the criterion remains low (< 15%).

The optimum cutting score of two or more symptom combinations for potential feigning provided valuable data on genuine patients (see Table 15.3). More specifically, this cutting score allowed us to rule out 109 of 140 (77.9%) of bona fide cases. Moreover, this cutting score identified for additional assessment 81.8% of suspected malingerers.

TABLE 15.3. Symptom Combinations in SADS Evaluations

| | Clinical samples | | | |
| | | | Jail referrals | |
Numbers and descriptors[a]	Forensic	Schizophrenic	Honest	Malingerers
317–239 Appetite and current worrying	8.3	2.2	10.0	40.9
317–243 Appetite and current feelings of inadequacy	7.4	4.4	4.0	22.7
317–245 Appetite and current discouragement	6.5	5.6	8.0	36.4
317–266 Appetite and current psychic anxiety	6.5	3.3	10.0	31.8
317–331 Appetite and current anger	6.5	2.2	4.0	40.9
317–419 Appetite and current distrustfulness	8.3	8.9	6.0	22.7
334–245 Agitation and current discouragement	8.3	6.7	12.0	59.1
334–266 Agitation and current psychic anxiety	9.3	6.7	12.0	40.9
428–239 Persecutory delusions and current worrying	9.3	13.3	0.0	36.4
428–245 Persecutory delusions and current discouragement	9.3	13.3	2.0	31.8
428–313 Persecutory delusions and current insomnia	7.4	7.8	2.0	36.4
428–331 Persecutory delusions and current anger	9.3	11.1	0.0	31.8
332–266 Overt irritability and psychic anxiety	>10.0	8.9	4.0	27.3
341–332 Current agitation and overt irritability	>10.0	3.3	8.0	54.5
419–324 Current distrustfulness and indecisiveness	>10.0	7.8	4.0	18.2

Note. For the clinical samples, Forensic = Rogers's (1988b) report on 104 forensic patients (suspected malingerers were removed); Schizophrenic = Duncan's (1995) study of 90 actively psychotic patients from partial hospitalization programs with extensive histories of schizophrenia; Jail referrals = Ustad's (1996) study of 122 inmates referred for psychological assessment with sample is divided into 22 suspected malingerers and 50 nonfeigning referrals based on the SIRS (50 referrals that were placed in the indeterminate category or had missing data were excluded).
[a]Symptom combinations are organized to facilitate rapid checking. If the patient has not endorsed appetite, psychomotor agitation, or persecutory delusions in the clinical range, then few symptom combinations will be found.

Symptom Severity. Genuine patients tend to endorse a relatively small proportion of symptoms on the SADS as "severe" (rating of 5) or "extreme" (rating of 6). This strategy is based on the premise that some malingerers will endorse an unrealistic number of symptoms as severe or extreme. As reported in Table 15.4, the upper ranges (i.e., top 5% and top 1%) of severe and extreme symptoms varied somewhat across clinical samples. Therefore, I computed the means across clinical samples for both the current episode/past week and the last week. I subsequently calculated percentages of malingerers that exceed these mean scores.

Various cutting scores are presented in Table 15.4. Use of the *M* scores for the top 5% and 1% gives strong indications of the upper limits of expected patterns with respect to symptom severity. A highly consistent finding was that approximately 20 symptoms with ratings ≥ 5 (current episode and last week) reflected the top 1% of clinical samples. In other words, 99% of the patients scored at or below this cutting score. Clinical referrals exceeding this cutting score should be further evaluated with respect to response style. Interestingly, a substantial minority (22.7%) of malingerers exceeded this criterion.

Assessment of the past week provides a useful index of whether a patient is reporting an unlikely number of symptoms in the severe or extreme range. Based on the schizophrenic and jail referral samples, endorsement of more than four symptoms at the severe or extreme severity might signal the need for further investigation. Approximately one-third (36.4%) of malingerers exceeded this criterion. However, I suspect that many genuine, acutely psychotic inpatients would also surpass this cutting score.

Indiscriminant Symptom Endorsement. Some malingerers are nonselective in their reporting and endorsement of psychological symptoms. As previously discussed, we expect that a disproportionate number of symptoms is likely to reflect feigning. For establishment of indiscriminant symptom endorsement, all ratings in the clinical range (≥ 3) were compiled for Part I of the SADS beginning with Item 234. Like symptom severity, the upper bounds (top 5% and top 1%) are reported. As summarized in Table 15.5, these cutting scores vary substantially across sample. However, the presence of 52 or more symptoms on Part I of the SADS rarely occurred (< 1%) in clinical populations. However, this same cutting score identified nearly half (45.5%) of the suspected malingerers for further investigation.

Cutting scores for the last week alone deemphasize psychotic symptoms (i.e., most psychotic symptoms are not recorded separately for the last week) and may be more vulnerable to individual variations in the course of the disorder. However, use of more than nine symptoms in the last week is likely to identify the majority (72.7%) of suspected malingerers.

Clinical Applications. An important component of this book is the establishment of when a response style should be evaluated (threshold model), and when a response style has been established (clinical decision model). Four SADS detection strategies proved useful in identifying atypical protocols for which fuller investigation of malingering is justified. These strategies and their optimum cutting scores are summarized in Table 15.6.

TABLE 15.4. Symptom Severity in SADS Evaluations

| | Clinical samples | | | | | | | | Malingerers % > M | |
| | Forensic | | Schizophrenic | | Jail honest | | Mean | | | |
Severity ratings	5%	1%	5%	1%	5%	1%	5%	1%	5%	1%
Both current episode and last week										
Number of severe symptoms (ratings ≥ 5)	16	19	14	20	20	20	16	20	31.8%	22.7%
Number of extreme symptoms (ratings ≥ 6)	9	11	5	10	11	15	8	11	19.2%	9.1%
Last week only										
Number of severe symptoms (ratings ≥ 5)	—	—	2	3	5	7	3	4	54.5%	36.4%
Number of extreme symptoms (ratings ≥ 6)	—	—	2	3	5	7	3	4	54.5%	36.4%

Note. For the clinical samples, Forensic = Rogers's (1988b) report on 104 forensic patients (suspected malingerers were removed); Schizophrenic = Duncan's (1995) study of 90 actively psychotic patients from partial hospitalization programs with extensive histories of schizophrenia; Jail honest = Ustad's (1996) study of 50 nonfeigning referrals; Malingerers = Ustad's (1996) study of 22 suspected malingerers. Persons exceeding the upper range (5% and especially 1%) should be further assessed relative to possible feigning. Percentages for malingerers represent the proportion of those feigning that exceeded the mean for 5% and 1%.

TABLE 15.5. Indiscriminant Symptom Endorsement in SADS Evaluations

	Clinical samples								Malingerers	
	Forensic		Schizophrenic		Jail honest		Mean		% > M	
Symptoms in the clinical range	5%	1%	5%	1%	5%	1%	5%	1%	5%	1%
Both current episode and last week	45	48	52	62	40	43	47	52	54.5	45.5
Current week only	—	—	9	14	9	11	9	12	72.7	54.5

Note. Symptoms in the clinical range = the number of symptoms on Part I of the SADS, beginning at Item 234, with ratings of ≥ 3. For the clinical samples, Forensic = Rogers's (1988b) report on 104 forensic patients (suspected malingerers were removed); Schizophrenic = Duncan's (1995) study of 90 actively psychotic patients from partial hospitalization programs with extensive histories of schizophrenia; Jail honest = Ustad's (1996) study of 50 nonfeigning referrals; Malingerers = Ustad's (1996) study of 22 suspected malingerers. Persons exceeding the upper range (5% and especially 1%) should be further assessed relative to possible feigning. Percentages for malingerers represent the proportion of those feigning that exceeded the mean for 5% and 1%.

Step 1 in the threshold model was designed to exclude from further consideration those persons whose SADS protocols had no evidence of feigning. If malingering appears to be unlikely in a particular setting, psychologists and other mental health professionals may wish to implement this step simply to rule out the possibility of malingering. Based on these data, we found that the exclusion rule eliminated 69.3% of bona fide patients from further consideration.

Step 2 in the threshold model should be utilized to identify potential malingerers. In settings in which a significant proportion of malingering is suspected, clinicians may find that the routine use of Step 2 saves time over the use of Step 1 and Step 2. With a limited sample of 22 suspected malingerers, Step 2 proved highly successful in identifying for full evaluation 95.5% of possible feigners.

TABLE 15.6. Threshold Model of Malingering in SADS Evaluation

Step 1: Criteria for exclusion of bona fide patients (optional)	Cutting score	Percentage excluded
Symptom severity: Current episode and last week "severe" (ratings ≥ 5)	< 3	31.4%
Indiscriminant symptom endorsement	< 13	16.6%
Combined percentage excluded		69.3%

Step 2: Criteria for identification of possible malingerers	Cutting score	Percentage of malingerers
Contradictory symptoms	≥ 1	68.2%
Symptom combinations	≥ 2	81.8%
Severe symptoms (episode and last week)	> 16	31.8%
Indiscriminant symptom endorsement	> 47	54.5%
Any single criterion in Step 2		95.5%

Note. Step 1 is included for settings in which malingering is likely to be rare. Depending on the setting and the expected prevalence of malingering, clinicians may wish to skip Step 1 and simply employ Step 2.

The overriding goal of the clinical decision model is to minimize false positives (i.e., genuine patients miscategorized as malingerers). The reasoning behind this goal is two-fold: (1) Suspected cases (i.e., persons that meet the threshold criteria) can be examined by more tailored measures of malingering; and (2) the cost of misclassifying a genuine patient as a malingerer can be catastrophic. Therefore, we should eschew overreliance on any single measure in making this crucial determination. As an exception, extreme scores on the SADS strategies, although not identifying a large proportion of malingerers, can establish with a high degree of probability the likelihood of feigning in a particular case.

The clinical decision model for the SADS in presented in Table 15.7. Only the presence of extreme elevations, exceeding the 99th percentile for clinical populations, are included in this model. In addition, clinicians must confirm these findings with corroborative data, based on either the patient's admission of malingering or clear evidence from other standardized measures.

Assessment of Defensiveness on the SADS

The assessment of defensiveness is typically measured by two basic methods: (1) the denial of common psychological problems, and (2) the endorsement of unrealistically positive attributes (see Chapter 1). Because SADS content focuses almost entirely on psychological symptoms and impairment, the latter method could not be examined. In operationalizing the first method, two strategies were identified, namely the denial of common symptoms and symptom underendorsement.

Denial of Common Symptoms. As a method of detecting defensiveness, I sought to identify symptoms that were endorsed in the clinical range (rating $\geq$ 3) by the majority of clinical referrals. For the purposes of establishing common symptoms, I employed the criterion that each selected symptom was endorsed by at least 50% of clinical samples. Inspection of common symptoms (see Table 15.8) revealed (1) four symptoms that exceeded this criterion in all three samples, and (2) an additional four that exceeded the criterion in two of the three samples. Combining across the 140 patients, the following benchmarks were established for these eight symptoms:

- 80% of the entire clinical sample has two or more symptoms.
- 94% of the entire clinical sample has one or more symptoms.

TABLE 15.7. Clinical Decision Model for Establishing Malingering in SADS Evaluations

---

A. Any combination of the following SADS criteria:
   1. Symptom combinations > 8
   2. Symptom severity > 20 symptoms scored 5 or greater (current episode and last week)
   3. Overendorsement of symptoms > 52 symptoms in the clinical range
B. Malingered presentation is corroborated by either:
   1. Patient's admission of malingering
   2. Clinical evidence of exaggeration and fabrication based on observation and/or psychometric data

---

TABLE 15.8. Commonly Reported Symptoms in SADS Evaluations

Number and descriptor	Clinical samples		
	Forensic	Schizophrenic	Jail referrals—Honest
All three samples			
234 Subjective feelings of depression	55.2	52.2	83.3
238 Worrying	55.7	55.5	63.0
265 Subjective feelings of anxiety	50.0	52.2	64.8
418 Antisocial behavior	55.7	64.4	100.0
Any two samples			
244 Discouragement	51.5	42.2	64.8
272 Sleep disturbance	51.5	44.4	75.9
330 Subjective feelings of anger	73.1	42.2	74.1
433 Severity of delusions	54.0	93.3	25.9

Note. For the clinical samples, Forensic evaluations = Rogers's (1988b) report on 104 forensic patients (suspected malingerers were removed); Schizophrenic sample = Duncan's (1995) study of 90 actively psychotic patients from partial hospitalization programs with extensive histories of schizophrenia; Jail honest = Ustad's (1996) study of 50 nonfeigning referrals based on the SIRS.

Defensiveness should be suspected in cases in which clinical referrals do not reach these benchmarks for common symptoms. In such cases, mental health professionals may wish to administer the MMPI-2, with its panoply of defensiveness scales (see Chapter 9), and investigate more fully the reasons for possibly denying and minimizing psychological impairment.

A closely related approach is the denial of symptoms within common symptom constellations. Rogers (1988b) developed two symptom constellations that occurred in the great majority of patients: (1) six symptoms representative of dysphoric feelings (i.e., subjective feelings of depression, worrying, feelings of discouragement, subjective feelings of anxiety, feelings of self-reproach, and subjective feelings of anger), and (2) six somatic complaints (i.e., somatic anxiety, sleep disturbance, hypersomnia, loss of appetite, increased appetite, and excessive concern with physical health). The following benchmarks were established. For the dysphoric constellation (Items 234, 238, 240, 244, 265, and 330):

- 83.3% of the entire clinical sample (i.e., 244 patients) has at least one symptom.
- The modal response to the dysphoric constellation is four.

For the somatic complaints constellation (Items 263, 272, 314, 317, 320, and 322):

- 74.9% of the entire clinical sample (i.e., 244 patients) has at least one symptom.
- The modal response to the somatic complaints constellation is two.

Common symptoms and common symptom constellations are closely related, largely due to item overlap. The use of one or more common symptoms appears to be the most stringent standard for identifying cases of possible defensiveness. Use of common symptom constellations is unlikely to add incremental validity. However, they may be valuable on a conceptual basis in providing defensive patients with reasons why their presentation appears to reflect an underreporting of common symptoms.

Symptom Underendorsement. The rationale for symptom underendorsement is that the great majority of clinical referrals will have at least a modest number of symptoms and associated features. This strategy is analogous to the indiscriminant symptom endorsement for malingering; for defensiveness, however, some individuals indiscriminantly deny and grossly minimize symptoms. Table 15.9 summarizes the minimum number of symptoms at the 93rd and 97th percentiles for symptoms in the clinical range (ratings ≥ 3). Across diverse clinical samples, the normative data indicate that most referrals (93%) endorse at least seven symptoms in the clinical range and nearly all (97%) endorse at least four symptoms.

I also attempted to establish symptom underendorsement for the last week, because some patients may be forthcoming about their last episode but actively deny current symptoms or problems. In cases in which the last episode is well documented (e.g., inpatient hospitalization), the minimization of current symptoms might serve the patient's goals (e.g., hospital discharge or discontinuance of medication). However, a substantial minority of patients (> 10%) did not report symptoms for the last week, although this finding may be an artifact of the SADS format.[5] Therefore, this strategy did not prove successful.

A final approach to symptom underendorsement was the absence of any symptom in the severe or extreme range. Simply put, it was expected that clinical referrals would experience urgency and symptom severity with respect to their presenting complaints. In this regard, we found that most patients, based on the Duncan and Ustad samples, had at least one severe symptom.

In summary, common symptoms and symptom underendorsement provide indirect evidence of defensiveness, based on the likelihood that most clinical referrals should

TABLE 15.9. Underendorsement of Symptoms: SADS Data from Forensic, Schizophrenic, and Jail Referral Samples

Number of symptoms	Current episode and past week	
	93%	97%
Clinical range (rating ≥ 3)	7	4
Severe (rating ≥ 5)	1	—

Note. The number of symptoms is computed from Part I of the SADS only, beginning with Item 234. Items prior to 234 do not address symptoms directly. Normative data combine the following clinical samples: Rogers's (1988b) report on 104 forensic patients (suspected malingerers were removed), Duncan's (1995) sample of 90 actively psychotic patients from partial hospitalization programs with extensive histories of schizophrenia, and Ustad's (1996) study of 50 jail referrals with all suspected malingerers removed.

be experiencing some psychological symptoms and distress. In addition, inspection of underendorsement of severe symptoms may afford some indication of systematic minimization. Of course, the small possibility exists that the referral is very well adjusted and essentially asymptomatic. With this alternative, the clinician must grapple with the question, "Why is such a well-adjusted person seeking assessment/treatment?"

Defensiveness is more likely to occur when the assessment is conducted at the behest of others (e.g., family members) than in cases of self-referral (see Chapter 1). In such instances, collateral interviews with informants may yield useful information for comparison purposes. Broadening the evaluation beyond the individual referral, clinicians may use data from the SADS to foster communication and clarify disagreements regarding symptomatology.

Dissimulation with Other Structured Interviews

Most of the detection strategies developed with the SADS are also applicable to other structured interviews. An important consideration is level of interrater reliability. If the reliability is marginal (e.g., Structured Clinical Interview for DSM-III-R Disorders [SCID]), then variations in reporting and even atypical endorsement patterns could be the result of measurement error. In addition, few measures beyond the SADS provide reliable gradations of symptom severity. Consequently, clinicians will not be able to use (1) symptom severity for malingering (severe or extreme symptoms) or (2) symptom underendorsement for defensiveness. Finally, the lack of accessible normative data on other structured interviews, as they relate to dissimulation, reduces their clinical applicability.

This section is highly focused on reporting studies of dissimulation with other structured interviews. Most apparent is the need for systematic research with children and adolescent populations. As summarized by Rogers (1995), discrepancies between children and parents' reports are very common. Even marked discrepancies cannot be construed as deliberate efforts at malingering and defensiveness, given the modest levels of child–parent agreement typically found on structured interviews for children.

Many structured interviews include either the requirement or the option for collateral interviews. Particularly with Axis II disorders, interviews with informants are recommended. In addition, persons with substance abuse problems are unlikely to be forthcoming in their presentation (see Chapter 6). For cases of suspected substance abuse, the Comprehensive Drinker Profile (CDP; Miller & Marlatt, 1984) recommends the use of a corroborative interview; surprisingly, informants appear as likely to overestimate as underestimate alcohol abuse (Miller, Crawford, & Taylor, 1979).

Diagnostic Interview Schedule

Erdman et al. (1992) compared the traditional Diagnostic Interview Schedule (DIS; Robins, Helzer, Cottler, & Goldring, 1989) to other computer-based versions. They also administered the Marlowe–Crowne Social Desirability Scale (Greenwald & Satow, 1978) and a research scale for atypical responding (Johnson, Williams, Klingler, & Gianetti, 1988). They found modest correlations between symptom endorsement and (1) social desirability ($r = -.30$) and (2) atypical responding ($r = .38$). These results suggest, even with basic screening measures, that patients may modify their response patterns.

Structured Clinical Interview for DSM-III-R Disorders

The Structured Clinical Interview for DSM-III-R Disorders (SCID; Spitzer, Williams, Gibbon, & First, 1990) was developed to assess a broad range of Axis I disorders. Unpublished SCID data by Rogers, Bagby, and Prendergast (1993; see Rogers, 1995) categorized 38 difficult-to-treat patients with schizophrenia as honest ($n = 30$) or suspected malingerers ($n = 13$) based on the SIRS. The groups appeared indistinguishable on most psychotic symptoms, although tactile hallucinations were more often reported by suspected malingerers than genuine patients. At best, these data are preliminary, given the atypical population (i.e., highly problematic patients in a specialized treatment program) and the small sample size.

NIMH Diagnostic Interview Schedule for Children

The Diagnostic Interview Schedule for Children (DISC; National Institute of Mental Health, 1991) was developed to improve diagnostic reliability in clinical and epidemiological settings. A virtually unexplored issue with the DISC and other child interviews is the presence of response styles in structured interviews for children. In a sample of 138 preadolescents, Zahner (1991) found substantial numbers engaged in less-than-forthright responses, as determined by the participating interviewers. More specifically, she found that a small number of children tended to engage in "yea-saying" (8.3%) or "nay-saying" (10.1%). In addition, some children appeared to be trying to please the interviewer (8%) or provided guarded responses (14%).

Structured Interview for DSM-III Personality Disorders

The Structured Interview for DSM-III Personality Disorders (SIDP; Pfohl, Stangl, & Zimmerman, 1982; Pfohl, Blum, Zimmerman, & Stangl, 1989) was developed to assess Axis II disorders, particularly in the presence of Axis I disorders. Only indirect evidence is available that hints at the vulnerability of the SIDP to response styles. Zimmerman and Coryell (1989) employed two rationally constructed and empirically unvalidated scales to investigate response styles on the SIDP. With the Lie and Social Desirability subscales, modest negative correlations ($< -.30$) were found with SIDP symptom ratings. At best, these findings suggest that response styles should be systematically investigated for Axis II disorders.

STRUCTURED INTERVIEW
OF REPORTED SYMPTOMS (SIRS)

Two recent summaries (Rogers, Bagby, & Dickens, 1992; Rogers, 1995) provide comprehensive coverage of the SIRS. The purpose of this current section is twofold:

(1) to provide distillation of findings as a resource to clinicians, and (2) to supplement existing knowledge with forthcoming research.

Development of the SIRS

The SIRS (Rogers, 1992) was first developed in 1985 and has gone through several important revisions. At present, the SIRS is a 172-item structured interview that is composed of (1) *Detailed Inquiries* that address specific symptomatology and its severity; (2) *Repeated Inquiries* that parallel the Detailed Inquiries and test for response consistency; and (3) *General Inquiries* that probe specific symptoms, general psychological problems, and symptom patterns. These items are organized into eight primary scales for the evaluation of feigning.

The SIRS is a structured interview that was designed to assess feigning and related response styles. The key difference between a structured and semistructured interview is that structured interviews do not allow clinicians their own clinical inquiries to clarify a patient's responses. The rationale for restricting the SIRS to a structured interview is the concern that the wording or tone of certain idiosyncratic questions may express incredulity, disbelief, or some other pejorative response—any of which is likely to alter the patient's presentation.

The eight primary strategies were selected from the empirical literature (Rogers, 1984b). From a pool of potential items, eight experts at malingering selected individual items that assessed a single strategy; the average concordance rate on single strategies for retained items was 88.2%. The next step was the transformation of strategies to scales. To enhance scale homogeneity, item-to-scale correlations were computed on combined data from seven samples. As a result, three items with item-to-scale correlations < .20 were dropped. Subsequently, alpha reliability coefficients were computed for six of the primary scales;[6] they ranged from .77 to .92, with a mean of .86 (see Table 15.10).

A brief description of the SIRS primary scales is presented in Table 15.10. The basic strategies underlying these scales have been described in earlier sections of this chapter, with the exception of Reported versus Observed (*RO*) scale. With the use of observable verbal and nonverbal behavior, marked discrepancies between reported and observed behavior is assessed on *RO* as indicative of feigning. The reliability estimates, summarized from Rogers, Bagby, and Dickens (1992), are uniformly high. More recently, Linblad (1994) investigated the SIRS interrater reliability with undergraduate research assistants; he found a very high level of agreement (median $r = .95$, range = .87–.97).

Validation of the SIRS

Validational studies reported by Rogers, Bagby, and Dickens (1992) have found consistent differences on SIRS primary scales between honest responders (i.e., community participants, outpatients, inpatients, and correctional residents) and feigners (simulators and suspected malingerers). Based on the normative data ($n = 403$), I computed effect sizes between honest and feigning groups (see Table 15.11); effect sizes are pre-

TABLE 15.10. SIRS Primary Scales: Composition and Description

Scale	Items	Alpha	Reliability	Description of scale strategy
RS	8	.85	.98	Symptoms that are infrequently endorsed in genuine patients
SC	10	.83	.97	Pairings of symptoms that are uncommon in genuine patients
IA	7	.89	.96	Fantastic and very atypical symptoms that, by definition, are unlikely to be true
BL	15	.92	.95	Disproportionate number of symptoms that are obvious signs of mental disorder
SU	17	.92	.96	Disproportionate number of symptoms that are likely to be viewed as everyday problems
SEL	32	na	1.00	Overall proportion of symptoms is higher than generally found in genuine patients
SEV	32	na	1.00	Disproportionate number of symptoms reported with extreme or unbearable severity
RO	11	.77	.91	Patient's self-reporting of observable behavior is more discrepant than most genuine patients

Note. Data are distilled from Rogers, Bagby, and Dickens (1992). *SEL* and *SEV* reflect the arithmetic summing of diverse items; therefore, alpha coefficients are inappropriate. Reliability estimates are the weighted means for interrater reliability coefficients (see p. 35). For more complete descriptions of the scales, see Rogers et al. (1992).

sented separately for clinical (inpatients and outpatients) and nonclinical (community and correctional) samples.

Effect sizes in Table 15.11 are substantial in magnitude. As noted in Chapter 19, the most rigorous validation of a malingering measure includes the combined use of known-groups comparison and simulation design. In this regard, Cohen's *d* was calculated between (1) clinical samples and suspected malingerers (i.e., known-groups comparison), and (2) clinical samples and simulators (i.e., simulation design). As noted in Table 15.11, both comparisons yielded similar results (i.e., identical *M*'s for Cohen's *d* of 1.74). As expected, effect sizes for comparisons to nonclinical samples were slightly higher for both suspected malingerers (2.19) and simulators (2.03).

Research by other investigators has demonstrated highly significant differences between honest and simulating samples. The following is a synopsis of their research findings:

• Connell (1991) tested the SIRS in a simulation design with offender and psychotic inpatient samples (*n* = 90). Despite a design issue that probably decreased accuracy,[7] the resulting discriminant analysis was highly accurate with 88.9% hit rate.

• Kropp (1992) examined the ability of psychopathic and nonpsychopathic offenders (*n* = 100) to feign mental disorders on the SIRS. All offenders had a history of mental health treatment and currently were receiving clinical services. Highly significant differences (*p* < .001) were found for all primary scales in the predicted direction. Psychopathy did not appear to improve the ability to feign successfully. On a multi-

TABLE 15.11. Effect Sizes for Rogers, Bagby, and Dickens (1992) SIRS Comparisons of Clinical and Nonclinical Samples to Suspected Malingerers and Simulators

Scales	Effect sizes				
	CL to MAL	CL to SIM	NON to MAL	NON to SIM	Mean
RS	2.31	1.83	2.52	1.95	2.15
SC	1.67	1.48	2.24	1.76	1.79
IA	1.60	1.20	1.90	1.32	1.51
BL	2.29	1.87	2.95	2.18	2.32
SU	1.40	1.79	1.85	2.25	1.82
SEL	1.59	1.98	1.93	2.59	2.02
SEV	1.65	1.95	2.24	2.15	2.00
RO	1.44	1.78	1.88	2.06	1.80
Mean	1.74	1.74	2.19	2.03	1.93

Note. Effect sizes were calculated with Cohen's *d*. CL = honest patients; MAL = suspected malingerers; SIM = simulators; NON = nonclinical honest participants.

variate basis (i.e., a MANCOVA with age as a covariate), the experimental condition (simulation vs. honest) was highly significant, $F(3,94) = 79.06$, $p < .001$; but the interaction of experimental condition × psychopathy was not, $F(3,94) = .25$, $p = .86$.

• Linblad (1991) examined three offender groups (Axis I, Axis II, and no mental disorder; $n = 66$) and their ability to feign in a within-subjects design. Strong and consistent effect sizes were found across the simulation and honest conditions for the three groups. More specifically, the Cohen's *d* ranged from 1.28 to 2.67 ($M = 1.95$). The SIRS combined with the MMPI-2 yielded a very accurate classification in a discriminant analysis (95.5%).

• Gothard (1993) conducted a simulation study of the SIRS, utilizing offender and patient groups ($n = 108$), and found highly significant differences. She found strong effect sizes between simulators and (1) patients found incompetent to stand trial ($M d = 1.99$; range from 1.60 to 2.56), (2) patients found competent to stand trial ($M d = 2.36$; range from 1.78 to 2.86), and (3) correctional controls ($M d = 2.99$; range from 2.18 to 3.88). For total SIRS scores, the effect sizes were also impressive (2.56, 2.86, and 3.76, respectively). Importantly, seven suspected malingerers evidenced a similar pattern of elevations to simulators.

• Kurtz and Meyer (1994) examined the efficacy of the SIRS in accurately classifying simulators as compared to correctional controls and psychiatric inpatients ($n = 140$). Combining across coached and uncoached simulators, they found that the SIRS was highly effective (88.8%) at classifying feigners and honest responders, despite its three-group classification.[8] Notably, the MMPI-2 was not as accurate as the SIRS (81.3%) and did not add incremental validity when combined with the SIRS.

• Ustad (1996) examined the convergent validity of SIRS primary scales with the Rule-In and Rule-Out scales of the M Test (Beaber, Marston, Michelli, & Mills, 1985) and the *NIM* scale of the Personality Assessment Inventory (PAI; Morey, 1991) in inmates ($n = 122$) referred for psychological consults. Solid evidence of convergent validity was provided with the Rule-In scale ($M r = .58$), Rule-Out scale ($M r = .60$), and *NIM* scale ($M r = .58$).

In summary, validation studies of the SIRS have demonstrated consistently its usefulness in classifying feigners and honest responders. Notably, these differences remain robust when used with inpatient samples in which some level of atypical responding is expected. Importantly, research (Gothard, 1993; Rogers, Bagby, & Dickens, 1992) had demonstrated a convergence across known-groups comparisons and simulation research in establishing the SIRS classificatory accuracy. In this regard, the SIRS is unequaled by other measures of feigned psychopathology (e.g., the MMPI/MMPI-2; see Rogers, Sewell, & Salekin, 1994) in its use of combined research methodology and standardized cutting scores.

New Developments

The SIRS has been extensively validated on adult populations for use in the classification of feigned psychopathology. As clearly documented in the test manual (Rogers, Bagby, & Dickens, 1992, p. 7), the SIRS was not validated with adolescent populations (i.e., less than 18 years old) or for the assessment of faked intellectual or neuropsychological impairment. In cases of purported deficits in concentration, memory, and thinking, other strategies (see Rogers, Harrell, & Liff, 1993) must be employed to assess dissimulation more directly. However, several recent studies (Hayes, Hale, & Gouvier, 1996; Rogers, Hinds, & Sewell, 1995) have examined the usefulness of the SIRS with adolescents and malingered mental retardation.

Adolescents

Rogers, Hinds, and Sewell (1995) examined the potential usefulness of the SIRS and the MMPI-2 with 53 dually diagnosed adolescents. They found that adult cutting scores (i.e., any primary scale in the definite range or three or more scales in the probable range) have superb negative predictive power (NPP; 1.00) and moderate positive predictive power (PPP; .66). With a slightly more liberal cutting score (i.e., two or more scales in the probable range), the NPP remained high (.98), with a substantial increase in the PPP (.79). An important limitation of the study was the absence of adolescents with psychotic disorders. Still, the SIRS can be used to provide corroborative data for adolescent populations, although it should not be employed as a primary determinant in the classification of malingering.

Malingered Mental Retardation

Hayes et al. (1996) performed a preliminary analysis of 9 suspected malingerers of mental retardation and 30 inpatients of limited intellectual ability via a known-groups comparison. All participants were selected from a forensic facility. The sample of inpatients had modest levels of education (8.4 years) and generally were classified in the range of mild mental retardation (M = 60.5; SD's = 4.9 and 5.6 for two subsamples of inpatients) on either the Wechsler Adult Intelligence Scale—Revised (WAIS-R) or the Shipley. Results of an initial discriminant analysis were promising (hit rate of 94.9%) but limited by the methodology.[9] Still, the study should serve as a stimulus for further investigations.

Clinical Applications

The SIRS appears to be established as a standard method for the assessment of malingering. The SIRS has a high level of reliability and well established validity (see Berry, Wetter, & Baer, 1995). In addition, the SIRS appears unparalleled in its ability to distinguish between feigned and genuine disorders (Rogers, 1995).

The SIRS manual does not present an explicit threshold model for when further investigations of feigning should be considered. Relying on Tables 16, 17, and 18 from the test manual (Rogers, Bagby, & Dickens, 1992, p. 24), three guidelines are proposed for when malingering should be more fully investigated (see Table 15.12). These guidelines are designed to identify protocols with relative few scales in the honest range (≤ 4) and those that nearly meet the criteria for feigning (i.e., two scales in the probable range or a markedly elevated total score).

The clinical decision model employs two main criteria and a supplementary criterion:

- *Any SIRS scale in the definite feigning range.* In summarizing across 290 clinical and nonclinical participants (Gothard, 1993; Rogers, Bagby, & Dickens, 1992), very high likelihood (99%) exists that persons exceeding the cutting score are feigning.
- *Three or more scales in the probable feigning range.* The probability of feigning at this criterion is very high: 97.4% (Gothard, 1993) and 97.9% (Rogers, Bagby, & Dickens, 1992).
- *Total SIRS score (all scores except Repeated Inquiries).* The cutting score for this supplementary criterion was set by Rogers, Bagby, and Dickens (1992) to represent a 100% likelihood of feigning.

The determination of malingering is a multimethod assessment that incorporates and integrates data from unstructured interviews, psychological tests, and collateral sources. Despite the unmatched accuracy of SIRS for the classification of feigned psychopathology, such an important determination should not rely solely on single measure. Therefore, the clinical decision model requires confirmatory data in addition to the SIRS.

Clinical decision models frequently overlook the issue of generalizability to minority populations (e.g., elevated scores by minorities on MMPI-2 validity scales; see Rogers & McKee, 1995). Available studies (Connell, 1991; Gothard, 1993) have yielded comparable findings across ethnic groups. For example, Connell (1991) performed a MANOVA on 30 African American and 60 White participants, and found no signifi-

TABLE 15.12. Threshold and Clinical Decision Models for the SIRS in the Assessment of Feigned Psychopathology

Threshold model

Any of the following:

1. Four or fewer SIRS scales in the honest range
2. Two SIRS scales in the probable feigning range
3. A total SIRS score of > 66[a]

Clinical decision model

A. Any of the following:
   1. Any SIRS scale in the definite feigning range
   2. Three or more SIRS scales in the probable feigning range
   3. A total SIRS score of > 76[b]

B. Corroborative data from self-reporting, collateral interviews, or psychometric measures.

[a]The cutting score is 2 SD's above the mean for clinical samples.
[b]The total SIRS score is generally employed when the first two decision rules yield an indeterminate classification.

cant differences due to race. Gothard (1993), although not formally analyzing race, achieved nearly perfect classification (97.4%) across a diverse sample that included 31 African Americans and 13 Hispanic Americans; clearly, the SIRS performed comparably across ethnic groups.

The Ustad (1996) study was the first SIRS investigation to evaluate consecutively an unselected sample of jail referrals for psychological consultation. Further inspection of her data allows direct comparisons between African Americans ($n = 51$) and Anglo Americans ($n = 60$) with respect to their classifications by the SIRS. She found nearly identical percentages for suspected malingering (21.2% vs. 20%), indeterminate group (27.5% vs. 25%), and honest responding (51% vs. 55%).[10] As expected, the resulting chi-square was nonsignificant, χ^2 (3, $n = 111$) = .18, $p = .92$. As a secondary analysis, Ustad performed ANOVAs on each of the primary scales. Only the IA scale evidenced significant differences, F (1, 109) = 7.40, $p < .01$, between African Americans ($M = 2.10$, $SD = 3.18$) and Anglo Americans ($M = .85$, $SD = 1.46$). Both M's fell in the honest range and reflected a relatively modest difference (Cohen's $d = .52$) when compared to differences between the criterion groups (see Table 15.11; Cohen's d range from 1.20 to 1.90; $M = 1.51$). Overall, these data would suggest no significant differences in SIRS classification and one modest difference in individual scale elevation for IA.

SUMMARY

Traditional interviews constitute an important element of diagnostic evaluations and provide an important, albeit idiosyncratic, basis for understanding a patient's motivations and possible response styles. Increasingly, structured interviews are forming a prominent role in psychological and psychiatric evaluations because of their standardization and validation (see Rogers, 1995). As noted in this chapter, the SADS provides a valuable avenue for evaluating patients' presentations by both nonempirical and empirical methods. In addition, the SIRS offers specialized data on the assessment of feigning that has been validated by both simulation design and known-groups comparison.

NOTES

1. Clinicians sometimes mistakenly believe that malingerers produce greater number of blatant (obvious) symptoms than subtle symptoms based on $O-S$ difference for the MMPI/MMPI-2 (see Chapter 9). These marked differences are produced by the T score transformations with the same number of obvious symptoms yielding higher T scores than subtle symptoms. For instance, 10 obvious symptoms on Scale 3 results in a T of 60; 10 subtle symptoms results in a T of 34.

2. Differences were also reported for mood symptoms; however, these comparisons are likely to be misleading, since the genuine patients were limited to primary diagnoses of psychotic disorders.

3. We did not have access to the raw data for the original Rogers (1988b) data; therefore, cutting scores were derived from the other two samples.

4. The unavailability of the raw data from the original forensic sample precluded an examination of the percentages for these three pairs.

5. Nearly all psychotic symptoms and a small number of other symptoms are not rated for the last week.

6. Two scales involve simply an arithmetic summing and, thus, are inappropriate for alpha coefficients.

7. Cornell utilized the SIRS both to discriminate (1) feigned from nonfeigned protocols and (2) psychotic from nonpsychotic protocols. Certainly, the SIRS was not developed for the latter classification.

8. The SIRS was not intended to discriminate between patient and control groups.

9. The discriminant function was constructed with three groups that attempted to distinguish (a) malingerers from genuine patients and (b) pretrial patients from patients found not guilty by reason of insanity. The SIRS was not intended for this latter purpose. In addition, the investigators did not limit the number of predictor variables. Therefore, the resulting discriminant function is likely to be unstable.

10. The number of Hispanic Americans ($n = 11$) was too small for a stable comparison but suggested that possibly smaller numbers fell in the suspected malingering and indeterminate groups.

16

Understanding and Detecting Dissimulation in Sex Offenders

KENNETH W. SEWELL, Ph.D.
RANDALL T. SALEKIN, M.S.

Outright denial and defensiveness are commonplace in the evaluations of sex offenders. Langevin (1988) found that approximately 50% of sex offenders denied or minimized their paraphiliac behavior, even following their conviction on these offenses. Even outside of evaluative settings, persons engaging in sexual behaviors deemed illegal and/or abhorrent by society are likely to misrepresent their own values, intentions, and behaviors. As Rogers and Dickey (1991) stated, "Sex offenders have learned to avoid both social censure and arrest by leading 'double lives' (p. 56).

The present chapter is organized into three major sections. First, the nature of dissimulation among sex offenders is examined, integrating recent theoretical and empirical contributions. Second, the clinical literature on detection methods of dissimulation is closely reviewed. Third, in keeping with this book's overall objectives, guidelines for threshold and clinical decision models are presented to assist mental health professionals in determining the potential and likelihood of dissimulation for individual sex offenders.

NATURE AND DIRECTION OF DISSIMULATION IN SEX OFFENDERS

Typology of Distortion

Happel and Auffrey (1995) described the most typical type of dissimulation associated with sex offenders as a "dance of denial" (p. 6) or a constellation of claims presented to deny culpability and to minimize the offender's behavior. This pattern of denial and

minimization might best be described as "defensiveness" on the part of many sex offenders (Rogers & Dickey, 1991). In this regard, Kennedy and Grubin (1992) offered
a number of specific denial patterns, based on their cluster analysis of 102 British males
convicted of sex offenses. The four resulting groups differed in their offense type and
past history of sexual offenses:

1. Pattern 1 (18%) was composed of men who admitted their offenses but denied causing any harm to their victims and instead claimed to have helped them in
some way. These individuals took a politicized stance toward the law, believing that
society should accommodate their sexual behaviors. A large proportion of Pattern 1
offenses were committed against children, particularly boys. These offenders tended
to resist treatments aimed at altering their sexual preferences, given that their preferences were valued more than social mores. Pattern 1 had the highest rate of recidivists.

2. Pattern 2 (20%) contained men who externalized responsibility for their sexual
behavior. Although they generally admitted to their behavior, they blamed either the
victims for the offense or others (e.g., their spouses). Thus, Pattern 2 offenders argued
that they were unjustly treated by the legal system. Pattern 2 offenders primarily targeted young females. A substantial minority of Pattern 2 offenders were recidivists.

3. Pattern 3 (27%) offenders denied the extent to which their sexually deviant
behaviors were ego-syntonic (labeled by the authors as "internalizers"). The group
included many heterosexual incest offenders who readily admitted their offense and
the harm that they had inflicted on the victim. However, these men presented a dissociative style of explanation; their actions attributed to a temporary aberration of
behavior or altered mental state.

4. Pattern 4 (35%) offenders were characterized by total denial of the offense.
These individuals were mostly convicted of offenses against adult females. Pattern 4
offenders were unlikely to feel that they would benefit from any sort of psychological treatment.

Kennedy and Grubin's (1992) four patterns correspond well with Langevin's (1988)
"degrees of admission" (in which Patterns 2 and 3 are collapsed). Thus, this typology
seems robust and applicable to a variety of clinical and forensic settings. Each pattern
has implications for dissimulation—both its prevention and detection. It is also clear
that the offense itself is not always the focus of the dissimulation. In Pattern 1, the
sexual behavior is acknowledged, but its consequences are denied, minimized, or distorted. In Patterns 2 and 3, the behavior is also acknowledged, but its "cause" is disavowed and attributed to some agent or process beyond the offender's control. Only
in Pattern 4 is the offense itself completely denied.

Sex offenders, at least in Pattern 4, are defensive specifically about sexual behaviors. For this group, specific assessments regarding their sexual preferences and arousal
patterns would seem maximally informative. However, sex offenders might attempt
to deny or minimize a wide array of psychological symptomatology (e.g., Grossman
& Cavanaugh, 1989, 1990; Haywood, Grossman, & Hardy, 1993; reviewed in more
detail later). Knowing this, clinicians need to evaluate not only specific indicators of

anomalous sexual behavior, but also general measures of defensiveness. Moreover, as noted by Haywood et al. (1993), some sex offenders may admit to the offense while malingering (or at least exaggerating) nonsexual psychopathology. This response style is consistent with Pattern 3 in its efforts to attribute the acknowledged offense to some mental disorder or impaired functioning beyond the offenders' control. Therefore, examining indices for malingering/exaggeration of psychopathology also is indicated.

Less commonly, alleged sex offenders might actually feign presence of a deviant sexual preference, even to the point of falsely admitting to an offense. Dwyer, Brockting, Robinson, and Miner (1994) reported a treatment case of a man who was charged with and admitted to sexual contact with his daughter from a previous marriage. After 2 years in therapy, he disclosed to his attorney that he had never committed the offense but, rather, had falsely claimed to have done so in order to "get on with his life" after a period of nonincarcerated treatment. He and his new wife reported spending hours in the library reading about sexual abuse in order to appropriately play their roles. Follow-up investigations included confusing and conflicting information regarding the mental status, personality, and behavior of the mother of the alleged victim (i.e., the complainant) as well as the behavior of the alleged victim and two male siblings. Clinicians involved in the case held markedly divergent views: (1) the children being sexual with each other, (2) the children being "brainwashed" by their mother, and (3) the father abusing one or more children. Such cases of feigned sexual abuse are admittedly rare. However, this extreme case illustrates the difficulty in determining historical truth when self-report is both central to the assessment and influenced by multiple motivations.

Explanatory Models of Dissimulation

The first step in preventing, detecting, or altering dissimulation among sex offenders is to develop an understanding of the motivations for the dissimulation. Three explanatory models (i.e., pathogenic, criminological, and adaptational) have been proposed that attempt to categorize motivations for malingering (Rogers, 1990a). Subsequently, these models have been applied to sex offenders' denial and minimization as well (Rogers & Dickey, 1991). In addition, we present the socioevaluative model that specifically targets a social point of reference, often relevant to sex offenders. Although clinicians tend to adhere to only one motivational model, we maintain that these models are not mutually exclusive. Rather than judge the models in abstract, we recommend that each be considered in the evaluation of individual sex offenders. In the paragraphs that follow, we will describe these four models and review some evidence for their applicability.

Pathogenic Model

Rogers and Dickey (1991) described the pathogenic model, in which denial and minimization among sex offenders is understood as reflecting the operation of a relatively primitive ego defense mechanism. Denial thus serves the function of protecting the individual from psychologically accepting responsibility for the offense, a state that would produce overwhelming guilt, shame, and anxiety. This perspective predicts the following sequence: If an individual adopts massive repression and denial as a defense to paraphiliac behaviors and then subsequently acknowledges these behaviors, psychological deterioration would be evident. Rogers and Dickey contended that psychodynamic formulations with splitting and loss of ego functions resulting in uncontrollable deceptions on the part of the offender largely have been refuted. They stated that many writers (e.g., Quinsey, 1984) have adequately argued against such conceptualizations as "denial" and "projection of blame" as unconscious processes in sex offenders. Moreover, some research has separated "self-deception" from "other-deception" and has demonstrated self-deception to be relatively stable across forensic populations, whereas other-deception is more frequent in violent and sex offenders (Gudjonsson, 1990).

In support of a pathogenic model, some investigators and clinicians maintain that at least some sex offenders do appear essentially to believe their own deceptions, with their denials serving psychic needs. For example, Ward, Hudson, and Marshall (1995) concluded that for a sex offender to admit the full scope of his behavior to others would be paramount to admitting it to himself, a condition that would be psychologically intolerable. Ward et al. argued that denial processes may be both precursors to offending as well as after-the-fact justifications to allow (1) offending to continue, (2) self-esteem to be maintained, and (3) negative self-evaluative cognitions to be disputed. After assessing cognitive distortions among sex offenders who either admitted or denied their alleged offense, Haywood, Grossman, Kravitz, and Wasyliw (1994) determined that a broader notion of pathogenic denial (beyond psychoanalytic concepts) merits consideration.

Two other presentations, beyond Rogers and Dickey, may be construed as falling within a pathogenic conception of sex offense denial/minimization: psychotic processing and neurological impairment. In the first instance, denial/minimization occasionally results directly from psychotic processing. Although the incidence of sex offenses by persons with psychoses is estimated to be quite low (Rice, Harris, & Quinsey, 1990), dissimulation within such cases could be unintentional distortions motivated by delusions or hallucinations. In addition, some neurological insults can result in both inhibition and memory deficits. Confabulation may result from such injuries. In both instances, the critical issue is the deliberativeness of the dissimulation. If the sex offender is unaware of the inaccuracies of his account (e.g., alcoholic blackout) yet believes these inaccuracies, no dissimulation or deception has occurred.

Criminological Model

Rogers and Dickey (1991) extended the criminological model of malingering (espoused by DSM-III, DSM-III-R, and DSM-IV) to the defensiveness of sex offenders. They argued that although antisocial characteristics can be related to deception, little empirical evidence exists that antisocial individuals malinger more frequently than others in similar circumstances, or are more successful in their efforts (see Chapter 4; Rogers, 1990a). Rogers and Dickey (1991) maintained, based on anecdotal information, that defensiveness about paraphiliac behavior is often determined by the situation and not a general characteristic of the offender.

Failure to participate fully in the forensic evaluation is viewed within the criminological model as evidence of dissimulation. As noted by Rogers and Dickey (1991), uncooperativeness also may result from a genuine disorder (e.g., eating disorders and borderline personality disorder), or from a rational appraisal of the circumstances. With reference to the latter, defendants may follow the advice of attorneys, resist the intrusiveness of the investigation (e.g., penile plethysmography, or PPG), or fear false positives. Thus, although uncooperativeness (e.g., muscle contractions producing artifact in PPG evaluations) may be an attempt to deliberately distort results, other explanations are also compelling.

These criticisms of the criminological model notwithstanding, several studies suggest that offenders with marked psychopathic traits and sadistic behaviors are more challenging to evaluate and treat (Chaplin, Rice, & Harris, 1995; Ogloff, Wong, & Greenwood, 1992). To address deliberate distortions among psychopathic persons, Barbaree, Seto, Serin, Amos, and Preston (1994) and Chaplin et al. (1995) concluded that more accurate outcomes can be achieved in these populations by using the Psychopathy Checklist—Revised (PCL-R) in combination with PPG data from appropriate stimuli. More specifically, these authors found improved classification rates for sex offenders denying particularly aggressive or sadistic arousal patterns when using phallometric test stimuli that included violent and sadistic components. In summary, the criminological model of dissimulation is a weak paradigm for most sex offenders, but appropriate for a small proportion high in psychopathic traits and the use deception as a pervasive interpersonal stance.

Adaptational Model

Rogers (1990a) proposed the adaptational model of malingering as an alternative to the pathogenic and criminological perspectives. Rogers and Dickey (1991) subsequently adapted this model of dissimulation to sex offenders. In the adaptational model, the male sex offender perceives himself to be in an adversarial situation, believes something might be gained by being defensive, and concludes that dissimulation is the most effective option. Avoiding pejorative attributions that the dissimulator is either "mad" (pathogenic) or "bad" (criminological), the adaptational model conceives denial/minimization as an effort to minimize the anticipated social and legal sanctions (Braginsky, Braginsky, & Ring, 1969; Rogers & Dickey, 1991; Walters, 1988; Wilcox & Kransnoff, 1967).

Socioevaluative Model

In the socioevaluative model, dissimulation is an attempt to constrict the extent to which the private world of the individual can be examined and made public, regardless of the reason for the examination. Dissimulation in these situations occurs with little thought or planning given to the outcome (i.e., consequences of positive or negative evaluation). Instead, the dissimulation is a learned response to any evaluative stimulus.

For many sex offenders, "evaluation" by others has been consistently and dramatically associated with failure, ostracism, stigmatization, and loss of freedoms and opportunities. Evidence of negative evaluation is the lack of academic accomplishment (i.e., most sex offenders report less than 11th-grade education) and the lack of close friendships and intimate relationships (social constriction of some, but certainly not all, persons with paraphilias; e.g., lack of satisfying romantic-relationship history). The socio-evaluative model might be seen as a special case of the adaptational model but has at least two points of departure. First, in the socioevaluative model, proposed calculation of risk versus benefit of dissimulation does not occur; rather, the constriction is relatively automatic. Second, socioevaluative constriction does not require an overtly adversarial situation, only the mere presence of evaluation. Evidence for the applicability of the socioevaluative model is inferential at present (e.g., higher than average likelihood of multiple academic and social failures among sex offenders); more specific research that addresses evaluative stance among sex offenders outside the forensic assessment setting is needed to determine the breadth of the model.

Assessment of Dissimulation among Sex Offenders

The models of dissimulation serve as a guide to the evaluator in answering the question, "For what purposes can this alleged sex offender be assessed?" Almost always, the clinician strives to determine the personality, sexual preferences, and degree of dissimulation of the alleged offender. But to what consequential ends? In clinical settings, three potential answers to this latter question are (1) to determine the likelihood of guilt or innocence with reference to the offense, (2) to determine the likelihood of recidivism, and/or (3) to offer guidance in the treatment of the alleged offender.

Guilt versus Innocence

First and foremost, no psychometric or phallometric instruments have been established as valid in the assessment of guilt versus innocence with respect to a particular sexual offense that is denied by the accused. Depending upon the degree to which the criminological model is ascribed legitimacy, the logic might be adopted (as the legal system often does) that if accused persons are deceptive about one or more aspects of their functioning (e.g., sexual arousal patterns or level of psychopathology), then they are likely to be lying with respect to the denied offenses. This apparent deduction is more prevalent if the phallometric data yield any indication of a deviant arousal pattern. Langevin (1988) and Freund and Blanchard (1989) have highlighted the dangers of treating phallometric results as "ground truth" or as a "sexual lie detector." Similarly, Murphy and Peters (1992) concluded that even state-of-the-art sex offender assessments are inadequate to address guilt versus innocence.

Most of the studies that address dissimulation among sex offenders classify the independent variable as "admitter" versus "denier." Although rarely addressed in the treatment and assessment literature, at least one presentation can easily be mistaken as defensiveness (i.e., false positives). That presentation is "innocent truth telling." The common assumption is that anything other than total acquiescence to the details as outlined by the complainant represents deception on the part of the accused. Another possibility is that the complainant is inaccurate—anywhere from distorted to completely false accounts (Everson & Boat, 1989; Mikkelsen, Gutheil, & Emens, 1992). Conversely, admitting to a particular offense is not a direct indication that the offender is being straightforward in the assessment process, or is not denying other levels of the offense (see Patterns 1–3; Kennedy & Grubin, 1992). Given these problems with the current research classifications and the lack of appropriate, controlled studies, the use of dissimulation methods to inform guilt assessments seems unwarranted and dangerous.

Recidivism Risk

Hanson, Cox, and Woszcyna (1991) listed denial/minimization as a variable relevant to estimating recidivism risk (see also Barbaree, 1991; Langevin, Wright, & Handy, 1990; Scully, 1990). However, more recent research has questioned this conclusion. Kennedy and Grubin (1992) found that the presence of denial per se did not appear to be an important predictor of recidivism. Rather, the overall degree of denial seemed to be least apparent in Pattern 1, the group with the greatest number of past sex offense convictions (a well-established predictor of reoffending). Pattern 4 (absolute denial) had recidivism rates comparable to the partial-denial groups. Thus, although denial/minimization as a global linear construct might not predict recidivism, these indirect findings suggest that the particular subtypes might represent different levels of risk. Along these same lines, Hanson, Steffy, and Gauthier (1993) concluded from a study of risk factors for recidivism in child sex offenders that denial and minimization (including MMPI validity indices) were not significant predictors. Thus, denial and minimization appear to have limited value in prediction of recidivism, with the possible exception of offenders who admit to the offense but minimize the value of society's sanctions against such offenses.

Treatment

Kennedy and Grubin (1992) contended that their different patterns of denial would be most useful in developing individual therapeutic programs and shaping the therapeutic and penal milieu. By measuring denial systematically and conducting studies of specific treatment methods, investigators could determine whether the denial patterns differentially impact treatment or predict treatment outcome. Then, treatment might accommodate dissimulation. For example, it might be found that Pattern 1 offenders are more cooperative in treatment when psychoeducational methods are employed, whereas Pattern 3 offenders might benefit more from group psychotherapy approaches.

Given this background, we examine the literature on identifying the denial as-, sessment of dissimulation among sex offenders. Based on empirical studies, we have organized this section in two parts. First, we discuss self-report personality measures with an emphasis on the MMPI. Second, we evaluate phallometric assessments, both their general validity and specific usefulness in the evaluation of dissimulation.

DISSIMULATION OF SEX OFFENDERS
ON SELF-REPORT PERSONALITY MEASURES

Various Self-Report Measures

A variety of self-report personality measures have been employed in the assessment of dissimulation among sex offenders. Haywood et al. (1993) examined 59 accused sex offenders with regard to denial of deviant sexual behaviors and bidirectional dissimulation on the Sixteen Personality Factor Questionnaire (16 PF) (Cattell, Eber, & Tatsuoka, 1970). Nonadmitters ($n = 26$) showed significantly more minimization of problems (Motivation Distortion scale), and admitters ($n = 33$) showed more exaggeration (Fake-Bad scale) on the 16 PF. According to the authors, minimization by the nonadmitters was evidenced by lower reports of anxiety and a presentation of self as "happy-go-lucky, venturesome, extroverted, and genuine" (p. 186). In contrast, exaggeration of psychological distress on the part of admitters was evidenced by greater reports of anxiety and a presentation of self as "reserved, dull, introspective, and liberal" (p. 187). Interpretation of these findings is hampered by the virtual absence of validity information related to these indices.

A potential problem with studies that interpret higher indices of fake-bad validity indicators as representing exaggeration (e.g., Haywood et al., 1993) is that fake-bad indices can be affected by levels of psychological impairment. In other words, persons with high levels of actual pathology tend to have higher fake-bad indices than those without significant pathology. Similarly, even given identical pathology in two groups and one group minimizing, the nonminimizing group will have higher fake-bad indices. This potential confound aside, Haywood et al. introduced the interesting issue of motivation during assessment for admitters. Evaluators often assume that once a sex offender admits to the alleged offense, he or she is likely to be forthright about associated issues including personality and pathology. This reasoning is not compelling; a person who has admitted an offense might be motivated to appear more psychopathological than is true (e.g., malingering) in order to garner such benefits as sympathy, medication, and less restrictive supervision. Thus, the validity of psychological assessment data of admitters might be as suspect as that of nonadmitters.

Minnesota Multiphasic Personality Inventory

The majority of studies investigating defensiveness among accused sex offenders has targeted personality assessment using the Minnesota Multiphasic Personality Inventory (MMPI; Hathaway & McKinley, 1951). This section reviews these studies and evaluates the extent to which they are informative in the detection of dissimulation in accused sex offenders in clinical/forensic settings. Table 16.1 contains a synopsis of the studies reviewed in this section.

MMPI assessments with sex offenders are often accompanied by a second inventory, the Multiphasic Sexual Inventory (MSI; Nichols & Molinder, 1984). To understand the convergent validity studies (MMPI and MSI), we describe the scales to assess dissimulation on the MSI. The Sexual Obsession scale of the MSI is interpreted as either

TABLE 16.1. MMPI Studies of Dissimulation among Sex Offenders

Study: Haywood, Grossman, Kravitz, & Wasyliw (1994)
Measures/samples: MMPI and MSI indices in 59 men (27 nonadmitters, 32 admitters) accused of child molesting.
Results: Most MSI validity indices were significantly correlated with *F-K* and *O-S*. Nonadmitters were differentiated from admitters on most MSI indices.

Study: Wasyliw, Grossman, & Haywood (1994)
Measures/samples: MMPI and Buss–Durkee Hostility Inventory (BDHI) with 82 alleged child molesters (45 admitters and 37 nonadmitters).
Results: MMPI indices *L, K, Mp, F-K, O-S,* and *Dsr* all significantly correlated with the BDHI. Admitters were higher on the BDHI than nonadmitters. Admitters appeared to exaggerate psychopathology on the MMPI.

Study: Grossman & Cavanaugh (1989, 1990)
Measures/samples: MMPI to accused sex offenders (30 admitters and 23 nonadmitters).
Results: MMPI *Mp, K, F, F-K, Ds,* and *O-S* all differed significantly in the expected direction between admitters and nonadmitters. Those offenders not facing legal charges endorsed more psychopathology than those facing charges.

Study: Haywood & Grossman (1994)
Measures/samples: MMPI and Pictorial Sexual Interest Card Sort to 75 alleged child molesters (45 admitters, 30 nonadmitters) and 41 normal controls.
Results: Low report of deviant sexual interest was correlated with minimization of psychopathology on the MMPI (*F-K, O-S,* and *Mp*).

Study: Bourget & Bradford (1995)
Measures/samples: MMPI to 20 amnesic nonadmitters, 20 nonamnesic nonadmitters, and 20 nonamnesic admitters charged with sex offenses.
Results: Amnesic nonadmitters show similar but more extreme patterns of defensiveness and symptom minimization than do accused offenders who simply deny the offense.

Study: Langevin, Wright, and Handy (1990)
Measures/samples: Analysis of 125 MMPI scales for 157 sex offenders.
Results: Discriminant analysis to classify admitters versus nonadmitters yielded the best discriminators to be the Homosexuality scale and Habitual Criminalism scale. Some defensiveness measures did discriminate at a weaker level (Repression, Projection, Admission to Minor Faults, Intellectualizing, and Suspicion scales).

Study: Lanyon (1993)
Measures/samples: MMPI to 130 male sex offenders (49 admitters, 52 part- or nonadmitters, and 29 indeterminate) and 239 nonoffenders, with subgroups thought to be forthcoming versus defensive.
Results: Nonadmitters were higher than nonadmitter controls on the *Pe, Sv,* and *Sm* scales, even with *K* covaried. The differentiation of nonadmitters was due to sexual deviance measures and not to overall defensiveness.

Study: Lanyon & Lutz (1984)
Measures/samples: MMPI with 90 men (divided into denier, partial-denier, and admitter groups) indicted or convicted for a sex-related felony.
Results: Predicted differences on the *L, K,* and *F* scales were found. Discriminant analysis between deniers and admitters, using the six validity scales of the MMPI yielded overall hit rate of 83%.

exaggeration of nondeviant sexual interest (high scores) or minimization of even nondeviant sexual interest (low scores). High scores on the Cognitive Distortion and Immaturity scale are interpreted as perceiving the self as a victim of circumstances. High scores on the Justification scale of the MSI reflect the use of rationalizations for the offense. The Treatment Attitudes scale, if elevated, is interpreted as openness to and motivation for treatment. Several content-specific Lie scales are also included in the MSI (e.g., Lie for Child Molest Scale; Lie for Incest Scale); these scales are included to measure defensiveness based on the assumption that the respondent actually committed the offense. The Social Sexual Desirability scale of the MSI is interpreted as representing "normal" adult heterosexual interests and drives (high scores) and minimizing even nondeviant sexual interest (low scores).

Haywood, Grossman, Kravitz, and Wasyliw (1994) examined the relation between MMPI and MSI indices in 59 men, accused child molesters. The Cognition Scale (Abel, Becker, & Cunningham-Rathner, 1984) was also employed as a comparison to the MSI. All but two MSI validity indices (i.e., Social Sexual Desirability and Lie for Incest) were significantly correlated with the MMPI indexes F-K and O-S. Significant correlations ranged from .21 (Lie for Child Molest with O-S) to .77 (Cognitive Distortion and Immaturity with O-S). Nonadmitters scores were significantly different from admitters on all MSI indices except the Sexual Obsessions, Social Sexual Desirability, and Cognitive Distortion and Immaturity scales. The Cognitive Distortion and Immaturity scale and the Justification scale of the MSI were correlated significantly with the Abel Cognition scale (.42 and .25, respectively). The Cognition scale also appeared susceptible to minimization (i.e., for F-K, $r = .30$; for O-S, $r = .33$). Haywood, Grossman, Kravitz, & Wasyliw (1994) concluded that the MSI has concurrent validity but should not be interpreted straightforwardly (if at all) with nonadmitters, given its obvious susceptibility to defensiveness.

Wasyliw, Grossman, and Haywood (1994) used the Buss–Durkee Hostility Inventory (BDHI) and the MMPI with 82 alleged child molesters. MMPI indices L, K, Mp, F-K, O-S, and Dsr all significantly correlated with the BDHI (absolute correlations ranging from .52 to .76). Admitters were higher on the BDHI than nonadmitters, mainly on Irritability and Guilt subscales. Admitters also appeared to exaggerate psychopathology on the MMPI, suggesting that some of the BDHI findings might have been affected by exaggeration among admitters as well as defensiveness among nonadmitters. The authors concluded that face-valid measures such as the BDHI are demonstrably susceptible to dissimulated response styles in child molesters.

Grossman and Cavanaugh (1989) found that nearly all MMPI scales differentiated between admitters and nonadmitters. Consistent with the adaptational model, they also found that those offenders not facing legal charges endorsed more psychopathology than those facing charges. In what appears to be an expansion of this study, Grossman and Cavanaugh (1990) reported almost identical findings on 53 accused sex offenders. The most frequent pathology patterns throughout these studies included elevations in antisocial attitudes, depressive features, somatization, and thought disorder. Based on these findings, Grossman and Cavanaugh (1989, 1990) concluded that many sex offenders deny and minimize many psychiatric symptoms.

Haywood and Grossman (1994) administered the Pictorial Sexual Interest Card Sort (PSICS; cited in Haywood, Grossman, & Cavanaugh, 1990) and the MMPI to 75 alleged child molesters and normal controls. Several findings supported the validity of the PSICS: (1) Molesters of boys reported more interest in boys and men than did molesters of girls and nonmolesting controls; (2) molesters of girls reported less interest in adult women than did controls; and (3) incest offenders reported less interest in children than did nonincest offenders. However, use of the PSICS with nonadmitters appeared to be problematic, given that nonadmitters reported lower interest in children than did admitters or controls. Also, low report of deviant sexual interest was correlated with minimization of psychopathology on the MMPI (F-K, O-S, and Mp). These findings were strongest for F-K and Mp, statistically significant even when using a Bonferroni adjustment (p ≤ .004). Although nonadmitters showed even less reported interest in girls and women than controls (not possible with boy interest due to a floor effect), cutting scores were not explored to determine diagnostic utility. Thus, the PSICS appears to yield useful information only when the offender admits to the offense. Nonadmitters appear to minimize both sexual interest on the PSICS and overall psychopathology on the MMPI.

Bourget and Bradford (1995) examined 20 sex offenders who claimed amnesia for the offense (i.e., amnesic nonadmitters) and compared them to 20 nonamnesic nonadmitters and 20 nonamnesic admitters. The investigators hypothesized that offenders claiming amnesia would look somewhat like nonadmitters but with higher degrees of psychopathology. Test and clinical findings yielded no intellectual, personality (MMPI), sexual functioning, testosterone, marital status, or employment status differences among the groups. The main, significant differences were that the claimed amnesia group reported higher use of alcohol at or around the time of offense and other differences in the nature of the offense. The authors suggested that the "amnestic offenders are different" (p. 305) than offenders with other presentations. However, a closer examination of the results reveals a consistent ordering from admitters to nonadmitters to amnestic nonadmitters. Stated differently, persons claiming amnesia for the offense show similar but more extreme patterns of defensiveness and symptom minimization than do accused offenders who simply deny the offense.

Langevin, Wright, and Handy (1990) divided 157 sex offenders into subgroups and examined 125 MMPI scales (as identified scales focusing on sexual behavior, substance abuse, personality, defensiveness, and brain damage) for internal consistency, factor structures, and discriminant validity. With reference to dissimulation, defensiveness measures, despite variable estimates of internal consistency, loaded via factor analysis so as to suggest unidimensionality of defensiveness. Discriminant analysis was conducted to distinguish admitters versus nonadmitters allowing any of the 125 scales to load. The best discriminators were special scales: Homosexuality scale (nonadmitters higher) and Habitual Criminalism scale (nonadmitters higher). Some defensiveness measures did discriminate at a weak level (nonadmitters were higher on Repression, Projection, and Admission to Minor Faults scales; and lower on Intellectualizing and Suspicion scales). This study presents a very mixed picture of defensiveness. Denying guilt of a sex offense appears partly comprised of general defensiveness and, perhaps, psychologically motivated denial processes. However, more variance appears to be accounted for by combinations of sexual deviation, criminal propensity, and substance abuse. Extrapolating from these data, criminological and adaptational models of dissimulation (Rogers & Dickey, 1990) appear applicable to explain portions of the overall pattern; pathogenic and socioevaluative appear relevant, but to a lesser degree. These findings are subject to all the cautions of other admitter–nonadmitter studies (e.g., absence of a "gold standard," types of minimization not captured by admission dichotomy). Additionally, there is a stark potential of overfitting the data when examining 125 scales in reference to 85 participants (even though only 16 scales discriminated with $p \leq .10$). Given this drawback, these findings need replication before they should be interpreted as stable.

Lanyon (1993) compared 130 male sex offenders (predominantly child molesters and exhibitionists) to (1) 122 nonoffenders that admitted to or slightly exaggerated their psychopathology and (2) 93 "nonadmitter controls" (i.e., persons apparently consciously defensive and not wanting to admit to obviously deviant but nonsexual behaviors). These groups were compared on the MMPI, including validity indices: L and K for defensiveness, F for overall psychopathology, and K-uncorrected Pd for "character disorder" (p. 304). Nonadmitters were higher than nonadmitter controls on sexual deviant scales: Pe, Sv, and Sm scales. Even when the K scale was covaried, the significant results remained. This finding was interpreted as evidence that the differentiation of nonadmitters was due to sexual deviance measures and not to overall defensiveness.

Because of the high proportion of child molesters in the Lanyon (1993) sample, these findings are applicable only to pedophiles. Comparisons of nonadmitters (sexual) to nonadmitter controls (nonsexual) suggest the possibility of "defensiveness norms" to assist in the evaluation of nonadmitters. Aside from pointing to such potential norms, the Lanyon findings offer corroboration that nonadmitters appear to show deviant sexual responding on the MMPI that is apart from their overall defensive stance.

Lanyon and Lutz (1984) examined the utility of the MMPI to assess defensiveness and denial with 90 men indicted or convicted for a sex-related felony. They hypothesized that participants, known to have denied the offense fully (i.e., deniers) or partially (i.e., part-deniers), would have higher elevations on MMPI indices of defensiveness than admitters. Predicted differences were found on the L scale with M's of 54.56 for deniers, 50.08 for part-deniers, and 45.71 for admitters. Likewise, K scale M's were 62 for deniers, 55.96 for part-deniers, and 48.15 for admitters. An opposite pattern was found for the F scale; interestingly a raw score index of $L + K - F$ showed the highest individual correlation ($r = .64$) with denial versus no denial. Despite these group differences, most profiles were not elevated, thereby limiting the clinical usefulness of these data.

Lanyon and Lutz (1984) conducted a discriminant analysis between the deniers and admitters, using the six validity scales as dependent variables. With an overall hit rate of 83%, they demonstrated that most alleged sex offenders who denied involvement could be classified by MMPI validity scales. A critical question remains: Do these findings say anything more than the obvious, namely that offenders deny their involvement? Perhaps they suggest that denial is being employed. But whether such a conclusion should add weight to the interpretation that the individual therefore is being "untruthful" with respect to the denied allegation is unaddressed. Arguably, the most informative conclusions would come from applying the results to treatment plans aimed at bringing the offender to an acknowledgment of his own personality and difficulties, rather than an admission per se.

PHYSIOLOGICAL ASSESSMENT OF SEX OFFENDERS

General Considerations of Phallometric Assessment

Penile plethysmography (PPG) is the assessment of sexual arousal via direct measurement of penile volume or circumference changes. Two recent meta-analytic reports (Hall, Shondrich, & Hirschman, 1993; Lalumière & Quinsey, 1994) have shown that phallometric data derived from PPG reliably correspond to sexual deviance with average effect sizes of .71 and .82, respectively. The only significant moderator variable noted by Lalumière and Quinsey was the level of graphic depictions in the stimulus sets; understandably, more graphic stimuli resulted in greater effect sizes.

PPG investigations have also stimulated concerted criticisms. For example, Simon and Schouten (1992) noted several limitations in PPG assessments that make their use in legal contexts "highly questionable" (p. 513). These limitations include (1) the ease with which PPG assessments can be faked, (2) the need for standardization of test protocols/stimuli, and (3) the lack of cumulative findings on subgroups of sex offenders. A more general problem is that the apparent directness of phallometric assessment yields a temptation to treat the PPG as a "sexual lie detector" (Rogers & Dickey, 1990), a use clearly not indicated by empirical studies. The following is a presentation of studies that illustrate use of PPG data, a discussion of their limitations, and a review of the PPG for detecting dissimulation.

Abel, Blanchard, and Barlow (1981) examined the effects of stimulus modality, instructional set, and stimulus content on sexual arousal for several paraphiliacs. The authors noted the use of slides, free fantasy, and audiotapes being used in some clinical and research settings. Little is known regarding the relative effectiveness or stability of these modalities. Therefore, sexual arousal was measured by various penile plethysmographic methods for groups of men with six different paraphilias. The authors found that videotape was the most powerful modality for generating erections (except with exhibitionists and male pedophiles). Abel et al. also compared the patterns of responses across the different offense groups. Rapists were typically more aroused than other groups. Exhibitionists were found to be generally lower in arousal level to both paraphiliac and nonparaphiliac stimuli than other groups. Both sadomasochists and fetishists showed less arousal to nonparaphiliac cues than to paraphiliac cues. Given that many studies combine sex offenders across a variety of offense/paraphiliac categories, there is reason to suspect that the particular combinations might produce confounded results. Further research is needed to understand fully the possible interactions between PPG stimulus modality and paraphiliac content.

Child Molestation

Chaplin et al. (1995) contended that child molesters can be differentiated from other offender and nonoffender groups by their PPG arousal to audiovisual stimuli in which extreme trauma is described from a victim's perspective. Likewise, Quinsey and Laws (1990) found highly reliable differences between child molesters' sexual response patterns and those of non-sex-offenders. In stark contrast, Hall, Proctor, and Nelson (1988) failed to obtain PPG differences between child molesters and other sex offenders.

Recent PPG research has indicated that stimuli emphasizing force and coercion effectively discriminated between sex offender and non-sex-offender groups. Based on initial findings, Chaplin et al. (1995) examined the discriminant validity of sexual responses to stories of child sexual assault when told from the point of view of the male perpetrator versus a female child victim. They found that depictions from the victim's perspective yielded more deviant arousal than the same actions from the perpetrator's vantage point. In addition, Chaplin et al. examined the effects of varying the level of immediate physical and psychological trauma suffered by the victim. Their results showed that all levels of trauma yielded excellent discrimination between the child molesters and nonoffender groups ($d = 4.10$; 93% sensitivity and 100% specificity). Discrimination was maximized by using stimuli that emphasized force and coercion (100% sensitivity and specificity). Their research suggests that when appropriate stimuli and procedures are used, child molesters' sexual responses are very different from those of normal men.

Adult Sexual Assault

Eccles, Marshall, and Barbaree (1994) evaluated whether stimuli that emphasize the degrading and humiliating aspects of rape would improve discriminability between 19 nonoffenders and 19 incarcerated male sex offenders. Three rape indices were obtained for each participant: (1) an Aggression Index, (2) a Degradation Index, and (3) a Neutral Index. None of the indices discriminated between rapists and nonrapists; thus, Eccles et al. questioned the utility of PPG for such purposes.

Limitations of PPG

The discriminant validity of PPG is often assumed to be a unitary concept. Simple dichotomies (sex offenders vs. others) are unlikely to be effective. Instead, we would argue that the validity of PPG assessment must be separately established for specific paraphilias (e.g., pedophilia and sexual sadism) and rape.

Another criticism of PPG assessment has been the use of the findings as ground truth in the absence of a "gold standard" (i.e., Rogers & Dickey, 1990). An illustration of this dubious assumption can be found in Freund and Watson's (1992) study exploring the differences between heterosexual pedophilia and homosexual pedophilia. On the assertion that not all sex offenders against children are pedophiles, they argued that "true" pedophilia could be established via PPG.

Other commentators are fully supportive of the use of PPG assessments in making forensic decisions regarding sex offenders. Annon (1988) reviewed the PPG literature and concluded that the methods and procedures have been sufficiently established so as to gain general acceptance in the fields of psychology and psychiatry. Annon appeared to fully support the use of PPG data in court to address issues of guilt and risk in rape and child molestation cases.

Usual PPG procedures assume that no systematic changes of penile responsivity occur throughout a testing session; thus, all measurements during one session are deemed to be comparable. Kolarsky and Madlafousek (1977) decided that this assumption required formal investigation. They studied the serial effect in PPG experiments in which several sexual stimuli were presented in different orders. They found the following serial effects: (1) Any stimulus presented first had a weaker effect in comparison to its later presentation; and (2) the effect of a stimulus is influenced by the preceding stimulus. The researchers did not observe a habituation effect to sexual stimuli. Based on these results, the authors suggested that it is advisable to apply some preliminary sexual stimuli prior to the PPG assessment.

In general, studies have found sex offender groups to be statistically distinguishable from control groups on the basis of PPG assessments. For example, Hinton, O'Neill, and Webster (1980) studied the sexual orientation and responses of sexual offenders in a maximum security hospital. Groups of sexual offenders, nonsexual assaulters of women, and nonoffending heterosexuals were compared on arousal patterns in reaction to video films that showed consenting adult heterosexual activity, adult homosexual activity, boy homosexual activity, girl abduction, and girl rape. No differences were found for consenting heterosexual material. However, nonoffending heterosexuals and nonsexual attackers of women showed significantly less response to depictions of girl abduction and rape than sex offenders in general. Because dissimulation is so common among sex offenders, Hinton et al. concluded that PPG assessments might be effectively used to differentiate globally sex offenders from non-sex-offenders. Such studies are generally seen as supporting the validity of the PPG. But critical questions remain. Because some measure can distinguish sex offenders from others, does that mean it can distinguish an individual sex offender, who is lying about the offense, from an admitting sex offender? In the following section, we review studies attempting to answer this question.

Detection of Dissimulation with PPG Assessment

Phallometric assessment has been shown to detect denied arousal in nonforensic cases. Blanchard, Racansky, and Steiner (1986) examined whether erotic response to cross-dressing fantasies could be detected in 37 heterosexual male cross-dressers who had denied any erotic arousal to cross-dressing. The results showed that all cross-dressers responded significantly more to cross-dressing than to neutral narratives, although controls evidenced no differences between conditions. Thus, the authors found discrepancies between the heterosexual male cross-dressers' self-reports and their more directly observed physiological responses.

Several researchers have noted the effectiveness of PPG assessments to detect dissimulation in forensic settings. Becker, Hunter, Stein, and Kaplan (1989) examined which variables are associated with erectile responding to "age-inappropriate" stimuli in the adolescent sex offender population. Variables included (1) level of denial or admission, (2) history of physical abuse, (3) history of sexual abuse, (4) history of non-sex-related arrests, (5) whether the subject's deviant sexual behavior was incestuous or nonincestuous, and (6) whether the child victim was less than 8 years of age or older. Participants included two samples of adolescent males, charged with sexual offenses against children. Two pedophile indices were used as relative measures of deviant and nondeviant arousal (the Pedophile Noncoercion Index and the Pedophile Coercion Index; Abel et al., 1981). Erectile responses were indicative of both noncoercive and coercive sexual interactions with children, irrespective of denial. This study offers support for the validity of the PPG in detecting denied arousal.

Freund, Chan, and Coulthard (1979) found that with standard PPG diagnostic procedures, 5% of "admitters" to arousal patterns involving children were missed on phallometric results. More inaccuracies occurred with nonadmitters: (1) "Almost one third" (p. 454) of the 18 nonadmitters were missed, and (2) an additional one-third of the nonadmitters were miscategorized by PPG results with respect to arousal interests in children (i.e., wrong gender or age range of attraction). In contrast, approximately one-fourth of the admitter group were miscategorized with respect to pedophiliac interests. In an attempt to improve detection rate, they developed a sequencing from adult to child stimulus that modestly improved classification.

Freund, Watson, and Rienzo (1988) tested the effectiveness of three potential signs of dissimulation during PPG assessment: (1) contractions of the abdominal and perineal musculature that is visible on the PPG; (2) showing highest or second-highest response to sexually neutral stimuli, when no deviant arousal is observed; and (3) having the highest arousal response involve a different gender than the second-highest arousal. Based on descriptive data alone, the following percentages were observed: muscle contractions (16.5%), abnormally high response to neutral images (7.7%). Almost all contractions occurred toward adult-female images, even though only 5 of the 164 participants had adult females as their highest response. This finding suggested that muscle contraction is not an artifact of high arousal, but possibly an attempt to feign arousal to socially desirable stimuli. The assumption that arousal to neutral stimuli is evidence of defensiveness is not compelling, because too large an inference is necessary to make the aforementioned connection without any clear evidence that the sex offender is actually attempting to be defensive. Finally, cross-gender arousal was higher for individuals who had molested males rather than females. Although possibly an indicator of defensiveness, offending against one gender does not rule out attraction to the other gender. However, "double-gender" arousal might have a differential base rate in males molesting girls versus boys.

As a further investigation, Freund et al. (1988) conducted a simulation study with 42 heterosexual, normal males coached and promised incentives for dissimulating interests in homosexuality and pedophilia on PPG testings. Results indicated that 30 of 42 (71.4%) produced arousals to children, whereas only 18 of 42 (42.9%) manifested arousal to same-sex stimuli. These studies clearly show that PPG responding is under at least partial control of the individual and, under certain conditions, can be dissimulated.

Freund and Blanchard (1989) developed a set of complex diagnostic rules for the PPG and then applied them to 40 child molesters who denied the offense. Of the 40 deniers, 22 had preferential arousal patterns to children (sensitivity = .55). In comparison, only 1 of 30 normal controls exhibited this arousal pattern (specificity = .97). The authors acknowledged that these results indicated that negative findings on the PPG are much less informative than positive results.

PPG has been found to bear no relationship to admission–denial of sex offenses, at least in one study. Haywood et al. (1990) compared 24 accused child molesters (11 nonadmitters, 13 admitters) and 23 normal controls on a PPG assessment as well as self-reported arousal and repulsion to the PPG stimulus slides. No differences were found between admitters and nonadmitters. Child molesters showed higher PPG and self-report response to children. Correlations were significant (1) for molesters' PPG and self-reported responses to children ($r = .43$), and (2) for controls' PPG and self-reported responses to adults ($r = .40$). All groups showed comparable instances of marked PPG response to slides judged as repulsive, and subjective arousal to slides evoking no PPG response. Thus, not only did the study fail to find a relationship between admission–denial and PPG-measured arousal, but it also failed to show the expected relationship between PPG and self-report. Moreover, cases of self-report and PPG disagreement were not related to admission–denial. These results beg the question of whether the PPG is providing reliable and unique information.

Combining the PPG with the MMPI

Comprehensive assessments commonly combine psychometric and PPG assessments. McAnulty, Adams, and Wright (1994) studied 90 men accused of child sexual abuse. Using the PPG as the "gold standard," 30 men showed pedophilic arousal, and 60 men showed adult-female arousal pattern. Importantly, although the "majority of subjects denied the allegations" (p. 182), no attempt was made to differentially investigate the relations among the MMPI and PPG indices and admission–denials. Instead, McAnulty et al. attempted to predict PPG status based on MMPI scale scores. A direct, discriminant analysis with all scales did not produce a significant function. However, a stepwise discriminant analysis with scales 7, K, L, 3, 1, 6 produced a significant function that correctly classified 63.3% of pedophilic responders and 75.4% of adult responders. However, the interpretability of the function is severely constrained, given the minuscule mean differences on scales contributing to the function. The function and its classification rate probably capitalized on chance relations. Although patterns of scores on MMPI scales separated alleged child molesters who exhibit deviant arousal from those who did not, one-third of the men were misclassified, based on MMPI scores. As summarized by the authors, "Attempts to identify men who display sexual attraction to children using the MMPI cannot be justified" (p. 184).

New "Physiological" Arousal Assessments

The explicitness of stimuli required for PPG assessments can be seen as impeding the standardization of the protocols (both the production and distribution of sexually explicit materials are illegal in some jurisdictions, especially when children are involved). Furthermore, the intrusiveness of PPG assessments likely inhibits large-scale participation. Moreover, this intrusiveness might also contribute to the frequent production of nonresponsive and thus invalid profiles. In an attempt to address both of these issues, a new physiometric procedure has been introduced by Abel (1995) that uses less explicit stimuli and less invasive physiological monitoring (i.e., no direct penile measure). Abel (1995; also see Abel, Lawry, Karlstrom, Osborn, & Gillespie, 1994) claimed that this new method promises to be comparable to PPG assessment in terms of the types of indices assessed and overall accuracy.

According to Abel et al. (1994), the Abel Screen works by matching arousal patterns and cognitions of men in the general population who deny any diagnosis of pedophilia. The individual first completes a questionnaire. The main aspect of the test involves viewing computer-driven slides of children, adolescents, and adults. The examinee reports his subjective sexual arousal to each slide in succession. In the first set of slides, the figures are partially dressed; in the subsequent set of slides, they are nude. Simultaneously, the examinee is to keep one hand resting on what is explained as a "psychophysiological hand monitor" reputed to be recording a physiological response to each slide. Apparently, the device (actually a computer mouse) is not connected to any physiological recording apparatus.

To empirically evaluate the efficacy of the Abel Screen, Abel et al. (1994) tested 101 control participants from the community as well as 30 pedophiles who had molested pubescent males, 25 molesters of prepubescent males, 57 molesters of pubescent girls, and 73 molesters of prepubescent girls. They conducted four separate discriminant function analyses for each of the pedophilic groups. When examining the measure's ability to discern pedophiles who had molested prepubesent males from normals, they found that the Abel Screen correctly classified 98% of the normals and 76% of the pedophiles. In discriminating pedophiles who had molested pubescent males from normal participants, the Abel Screen correctly classified 98% of the normals and 90% of the pedophiles. In discerning pedophiles who had molested preadolescent girls from the normal participants, the screen correctly classified 77% of the normals and 91% of the pedophiles. Finally, in discriminating pedophiles who had molested pubescent girls from normal participants, the Abel Screen correctly classified 77% of the normals and 86% of the pedophiles. These classifications were similar to those produced by PPG data from the same sample.

Abel et al. (1994) suggested that the Abel Screen is difficult to fake. They reported that preliminary data showed no differences on measures of pedophiles instructed to reveal versus those instructed to conceal their deviant sexual interests. In addition, using discriminant function analyses, Abel et al. examined the efficacy of the Abel Screen at discerning 13 deniers from the control group. The authors found that the Abel Screen correctly classified 88% of the normals and 100% of the deniers. The authors noted the small sample and suggested that the results are promising but only preliminary.

CONCLUSIONS AND APPLICATIONS

In the nomothetic sense, the studies reviewed in the preceding sections tend to indicate that groups of accused sex offenders who deny the offense can be statistically distinguished from those who admit the offense. However, the absence of consistent and acceptable classification rates would suggest that the ability to classify individuals into these two groups based on psychometric and phallometric assessment is relatively poor. Regardless, the forensic clinician is *never* faced with the following demand: Use psychometric and phallometric assessment tools to estimate whether the examinee will deny or admit to the offense. Such information is readily available simply by questioning the sex offender. Instead, the question we believe to be more important and appropriate is directly addressed nowhere in current literature: "Can assessment tools distinguish a sex offender who is lying about the offense from a person falsely accused?" The answer to this question is unknown. There is yet another question faced by the clinician: "Is this particular accused sex offender, whether admitting to the offense or not, dissimulating in his presentation?" Although the extant research does not allow us to make direct actuarial predictions in answering this question, the studies do yield some generalities regarding how deception and dissimulation are expressed by accused sex offenders in an assessment context.

Murphy and Peters (1992) contended that little empirical support exists regarding the adequacy of data to allow the clear profiling of sex offenders. They argued that when judged against the legal requirements for expert testimony, psychological profiles developed from existing tools are *unlikely* to be helpful in a criminal trial in the decision process of guilt or innocence. Specifically, Murphy and Peters stated that the research evidence does not demonstrate that clinicians can profile sexual offenders with sufficient reliability and validity, even when using all the tools available. However, they emphasize that once guilt or innocence has been decided, such evaluation is useful for treatment purposes.

With regard to the MMPI, Murphy and Peters (1992) raise several important concerns outlined below:

• Commonly reported (e.g., Anderson & Kunce, 1979; Swenson & Grimes, 1969) 4–9 or 4–8 profiles with sex offenders often occur in other forensic populations (see Quinsey, Arnold, & Pruess, 1980), including murderers, arsonists, and property offenders. In addition, Dahlstrom, Welsch, and Dahlstrom (1972) reported that 4–9 profiles are commonly seen in prison populations and 4–8/8–4 profiles are observed in a number of psychiatric populations and prison populations.

• Many sex offender MMPI studies report mean or modal profiles, which create the illusion of homogeneity. Murphy and Peters (1992) noted that in several large-scale studies (Erikson, Luxenberg, Walbek, & Seely, 1987; Hall, 1989; Hall, Maiuro,

Vitaliano, & Proctor, 1986), almost every imaginable MMPI profile was observed; more specifically, 43 of the 45 theoretically possible 2-point codes were observed by Erickson et al. (1987).

• The ability of offenders to dissimulate on the MMPI was noted as a major problem. Murphy and Peters (1992) pointed to studies (e.g., Lanyon & Lutz, 1984) to conclude that accused offenders who either partially or fully deny the offense can produce basically normal profiles.

With regard to penile plethysmography, Murphy and Peters (1992) concluded from their literature review that, despite some inconsistent findings, consistent patterns were generally found. However, we have shown throughout the present chapter that classification of offenders is not particularly accurate using these data. The evidence (Abel, Barlow, Blanchard, & Mavissakalian, 1975; Freund, 1963; Laws & Holmen, 1978; Laws & Rubin, 1969; Quinsey & Bergersen, 1976; Wydra, Marshall, Earls, & Barbaree, 1983) that individuals can fake and suppress erection responses raises important validity concerns. Because many individuals are able to control their erectile responses, a person's failure to respond may result from either intentional suppression or a genuine disinterest in the presented stimuli. In addition, as Murphy and Peters (1992) argued, even though group differences might be reliably found, use of the PPG to classify an individual produces error rates that are unacceptably high for courtroom applications.

After reviewing the literature, both preceding and following Murphy and Peters (1992), we agree with their conclusions. More specifically, we do not endorse the use of psychological and PPG assessment data to assist in the determination of guilt or innocence, even when the accused has attempted to dissimulate presentation in one or more aspects of the assessment. The absence of a consensually accepted "gold standard" makes the likelihood of ameliorating our methodological concerns in the near future quite slim. Furthermore, the difficulty in providing sufficient experimental controls—most notably, groups of accused sex offenders who deny the offense and are subsequently established to have been telling the truth—prevents drawing firm conclusions.

The linking of dissimulation to recidivism risk has yet to be sufficiently validated. However, this connection holds considerable promise, particularly as dissimulation assessment relates to treatment. Many kinds of psychological interventions are aimed at producing empathy, insight, and assumption of personal responsibility. If dissimulation can be effectively measured and studied, it seems highly likely that stable relations will be established between the degree of dissimulation and the effectiveness of such interventions. At present, the detection of dissimulation remains important, both to guide individual treatment planning and further understand its relationship to recidivism.

An overriding goal of this book is the application of applied research to clinical practice. Toward this end, we provide threshold and clinical decision models for the detection of dissimulated presentations when assessing accused or adjudicated sex offenders.

Threshold Model

A threshold model addresses the question, "What should alert the clinician to the potential for dissimulation in a particular case?" Given the societal and legal ramifications of admitting to a sex offense, with its social sanctions and criminal penalties, dissimulation should be considered in every case of a person accused of a sex offense, whether or not the individual admits to the offense. Therefore, we are suggesting that any accusations of sex offenses be sufficient to meet the threshold criterion.

The rationale for the threshold criterion is based on studies showing minimization of psychological and sexual deviance among individuals who deny purported sex offenses, as well as the studies showing exaggeration of psychological–substance-abuse pathology among individuals admitting to a sex offense. Moreover, an admission to a particular sex offense has never been established as meaning that the offender is being honest about other offenses, many of which might never have been reported. In addition, most sex offender cases are not self-referred for evaluation or treatment; more typically, such referrals originate in the criminal justice system where, understandably, punitive rather than treatment interventions are the norm. Therefore, dissimulation must be considered in any case in which the issue of a sex offense is raised.

This threshold model should not be interpreted as a pejorative stance toward accused sex offenders or as an implicit assumption that they are always dissimulating. Rather, it is a recognition that dissimulation is frequently present in this domain, where the stakes for sex offenders are especially high. It is also an admission that our assessment methods cannot provide an accurate screening measure of which sex offenders are dissimulating. Therefore, the presentation of an accused or admitted sex offender is considered sufficient to meet the threshold model for dissimulation.

Clinical Decision Model

The clinical decision model is used to determine dissimulation among sex offenders. Given the admittedly wide net cast by the threshold model, components of the clinical decision model need to be thoroughly integrated with the clinical/forensic assessment process with sex offense referrals. Figure 16.1 represents our recommended clinical model for determining the probability of dissimulation in sex offense cases. The first critical question to assess is the examinee's admission status. As emphasized throughout this chapter, whether an accused person admits to the offense should not be interpreted in terms of dissimulation. Instead, as presented in Figure 16.1, the answer to this question directs the evaluation toward malingering/exaggeration versus denial/minimization of sexual deviance and/or general psychopathology.

For those examinees admitting to the offenses, an evaluation of malingering/exaggeration is recommended. One possible motivation for malingering is the assumption that more general pathology will reduce perceived culpability for the offense. Even when the offense is admitted, denial/minimization might still be a point of evaluation, depending upon consistency between interviews, test results, and collateral information.

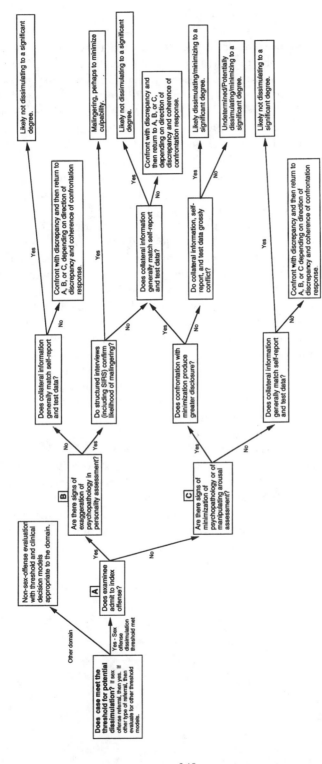

FIGURE 16.1. Clinical decision model.

Likewise, an examinee who denies the offense might be telling the truth, unwilling to tell the truth, or unable to tell the truth. Therefore, the most immediate evaluation need is the possibility that the examinee is denying or minimizing sexual arousal patterns (as evidenced by apparently manipulated PPG data) or psychopathology (as evidenced by defensive profiles on personality assessment tools). Still, depending upon the consistency between these findings and collateral data, clinicians might turn their attention to potential malingering/exaggeration.

The general progression of the model is as follows: (1) Determine direction of most likely dissimulation via admission status; (2) assess personality (e.g., MMPI-2), sexual arousal patterns (e.g., PPG) and psychopathology (e.g., structured interviews); (3) depending upon apparent signs of dissimulation, confront and/or perform more specialized assessments (e.g., Structured Interview of Reported Symptoms [SIRS]; Rogers, 1992); (4) collect collateral information; (5) depending on consistency and conclusiveness of cumulative data, either determine probability and direction of dissimulation, or confront examinee with inconsistencies and refocus assessment accordingly.

Given the inconclusive status of the literature on dissimulation, no explicit decision rules are indicated by current empirical knowledge. We cannot say, for example, exactly what MMPI K scale or F-K + L index score constitutes firm grounds for deciding that a sex offender's personality profile is defensive, or precisely what proportion of total PPG arousal attained by neutral stimuli constitutes a defensive phallometric assessment. Nor can we say definitely what kind of collateral information from which sources constitutes veridical data. Instead, consistency–inconsistency of "clinically judged" factors across these instruments and assessment modalities must be evaluated at each point in the model, before determining dissimulation or even moving to another level in the model. Fortunately, some aspects of the model can be slightly more straightforward (e.g., admission status and SIRS outcome). Still, these data must be interpreted in the context of the entire case, which will almost always contain some amount of conflicting data. The model relies on the experienced professional's interpretation of broad levels of data of varying reliability and validity. The present clinical decision model is thus intended to serve as a template to assist the clinician in organizing both the assessment process and the eventual clinical determination of dissimulation.

17

Assessment of Malingering with Self-Report Instruments

GLENN P. SMITH, Ph.D.

"Malingering" is defined by the fourth edition of the *Diagnostic and Statistical Manual of Mental Disorders* (DSM-IV) as "the intentional production of false or grossly exaggerated physical or psychological symptoms, motivated by external incentives" (American Psychiatric Association, 1994a, p. 683). Although easily defined, malingering has proven far more difficult to detect. Generally, three approaches have been utilized. The first method employs existing intelligence or personality measures (for review, see Schretlen, 1988). The underlying logic has been that malingerers respond in a distinctly aberrant manner to these standardized assessment devices (e.g., interitem scatter, significantly different scores across administrations, and "near miss" responses). Although sometimes effective, the time of administration can be lengthy, and the effectiveness of certain tests vary markedly between populations (e.g., the Minnesota Multiphasic Personality Inventory [MMPI]; see Berry, Baer, & Harris, 1991). Interview techniques and observational strategies are the second general approach to the detection of malingering. Resnick (1984, 1993), for example, noted the distinct qualitative characteristics of malingerers found in traditional interviews. In this regard, the Structured Interview of Reported Symptoms (SIRS; Rogers, Bagby, & Dickens, 1992) operationalized detection strategies and standardized the interview format (see Chapter 15).

The third approach, which is the focus of this chapter, involves the use of screening instruments specifically designed for the detection of malingering. This approach is derived from a practical consideration (e.g., limited time) as well as an assessment vantage point (e.g., some conditions are not detectable through standardized tests). Conceptually, screening measures should provide a threshold method for malingering, when used alone. In combination with additional testing, they may serve as a source of confirmatory data.

The reader is cautioned that these screening measures were designed only to detect feigned psychopathology. Feigned cognitive and neuropsychological deficits generally require entirely different strategies. For a discussion of measures used in the evaluation of feigned neuropsychological deficits, please refer to Chapters 5 and 11.

This chapter is organized into four major sections. The first section is devoted to the M Test and the Malingering Scale, both of which are discussed in some depth. These instruments represent two sustained efforts to validate a brief screen for malingering by using both simulation design (i.e., research participants instructed to feign psychopathology) and known-groups comparisons (i.e., suspected malingerers contrasted with genuine patients). The second section reviews more recently developed instruments, often in their initial stages of validation. Consistent with the book's objectives, the third section discusses the use of the threshold and clinical decision models for malingering. The fourth and final section addresses research directions for these screening measures.

ESTABLISHED SCREENS

M Test

The M Test (Beaber, Marston, Michelli, & Mills, 1985) was among the first attempts in recent years to develop a screening measure specifically to detect the presence of malingering. The M Test was also innovative. Unlike previous research into an undifferentiated "faking-bad" condition (e.g., Grow, McVaugh, & Eno, 1980), the purpose of the M Test was to detect malingering of a specific mental condition, namely schizophrenia.

The M Test consists of 33 true–false items organized on three scales. The first eight questions comprise the C (Confusion) scale. None of the C scale items involve symptom endorsement associated with a mental disorder. Rather, questions are purported to reflect "attitudes" or "beliefs." Consequently, the respondent's endorsement was in an expected direction to provide an assessment of comprehension regardless of the diagnostic category. The M (Malingering) and S (Schizophrenia) scales constitute the body of the test. The ten items of the S scale are genuine DSM-III symptoms associated with schizophrenia, whereas the M scale is composed of 15 bogus questions. The strategies used in the construction of these M-scale items included endorsement of nonexistent entities, atypical hallucinations, extremely severe symptoms not characteristic of actual illness, and atypical delusions. Beaber et al. (1985) hypothesized that those participants attempting to malinger schizophrenia would not be able to differentiate between actual schizophrenic items contained on the S scale and those apparently genuine symptoms on the M scale. In short, the M Test attempts to assess the malingering participants' knowledge base with regard to genuine pathological signs/symptoms.

The original validation study (Beaber et al., 1985) consisted of three phases. First, a pretest sample of undergraduates completed the M Test under honest instructions to ensure that none of the individual items were endorsed by more than 10% of respondents. Second, 104 male undergraduate students completed the M Test under both honest and malingering instructions (i.e., "Pretend you are in a situation where it would be to your advantage to look crazy"; p. 1479). Prior to the second administration, participants read a description of the DSM-III criteria for schizophrenia to help them distinguish between genuine and malingering items. Third, 65 male Veterans Administration inpatients with diagnoses of schizophrenia completed the M Test under standard instructions.

Simulators (i.e., students feigning schizophrenia) scored consistently higher than psychiatric inpatients on all three M Test scales. This finding suggests that feigning participants either did not differentiate between scale items or adopted a relatively indiscriminant pattern of endorsement. Based on the cutting scores using the *C* and *M* scales, 78.2% of simulators and 87.3% of the inpatients were correctly classified.

Although subsequent studies have replicated these findings in simulation research (see Table 17.1), the M Test has not proven effective in known-groups comparison (i.e., application to suspected malingerers). Gillis, Rogers, and Bagby (1991) recruited 124 individuals from community, university, and correctional populations; simulators completed the M Test under feigning instructions. Comparable to Beaber et al. (1985), 79.8% of the simulators were correctly identified. However, when these same researchers applied the original scoring criteria to suspected malingerers from a pretrial forensic unit, the accuracy of classification dropped precipitously to 40%. Assignments to the suspected malingerer and clinical comparison samples were based on the independent findings of a pretrial evaluation.

More recent studies have yielded variable results for the M Test with suspected malingerers. Two studies reported moderate rates: Smith and Borum (1992) identified 69.6% of their malingering group, while Schretlen, Neal, and Hochman (1995) detected 72.8% of suspected malingerers with the *M* scale of the M Test using the criteria proposed by Beaber et al. (1985). In stark contrast, Hankins, Barnard, and Robbins (1993) found that only 30.8% of the malingering group was correctly classified. In the latter two studies, the *C* scale was omitted in the hopes of shortening the M Test without sacrificing its effectiveness.

Rogers, Bagby, and Gillis (1992) attempted to improve the utility of the M Test by introducing a new scoring system: the Rule-Out and Rule-In scales. This method involves a two-step process. The investigators first "ruled out" those individuals who responded in a scoreable direction to 10 items with the highest negative predictive power (i.e., NPP; eliminating bona fide psychiatric patients, based on a believable number of actual symptoms). The remaining individuals were then evaluated based on their responses to the 10 items with the most positive predictive power (i.e., PPP; classified as malingerers based on bogus symptoms).

In addition, these researchers provided two Rule-Out and Rule-In options. Option A was designed for general clinical practice because of a higher sensitivity for genuine patients. Option B was recommended for forensic work because of its higher hit rates for malingerers. Applying these options to the data set of Gillis et al. (1991), Rogers, Bagby, & Gillis (1992) were able to correctly classify 83.6% of the genuine psychiatric patients under Option A and 95.2% of the suspected malingering group under Option B.

TABLE 17.1. Design Features and Study Outcomes Using the M Test

Study	Subject groups			Scoring system	Percentage correctly classified		
	Simulators	Mentally disordered	Controls		Simulators	Mentally disordered	Controls
Beaber et al. (1985)	n = 104 Simulating students	n = 65 Psychiatric inpatients	n = 104 Honest college students	Original	78.2	87.3	> 90
Gillis, Rogers, & Bagby (1991)	n = 124 Simulating community, correctional, and students	n = 72 Psychiatric outpatients and forensic inpatients	n = 97 Community, correctional, and student subjects	Original	79.8	86.1	92.3
	n = 25 Suspected malingerers	n = 72 Psychiatric outpatients and forensic inpatients	n = 97 Community, correctional, and student subjects	Original	40.0	86.1	92.3
Smith & Borum (1992)	n = 23 Suspected malingerers	n = 62 Psychiatric inmates	—	Original	69.6	66.1	—
Hankins, Barnard, & Robbins (1993)	n = 13 Suspected malingerers[a]	n = 66 Forensic residential	—	Original	30.8	69.7	—
Schretlen, Neal, & Hochman (1995)	n = 11 Suspected malingerers	n = 86 Forensic psychiatric inmates	—	Original[b]	54.5	98.8	—
Rogers, Bagby, & Gillis (1992)	n = 21 Suspected malingerers	n = 68 Psychiatric outpatients and forensic inpatients	—	Rule Out/Rule In Option A Option B	81.0 95.2	83.8 70.6	—
Hankins, Barnard, & Robbins (1993)	n = 13 Suspected malingerers	n = 66 Forensic residential	—	Rule Out/Rule In Option A Option B	61.5 69.2	63.6 51.5	—
Smith, Borum, & Schnika (1993)	n = 23 Suspected malingerers	n = 62 Forensic psychiatric inmates	—	Rule Out/Rule In Option A Option B	68.2 72.7	65.6 49.2	—

[a]Based on primary therapists' judgment of global malingering.
[b]C Scale omitted and the M scale criterion was a score > 5.

Attempts at cross-validation of this revised scoring strategy have not been entirely successful. Hankins et al. (1993) applied the Rule-Out/Rule-In system to their residential forensic population. Option A increased the M Test's sensitivity to 62% but at the cost of misclassifying 36.4% of those with genuine mental disorders. Option B increased the correct classification of malingerers (69.0%), but even more patients were incorrectly identified (48.5%). Smith, Borum, and Schinka (1993) were able to eliminate 65.6% of nonmalingering prisoners and retained 68.2% of malingerers under Option A. Using Option B, 49.2% of patients were eliminated and 72.7% of malingerers were retained.

One explanation for the discrepancy in these results might be due to the issue of the varying base rates/prevalence among the samples. Research into the detection of malingering often makes use of measures of sensitivity (i.e., the percentage of participants correctly identified as having a particular condition) and specificity (i.e., percentage of participants correctly identified as not having a particular condition) in order to evaluate the effectiveness of an instrument. Group membership is established beforehand, and the power of the instrument to detect a condition is determined by comparing the known group membership to classifications by the test. Although a reasonable approach, studies often vary in terms of the proportion of malingerers. Increasing the percentage of malingerers maximizes the chances of detection and increases measures of sensitivity. A review of Table 17.2 would seem to suggest a general trend toward a reduction in sensitivity, with decreased base rate of malingerers when using the M Test.

Because estimates of sensitivity vary with different base rates, comparisons across studies are difficult based solely on measures of sensitivity and specificity. In addition,

TABLE 17.2. Interrelationship of Sensitivity and Baserate in M Test Research

Study	Scoring system	Sensitivity	Baserate
Beaber, Marston, Michelli, & Mills (1985)	Original	78.2	61.5
Gillis, Rogers, & Bagby (1991)	Original	79.8	63.3
	Original	40.0	25.8
Smith & Borum (1992)	Original	69.6	27.1
Hankins, Barnard, & Robbins (1993)	Original	30.8	16.4
Schretlen, Neal, & Hochman (1995)	Original	54.5	11.3
Rogers, Bagby, & Gillis (1992)	Rule Out/Rule In		
	Option A	81.0	23.6
	Option B	95.2	23.6
Hankins, Barnard, & Robbins (1993)	Rule Out/Rule In		
	Option A	61.5	16.5
	Option B	69.2	16.5
Smith, Borum, & Schnika (1993)	Rule Out/Rule In		
	Option A	68.2	27.1
	Option B	72.7	27.1

practitioners are unlikely to know the base rate of dissimulation for specific segments of their clinical setting. Because of these limitations, researchers (e.g., Browner, Newman, & Cummings, 1988) have used other estimates of diagnostic efficiency, namely, PPP and NPP. In brief, PPP is the likelihood that high or deviant scores correctly identify feigners. Conversely, NPP is the likelihood that low or nondeviant scores correctly identify nonfeigners (see Browner et al., 1988; Retzlaff & Gibertini, 1994). The importance of calculating both the PPP and NPP lies in the certainty with which the examiner can make a classification regarding a particular individual. In other words, given the base rate in a particular population, what are the chances or probability that the individual scoring above a certain level is malingering?

A review of Table 17.2 reveals that the ratio of simulators and suspected malingerers to genuine patients varied across studies. For example, the ratio of malingerers to the total sample was 61.5% (i.e., 104/169) in Beaber et al. (1985). The PPP for Beaber et al. is 93.1% (see Table 17.3). Although a 93.1% certainty is impressive, the base rate of malingering is dramatically higher than those typically found in clinical samples. For example, Rogers, Sewell, and Goldstein (1994) surveyed a sample of 320 forensic experts and reported an estimated base rate for malingering of 15.7% of forensic and 7.4% of nonforensic patients. As a result, the studies by Hankins et al. (1993) and Schretlen et al. (1995) appear to better reflect the base rate of malingering in these populations. Hankins et al. (1993) reported a PPP of only 16.7%. Although Schretlen et al. (1995) demonstrated a substantially higher PPP (85.7%), participants in their study were not administered the C scale of the M Test, and the M-scale cut score was higher than that proposed by Beaber et al. (1985). Although Hankins et al. (1993) were able to improve the sensitivity by using Option B of the Rule-Out/Rule-In System, the PPP remained disappointingly low (i.e., 21.9%).

Besides the issue of base rates within the sample, conflicting results may be explained by the potential confound between test demands and level of psychiatric impairment. Specifically, when the clinical comparison samples are composed of higher functioning individuals, then malingerers are easier to detect. Hankins et al. (1993), for example, noted that most of the variance in participants' responses could be accounted for by measures of clinical status. Schretlen et al. (1995) found that when mentally disordered participants were rated as moderate or severe in the level of genuine mental disorder, they endorsed significantly more M-scale items than those judged only mildly disturbed. The level of item endorsement more closely approximated that of suspected malingerers, making the differentiation between groups more difficult. Endorsement of "bogus" symptoms by persons with severe impairment raises questions (1) whether these symptoms are bogus, and (2) whether severe impairment compromises the ability to comprehend questions (see Hankins et al., 1993). In summary, genuinely disturbed individuals may endorse similar numbers of "bogus" symptoms as their feigning counterparts. Consequently, the assessment of malingering is confounded by functional impairment.

The M Test may also be confounded by the educational level of research participants. Participants with less formal education tend to be more difficult to distinguish

TABLE 17.3. Interrelationship of Positive–Negative Predictive Power and Base Rate in M Test Research

Study	Base rate	Positive predictive power (PPP)	Negative predictive power (NPP)
Beaber, Marston, Michelli, & Mills (1985)	61.5	93.1	71.9
Gillis, Rogers, & Bagby (1991)	63.3	90.8	71.3
	25.8	50.0	80.5
Smith & Borum (1992)	27.1	43.2	85.4
Hankins, Barnard, & Robbins (1993)	16.4	16.7	83.6
Schretlen, Neal, & Hochman (1995)	11.3	85.7	94.4
Rogers, Bagby, & Gillis (1992)	23.6	60.7	93.4
	23.6	50.0	97.9
Hankins, Barnard, & Robbins (1993)	16.5	25.0	89.4
	16.5	21.9	89.5
Smith, Borum, & Schinka (1993)	27.1	43.2	85.4
	27.1	34.7	83.3

from malingering individuals. For example, Gillis et al. (1991) employed an outpatient clinic sample with a relatively high level of education (i.e., 16.2 years) compared to suspected malingerers (i.e., 9.2 years). The M Test sensitivity in this study was high (i.e., 79.8%). Similarly, Schretlen et al. (1995) employed a clinical comparison sample with a greater number of years of education than feigners and yielded very positive results. However, when clinical comparison and suspected malingerers have comparable education, the M Test appears to be less effective (e.g., Hankins et al., 1993; Smith & Borum, 1992). In other words, the discriminability of the M Test could be partially attributable to differences in educational levels rather than the presence of malingering.

A final possible explanation for these discrepant findings may be race effects. The malingering sample of Gillis et al. (1991) was predominantly White (84.0%). On the other hand, Hankins et al. (1993) and Smith and Borum (1992) enlisted over 60% of minority-group participants in their samples. Hypothesized racial effects were further supported by the noted significant correlation between racial background and test scores. Smith et al. (1993) found that, regardless of group classification, African American participants scored lower than White participants.

Despite these potential threats to the external validity of the instrument, the M Test remains an important screening measure in the growing body of research on the detection of malingering. Among screening measures, the M Test has been subjected to the most rigorous research. In addition, the M Test has utilized both known-groups and simulation designs. Its psychometric characteristics have been explored, demonstrating acceptable internal reliabilities and consistency. Furthermore, the M Test has guided the direction of subsequent investigations from global "faking-bad" to a more focused investigation of malingering a particular condition. Finally, the instrument has demonstrated some utility in distinguishing malingerers in a forensic setting using an improved scoring system. However, additional research is indicated to explore the possibility of race effects as well as the potential impact of cognitive impairment on test scores. At the present time, as Hankins et al. (1993) noted, there are "insufficient data to support recommending it for routine clinical use" (p. 121).

Malingering Scale

The Malingering Scale (MS; Schretlen & Arkowitz, 1990) is another brief inventory developed to detect the presence of feigned psychopathology. Like the M Test, the MS was designed to detect malingering of specific conditions: "insanity" (the authors' term) and mental retardation. The MS is a 90-item test that combines a paper-and-pencil format with examiner inquiry. The MS is composed of four subtests. Two subtests are two–alternative forced choices (Abstraction with 20 questions and Vocabulary with 26 questions), and two subtests consist of open-ended items presented by the examiner (Arithmetic with 20 questions and Information with 24 questions). Many of the MS items were adapted from existing intelligence measures. The remainder of the test questions were rationally derived.

The original research (Schretlen & Arkowitz, 1990) employed two groups of simulators (i.e., prisoners instructed to feign mental retardation or insanity), two clinical comparison groups (i.e., inpatients with severe psychopathology and outpatients diagnosed with mental retardation), and a control group (i.e., honestly responding prisoners) in a fully controlled design. The MS was administered to these five groups (n = 20) as part of a battery that included the MMPI and Bender–Gestalt. Participants were paid for their participation, and an additional monetary incentive was awarded to successful simulators. An analysis of the psychometric properties of the instrument was conducted and demonstrated good scale characteristics. Internal consistency coefficients were calculated for each scale: Vocabulary (.92), Abstraction (.88), Arithmetic (.97), and Information (.95). With the base rate lowered to 20%, discriminant analyses conducted using the test battery correctly identified 85% of participants simulating "insanity" and 80% of those feigning mental retardation.

In cross-validation research by Schretlen, Wilkins, Van Gorp, and Bobholz (1992), discriminant scores were derived and applied to a sample of 22 simulators of "insanity." These simulators were diagnosed with substance abuse disorders and their responses were compared to 20 inpatients on a mental health unit. Unlike the original study (Schretlen & Arkowitz, 1990), no significant differences occurred between the two groups on demographic variables. Results indicated that only one of the simulators was misclassified yielding an overall hit rate of 97.6% (i.e., 41 out of 42 participants). Pooling these participants with the earlier data (Schretlen & Arkowitz, 1990), the investigators classified 79.5% of the simulators and 98.3% of the criterion group using the Vocabulary and Arithmetic subtests alone. The authors attribute the lack of expected shrinkage in the overall hit rate between the samples to differential incentives (i.e., the original validation sample could receive as much as $15, whereas the second received only $5). It should be noted that no cross-validation was conducted on the ability of the MS to detect feigned mental retardation in this study.

Finally, Schretlen, Neal, and Hochman (1995) investigated the utility of the MS in a naturalistic design. A total of 97 consecutive referrals for court-ordered evaluations served as the final sample. Participants were rated by the examiners as to the presence of malingering on a 4-point scale from "very unlikely" to "very likely." The type of feigning was not specified in this study. Persons judged either "likely" or "very likely" were placed in the malingering category; this grouping resulted in a prevalence rate of 11.3%, similar to that of other research (e.g., Hankins et al., 1993). All participants were administered the M Test (excluding the C-scale items) and the Vocabulary subtest of the MS. Using the original cut score correctly identified 72.7% of the simulators (8 out of 11) while misidentifying only 6 of 86 (7%) genuine patients. Combining the MS and M Test scores into a "Malingering Index" (i.e., the total number of correct MS Vocabulary items minus the number of items endorsed on the *M* Scale) improved the predictive ability. With a Malingering Index greater than 15, 7 of 11 malingerers and 85 of 86 genuine patients were correctly identified. More explicitly, the PPP (i.e., the certainty that an individual exceeding this score falls in the malingering group) was 87.5% and NPP (i.e., the probability that the individual below this score does not fall in the malingering group) was 95.6%.

The research on the MS has several limitations. First, studies have used generally small sample sizes, thus leaving the research open to potential selection biases. Second, only males were involved in the first two investigations (i.e., Schretlen & Arkowitz, 1990; Schretlen et al., 1992) and constituted the bulk of participants (i.e., 87.6%) in the third study (Schretlen et al., 1995). Third, estimated IQ scores fell only within the average range, preventing exploration of possible confounding effects of this variable. With respect to the final issue, the most recent investigation (Schretlen et al., 1995) found significant differences in years of education between the criteria group and suspected malingerers.

Despite these shortcomings, the MS shows some promise in the detection of malingering. Its contributions to the growing body of research include the greater generalizability across feigned psychopathology and simulated conditions. The MS also demonstrated that a single instrument could be used simultaneously to detect feigned psychopathology and cognitive deficits. In addition, the MS employs varied detection strategies within a single test. It also represents one of the few attempts to investigate the usefulness of an instrument employing a known-groups design with suspected malingerers. Finally, the use of the MS Vocabulary in combination with the *M* scale of the M Test represents a particularly encouraging strategy that should receive the attention of future research.

Although the M Test and the MS were among the first instruments designed for the assessment of malingering, subsequent researchers have constructed additional self-report measures and behavioral checklists to assist in the detection process. A review of the current research revealed six more recently developed instruments. I review individually the current development and validation of each measure.

NEW GENERATION SCREENS

Tehachapi Malingering Scale

The Tehachapi Malingering Scale (TMS; Haskett, 1995) is a behavioral checklist designed to assist in the detection of malingering in a correctional setting. The scale itself consists of 20 items. The first 11 items are scored during the earlier stages of the interview. These items include the nature of presenting difficulties (e.g., poor memory, rocking movements, and vague hallucinations) and aspects of history (e.g., use of psychiatric medication and drug dependence). The remaining items are completed at the end of the interview and focus on the qualitative features of the individual's presentation (e.g., irritable), statements of the examinee (e.g., "I'm not responsible"), and the presence of potential incentive to malingering. The TMS is a brief instrument, requiring approximately 1 minute to score. The TMS also offers items with unique content that may provide additional cues for the detection of malingering (e.g., sleep problems are repeatedly emphasized). Each of the 20 TMS items is awarded a score of .05 when endorsed in the malingering direction. With a range of scores from 0 to 1, a cut score of $\geq .30$ is used for suspected malingering (J. Haskett, personal communication, April 19, 1995).

Items were developed based on clinical experience and previous research (e.g., Resnick, 1984). Questions tap aspects of behavioral presentation, history, and nature of presenting complaints. The examiner is also asked to indicate the presence of any motivation to malinger. The criterion for final inclusion of items on the scale was the frequency of occurrence among the malingering sample. Nine of the 62 inmates identified as malingerers completed the MMPI-2. Based on an inspection of the MMPI-2 results, their profiles "approximated the classic 'Fake Bad' configuration that is associated with malingering" (Haskett, 1995, p. 20).

In the formal validation (Haskett & Lender, 1995), a sample of inmates detained between July and December 1994 were administered the TMS. Despite some logistical problems, participants were recruited "as randomly as we were able" (Haskett, 1995, p. 21), with an effort to approximate the ethnic groups typically seen in the Reception Center's population. Inmates without any reported symptoms were assigned to the asymptomatic group. Those admitting to symptoms were placed either in the malingering or clinical comparison groups, based on their scores on the TMS. Interrater reliability was very high ($r = .96$) for total scores. All participants were administered the MMPI-2 for comparison purposes, although no statistical analyses were reported comparing the results of the TMS and the MMPI-2. Rather, analyses were confined to a review of the mean raw and T scores between the three groups (i.e., suspected malingerers, symptomatic inmates, and asymptomatic inmates). The malingering group scored higher in an expected direction on other MMPI validity indicators, such as the F-K index, the L scale, and K scale.

Haskett (1995) noted that some inmates scored below criterion on the TMS but provided invalid MMPI profiles. This counterintuitive finding was attributed to several factors, such as cultural differences producing elevated F-scale scores. In addition,

African Americans were disproportionately represented in the malingering group. Haskett speculated whether this finding might be the result of a differential drug usage (i.e., phencyclidine, or PCP) between ethnic groups.

The validation of the TMS is based primarily on differences observed on the MMPI-2. The use of this as a criterion is very much open to question (Chapter 19), especially in the absence of any statistical analyses. The generalizability of the TMS is circumscribed, and the ethnic composition was intended only to approximate the proportions found within this particular forensic setting. The research is also limited by the fact that the clinicians served as the external criterion for classification into the malingering group. Additionally, the authors do not seem to take into account other factors potentially influencing test scores (e.g., level of severity of psychopathology, intelligence, race, or irrelevant/random responding). Although they admit that factors (e.g., head injury or antisocial personality factors) may effect MMPI-2 results and not be tapped by the TMS, no apparent effort was made to screen for these potentially confounding variables. Finally, the authors conjectured that the high percentage of malingering among African American participants was due to the use of PCP. However, the reason for this putative correlation remains unclear. As an alternative explanation, Cornell and Hawk (1989) observed that built-in biases in the referral process may account for cultural differences.

Malingering Detection Scale

The Malingering Detection Scale (MDS) is a 29-item, examiner-scored instrument designed to distinguish between neurology clinic patients with demonstrable organic disease and malingerers (Barkemeyer & Callon, 1989). The MDS is divided into two major sections: interview behaviors and apparent goals for patients' behavior. Under the interview behavior section, the items require the professional to note the presence of characteristics (e.g., the patient spontaneously expressed exaggerated confidence in the examiner's ability) during the psychiatric evaluation process. Other examples of scoreable characteristics include the patient's presentation, manipulation attempts, specific responses to questions, and reactions to disagreement. The examiner also rates the potential goals of patients' behavior in terms of avoidance of normal responsibility as well as securing a concrete entity (e.g., monetary gain).

The questions were developed based on their "high positive correlation with malingering" (Callon, Jones, Barkemeyer, & Brantley, 1990, p. 3). Scoring of the instrument follows the examination by the attending professional. Initially designed for use by physicians and psychologists, the MDS reportedly can be used by individuals without extensive professional training. However, two of the questions require some medical knowledge. A cut score of 8 or higher "is associated with at least a 95% chance of malingering" (Callon et al., 1990, p. 4).

Some items appear to be based on previously noted characteristics of malingerers. For example, Resnick (1984) notes that malingerers' presentation often fit no known diagnostic entity. This feature is captured by several of the MDS items. Other strategies are intriguing: (1) rejection of alternative explanations regarding the etiology of current difficulties, (2) manipulation of the examiner, and (3) expressed ignorance for aggravating factors.

In the initial validation study, the MDS was completed by 122 adult neurology clinic patients. The senior author classified participants into groups based on certain features (e.g., inconsistency between presenting complaints and defined symptoms complex, failure of the examination to support complaints, and failure of laboratory results to support complaints). If at least two of these three criteria were met, the participant was placed in the malingering group ($n = 30$). Internal consistency was determined to be .93; interrated reliabilities with two independent examiners were reported to be .94. A subsequent discriminant analysis yielded a cut score of 7.6 on the MDS that correctly classified 95.1% of the participants. Three malingerers (10%) and three genuine patients (3.3%) were misclassified. The authors attempted to cross-validate these results using an additional 66 patients: 17 malingerers and 49 genuine patients. Overall, 98.5% of participants were correctly classified, with none of the genuine patients placed in the malingering group.

The MDS has the advantage of a known-groups comparison. It also provides a qualitative description of the patient's presentation relative to malingering (e.g., attempts at manipulation). However, the demographic variables of the samples were not reported. As a result, first, it is uncertain whether these features could have accounted for differential response patterns. Second, the basis for items is unclear. The validation indicates that these items "described specific behaviors that detract from objective examination of the patient" (Callon et al., 1990, p. 3). Some of these items were not operationally defined. For example, one of the listed goals is the gain or retention of an "abstract quality." Third, at least the potential for contamination is present between predictors and criteria (Lanyon, Almer, & Curran, 1993); that is, the professional classifying individuals into groups also served in the development of the instrument. Finally, as the authors suggest, additional research is required with additional populations to determine the scale's generalizability across different samples.

Malingering Probability Scale

The Malingering Probability Scale is a 140-item self-report inventory written in a true–false format for use within an outpatient and forensic population (Silverton & Gruber, in press). Items are organized on four different scales intended to represent those conditions likely to be malingered: depression (DEP), dissociative disorder (DIS), post-traumatic stress disorder (PTS), and schizophrenia (SCH). Items on these scales are of two different types, namely actual symptoms and malingering items. The 77 "actual symptom items" were drawn from the DSM-III-R criteria. The general rationale for "pseudo-item" (i.e., malingering question) construction was to develop inquiries that ostensibly appeared to be genuine symptoms but were overly specific or absurd (C. Gruber, personal communication, July 19, 1995). A total of 55 malingering questions were included in the final measure, providing 12 to 15 pseudo-items for each of the areas of psychopathology covered by the MPS. One additional scale, the INC, was developed to identify random response protocols. *INC* consists of 20 item pairs that showed the highest correlations.

Psychometrically, the instrument appears to have reasonably good scale characteristics using honestly responding students, outpatients, forensic participants, and prisoners. Internal consistency of the scales with alpha reliabilities were generally high (.77 to .89) with the exception of the *SCH* (i.e., .56 with prisoners to .69 with outpatients). This scale was, however, retained to "preserve the overall rational design of the MPS" (p. 4). The interscale correlations across validation samples had a median value of .60.

Measures of convergent validity were also obtained using the outpatient and forensic sample. The authors calculated the first-order correlations between the MMPI *D, Sc,* and *A* scales and the *DEP, SCH,* and *PTS* scales of the MPS. In addition, the MPS *DIS* scale correlations were evaluated in light of its correlation with two MMPI scales of dissociative tendencies: the Perceptual Alteration Scale (Sanders, 1986) and the Depersonalization-Derealization-Dissociation (D. S. Nichols, personal communication to C. Gruber, April 18, 1994). The *DEP* scale of the MPS was more highly correlated with the *D* scale of the MMPI (i.e., .77) than any of the other scales. Similarly, the *DIS* scale correlation with the Perceptual Alteration Scale was larger than any other (i.e., .75). However, the *PTS* and *SCH* correlations were less compelling. The *PTS* scale and the *A* scale of the MMPI correlation was .66, and the *SCH* scale and *Sc* scale of the MMPI was .56. The magnitude of these correlations would suggest little utility of these scales as indicators of posttraumatic stress disorder (PTSD) or schizophrenia.

As a discriminative tool, the MPS also demonstrated good specificity and sensitivity in an analogue design. The authors first administered the MPS under honest and simulation conditions to 131 students with a small incentive (i.e., movie tickets) provided to simulators. The distribution of scores was plotted and *T* scores formulated for the *INC, MAL,* and four clinical scales. Using a cutoff of ± 70*T* on both the *INC* and *MAL* scales yielded a sensitivity of 94% and a specificity of 88%. Next, attempts were made to replicate these findings with four groups: prisoners (*n* = 80) under honest and simulating conditions, students (*n* = 28) asked to malinger "symptoms associated with PTSD," and 150 honestly responding outpatients involved in psychological evaluations without any forensic involvement. Simulating prisoners received vouchers amounting to about $10 for their participation. Using the same criteria, the MPS achieved a sensitivity of 94% and a specificity of 86% across all four groups.

The authors point out a number of limitations with regard to the MPS. A particular caution involved the use of the instrument alone as a diagnostic tool. Rather, they strongly encourage the use of the MPS in combination with other assessment devices before rendering a classification of malingering. In addition, they note that the MPS does not assess defensiveness (faking-good) or malingering of neuropsychological or cognitive deficits.

Other potential limitations of the instrument include results based only on a simulation design. As yet, no investigations have been conducted with MPS using suspected malingerers. Although the use of simulating participants is an appropriate first step in the development of a new instrument, the lack of known-groups design limits the generalizability of the research findings (see Chapter 19).

The clinical comparison group constrains the generalizability of the MDS. Without any inpatients, the crucial task of differentiating genuine and bogus disorders is obscured. The critical issue is whether patients with severe impairment are distinguished on the MDS. Other limits on clinical comparison group are ethnicity (92.0% White) and education (M years of education = 13.4).

The presentation of decision rules based on assumed prevalence rates may create more problems than it resolves. Because clinicians are unaware of the base rates in their particular setting, assumptions of 10% or 50% base rates are likely to be spurious. Although highlighting the problems associated with varying base rates, the multiple decision rules presently do not appear to be a viable solution.

Despite these limitations, the MPS has demonstrated some encouraging early results in terms of its sensitivity and specificity. Among its strengths is the inclusion of the *INC* that increases its sensitivity to alternative explanations for apparent malingering (e.g., reading problems). In addition, because the materials provided by the authors are from an early, prepublication version of the MPS, many of these potential limitations may be addressed in the final edition of the instrument.

SIMS

The Structured Inventory of Malingered Symptomatology (SIMS; Smith, 1992; Smith & Burger, in press) is a 75-item true–false test constructed to detect the presence of malingering of several specific conditions. Items were drawn from two different sources. First, questions were selected from existing measures such as the MMPI, SIRS, and the Wechsler Adult Intelligence Scale—Revised (WAIS-R) that had demonstrated some utility in detecting malingering in past research. These items were then edited to incorporate a particular detection strategy (e.g., approximate answers) as well as to increase their sensitivity to the feigning of a particular condition. Second, additional questions were written to reflect the qualitative characteristics of malingerers noted in previous research (e.g., Resnick, 1984; Rogers, 1984; Seamons, Howell, Carlisle, & Roe, 1981). All items were then organized into five scales of 15 questions each, designed to reflect what was judged to be the most commonly malingered conditions: low intelligence (*LI*), affective disorders (*AF*), neurological impairment (*N*), psychosis (*P*), and amnesia (*AM*). Expert raters served to confirm item placement in each scale.

The initial research (Smith, 1992; Smith & Burger, in press) was conducted using 476 students divided into a developmental and cross-validational samples. In each sample, participants were assigned to a specific experimental condition reflecting a disorder to be simulated. In addition to the SIMS, participants completed the *F* and *K* scales of the MMPI as well as the Sixteen Personality Factor Questionnaire (16 PF) Faking-Bad scale and portions of the Malingering Scale that could be administered in a paper-and-pencil fashion. Cut scores were developed for each of the scales of the SIMS as well as the Total Score (i.e., sum of the five scales) that maximized the discrimination between each group and controls. These cut scores were then applied to the responses of the cross-validation sample.

Results of the cross-validation demonstrated good internal reliabilities for individual scales, ranging from .80 to .88. In addition, intercorrelations among the scales were generally low, and an exploratory factor analysis indicated unique loadings on expected scales. Univariate ANOVAs yielded significant differences among the groups for all scales, with all *p* levels less than .0001.

The Total Score for the SIMS proved to be the most efficient indicator of malingering. It accurately identified 95.6% of the simulators and 87.9% of the honestly responding participants. The other scales varied in terms of their sensitivity from a low of 74.6% using the *AF* to a high of 88.3% using the *AM*. Even though they proved less successful to detect malingering individually, the scales of the SIMS suggested certain profile patterns within each of the malingering groups. For example, participants asked to malinger psychosis also tended to endorse items consistent with low intelligence.

The MMPI *F* scale was the most effective measure among the other validity indices to detect simulators. In fact, the percentage of simulators correctly classified by the *F* scale fell only slightly below the SIMS (i.e., 94.6%). However, classification was obtained by substantially reducing the cut score to 10; in contrast, Graham (1987) proposed a cut score of 27. When higher cut scores were used, the accuracy of *F* was markedly diminished.

Rogers, Hinds, and Sewell (1995) investigated the usefulness of the SIMS to detect the presence of feigned response patterns in an adolescent treatment setting. A total of 53 participants, court-ordered into treatment, completed the SIMS, the MMPI-A, and SIRS under honest and malingering conditions. For the latter, the participants were randomly assigned to feign either schizophrenia, major depression, or generalized anxiety disorder. A financial incentive was offered for successful feigning. Not surprisingly, given the nature of the feigned conditions, the *AF* scale emerged as the most sensitive indicator using the established cut score. The Total Score also possessed comparable sensitivity rates (i.e., 87%). The authors recommended that because of its easy reading comprehension level, sensitivity, and brevity, the SIMS be used as a screening measure. However, they cautioned that the instrument be used only for its intended purpose (i.e., triggering a more complete evaluation) and not to render a diagnosis of malingering.

Perhaps the greatest limitation of the SIMS is the analogue nature of its current research. No data beyond that of Rogers, Hinds, and Sewell (1995) exist on clinical comparison samples. Although work is currently under way to address these shortcomings (D. Nussbaum, personal communication, January 23, 1995), the ultimate power of the instrument to detect actual malingering participants is uncertain. Other shortcomings include a predominantly White (90%) and female (71%) validation sample, questionable incentive to malinger (i.e., college extra credit), failure to assess participants for psychopathology, and the untested ability of the SIMS to detect random response patterns.

Despite these restrictions, the SIMS shows some promise for the future. The level of reading comprehension and brief administration time makes it applicable across a wider range of settings. It has demonstrated satisfactory levels of sensitivity. In addition, the SIMS is one of the few instruments to date that has been investigated with an adolescent population.

Inventory of Problems

The Inventory of Problems (IOP; Viglione & Landis, 1995) is another brief, self-report indicator of malingered symptomatology designed for use across a wide range of clinical settings (e.g., workers' compensation and forensic). The IOP consists of 162 items organized on 19 scales. These scales, in turn, are grouped under categories of Symptom Endorsement, Symptom Attributes, Test Behavior, and Empirical Scales.

According to the authors, malingering participants are detected through greater symptom density (endorsement of symptoms), dispersion (symptom endorsement across diagnostic categories), and atypicality (extreme or unrealistic symptoms) than those who are psychiatrically involved. The time for completion of the IOP was estimated to be 45–90 minutes.

The IOP presents a somewhat unique approach compared with other measures, as it integrates detection strategies from both interview and objective measurement. For example, instead of a traditional true–false format, a third option ("doesn't make sense") was added. Presumably this alternative would be sensitive to the malingerer's reluctance to respond to confusing or flawed questions. Because the IOP is administered via a computer, it also has the ability to measure response latencies.

At present, no research is available on the computerized version. However, an earlier draft of the IOP was administered in a paper-and-pencil format to honest nonpatients, psychiatric inpatients, psychopathology simulators, and three suspected malingerers (Viglione & Landis, 1994). Although rates of test sensitivity and specificity were not reported, score differences between honestly responding participants (i.e., $n = 87$; combining under honest instructions: psychology graduate students, prisoners, and community participants) and simulators (i.e., $n = 49$; combining under feigning instructions: psychology graduate students, prisoners, and community participants) were significantly different for 20 of 22 scales. It is important to note that a variety of conditions were feigned, including depression and "incompetent to stand trial" (D. Viglione, personal communication, June 5, 1995). Introducing a group of mentally disordered patients (i.e., $n = 90$; drawn from residential care, acute care inpatients, and outpatient offenders convicted of violent crimes), however, reduced the instrument's ability to discriminate the combined groups significantly. Hit rates for the three suspected malingerers were not reported.

Importantly, simulators did not differ from psychiatric inpatients in residential care. This lack of significant differences was attributed to the level of severity among the inpatient participants (D. Viglione, personal communication, April 17, 1995). In other words, the severity of pathology in the psychiatric inpatients was comparable to the rate of endorsement among simulators exaggerating pathology.

On the other hand, the authors found that those feigning a particular condition responded differently to items concerning symptom attribution, test behaviors, use of the "doesn't make sense" alternative, and reference to past incidents. Specifically, simulators were reticent to admit to any success in controlling symptoms. They were also more likely to indicate a marked reaction to the test situation. While patient and nonpatient groups endorsed purposefully confusing test items by indicating "doesn't make sense," those feigning pathology provided either a "true" or "false" response. Finally, simulators tended to externalize the responsibility of their difficulties by endorsing items that suggested an outside incident or traumatic event was critical to their current condition.

The IOP has certain innovative strategies, such as the inclusion of an additional response option (i.e., "doesn't make sense") as well as attempts to integrate response latencies. Also, because it includes questions tapping cognitive abilities and graphical interactive tasks, it has the potential for discriminating those feigning neuropsychological deficits.

However, the ability of the IOP to detect malingerers is unclear at this point, given the analogue nature of the research and the fact that the final version has not been investigated. Furthermore, the discriminability of the scales is a question for both realistic and unrealistic symptoms (i.e., atypical, overly specific, or exaggerated). The increased severity of the clinical comparison group might explain the lack of differences for realistic symptoms but may not fully account for unrealistic symptoms. Subsequent research may further refine these scales through more stringent statistical analyses. In addition, the possible impact of other potentially confounding variables, such as severity of impairment, age, race, and intelligence apparently were not addressed.

Sentence Completion Test

The Sentence Completion Test (SCT-136) consists of 136 stems selected because of their relevance to "physical disability, psychiatric disability, work adjustment, life attitudes, and general honesty" (Timmons, Lanyon, Almer, & Curran, 1993, p. 26). The scoring system is based on categories or features of malingerers noted by previous authors (i.e., Barkemeyer & Callon, 1989), such as denigration of the examiner. The remaining scoring categories were the result of the responses among malingerers in the sample. Individual items are scored from 0 to 2, based on the degree to which they reflected one of the 12 categories.

In the original validation work, 51 personal injury claimants completed the SCT-136 after undergoing a psychiatric evaluation and MMPI administration. An exploratory factor analysis revealed a 3-factor solution representing angry negativity (Factor I), disability exaggeration (Factor II), and excessive honesty/virtue (Factor III). These dimensions were believed to represent three recognizable strategies for malingering (Lanyon et al., 1993, p. 496).

The strongest correlations were observed between the total malingering score and Factor I and MMPI scales. The total malingering score of the SCT-136 correlated with both the *Hs* (.48) and *Hy* (.51) scales of the MMPI. This finding was interpreted as evidence that the measure was sensitive to claims of physical symptoms in the service of personal goals. Factor I (angry negativity) was significantly correlated with the *F* (.44), *Dsr* (.47), *Hs* (.39), *Hy* (.32), *ORG* (.37), and *HEA* (.44) scales. Timmons et al. (1993) saw Factor I as reflective of an indiscriminant faking-bad strategy.

In an effort to improve the ease of administration, the authors reduced the length of the instrument. The result was a 39-item instrument, with 35 items loading on the three factors plus four additional stems developed to "complete the representation" on all factors (p. 31). This SCT-39 was administered in a simulation design to introductory college students under instructional sets reflecting the type of malingering strategy noted in the factor analysis of the SCT-136 (i.e., angry negativity, disability exaggeration, and excessive honesty/virtue). Planned comparisons revealed significant mean differences between groups at the .001 level with much higher scores for each relevant group.

Although an interesting adaptation to an established form of assessment (i.e., sentence completion), the current research is limited by a number of concerns. These concerns include an inadequate subject-to-factor ratio and the possibility of additional malingering response sets beyond the three highlighted in the present investigation. The shortened version also lacks a clinical comparison group. Although litigating participants were used in the development of the earlier SCT-136, their relevance is constrained by (1) the unknown generalizability to the shorter SCT-39 version, and (2) the apparent mixture of genuine and feigning patients.

Additional research will be needed to address other important considerations. First, the use of incentives is likely to improve the real-world application of the simulation research. Second, a known-groups comparison is critical to the SCT-39 cross-validation. Third, additional research is needed to investigate the SCT-39's usefulness in classification. At present, the authors demonstrated a statistical relationship with some of the validity and clinical scales of the MMPI using the longer version, but not the SCT-39. Further studies with an emphasis on external validity are strongly encouraged.

THRESHOLD AND CLINICAL DECISION MODELS

The two issues in determining the usefulness of these measures involve threshold and clinical decision models. The threshold model proposes guidelines that would trigger a more thorough assessment into suspected malingering. The purpose of the clinical decision model is to provide specific criteria to direct the professional in rendering a decision about the presence or absence of malingering.

The state of the current research does not support the use of brief screening instruments as the sole basis to render a clinical decision as to the presence of malingering. Although a number of the studies, cited throughout this chapter, have noted high levels of sensitivity and specificity, many of the authors themselves (e.g., Rogers, Bagby, & Gillis, 1992; Silverton & Gruber, 1995; Smith & Borum, 1992) caution against relying solely on these types of tests to make such classifications in the absence of other confirmatory data (e.g., history and findings of other objective measures). Furthermore, making such a diagnosis on a strictly *actuarial* basis would be ill-advised in light of the limited research. At best, these instruments could be used as a source of confirmatory evidence within a battery of tests to provide a clinical decision of malingering. Again, this approach is recommended by several of the authors of these screening measures (e.g., Haskett & Lender, 1995; Schretlen et al., 1992). In short, these instruments should *not* be used for diagnostic purposes.

As opposed to the clinical decision model, I argue for a threshold model in the use of these instruments. This approach is clinically appropriate; screening measures, by definition, are a way of operationally defining the threshold model (i.e., identifying the need for a more thorough investigation into the possible presence of malingering). Table 17.4 provides a listing of the available criteria for those instruments reviewed and their respective cut scores. These cut scores were drawn from the review studies in which an excess of 90% of feigning participants have been correctly identified.

DIRECTIONS FOR FUTURE RESEARCH

Chapter 19 provides a comprehensive review of research models as they apply to response styles. The purpose of this section is to highlight research needs related specifically to screening measures for malingering. I have enumerated the primary concerns below:

1. *Overly specialized measures.* Initially, the M Test was constructed in order to tap malingering of one condition, namely schizophrenia. However, malingerers are likely not to limit their feigning to a single diagnostic entity. Therefore, screening measures should attempt to represent a spectrum of feigned disorders, both in item development and subsequent validation.

2. *Irrelevant responding.* Random or irrelevant responding often results in a highly atypical response pattern that overlaps with malingering (see Chapter 9). Screening measures need to distinguish irrelevant responding from feigning; at present, only the MPS makes use of an inconsistency scale for this purpose.

3. *Multiple detection strategies.* Screening measures have adopted a number of strategies for the detection of feigning that are summarized in Table 17.5. The use of multiple strategies is justified on classification (Schretlen et al., 1995) and theoretical (Rogers, Bagby, & Chakraborty, 1993) grounds. The next logical step is to assess the comparative utility of specific strategies across measures. The objectives of such research are the investigation of (1) which strategies are robust, and (2) what combinations of strategies are the most effective.

TABLE 17.4. Proposed Criteria for Screening Measures of Malingering

Instrument	Scale	Cutoff
M Test	Rule Out	< 4
	Rule In	< 2
MS	Vocabulary	< 21
TMS	Total score	> .30
MDS	Total score	≥ 8
MPS	*MAL*	≥ 70*T*
	INC	≥ 70*T*
SIMS	Total score	> 15

TABLE 17.5. Current Research Detection Strategies

Category	Characteristic	Instrument
Extratest data	Drug abuse/dependence	TMS
Intraitem characteristics	Approximate answers	IOP, SIMS
	Rare symptoms	MPS, SIMS
	Atypical symptoms	M Test, SIMS
	Exaggerated symptoms/impairment	M Test, SIMS, TMS
	Inconsistent combinations	SIMS
	Vague complaints	TMS
	Overly specific symptoms	M Test
	Reaction times	IOP
Interitem characteristics	Scatter	MS
	Symptom validity testing	MS
	Overendorsement/High total score	IOP, M Test, MDS, MS,
	Inconsistency	MPS SIMS, TMS
	Changing task demands	MPS, TMS
	Emphasizes certain problems	IOP, MS
	Low intelligence	TMS
	Muteness	TMS
	Sleep problems	TMS
	Paranoia	TMS
Test behaviors	Exaggerated confidence (or lack of it) in examiner	MDS, SCT
	Self-enhancing statements	MDS, SCT
	Denigration of others	MDS, SCT
	Severity in nonspecific terms	MDS
	Disregarding alternative explanations	MDS, SCT
	Atypical response to treatment	MDS
	Externalizes/Denies responsibility	IOP, MDS
	Denies ability to cope	IOP, MDS
	Threatens harm/Retaliation against self or others	MDS, SCT, MDS
	Overreactivity to testing situation	IOP
	Responds to confusing/Leading questions	IOP, MDS
	Irritable/Hostile/Lack of cooperation	MDS, TMS, DSM-IV

4. *Confounds to classification.* Cultural background and educational status both require fuller study with screening measures. Current studies have found significant differences that need further investigation on how they affect classification rates. In addition, research with very high base rates of malingering (> 50%) do not represent most clinical settings and likely skew any subsequent classification.

5. *Known-groups comparisons.* Results from simulation research need to be cross-validated using a variety of clinical comparison samples. In addition, simulation research also should be validated with known-groups comparison. In this case, results of suspected malingerers are compared to bona fide patients. As discussed previously, the M Test is an excellent illustration of the need for both types of validation with screening measures of malingering.

IV

SUMMARY

18

Current Status of Clinical Methods

RICHARD ROGERS, Ph.D.

Important advances in the clinical assessment of response styles have ensued between the first and current editions of this book. Substantial progress has occurred on both the conceptualization of response styles and development of empirically validated methods for their detection. The purpose of this chapter is a synthesis of clinically relevant methods. Toward that objective, close attention is paid to detection strategies, including their conceptual underpinnings and clinical relevance. Subsequent sections address the integration of clinical methods and their pertinence to professional practice.

This chapter examines conceptually the diverse detection strategies used with specific forms of dissimulation. It integrates threshold and clinical decision models presented throughout earlier chapters as they relate to malingering and defensiveness. It discusses the clinical relevance of dissimulation in making treatment and nontreatment interventions, and considers its significance to referral questions. The chapter is organized into five major sections: (1) detection strategies, (2) usefulness of individual diagnostic methods, (3) clinical relevance, (4) confrontation of suspected dissimulation, and (5) synthesis of clinical data.

DETECTION STRATEGIES

Rogers (1984b) proposed the first systematic model for the detection of dissimulation. Based on the existing literature, he suggested that five response styles (i.e., honest, malingered, defensive, irrelevant, and deceptive) be considered on 17 indicators drawn from case studies and distilled from psychometric and social psychological research. Perhaps the most salient observation by Rogers's summary (1984b, p. 106) was the paucity of research cross-validating results for specific response styles across different research paradigms.

Rogers (1990b) established three stringent criteria for the validation of detection strategies. The first two criteria involved the convergence of findings across (1) research designs (i.e., simulation and known-groups comparisons) and (2) methods of assessment (e.g., structured interviews and multiscale inventories). The third criterion is that detection strategies must be carefully cross-validated on clinically diverse samples. Only when these three criteria are met can practitioners and researchers have a high level of confidence in the usefulness of a general *detection strategy* for dissimulation. In contrast, when only the first and third criteria are satisfied, then the effectiveness of a *specific scale* is demonstrated. At the time of the first review (Rogers, 1984b), none of the detection strategies fulfilled these criteria.

Feigned Psychopathology

At present, four detection strategies for feigned psychopathology have been cross-validated across research designs and methods of assessment (see Table 18.1); these strategies are composed of rare symptoms, indiscriminant symptom endorsement, obvious symptoms, and improbable symptoms. Two additional strategies, which nearly meet these criteria, are symptom combination and symptoms of extreme severity. These strategies appear promising across interview-based measures but need validation with self-report instruments. For a detailed discussion of these strategies and their applications to traditional interviews and structured interviews (i.e., Schedule of Affective Disorders and Schizophrenia [SADS] and Structured Interview of Reported Symptoms [SIRS]), please refer to Chapter 15.

Use of these four strategies is strongly recommended in clinical practice. Psychologists and psychiatrists should employ standardized measures that incorporate these strategies whenever feigned psychopathology is suspected. In addition, clinicians are urged to construct their own inquiries based on these strategies. In general, determinations of malingered psychopathology should not be rendered without the incorporation of one, and preferably several, of these four strategies.

Other strategies that deserve our attention are those based on extreme severity, unusual combination of symptoms, and stereotypes about mental disorders. Symptoms of extreme severity provide the most direct evidence of "gross exaggeration," a primary component of malingering. When a wide range of psychopathology is considered and the patient endorses the majority of symptoms at an extreme severity, the likelihood of gross exaggeration increases substantially. Symptom combinations require an unparalleled level of sophistication on the part of malingerers. Malingerers need to make multiple decisions about what symptom pairs are common in mentally disordered patients and what pairs are very atypical. Stereotypes and misconceptions of mental disorders constitute an ingenious strategy that could easily be applied to specific disorders or settings.

Projective measures have a very circumscribed role in the assessment of malingered psychopathology. The expert consensus is that the Rorschach and other projectives are fakable. As summarized in Chapter 10, cross-validated methods for the detection of malingering have yet to be forthcoming. However, preliminary research with the use of forced choices appears to have merit both with the Rorschach (Pettigrew,

TABLE 18.1. Detection Strategies for Malingered Psychopathology

Strategy/definition	Validation			Representative measures
	Sim	K–G–C	M–M	
Rare symptoms that occur only infrequently in clinical populations	Y	Y	Y	*F* and *Fb* (MMPI-2); *RS* (SIRS); *NIM* (PAI)
Indiscriminant symptom endorsement	Y	Y	Y	*LW* (MMPI-2); *SEL* (SIRS)
Overendorsement of obvious symptoms	Y	Y	Y	*O-S* (MMPI-2); *BL* (SIRS)
Improbable or preposterous symptoms	Y	Y	Y	*IA* (SIRS); *VI* (MCMI); M Test
Symptom combination—atypical pairings of otherwise common symptoms	Y	Y		*SC* (SIRS); Symptom combination (SADS)
Unusual number of symptoms with extreme severity	Y	Y		*SEV* (SIRS); Symptom severity (SADS)
Endorsed symptoms highly discrepant from observed symptoms in the pathological direction	Y	Y	.	*RO* (SIRS)
Relative absence of any socially desirable responses	Y			*Gi* (CPI)
Reported symptoms reflecting erroneous stereotypes or misconceptions about mental disorders	Y			*Ds* and *Dsr* (MMPI-2)
Highly bizarre responses to neutral stimuli	Y			Bizarre content on the Rorschach

Note. For validation, Sim = simulation design; K–G–C = known–groups comparison; M–M = multimethod validation (i.e., convergent evidence across different assessment domains, such as multiscale inventories and structured interviews).

Tuma, Pickering, & Whelton, 1983), and more recently, a combination of human figure drawings, word associations, and Rorschach responses (Fauteck, 1995).

Feigned Cognitive Deficits

Detection strategies for feigned cognitive deficits generally differ from those employed with malingered psychopathology. Unlike the fabrication of a mental disorder (e.g., a constellation of symptoms and associated features with a convincing onset and course), feigned cognitive deficits do not require the creation of anything. Instead, malingerers simply can claim "not to know" or appear to expend effort but provide an incorrect response. On timed measures (e.g., Digit Symbol subtest of the Wechsler Adult Intelligence Test—Revised [WAIS-R]), deliberate performance at just a slower rate may appear to be a cognitive deficit. Although not necessary, some persons feigning intellectual or neuropsychological impairment may concoct psychological sequelae to their putative cognitive deficits (see Rogers, Harrell, & Liff, 1993).

Symptom validity testing[1] (SVT) with below-chance performance is the best validated detection strategy for feigned cognitive impairment (see Table 18.2). SVT has been tested on sensory and memory deficits. Although not cross-validated with known-groups comparisons, the mathematical probability of a bona fide impairment can be firmly established. Therefore, any possible differences between simulation design and known-groups comparison would not affect the misclassification of genuine patients (i.e., false positives). More recent efforts to apply SVT methods to persons that perform above chance

TABLE 18.2. Detection Strategies for Malingered Cognitive Impairment

Strategy/definition	Validation			Representative measures
	Sim	K-G-C	M-M	
Symptom validity testing (SVT): comparisons of forced choice performance to chance probability	Y		Y	PDRT
Performance consistency: similar success on items of comparable difficulty	Y			Modified TONI[a]
Performance curve: increasing success with items of decreased difficulty	Y		Y	Modified TONI; Ravens[b]
Floor effect: failure on very simple items that most impaired persons get correct	Y			Rey-15[c]; PHI[d]
Magnitude of error: wrong answers that are atypical (e.g., near misses or gross errors)				Available but not tested (e.g., WAIS-NI[e] and Ravens)
Memory deficits inconsistent with learning principles	Y		Y	Recall–Recognition Test[f]; AVLT[g]
Increased latency on feigned protocols	Y			Incorporated into the PDRT[h]

Note. For validation, Sim = simulation design; K-G-C = known-groups comparison; M-M = multimethod validation (i.e., convergent evidence from different assessment domains, such as multiscale inventories and structured interviews).
[a]Frederick and Foster (1991) devised a two-choice version of the TONI with a randomization of item difficulty.
[b]Gudjonsson and Shackleton (1986) compared performances on the Standard Raven Matrices.
[c]Rey-15 refers to Rey's 15-Item Test (see Chapters 5 and 11).
[d]PHI is the Personal History Interview (see Chapter 5).
[e]The WAIS-NI is a modification of the WAIS-R with forced-choice items.
[f]The Recall–Recognition Test was developed by Brandt, Rubinsky, and Lassen (1985; see Chapter 5).
[g]The AVLT is Rey Auditory Verbal Learning Test (Rey, 1964).
[h]A computer-administered version with response latencies has been tested preliminarily (Rose, Hall, & Szalda-Petree, 1995).

but lower than brain-injured groups are much more open to criticism: (1) Studies with known-group comparisons have yet to be conducted; and (2) available simulation studies do not take into account genuine patients with both functional disorders (e.g., schizophrenia) and cognitive impairment. I recommend that only below-chance performances on the SVT be employed for the determination of feigning; other atypical performances on SVT measures are used more properly as part of a threshold model.

Table 18.2 summarizes the detection strategies for feigned cognitive deficits. The strategies are discussed in Chapter 11 and examined in considerable detail by Rogers, Harrell, and Liff (1993). In addition to SVT, the seminal work by Frederick and Foster (1991) on performance consistency and performance curve deserves particular attention. They have modified the Test of Nonverbal Intelligence (TONI) to assess feigned cognitive impairment. Work with the floor effect appears to be most appropriate with brief screening measures (e.g., the Rey 15-Item Memory Test [Rey-15]).

Defensiveness

Strategies for the detection of defensiveness have remained relatively constant during the last decade. Psychometrically based strategies (see Table 18.3) have typically involved some combination of idealized attributes, denial of common psychological problems, and overendorsement of socially desirable responses. As noted in Chapter 9 (see Table 9.9), MMPI-2 scales measuring these strategies are not highly correlated. In other words, although the concepts appear to be closely related, they are apparently assessing different dimensions. This point is supported by recent research (Baer, Wetter, Nichols, Greene, & Berry, 1995) that demonstrated incremental validity for these scales in the assessment of defensiveness. These three strategies need to be fully investigated for other psychometric measures and cross-validated with known-groups comparisons.

The meta-analysis of MMPI-2 measures of defensiveness (Baer, Wetter, & Berry, 1992) is instructive on several grounds. First, the standard indices of defensiveness (i.e., scales *L* and *K*) were not as effective as specialized measures. Second, indices that assessed social desirability (scales *Wsd* and *Mp*) appeared more effective than those employing idealized attributes (*L*) or denial of common foibles (*K*). Clinicians should routinely score these specialized scales in cases of suspected defensiveness.

Significant progress has been made with the use of physiological markers for certain disavowed behaviors. Of these, the detection of denied substance abuse, especially through the application of hair analysis, has proven to be highly effective. In contrast, the use of global measures of defensiveness and deceit (e.g., polygraph and integrity testing) appears less accurate and more vulnerable to false positives (i.e., misclassifying an honest person as defensive/deceptive). In summary, the value of physiological markers is method-specific; atypical findings on physiological markers must be evaluated in light of the particular method and referral issue.

Irrelevant Responding

Irrelevant or inconsistent responding has received increased attention by both clinicians and researchers. Carlin and Hewitt (1990) demonstrated that experienced psychologists often miss irrelevant profiles, if they do not inspect scales designed to measure response consistency. In particular, practitioners increasingly realize the dangers of not discovering irrelevant responders. On multiscale inventories, irrelevant responders can produce a clinical profile that does not represent their current psychological func-

TABLE 18.3. Detection Strategies for Defensiveness

Strategy/definition	Validation			Representative measures
	Sim	K-G-C	M-M	
Idealized attributes (highly desirable but rare human qualities)	Y			*L* and *S* (MMPI-2)
Denial of common foibles and problems	Y			*K* (MMPI-2)
Socially desirable responses	Y			*Wsd, Esd, Mp* (MMPI-2)
Physiological markers inconsistent with denied behaviors	Y	Y	Y	hair analysis; phallometric testing

Note. For validation, Sim = simulation design; K-G-C = known-groups comparison; M-M = multimethod validation (i.e., convergent evidence from different assessment domains, such as multiscale inventories and structured interviews).

tioning. In addition, some persons responding irrelevantly will appear to be malingering on most feigning indicators.

The most common form of irrelevant responding is a disengagement from the assessment. As a result of this disengagement, answers are often inconsistent. Therefore, research and clinical efforts have been devoted to inconsistent responses. Although known-groups comparisons have not been employed, a reasonable alternative is the use of fully and partially random profiles to approximate this particular form of inconsistent responding. Repeating of identical items is the purest measure of item consistency and requires no inference on the part of clinicians. By definition, a person that misses a substantial proportion of repeated items is responding inconsistently. Close approximations to repeated items involve two distinct categories: (1) items of similar and opposite content and (2) highly correlated item pairs.[2] Other measures sometimes employed for irrelevant responding include infrequent items and reaction times; however, these strategies are open to alternative explanations, such as severe psychopathology, marked decrements in concentration, and attempts to malinger. Table 18.4 provides a distillation of detection strategies for irrelevant responding.

Role playing constitutes another form of irrelevant responding that is rarely addressed. Kroger and Turnbell (1975) demonstrated that normal participants could adopt roles (e.g., air force officer or creative artist) and thereby alter substantially their MMPI profiles. These roles, although not necessarily inconsistent in presentation, were irrelevant to the person. It is surmised that relatively few individuals would engage in role playing without a specific motivation (e.g., malingering or defensiveness).

In summary, substantial progress has been made with the development of detection strategies for malingering, defensiveness, and irrelevant responding. Of these, malingering strategies appear to be the most sophisticated and best validated. Defensiveness and its variants (social desirability and impression management) tend to be situationally specific and, therefore, challenging to assess. Irrelevant responding is typically measured with reference to response consistency, although a number of innovative strategies have been introduced. In the next section, I examine specific measures used by practitioners and evaluate their efficacy.

TABLE 18.4. Detection Strategies for Irrelevant Responding

Strategy/definition	Validation Sim	K-G-C	M-M	Representative measures
Repeating of identical items	Y			*TR* index (MMPI)
Repeating of item either similar or opposite in content	Y			*VRIN* and *TRIN* (MMPI-2); *CLS* (MMPI)
Use of highly correlated item pairs	Y			*INC* (PAI)
Use of infrequent items that are unrelated to psychopathology	Y			*VI* (MCMI)
Reaction time				Computerized MMPI-2s

Note. For validation, Sim = simulation design; K-G-C = known-groups comparison; M-M = multimethod validation (i.e., convergent evidence from different assessment domains, such as multiscale inventories and structured interviews).

USEFULNESS OF INDIVIDUAL DIAGNOSTIC METHODS

Mental health professionals are often confronted with highly atypical or anomalous findings based on individual interviews and single measures. Of critical importance is the relationship between these findings and response styles. This section provides a summary of the principal findings for the use of specific diagnostic methods.

Clinical methods can be conceptualized in relationship to dissimulation on four levels: susceptibility, detection, detection—coached, and interpretability. These four levels are outlined here.

1. *Susceptibility*. The most basic consideration is whether a particular method is vulnerable to dissimulation. For example, projective methods once were viewed as inaccessible to feigning, but this notion subsequently has been disproved (see Chapter 10). When methods are susceptible to feigning, then the crucial issue is detection.

2. *Detection*. The second consideration is whether a measure includes *systematic* methods for the identification of dissimulation. Unfortunately, many of the most commonly used assessment methods (e.g., intelligence testing, projectives, and structured interviewing) largely ignore the issue of response styles and their detection. As operationally defined, *detection* is standardized and validated procedures for the assessment of specific response styles.

3. *Detection—Coached*. Clinicians and researchers during the last decade have become poignantly aware that dissimulating persons are not necessarily naive and unprepared. On the contrary, some dissimulators have ample knowledge of disorders, based on direct observation or personal experiences, and considerable sophistication regarding the purpose and design of assessment methods. Therefore, the third consideration is whether the detection methods remain effective, despite coaching and other forms of preparation.

4. *Interpretability*. Most early research designs implicitly assumed an either–or paradigm for response styles (e.g., malingering *or* mentally disordered). In the face of such simplistic dichotomization, researchers found no need to investigate the interpretability of dissimulated profiles. More recently, spurred by research on the MMPI *K*-correction, investigators are beginning to explore the issue of interpretability. Simply put, what clinical conclusions can be rendered, despite the dissimulation.

Tables 18.5 and 18.6 provide a distillation of clinical methods by susceptibility, detection, detection—coached, and interpretability. These tables are intended as an initial reference point; readers should refer to specific chapters for their relative effectiveness of particular methods. Even though most measures are susceptible to dissimulation and lack interpretability, I have included this information on each category to emphasize their importance to clinical practice.

Susceptibility to Dissimulation

Rogers (1984b) summarized the empirical literature through the early 1980s and concluded that nearly all measures are susceptible to response styles. More recent research

TABLE 18.5. Usefulness of Clinical Methods in the Assessment of Dissimulation

	Assessment issues			
Clinical methods	Susceptibility	Detection	Detection— Coached	Interpretability
A. Diagnostic interviews				
1. Malingering	Yes	Variable[a]	No	No
2. Defensiveness	Yes	No	No	No
B. SADS				
1. Malingering	Yes	Yes[b]	No	Partial[c]
2. Defensiveness	Yes	Yes	No	Partial[c]
C. SIRS				
1. Malingering	Yes	Yes	Yes	Partial[d]
2. Defensiveness	Yes	Partial[e]	No	No
D. Hypnosis				
1. Deception	Yes	No	No	No
E. Drug-assisted interviews				
1. Deception	Yes	Partial[f]	No	No[g]
F. Plethysmography				
1. Defensiveness	Yes	Partial[h]	Partial[i]	Partial[j]
G. Polygraphs				
1. Deception	Yes	Partial[k]	No	Variable[l]
H. Integrity testing	Yes	No	No	No

[a]Clinician who systematically probes for malingering may identify more blatant cases.
[b]Only if specific procedures are employed (see Chapter 14).
[c]Use of the multiple SADS with informants.
[d]A review of SIRS scales can give information about the type of feigning (e.g., endorsement of symptoms with extreme severity) but not genuine disorders.
[e]Normative data are available on the endorsement of common psychological problems by clinical and nonclinical samples; substantially lower levels of endorsement signal the need to assess defensiveness comprehensively.
[f]Cases identified are probably accurate; a substantial proportion are not identified.
[g]Rare cases may occur where previously unknown details are provided that can be confirmed by independent sources.
[h]Some patients are identifiable that suppress deviant sexual arousal.
[i]At least some offenders that attempt to use countermeasures are identifiable.
[j]By inference, it may be possible to identify suppressed arousal, but not necessarily paraphiliac behavior.
[k]GKT is very accurate but rarely employed; CQT tends to have an unacceptably high rate of false positives.
[l]Only with GKT.

has generally confirmed this conclusion. For example, extensive investigations of the MMPI (Berry, Baer, & Harris, 1991; Baer et al., 1992) and the MMPI-2 (Rogers, Salekin, & Sewell, 1994) have demonstrated amply their vulnerability to malingering and defensiveness. Rare exceptions involve physiological measures of denied substance abuse (e.g., hair analysis) and defensiveness on cognitive measures (e.g., intelligence).

Denial or gross minimization are common response styles of substance abusers. As summarized in Chapter 6, even specialists in chemical dependence are often inaccurate in their judgments. In addition, commonly used psychometric measures are

TABLE 18.6. Clinical Usefulness of Psychometric Methods in the Assessment of Dissimulation

Clinical methods	Assessment issues			
	Susceptibility	Detection	Detection—Coached	Interpretability
A. Rorschach				
1. Malingering	Yes	Variable[a]	No[b]	No
2. Defensiveness	Yes	No[c]	No	No
B. Other projectives				
1. Malingering	Yes	No	No	No
2. Defensiveness	Yes	No	No	No
C. MMPI/MMPI-2				
1. Malingering	Yes	Yes[d]	Variable[e]	No
2. Defensiveness	Yes	Yes	No	Yes[f]
3. Irrelevant responding	Yes	Yes	No	No
D. PAI				
1. Malingering	Yes	Yes[g]	Partial[h]	No
2. Defensiveness	Yes	Yes	No	No
E. CPI/CPI-R				
1. Malingering	Yes	Partial[i]	No	No
2. Defensiveness	Yes	Partial[i]	No	No
F. MCMI-II/MCMI-III				
1. Malingering	Yes	Yes[j]	No	No
2. Defensiveness	Yes	No[k]	No	No
G. Intelligence				
1. Malingering	Yes	No[l]	No	No
2. Defensiveness[m]	No	N/A	N/A	N/A
H. Neuropsychological batteries				
1. Malingering	Yes	Variable[n]	No	No
2. Defensiveness[o]	No	N/A	N/A	N/A

[a]Only modestly effective, with the exception of the Pettigrew procedure.
[b]Coaching markedly reduces detection.
[c]Only exception is psychotics who can be readily identified.
[d]Variability in cutting scores means that confidence can only be established for extreme scores.
[e]Coaching about disorders does not appear to affect detection; coaching about validity scales has a marked effect.
[f]Limited in applicability to inpatient samples.
[g]A discriminant function appears more effective than *NIM* scale elevations.
[h]*NIM* is apparently ineffective with highly sophisticated simulators, but a discriminant model maintains its efficacy.
[i]Very little research focused on the original CPI.
[j]No research is available on the MCMI-III.
[k]Very mixed results contraindicate the use of Scale *Y*.
[l]The notable exception is the modified TONI by Frederick and Foster (1991).
[m]Evaluated persons cannot minimize intellectual deficits, unless they "train for the test" by gaining access to information or test protocols.
[n]Depending on the specific neuropsychological measures, some data are available.
[o]See note *m*.

typically face valid and very vulnerable to distortion. More sophisticated measures are also susceptible to denial and distortion. In contrast to this bleak landscape, physiological measures provide a reliable means of assessing substance abuse that is relatively impervious to patient manipulation: Breathalyzer and hair analysis. Unfortunately, physiological measures provide little data on psychological functioning and general behavior—issues of central importance to mental health professionals.

Defensiveness on cognitive measures is often unsuccessful. For example, a memory-impaired person may attempt to minimize amnesia but is unlikely to be successful in light of neuropsychological testing. The sole exception is "training for the test" in which the person practices either on actual test items or similar tasks. As an illustration, the Similarities subtest of the Weschler Intelligence Scale for Children—Third Edition (WISC-III) could easily be coached without using any "protected" items from the test. Our views of coaching may be determined more by the setting than the actual activity. We are likely to view coaching a child on items similar to intelligence tests for the purpose of seeking admission into a school for the gifted as reprehensible and unethical. Paradoxically, coaching students on items similar to general aptitude tests for the purpose of seeking admission to a university may be viewed as acceptable, if not laudable.

Detection

The litmus test of any dissimulation measure is its classification rates. In this regard, Tables 18.5 and 18.6 should be construed as summaries for threshold models (i.e., anomalous findings that trigger a full investigation) rather than clinical decision models. If we hold to the criteria established in Chapter 1 (see Table 1.2), then most clinical research reaches the tentative and probable levels of certainty in classifying dissimulators. However, even with less robust measures, extremely deviant scores may be interpretable. For example, although the Personality Assessment Inventory (PAI) *NIM* scale does not appear to be highly accurate in the detection of feigning, a marked elevation (e.g., $T = 90$) is likely to be useful for classification (see Rogers, Sewell, Morey, & Ustad, 1996).

Interview methods vary considerably in their usefulness with dissimulation. Skilled clinicians can sometimes detect more obvious attempts at feigned psychopathology. Unfortunately, many clinicians do not include sufficient probes, based on established detection strategies (e.g., rare symptoms), to maximize the effectiveness of this approach. Structured interviews (see Chapter 15) provide a standardized methodology for assessing response styles. Of these, the SIRS was developed specifically for the evaluation of feigning and related response styles. As such, the SIRS provides data on detection that can be related to a variety of settings and faked presentations.

Specialized methods for the detection of deception and dissimulation include hypnosis, drug-assisted interviews, penile plethysmography (PPG), polygraphs, and integrity testing. Of these, hypnosis, polygraphs, and integrity testing appear to have enduring problems in the detection of deception. Conceivably, the vagueness and breadth of the criterion (i.e., general deception) augurs against classificatory accuracy.

As discussed in Chapter 13, the usefulness of polygraphs is constrained by the prevailing method; the control question technique (CQT) has only moderate classification rates (biased against honest persons) that are often based on faulty research designs that overestimate its accuracy. In addition, drug-assisted interviews are best conceptualized as a challenge test. In other words, a marked alteration in the person's account during the drug-assisted interview, subsequently confirmed in follow-up interviews or from other sources, can provide evidence of deception. However, the absence of such findings is uninformative, because many dissemblers are able to maintain their misrepresentations during the drug-assisted interview.

Psychometric methods (see Table 18.6) vary widely in the breath and sophistication of their dissimulation research. In general, multiscale inventories are the best-validated category of psychological testing. Unlike other testing, measures of response styles were developed as a component of scale development. Not surprisingly, this foresight has paid valuable dividends in the classifying of persons with fabrication or denial of psychopathology on multiscale inventories. In stark contrast, little systematic attention was paid in the construction of intellectual and neuropsychological measures to motivation and response style. For example, specific indicators could be developed for the Wechsler Memory Scale—Revised (WMS-R) based on performance curve and magnitude of error for both learning and recall.

The MMPI and MMPI-2 are the best validated multiscale measures for irrelevant responding, malingered psychopathology, and defensiveness. Chapter 9 provides a comprehensive review of validity indicators; this chapter's greatest strength is the inclusion of unparalleled normative data on clinical and nonclinical samples. In addition, recent meta-analyses of the MMPI-2 (e.g., Baer, Wetter, & Berry, 1992; Rogers, Sewell, & Salekin, 1994) offer clinical guidelines on the likelihood that anomalous scores reflect defensiveness or malingering. Strong evidence of dissimulation is provided by (1) scores that substantially exceed clinical and nonclinical norms (see Chapter 9), and (2) scores that exceed the majority of simulation studies for a specific response style (see Baer, Wetter, & Berry, 1992; Rogers, Sewell, & Salekin, 1994).

Detection of Coached Dissimulation

The implicit and untenable assumption in early studies was that prospective dissimulators would not prepare for their deceptive presentations. For example, many malingering studies ask apparently unimpaired persons to feign a mental disorder without providing sufficient time or materials for preparation. Obviously, this design is limited in its generalizability to naive persons that do not attempt to prepare their dissimulations.

Two measures have been well validated with coached malingering: the SIRS and the MMPI-2. In general, coaching about specific disorders (e.g., DSM-IV symptoms) has relatively little effect on classification rates on both measures. In contrast, coaching about detection strategies is likely to reduce scores on validity indicators, although the majority of simulators continue to be classified as feigning on the SIRS. Use of both measures is strongly recommended for cases of suspected malingering because of their (1) extensive validation and (2) relative robustness in light of coaching and other forms of preparation.

Interpretability

Relatively little progress has occurred during the last decade on correction formulas for the interpretation of dissimulated protocols. The simple conclusion that an individual is feigning or defensive is very useful information. However, dissimulation and genuine impairment are not mutually exclusive. Therefore, the interpretability of dissimulated protocols is important. The original work by Meehl and Hathaway (1946) on K correction for defensiveness was seminal in establishing the interpretability of these profiles. Unfortunately, the last three decades have yielded few additional studies on either inpatients or outpatients.

Rogers and Nussbaum (1991) provided circumscribed data on the interpretation of inconsistent MMPI/MMPI-2 profiles. For profiles with elevated measures of inconsistency (e.g., TR index), they calculated the probability that inconsistent profiles were an attempt at feigning. In other words, extreme elevations of clinical scales would not occur simply by chance (i.e., 50% endorsement) but would reflect a highly selective pattern of responding. For instance, an MMPI-2 profile may provide evidence of feigning, irrespective of elevations on $VRIN$ and $TRIN$. In this regard, elevated indicators of feigning coupled with several clinical scales of extreme endorsement (e.g., ≥ 75% of the items endorsed in the psychopathological direction) would not occur by chance and are likely to reflect a deliberate effort to malinger.[3]

Structured interviews, such as the SADS, provide an interesting basis for evaluating genuine disorders in dissimulating persons through the use of collateral interviews. By systematically asking and rating identical questions with the patient and significant others, consistent patterns sometimes emerge that are interpretable, despite attempts at defensiveness or malingering. The SIRS provides different information about feigners; it allows the examiners to more fully understand the way in which the person appears to simulating. This information may be relevant for treatment interventions by discussing with the patient his or her needs and the purposes served by dissimulation. For example, a patient indiscriminantly endorsing symptoms obscures treatment priorities and may blunt focused efforts to reduce acute distress.

Attempts at denial on physiological measures may provide limited information about the denied behavior but has little generalizability to other behaviors, attitudes, or emotions. For instance, the Guilty Knowledge Test (GKT) can furnish useful information that a person may have knowledge about a specific incident, despite vigorous denials. However, the extent of this information is much more difficult to ascertain. By the same token, an atypical arousal pattern on penile plethysmography may denote paraphiliac urges but offers little data on sexual fantasies or behavior.

CLINICAL RELEVANCE

The clinical relevance of dissimulation varies directly with the degree of distortion, the type of dissimulation, and the specific referral question. For example, a person with paranoid schizophrenia and an extensive history of auditory hallucinations may attempt to feign command hallucinations. The clinical relevance of such fabrications would depend greatly on the referral question and vary considerably in relevance depending on whether the patient is seeking voluntary hospitalization or attempting an insanity plea. Indeed, the relevance of any type of dissimulation can only be established with reference to a specific referral question.

Empirical data are not available on the prevalence of dissimulation by referral questions. Surveys (Rogers, Salekin, Sewell, & Goldstein, 1996; Rogers, Sewell, & Goldstein, 1994) of forensic experts suggested that only a small proportion of clinical populations are likely to malinger (15.7% and 17.4% of forensic, and 7.4% and 7.8% of nonforensic cases). The estimates for nonforensic cases are possibly inflated because forensic experts may be asked to consult on more adversarial evaluations than most psychologists and psychiatrists. Prevalence estimates for nonforensic evaluations are surprisingly absent. Mental health professionals assigned to emergency rooms attest to both (1) malingering by voluntary patients seeking admission (especially during severe winters) and (2) defensiveness among involuntary patients denying or refusing to discuss their psychopathology as well as the events precipitating their admission. Beyond these anecdotal data, a dearth of information exists on dissimulation in relation to inpatient or outpatient treatment.[4]

Vocational assessments have the obvious potential for dissimulation. The determination of benefits as related to rehabilitation efforts may provide motivation in a minority of cases for suboptimal performance. In contrast, job applicants are likely to be motivated to present themselves in the best possible light. With reference to psychological impairment, some degree of defensiveness would be understandable, despite protection from the Americans with Disabilities Act (ADA). The ADA appears to be responsible for increasing numbers of persons seeking special accommodation in higher education. Although many requests for special accommodation appear unwarranted, the overall proportion of persons fabricating symptoms to circumvent academic requirements is not likely to be large.[5] Special education placements often vary in the quality of services provided but almost always carry a social stigma. We should therefore expect the proportion of defensiveness to vary according to these same two parameters (i.e., quality of services and stigmatization).

A substantial number of forensic evaluations yield atypical results (e.g., Heaton, Smith, Lehman, & Vogt, 1978; Heilbrun, Bennett, White & Kelly, 1990) that are possibly indicative of malingering. Clinicians must avoid the facile conclusion that atypical results combined with putative external motivation and buttressed by DSM-IV indices (e.g., APD and medicolegal evaluation) are tantamount to malingering. Our best available data suggest that (1) forensic settings vary in their prevalence rates, and (2) most forensic evaluatees, despite potential rewards, do not malinger.

An obvious motivation for parents in child-custody cases would be to minimize their psychological impairment. However, parents with known mental health histories may decide to be forthcoming in their presentations, since denials would be damaging. Analogous MMPI data from adopting parents (Dalton, 1994) would suggest a moderate degree of defensiveness among parents in custody cases.

A commonsensical review of the forensic issues suggests that dissimulation is highly dependent on the legal issues and the specifics of the case. Although plaintiffs in personal injury cases may have something to gain from feigned deficits, the amount of gain varies directly with the degree of genuine disorder. For example, a person with unequivocal memory impairment coupled with major depression is not likely to be compensated more for the fabrication of additional symptoms. Insanity cases may provide an apparent motivation to malinger. However, this apparent motivation may evaporate in noncapital cases when the length and conditions of institutionalization (prison vs. maximum-security hospital) are considered.

In summary, Table 18.7 provides a heuristic framework for estimating the expected likelihood of malingering and defensiveness by the type of assessment being conducted. As noted in Chapter 1 (see Table 1.2), the patient's degree of choice and the congruence of his or her goals with those of the mental health professionals are also likely to be influential.

The relevance of dissimulation ranges widely with the degree of distortion and the referral question. One pivotal consideration underlying the analysis of clinical relevance is if the dissimulation were true, what appreciable difference would it make to intervention or disposition? For instance, a psychotically depressed woman who feigns suicidal ideation to ensure her hospitalization in a crowded public facility likely should be hospitalized irrespective of her malingering. Likewise, a job applicant who minimizes past episodes of anxiety out of fear of stigmatization ought to be considered for

TABLE 18.7. Potential for Dissimulation by Types of Clinical Evaluation

Type of assessment	Expected likelihood of dissimulation	
	Malingering	Defensiveness
A. Treatment		
1. Voluntary outpatient	Low	Low
2. Voluntary inpatient	Variable[a]	Low
3. Involuntary inpatient	Low	Moderate
B. Vocational		
1. Rehabilitation assessments	Moderate	Low
2. Job placement/performance	Low	Moderate
C. School		
1. Special education placement	Low	Variable
2. Special accommodation under ADA	Variable	Low
D. Forensic		
1. Child custody	Low	High
2. Personal injury	High	Low
3. Insanity	High	Low
4. Presentence	Low	Variable[b]

[a]Where inpatient resources are scarce, voluntary patients may feel compelled to malinger in order to qualify for services.
[b]In minor offenses, defendants may hope for treatment alternatives to incarceration by appearing mentally ill. In other cases, defendants may worry that the appearance of mental illness will lead to a harsher sentence.

most positions, irrespective of past anxiety episodes. In such cases, the dissimulation may have only a minor influence on the clinical opinion and subsequent decision making. Each case of suspected dissimulation must be evaluated thoroughly, since the clinician cannot determine *prior* to his or her assessment what the potential relevance of malingering and defensiveness might be in an individual case. The issue of relevance must be raised following each assessment in assigning importance of the dissimulation to the overall evaluation of the patient.

Treatment Considerations

The majority of clinical assessments address related issues of treatment recommendations and likely treatment outcomes. Little research exists on the relationship of specific styles of dissimulation to treatment response. Clinical interpretations based on the MMPI would suggest that a mild to moderate degree of defensiveness may be evidence of ego strength and positive treatment outcome (e.g., Marks, Seeman, & Haller, 1974). Paradoxically, some exaggeration of psychological impairment as measured by the *F* scale of the MMPI has been commonly labeled as a "cry for help" and a sign of increased motivation. Available research would question this latter assumption with empirical evidence that *F* elevations are associated with poor treatment outcome (see Chapter 9; see also Berry et al., 1996). Despite these clinical interpretations, little is known regarding the relationship of malingering, defensiveness, or irrelevant responding to the (1) type of treatment that should be recommended and (2) likelihood of treatment compliance and favorable outcome. Certainly, patients with extreme presentations of dissimulation would appear to be poor treatment candidates. Individuals who are either categorically denying any psychological difficulties or unfalteringly malinger pervasive problems that do not exist would not appear, on an intuitive basis, to be amenable to treatment. Mild to moderate degrees of malingering and defensiveness present a more complicated picture. Certainly a common ground may exist with less severe dissimulation for treatment of "real" problems while trust and rapport are being established.

A difficult issue to establish is the patient's motivation for dissimulation and the relevance of this motivation for treatment recommendations. A parent in a child–custody dispute may have a strong motivation to deny problems prior to the child-custody hearing, but manifest strong motivation for treatment, if treatment is a condition of the custody. Similarly, an involuntary patient may be markedly defensive during the civil commitment proceedings, yet show at least some motivation to participate in treatment once the decision to hospitalize has been determined judicially. Simply put, any striking change in life circumstances signals the need to reevaluate the relationship of response styles to clinical interventions.

Treatment compliance is an important element in the assessment of treatment recommendations for malingering and defensive individuals. By definition, malingering and defensive individuals must be viewed as being at cross-purposes with their evaluators, although not necessarily with subsequent treatment. Without minimizing the confounding effects of dissimulation, many "presenting complaints" by nondissimulating patients are deliberate gambits to test the trustworthiness and competence of the clinician. In other words, trust and the development of shared goals are necessary components of most treatment interventions. From this perspective, the treating clinician may attempt to define a dissimulator's objectives and to assess to what extent the proposed treatment would assist the dissimulator in meeting these objectives. These objectives likely include the nature of the therapeutic relationship and concomitant feelings of vulnerability and dependency. The concerns underlying these objectives may extend beyond the therapeutic process and have real-world implications. A pedophiliac parent *does* have something to fear from therapy. An unskilled laborer, whether deserving Workers' Compensation or not, is likely to be threatened by discussions of exaggerated symptoms of depression and his or her apparent impairment.

The assessment of treatability is at best an imprecise process, which relies heavily on trial and error (see Rogers & Webster, 1989). No empirical studies have been found that specifically compare the treatment response of dissimulators with nondissimulating patients. Perhaps the most fruitful approach would be to attempt a contractual arrangement with a dissimulating patient for an explicit treatment intervention over a specified time period. In cases in which treatment is deemed essential and nonoptional, enforced treatment would be strictly controlled by statutory requirements, with a treatment outcome often limited to the reduction of imminent dangerousness. In these latter cases, the focus is more on the appropriate case management with less attention paid to treatment compliance or outcome.

Nontreatment Considerations

Psychologists and other mental health professionals often engage in consultations that involve nontreatment decisions. In a classic study, Lorei (1970) surveyed VA hospitals and found that the determination of malingering was second only to dangerousness in importance when assessing the potential dischargeability of inpatients. Patients in preparation for discharge may manifest a strong desire to remain in the hospital or to receive a favorable community placement. Furthermore, outpatients may wish to present themselves as sufficiently impaired to warrant certain benefits (e.g., insurance reimbursement and workers' compensation) but not so impaired as to risk certain privileges (e.g., permanent loss of employment, hospitalization, or termination of parental rights; see Rogers & Cavanaugh, 1983). Military personnel may seek discharge from armed forces or noncombat placements (Rabinowitz, Mark, Modai, & Margalit, 1990). Vocational, school, and forensic assessments frequently include such nontreatment dispositions. Such cases tend to be perceived as more adversarial than simple treatment decisions, since the clinician is likely to be seen as a means to an end (e.g., selection of the best candidate for a managerial position) and have goals that differ from the client (e.g., furthering the company's objectives, not the client's career).

The risk and potential benefits accrued from psychiatric/psychological assessment are often explicit and legally sanctioned. In nontreatment assessments, the clinician does not often have the luxury of a reassessment, because a lasting determination must be rendered. As the potential benefits increase, the likelihood of dissimulation should also increase. The extent to which potential dissimulators weigh the risks of detection is not known, although awareness of risk should have a moderating effect on the probability of dissimulation.

Nontreatment dispositions typically require the clinician to examine a patient according to a specific legal or administrative standard. This standard reflects decisions, often made by agencies, schools, or the courts, that may not be perceived by the client as either beneficial or benevolent. Although the emphasis of such assessments is a particular standard, deception and dissimulation must also be considered. Within a nontreatment context, the use of corroborative data becomes increasingly important in making the appropriate recommendations or dispositions because no prior or ongoing professional relationship exists.

Motivational Considerations

A final issue in considering the clinical relevance of dissimulation is to understand its adaptive functions for the dissimulator (see also the discussion of the adaptational model in Chapter 1). Although clinicians frequently view dissimulation as a negative and complicating factor in clinical assessment, this same behavior may be viewed as positive and adaptive by the dissimulator. Goals of dissimulation may include the maintenance of an individual's sense of autonomy, securing denied benefits, avoidance of painful circumstances, and avoidance or disengagement from a difficult or nonvoluntary process.

Such objectives, from the perspective of the dissimulator, may be viewed as attempts (successful or otherwise) to maintain a sense of worth or competence, and to minimize avoidable pain or coercion. For example, patients who resist involuntary hospitalization or mandatory treatment may be defending, whether correctly or not, their own right to self-determination. Individuals who deny disabling psychological disorders may be struggling to maintain their sense of competence either through work or the continued custody of their children. Other dissimulators, who have experienced physical and/or psychological injuries through the negligence of others, may exaggerate their impairment from their own perspective of justice, believing that no financial compensation can ever equal the losses that they have incurred. Finally, dissimulators may be motivated by an understandable desire to avoid painful or coercive circumstances that may be a factor in presentence evaluations or civil commitment proceedings.

A clinician's responsibility goes beyond the mere identification of dissimulators and extends to his or her understanding of their motivations for these deliberate distortions. Inquiry into patients' perceived risks and benefits may be useful in understanding their motivations. In most cases, this motivation probably extends beyond tangible rewards and punishment of the immediate circumstances and is related to an individual's self-image. Simply presented as an inquiry, "What are the different outcomes of this assessment, and what do they mean to this individual's self-perception?" For example, the acknowledgment of a severe mental disorder may well be devastating and unacceptable to a particular person's self-image of being strong and capable. Thus, the role that motivation plays in dissimulation must be considered for each individual and addressed within a possibly adversarial context and in relationship to a specific referral question.

An informal review of clinical reports suggests that some clinicians attempt to go one step further and make statements regarding an individual's personality on the basis of his or her specific dissimulative style. Reports may describe dissimulating patients as manipulative, self-serving, dishonest, noncooperative, and oppositional. Such inferences should never be generated on the basis of malingering and defensiveness alone. As a rule, such attempts to link response styles with personality characteristics should be avoided, since an underlying premise of such, often pejorative, interpretations is that only "bad" persons dissimulate. A preferable approach is to describe a patient's apparent motivation rather than make unsupported inferences regarding character or personality.

CONFRONTATION OF SUSPECTED DISSIMULATION

An important and perhaps essential component in the clinical determination of dissimulation is to offer the patient some feedback regarding his or her presentation. This process might well include a summary of the patient's presentation and the difficulties or problems that the clinician has in accepting the patient's accounts at face value. Feedback on the patient's response style requires sensitivity, tact, and timing from the clinician.

As a general principle, clinicians should be parsimonious in their feedback and judicious in their confrontation of patients seen for evaluation. The goals of providing feedback may range from (1) informing the patient of the status of the evaluation, (2) asking the patient for assistance in clarifying incongruities, (3) eliciting more complete information, and (4) giving the patient an opportunity to change his or her self-report. Except under unusual circumstances, the purpose of such feedback/confrontation should not be to extract from the patient an "admission of dissimulation." The clinician should attempt to establish his or her conclusions prior to any discussion of dissimulation. Rather, the purpose is to give the patient an opportunity to clarify areas of ambiguity and, more important, to offer insight into possible motivation for the dissimulation. An additional goal, which may be occasionally realized, is for the patient to spontaneously provide a more accurate description of his or her psychological impairment. Such revisions of self-reports must, of course, be carefully scrutinized, since they may represent simply another attempt at malingering or defensiveness.

Confrontation with, and feedback to, a defensive patient typically require the use of corroborative data. Naturally, the clinician should attempt to present his or her observations in a straightforward and nonpejorative manner. The following are examples of feedback and confrontation with a defensive patient:

1. "Although you are telling me that everything is going fine, when I hear about . . . (i.e., description of current problems), I am having some trouble understanding this."
2. "I know how much you want me to believe that you have your problems well under control, but when I see you . . . (i.e., clinical observations of the patient), I don't think this is the case."

3. "Life is not all black and white. Whenever someone tells me only the good side, I become interested in what is being left out. . . ."
4. "According to you, you are having no difficulty handling . . . (i.e., describe a specific problem), but according to . . . (i.e., a reliable informant) you are experiencing. . . ."

Malingering patients, unlike their defensive counterparts, are commonly either inconsistent or improbable in their clinical presentation. Therefore, the clinician needs a wider range of probes in discussing dissimulation with malingerers. Representative probes include the following:

1. "Some of the problems you describe are rarely seen in patients with mental disorders. I am worried that you might be trying to make things seem worse than they are."
2. "Earlier in the evaluation you told me . . . , now you are telling me. . . . I am having trouble putting this together."
3. "Although you have told me about . . . (i.e., description of current problems), when I observed you, you have not appeared. . . ."
4. "I don't want to hurt your feelings, but I just don't think things are quite as bad as you tell me they are."
5. "According to you, you have . . . (i.e., current problems), but according to . . . (i.e., a reliable informant) you are. . . . Can you help me understand this?"

Irrelevant responders typically are disengaged from the assessment process. This disengagement makes feedback or confrontation particularly difficult, because the patient is uninvolved and emotionally distant from the clinician. The clinician must weigh the merits of direct confrontation with irrelevant responders against the possibility that such confrontation may only further alienate the patient. Representative probes include the following:

1. "I don't think we got off on the right foot. Can we start again? Tell me in your words what you see as your problems."
2. "I don't think you're listening to what I have to say, and I know that you're not particularly pleased about being here. How can we make sure that this is not a waste of time for you?"
3. "I know you took these . . . (i.e., psychological tests) for me, but I don't think you paid much attention to how you answered them. What about . . . (i.e., specific test items), which you gave different answers to at different times?"

As discussed earlier, the purpose of feedback and discussion is to provide a greater understanding of the patient's motivation. Experienced clinicians have found that matter-of-fact confrontation with respect for the patient's personal dignity and efforts at dissimulation often provides an avenue for further understanding of that patient. Not giving the patient an opportunity to address ambiguities and incongruities within the assessment process may well shortchange the evaluation itself.

An alternative to direct feedback is to offer the patient possible motivations for dissimulation. In a child-custody case, the clinician might remark, "Many parents do themselves more harm than good by trying to appear perfect." For a chronic patient feigning hallucinations, the clinician might caution indirectly, "Sometimes patients make up symptoms to get special attention or more medication. The danger in doing this is that no one believes fakers, even when they are really in crisis." The indirect discussion of possible motivation has the advantage of providing a face-saving method of discussing and possibly changing dissimulation. The drawback is that the clinician's construal of motivation is likely to impede any open discussion of alternative motivations.

SYNTHESIS OF CLINICAL DATA

The clinician must integrate an array of clinical findings on the issue of dissimulation and discuss these findings in terms of both the referral question and clinical relevance. Such synthesis of dissimulation material requires the examination of the following dimensions: (1) the strength and consistency of results across psychological measures, (2) the absence of alternative explanations, (3) the possibility of hybrid styles of dissimulation, and (4) the methods of reporting dissimulation. Each of these dimensions is discussed individually.

Strength and Consistency of Findings

Among the dozens of standardized methods and specific techniques, the strength and robustness of measures must be considered in the determination of response styles. Several methods are particularly robust and produce very few false positives. For feigned psychopathology, the SIRS and occasionally the MMPI-2[6] provide highly robust findings. For feigned cognitive impairment, below-chance performance on SVT may furnish conclusive evidence. For defensiveness and deception, anomalous findings on urinalysis, hair analysis, GKT, and penile plethysmography provide confirmation. Even with these measures, corroborative data should be actively sought.

Given the fallibility of individual diagnostic methods in accurately identifying malingering and defensiveness, the degree of consistency among measures is crucial. If a clinician has ample data based on pencil-and-paper measures, clinical interviews, and corroborative sources regarding a patient's inconsistent or improbable presentation, then the determination of malingering, defensiveness, or irrelevant responding is a relatively straightforward matter. Unpublished data by Rogers and Dickens (1987) would suggest, however, that there may be marked discrepancies between results of psychological testing (e.g., the MMPI) and clinical interviews. Within a pretrial sample, they found approximately 9.4% of forensic patients had fake-bad MMPI profiles, but only 3.2% of forensic cases were suspected of definite malingering in independent diagnostic interviews. In other words, almost three times as many defendants were identified by one method (MMPI) than by other methods (diagnostic interviews and corroborative data). What should the clinician do if the patient appears reliable on the basis of clinical and corroborative data and yet presents a malingered profile on the MMPI? At minimum, such inconsistencies reduce the degree of certainty in the diagnostic conclusions. Such inconsistencies will be discussed further within the examination of hybrid styles of dissimulation. The absence of such consistency, depending on the particular clinical presentation, may argue for the *unreliable* designation. Suffice it to say that highly consistent results from different sources of clinical investigation are invaluable in making definite conclusions regarding a specific dissimulative style.

Absence of Alternative Explanations

Specific indicators of dissimulation can be ranked on the degree to which they may be open to alternative interpretations. For example, rare symptoms are, by definition, infrequently seen in the clinical population; the presence of several such symptoms, although perhaps indicative of malingering, does not preclude other interpretations. In comparison, a large number of improbable symptoms or symptom combinations are extremely unlikely in bona fide patients.

As an illustration, overly dramatic presentation has been described in case studies to signify feigning. Alternative explanations might include Axis I symptoms (e.g., grandiose delusions) or Axis II symptomatology (e.g., histrionic personality disorder). Other alternatives must be considered explicitly. Evaluations with conclusions about dissimulation are sometimes strengthened by the inclusion of these alternatives and the reasons why they are not compelling.

Standardized measures, such as the SIRS, can provide specific probability estimates that a particular presentation is feigned. For example, three or more SIRS primary scales in the probable range reflects a very high probability (.98) of feigning. With such data, alternative explanations are unlikely to be viable. Although less clear with the MMPI-2 because of the variability in cut scores, extreme elevations on validity indicators (e.g., raw $F > 30$) with an unelevated *VRIN* can also signal a high likelihood of feigning.

Below-chance performance on SVT provides the most compelling evidence of feigning and the virtual exclusion of other explanations. When a sufficient number of trials are given and the scores are markedly below persons with *no* ability (i.e., chance performance), the likelihood of feigning is maximized. Although other factors may be present (e.g., fatigue and depression), they are insufficient to produce these abysmal results.

Hybrid Styles of Dissimulation

An important task in the clinical determination of dissimulation is whether a patient presenting with a mixed response style should be considered as a hybrid style or an ambiguous clinical presentation. The clinician must be careful not to overinterpret contradictory findings, particularly when the indicators are gathered from distinct sources of clinical data. Two conditions under which diagnostic conclusions regarding hybrid styles may be justified are (1) on circumscribed issues and (2) within specified time periods. An example of circumscribed issues would be the assessment of a suspected child molester who appeared open and honest in the description of his day-to-day functioning, with the notable exception of any discussion of pedophilia or other paraphilias. Depending on the quality of the clinical data, the clinician might well conclude that the patient has an honest/defensive response style and provide a thorough description of what is meant by this term.

The second condition would relate to specific periods. Borrowing from forensic assessments, in occasional personal injury evaluations, the patient is seen as defensive regarding his or her functioning prior to the injury (i.e., no problems at all) and malingering following the injury. Such clinical presentation would be characterized as a defensive/malingering response style requiring careful explanation to the referral source. However, many persons involved in personal injury cases appear to polarize their perspectives (i.e., the untroubled past vs. the problem-ridden present; Rogers, 1995). Care must be taken to differentiate this common process of polarization from deliberate attempts to conceal the past and fabricate current psychopathology.

The general guideline for addressing such clinical ambiguities is that when any substantial doubt exists, yet motivation is unclear, the case should be labeled "unreliable." Furthermore, when the clinician is convinced that the patient is deliberately distorting his or her self-report, if not clearly malingering, defensive, or irrelevant, the clinician may characterize this as *dissimulation*. Hybrid response styles should be reserved for cases in which the clinical data are internally consistent and understandable either with respect to circumscribed issues or specific periods.

Reporting Dissimulation

Chapter 1 provides three gradations of malingering and defensiveness: mild, moderate, and severe. In synthesizing the clinical data, the clinician should attempt to describe the patient's malingering or defensiveness in terms of its severity. Such terms should be reserved for assessment cases in which the distortions consistently meet these criteria. Table 18.8 presents the three gradations of malingering and defensiveness, with sample descriptions for their inclusion in clinical reports.

The clinician must decide, for the purposes of synthesizing clinical data into a relevant report, what observations of the patient's response style should be included. As noted earlier, the clinical relevance of a patient's dissimulative style must be examined with reference to the referral question. With certain referral questions, discussion of the response style may have little direct bearing on the referral question, and therefore the clinician would have the option of briefly reporting or withholding his or her clinical observations. In the majority of cases, however, the patient's dissimulative style is relevant to the referral question, diagnosis, and capacity to form a therapeutic relationship. In such cases, the clinician should describe the patient's response style, including its severity. Although clinicians are encouraged to use the terms employed throughout this book, such terms are in no way a substitution for a thorough description of the patient's response style and its relevance to the assessment. The clinician must address the patient's deliberateness, type of distortion, and degree of distortion. In supporting his or her diagnostic conclusions, the clinician should provide specific

TABLE 18.8. Reporting Dissimulation: A Sampling of Descriptive Statements

A. Mild dissimulation (malingering or defensiveness)
1. Although minor distortions were observed in the patient's presentation, these are expected, given the context of the evaluation.
2. Although the patient manifested a slight tendency to minimize (or amplify) his or her self-report, no major distortions were observed.
3. Although some variations were noted in the patient's self-report, they have no (or little) bearing on diagnosis and disposition.

B. Moderate malingering
1. Clinical findings clearly indicate that the patient was exaggerating (and/or fabricating) his or her psychological impairment. This was observed in . . . (descriptive examples).
2. The patient has fabricated several important symptoms including . . . (descriptive examples); these symptoms have direct bearing on the patient's diagnosis and disposition.
3. The patient has evidenced a moderate degree of malingering as observed in . . . (descriptive examples). This attempt to manipulate the evaluation raises some concern about motivation for treatment.
4. The patient's self-report appears to be exaggerated (and/or fabricated) with . . . (descriptive examples). Difficulty in assessing the patient's motivation leaves unanswered what is his or her intended goal; the unresolved diagnosis is between factitious disorder and malingering.

C. Severe malingering
1. The patient is attempting to present himself or herself as severely disturbed by fabricating many symptoms including . . . (descriptive examples).
2. The patient has evidenced severe malingering by presenting . . . (strategies of malingering, e.g., "rare and improbable symptoms, uncorroborated by clinical observation"). Most notable examples of fabrication are . . . (descriptive examples).

D. Moderate defensiveness
1. Clinical findings clearly indicate that the patient was minimizing (and/or denying) his or her psychological impairment. The defensiveness was observed in . . . (descriptive examples).
2. The patient has denied several important symptoms including . . . (descriptive examples); these denied symptoms have direct bearing on the patient's diagnosis and disposition.
3. The patient has evidenced a moderate degree of defensiveness as observed in . . . (descriptive examples). Such defensiveness is fairly common in patients being assessed for treatment.

E. Severe defensiveness
1. The patient is attempting to present him- or herself as well adjusted by denying many observed symptoms including . . . (descriptive examples).
2. The patient has evidenced severe defensiveness by presenting . . . (strategies of defensiveness, e.g., "denial of everyday problems, endorsement of overly positive attributes, and denial of psychological impairment despite overwhelming clinical data to the contrary"). Most notable examples are . . . (descriptive examples).
3. The patient's self-report includes the denial of any psychiatric difficulties, despite convincing evidence of . . . (DSM-IV diagnosis). This severe defensiveness raises some concern about motivation for treatment.

examples, preferably employing direct quotes from the patient. In summary, the clinical report should include a detailed description of how the patient is responding, and how this response style relates to both diagnostic issues and the referral question.

CONCLUSION

The strength of clinical assessment in the evaluation of malingering and defensiveness remains chiefly in the use of well-validated individual measures (see, e.g., Borg, Connor, & Landis, 1995). The synthesis of these measures must take into account validation of each measure for the purpose of assessing dissimulation. As noted in other diagnostic issues (Sechrest, 1963), the accuracy of clinical judgment does not improve incrementally with the number of measures employed. However, discriminant models have proven effective in maximizing hit rates and reducing redundant and potentially irrelevant data in the clinical determination of malingering and defensiveness.

A review of clinical methods by the four criteria of susceptibility, detection, detection—coached, and interpretability delineates clearly the strengths and limitations in our current knowledge of dissimulation. Perhaps the weakest link of this decision process is in establishing the intention and motivation of the patient. As noted in Chapter 2, the degree of consciousness and deliberateness can only be clearly understood when presented in a consistent and unambiguous manner. In less obvious cases, the clinician is compelled to describe the suspected dissimulation and discuss openly the alternative diagnoses.

The assessment of response styles continues to be an essential component of clinical assessment. Although challenging to assess, the patient's presentation deserves our attention. The evaluation of malingering and defensiveness has become increasingly sophisticated during the last decade. Psychologists and other mental health professionals must employ the same degree of thoroughness in the assessment of malingering and defensiveness as they would in establishment of any diagnosis. Their clinical reports should include not only the diagnostic conclusions regarding patient's response style, but also provide the basis of this determination. Assessment methods must be delineated and the resulting conclusions framed in patient data (scales and specific examples, preferably quotes). The relevance of the response style, as well as its severity, should be related to the referral question. Unsupported and insupportable conclusions regarding dissimulation represent substandard practice, given the importance of such assessments to the diagnosis and disposition of psychiatric patients.

NOTES

1. Pankratz and Binder (Chapter 11) have chosen to refer to symptom validity testing (SVT) by a less-descriptive term, "forced-choice testing." Because this latter term has several meanings unrelated to dissimulation, the other authors and I prefer SVT.

2. A potential advantage would be the use of correlated pairs with unrelated (i.e., neither same, similar, or opposite) content. Even sophisticated persons that attempt to foil the test by

appearing too confused to respond consistently would have trouble recognizing this strategy. At present, we do not know whether an *intentional attempt* to invalidate the test by responding inconsistently is reflected in a combination of (1) unremarkable scores on correlated pairs of related content and (2) highly atypical scores on correlated pairs of unrelated content.

3. The answers must also be reviewed for the proportion of "trues"; indiscriminant endorsement of "true" responses may result in extreme elevations on Scales *7, 8,* and *9*.

4. As indirect evidence, Logan, Reuterfors, Bohn, and Clark (1984) found that 14.3% of the persons threatening the President were motivated by the desire for institutionalization. The involvement of the Secret Service apparently assisted inpatient hospitalization, whereas feigned homicidal ideation toward ordinary citizens might not produce the desired result.

5. More often, students present at our university clinic with the clearly stated objective (e.g., "I don't want to take math") but no apparent attempt to feign.

6. Use of typical cutting scores often produce an unacceptable proportion of false positives. However, a few malingerers produce such extreme elevations on multiple indices that likelihood of a misclassification is remote.

19

Researching Dissimulation

RICHARD ROGERS, Ph.D.

Research methodology for the assessment of response styles has become more firmly established since the publication of the first edition. In particular, considerable attention currently is paid to simulation research in an effort to improve its external validity. For instance, simulation studies carefully gauge whether instructional sets for simulators correspond to real-world situations. Other considerations include the use of tangible incentives, warnings regarding the detection of dissimulation, and the provision of relevant clinical information. Moreover, a concerted effort has been made in the selection of clinical comparison groups by selecting either diagnostically heterogeneous samples for improved generalizability or particular diagnostic groups for specialized investigations. What was described in the first edition as a bridgeable division between clinical practice and applied research has narrowed considerably.

An important element in the integration of clinical practice and applied research is offering researchers an opportunity to grapple with the clinical issues facing practitioners. Often the research questions posed by the academic community, although of intrinsic interest, do not adequately address the realities of clinical practice. For example, I see no need for additional research to demonstrate, yet again, that nearly all measures are susceptible to malingering and defensiveness (see Rogers, 1984b). Studies should instead be focused on constructive approaches to the assessment of dissimulation under conditions similar to those faced by clinicians. By outlining these relevant clinical issues, an invitation is extended for more applied research to solidify the foundation of our knowledge for the assessment of malingering and deception.

This chapter serves two primary purposes. First, the chapter examines the current research designs and methodology. This portion of the chapter provides major sections on the elements of dissimulation research and a delineation of research models. Second, the chapter pays close attention to unresolved clinical issues and grapples with methodological advances and fundamental questions.

ELEMENTS OF DISSIMULATION RESEARCH

Despite the rich diversity of research methodology and objectives in the study of dissimulation, common elements can be found in most research. Such elements include instructions, preparation/participation, incentives, standardization of measures, and debriefing. The emphasis of this section will be on the commonalities among research methods. Dissimilarities will be subsequently addressed in the individual examination of specific research designs.

Instructions

Simulation studies rely heavily on the use of instructions to create discrete experimental conditions. In spite of their importance, instructions, as described in many research articles, are brief and nonspecific. Participants simply may be asked to appear "mentally ill" or "well adjusted." How these instructions are interpreted, or whether they are considered seriously, remain unanswered empirical questions.

Six elements must be considered in construction of experimental instructions with respect to dissimulation (Rogers, Cruise, & Sewell, 1996). These elements are delineated as follows:

Comprehensibility

The overriding issue is whether participants have a clear understanding of what is expected of them. Beyond verbal recall, can they grasp the true nature of the task and their role?

Specificity

The instructions must be sufficiently explicit that researchers will be able to make a meaningful interpretation of the resulting data. Of course, circumstances do occur in which a proportion of persons engages in a global, indiscriminant response style (e.g., denial of any faults when applying to be adoptive parents). In such atypical cases, more global instructions may parallel real-world applications. With highly specific instructions, care must be taken that participants can understand complex instructions and competently apply them in their research participation.

Contextuality

Many studies offer participants a scenario or choice of scenarios in an attempt to improve external validity. The inclusion of scenarios likely will limit the generalizability of results. For instance, instructions on defensiveness probably will be interpreted differently if the circumstances involve a suicide attempt with street drugs as part of (1) a police investigation or (2) a teenager residing at home. These examples illustrate a related problem: Can the participants identify with the scenarios? If not, the scenarios *dimin-*

ish rather than *augment* the external validity. I strongly recommend that debriefing questions address participants' experience and knowledge of experimental scenarios so that differences among participants can be investigated.

Relevance

Data from research participants may have limited generalizability simply because these individuals trivialized their involvement as a necessary chore (e.g., extra credit for routine participation). Several empirically untested possibilities include (1) heightening the relevance and (2) challenging the participants. For example, research on malingering might emphasize the magnitude of the problem, especially the tax dollars (including the participant's) spent on bogus disorders and the subsequent curtailment of health services available to the participant and his or her family. Alternatively, participants could be challenged to see if they are skilled or adept enough to "beat" a test.

Motivation

Motivation, while taking into account the relevance of the simulation task, must also grapple with external incentives that are frequently present in applied settings. For the job applicant, the incentive is readily apparent and heartfelt. How can studies of dissimulation mirror the importance and immediacy of securing a desirable position? Likewise, parents in child-custody evaluations may dramatically limit their self-disclosure and attempt to enhance their social desirability in an effort to secure favorable custody decisions. The motivation to maintain one's family may well exceed any incentive available to researchers. Two aspects of incentives must be differentiated: the *type* of incentive from the *magnitude* of the incentive. Researchers are typically limited on both dimensions.

Credibility and the assumed motivation to appear credible are posited as powerful incentives for actual dissimulators. Not only is the loss of credibility likely to be associated with failure to achieve the goals of dissimulation, but this loss may result in very negative social consequences. For example, a borderline patient that feigns a bogus suicide attempt (e.g., no drugs were ingested in an "overdose") loses not only the immediate goal (e.g., hospitalization and medical attention) but also may jeopardize future treatment, funding associated with disability status, and credibility among health care professionals and fellow patients. A criminal defendant feigning insanity places his or her future, if not life, at risk, since an insanity plea includes an admission of the crime.

Can research capture the negative social consequences of a bungled dissimulation? Designs might include some form of public disapproval (e.g., publishing failed attempts by research participants; see Patrick & Iacono, 1986). However, such studies must grapple with both the troubling ethical concerns and the untested possibility of participant attrition.

Believability

More recent dissimulation research typically includes an admonition to the participants to make their presentations believable. Participants commonly are warned that the test or procedure has indicators of dissimulation. Thus, the task becomes clearly defined: Dissimulation must be sufficiently believable to elude detection.

Preparation and Participation

Studies of dissimulation are often limited in their clinical usefulness by minimal levels of preparation and questionable commitment by research participants. Persons are rarely given any preparation time or opportunities to plan their strategy of deception. Researchers may wish to plan a preparation time and give participants specific tasks to complete, such as writing down the strategies they intend to employ. In addition, the provision of preparation materials may enhance participants' overall performance, including both their level of involvement and their effectiveness.

Preparation materials must be easy to comprehend and highly pertinent to the dissimulation task. For instance, presenting participants with unedited sections of the fourth edition of the *Diagnostic and Statistical Manual of Mental Disorders* (DSM–IV) is unlikely to enhance their understanding of a feigned disorder. Indeed, reading unfamiliar technical terms about sophisticated psychological constructs may lead to frustration and disaffiliation from the study's objectives. A possible innovation would be to test participants immediately following the preparation period regarding their understanding of the supplied materials.

Deception studies often cast clinicians and lay judges into the roles of passive observers (Rogers, 1987). Brief videotaped segments are presented so that observers can make judgments regarding the veracity of one or more persons. While maintaining an admirable degree of experimental rigor, this methodology does not allow for the study of either interactions or clinicians' own decision processes in evaluating the malingering or defensiveness of a particular patient. Research designs could be devised, however, that would allow for much higher levels of participation at an acceptable trade-off in experimental rigor. One alternative is to institute pseudo-naturalistic studies in which research participants present themselves in actual diagnostic settings. Although this design is not without methodological problems (Spitzer, 1974) and ethical concerns, certainly the research by Rosenhan (1973) attested to the usefulness of this technique in assessing clinicians' ability to identify malingerers, based on their customary assessment methods. A variation of the pseudo-naturalistic design would be the use of highly trained confederates that could offer relatively standardized presentations while being assessed by different clinicians. In this design, the confederates would be thoroughly prepared regarding their personal and psychiatric history and current psychological problems; this approach would allow the participating clinicians to employ an array of clinical skills in the assessment of dissimulation. With sufficient samples, both the effectiveness of particular clinicians the relative efficacy of their respective methods could be ascertained.

Research might also present videotaped assessments conducted by experienced clinicians that represent a range of diagnostic styles and dissimulating patients (Resnick, 1987). These videotapes would then be shown to samples of clinicians (1) to test their overall ability to identify dissimulators, and (2) to determine which diagnostic style is most effective at making such an assessment. Although not generalizable to clinicians' own diagnostic methods, the design has two distinct advantages over pseudo-naturalistic research: (1) standardization of experimental conditions and (2) capacity for group administration. A sophisticated variant of this design is found in on-line medical education, whereby the clinician can request additional information to facilitate his or her decision process; both standardization of clinical data and active participation of the clinicians are achievable.

Coaching

Coaching is an element of preparation. I have purposefully set coaching apart because of its importance to dissimulation and possible ethical concerns. Coaching involves the education of simulators to facilitate their avoidance of detection. As noted by Rogers, Bagby, and Chakraborty (1993), the unspoken assumption of much dissimulation research is that malingerers and defensive persons will not prepare and remain naive to the purposes of testing. I think this assumption is untenable for two reasons. First, persons being evaluated must give informed consent based on the nature and goals of the evaluation. Second, these same persons have easy access to books that describe psychological tests, including descriptions of validity scales.

Two distinct strategies have been employed in coaching studies; these involve providing information about (1) genuine disorders and (2) detection strategies. Current research data (see Lamb, Berry, Wetter, & Baer, 1994; Rogers, Bagby, & Chakraborty, 1993; Wetter, Baer, Berry, & Reynolds, 1994) suggest that information about disorders is relatively ineffective, whereas information about detection strategies is very useful (see also Baer, Wetter, & Berry, 1995). These findings are intuitively appealing. Since bona fide disorders often manifest heterogenous clinical profiles, the fabrication of a "genuine" profile is unnecessary. However, the validity scales are discriminating between actual and feigned disorders. Therefore, information about detection strategies substantially affects detection rates. An interesting question is whether these findings generalize to defensiveness with the provision of analogous information on (1) adjustment and (2) detection strategies.

A small controversy has simmered over the ethical implications of coached research, particularly as it relates to the subsequent publication of results. Institutional review boards may scrutinize research proposals that aim at educating persons in feigning as possibly offering skills to be used in future fraudulent activity. The publication of coached studies poses another dilemma: Does adequately explaining the procedures (i.e., coached feigning conditions) compromise test security? Rogers, Bagby, and Chakraborty (1993), following the accepted standards for describing experimental conditions, included paragraph descriptions of each detection strategy implicit in commonly used validity scales. Subsequent commentaries (Ben-Porath, 1994; Berry et al., 1994) have underscored to varying degrees the potential misuse of this information.

In hindsight, I believe these criticisms have some merit and would not publish such detailed descriptions in the future. However, these criticisms truly underscore the weakness of the measures in question. If a 2-minute overview of detection strategies is sufficient to lower dramatically validity scale elevations, how can we ever feel safe in using them? I also wonder if a description in the appendix of a professional journal is more accessible than widely available texts that include not only descriptions of the strategies but also enumerate which items are potentially bogus. In other words, this information is accessible, whether or not it is described in professional journals.

I am concerned with misplaced efforts to protect fragile secrets. The accessibility of information continues to grow exponentially and is unlikely to be curtailed, especially when the potential stakes of dissimulation remain so high. My personal view is that the goal of coached studies should be to develop robust strategies that can withstand rudimentary knowledge of their general intent.

An important alternative to fragile, simple secrets (e.g., primacy effect in learning tasks) and their vulnerability to coaching is the development of *intricate strategies*. One intricate strategy that I find particularly appealing is multiple tasks. The purpose of multiple tasks is to provide all respondents with a caution against dissimulation and a description of at least two detection strategies (i.e., multiple tasks). The multiple tasks ask the simulator to consider two (or possibly more) detection strategies simultaneously. These strategies require the simulator to attempt to accommodate seemingly incompatible concepts (e.g., performance curve and reaction time). As an illustration, I have included a sample of instructions for feigned cognitive impairment:

> Please do your very best job on this test. For the test to be accurate, you have to try your best. *Warning*: Every now and then, someone tries to fool the test. He or she pretends to have problems that really don't exist. The test has safeguards against faking. First, the test keeps tracks of the answers you get wrong to see if they are easy items or hard items. Second, the test keeps tracks of how many seconds you use on items. If you take the same amount of time on easy and hard items, you are not trying your best. Third, the test looks at your wrong answers to see if you make the same kind of mistakes as people that really have problems.

Incentives

Rogers, Harrell, and Liff (1993) reviewed the role of incentives in malingering research. They found that few studies have directly compared the effect of incentives on simulators' performance. An unexpected finding by Wilhelm, Franzen, Grinvalds, and Dews (1991) was that undergraduates produced more extreme scores on several cognitive measures when offered a $20 incentive as compared to those without an incentive. Logically, the extremeness of scores increased the likelihood of detection. In other words, the desire for the award apparently increased the *motivation* to feign, possibly at the expense of believability. Similarly, Bernard (1990) had an incentive (i.e., the two best feigners received $50) and nonincentive (i.e., no rewards) groups feigning cognitive impairment. In contrast to Wilhelm et al., he found a mixed pattern of results: Participants with incentives performed worse on three, and better on two subtests than their nonincentive counterparts. Obviously, further research is needed both to clarify the aforementioned results and examine their generalizability to other forms of malingering.

The effects of incentives on defensiveness remain unexplored. As noted previously, many of the potential rewards (securing a favorable position and custody of one's children) cannot be paralleled in dissimulation research. An interesting research possibility would be to assess the effects of incentives on defensiveness in comparison to social desirability and impression management. For example, job applicants, attempting to make a favorable impression, may be more detectable on measures of social desirability than defensiveness.

The previous discussion of motivation (see Instructions section) provides a practical overview of incentives and their potential role in dissimulation research. The following elements should be considered:

Magnitude of the Incentive

Simply put, is the incentive really an incentive? If the goal of winning is emphasized, then even symbolic rewards may suffice. Financially successful persons can become highly motivated by negligible rewards (e.g., penny poker) that have symbolic value (e.g., "best" gambler). On the other hand, research sites do exist in which small monetary incentives are likely to represent a tangible reward. For example, correctional settings typically reimburse inmates at a nominal rate. In such settings, $5–$10 incentives may equal a week's pay (see, e.g., Bickart, Meyer, & Connell, 1991; Connell, 1991; Kropp, 1992; Rogers, Kropp, Bagby, & Dickens, 1992).

Type of Incentive

Monetary incentives are the most easily implemented rewards in most research settings. Would offering nonmonetary rewards produce either (1) different results or (2) increase the external validity of the results? For example, would a weekend getaway at a nice hotel more closely approximate the "better life" sought in personal injury fraud than the typical financial incentive?

Probability of the Incentive

Dissimulation research is typically underfunded in terms of financial incentives. Although some researchers offer very modest incentives (e.g., $5) to each simulator, other investigators use a selection procedure (lottery system or "best" simulator) to provide more substantial rewards (e.g., $50–$100) to a very small number of simulators. We simply do not know which alternative (high probability of a low incentive or low probability of a high incentive) provides the greater motivation.

Negative Incentives

Researchers studying incentives may wish to consider the use of negative incentives to parallel real-world applications. For example, researchers could offer credit simply for participation in series of studies. The credit would be "taken away" if the participants were detected. Naturally, informed consent would have to delineate these conditions, especially if more credit could be lost than gained from participation. A variation of this design with few ethical constraints would be research whereby participants select for themselves different conditions ranging from high-risk/high-gain to low-risk/low-gain.

Debriefing

Debriefing is often employed in dissimulation research. First and foremost, debriefing can serve as a manipulation check to ensure that participants understand and comply with the experimental instructions. Three related elements must be considered: *recall, comprehension,* and *compliance*. More specifically, researchers must ascertain whether the participants remember the instructions and what they understand them to mean. Although vulnerable to social desirability, some effort should be made to determine the extent to which participants follow the instructions. As a corollary to comprehension, researchers may also wish to discern the *relevance* of the instructions. If the instructional set involves circumstances or psychological conditions completely alien to the participant, his or her performance will be severely constrained.

The manipulation check can also be applied to preparation materials supplied to research participants. Like the instructions, investigators can assess participants' recall and comprehension of these materials. If materials are not remembered or adequately understood, then efforts to inform the participants suffer accordingly. At present, dissimulation research commonly overlooks this critical component of debriefing.

Beyond manipulation checks, debriefing can be used to assess (1) motivation to succeed and (2) limits on participation. Participants' motivation may be affected by the incentive and the strength of their desire (depending on the instructions) to appear credible and elude detection. Other factors possibly limit involvement in the study. Participants may believe that they are unable to suppress their "true" selves or feel less capable to do to because of moral reasons (e.g., it is immoral to deceive; a good liar is a bad person), psychological problems (e.g., emotional interference with following the instructions), or distrust of the experimenter (e.g., the results will reflect negatively on the participant).

Researchers have also used the debriefing phase to survey participants' beliefs about their success at dissimulation. Results have varied across studies. For example, Kropp (1992) found that 90% of simulators on the Structured Interview of Reported Symptoms (SIRS) believed they were successful; this belief was unrelated to their ability to elude detection. In contrast, Gothard (1993) found that 24% believed they had successfully feigned on the SIRS; again, the belief was unrelated to the performance. The relationship between the perceived innocuousness of a measure and its effectiveness at detecting dissimulation deserves formal investigation.

I believe that much more attention should be paid to the debriefing phase of dissimulation studies. Table 19.1 provides an elaborate model that might serve to standardize elements of debriefing inquiries. Researchers will need to be selective in their choice of what elements to include, although recall, comprehension, and compliance are essential. Moreover, some attention should be paid to participants' motivation to succeed and limits on their involvement.

TABLE 19.1. An Overview of Debriefing Instructions in Dissimulation Research

Facets of the research	Example questions
A. Instructional sets	
1. Recall of instructions	What were you told to do? What were your instructions?
2. Comprehension of instructions	What do these instructions mean to you?
3. Compliance with instructions	Some people always do what they are told, while others prefer to improvise. . . . Which do you prefer? No one is perfect. What percentage of the time did you *carefully* follow instructions?
4. Relevance of the instructions	Have you ever been faced with a situation like the one described in the instructions? Could you relate to this scenario? Of course this was just an experiment; could you imagine yourself doing what you were asked to do, if the situation warranted it?
B. Preparation	
1. Preparation effort	What did you do during the preparation time?
2. Knowledge of preparation materials	What do you remember from the preparation materials?
3. Relevance of preparation materials	How did the preparation materials help you?
C. Motivation to succeed	
1. Importance of the incentive	Did you try any harder because there was an incentive?
2. Magnitude of the incentive	In this study the rewards were fairly small, how much _____ (e.g., money) would it take for you to put forward your very best effort?
3. Belief in the incentive	Some people worry that researchers make promises, like rewards, for the sake of the experiment, but won't really follow through. Do you have any worries that the reward might be just a gimmick?
4. Credibility	Were you concerned that the experimenter might not believe you?
5. Detection of dissimulation	Were you aware that there were items on the _____ (e.g., test) designed to trip you up? Can you give us any specific examples?
D. Limits to participation	
1. Self disclosure	Despite your efforts to appear different than you actually are, how much of the real you showed through?
2. Morality	Were there any moral or ethical reasons why you didn't participate fully in the study? What were they?
3. Emotional interference	Sometimes when people are going through a difficult time, they find it hard to really participate; did this happen to you?
4. Fear of success	Were you concerned that if you succeeded at fooling the test, this might mean that you are good at deceiving others?
5. Purpose of the study	Were you worried that the purpose of the study was something different than you were told?
E. Other issues associated with deception	
1. Perceived success	How successful were you at fooling the _____ (e.g., test)?
2. Experience with dissimulation	How good are you at fooling others?
3. Types of deception	Some people are better at hiding their feelings while others do a better job at keeping their past private; which fits you?

CURRENT RESEARCH MODELS

Dissimulation research is composed of four basic designs: case study, simulation, known-groups, and differential prevalence. Two competing dimensions, important in reviewing these designs, are *clinical relevance* and *experimental rigor*. In certain respects, these dimensions are inversely related, so that it often infeasible to achieve high levels of clinical relevance and experimental rigor within the same study. However, exceptions may occur, particularly when known-groups comparisons are augmented with sophisticated laboratory procedures (e.g., the use of hair analysis to verify denied substance abuse; see Chapter 7). Despite the likely trade-off between relevance and rigor, most research on dissimulation could be improved on one or both of these dimensions. Thus, an objective of this section is to review current research designs and to offer recommendations with respect to both clinical relevance and experimental rigor.

Case Study Approaches

Case study design in psychiatry and clinical psychology has fallen into disfavor over the last several decades. Despite past debates over the relative merits of idiographic and nomothetic research models (e.g., Dukes, 1965; Eysenck, 1954; Marceil, 1977), clinical journals have opted for much greater emphasis on nomothetic research than on single case descriptions. Insistent demands for greater experimental rigor (e.g., Campbell & Stanley, 1966) and the decreased popularity of psychoanalytical thought are largely responsible for this change. Notwithstanding its diminished role in clinical research, the real value of the case study approach is in providing a rich panoply of clinical observations unfettered by research protocols (Scriven, 1976). Such detailed clinical observations on a highly relevant topic offer two decided advantages over other research designs. First, case studies generate a variety of relevant hypotheses to be tested by more rigorous designs (Cook, Levitou, & Shadish, 1985; Davison & Lazarus, 1994). Second, case studies represent the only practical design in the study of rare syndromes such as Munchausen-by-proxy syndrome.

Case study approaches to dissimulation should therefore be encouraged in order to further these relevant goals. For example, the diagnosis of Munchausen syndrome was originally stimulated through a series of case studies initiated by Asher (1951), which eventually led to its current syndromal status (Stern, 1980). A prime example of how a single case study may stimulate further applied research and improvements in clinical practice is observed in the development of symptom validity testing (SVT). Pankratz, Fausti, and Peed (1975) devised this approach to assess the purported loss of hearing in a 27-year-old man. Additional research based on this single case study has led to a highly useful technique in detecting individuals feigning intellectual and neuropsychological deficits (Pankratz, 1979; see also Chapter 10). More recently, Frederick, Carter, and Powel (1995) reported several cases in which they attempted to broaden the clinical applications of the SVT to assessing purported loss of personal memory.

Case study approaches to dissimulation have focused almost exclusively on malingering. Early case studies (e.g., Davidson, 1949; Ossipov, 1944) as well as more recent work (Hay, 1983; Ritson & Forrest, 1970; Sadow & Suslick, 1961; Wachspress, Berenberg, & Jacobson, 1953) have a severe methodological limitation in that they lack any independent criterion for establishing dissimulation. In other words, the clinicians who evaluated these cases employed detailed observations of dissimulating patients to make the determination of malingering. They subsequently reversed the process in providing the same detailed observations that could be used to characterize malingerers. This circularity could be easily modified by employing clinical staff, masked to the diagnostic issues regarding dissimulation, to make standardized observations of the cases. Similarly, the degree of confidence in the diagnosis of malingering or defensiveness could be improved if the classification were based on two independent evaluations. These two procedures combined would offer some assurance that (1) the dissimulation was reliably established, and (2) the clinical observations were not confounded by interviewer bias.

A second methodological issue involves sampling. Available case studies typically are limited to psychiatric inpatients suspected of malingering. Although these samples are, by necessity, nonrandom, it is possible that nonmalingering comparison groups could be employed with patients matched for sociodemographic background and psychiatric history. The advantages of such comparison groups would be to assess, on a preliminary basis, whether the suspected dissimulators' presentations differed significantly from psychiatric patients with atypical presentations (e.g., Hay, 1983). For example, Pope, Jonas, and Jones (1982) studied 9 patients presenting with factitious psychosis and severe character pathology; the ideal clinical comparison group would be genuinely psychotic patients with similar character pathology. Otherwise, researchers are uncertain whether the "factitial characteristics" differentially classify factitious patients from genuine patients with Axis I–Axis II interactions. In addition, other samples of suspected dissimulators, including outpatients and forensic patients, could also be studied to improve generalizability. These and other methodological issues are summarized in Table 19.2.

TABLE 19.2. Case Study Approaches to Dissimulation

Methodological issues	Research practices Current	Proposed
1. Sampling	Nonrandom psychiatric inpatients suspected of malingering	In addition, outpatients and forensic patients
2. Comparison groups	Not employed	Matched comparison groups should be employed
3. Independent criterion	Rarely employed	Evaluators masked to the suspected response style
4. Standardized measures	Psychological testing	In addition, structured interviews and histories
5. Corroborative data	Variable	Independent observations of clinicians not involved in the assessment
6. Study of admitters	Clinical presentation	In addition, study their strategies for dissimulation

Two additional methodological issues are worthy of comment. First, case studies could be improved by further standardizing the assessment procedures. In addition to reporting psychological test results, such studies might also include structured diagnostic interviews (see Rogers, 1995) for both Axis I (e.g., Schedule of Affective Disorders and Schizophrenia [SADS] and Structured Clinical Interview for DSM-III-R [SCID]) and Axis II (e.g., Personality Disorder Examination [PDE] and Structured Interview for DSM-III Personality Disorders [SIDP]). Such data, along with additional corroborative information, would allow for a more systematic investigation of the suspected dissimulation. Second, case studies could be focused on "admitters" (i.e., persons who acknowledge their past dissimulation).[1] One potential avenue of research would be to compare their performance before and after admitting their deception. For example, differences between phallometric results before and after conceding sexual deviance might be a profitable resource in developing new methods for the detection of denied paraphiliac behavior.

Simulation Studies

Simulation or analogue research on dissimulation implements a quasi-experimental design with participants randomly assigned to experimental and control conditions. Participants in the experimental conditions are given instructions to dissimulate, whereas those in the control group are given standard instructions for the assessment measures and are often asked to be honest and forthright in their responding. Such research generally does not address the critical issue of whether a measure can distinguish dissimulating persons from other persons (1) likely to be found in that setting and (2) faced with similar circumstances. For example, most studies of malingering employ nonclinical samples (i.e., persons presumed not to have mental disorders) in a nonthreatening situation. Differences found in simulation research between experimental and control groups are, by themselves, inapplicable to actual settings. Simply put, how do we know whether "bogus" psychotic symptoms would not be found in persons with genuine schizophrenia? Or, that most legitimate patients would not respond differently when placed in adversarial or hostile circumstances than when voluntarily receiving mental health services?

The crucial matter for simulation research is generalizability. For malingering, most research is designed to assess feigning in persons without mental disorders. Therefore, clinical samples typically are not used for random assignment to experimental and control conditions. In such cases, the simulation design must be augmented by the addition of nonrandom *clinical comparison* groups. Care must be taken that clinical comparison groups represent symptom patterns and level of impairment that are comparable to clinical settings in which dissimulation is suspected. Obviously, the use of clinical comparison samples increases the clinical relevance at a modest cost to experimental rigor.

Persons with mental disorders may also malinger. The simulation design must be modified to address the specific question, "Can measures detect malingering in mentally disordered persons?" In this case, clinical samples must be randomly assigned to experimental and control conditions. Ideally, the use of four groups (i.e., clinical–

experimental, clinical–control, nonclinical–experimental, and nonclinical–control) could address the relative efficacy of detection methods for disordered and nondisordered samples.

Several issues must be considered in the use of clinical–experimental groups. First, if patients are severely impaired, their ability to follow conscientiously simulation instructions may be compromised.[2] In early research, Rogers (1988b) found that nearly half of psychiatric inpatients either did not remember or did not follow instructions to feign. In the same vein, some patients experiencing severe distress may encounter a ceiling effect. In other words, these patients perceive, at least from their viewpoint, extreme impairment and cannot imagine, let alone simulate, even greater impairment. As a parallel, test measures may also be limited by a ceiling effect. For example, patients with severe depression may not be able to feign on the Beck Depression Inventory, if they warrant close to the maximum score under honest instructions. As partial solutions, several methodological changes can be implemented: (1) debriefing to ensure memory, comprehension, and compliance with experimental instructions; (2) screening of persons in the clinical–experimental group, prior to their participation, to exclude patients in severe distress; and (3) selection of measures that do not have a circumscribed clinical range.

A different problem with generalizability commonly occurs in the study of defensiveness. Because participants are often selected in college or employment settings, many will not have any significant impairment. In contrast to malingering, many participants may experience a floor effect; they simply do not have any significant distress/impairment. Therefore, they are unable to respond defensively but may attempt an idealistic presentation in an effort to comply with experimental instructions. Such a presentation is unrealistically positive and, thus, may be relatively easy to detect. As a related issue, many individuals are aware of the stigmatization associated with mental disorders. Their characteristic response to unfamiliar researchers probing their mental health might be a defensive posture. Researchers need to screen participants to ensure that they currently experience some troubling psychological problems and to test their characteristic openness–defensiveness with respect to these problems.

One remedy to generalizability problems with studies of defensiveness is the use of a within-subjects design. For example, Cashel et al. (1995) examined clinical elevations of students and offenders on the Personality Assessment Inventory (PAI) under both honest and defensive instructions. They were able to assess changes in clinical elevations as well as characteristic defensiveness. Interestingly, their results revealed an ordering effect, with persons taking the PAI under honest instructions first having higher clinical scores. Conceivably, the use of defensiveness instructions first had a lasting influence, even though the two administrations were on separate days.

Simulation studies of social desirability and defensiveness have typically taken less care methodologically than parallel research on malingering. Many studies have not included cautionary instructions on believability, with information about the presence of scales to detect either social desirability or defensiveness. In addition, researchers apparently have assumed that participants would not need to be coached regarding the simulation of adjustment. Although this supposition probably has some justification in studies of nonclinical samples, it appears less defensible for persons with either severe disorders or chronic impairment. Moreover, malingering research clearly indicates that knowledge of detection strategies is a key element of successful feigning. Given this important finding, coached studies with knowledge of detection strategies clearly are needed for defensiveness and social desirability.

A second, virtually unexplored facet of simulation research is the interpretability of dissimulated results. For example, can we assume that a defensive person has psychological problems? If so, what are they? By the same token, can we conclude anything about a malingerer, besides the simple fact that he or she is feigning? The most frightening prospect is the assumption of mutual exclusivity: The presence of feigning precludes a mental disorder (Rogers, 1994). The solution is the development of correction formulas.

The challenge of the first edition for the development of correction formulas has gone unheeded. McKinley, Hathaway, and Meehl (1948) developed for the MMPI a "*K*-correction" formula to approximate the degree of impairment, taking into account the patient's degree of defensiveness. Now, more than four decades latter, few replication studies have been forthcoming (see McCrae et al., 1989; Yonge, 1966) while thousands of MMPI *K*-corrected profiles continue to be interpreted. Parallel efforts with the MMPI-A have met with limited success (see Alperin, Archer, & Coates, 1996). Research is also needed to establish an "*F*-correction" to determine genuine disorders among those feigning. Within-subjects simulation design appears well suited for the development of correction formulas. For malingering, patients could be administered the MMPI under standard and feigning instructions. Systematic differences could be explored and concomitant adjustments made in the interpretation of "invalid" profiles. For defensiveness, clinical samples could also be employed with similar strategies implemented. Despite the remarkable advances in dissimulation research, the absence of any systematic investigation on correction formulas is especially regrettable.

In summary, simulation research is the predominant design in the study of response styles. The great strength of this design is it experimental rigor, which is sometimes achieved at the expense of its clinical relevance. In Table 19.3, I summarize salient issues in simulation research that can improve its generalizability to real-world applications.

Methodological improvements in simulation research focus primarily on improving its clinical relevance and overall generalizability. Current sampling techniques involve random samples of usually nonpsychiatric participants in both experimental and control groups. This design can be augmented by the use of patients with mental disorders in experimental, control, and comparison groups. This modification would allow dissimulation research to address two important considerations: (1) How effectively can participants with mental disorders dissimulate? and (2) Do clinical decision rules work effectively for simulators with mental disorders? Debriefing and instructional sets were discussed extensively in prior sections. However, the stability of dissimulation remains to be explored. Some clinicians appear to assume almost a trait model of dissimulation (e.g., "once a malingerer, always a malingerer") and that patterns of dissimulation do not change. From a different perspective, clinicians may posit that

TABLE 19.3. Simulation or Analogue Designs for Dissimulation

Methodological issues	Research practices	
	Current	Proposed
1. Sampling	Random, usually nonpsychiatric participants	In addition, participants with mental disorders
2. Control groups	Usually normal individuals	In addition, comparison samples of psychiatric groups
3. Decision rules	Cutting scores for the MMPI, rare for other measures	Discriminant functions and/or cutting scores for all measures
4. Participants' compliance	Rarely have follow-up	Collect data on participants' compliance
5. Simulation instructions	Often general and vague	Make specific, emphasize a "believable" response style
6. Coaching instructions	Rarely used	Study both experimental conditions and knowledge of detection strategies
7. Participants' motivation	Usually no incentives to succeed	Incentives for successful dissimulation
8. Stability of dissimulation	Not assessed	Assess across time intervals and situations

differences between administrations signify some form of dissimulation. For example, Moses, Golden, Wilkening, McKay, and Ariel (1983) recommended repeat administrations of the Luria–Nebraska with inconsistencies seen as evidence of malingering; however, without knowing the expected variability found with genuine patients, clinicians are severely hampered in their interpretation of inconsistent results. This postulation requires investigations to establish differences found with bona fide patients on repeat administrations as compared to simulators.

Social Psychological Studies of Dissimulation

Social psychological studies on deception are a component of simulation research. I have discussed them separately, because they often include specific elements not found in other simulation studies. These studies typically address some form of deception that may range from suppressed emotions to deliberate misstatements. As a rule, these studies use untrained confederates who simulate deception while passive untrained observers render judgments about their honesty (e.g., Littlepage & Pineault, 1978; Maier & Thurber, 1968; Miller et al., 1981). With substantial modifications, these studies could be redesigned to increase their usefulness and applicability to clinical and other professional settings.

The clinical relevance of social psychological research could be greatly improved without substantively affecting its experimental rigor. The current practice of using only normal participants could be augmented with psychiatric patients in both honest and deceptive conditions. Moreover, experimental conditions could include trained persons, such as mental health professionals and persons coached in dissimulation. These modifications would allow researchers to address more closely the applicability of research findings to clinical settings (see Table 19.4).

Studies of deception could be enhanced by the use of mental health professionals as evaluators. This modification would allow researchers to address what effect, if any, professional training has on the detection of dissimulation. An important alteration in social psychological research would be the study of specific forms of dissimulation, namely, malingering and defensiveness. Unspecified deception has, at best, only limited relevance to the clinical and other professional contexts. In addition, social psychological methodology, when applied to clinical practice, should have as its goal the development of explicit decision rules that may be consistently applied in classifying dissimulative response styles.

Other proposed modifications in social psychological research would focus on the same goal of improving its relevance to professional practice. At present, evaluators are limited to brief periods of passive observation (Rogers, 1984b). Extensive or multiple observation periods would correspond more closely to clinical practice. Moreover, the format of the observed material could be altered so that the structure was similar to a diagnostic interview or psychological history. Such formats would parallel clinical assessment. Furthermore, the motivation of confederates and participants may play a determinative role in whether deception is detected. For example,

TABLE 19.4. Social Psychological Studies of Deception

Methodological issues	Research practices	
	Current	Proposed
1. Sampling—confederates	Normal participants	In addition, psychiatric patients and coached persons
2. Sampling—observers	Random; nonprofessionals	In addition, mental health professionals
3. Comparison groups	Normal participants	In addition, psychiatric patients and participants trained in dissimulation
4. Criterion studied	Unspecified deception	Specific styles of dissimulation
5. Decision rules	Not employed	Cutting scores for classifying response styles
6. Level of participation	Brief periods; passive observers	Extensive periods; some studies allowing interactions
7. Motivation	Variable for confederates and participants	Offer incentives for both deception and detection

DePaulo and her associates (DePaulo, Lanier, & Davis, 1983; DePaulo, Stone, & Lassiter, 1985) found that participants' motivation to deceive was an important factor in nonprofessionals' judgments regarding honesty/deception. She concluded that highly motivated participants were more successful at concealing their dishonesty and were less likely to be detected than their poorly motivated counterparts. Thus, the degree of motivation must be considered in applying social psychological studies to the clinical assessment of dissimulation.

An interesting application of confederates to professional practice involves a deviation from the typical social psychology experiment that has commonalities with Rosenhan's (1973) pseudo-naturalistic research. For malingering, confederates could be trained with a basic understanding of mental disorders and sent as clients to various clinical settings. Differences among clinical presentations (e.g., depression vs. psychosis), putative motivations (e.g., worker's compensation vs. special accommodations under the American Disability Act), and background history (e.g., antisocial vs. prosocial behavior) could be systematically studied. In addition, the ability of clinicians to detect feigning could be examined, based on their training and assessment methods.

Psychophysiological Studies

Laboratory methods sometimes embody an image of unmatched scientific objectivity. With respect to dissimulation, this image typically has only a sliver of truth. Laboratory procedures for the assessment of dissimulation may provide very precise measurements. Yet, even this precision may be illusory. Although the *measurement* of sexual arousal may be highly accurate, the *meaning* of this finding is not. First, persons without any known sexual deviations may evidence varying degrees of sexual arousal to atypical stimuli. Second, persons with paraphilias do not necessarily evidence deviant sexual arousal. Even when deviant sexual arousal is found, "precise" differences in sexual stimuli do not translate into specific deviations.

Deviant response patterns are likely to be interpreted differently, depending on the physiological method used. For defensiveness regarding paraphilac behavior, researchers have posited a "trait" model and typically assumed that denied sexual interests are indicative of characteristic sexual response patterns. In stark contrast, polygraphy research has postulated a "state" model and assumed that deception was generally situational. Both assumptions deserve further testing.

Much of the research on physiological measures has adopted known-groups comparison, which is described in the next section. However, simulation research is particularly useful for studying the effects of coaching, preparation, and countermeasures on the detection of dissimulation. Coaching and preparation correspond to other forms of simulation research. In contradistinction, countermeasures sometimes involve the use of chemicals (e.g., medications in polygraphy evaluations) or behavioral interventions designed to modify physiological responses (e.g., repeated masturbation prior to penile plethysmography). The effectiveness of these efforts deserves further inquiry.

Simulation studies may prove successful in determining the most efficacious methods of detecting dissimulation. As noted in Chapter 13, polygraphy is not a single, standardized measure but three separate major techniques with countless variations in administration. Comparative studies could assess the relative merit of each technique. Moreover, the decision process (e.g., human judgment vs. computer models) also could be evaluated. Similarly, the stimulus materials used in phallometric methods vary widely across laboratories. The comparative usefulness of different stimuli could be gauged.

Psychophysiological studies of dissimulation could be improved through the examination of specific populations. To what extent do mental disorders affect responses on the polygraph? Without sizable clinical samples, polygraphers have no way of knowing whether a deviant response in indicative of dishonesty or psychological impairment. Likewise, how do nonsexually violent individuals respond on the rape index and the aggression index? Clinical comparison groups are essential to establishing the discriminant validity of these indexes. Although previous research has occasionally compared "violent" offenders with others, no attempt has been made to match samples on the frequency or type of violent behavior (e.g., child molesters vs. physical abusers of children).

Table 19.5 summarizes current and proposed methodology for psychophysiological studies of dissimulation. The emphasis is twofold. First, increased generalizability is encouraged through sampling and comparison group modifications. Second, increased standardization is recommended with respect to procedures, decision rules, and the stability of these rules. These modifications are likely to improve both the clinical relevance and experimental rigor of psychophysiological studies.

Known-Groups Comparison

Known-groups comparisons are composed of two discrete and independent phases: (1) establishment of criterion groups (e.g., bona fide patients and malingerers) and (2) systematic analysis of similarities and dissimilarities between criterion groups. The

TABLE 19.5. Psychophysiological Approaches to Dissimulation

Methodological issues	Research practices	
	Current	Proposed
1. Sampling	Normal individuals and suspected offenders	In addition, psychiatric samples
2. Comparison groups	Rarely used in polygraphy	Compare groups across specific measures
3. Specific criterion	Usually unspecified deception	Specific styles of dissimulation
4. Decision rules	Variable	Cutting scores for classifying response styles
5. Standardized procedures	Typically in drug-assisted interviews; not in polygraphy	Standardize all phases of the study
6. Stability of dissimulation	Not assessed	Assess across time intervals and situations

primary challenge of known-groups comparisons is the first phase, namely the reliable and accurate classification of criterion groups. Because of this challenge, known-groups comparisons are relatively rare in dissimulation research.

Employment of known-groups comparisons addresses fully the clinical relevance of dissimulation research. First, the research typically is conducted in clinical or other professional settings where dissimulation is expected to occur. Second and more important, the persons engaging in dissimulation are doing so for real-world reasons. The generalizability of their findings, at least to a portion of dissimulating persons, is well established; they obviously have the necessary background, antecedent events, personality variables, and motivation to participate in dissimulation. As with any design, researchers must consider the representativeness of one dissimulating sample to the population of dissimulating persons. Although the combination of different samples dramatically improves the generalizability of known-groups comparisons, all investigations are limited to the unsuccessful (i.e., detected) persons.

The critical task in known-groups comparisons is the establishment of criterion groups. This task is generally reserved for highly trained experts (e.g., forensic psychologists and psychiatrists) and based on full evaluations. In this regard, Viglione, Fals-Stewart, and Moxham (1995) provide an instructive example of systematically determining suspected malingerers in a military setting through the implementation of standardized criteria. Several pitfalls occur when either the classification system or the criteria are vitiated. These pitfalls are outlined below:

• *Questionable criteria.* For example, Ganellen (1994) and his colleagues (Ganellen, Wasyliw, Haywood, & Grossman, 1996) attempted to use a combination of the referral question and MMPI validity indices to establish criterion groups. To use malingering as an example (see Ganellen, 1996), existing data suggest that the majority of criminal defendants *do not* feign (Rogers, Sewell, & Goldstein, 1994) and that application of the traditional MMPI *F* scale results in substantial misclassifications (Berry, Baer, & Harris, 1991). Use of questionable criteria seriously attenuates the clinical relevance of known-groups comparisons.

• *Broadened criteria.* As an example, Hankins, Barnard, and Robbins (1993) adopted a less stringent criterion for the determination of malingering than used by most clinicians. He utilized a minimal standard: As few as *one* bogus symptom would result in this classification. The temptation always exists with infrequent disorders/response styles to broaden and thereby weaken the criterion groups.

The application of known-groups comparisons to individual response styles deserves specific comments. For easy reference, I have captioned each response style in the following paragraphs:

Malingering

An avoidable problem with malingering research is the use of DSM indices to establish criterion groups. As noted in DSM-IV (American Psychiatric Association, 1994a,

p. 683) these indices are intended as a threshold model (i.e., "strongly suspected") and not a clinical decision model. The sole effort (Rogers, 1990b) to implement this threshold model resulted in an unacceptably low sensitivity rate.

Deception

A major weakness of polygraph research is the absence of an independent criterion for establishing deception. Most polygraphy studies rely on the examiner who administers the polygraph to extract a confession, which is then used to validate the efficacy of that procedure (Rogers, 1987). Such nonindependence unnecessarily confounds research findings on polygraph techniques.

Denied Substance Abuse

A "gold standard" does exist for denied drug use, namely, hair analysis. The highly reliable classification can be employed for both current (i.e., last month) and longitudinal (e.g., last year) substance abuse. As of yet, hair analysis has not been used in known-groups comparisons for dissimulation on psychological measures.

General Defensiveness

Researchers often have missed opportunities for known-group comparisons with persons minimizing psychological problems. Circumstances occur (e.g., review hearings for the release of involuntary patients or background investigations on criminal defendants seeking probation) in which documented evidence of denied psychopathology is available. Such research is urgently needed.

Defensiveness among Sex Offenders

Plethysmographic studies have demonstrated that a high proportion of paraphiliac patients consciously minimize their aberrant sexual interests and activities (Abel, Rouleau, & Cunningham-Rathner, 1986; see Chapter 16). Phallometric procedures have been useful in identifying comparative arousal patterns to a variety of erotic and aggressive stimuli. However, the relationship of these arousal patterns to subsequent sexual behavior requires further investigation. It is unclear, for example, whether individuals exist in the normal population who have never engaged in deviant sexual behavior, regardless of any anomalous phallometric results or unusual sexual interests they might have. More extensive work on nonreferred populations may be useful in establishing this relationship.

Research is also needed on laboratory methods to delineate their stability in a test–retest paradigm for clinical and nonclinical participants. Many clinicians treating sex offenders believe that the effectiveness of penile plethysmography as an assessment method attenuates over subsequent administrations. Of course, an alternative explanation is that treatment is successful. This conundrum could be explored by dividing patients with paraphilias into two groups, responsive and nonresponsive to treatment, and testing these two groups with the same or novel stimuli.

Differential Prevalence Design

Rogers, Harrell, and Liff (1993) first described the differential prevalence design and carefully distinguished it from known-groups comparisons. In a differential prevalence design, the researcher *assumes* that two samples will have different proportions of dissimulating persons. The assumption is generally based on perceived incentives for deception; most commonly, persons involved in criminal proceedings or civil litigation are presumed more likely to dissemble than persons from other contexts.

The differential prevalence design, although offering indirect evidence of construct validity, has no practical value in establishing criterion-related validity and is inutile for clinical classification. Why such harsh criticism?

Differences in prevalence rates are inferred, not measured. Inferences are founded on commonsensical beliefs or survey data, rather than on estimates derived from the specific samples under investigation. Moreover, no data are available that suggest prevalence rates of dissimulation, irrespective of the referral question or setting, even approach 50%. Therefore, we cannot assume that any particular sample is composed largely of dissimulating persons. On the contrary, even when the stakes are very high (e.g., insanity evaluations; see Rogers, 1986), only a minority appear to feign or otherwise engage in deception.

We learn very little from differential prevalence designs. By design, we do not know *who* is dissimulating in each group. Logically, we do not know *how many* are dissimulating in each group. Even when groups yield predicted differences, we do not know *what meaning* should be assigned to deviant or atypical scores. For all we know, every "deviant" or "atypical" score could be indicative of honest responding. We also do not know *how comparable* the different samples are on many important dimensions, beyond conjectured incentives. For the sake of illustration, criminal defendants who are referred for psychological evaluations may differ from voluntary patients on many parameters, including symptomatology, level of psychological impairment, socioeconomic status, and extreme distress (e.g., stemming from both incarceration and the pending trial). Likewise, brain-injured patients seeking compensation may be more impaired, cognitively or emotionally, that those not seeking compensation (see Chapter 5).

Differential prevalence designs are often misconstrued by practitioners as known-groups comparisons. The key difference is the use by known-groups comparisons of an established external criterion for determining who is dissimulating. In contrast, the classification is vaguely inferred in differential prevalence design studies. As a concrete example, the best available estimate from 320 experts is that malingering, although fluctuating widely across sites, occurs in 15.7% of forensic and 7.4% on nonforensic cases. If these percentages were assumed to be true for a particular study, then 8.3% more feigners are present in the forensic than nonforensic samples. Knowing that roughly one-fifteenth of the nonforensic and one-sixth of the forensic samples are malingering is to know very little of theoretical value or practical utility. Ironically, marked differences between samples, even in the predicted direction, are likely to be measuring something other than malingering. With a mere 8% more malingerers in the forensic sample, the "true" differences should hardly be dramatic and are apt to be insignificant.

In summary, findings from differential prevalence design (1) offer practitioners and researchers little assistance in understanding dissimulation, and (2) do not aid in its classification. Professionally, we share the obligation of ensuring that results from this deficient design are not misunderstood by our colleagues and misapplied to their clients.

Combined Research Models

Rogers (1995) advocated the combination of simulation design and known-groups comparison in the validation of assessment methods for dissimulation. The respective strengths of both designs are complementary. Well-designed simulation studies address satisfactorily the need for experimental rigor. Specific response styles can be investigated as they relate to assessment methods, characteristics/abilities of simulators, and incentives. Moreover, within-subject designs allow for the comparison of response style and provide an opportunity to research correction formulas for dissimulation. In contrast, known-groups comparisons address sufficiently the need for clinical relevance. Dissimulating persons can be examined in the most relevant professional settings with all the external motivations in place.

Research on the M Test (Beaber, Marston, Michelli, & Mills, 1985) illustrates the need for combined research models (i.e., simulation design plus known-groups comparison). The original simulation study appeared very promising with initial classification rates approaching 90%. A second study by different investigators (Gillis, Rogers, & Bagby, 1991) also yielded very positive results for the simulation design but not for known-groups comparison. Indeed, cross-validation of the original rules suggest they are not effective across both research designs (Hankins, Barnard, & Robbins, 1993; Smith & Borum, 1992). As a result, Rogers, Bagby, and Gillis (1992) revised the decision rules based on a combined research design (see Chapter 17).

The logical sequence is the development of an assessment method with simulation studies followed by known-groups comparisons. The key to this sequencing is twofold: (1) the comparative availability of participants for simulation research, and (2) the ability to refine measures systematically based on simulation design. Known-group comparisons are challenging to implement because of the relative infrequency of specific response styles. They are best used to cross-validate results of simulation studies.

Conclusions on Research Designs

I outline here the basic conclusions regarding research designs for dissimulation studies:

- *Case studies* are useful for hypothesis generation, but generally lack the necessary rigor for clinical or other professional applications.

- *Simulation designs* are very effective, when appropriate methodology is used, at developing and testing methods for detection of dissimulation.
- *Known-groups comparisons* are essential, because of their clinical/applied relevance, at cross-validating results established by simulation studies.
- *Differential prevalence design* is often mistaken for known-groups comparison but is inadequate as a research design to provide any useful data for classification purposes.

The scope of dissimulation research deserves brief comment. The vast majority of dissimulation studies have focused on a single response style (e.g., malingering, defensiveness, or unspecified deception) and the use of a solitary technique (e.g., the MMPI). The classic study by Johnson, Klingler, and Williams (1977) offers strong evidence for why single-measure studies may be vulnerable; they found negligible correlations between interview and MMPI data for malingering ($r = .15$) and defensiveness ($r = .01$). Research with multiple measures assessing multiple response styles could augment our understanding of dissimulation as well as increase the sophistication of our assessment methods. For example, the bipolarity of dissimulation scales (e.g., malingering vs. defensiveness) has been investigated for some MMPI indicators, but generally not in the same study. As a specific illustration, is the *absence* of F an indication of defensiveness in normal and clinical populations?

STATISTICAL AND METHODOLOGICAL APPLICATIONS

Research methodology for the assessment of deception and dissimulation increasingly has been standardized. Despite its obvious advantages, this standardization carries its own risk, namely, an unnecessary narrowing of research methods and a disinclination to explore alternative approaches. This brief section overviews several research methods, well established in other areas of psychological research, that are beginning to be applied to dissimulation research.

Receiver Operating Characteristic Analysis

Receiver operating characteristic (ROC) analysis was developed in the 1950s in research centering on signal detection across a range of applications (e.g., radar and memory vigilance tasks; see Swets, 1973). Although the potential applications of ROC analyses are relatively complex[3], a primary use in behavioral sciences is a plotting of sensitivity by the false-positive rate (Murphy et al., 1987). This graphic display allows the practitioner to immediately assess the accuracy of the measure in terms of sensitivity and specificity. As noted by Swets (1988), one early application of ROC analysis was to examine the accuracy of polygraph examinations. Swets provided a penetrating analysis of the measured values for the polygraph, with marked differences reported by the source of the study (e.g., commercial polygraphers vs. university researchers).

Swets also observed that the use of confessions as a criterion was likely to overestimate accuracy (e.g., data on confessing suspects are unlikely to generalize to nonconfessing suspects; nonconfessing suspects are likely to include an unknown percentage of deceptive persons). More recently, Mouton, Peterson, Nicholson, and Bagby (1995) applied ROC analysis to malingered MMPI-2 profiles in order to assess the relative accuracy of different validity scales and indexes.

The graphed results of ROC analysis allow the researcher to optimize the overall accuracy ("elbow" of the curve) or to modify the cut score to increase either sensitivity or specificity (Fombonne, 1991). Because this technique was developed for large samples, an important consideration is whether there are sufficient data to represent the numerous intermediate points of the graph adequately. For instance, if only two research participants had an F-scale elevation of 23, would we be justified in interpreting the sensitivity and specificity rates for this cut score? Some researchers may opt for tables that include a broader representation of diagnostic efficiency estimates (e.g., positive and negative predictive power) than typically found in ROC analysis.

Taxonometric Analysis

Frederick (1995) is the first investigator to apply taxonometric analysis to dissimulation. He applied this analysis to the feigning of cognitive impairment on a large sample ($n = 774$) of honest and malingering participants. The value of taxonometric analysis is the identification of underlying "taxons," or categories, that might not otherwise be observed by clinicians. This analysis requires very large samples and the administration of at least three related measures. Although ambitious, such efforts may assist in elucidating the "true" nature of specific response styles.

Latent Trait Analysis

Carter and Wilkinson (1984) utilized latent trait analysis to examine the cumulative probability of individual items on MMPI scales in what is referred to as the "item characteristic curve." For the validity scales, they found five items on scale F and four items on scale K that evidenced poor fit with the latent construct. One major use of latent trait analysis is to investigate the probability that participants with a given trait will endorse a particular item; the resulting data can examine the discriminability of individual items and the construction of briefer and more accurate scales (Grayson, 1986). The full application of latent trait analysis to response styles has yet to be explored.

FUNDAMENTAL QUESTIONS

The first and second editions of this book represent only a beginning in mapping out the future directions for dissimulation research. What is immediately apparent from a comprehensive review of the dissimulation literature is the range of unresearched and underresearched topics. Little is known, for example, about the background and characteristics of dissimulators in clinical settings. Although the motivation of dissimulators is often inferred, the multidetermined nature of behavior belies the simplicity of these inferences. Simply put, the motivation of dissimulators is poorly understood. In addition, the influence of situational and interactional variables on the frequency and severity of dissimulation has not been adequately studied. Finally, virtually no studies exist that examine the significance of dissimulation in the assessment of treatability and legal issues. The following sections will outline briefly fundamental questions in the study of dissimulation.

The Study of Dissimulators

Research has not addressed the sociodemographic variables, clinical characteristics, or psychosocial backgrounds of defensive and malingering persons. As an example, Lees-Haley (1992) examined the sociodemographic backgrounds and clinical presentations of persons making spurious posttraumatic stress disorder (PTSD) claims. Although the consecutive sampling of 55 pseudo-PTSD patients and 64 personal injury claimants as controls is not ideal, the data suggest that women may be represented more frequently than thought by some clinicians (41.8%), and that spurious claims, at least in this sample drawn primarily from Los Angeles, were widely distributed across ethnic groups (27.3% African American, 52.7% Anglo American, 16.4% Hispanic American, and 3.6% other). Although the data offer several tantalizing speculations about differences between spurious PTSD claims and genuine personal injury cases, the sampling procedure does not allow their exploration.[4] Moreover, initial data by DuAlba and Scott (1993) suggested possible differences in malingering and somatization for Anglo American and Hispanic American applicants for workers' compensation, although any disparities may reflect cultural bias in the test measure. Listed here is a sampling of related research questions:

1. What is the prevalence of malingering and defensiveness established by clinical settings or referral questions?
2. What proportion of dissimulators have coexisting mental disorders?
3. Are there "pure" or "trait-based" dissimulators who consistently deceive, regardless of the situation or any expected payoffs?
4. What are dissimulators' reported motivations for their intentional distortions?
5. Can degrees of intent be established by dissimulators?

Research on Decision Models

Most decision rules in dissimulation research favor simple decision rules, typically dichotomous in nature. For instance, the bulk of MMPI/MMPI-2 research on defensiveness is consistent with this approach; such models do not allow conclusions regarding the "gradations of dissimulation" (see Chapter 1). Moreover, the lack of an indeterminant category means that misclassifications are inevitable, because such decision rules do not take into account (1) the capitalization on chance variation or (2) the standard error of measurement. One simple but profound improvement would be the adoption of polychotomous classification with three groups: dissimulating, indeterminant, and nondissimulating. Please note the obvious pitfalls of treating these three categories as ordinal: Indeterminant is no longer indeterminant but is unwittingly transformed into a gradation of dissimulation.

A variation of dichotomous decision rules is found in the Malingering Probability Scales (MPS; Silverton & Gruber, in press). They provide different decision rules based on assumed base rates of malingering at 10%, 20%, and 50%. Although intellectually appealing, the resulting classifications are likely to be spurious, simply because the base rates are not known, either for specific settings or particular referral questions.

Recent meta-analytic studies (e.g., Berry, Baer, & Harris, 1991; Rogers, Sewell, & Salekin, 1994) sometimes have encouraged the use of multiple decision rules. In many cases, an individual may exhibit moderately high elevations on some validity indicators and extreme elevations on others. Research is needed to know which combination of decision rules increases accuracy. Multiple decision rules can also be organized in a hierarchical order. In such cases, very large samples are required to test the permutations inherent in these models. For example, Rogers, Cashel, Johansen, Sewell, and Gonzalez (in press) found that two of the five Substance Abuse Subtle Screening Inventory (SASSI) steps did not appear to affect classification.

Multivariate models, such as discriminant functions, have a potential to optimize classification. This advantage may prove to be a liability if not cross-validated on substantial samples, because shrinkage in classification is very common, given the likelihood of capitalizing on chance variation. For example, Rogers, Sewell, Morey, and Ustad (1995) performed a two-stage discriminant analysis on 204 participants in the calibration sample and 199 participants in the cross-validation sample, with shrinkage in classification from 92.2% to 80.4%. Multivariate models often require extensive computations, ideally suited for computer scoring.

Many research questions emerge from the previous discussion that are worthy of fuller inquiry:

1. What are the *misclassification* rates based on different types (e.g., dichotomous, polychotomous, or hierachical) of decision rules?
2. Can decision rules be developed to categorize gradations of dissimulation?
3. What are the advantages and disadvantages of multivariate models of classification?

Situational and Interactional Factors

Dissimulation within clinical and other applied settings is not an isolated event but an important element of an interactive process. The role of clinicians, for example, in unintentionally encouraging or discouraging dissimulation remains unknown. More to this point, the intensity of an adversarial situation as perceived by the potential dissimulator is likely to have an important influence on his or her presentation. For instance, it is not surprising that Audubon and Kirwin (1982) found that patients evaluated prior to trial tended to exaggerate their symptoms, but the same individuals, during a postacquittal assessment, tended to minimize them. As part of an interpersonal process, clinicians are not exempt from inquiry; Rogers, Sewell, and Goldstein (1994) found that psychologists' estimates for the prevalence of malingering ranged more than 50%; how much of this variability is accounted for by (1) differences among forensic settings or (2) the proclivities/presumptions of the psychologists remains to be investigated. Research questions that deserve empirical inquiry include the following:

1. What are mental health professionals' attitudes toward dissimulation?
2. Are differences in professionals' attitudes reflected in either (1) the *actual* frequency of dissimulation or (2) the *perceived* frequency of dissimulation?
3. Can environmental variables (e.g., a hostile or adversarial climate) be identified that significantly influence patients to dissimulate?
4. Do alternatives exist within the clinical setting for dissimulators to achieve their goals without deception?
5. Do clinical settings exist in which the majority of those being evaluated engage in some level of dissimulation?

Dissimulation and Treatability

The role of dissimulation in the assessment of patients' treatability has not been examined empirically. In clinical practice, psychologists sometimes interpret mild defensiveness as a sign of ego strength (i.e., a positive indicator of treatment success), and alternatively, that an exaggeration of symptoms may be a "cry for help." Research (Greene, 1988b; Hale, Zimostrad, Duckworth, & Nicholas, 1986; see Chapter 9) did not find empirical support for the "plea for help" hypothesis. Research is needed to test under what conditions either of these two hypotheses is true and how the presence of dissimulation affects clinical decision making on treatment recommendations. In this regard, Rogers, Sewell, and Goldstein (1994) found that our understanding of malingerers' motivation strongly affect our perceptions of treatability. Psychologists that view malingering as motivated by primarily a criminological impetus saw little need for treatment. Several research questions emerge on the relationship of dissimulation to patients' treatment responses.

1. To what extent do dissimulators comply with and follow treatment recommendations?
2. What are the treatment outcomes for dissimulating patients? In other words, do malingering or defensive patients with coexisting mental disorders respond as well as nondissimulators with similar disorders?
3. How do mental health professionals view dissimulators as treatment candidates?

As a related matter, researchers should consider whether the dissimulation itself can be treated or modified. From an adaptational model (see Chapter 1), a modification of the incentives for dissimulation should alter the response style. In the case of malingering, direct feedback on this response style is likely to have a direct effect in changing the incentive from the desired goal (e.g., financial gain in a personal-injury case) to the avoidance of further harm (e.g., social disapprobation and the possibility of keeping fraud charges from being discovered). No research to date has examined the usefulness of direct or indirect interventions in modifying a response style.

Dissimulation and Legal Issues

Rogers (1990a, 1990b) observed the potential dangers inherent in the DSM threshold model of malingering as applied to forensic cases. For instance, all criminal defendants with extensive antisocial histories are likely to meet the threshold criteria (i.e., "two or more indices" are satisfied by antisocial personality disorder [APD] and medicolegal evaluations). As a second example, some practitioners treat any complaint of intrafamilial sexual abuse as veridical and parents' subsequent disavowals as defensiveness. Research is urgently needed to test the effects of these assumptions on differences among mental health professionals and their decisions in clinical practice. Relevant investigations are required to address the role of dissimulation within forensic reports and legal outcome. Research questions include the following:

1. In what proportion of forensic cases is the issue of dissimulation determinative of clinicians' psycholegal conclusions?
2. Given the far-reaching consequences of forensic evaluations, are different clinical criteria needed to differentiate dissimulators from others?
3. What influences do descriptions of dissimulation within clinical reports have on the legal disposition?
4. In public policy terms, what errors (false positives or false negatives) is the criminal justice system willing to tolerate with respect to malingering and defensiveness?

CONCLUSION

Research on dissimulation can be roughly categorized in three phases: (1) early case studies on which much of clinical practice is based, (2) sustained interest in psychometric and social psychological research emphasizing group differences within simulation design, and (3) a gradually increasing focus on cross-validating simulation studies with known-groups comparisons. In addition, research has flourished on developing specialized measures of dissimulation. These measures range from structured interviews (e.g., SIRS) to self-report scales (e.g., M Test, SASSI, and Structured Inventory of Malingered Symptomatology) and laboratory tests (e.g., hair analysis). Large gaps, as highlighted by the fundamental questions posed in this chapter, remain in our understanding of dissimulation and its reliable assessment. As affirmed in the first edition, clinicians and researchers alike must actively resist the *woozle effect* (i.e., the frequent citing of the same substandard research until it obtains a reputable "scientific" status; Gelles, 1980) in cases in which the professional knowledge base is simply lacking.

Methodology for the study of malingering and defensiveness, although somewhat fragmented by its diverse origins, is well developed and understood. The impetus for more sophisticated research, combining methodologies, must include practitioners in both design and implementation to ensure the direct clinical relevance worthy of our empirical efforts.

NOTES

1. Of course, the admission of deception is not a faultless measure of dissembling. Cases occur in which the "acknowledgment of deception" is itself a fabrication.

2. The inability to follow experimental instructions to simulate should not be confused with an inability to malinger. Even grossly impaired individuals are sometimes capable of fabricating symptoms for a strongly desired goal. The task and concomitant motivation are quite different from simulation studies that impose an extrinsic instructional set that may be incompatible with their own goals.

3. A range of computational methods and statistics are available (see, e.g., Donaldson, 1993; Reales & Ballesteros, 1994; Simpson & Fritter, 1973).

4. Since the control group excluded all persons with PTSD, differences between the two samples may be attributable to either spurious or genuine PTSD.

References

Abbey, S. E., & Garfinkel, P. E. (1991). Neurasthenia and chronic fatigue syndrome: The role of culture in the making of a diagnosis. *American Journal of Psychiatry, 148,* 1638–1646.

Abel, G. G. (1995). *The comparison of the Abel Assessment with penile plethysmography.* Unpublished manuscript, Behavioral Medicine Institute, Atlanta, GA.

Abel, G. G., Barlow, D. H., Blanchard, E. B., & Mavissakalian, M. (1975). Measurement of sexual arousal in male homosexuals: Effects of instructions and stimulus modality. *Archives of Sexual Behavior, 4,* 623–630.

Abel, G. G., Becker, J. V., & Cunningham-Rathner, J. (1984). Complications, consent and cognitions in sex between children and adults. *International Journal of Law and Psychiatry, 7,* 89–103.

Abel, G. G., Blanchard, E. B., & Barlow, D. H. (1981). Measurement of sexual arousal in several paraphilias: The effects of stimulus modality, instructional set and stimulus content on the objective. *Behaviour Research and Therapy, 19,* 25–33.

Abel, G. G., Lawry, S. S., Karlstrom, E., Osborn, C. A., & Gillespie, C. F. (1994). Screening tests for pedophilia. *Criminal Justice and Behavior, 21,* 115–131.

Abel, G. G., Rouleau, J. L., & Cunningham-Rathner, J. (1986). Sexually aggressive behavior. In W. J. Curran, A. L. McGarry, & S. A. Shah (Eds.), *Forensic psychiatry and psychology* (pp. 289–314). Philadelphia: F. A. Davis.

Abeles, M., & Schilder, P. (1935). Psychogenic loss of personal identity. *Archives of Neurology and Psychiatry, 34,* 587–604.

Abrams, S. (1989). *The complete polygraph handbook.* Lexington, MA: Lexington Books.

Achenbach, T. M., & Edelbrock, C. S. (1983). *Manual for the Child Behavior Checklist and Revised Child Behavior Profile.* Burlington, VT: University Associates in Psychiatry.

Achenbach, T. M., McConaughy, S. H., & Howell, C. T. (1987). Child/adolescent behavioral and emotional problems: Implications of cross-informant correlations for situational specificity. *Psychological Bulletin, 101,* 213–232.

Adatto, C. P. (1949). Observations on criminal patients during narcoanalysis. *Archives of Neurology and Psychiatry, 69,* 82–92.

Adelman, R. M., & Howard, A. (1984). Expert testimony on malingering: The admissibility of clinical procedures for the detection of deception. *Behavioral Sciences and the Law, 2,* 5–20.

Aduan, R. P., Fauci, A. S., Dale, D. C., Herzberg, J. H., & Wolff, S. M. (1979). Factitious fever and self-induced infection. *Annals of Internal Medicine, 90,* 230–242.

Albert, S., Fox, H. M., & Kahn, M. W. (1980). Faking psychosis on a Rorschach: Can expert judges detect malingering? *Journal of Personality Assessment, 44,* 115–119.

Alderman v. Zant, 22 F.3d 1541 (11th Cir. 1994).

Alexander, M. P. (1995). Mild traumatic brain injury: Pathophysiology, natural history, and clinical management. *Neurology, 45,* 1253–1260.

Allan, C. A. (1991). Acknowledging alcohol problems: The use of a visual analogue scale to measure denial. *Journal of Nervous and Mental Disease, 179,* 620–625.

Allen, J. J., Iacono, W. G., & Danielson, K. D. (1992). The identification of concealed memories using the event-related potential and implicit behavioral measures: A methodology for prediction in the face of individual differences. *Psychophysiology, 29,* 504–522.

Allen, V. L., & Atkinson, M. L. (1978). Encoding of nonverbal behavior by high-achieving and low-achieving children. *Journal of Educational Psychology, 70,* 298–305.

Alliger, G. M., Lilienfeld, S. O., & Mitchell, K. E. (1996). The susceptibility of overt and covert integrity tests to coaching and faking. *Psychological Science.*

Allison, R. B. (1984). Difficulties diagnosing the multiple personality syndrome in a death penalty case. *International Journal of Clinical and Experimental Hypnosis, 32,* 102–117.

Alperin, J. J., Archer, R. P., & Coates, G. D. (1996). Development and effects of an MMPI-A K-correction procedure. *Journal of Personality Assessment, 67,* 155–168.

Alpert, M., & Silvers, K. N. (1970). Perceptual characteristics distinguishing auditory hallucinations in schizophrenia and acute alcoholic psychoses. *American Journal of Psychiatry, 127,* 298–302.

Altarriba, J., & Santiago-Rivera, A. L. (1994). Current perspectives on using linguistic and cultural factors in counseling the Hispanic client. *Professional Psychology: Research and Practice, 25,* 388–397.

Altshuler, L. L., Cummings, J. L., & Mills, M. J. (1986). Mutism: Review, differential diagnosis and report of 22 cases. *American Journal of Psychiatry, 143,* 1409–1414.

American Medical Association. (1985). Scientific status of refreshing recollection by the use of hypnosis. *Journal of the American Medical Association, 253,* 1918–1923.

American Medical Association Council on Scientific Affairs. (1986). Scientific status of refreshing recollection by the use of hypnosis. *International Journal of Clinical and Experimental Hypnosis, 34,* 1–12.

American Psychiatric Association. (1952). *Diagnostic and statistical manual of mental disorders.* Washington, DC: Author.

American Psychiatric Association. (1968). *Diagnostic and statistical manual of mental disorders* (2nd ed.). Washington, DC: Author.

American Psychiatric Association. (1980). *Diagnostic and statistical manual of mental disorders* (3rd ed.). Washington, DC: Author.

American Psychiatric Association. (1987). *Diagnostic and statistical manual of mental disorders* (3rd ed., rev.). Washington, DC: Author.

American Psychiatric Association. (1994a). *Diagnostic and statistical manual of mental disorders* (4th ed.). Washington, DC: Author.

American Psychiatric Association. (1994b, April). *Fact sheet: Memories of sexual abuse.* Washington, DC: Author.

American Psychological Association. (1985). *Standards for educational and psychological testing.* Washington, DC: Author.

Anastasi, A. (1988). *Psychological testing* (6th ed.). New York: Macmillan.

Anderson, E. W., Trethowan, W. H., & Kenna, J. C. (1959). An experimental investigation of simulation and pseudo-dementia. *Acta Psychiatrica et Neurologica Scandinavica, 34,* (132; whole issue).

Anderson, W. P., & Kunce, J. T. (1979). Sex offenders: Three personality types. *Journal of Clinical Psychology, 35,* 671–676.

Andreyev, L. (1902). *The dilemma.* In L. Hamalian & V. Von Wiren-Garczynski (Eds.), *Seven Russian short novel masterpieces.* New York: Popular Library.

Annon, J. S. (1988). Reliability and validity of penile plethysmography in rape and child molestation cases. *American Journal of Forensic Psychology, 6,* 11–26.

Annotation. (1986). Admissibility of physiological or psychological truth and deception test or its results to support physicians' testimony. *American Law Reports, 41,* 1369–1385.

Arbisi, P. A., & Ben-Porath, Y. S. (1995). On MMPI-2 infrequent response scale for use with psychopathological populations: The Infrequency Psychopathology Scale F(p). *Psychological Assessment, 7,* 424–431.

Arnett, P. A., Hammeke, T. A., & Schwartz, L. (1995). Quantitative and qualitative performance on Rey's 15-item test in neurological patients and dissimulators. *Clinical Neuropsychologist, 9,* 17–26.

Arnold, D. W. (1991). To test or not to test: Legal issues in integrity testing. *Forensic Reports, 4,* 213–224.

Arons, H. (1967). *Hypnosis in criminal investigation.* Springfield, IL: Charles C Thomas.

Asher, R. (1951). Munchausen's syndrome. *Lancet, 1,* 339–341.

Asher, R. (1972). *Richard Asher talking sense.* London: University Park Press.

Ashlock, L., Walker, J., Starkey, T. W., Harmand, J., & Michel, D. (1987). Psychometric characteristics of factitious PTSD. *VA Practitioner, 4,* 37–41.

Assad, G., & Shapiro, B. (1986). Hallucinations: Theoretical and clinical overview. *American Journal of Psychiatry, 143,* 1088–1097.

Association for Personnel Test Publishers. (1990). *Model guidelines for preemployment integrity testing programs.* Washington, DC: Author.

Atkins, E. L. (1991). Use of sodium amytal in an insanity and diminished capacity defense of a capital murder case. *American Journal of Forensic Psychology, 9,* 41–53.

Atkinson, R. M., Henderson, R. G., Sparr, L. F., & Deale, S. (1982). Assessment of Vietnam veterans for post-traumatic stress disorder in Veterans Administration disability claims. *American Journal of Psychiatry, 139,* 1118–1121.

Aubrey, J. B., Dobbs, A. R., & Rule, B. G. (1989). Persons' knowledge about the sequelae of minor head injury and whiplash. *Journal of Neurology, Neurosurgery, and Psychiatry, 52,* 842–846.

Audubon, J. J., & Kirwin, B. R. (1982). Defensiveness in the criminally insane. *Journal of Personality Assessment, 45,* 304–311.

Auerbach, A. H., Schefflen, N. A., & Scholz, C. K. (1967). A questionnaire survey of the posttraumatic syndrome. *Diseases of the Nervous System, 28,* 110–112.

Austin, J. S. (1992). The detection of fake good and fake bad on the MMPI-2. *Educational and Psychological Measurement, 52,* 669–674.

Averbach, A. (1963). Medical arsenal of a personal injury lawyer. *Cleveland Marshall Law Review, 12,* 195–207.

Babor, T. F., Stephens, R. S., & Marlatt, G. A. (1987). Verbal report methods in clinical research on alcoholism: Response bias and its minimization. *Journal of Studies on Alcohol, 48,* 410–424.

Bachman, J. G., & O'Malley, P. M. (1981). When four months equal a year: Inconsistencies in student reports of drug use. *Public Opinion Quarterly, 45,* 536–548.

Baddeley, A. D., & Warrington, E. K. (1970). Amnesia and the distinction between long- and short-term memory. *Journal of Verbal Learning and Verbal Behavior, 9,* 176–189.

Baer, J. D., Baumgartner, W. A., Hill, V. A., & Blahd, W. H. (1991). Hair analysis for the detection of drug use in pretrial probation and parole populations. *Federal Probation, 55,* 3–10.

Baer, R. A., Wetter, M. W., & Berry, D. T. R. (1992). Detection of underreporting of psychopathology on the MMPI: A meta-analysis. *Clinical Psychology Review, 12,* 509–525.

Baer, R. A., Wetter, M. W., & Berry, D. T. R. (1995). Effects of information about validity scales on underreporting of symptoms on the MMPI-2: An analogue investigation. *Assessment, 2,* 189–200.

Baer, R. A., Wetter, M. W., Nichols, D. S., Greene, R., & Berry, D. T. R. (1995). Sensitivity of MMPI-2 validity scales to underreporting of symptoms. *Psychological Assessment, 7,* 419–423.

Bagby, R. M., Gillis, J. R., Toner, B. B., & Goldberg, J. (1991). Detecting fake-good and fake-bad responding on the Millon Clinical Multiaxial Inventory–II. *Psychological Assessment, 3,* 496–498.

Bagby, R. M., Rogers, R., & Buis, T. (1994). Detecting malingered and defensive responding on the MMPI-2 in a forensic inpatient sample. *Journal of Personality Assessment, 62,* 191–203.

Bagby, R. M., Rogers, R., Buis, T., & Kalemba, V. (1994). Malingered and defensive response styles on the MMPI-2: An examination of validity scales. *Assessment, 1,* 31–38.

Baile, W. F., Kuehn, C. V., & Straker, D. (1992). Factitious cancer. *Psychosomatics, 33,* 100–105.

Bailey, S. L., Flewelling, R. L., & Rachal, J. V. (1992). The characterization of inconsistencies in self-reports of alcohol and marijuana use in a longitudinal study of adolescents. *Journal of Studies on Alcohol, 53,* 636–647.

Baker, G. A., Hanley, J. R., Jackson, H. F., Kimmance, S., & Slade, P. (1993). Detecting the faking of amnesia: Performance differences between simulators and patients with memory impairment. *Journal of Clinical and Experimental Neuropsychology, 15,* 668–684.

Baker, J. N. (1967). Effectiveness of certain MMPI dissimulation scales under "real-life" conditions. *Journal of Counseling Psychology, 14,* 286–292.

Baldesserini, R. J., Finkelstein, S., & Arona, G. W. (1983). The predictive power of diagnostic tests and the effects of prevalence of illness. *Archives of General Psychiatry, 40,* 569–573.

Balla, J. I., & Moraitis, S. (1970). Knights in armour: A follow-up study of injuries after legal settlement. *Medical Journal of Australia, 2,* 355–361.

Ballinger, B. R., Simpson, E., & Stewart, M. J. (1974). An evaluation of a drug administration system in a psychiatric hospital. *British Journal of Psychiatry, 125,* 202–207.

Bandura, A. (1991). Social cognitive theory of moral thought and action. In W. M. Kurtines & J. L. Gerwirtz (Eds.), *Moral behavior and development: Advances in theory, research and applications* (Vol 1., pp. 451–453). Hillsdale, NJ: Erlbaum.

Barbaree, H. E. (1991). Denial and minimization among sexual offenders: Assessment and treatment outcome. *Forums on Corrections Research, 3,* 30–33.

Barbaree, H. E., Seto, M. C., Serin, R. C., Amos, N. L., & Preston, D. L. (1994). Comparisons between sexual and nonsexual rapist subtypes: Sexual arousal to rape, offense precursors, and offense characteristics. *Criminal Justice and Behavior, 21,* 95–114.

Barber, T. X. (1962). Experimental controls and the phenomenon of "hypnosis": A critique of hypnotic research methodology. *Journal of Nervous and Mental Disease, 134,* 493–505.

Barber, T. X. (1965). Measuring "hypnotic-like" suggestibility with and without "hypnotic induction": Psychometric properties, norms, and variables influencing response to the Barber Suggestibility Scale. *Psychological Reports, 16,* 809–844.

Barber, T. X. (1972). Suggested ("hypnotic") behavior: The trance paradigm versus an alternative paradigm. In E. Fromm & R. E. Shor (Eds.), *Hypnosis: Research developments and perspectives* (pp. 115–182). Chicago: Aldine–Atherton.

Barber, T. X., & Calverly, D. S. (1963). "Hypnotic-like" susceptibility in children and adults. *Journal of Abnormal and Social Psychology, 66,* 589–597.

Barber, T. X., & Calverly, D. S. (1964). Empirical evidence for a theory of hypnotic behavior: Effects of pretest instructions on response to primary suggestions. *Psychological Records, 14,* 457–467.

Barber, T. X., & Glass, L. B. (1962). Significant factors in hypnotic behavior. *Journal of Abnormal and Social Psychology, 64,* 222–228.

Barber, T. X., Spanos, N. P., & Chaves, J. F. (1974). *Hypnotism: Imagination, and human potentialities.* New York: Pergamon Press.

Barber, T. X., & Wilson, S. C. (1977). Hypnosis, suggestions, and altered states of consciousness: Experimental evaluation of the new cognitive-behavioral theory and the traditional trance-state theory of "hypnosis." *Annals of the New York Academy of Sciences, 296,* 34–47.

Barkemeyer, C. A., & Callon, E. B. (1989). *Malingering Detection Scale.* Baton Rouge, LA: North Street.

Barlow, D. H. (1994). Psychological interventions in the era of managed competition. *Clinical Psychology: Science and Practice, 1,* 109–122.

Barnier, A. L., & McConkey, K. M. (1992). Reports of real and false memories: The relevance of hypnosis, hypnotizability, and context of memory test. *Journal of Abnormal Psychology, 101,* 521–527.

Baro, W. Z. (1950). Industrial head and back injuries. *Industrial Medical Surgery, 19,* 69–71.

Barrick, M. R., & Mount, M. K. (1991). The Big Five personality dimensions and job performance: A meta-analysis. *Personnel Psychology, 41,* 1–26.

Barry, H., Jr., MacKinnon, D. W., & Murray, H. A. (1931). Studies in personality: A. Hypnotizability as a personality trait and its typological relations. *Human Biology, 3,* 1–36.

Barth, J. T., Macciocchi, S. N., Giordani, B., Rimel, R., Jane, J. A., & Boll, T. J. (1983). Neuropsychological sequelae of minor head injury. *Neurosurgery, 13,* 529–533.

Bartlett, F. C. (1932). *Remembering: A study in experimental and social psychology.* Cambridge, UK: Cambridge University Press.

Bash, I. Y., & Alpert, M. (1980). The determination of malingering. *Annals of New York Academy of Sciences, 347,* 86–99.

Bass, E., & Davis, L. (1988). *The courage to heal.* New York: Harper & Row.

Bass, E., & Davis, L. (1994). *The courage to heal* (3rd ed.). New York: Harper Perennial.

Baumgartner, W. A., Hill, V. A., & Blahd, W. H. (1989). Hair analysis for drugs of abuse. *Journal of Forensic Sciences, 34,* 1433–1453.

Beaber, R. J., Marston, A., Michelli, J., & Mills, M. J. (1985). A brief test for measuring malingering in schizophrenic individuals. *American Journal of Psychiatry, 142,* 1478–1481.

Beachum v. Tansy, 903 F.2d 1321 (10th Cir. 1990).

Beck, J., & Harris, M. J. (1994). Visual hallucinations in non-delusional elderly. *International Journal of Geriatric Psychiatry, 9,* 531–536.

Becker, J. V., Hunter, J. A., Stein, R. M., & Kaplan, M. S. (1989). Factors associated with erection in adolescent sex offenders. *Journal of Psychopathology and Behavioral Assessment, 11,* 353–362.

Beetar, J. T., & Williams, J. M. (1995). Malingering response styles on the Memory Assessment Scales and symptom validity tests. *Archives of Clinical Neuropsychology, 10,* 57–72.

Behar, L. (1977). The Preschool Behavior Questionnaire. *Journal of Abnormal Child Psychology, 5,* 265–275.

Bejerot, N. (1972). A theory of addiction as an artificially induced drive. *American Journal of Psychiatry, 128,* 842–846.

Bell, I. R., Peterson, J. M., & Schwartz, G. E. (1995). Medical histories and psychological profiles of middle-aged women with and without self-reported illness from environmental chemicals. *Journal of Clinical Psychiatry, 56,* 151–160.

Belli, R. F. (1989). Influences of misleading postevent information: Misinformation interference and acceptance. *Journal of Experimental Psychology: General, 121,* 326–351.

Ben-Porath, Y. S. (1994). The ethical dilemma of coached malingering research. *Psychological Assessment, 6,* 14–15.

Ben-Shakar, G., & Furedy, J. J. (1990). *Theories and applications in the detection of deception.* New York: Springer-Verlag.

Benton, A. L. (1945). Rorschach performances of suspected malingerers. *Journal of Abnormal and Social Psychology, 40,* 94–96.

Bergmann, T. J., Mundt, D. H., Jr., & Illgen, E. J. (1990). The evolution of honesty tests and means for their evaluation. *Employee Responsibilities and Rights Journal, 3,* 215–223.

Berman, E. (1987, March 25). *USA Today,* p. 10A.

Bernard, L. C. (1990). Prospects for faking believable memory deficits on neuropsychological tests and the use of incentives in simulation research. *Journal of Clinical and Experimental Neuropsychology, 12,* 715–728.

Bernard, L. C. (1991). The detection of faked deficits on the Rey Auditory Verbal Learning Test: The effect of serial position. *Archives of Clinical Neuropsychology, 6,* 81–88.

Bernard, L. C., & Fowler, W. (1990). Assessing the validity of memory complaints: Performance of brain-damaged and normal individuals on Rey's task to detect malingering. *Journal of Clinical Psychology, 46,* 432–436.

Bernard, L. C., Houston, W., & Natoli, L. (1993). Malingering on neuropsychological tests: Potential objective indicators. *Journal of Clinical Psychology, 49,* 45–53.

Bernard, L. C., McGrath, M. J., & Houston, W. (1993). Discriminating between simulated malingering and closed head injury on the Wechsler Memory Scale—Revised. *Archives of Clinical Neuropsychology, 8,* 539–551.

Berney, T. P. (1973). A review of simulated illness. *South African Medical Journal, 47,* 1429–1434.

Bernheim, H. M. (1964). *Hypnosis and suggestion in psychotherapy: A treatise on the nature and use of hypnotism* (C. A. Herter, Trans.). New Hyde Park, NY: University Books. (Original work published 1884)

Berrios, G. E. (1991). Musical hallucinations: A statistical analysis of 46 cases. *Psychopathology, 24,* 356–360.

Berry, D. T. R. (1995). Detecting distortion in forensic evaluations with the MMPI-2. In Y. S. Ben-Porath, J. R. Graham, G. C. N. Hall, R. D. Hirschman, & M. S. Zaragoza (Eds.), *Forensic applications of the MMPI-2* (pp. 82–102). Thousand Oaks, CA: Sage.

Berry, D. T. R., Adams, J. J., Clark, C. D., Thacker, S. R., Burger, T. L., Wetter, M. W., Baer, R. A., & Borden, J. W. (1996). Detection of a cry for help on the MMPI-2: An analog investigation. *Journal of Personality Assessment, 67,* 26–36.

Berry, D. T. R., Baer, R. A., & Harris, M. J. (1991). Detection of malingering on the MMPI: A meta-analytic review. *Clinical Psychology Review, 11,* 585–598.

Berry, D. T. R., Lamb, D. G., Wetter, M. W., Baer, R. A., & Widiger, T. A. (1994). Ethical considerations in research on coached malingering. *Psychological Assessment, 6,* 16–17.

Berry, D. T. R., Wetter, M. W., & Baer, R. A. (1995). Assessment of malingering. In J. N. Butcher (Ed.), *Clinical personality assessment: Practical approaches* (pp. 236–248). New York: Oxford University Press.

Berry, D. T. R., Wetter, M. W., Baer, R. A., Larsen, L., Clark, C., & Monroe, K. (1992). MMPI-2 random responding indices: Validation using a self-report methodology. *Psychological Assessment, 4,* 340–345.

Betts, G. L. (1947). The detection of incipient army criminals. *Science, 106,* 93–96.

Betts, T., & Boden, S. (1992). Diagnosis, management and prognosis of a group of 128 patients with non-epileptic attack disorder: Part I. *Seizure, 1,* 19–26.

Bickart, W. T., Meyer, R. G., & Connell, D. K. (1991). The symptom validity technique as a measure of feigned short-term memory deficit. *American Journal of Forensic Psychology, 9,* 3–11.

Binder, L. M. (1986). Persisting symptoms after mild hear injury: A review of the post-concussive syndrome. *Journal of Clinical and Experimental Neuropsychology, 8,* 323–346.

Binder, L. M. (1990). Malingering following minor head trauma. *Clinical Neuropsychologist, 4,* 25–36.

Binder, L. M. (1992). Forced-choice testing provides evidence of malingering. *Archives of Physical Medicine and Rehabilitation, 72,* 377–380.

Binder, L. M. (1993). Assessment of malingering after mild head trauma with the Portland Digit Recognition Test. *Journal of Clinical and Experimental Neuropsychology, 15,* 170–183.

Binder, L. M., & Kelly, M. P. (1996). Portland Digit Recognition Test performance by brain dysfunction patients without financial incentives. *Assessment, 3,* 403–409.

Binder, L. M., & Pankratz, L. (1987). Neuropsychological evidence of a factitious memory complaint. *Journal of Clinical and Experimental Neuropsychology, 9,* 167–171.

Binder, L. M., & Rohling, M. L. (1996). Money matters: A meta-analytic review of the relationship between financial incentives. *American Journal of Psychiatry, 153,* 7–10.

Binder, L. M., & Thompson, L. L. (1995). The ethics code and neuropsychological assessment practices. *Archives of Clinical Neuropsychology, 10,* 27–46.

Binder, L. M., Villanueva, M. R., Howieson, D., & Moore, R. T. (1993). The Rey AVLT recognition memory task measures motivational impairment after mild head trauma. *Archives of Clinical Neuropsychology, 8,* 137–147.

Binder, L. M., & Willis, S. C. (1991). Assessment of motivation after financially compensable minor head trauma. *Psychological Assessment: A Journal of Consulting and Clincal Psychology, 3,* 175–181.

Binder, R. L., Trimble, M. R., & McNiel, D. E. (1991). The course of psychological symptoms after resolution of lawsuits. *American Journal of Psychiatry, 148,* 1073–1075.

Binet, A. (1905). La science du témoinage. *Annales de Psychologie, 11,* 128–136.

Biskup v. McCaughtry, 20 F.3d 245 (7th Cir. 1994).

Bishop, E. R., & Holt, A. R. (1980). Pseudopsychosis: A reexamination of the concept of hysterical psychosis. *Comprehensive Psychiatry, 21,* 150–161.

Bitzer, R. (1980). Caught in the middle: Mentally disabled veterans and the Veterans Administration. In C. R. Figley & S. Leventman (Eds.), *Strangers at home: Vietnam veterans since the war* (pp. 305–323). New York: Praeger.

Bitzer, R. (1990). Caught in the middle: Mentally disabled veterans and the Veterans Administration. In C. R. Figley & S. Leventman (Eds.), *Strangers at home: Vietnam veterans since the war* (pp. 305–323). New York: Brunner/Mazel. (Original work published 1980, Praeger)

Bjork, R. (1989). Retrieval inhibition as an adaptive mechanism in human memory. In F. I. M. Craik & H. L. Roediger, III (Eds.), *Varieties of memory and consciousness* (pp. 309–330). Hillsdale, NJ: Erlbaum.

Blanchard, E. B., Kolb, L. C., Pallmeyer, T. P., & Gerardi, R. J. (1982). A psychophysiological study of post-traumatic stress disorder in Vietnam veterans. *Psychiatric Quarterly, 54,* 220–229.

Blanchard, R., Racansky, I. G., & Steiner, B. W. (1986). Phallometric detection of fetishistic arousal in heterosexual male cross-dressers. *Journal of Sex Research, 22,* 452–462.

Bloom, P. B. (1994). Clinical guidelines in using hypnosis in uncovering memories of sexual abuse: A master class commentary. *International Journal of Clinical and Experimental Hypnosis, 42,* 173–178.

Boffeli, T. J., & Guze, S. B. (1992). The simulation of neurologic disease. *Psychiatric Clinics of North America, 15,* 301–310.

Bohn, R. W. (1932). Sodium amytal narcosis as a therapeutic aid in psychiatry. *Psychiatric Quarterly, 6,* 301–309.

Bohnen, N., Twijnstra, A., Wijnen, G., & Jolles, J. (1991). Tolerance for light and sound of patients with persistent post-concussional symptoms six months after mild head injury. *Journal of Neurology, 238,* 443–446.

Bolton, B. (1985). Review of Inwald Personality Inventory. In J. V. Mitchell, Jr. (Ed.), *The ninth mental measurements yearbook* (pp. 711–713). Lincoln, NE: Buros Institute of Mental Measurements.

Bongartz, W. (1985). German norms for the Harvard Group Scale of Hypnotic Susceptibility, Form A. *International Journal of Clinical and Experimental Hypnosis, 33,* 131–138.

Borg, S., Connor, E. J., & Landis, E. E. (1995). *Impact of expertise and sufficient information on psychologists' ability to detect malingering.* Unpublished manuscript, Federal Bureau of Prisons, Butner, NC.

Bourget, D., & Bradford, J. M. W. (1995). Sex offenders who claim amnesia for their alleged offense. *Bulletin of the American Academy of Psychiatry and Law, 23,* 299–307.

Bowman, E. S. (1993). Etiology and clinical course of pseudoseizures. *Psychosomatics, 34,* 333–342.

Bradford, J. W., & Smith, S. M. (1979). Amnesia and homicide: The Padola case and a study of thirty cases. *Bulletin of the American Academy of Psychiatry and the Law, 7,* 219–231.

Bradley, M. T., MacDonald, P., & Fleming, I. (1989). Amnesia, feelings of knowing, and the guilty knowledge test. *Canadian Journal of Behavioural Science, 21,* 224–231.

Bradley v. Preston, 263 F.Supp. 283 (D.D.C. 1967), *cert. denied,* 390 U.S. 990 (1968).

Braginsky, D. D. (1970). Machiavellianism and manipulative interpersonal behavior in children. *Journal of Experimental and Social Psychology, 6,* 77–99.

Braginsky, B. M., & Braginsky, D. D. (1967). Schizophrenic patients in the psychiatric interview: An experimental study of their effectiveness at manipulation. *Journal of Consulting Psychology, 31,* 543–547.

Braginsky, B. M., Braginsky, D. D., & Ring, K. (1969). *The mental hospital as a last resort.* New York: Holt, Rinehart & Winston.

Brahams, D. (1989, June 10). Benzodiazepine sedation and allegations of sexual assault. *Lancet, i,* 1339–1340.

Brahams, D. (1990a). Benzodiazepines and sexual fantasies. *Lancet, 335,* 157.

Brahams, D. (1990b). Benzodiazepine sexual fantasies: Acquittal of dentist. *Lancet, 335,* 403–404.

Brahams, D. (1991). Benzodiazepines and sexual assault, Canada. *Lancet, 337,* 291–292.

Brandt, J. (1988). Malingered amnesia. In R. Rogers (Ed.), *Clinical assessment of malingering and deception* (1st ed., pp. 65–83). New York: Guilford Press.

Brandt, J. (1992). Detecting amnesia's imposters. In L. R. Squire & N. Butters (Eds.), *Neuropsychology of memory* (2nd ed., pp. 156–165). New York: Guilford Press.

Brandt, J., Rubinsky, E., & Lassen, G. (1985). Uncovering malingered amnesia. *Annals of the New York Academy of Sciences, 444,* 502–503.

Braverman, M. (1978). Post-injury malingering is seldom a calculated ploy. *Occupational Health and Safety, 47,* 36–48.

Brems, C., & Johnson, M. E. (1991). Subtle–obvious scales of the MMPI: Indicators of profile validity in a psychiatric population. *Journal of Personality Assessment, 56,* 536–544.

Breslau, N. (1987). Inquiring about the bizarre: False positives in Diagnostic Interview Schedule for Children (DISC)—Ascertainment of obsessions, compulsions, and psychotic symptoms. *Journal of the American Academy of Child and Adolescent Psychiatry, 26,* 639–644.

Breslau, N., & Davis, G. C. (1987). Post-traumatic stress disorder: The etiologic specificity of wartime stressors. *American Journal of Psychiatry, 144,* 289–297.

Breuer, J., & Freud, S. (1955). Studies on hysteria. In J. Strachey (Ed.), *Standard edition of the complete psychological works of Sigmund Freud* (Vol. 2, pp. 1–305). London: Hogarth. (Original work published in 1895)

Brewin, E., Andrews, B., & Gotlib, I. (1993). Psychopathology and early experience: A reappraisal of retrospective reports. *Psychological Bulletin, 113,* 82–98.

Brittain, R. P. (1966). The history of legal medicine: The assizes of Jerusalem. *Medicolegal Journal, 34,* 72–73.

Brodsky, S. L. (1978). Reid Report. In O. K. Buros (Ed.), *The eighth mental measurements yearbook* (pp. 1025–1026). Highland Park, NJ: Gryphon Press.

Browner, W. S., Newman, T. B., & Cummings, S. R. (1988). Designing a new study: III. In S. B. Hulley & S. R. Cummings (Eds.), *Diagnostic tests in designing clinical research* (pp. 87–97). Baltimore: Williams & Wilkins.

Brozovich, R. (1970). Fakability of scores on the Group Personality Projective Test. *Journal of Genetic Psychology, 117,* 143–148.

Bruhn, A. R., & Reed, M. R. (1975). Simulation of brain damage on the Bender–Gestalt test by college subjects. *Journal of Personality Assessment, 39,* 244–255.

Bryan, W. (1962). *Legal aspects of hypnosis.* Springfield, IL: Charles C Thomas.

Bryer, J. B., Martines, K. A., & Dignan, M. A. (1990). Millon Clinical Multiaxial Inventory alcohol abuse and drug abuse scales and the identification of substance-abuse patients. *Psychological Assessment: A Journal of Consulting and Clinical Psychology, 2,* 438–441.

Buck, O. D. (1983). Multiple personality as a borderline state. *Journal of Nervous and Mental Disease, 171,* 62–65.

Buckhout, R. (1974). Eyewitness testimony. *Scientific American, 231,* 23–31.

Buckman, J., Hain, J. D., Smith, B. M., & Stevenson, I. (1973). Controlled interview using drugs: II. Comparisons between restricted and freer conditions. *Archives of General Psychiatry, 29,* 623–627.

Bukalew, L. W., & Cotfield, K. E. (1982). An investigation of drug expectancy as a function of capsule color and size and preparation form. *Journal of Clinical Psychopharmacology, 2,* 245–248.

Bulman, R. J., & Wortman, C. B. (1977). Attributions of blame and coping in the real world: Severe accident victims to their lot. *Journal of Personnel and Social Psychology, 33,* 351.

Burgoon, J. K., & Buller, D. B. (1994). Interpersonal deception: III. Effects of deceit on perceived communication and nonverbal behavior dynamics. *Journal of Nonverbal Behavior, 18(2),* 155–184.

Burgoon, M., Callister, M., & Hunsaker, F. G. (1994). Patients who deceive: An empirical investigation of patient–physician communication. *Journal of Language and Social Psychology, 13(4),* 443–468.

Bursten, B. (1965). On Munchausen's syndrome. *Archives of General Psychiatry, 13,* 261–268.

Bussey, K. (1992). Children's lying and truthfulness: Implications for children's testimony. In S. J. Ceci, M. D. Leichtman, & M. E. Putnick (Eds.), *Cognitive and social factors in early deception* (pp. 89–109). Hillsdale, NJ: Erlbaum.

Bustamante, J. P., & Ford, C. V. (1977). Ganser's syndrome. *Psychiatric Opinion, 14,* 39–41.

Butcher, J. N., Dahlstrom, W. G., Graham, J. R., Tellegen, A., & Kaemmer, B. (1989). *MMPI-2: Manual for administration and scoring.* Minneapolis: University of Minnesota Press.

Butcher, J. N., & Han, K. (1995). Development of an MMPI-2 scale to assess the presentation of self in a superlative manner: The *S* scale. In J. N. Butcher & C. D. Spielberger (Eds.), *Advances in personality assessment* (Vol. 10, pp. 25–50). Hillsdale, NJ: Erlbaum.

Butcher, J. N., & Tellegen, A. (1967). Objections to MMPI items. *Journal of Consulting Psychology, 30,* 527–534.

Butcher, J. N., & Williams, C. L. (1992). *Essentials of MMPI-2 and MMPI-A interpretation.* Minneapolis: University of Minnesota Press.

Butcher, J. N., Williams, C. L., Graham, J. R., Archer, R. P., Tellegen, A., Ben-Porath, Y. S., & Kaemmer, B. (1992). *MMPI-A: Manual for administration, scoring and interpretation.* Minneapolis: University of Minnesota Press.

Butters, N., Miliotis, P., Albert, M. S., & Sax, D. S. (1984). Memory assessment: Evidence of heterogeneity of amnesic symptoms. In G. Goldstein (Ed.), *Advances in clinical neuropsychology* (pp. 127–159). New York: Plenum Press.

Caine, E. D. (1993). Amnesic disorders. *Journal of Neuropsychiatry and Clinical Neurosciences, 5,* 6–8.

Caldwell, A. B. (1969). *MMPI critical items.* Unpublished mimeograph. (Available from Caldwell Report, 1545 Sawtelle Boulevard, Los Angeles, CA 90025)

Callon, E. B., Jones, G. N., Barkemeyer, C. A., & Brantley, P. J. (1990, August). *Validity of a scale to detect malingering.* Paper presented at the 98th annual meeting of the American Psychological Association, Boston, MA.

Camara, W. J., & Schneider, D. L. (1994). Integrity tests: Facts and unresolved issues. *American Psychologist, 49,* 112–119.

Camara, W. J., & Schneider, D. L. (1995). Questions of construct breadth and openness of research in integrity testing. *American Psychologist, 50,* 459–460.

Campbell, D. T., & Stanley, J. C. (1966). *Experimental and quasi-experimental designs for research.* Chicago: Rand McNally.

Cantwell, H. B. (1981). Sexual abuse of children in Denver, 1979: Reviewed with implications for pediatric intervention and possible prevention. *Child Abuse and Neglect, 5,* 75–85.

Caradoc-Davies, G. (1988). Feigned alcohol abuse. *British Journal of Psychiatry, 152,* 418–420.

Carlin, A. S., & Hewitt, P. L. (1990). The discrimination of patient-generated and randomly generated MMPIs. *Journal of Personality Assessment, 54,* 24–29.

Carlson, R. J. (1985). Factitious psychiatric disorders: Diagnostic and etiologic considerations. *Psychiatric Medicine, 2,* 383–388.

Carney, M. W., & Brown, J. P. (1983). Clinical features and motives among 42 artifactual illness patients. *British Journal of Medical Psychology, 56,* 57–66.

Carp, A. L., & Shavzin, A. R. (1950). The susceptibility to falsification of the Rorschach psychodiagnostic technique. *Journal of Consulting Psychology, 14,* 115–119.

Carsky, M., Selzer, M. A., Terkelson, K., & Hurt, S. W. (1992). The PEH: A questionnaire to assess acknowledgement of psychiatric illness. *Journal of Nervous and Mental Disease, 180,* 458–464.

Carter, J. E., & Wilkinson, L. (1984). A latent trait analysis of the MMPI. *Multivariate Behavioral Research, 19,* 385–407.

Cash, W. S., & Moss, A. J. (1972). *Optimum recall period for reporting persons injured in motor vehicle accidents* (DHEW Publication No. HSM72-1050). Washington, DC: U.S. Government Printing Office.

Cashel, M. L., Rogers, R., & Sewell, K. W. (1995). The Personality Assessment Inventory (PAI) and the detection of defensiveness. *Assessment, 2,* 333–342.

Cattell, R. B. (1949). *Manual for Forms A and B: Sixteen Personality Factor Questionnaire.* Champaign, IL: Institute for Personality and Ability Testing.

Cattell, R. B., Eber, H. W., & Tatsuoka, M. M. (1970). *Handbook for the 16 PF.* Champaign, IL: Institute of Personality and Abilty Testing.

Ceci, S. J., & Bruck, M. (1993). Suggestibility of the child witness: A historical review and synthesis. *Psychological Bulletin, 113,* 403–439.

Ceci, S. J., Loftus, E. F., Leichtman, M. D., & Bruck, M. (1994). The possible role of source misattributions in the creation of false beliefs among preschoolers. *International Journal of Clinical and Experimental Hypnosis, 42,* 304–320.

Ceci, A., Ross, D., & Toglia, M. (1987). Age differences in suggestibility: Narrowing the uncertainties. In S. Ceci, M. Toglia, & D. Ross (Eds.), *Children's eyewitness memory* (pp. 79–91). New York: Springer-Verlag.

Cercy, S. P., Radtke, R. C., & Chittum, R. (1995). *Integrating memory theory in the detection of dissimulated amnesia: The application of proactive interference.* Under editorial review.

Chandler, M., Fritz, A. S., & Hala, S. (1989). Small-scale deceit: Deception as a marker of two-, three-, and four-year-olds' early theories of mind. *Child Development, 60,* 1263–1277.

Chaney, H. S., Cohn, C. K., Williams, S. G., & Vincent, K. R. (1984). MMPI results: A comparison of trauma victims, psychogenic pain, and patients with organic disease. *Journal of Clinical Psychology, 40,* 1450-1454.

Chaplin, T. C., Rice, M. E., & Harris, G. T. (1995). Salient victim suffering and the sexual responses of child molesters. *Journal of Consulting and Clinical Psychology, 63,* 249–255.

Chapman, S. L., & Brena, S. F. (1990). Patterns of conscious failure to provide accurate self-report data in patients with low back pain. *Clinical Journal of Pain, 6,* 178–190.

Charcot, J. M. (1886). *Oeuvres complètes [Complete works].* Paris: Aux Bureau de Progres Medical.

Choca, J. P., Shanley, L. A., & Van Denburg, E. J. (1992). *Interpretative guide to the Millon Multiaxial Inventory.* Washington, DC: American Psychological Association.

Clark v. State, 379 So.2d 372 (Fla. Dist. Ct. App. 1979).

Cleckley, H. (1976). *The mask of sanity* (5th ed.). St. Louis, MO: Mosby.

Clevenger, S. V. (1889). *Spinal concussion.* London: F. A. Davis.

Clopton, J. R. (1978). Alcoholism and the MMPI: A review. *Journal of Studies on Alcohol, 39,* 1540-1558.

Cogburn, R-. A. K. (1993). A study of psychopathy and its relation to success in interpersonal deception. *Dissertation Abstracts International, 54,* 2191-B.

Coe, W. C. (1964). Further norms on the Harvard Group Scale of Hypnotic Susceptibility, Form A. *International Journal of Clinical and Experimental Hypnosis, 12,* 184–190.

Coe, W. C. (1989). Posthypnotic amnesia: Theory and research. In N. P. Spanos & J. F. Chaves (Eds.), *Hypnosis: The cogitive-behavioral perspective.* Buffalo, NY: Prometheus Books.

Cofer, C. N., Chance, J., & Judson, A. J. (1949). A study of malingering on the MMPI. *Journal of Psychology, 27,* 491–499.

Cohen, J. B. (1990). Misuse of computer software to detect faking on the Rorschach: A reply to Kahn, Fox, and Rhode. *Journal of Personality Assessment, 54,* 58–62.

Cohen, N. J. (1984). Preserved learning capacity in amnesia: Evidence for multiple memory systems. In L. Squire & N. Butters (Eds.), *Neuropsychology of memory* (pp. 83–103). New York: Guilford Press.

Cohen, S. (1984). Drugs in the workplace. *Journal of Clinical Psychiatry, 45,* 4–8.

Colby, F. (1989). Usefulness of the *K* correction in the MMPI profiles of patients and non-patients. *Psychological Assessment, 1,* 142–145.

Cole, E. S. (1970). Psychiatric aspects of compensable injury. *Medical Journal of Australia, 1,* 93–100.

Cole, P. M. (1986). Children's spontaneous control of facial expression. *Child Development, 57,* 1309–1321.

Cole, P. M., Barrett, K. C., & Zahn-Waxler, C. (1992). Emotion displays in two-year-olds during mishaps. *Child Development, 63,* 314–324.

Collie, J. (1917). *Malingering and feigned sickness.* London: Edward Arnold.

Collinson, G. D. (1812). *A treatise on the law concerning idiots, lunatics, and other persons non compo mentis.* London: W. Reed.

Commonwealth ex rel. Cummins v. Price, 218 A.2d 758 (1966).

Connell, D. K. (1991). *The SIRS and the M test: The differential validity and utility of two instruments designed to detect malingered psychosis in a correctional sample.* Unpublished dissertation, University of Louisville.

Cook, T. D., & Campbell, D. T. (1979). *Quasi-experimentation: Design and analysis issues for field settings.* Boston: Houghton Mifflin.

Cook, T. D., Levitou, L. C., & Shadish, W. R. (1985). Program evaluation. In G. Lindzey & E. Aronson (Eds.), *Handbook of social psychology* (Vol. 1, pp. 699–777). New York: Random House.

Coons, P. M. (1991). Iatrogenesis and malingering of multiple personality disorder in the forensic evaluation of homicide defendants. *Psychiatric Clinics of North America, 14,* 757–768.

Coons, P. M. (1993). Use of the MMPI to distinguish genuine from factitious multiple personality disorder. *Psychological Reports, 73,* 401–402.

Coons, P. M. (1994). Reports of satanic ritual abuse: Further implications about pseudo-memories. *Perceptual and Motor Skills, 78*(3, Pt. 2), 1376–1378.

Corcoran, K., & Winslade, W. J. (1994). Eavesdropping on the 50-minute hour: Managed mental health care and confidentiality. *Behavioral Sciences and the Law, 12,* 351–365.

Cornelius, J. R., Mezzich, J., Fabrega, H., Cornelius, M. D., Myer, J., & Ulrich, R. F. (1991). Characterizing organic hallucinosis. *Comprehensive Psychiatry, 32,* 338–344.

Cornell, D. G., & Hawk, G. L. (1989). Clinical presentation of malingerers diagnosed by experienced forensic psychologists. *Law and Human Behavior, 13,* 374–383.

Cornell v. Sup. Ct., 338 P.2d 447 (1959).

Corradi, R. B. (1983). Psychological regression with illness. *Psychosomatics, 24,* 353–362.

Costa, P. T., Jr., & McCrae, R. R. (1985). *The NEO Personality Inventory manual.* Odessa, FL: Psychological Assessment Resources.

Cotterill, J. A. (1992). Self-stigmatization: Artefact dermatitis. *British Journal of Hospital Medicine, 47,* 115–119.

Cox, B. J., Swinson, R. P., Direnfeld, D. M., & Bourdeau, D. (1994). Social desirability and self-reports of alcohol abuse in anxiety disorder patients. *Behaviour Research and Therapy, 32,* 175–178.

Coyne, J. C. (1976). Toward an interactional description of depression. *Psychiatry, 39,* 28–40.

Craig, J. R. (1986). Personnel Selection Inventory. In D. J. Keyser & R. C. Sweatland (Eds.), *Test critiques* (Vol. 3, pp. 510–520). Kansas City, MO: Test Corporation of America.

Craig, R. J., Kuncel, R., & Olson, R. E. (1994). Ability of drug abusers to avoid detection of substance abuse on the MCMI-II. *Journal of Social Behavior and Personality, 9,* 95–106.

Craig, R. J., & Weinberg, D. (1992). Assessing drug abusers with the Millon Clinical Multi-axial Inventory: A review. *Journal of Substance Abuse Treatment, 9,* 249–255.

Cramer, B., Gershberg, M. R., & Stern, M. (1971). Munchausen syndrome. Its relationship to malingering, hysteria, and the physician–patient relationship. *Archives of General Psychiatry, 24,* 573–578.

Crockett v. Haithwaite et al., No. 297/73 (Sup. Ct. B.C. Can., February 10, 1978).

Croft, R. D., & Jervis, M. (1989). Munchausen's syndrome in a 4-year-old. *Archives of Disease in Childhood, 63,* 740–741.

Cronbach, L. J. (1949). Statistical methods applied to Rorschach scores: A review. *Psychological Bulletin, 46,* 393–429.

Cronbach, L. J., & Meehl, P. E. (1955). Construct validity in psychological tests. *Psychological Bulletin, 52,* 281–302.

Crowley, M. E. (1952). The use of the Kent EGY for the detection of malingering. *Journal of Clinical Psychology, 8,* 332–337.

Crowne, D. P., & Marlowe, D. (1960). A new scale of social desirability independent of psychopathology. *Journal of Consulting Psychology, 24,* 349–354.

Cummings, J. L. (1994, November). Mutism: Evaluation and differential diagnosis. *Psychiatric Times,* pp. 24–25.

Cummings, J. L., & Miller, B. L. (1987). Visual hallucinations: Clinical occurrence and use in differential diagnosis. *Western Journal of Medicine, 146,* 46–51.

Cunnien, A. J. (1988). Psychiatric and medical syndromes associated with deception. In R. Rogers (Ed.), *Clinical assessment of malingering and deception* (1st ed., pp. 13–33). New York: Guilford Press.

Curran, W. J. (1983). The acceptance of scientific evidence in the courts. *New England Journal of Medicine, 309,* 713–714.

Dahlstrom, W. G. (1991, July). *Correlates of each of the subtle and obvious subscales of D, Hy, Pd, Pa, and Ma (Wiener & Harmon).* Paper presented at the MMPI-2 Summer Institute, Colorado Springs, CO.

Dahlstrom, W. G., Welsh, G. S., & Dahlstrom, L. E. (1972). *An MMPI handbook: Vol. I. Clinical interpretation* (rev. ed.). Minneapolis: University of Minnesota Press.

Dahlstrom, W. G., Welsh, G. S., & Dahlstrom, L. E. (1975). *An MMPI handbook: Vol. II. Research applications* (rev. ed.). Minneapolis: University of Minnesota Press.

Dahmus, S., Bernardin, H. J., & Bernardin, K. (1992). Test review: Personal Experience Inventory. *Measurement and Evaluation in Counseling and Development, 25,* 91–94.

Dale, P. S., Loftus, E. F., & Rathbun, L. (1978). The influence of the form of the question on the eyewitness testimony of preschool children. *Journal of Psycholinguistic Research, 7,* 269–277.

Dalton, J. E. (1994). MMPI-168 and Marlowe-Crowne profiles of adoption applicants. *Journal of Clinical Psychology, 50,* 863–866.

Dalton, J. E., Tom, A., Rosenblum, M. L., Garte, S. H., & Aubuchon, I. N. (1989). Faking on the Mississippi Scale for combat-related posttraumatic stress disorder. *Psychological Assessment: A Journal of Consulting and Clinical Psychology, 1,* 56–57.

Damasio, A. R., Graff-Radford, N. R., & Damasio, H. (1983). Transient partial amnesia. *Archives of Neurology, 40,* 656–657.

Daniel, A. E., & Resnick, P. J. (1987). Mutism, malingering and competency to stand trial. *Bulletin of the American Academy of Psychiatry and the Law.*

Dannenbaum, S. E., & Lanyon, R. I. (1993). The use of subtle items in detecting deception. *Journal of Personality Assessment, 61*, 501–510.

Darton, N. (1991, October 7). The pain of the last taboo. *Newsweek*, pp. 70–72.

Daubert v. Merrell Dow Pharmaceuticals, 113 S. Ct. 2786 (1993).

Davidson, H., Suffield, B., Orenczuk, S., Nantau, K., & Mandel, A. (1991, February). *Screening for malingering using the memory for fifteen items test (MFIT)*. Paper presented at the annual meeting of the International Neuropsychological Society, San Antonio, TX.

Davidson, H. A. (1949). Malingered psychosis. *Bulletin of the Menninger Clinic, 13*, 157–163.

Davidson, H. A. (1952). *Forensic psychiatry* (2nd ed.). New York: Ronald Press.

Davidson, J. (1993). Issues in the diagnosis of posttraumatic stress disorder. In J. M. Oldham, M. B. Riba, & A. Tasman (Eds.), *Review of psychiatry*. Washington, DC: Author.

Davis, J. W., & Small, G. W. (1985). Munchausen's syndrome in an 85-year-old man. *Journal of the American Geriatrics Society, 33*, 154–155.

Davis, L. W., & Husband, R. W. (1931). A study of hypnotic susceptibility in relation to personality traits. *Journal of Abnormal and Social Psychology, 26*, 175–182.

Davis v. State, 354 So.2d 334 (Ala. Crim. App. 1978).

Davison, G. C., & Lazarus, A. A. (1994). Clinical innovation and evaluation: Integrating practice with inquiry. *Clinical Psychology: Science and Practice, 1*, 157–168.

deGroot, H. P., & Gwynn, M. I. (1989). Trance logic, duality and hidden observer responding. In N. P. Spanos & J. F. Chaves (Eds.), *Hypnosis: The cogitive-behavioral perspective*. Buffalo, NY: Prometheus Books.

Delis, D. C., Kramer, J. H., Kaplan, E., & Ober, B. A. (1987). *The California Verbal Learning Test: Research edition*. New York: Psychological Corporation.

Dell, P. F. (1988). Professional skepticism about multiple personality. *Journal of Nervous and Mental Disease, 176*, 528–531.

Denker, P. G., & Perry, G. F. (1954). Postconsussion syndrome in compensation and litigation. *Neurology, 4*, 912–918.

Denney, R. L. (in press). Symptom validity testing of remote memory in a criminal forensic setting. *Archives of Clinical Neuropsychology*.

Denney, R. L., & Wynkoop, T. F. (1995, August). *Exaggeration of neuropsychological deficits in pretrial evaluation: A case presentation*. Paper presented at the 103rd annual meeting of the American Psychological Association, New York.

Department of Health and Human Services. (1989). *Interagency head injury task force report*. Washington, DC: Author.

DePaulo, B. M., Lanier, K., & Davis, T. (1983). Detecting the deceit of the motivated liar. *Journal of Personality and Social Psychology, 45*, 1096–1103.

DePaulo, B. M., Stone, J. I., & Lassiter, G. D. (1985). Deceiving and detecting deceit. In B. R. Schlenker (Ed.), *Self and identity: Presentations of self in social life* (pp. 323–370). New York: McGraw-Hill.

De Puysegur, A. M. (1943). On the discovery of artificial somnambulism. In A. Teste (Ed.), *Practical manual of animal magnetism* (D. Spillan, Trans.). London: H. Bailliere. (Original work published 1784)

Deutsch, H. (1982). On the pathological lie. *Journal of the American Academy of Psychoanalysis, 10*, 369–386.

de Wit, H., Uhlenhuth, E. H., Pierri, J., & Johanson, C. E. (1987). Individual differences in behavioral and subjective responses to alcohol. *Alcoholism: Clinical and Experimental Research, 11*(1), 52–59.

Diamond, B. (1956). The simulation of insanity. *Journal of Social Therapy, 2*, 158–165.

Diamond, B. L. (1980). Inherent problems in the use of pretrial hypnosis on a prospective witness. *California Law Review, 68,* 313–349.

Dicken, C. F. (1960). Simulated patterns on the California Psychological Inventory. *Journal of Consulting Psychology, 7,* 24–31.

Dikmen, S. S., Machamer, J. E., Winn, H. R., & Temkin, N. R. (1995). Neuropsychological outcome at 1-year post head injury. *Neuropsychology, 9,* 80–90.

Dikmen, S. S., Ross, B. L., Machamer, J. E., & Temkin, N. R. (1995). One year psychosocial outcome in head injury. *Journal of the International Neuropsychological Society, 1,* 67–77.

Dilloff, N. J. (1977). The admissibility of hypnotically influenced testimony. *Ohio Northern University Law Review, 4,* 1–23.

Donaldson, W. (1993). Accuracy of *d'* and *A'* as estimates of sensitivity. *Bulletin of the Psychonomic Society, 31,* 271–274.

Doren, D. M. (1987). *Understanding and treating the psychopath.* New York: Wiley.

Downing, J. (1942). *Science News Letter, 55,* 392.

Druss, R. G., & Douglas, C. J. (1988). Adaptive responses to illness and disability: Healthy denial. *General Hospital Psychiatry, 10,* 163–168.

DuAlba, L., & Scott, R. L. (1993). Somatization and malingering for workers' compensation applicants: A cross-cultural study. *Journal of Clinical Psychology, 49,* 913–917.

Dubinsky, S., Gamble, D. J., & Rogers, M. L. (1985). A literature review of subtle–obvious items on the MMPI. *Journal of Personality Assessment, 49,* 62–68.

Duckworth, J., & Barley, W. D. (1987). Normal limit profiles. In R. Greene (Ed.), *The MMPI: Its use in specific diagnostic groups* (pp. 278–315). Orlando, FL: Grune & Stratton.

Duffy, J. B., & Martin, P. P. (1973). The effects of direct and indirect teacher influence student trait anxiety on the immediate recall of academic material. *Psychology in the Schools, 10,* 233–237.

Duffy, T. P. (1992). The red baron. *New England Journal of Medicine, 327,* 408–411.

Dukes, W. F. (1965). $N = 1$. *Psychological Bulletin, 64,* 74–79.

Duncan, J. (1995). *Medication compliance in schizophrenic patients.* Unpublished dissertation, University of North Texas, Denton.

Dunn, J. T., Lees-Haley, P. R., Brown, R. S., Williams, C. W., & English, L. T. (1995). Neurotoxic complaint base rates of personal injury claimants: Implications for neuropsychological assessment. *Journal of Clinical Psychology, 51,* 577–584.

Dush, D. M., Simons, L. E., Platt, M., Nation, P. C., & Ayres, S. Y. (1994). Psychological profiles distinguishing litigating and nonlitigating pain patients: Subtle, and not so subtle. *Journal of Personality Assessment, 62,* 299–313.

Dworkin, R. H., Handlin, D. S., Richlin, D. M., Brand, L., & Vannucci, C. (1985). Unraveling the effects of compensation, litigation, and employment on treatment response in chronic pain. *Pain, 23,* 49–59.

Dwyer, S. M., Brockting, W. O., Robinson, B., & Miner, M. H. (1994). Sex offender case study: The truth? *Journal of Forensic Sciences, 39,* 241–245.

Dysken, M. W., Chang, S. S., Casper, R. C., & Davis, J. M. (1979). Barbiturate-facilitated interviewing. *Biological Psychiatry, 14,* 421–432.

Dysken, M. W., Kooser, J. A., Haraszti, J. S., & Davis, J. M. (1979). Clinical usefulness of sodium amobarbital interviewing. *Archives of General Psychiatry, 36,* 789–794.

Dysken, M. W., Steinberg, J., & Davis, J. M. (1979). Sodium amobarbital response during simulated catatonia. *Biological Psychiatry, 14,* 995–1000.

Earhart v. State, 823 S.W.2d 607 (Tex. Ct. App. 1991).

Earls, F., Smith, E., Reich, W., & Jung, K. G. (1988). Investigating psychopathological consequences of a disaster in children: A pilot study incorporating a structured diagnostic interview. *Journal of the American Academy of Child and Adolescent Psychiatry, 27,* 90–95.

Early, E. (1984). On confronting the Vietnam veteran [Letter to the editor]. *American Journal of Psychiatry, 14,* 472–473.

East, N. W. (1927). *An introduction to forensic psychiatry in the criminal courts.* London: J. A. Churchill.

Easton, K., & Feigenbaum, K. (1967). An examination of an experimental set to fake the Rorschach test. *Perceptual and Motor Skills, 24,* 871–874.

Eccles, A., Marshall, W. L., & Barbaree, H. E. (1994). Differentiating rapists and non-offenders using the rape index. *Behaviour Research and Therapy, 32,* 539–546.

Eckblad, M., & Chapman, L. J. (1983). Magical ideation as an indicator of schizotypy. *Journal of Consulting and Clinical Psychology, 51,* 215–225.

Eckenhoff, M. F., & Rakic, P. (1991). A quantitative analysis of synaptogenesis in the molecular layer of the dentate gyrus in the rhesus monkey. *Developmental Brain Research, 64,* 129–135.

Eisendrath, S. J. (1984). Factitious illness: A clarification. *Psychosomatics, 25,* 110–117.

Eisendrath, S. J. (1989). Factitious physical disorders: Treatment without confrontation. *Psychosomatics, 30,* 383–387.

Eisendrath, S. J. (1994). Factitious physical disorders. *Western Journal of Medicine, 160,* 177–179.

Eissler, K. R. (1951). Malingering. In G. B. Wilbur & W. Muensterberger (Eds.), *Psychoanalysis and culture* (pp. 218–253). New York: International Universities Press.

Ekman, P. (1985). *Telling lies: Clues to deceit in the marketplace, politics and marriage.* New York: W. W. Norton.

Ekman, P. (1991). *Telling lies: Clues to deceit in the marketplace, politics, and marriage.* New York: W. W. Norton.

Ekman, P., Friesen, W. V., & O'Sullivan, M. (1988). Smiles when lying. *Journal of Personal and Social Psychology, 54,* 414–420.

Elaad, E. (1990). Detection of guilty knowledge in real life criminal investigations. *Journal of Applied Psychology, 75,* 521–529.

Elaad, E., Ginton, A., & Jungman, N. (1992). Detection measures in real-life guilty knowledge tests. *Journal of Applied Psychology, 77,* 757–767.

Ellinwood, E. N., Jr. (1972). Amphetamine psychosis: Individuals, settings, and sequences. In E. H. Ellinwood, Jr. & S. Cohen (Eds.), *Current concepts on amphetamine abuse* (pp. 145–157). Rockville, MD: National Institute of Mental Health.

Emerson, J., Pankratz, L., Joos, S., & Smith, S. (1994). Personality disorders in problematic medical patients. *Psychosomatics, 35,* 469–473.

Endicott, J., & Spitzer, R. L. (1978). A diagnostic interview. *Archives of General Psychiatry, 35,* 837–844.

Enelow, A. J. (1971). Malingering and delayed recovery from injury. In J. J. Leedy (Ed.), *Compensation in psychiatric disability and rehabilitation* (pp. 42–46). Springfield, IL: Charles C Thomas.

Engel, G. L. (1970). Conversion symptoms. In C. M. MacBryde & R. S. Blacklow (Eds.), *Signs and symptoms* (5th ed.). Philadelphia: Lippincott.

Erdelyt, M. H. (1994). Hypnotic hypermnesia: The empty set of hypermnesia. *International Journal of Clinical and Experimental Hypnosis, 42,* 379–390.

Erdman, H. P., Klein, M. H., Greist, J. H., Skare, S. S., Husted, J. J., Robins, L. N., Helzer, J. E., Goldring, E., Hamburger, M., & Miller, J. P. (1992). A comparison of two computer-administered versions of the NIMH Diagnostic Interview Schedule. *Journal of Psychiatric Research, 26,* 85–95.

Erickson, M. H. (1939). The induction of color blindness by a technique of hypnotic suggestion. *Journal of General Psychology, 20,* 64–69.

Erickson, M. H., & Kubie, L. S. (1941). The successful treatment of a case of acute hysterical depression by a return under hypnosis to a critical phase of childhood. *Psychoanalytic Quarterly, 10,* 583–609.

Erickson, W. D., Luxenberg, M. G., Walbek, N. H., & Seely, R. K. (1987). Frequency of MMPI two-point code types among sex offenders. *Journal of Consulting and Clinical Psychology, 55,* 566–570.

Evans, F. I., & Schmeidler, D. (1966). Relationships between the Harvard Group Scale of Hypnotic Susceptibility and the Stanford Hypnotic Susceptibility Scale, Form C. *International Journal of Clinical and Experimental Hypnosis, 14,* 333–343.

Evans, I. M., & Nelson, R. O. (1977). Assessment of child behavior problems. In A. R. Ciminero, K. S. Calhoun, & H. E. Adams (Eds.), *Handbook of behavioral assessment* (pp. 603–681). New York: Wiley.

Evans, J., Wilson, B., Wraight, E. P., & Hodges, J. R. (1993). Neuropsychological and SPECT scan findings during and after transient global amnesia: Evidence for the differential impairment of remote episodic memory. *Journal of Neurology, Neurosurgery, and Psychiatry, 56,* 1227–1230.

Evans, R. G., & Dinning, W. D. (1983). Response consistency among high *F* scale scorers on the MMPI. *Journal of Clinical Psychology, 39,* 246–248.

Everson, M. D., & Boat, B. W. (1989). False allegations of sexual abuse by children and adolescents. *Journal of the American Academy of Child and Adolescent Psychiatry, 28,* 230–235.

Exner, J. E. (1974). *The Rorschach: A comprehensive system.* New York: Wiley.

Exner, J. E. (1978). *The Rorschach: A comprehensive system: Vol. 2. Interpretation.* New York: Wiley.

Exner, J. E. (1985). *Systematic interpretation of the Rorschach protocol utilizing the comprehensive system.* Minneapolis: National Computer Systems.

Exner, J. E. (1991). *The Rorschach: A comprehensive system: Vol. 2. Interpretation* (2nd ed.). New York: Wiley.

Exner, J. E., & Sherman, J. (1977). *Rorschach performance of schizophrenics asked to improve their protocols: Workshops Study No. 243.* Unpublished manuscript.

Exner, J. E., Viglione, D. J., & Gillespie, R. (1984). Relationships between Rorschach variables as relevant to the interpretation of structural data. *Journal of Personality Assessment, 48,* 65–69.

Eysenck, H. J. (1954). The science of personality: Nomothetic! *Psychological Review, 61,* 339–342.

Fabian, C. A., & Billick, S. B. (1986, October). *Ethical and forensic issues in general psychiatry narcoanalysis.* Paper presented at annual convention of the American Academy of Psychiatry and Law, Philadelphia.

Fairbank, J. A., McCaffrey, R. J., & Keane, T. M. (1985). Psychometric detection of fabricated symptoms of posttraumatic stress disorder. *American Journal of Psychiatry, 142,* 501–503.

Fairbank, J. A., McCaffrey, R. J., & Keane, T. M. (1986). Letters to the Editor—On simulating post-traumatic stress disorder—Dr. Fairbank and associates reply. *American Journal of Psychiatry, 143,* 268–269.

Falloon, I., & Talbot, R. (1981). Persistent auditory hallucinations: Coping mechanisms and implications for management. *Psychological Medicine, 11,* 329–339.

False Memory Syndrome Foundation. (1994). *Frequently asked questions.* Philadelphia: Author.

Fals-Stewart, W. (1995). The effect of defensive responding by substance-abusing patients on the MCMI. *Journal of Personality Assessment, 64,* 540–551.

Fantoni-Salvador, P., & Rogers, R. (in press). Spanish versions of the MMPI-2 and PAI: An investigation of concurrent validity with Hispanic patients. *Journal of Personality Assessment.*

Farwell, L. A., & Donchin, E. (1991). The truth will out: Interrogative polygraphy ("lie detection") with event related potentials. *Psychophysiology, 28,* 531–547.

Faust, D., Hart, K., & Guilmette, T. J. (1988). Pediatric malingering: The capacity of children to fake believable deficits of neuropsychological testing. *Journal of Consulting and Clinical Psychology, 56,* 578–582.

Faust, D., Hart, K., Guilmette, T. J., & Arkes, H. R. (1988). Neuropsychologists' capacity to detect adolescent malingerers. *Professional Psychology: Research and Practice, 19,* 508–515.

Fauteck, P. K. (1995). Detecting the malingering of psychosis in offenders: No easy solutions. *Criminal Justice and Behavior, 22,* 3–18.

Fekken, G. C. (1986). The Inwald Personality Inventory. In D. J. Keyser & R. C. Sweatand (Eds.), *Test critiques* (Vol. 6, pp. 265–276). Kansas City, MO: Test Corporation of America.

Fekken, G. C., & Holden, R. R. (1987). Assessing the person reliability of an individual MMPI protocol. *Journal of Personality Assessment, 51,* 123–132.

Feldman, M. D., & Ford, C. V. (with Reinhold, T.). (1994). *Patient or pretender: Inside the strange world of factitious disorders.* New York: Wiley.

Feldman, M. D., Ford, C. V., & Stone, T. (1994). Deceiving others/deceiving oneself: Four cases of factitious rape. *Southern Medical Journal, 87,* 736–738.

Feldman, M. D., & Russell, J. L. (1991). Factitious cyclic hypersomnia: A new variant of factitious disorder. *Southern Medical Journal, 84,* 379–381.

Feldman, M. J., & Graley, J. (1954). The effects of an experimental set to simulate abnormality on group Rorschach performance. *Journal of Projective Techniques, 18,* 326–334.

Feldman, R., & White, J. (1980). Detecting deception in children. *Journal of Communication, 30,* 350–355.

Fenichel, O. (1945). *The psychoanalytic theory of neurosis.* New York: W. W. Norton.

Ferguson, L. R., Partyka, L. B., & Lester, B. M. (1974). Patterns of parent perception differentiating clinic from non-clinic children. *Journal of Abnormal Child Psychology, 2,* 169–181.

Feucht, T. E., Stephens, R. C., & Walker, M. L. (1994). Drug use among juvenile arrestees: A comparison of self-report, urinalysis and hair assay. *Journal of Drug Issues, 24,* 99–116.

Fink, P. (1992). Physical complaints and symptoms of somatizing patients. *Journal of Psychosomatic Research, 36,* 125–136.

Folks, D. G., & Freeman, A. M. (1985). Munchausen's syndrome and other factitious illness. *Psychiatric Clinics of North America, 8,* 263–278.

Folstein, M. F., Folstein, S. E., & McHugh, P. R. (1975). Mini-mental state: A practical method of grading cognitive state of patients for the clinician. *Journal of Psychiatric Research, 12,* 189–198.

Fombonne, E. (1991). The use of questionnaires in child psychiatry research: Measuring their performance and choosing an optimal cutoff. *Journal of Child Psychology and Psychiatry, 32,* 677–693.

Fontana, A. F., Klein, E. B., Lewis, E., & Levine, L. (1968). Presentation of self in mental illness. *Journal of Consulting and Clinical Psychology, 32,* 110–119.

Ford, C. V., King, B. H., & Hollender, M. H. (1988). Lies and liars: Psychiatric aspects of prevarication. *American Journal of Psychiatry, 145,* 554–562.

Fordyce, W. E., Roberts, A. H., & Sternbach, R. A. (1985). The behavioral management of chronic pain: A response to critics. *Pain, 22,* 113–125.

Fosberg, I. A. (1938). Rorschach reactions under varied instructions. *Rorschach Research Exchange, 3,* 12–30.

Fosberg, I. A. (1941). An experimental study of the reliability of the Rorschach Psychodiagnostic Technique. *Rorschach Research Exchange, 5,* 72–84.

Fosberg, I. A. (1943). How do subjects attempt to fake results on the Rorschach test? *Rorschach Research Exchange, 7,* 119–121.

Fox, D. D., Gerson, A., & Lees-Haley, P. R. (1995). Interrelationships of MMPI-2 validity scales in personal injury claims. *Journal of Clinical Psychology, 51,* 42–47.

Francis, L. J., Lankshear, D. W., & Pearson, P. R. (1989). The relationship between religiosity and the short form JEPQ (JEPQ-S) indices of *E, N, L,* and *P* among eleven year olds. *Personality and Individual Differences, 19,* 763–769.

Frank, L. K. (1939). Projective methods for the study of personality. *Journal of Psychology, 8,* 389–413.

Frankel, F. H. (1976). *Hypnosis: Trance as a coping mechanism.* New York: Plenum.

Frankel, F. H. (1993). Adult reconstruction of childhood events in the multiple personality literature. *American Journal of Psychiatry, 150,* 954–958.

Franzen, M. D., Iverson, G. L., & McCracken, L. M. (1990). The detection of malingering in neuropsychological assessment. *Neuropsychology Review, 1,* 247–279.

Frederick, R. I. (1995, August). *Taxonometric analysis of malingering.* Paper presented at the 101st annual meeting of the American Psychological Association, New York.

Frederick, R. I., & Carter, M. (1993, August). *Detection of malingered amnesia in a competency evaluee.* Paper presented at the annual meeting of the American Psychological Association, Toronto.

Frederick, R. I., Carter, M., & Powel, J. (1995). Adapting symptom validity testing to evaluate suspicious complaints of amnesia in medicolegal evaluations. *Bulletin of the American Academy of Psychiatry and the Law, 23,* 231–237.

Frederick, R. I., & Foster, H. G. (1991). Multiple measures of malingering on a forced-choice test of cognitive ability. *Psychological Assessment: A Journal of Clinical and Consulting Psychology, 3,* 596–602.

Frederick, R. I., Sarfaty, S. D., Johnston, J. D., & Powel, J. (1994). Validation of a detector of response bias on a forced-choice test of nonverbal ability. *Neuropsychology, 8,* 118–125.

Freund, K. (1963). A laboratory method for diagnosing predominance of homo- and hetero-erotic interest in the male. *Behaviour Research Therapy, 1,* 85–93.

Freund, K., & Blanchard, R. (1989). Phallometric diagnosis of pedophilia. *Journal of Consulting and Clinical Psychology, 57,* 100–105.

Freund, K., Chan, S., & Coulthard, R. (1979). Phallometric diagnosis with "nonadmitters." *Behaviour Research and Therapy, 17,* 451–457.

Freund, K., & Watson, R. J. (1992). The proportions of heterosexual and homosexual pedophiles among sex offenders against children: An exploratory study. *Journal of Sex and Marital Therapy, 18,* 34–42.

Freund, K., Watson, R., & Rienzo, D. (1988). Signs of feigning in the phallometric test. *Behaviour Research and Therapy, 26,* 105–112.

Friedlander, J. W., & Sarbin, T. R. (1938). The depth of hypnosis. *Journal of Abnormal and Social Psychology, 33,* 453–475.

Friedman, M. J. (1981). Post-Vietnam syndrome: Recognition and Management. *Psychosomatics, 22,* 931–943.

Fritz, G. K., Spirito, A., & Yeung, A. (1994). Utility of the repressive defense style construct in childhood. *Journal of Clinical Child Psychology, 23,* 306–313.

Frueh, B. C., & Kinder, B. N. (1994). The susceptibility of the Rorschach Inkblot Test to malingering of combat-related PTSD. *Journal of Personality Assessment, 62,* 280–298.

Frumkin, L. R., & Victoroff, J. I. (1990). Chronic factitious disorder with symptoms of AIDS. *American Journal of Medicine, 88,* 694–696.

Fuchs, D., & Thelen, M. (1988). Children's expected interpersonal consequences of communicating their affective states and reported likelihood of expression. *Child Development, 59,* 1314–1322.

Gacano, C. B., Meloy, J. R., Sheppard, K., Speth, E., & Roske, A. (1995). A clinical investigation of malingering and psychopathy in hospitalized insanity acquittees. *Bulletin of the American Academy of Psychiatry and Law, 23,* 387–397.

Gade, A., & Mortensen, E. L. (1990). Temporal gradient in the remote memory impairment of amnesic patients with lesions in the basal forebrain. *Neuropsychologia, 28,* 985–1001.

Gallucci, N. T. (1985). Influence of dissimulation on indexes of response consistency for the MMPI. *Psychological Reports, 57,* 1013–1014.

Ganellen, R. J. (1994). Attempting to conceal psychological disturbance: MMPI defensive response sets and the Rorschach. *Journal of Personality Assessment, 63,* 423–437.

Ganellen, R. J., Wasyliw, O. E., Haywood, T. W., & Grossman, L. S. (1996). Can psychosis be malingered on the Rorschach?: An empirical study. *Journal of Personality Assessment, 66,* 65–80.

Ganguli, H. C. (1985). Review of the Stanton Survey and the Stanton Survey Phase II. In J. V. Mitchell, Jr. (Ed.), *The ninth mental measurements yearbook* (pp. 1470–1472). Lincoln, NE: Buros Institute of Mental Measurements.

Ganter, A. B., Graham, J. R., & Archer, R. A. (1992). Usefulness of the MAC scale in differentiating adolescent in normal, psychiatric, and substance abuse settings. *Psychological Assessment, 4,* 133–137.

Garfield, P. (1987). Nightmares in the sexually abused female teenager. *Psychiatric Journal of the University of Ottawa, 12,* 93–97.

Garry, M., & Loftus, E. F. (1994). Pseudomemories without hypnosis. *International Journal of Clinical and Experimental Hypnosis, 42,* 363–378.

Gaston, L., & Sabourin, S. (1992). Client satisfaction and social desirability in psychotherapy. *Evaluation and Program Planning, 15,* 227–231.

Gavin, D. R., Ross, H. E., & Skinner, H. A. (1989). Diagnostic validity of the drug abuse screening test in the assessment of DSM-III drug disorders. *British Journal of Addictions, 84,* 301–307.

Gelles, R. J. (1980). Violence in the family: A review of research in the seventies. *Journal of Marriage and the Family, 42,* 873–885.

Gerson, M. J., & Victoroff, V. M. (1948). Experimental investigation into the validity of confessions obtained under sodium Amytal narcosis. *Clinical Psychopathology, 9,* 359–375.

Gibson, G. S., & Manley, S. (1991). Alternative approaches to urinalysis in the detection of drugs. *Social Behavior and Personality, 19,* 195–204.

Gill, M. M., & Brenman, M. (1959). *Hypnosis and related states: Psychoanalytic studies in regression.* New York: International Universities Press.

Gillis, J. R., Rogers, R., & Bagby, R. M. (1991). Validity of the M Test: Simulation-design and natural-group approaches. *Journal of Personality Assessment, 57*(1), 130–140.

Glisky, E. L., Polster, M. R., & Routhieaux, B. C. (1995). Double dissociation between item and source memory. *Neuropsychology, 9,* 229–235.

Goebel, R. A. (1983). Detection of faking on the Halstead–Reitan neuropsychological test battery. *Journal of Clinical Psychology, 39,* 731–742.

Goldberg, E., Hughes, J. E. O., Mattis, S., & Antin, S. P. (1982). Isolated retrograde amnesia: Different etiologies, same mechanisms? *Cortex, 18,* 459–462.

Goldberg, J. D., & Miller, A. R. (1986). Performance of psychiatric inpatients and intellectually deficient individuals on a task assessing thr validity of memory impairments. *Journal of Clinical Psychology, 42,* 792–795.

Goldberg, L. R., Grenier, J. R., Guion, R. M., Sechrest, L. B., & Wing, H. (1991). *Question-*

naires used in the prediction of trustworthiness in preemployment selection decisions. Washington, DC: American Psychological Association.

Goldstein, F. C., Levin, H. S., & Boake, C. (1989). Conceptual encoding following severe closed head injury. *Cortex, 25,* 541–554.

Golechha, G. R., Sethi, I. C., Misra, S. L., & Jayaprakash, N. P. (1986). Ketamine abreaction: A new approach to narcoanalysis. *Indian Journal of Psychiatry, 28,* 297–304.

Goodman, G. S. (1984). The child witness: Conclusions and future directions for research and legal practice. *Journal of Social Issues, 40,* 157–175.

Goodman, G. S., & Clarke-Stewart, A. (1991). Suggestibility in children's testimony: Implications for sexual abuse allegations. In J. Doris (Ed.), *The suggestibility of children's recollections* (pp. 92–105). Washington, DC: American Psychological Association.

Goodnow, J. J. (1988). Parents' ideas, actions, and feelings: Models and methods from developmental and social psychology. *Child Development, 59,* 286–320.

Goodwin, D. W., Alderson, P., & Rosenthal, R. (1971). Clinical significance of hallucinations in psychiatric disorders: A study of 116 hallucinatory patients. *Archives of General Psychiatry, 24,* 76–80.

Goodwin, J. (1988). Munchausen's syndrome as a dissociative disorder. *Dissociation, 1,* 54–60.

Goodwin, J., Sahd, D., & Rada, R. T. (1978). Incest hoax: False accusations, false denials. *Bulletin of the American Academy of Psychiatry and the Law, 6,* 269–276.

Gorman, W. F. (1984). Neurological malingering. *Behavioral Sciences and the Law, 2,* 67–73.

Gorman, W. F., & Winograd, M. (1988). Crossing the border from Munchausen to malingering. *Journal of the Florida Medical Association, 75,* 147–150.

Gothard, S. (1993). *Detection of malingering in mental competency evaluations.* Unpublished dissertation, California School of Professional Psychology, San Diego.

Gothard, S., Viglione, D. J., Meloy, J. R., & Sherman, M. (1995). Detection of malingering in competency to stand trial evaluations. *Law and Human Behavior, 19,* 493–505.

Gottesman, I. I., & Prescott, C. A. (1989). Abuses of the MacAndrew MMPI alcoholism scale: A critical review. *Clinical Psychology Review, 9,* 223–258.

Gough, H. G. (1947). Simulated patterns on the MMPI. *Journal of Abnormal and Social Psychology, 42,* 215–225.

Gough, H. G. (1950). The *F* minus *K* dissimulation index for the MMPI. *Journal of Consulting Psychology, 14,* 408–413.

Gough, H. G. (1954). Some common misconceptions about neuroticism. *Journal of Consulting Psychology, 18,* 287–292.

Gough, H. G. (1957). *Manual for the California Psychological Inventory.* Palo Alto, CA: Consulting Psychologists Press.

Gough, H. G. (1971). The assessment of wayward impulse by means of the Personnel Reaction Blank. *Personnel Psychology, 24,* 669–677.

Gough, H. G. (1972). *Manual for the Personnel Reaction Blank.* Palo Alto, CA: Consulting Psychologists Press.

Gough, H. G. (1987a). *Manual for the California Psychological Inventory* (2nd ed.). Palo Alto, CA: Consulting Psychologists Press.

Gough, H. G. (1987b). *Administrator's guide for the California Psychological Inventory.* Palo Alto, CA: Consulting Psychologists Press.

Gough, H. G. (1989). The California Psychological Inventory. In C. S. Newmark (Ed.), *Major psychological assessment instruments* (Vol. 2, pp. 67–98). Boston: Allyn & Bacon.

Graber, R. A., & Miller, W. R. (1988). Abstinence or controlled drinking goals for problem drinkers: A randomized clinical trial. *Psychology of Addictive Behaviors, 2,* 20–33.

Graf, P., Squire, L. R., & Mandler, G. (1984). The information that amnesic patients do not forget. *Journal of Experimental Psychology: Learning, Memory, and Cognition, 10,* 164–178.

Graham, J. R. (1987). *The MMPI: A practical guide* (2nd ed.). New York: Oxford University Press.

Graham, J. R. (1993). *MMPI-2: Assessing personality and psychopathology* (2nd ed.). New York: Oxford University Press.

Graham, J. R., Watts, D., & Timbrook, R. E. (1991). Detecting fake-good and fake-bad MMPI-2 profiles. *Journal of Personality Assessment, 57,* 264–277.

Graham, N., & Wish, E. D. (1994). Drug use among female arrestees: Onset, patterns, and relationships to prostitution. *Journal of Drug Issues, 24*(2), 315–329.

Grayson, D. A. (1986). Latent trait analysis of the Eysenck Personality Questionnaire. *Journal of Psychiatric Research, 20,* 217–235.

Grayson, H. M. (1951). *A psychological admissions testing program and manual.* Los Angeles: Veterans Administration Center, Neuropsychiatric Hospital.

Green, J. P., Lynn, S. J., Weekes, J. R., Carlson B. W., Brentar, J., Latham, L., & Kurzhals, R. (1990). Literalism as a marker of hypnotic "trance": Disconfirming evidence. *Journal of Abnormal Psychology, 99,* 16–21.

Greene, E., Flynn, M., & Loftus, E. F. (1982). Inducing resistance to misleading information. *Journal of Verbal Learning and Verbal Behavior, 21,* 207–219.

Greene, R. L. (1978). An empirically derived MMPI carelessness scale. *Journal of Clinical Psychology, 34,* 407–410.

Greene, R. L. (1980). *The MMPI: An interpretive manual.* New York: Grune & Stratton.

Greene, R. L. (1988a). Assessment of malingering and defensiveness by objective personality measures. In R. Rogers (Ed.), *Clinical assessment of malingering and deception* (1st ed., pp. 123–158). New York: Guilford Press.

Greene, R. L. (1988b). The relative efficacy of *F–K* and the obvious and subtle scales to detect over-reporting of psychopathology on the MMPI. *Journal of Clinical Psychology, 44,* 152–159.

Greene, R. L. (1991). *The MMPI-2/MMPI: An interpretive manual.* Boston: Allyn & Bacon.

Greene, R. L. (1995). [MMPI-2 data research file for psychiatric inpatients and outpatients.] Unpublished raw data.

Greene, R. L., Arredondo, R., & Davis, H. D. (1990, August). *The comparability of the MacAndrew Alcoholism Scale—Revised (MMPI-2) and the MacAndrew Alcoholism Scale (MMPI).* Paper presented at the annual meeting of the American Psychological Association, Boston.

Greene, R. L., Weed, N. C., Butcher, J. N., Arredondo, R., & Davis, H. G. (1992). A cross-validation of the MMPI-2 substance abuse scales. *Journal of Personality Assessment, 58,* 405–410.

Greenfield v. Commonwealth, 204 S.E.2d 414 (1974).

Greenfield, D. (1987). Feigned psychosis in a 14-year-old girl. *Hospital and Community Psychiatry, 38,* 73–77.

Greenwald, J., & Satow, Y. (1978). A short social desirability scale. *Psychological Reports, 27,* 131–135.

Greiffenstein, M. F., Baker, W. J., & Gola, T. (1994). Validation of malingered amnesia measures with a large clinical sample. *Psychological Assessment, 6,* 218–224.

Griffin, M. L., Weiss, R. D., Mirin, S. M., Wilson, H., & Bouchard-Voelk, B. (1987). The use of the Diagnostic Interview Schedule in drug-dependent patients. *American Journal of Drug and Alcohol Abuse, 13,* 281–291.

Griffith, J. L., & Slovik, L. S. (1989). Munchausen syndrome by proxy and sleep disorders medicine. *Sleep, 12,* 178–183.

Grillo, J., Brown, R. S., Hilsabeck, R., Price, J. R., & Lees-Haley, P. R. (1994). Raising doubts about claims of malingering: Implications of relationships between MCMI-II and MMPI-2 performances. *Journal of Clinical Psychology, 50,* 651–655.

Gripshover, D. L., & Dacey, C. M. (1994). Discriminative validity of the MacAndrew scale in settings with a high base rate of substance abuse. *Journal of Studies on Alcohol, 55,* 303–308.

Gronwall, D. M. A., & Wrightson, P. (1974). Cumulative effects of concussion. *Lancet, 2,* 995–997.

Grossman, L. S., & Cavanaugh, J. L. (1989). Do sex offenders minimize psychiatric symptoms? *Journal of Forensic Sciences, 34,* 881–886.

Grossman, L. S., & Cavanaugh, J. L. (1990). Psychopathology and denial in alleged sex offenders. *Journal of Nervous and Mental Disease, 178,* 739–744.

Grossman, L. S., & Wasyliw, O. E. (1988). A psychometric study of stereotypes: Assessment of malingering in a criminal forensic group. *Journal of Personality Assessment, 52,* 549–563.

Grow, R., McVaugh, W., & Eno, T. D. (1980). Faking and the MMPI. *Journal of Clinical Psychology, 36*(4), 910–917.

Grunberger, G., Weiner, J. L., Silverman, R., Taylor, S., & Gorden, P. (1988). Factitious hypoglycemia due to surreptitious administration of insulin. *Annals of Internal Medicine, 108,* 252–257.

Guastello, S. J., & Rieke, M. L. (1991). A review and critique of honesty test research. *Behavioral Sciences and the Law, 9,* 501–523.

Guberman, A. (1982). Psychogenic pseudoseizures in non-epileptic patients. *Canadian Journal of Psychiatry, 27,* 401–404.

Gudjonsson, G. H. (1990). Self-deception and other-deception in forensic assessment. *Personality and Individual Differences, 11,* 219–225.

Gudjonsson, G. H., & Shackleton, H. (1986). The pattern of scores on Raven's matrices during "faking bad" and "non faking" performance. *British Journal of Clinical Psychology, 25,* 35–41.

Gudjonsson, G. H., & Taylor, P. J. (1985). Cognitive deficit in a case of retrograde amnesia. *British Journal of Psychiatry, 147,* 715–718.

Guilmette, T. J., Hart, K. J., & Giulianao, A. J. O. (1993). Malingering detection: The use of a forced-choice method in identifying organic versus simulated memory impairment. *Clinical Neuropsychologist, 7,* 59–69.

Guilmette, T. J., Hart, K. J., Giuliano, A. J., & Leininger, B. E. (1994). Detecting simulated memory impairment: Comparison of the Rey 15-Item Test and the Hiscock Forced-Choice Procedure. *Clinical Neuropsychologist, 8,* 283–294.

Guilmette, T. J., Whelihan, W., Sparadeo, F. R., & Buongiorno, G. (1994). Validity of neuropsychological test results in disability evaluations. *Perceptual and Motor Skills, 78,* 1179–1186.

Guthmann, D. R., & Brenna, D. C. (1990). The Personal Experience Inventory: An assessment of the instrument's validiy among a delinquent population in Washington State. *Journal of Adolescent Chemical Dependency, 1,* 15–24.

Guttmacher, M. S., & Weihofen, H. (1952). *Psychiatry and the law.* New York: W. W. Norton.

Hain, J. D., Smith, B. M., & Stevenson, I. (1966). Effectiveness and processes of interviewing with drugs. *Journal of Psychiatric Research, 4,* 95–106.

Haines, M. E., & Norris, M. P. (1995). Detecting the malingering of cognitive deficits: An update. *Neuropsychology Review, 5,* 125–148.

Hale, G., Zimostrad, S., Duckworth, J., & Nicholas, D. (1986, March). *The abusive personality: MMPI profiles of male batterers.* Paper presented at the 21st Annual Symposium on Recent Developments in the Use of the MMPI, Clearwater, FL.

Hall, C. G. N. (1989). WAIS-R and MMPI profiles of men who have assaulted children: Evidence of limited utility. *Journal of Personality Assessment, 53,* 404–412.

Hall, C. G. N., Maiuro, R. D., Vitaliano, P. P., & Proctor, W. D. (1986). The utility of the

MMPI with men who have sexually assaulted children. *Journal of Consulting and Clinical Psychology, 54,* 493–496.

Hall, C. G. N., Proctor, W. C., & Nelson, G. M. (1988). Validity of physiological measures of pedophilic sexual arousal in a sexual offender population. *Journal of Consulting and Clinical Psychology, 56,* 118–122.

Hall, G. C. N., Shepherd, J. B., & Mudrak, P. (1992). MMPI taxonomies of child sexual and nonsexual offenders: A cross-validation and extension. *Journal of Personality Assessment, 58,* 127–137.

Hall, G. C., Shondrick, D. D., & Hirschman, R. (1993). The role of sexual arousal in sexually aggressive behavior: A meta-analysis. *Journal of Consulting and Clinical Psychology, 61,* 1091–1095.

Hall, H. V. (1982). Dangerousness predictions and the maligned forensic professional. *Criminal Justice and Behavior, 9,* 3–12.

Halleck, S. (1975). The criminal's problem with psychiatry. In R. C. Allen (Ed.), *Readings in law and psychiatry* (pp. 51–54). Baltimore: Johns Hopkins University Press.

Halleck, S. L. (1971). *The politics of therapy.* New York: Harper and Row.

Hamilton, J. D. (1985). Pseudo-posttraumatic stress disorder. *Military Medicine, 150,* 353–356.

Hamilton, J. E. (1906). *Railway and other accidents.* London: Bailliere, Tindall & Co.

Hamsher, J. H., & Farina, A. (1967). "Openness" as a dimension of projective test responses. *Journal of Consulting Psychology, 31,* 525–528.

Hankins, G. C., Barnard, G. W., & Robbins, L. (1993). The validity of the M Test in a residential forensic facility. *Bulletin of the American Academy of Psychiatry and the Law, 21,* 111–121.

Hanson, R. K., Cox, B., & Woszcyna, C. (1991). Assessing treatment outcome for sexual offenders. *Annals of Sex Research, 4,* 177–208.

Hanson, R. K., Steffy, R. A., & Gauthier, R. (1993). Long-term recidivism of child molesters. *Journal of Consulting and Clinical Psychology, 61,* 646–652.

Happel, R. M., & Auffrey, J. J. (1995). Sex offender assessment: Interrupting the dance of denial. *American Journal of Forensic Psychology, 13,* 5–22.

Harding v. State, 230, 246 A.2d 302 (1968); *cert. denied,* 395 U.S. 949 (1968).

Hare, R. D. (1970). *Psychopathy: Theory and research.* New York: Wiley.

Hare, R. D. (1991). *Manual for the Revised Psychopathy Checklist.* Toronto: Multihealth Systems.

Hare, R. D., Cox, D. N., & Hart, S. D. (1989). *Preliminary manual for the Psychopathy Checklist: Clinical Version (PCL:CV).* Unpublished manuscript, University of British Columbia, Vancouver.

Harford, R. J., & Kleber, H. D. (1978). Comparative validity of random-interval and fixed-interval urinalysis schedules. *Archives of General Psychiatry, 35,* 356–359.

Harpur, T. J., Hakstian, A. R., & Hare, R. D. (1988). Factor structure of the psychopathy checklist. *Journal of Consulting and Clinical Psychology, 56,* 741–747.

Harpur, T. J., Hare, R. D., & Hakstian, A. R. (1989). Two-factor conceptualization of psychopathy: Construct validity and assessment implications. *Psychological Assessment: A Journal of Consulting and Clinical Psychology, 1,* 6–17.

Harris, W. G. (undated). *An investigation of the Stanton Survey using a validity generalization model.* Charlotte, NC: Stanton Corporation.

Harrell, A. V., & Wirtz, P. W. (1989). *Adolescent Drinking Inventory professional manual.* Odessa, FL: Psychological Assessment Resources.

Harter, S. (1983). The development of the self-system. In M. Hetherington (Ed.), *Handbook of child psychology: Social and personality development* (Vol. 4, pp. 275–385). New York: Wiley.

Hartshorne, H., & May, M. A. (1928). *Studies in deceit.* New York: Macmillan.

Hasher, L., & Zacks, R. T. (1979). Automatic and effortful processes in memory. *Journal of Experimental Psychology: General, 108,* 356–388.

Hasin, D. S., & Grant, B. F. (1987). Assessment of specific drug disorders in a sample of substance abuse patients: A comparison of the DIS and the SADS-L procedures. *Drugs and Alcohol Dependence, 19,* 165–176.

Haskett, J. (1995). *Tehachapi Malingering Scale: Research revision No. 5 Manual.* Modesto, CA: Logocraft.

Haskett, J., & Lender, J. (March, 1995). *Deception at reception: The Tehachapi Malingering Scale.* Paper presented at the 20th annual conference of the Forensic Mental Health Association of California, Asilomar, CA.

Hathaway, S. R., & McKinley, J. C. (1951). *The Minnesota Multiphasic Personality Inventory Manual* (rev.). New York: Psychological Corporation.

Hathaway, S. R., & McKinley, J. C. (1967). *MMPI manual.* New York: Psychological Corporation.

Hawkins, K. A., Sledge, W. H., Orleans, J. F., Quinlan, D. M., Rakfeldt, J., & Hoffman, R. E. (1995). Can digit symbol–verbal fluency comparisons facilitate detection of pseudodementia? *European Archives of Psychiatry and Clinical Neuroscience, 244,* 317–319.

Hay G. G. (1983). Feigned psychosis—A review of the simulation of mental illness. *British Journal of Psychiatry, 143,* 8–10.

Hayes, J. S., Hale, D. B., & Gouvier, W. D. (1996, February). *Tests of malingering: Do they discriminate malingering in defendants with mental retardation?* Paper presented at the meeting of the International Neuropsychological Society, Chicago.

Hays, J. R., Emmons, J., & Lawson, K. A. (1993). Psychiatric norms for the Rey 15-Item Visual Memory Test. *Perceptual and Motor Skills, 76,* 1331–1334.

Hays, R. D., & Ware, J. E., Jr. (1986). My medical care is better than yours: Social desirability and patient satisfaction ratings. *Medical Care, 24,* 519–524.

Haywood, T. W., & Grossman, L. S. (1994). Denial of deviant sexual arousal and psychopathology in child molesters. *Behavior Therapy, 25,* 327–340.

Haywood, T. W., Grossman, L. S., & Cavanaugh, J. L. (1990). Subjective versus objective measurement of deviant sexual arousal in clinical evaluations of alleged child molesters. *Journal of Consulting and Clinical Psychology, 2,* 269–275.

Haywood, T. W., Grossman, L. S., & Hardy, D. W. (1993). Denial and social desirability in clinical examinations of alleged sex offenders. *Journal of Nervous and Mental Diseases, 181,* 183–188.

Haywood, T. W., Grossman, L. S., Kravitz, H. M., & Wasyliw, O. E. (1994). Profiling psychological distortion in alleged child molesters. *Psychological Reports, 75,* 915–927.

Heaton, R. K., Smith, H. H., Lehman, R. A. W., & Vogt, A. T. (1978). Prospects for faking believable deficits on neuropsychological testing. *Journal of Consulting and Clinical Psychology, 46,* 892–900.

Heilbrun, K., Bennett, W. S., White, A. J., & Kelly, J. (1990). An MMPI-based empirical model of malingering and deception. *Behavioral Sciences and the Law, 8,* 45–53.

Heins v. Commonwealth of Pennsylvania, Unemployment Compensation Board of Review. 534 A.2d 592 (1987).

Hellerstein, D., Frosch, W., & Koenigsberg, H. W. (1987). The clinical significance of command hallucinations. *American Journal of Psychiatry, 144,* 219–225.

Henderson, J. (1986, October). *Psychic trauma claims in civil and administrative law.* Panel Presentation at the 17th American Academy of Psychiatry and the Law Meeting, Philadelphia.

Henly, G. A., & Winters, K. C. (1988). Development of problem severity scales for the assessment of adolescent alcohol and drug abuse. *International Journal of the Addictions, 23,* 65–85.

Herman, J. L., & Harvey, M. R. (1993). The false memory debate: Social science or social backlash. *Harvard Mental Health Letter.*

Herman, M. (1985). Amytal and the detection of deception. In R. Rosner (Ed.), *Critical issues in American psychiatry and law* (Vol. 2, pp. 187–194). New York: Plenum.

Hilgard, E. R. (1965). *Hypnotic susceptibility.* New York: Harcourt, Brace, Jovanovich.

Hilgard, E. R. (1967). A quantitative study of pain and its reduction through hypnotic suggestions. *Proceedings of the National Academy of Sciences, 57,* 1581–1586.

Hilgard, E. R. (1973). Dissociation revisited. In M. Henle, J. Jaynes, & J. J. Sullivan (Eds.), *Historical conceptions of psychology* (pp. 205–219). New York: Springer.

Hilgard, E. R. (1977). *Divided consciousness: Multiple controls in human thought and action.* New York: Wiley.

Hilgard, E. R. (1979). The Stanford Hypnotic Susceptibility Scales as related to other measures of hypnotic responsiveness. *International Journal of Clinical and Experimental Hypnosis, 21,* 68–82.

Hilgard, E. R. (1982). Hypnotic susceptibility and implications for measurement. *International Journal of Clinical and Experimental Hypnosis, 30,* 294–403.

Hilgard, E. R., & Loftus, E. F. (1979). Effective interrogation of the eyewitness. *International Journal of Clinical and Experimental Hypnosis, 27,* 342–357.

Hinojosa, L. (1993). The MMPI-2 and malingering: A study aimed at refining the detection of deception. *Dissertation Abstracts International, 54,* 2203-B.

Hinton, J. W., O'Neill, M. T., & Webster, S. (1980). Psychophysiological assessment of sex offenders in a security hospital. *Archives of Sexual Behavior, 9,* 205–216.

Hintzman, D. L. (1988). Judgments of frequency and recognition memory in a multiple-trace memory model. *Psychological Review, 95,* 528–551.

Hirschel, J. D., & McCarthy, B. R. (1983). The TASC–drug treatment program connection: Cooperation, cooptation or corruption of treatment objectives? *Journal of Offender Counseling, Services and Rehabilitation, 8,* 117–131.

Hiscock, M., & Hiscock, C. K. (1989). Refining the forced-choice method for the detection of malingering. *Journal of Clinical and Experimental Neuropsychology, 11,* 967–974.

Hofling, C. K. (1965). Some psychologic aspects of malingering. *GP, 31,* 115–121.

Holden, R. R., & Kroner, D. G. (1992). Relative efficacy of differential response latencies for detecting faking on a self-report measure of psychopathology. *Psychological Assessment, 4,* 170–173.

Hollrah, J. L., Schlottmann, R. S., Scott, A. B., & Brunetti, D. G. (1995). Validity of the MMPI subtle items. *Journal of Personality Assessment, 65,* 278–299.

Holmes, D. S. (1974). The conscious control of thematic projection. *Journal of Consulting and Clinical Psychology, 42,* 323–329.

Holmes, G. P., Kaplan, J. E., Gantz, N. M., Komaroff, A. L., Schonberger, L. B., Straus, S. E., Jones, J. F., Dubois, R. E., Cunningham-Rundles, C., Pahwa, S., Tosato, G., Zegans, L. S., Purtilo, D. T., Brown, N., Schooley, R. T., & Brus, I. (1988). Chronic fatigue syndrome: A working case definition. *Annals of Internal Medicine, 108,* 387–389.

Honts, C. R., Hodes, R. L., & Raskin, D. C. (1985). Effects of physical countermeasures on the physiological detection of deception. *Journal of Applied Psychology, 70,* 177–187.

Honts, C. R., Raskin, D. C., & Kircher, J. C. (1987). Effects of physical countermeasures and their electromyographic detection during polygraph tests for deception. *Journal of Psychophysiology, 1,* 241–247.

Honts, C. R., Raskin, D. C., & Kircher, J. C. (1994). Mental and physical countermeasures reduce the accuracy of polygraph tests. *Journal of Applied Psychology, 79,* 252–259.

Horn, J. L., Wanberg, K. W., & Foster, F. M. (1990). *Guide to the Alcohol Use Inventory*. Minneapolis: National Computer Systems.

Horsley, J. S. (1936). Narcoanalysis. *Journal of Mental Sciences, 82,* 416.

Horton, K. D., Smith, S. A., Barghout, N. K., & Connolly, D. A. (1992). The use of indirect memory tests to assess malingered amnesia: A study of metamemory. *Journal of Experimental Psychology: General, 121,* 326–351.

Horvath, F. (1977). The effect of selected variables on interpretation of polygraph records. *Journal of Applied Psychology, 62,* 127–136.

Hough, L. M. (1986). Personnel Reaction Blank (1988 Edition). In D. J. Keyser & R. C. Sweatland (Eds.), *Test critiques* (Vol. 8, pp. 563–569). Kansas City, MO: Test Corporation of America.

House v. State, 445 So.2d 815 (Miss. 1984).

Huba, G. J. (1986). The use of the runs test for assessing response validity in computer scored inventories. *Educational and Psychological Measurement, 46,* 929–932.

Huddleston, J. H. (1932). *Accidents, neuroses and compensation.* Baltimore: Williams & Wilkins.

Hunt, W. A. (1946). The detection of malingering: A further study. *Naval Medical Bulletin, 46,* 249–254.

Hunter, J. E., & Schmidt, F. L. (1990). *Methods of meta-analysis: Correcting error and bias in research findings.* Newbury Park, CA: Sage.

Hurwitz, T. A. (1989). Ideogenic neurological deficits: Conscious mechanisms in conversion symptoms. *Neuropsychiatry, Neuropsychology, and Behavioral Neurology, 4,* 301–308.

Hyer, L., Fallon, J. H., Harrison, W. R., & Boudewyns, P. A. (1987). MMPI overreporting by Vietnam combat veterans. *Journal of Clinical Psychology, 43,* 79–83.

Hyler, S. E., & Sussman, N. (1981). Chronic factitious disorder with physical symptoms (Munchausen syndrome). *Psychiatric Clinics of North America, 4,* 365–377.

Iacono, W. G. (1991). Can we determine the accuracy of polygraph tests? In J. R. Jennings, P. K. Ackles, & M. G. H. Coles (Eds.), *Advances in psychophysiology* (Vol. 4, pp. 201–207). London: Jessica Kingsley.

Iacono, W. G. (1995). Offender testimony: The detection of deception and guilty knowledge. In N. Brewer & C. Wilson (Eds.), *Psychology and policing* (pp. 155–171). Hillsdale, NJ: Erlbaum.

Iacono, W. G., Boisvenu, G. A., & Fleming, J. A. (1984). The effects of diazepam and methylphenidate on the electrodermal detection of guilty knowledge. *Journal of Applied Psychology, 69,* 289–299.

Iacono, W. G., & Lykken, D. T. (1983). The effects of instructions on electrodermal habituation. *Psychophysiology, 20,* 71–80.

Iacono, W. G., & Lykken, D. T. (1997). The scientific status of research on polygraph tests: The case against polygraph tests. In D. L. Faigman, D. Kaye, M. J. Saks, & J. Sanders (Eds.), *The West companion to scientific evidence.* St. Paul, MN: West.

Iacono, W. G., & Patrick, C. J. (1987). What psychologists should know about lie detection. In I. B. Weiner & A. K. Hess (Eds.), *Handbook of forensic psychology* (pp. 460–489). New York: Wiley.

Iacono, W. G., & Patrick, C. J. (1988). Assessing deception: Polygraph techniques. In R. Rogers (Ed.), *Clinical assessment of malingering and deception* (1st ed., pp. 205–223). New York: Guilford Press.

Imboden, J. B., Canter, A., & Cluff, L. (1961). Symptomatic recovery from medical disorders. *Journal of the American Medical Association, 178,* 1182–1184.

Inbau, F. E., & Reid, J. E. (1967). *Criminal interrogation and confessions* (2nd ed.). Baltimore: Williams & Wilkins.

Iverson, G. L. (1995). Qualitative aspects of malingered memory deficits. *Brain Injury, 9,* 35–40.

Iverson, G. L., Franzen, M. D., & Hammond, J. A. (1995). Examination of inmates' ability to malinger on the MMPI-2. *Psychological Assessment, 7,* 118–121.

Iverson, G. L., Franzen, M. D., & McCracken, L. M. (1991). Evaluation of an objective assessment technique for the detection of malingered memory deficits. *Law and Human Behavior, 15,* 667–676.

Iverson, G. L., Franzen, M. D., & McCracken, L. M. (1994). Application of a forced choice memory procedure designed to detect experimental malingering. *Archives of Clinical Neuropsychology, 9,* 437–450.

Jackson, D. N. (1971). The dynamics of structured personality tests: 1971. *Psychological Review, 78,* 229–248.

Jackson, D. N. (1976). *Basic Personality Inventory.* London, Ontario: Author.

Jacobson, S. A. (1969). Mechanisms of sequelae of minor crainocervical trauma. In A. E. Walker, W. F. Caveness, & M. Critchley (Eds.), *Late effects of head injury* (pp. 35–45). Springfield, IL: Charles C Thomas.

Jaffe, L. T., & Archer, R. P. (1987). The prediction of drug use among college students from MMPI, MCMI, and sensation seeking scales. *Journal of Personality Assessment, 51,* 243–253.

Jalazo, J., Steer, R. A., & Fine, E. W. (1978). Use of breathalyzer scores in the evaluation of persons arrested for driving while intoxicated. *Journal of Studies on Alcohol, 39*(7), 1304–1307.

Janet, P. (1903). *Les obsessions et la psychasthénie* [Obsessions and psychasthenia]. Paris: Alcan.

Janowsky, J. S., Shimamura, A. P., & Squire, L. R. (1989). Source memory impairments in patients with frontal lobe lesions. *Neuropsychologia, 27,* 1043–1056.

Jauch, T. E., Loch, J., Earl, J., & Bauer, W. (1993). Droperidol: A preferred neuroleptic in narcoanalysis. *Diseases of the Nervous System, 57,* 259–262.

Jellinek, E. M. (1960). *The disease concept of alcoholism.* New Haven, CT: Hillhouse Press.

Johnson, J. A. (1986). PDI Employment Inventory. In D. J. Keyser & R. C. Sweatland (Eds.), *Test critiques* (Vol. 8, pp. 548–556). Kansas City, MO: Test Corporation of America.

Johnson, J. H., Klingler, D. E., & Williams, T. A. (1977). The external criterion study of the MMPI validity indices. *Journal of Clinical Psychology, 33,* 154–156.

Johnson, M. M., & Rosenfeld, J. P. (1992). Oddball-evoked P300-based method of deception detection in the laboratory. II: Utilization of non-selective activation of relevant knowledge. *International Journal of Psychophysiology, 12,* 289–306.

Johnson, J. H., Williams, T., Klingler, D., & Gianetti, R. (1988). Interventional relevance and retrofit programming: Concepts for the improvement of clinical acceptance of computer-generated assessment reports. *Behavioral Research Methods and Instrumentation, 9,* 123–132.

Jonas, J. M., & Pope, H. G. (1985), The dissimulating disorders: A single diagnostic entity? *Comprehensive Psychiatry, 26,* 58–62.

Jones, A. B., & Llewellyn, J. (1917). *Malingering.* London: Heinemann.

Jones, J. W., Arnold, D., & Harris, W. G. (1990). Introduction to the model guidelines for preemployment integrity testing. *Journal of Business and Psychology, 4,* 525–532.

Jourard, S. M. (1971). *Self-disclosure: An experimental analysis of the transparent self.* New York: Wiley–Interscience.

Junginger J. (1990). Predicting compliance with command hallucinations. *American Journal of Psychiatry, 147,* 245–247.

Junginger, J. (1995). Command hallucinations and the prediction of dangerousness. *Psychiatric Services, 46,* 911–914.

Junginger, J., & Frame, C. L. (1985). Self-report of the frequency and phenomenology of verbal hallucinations. *Journal of Nervous and Mental Disease, 173,* 149–155.

Juni, S. (1992). Review of the Inwald Personality Inventory. In J. J. Kramer & J. C. Conoley (Eds.), *The eleventh mental measurements yearbook* (pp. 415–418). Lincoln, NE: Buros Institute of Mental Measurements.

Jureidini, J. (1993). Obstetric factitious disorder and Munchausen syndrome by proxy. *Journal of Nervous and Mental Disease, 181,* 135–137.

Kahn, M. W., Fox, H., & Rhode, R. (1988). Detecting faking on the Rorschach: Computer versus expert clinical judgment. *Journal of Personality Assessment, 52,* 516–523.

Kalas, R. (1986). Parent–child agreement on child psychiatric symptoms assessed via structured interview. *Journal of Child Psychology and Psychiatry, 27,* 181–190.

Kalman, G. (1977). On combat neurosis. *International Journal of Social Psychiatry, 23,* 195–203.

Kaminer, Y., Bukstein, O., & Tarter, R. E. (1991). The Teen-Addiction Severity Index: Rationale and reliability. *International Journal of Addictions, 26,* 219–226.

Kaminer, Y., Wagner, E., Plummer, B., & Seifer, R. (1993). Validation of the Teen-Addiction Severity Index (T-ASI): Preliminary findings. *American Journal of Addictions, 2,* 250–254.

Kanas, N., & Barr, M. A. (1984). Self-control of psychotic productions in schizophrenics [Letter to the editor]. *Archives of General Psychiatry, 41,* 919–920.

Kanin, E. J. (1994). False rape allegations. *Archives of Sexual Behavior, 23,* 81–91.

Kanovitz, J. (1992). Hypnotic memories and civil sexual abuse trials. *Vanderbilt Law Review, 45,* 1185–1262.

Kanzer, M. (1939). Amnesia: A statistical study. *American Journal of Psychiatry, 96,* 711–716.

Kaplan, H. I., & Sadock, B. J. (1988). *Synopsis of psychiatry, behavioral sciences, clinical psychiatry* (5th ed.). Baltimore: Williams & Wilkins.

Kaplan, M. F., & Eron, L. D. (1965). Test sophistication and faking in the TAT situation. *Journal of Projective Techniques and Personality Assessment, 29,* 498–503.

Kapur, B. (1994). Drug testing methods and interpretations of test results. In S. MacDonald & P. Roman (Eds.), *Drug testing in the workplace* (pp. 103–120). New York: Plenum.

Kapur, N. (1993). Focal retrograde amnesia in neurological disease: A critical review. *Cortex, 29,* 217–234.

Kapur, N., Ellison, D., Smith, M. P., McLellan, D. L., & Burrows, E. H. (1992). Focal retrograde amnesia following bilateral temporal lobe pathology. *Brain, 115,* 73–85.

Kapur, N., Young, A., Bateman, D., & Kennedy, P. (1989). Focal retrograde amnesia: A long-term clinical and neuropsychological follow-up. *Cortex, 25,* 387–402.

Karson, S., & O'Dell, J. W. (1976). *A guide to the clinical use of the 16 PF.* Champaign, IL: Institute for Personality and Ability Testing.

Kasper, M. E., Rogers, R., & Adams, P. A. (1996). Clinical characteristics of psychiatric patients with command hallucinations. *Bulletin of the American Academy of Psychiatry and Law, 24,* 219–224.

Katon, W., Egan, K., & Miller, D. (1985). Chronic pain: Lifetime psychiatric diagnoses and family history. *American Journal of Psychiatry, 142,* 1156–1160.

Kazdin, A. E., Colbus, D., & Rodgers, A. (1986). Assessment of depression and diagnosis of depressive disorder among psychiatrically disturbed children. *Journal of Abnormal Child Psychology, 14,* 499–515.

Kazdin, A. E., French, N. H., Unis, A. S., & Esveldt-Dawson, K. (1983). Assessment of childhood depression: Correspondence of child and parent ratings. *Journal of the American Academy of Child Psychiatry, 22,* 157–164.

Keane, T. M., Caddell, J. M., & Taylor, K. L. (1988). Mississippi Scale for Combat-Related

Post-Traumatic Stress Disorder: Three studies in reliability and validity. *Journal of Consulting and Clinical Psychology, 56,* 85–90.

Keane, T. M., Kolb, L., & Thomas, R. G. (1991). *Cooperative study #334: A psychophysiological study of chronic PTSD.* Interim Progress Report to the Study Group and Executive Committee, Veterans Health Administration Medical Research Service Report.

Keane, T. M., Malloy, P. R., & Fairbank, J. A. (1984). Empirical development of an MMPI subscale for the assessment of combat-related posttraumatic stress disorder. *Journal of Consulting and Clinical Psychology, 52,* 888–891.

Keiser, H. R. (1991). Surreptitious self-administration of epinephrine resulting in "pheochromocytoma." *Journal of the American Medical Association, 266,* 1553–1555.

Keiser, L. (1968). *The traumatic neurosis.* Philadelphia: J. B. Lippincott.

Kelly, K., & Rogers, R. (1996). Detection of misreported drug use in forensic populations: An overview of hair analysis. *Bulletin of the American Academy of Psychiatry and Law, 24,* 85–94.

Kelly, R. (1975). The post-traumatic syndrome: An iatrogenic disease. *Forensic Science, 6,* 17–24.

Kelly, R. (1981). The post-traumatic syndrome. *Journal of the Royal Society of Medicine, 74,* 242–245.

Kelly, R., & Smith, B. N. (1981). Post traumatic syndrome: Another myth discredited. *Journal of the Royal Society of Medicine, 74,* 275–278.

Kennedy, B. P., & Minami, M. (1993). The Beech Hill Hospital/outward bound adolescent chemical dependency treatment program. *Journal of Substance Abuse Treatment, 10,* 395–406.

Kennedy, F. (1946). The mind of the injured worker: Effect on disability periods. *Comprehensive Medicine, 1,* 19–24.

Kennedy, H. G., & Grubin, D. H. (1992). Patterns of denial in sex offenders. *Psychological Medicine, 22,* 191–196.

Kennedy, J., & Coe, W. C. (1994). Nonverbal signs of deception during posthypnotic amnesia. *International Journal of Clinical and Experimental Hypnosis, 42,* 13–19.

Keschner, M. (1960). Simulation (malingering) in relation to injuries of the brain and spinal cord and their coverings. In S. Brock (Ed.), *Injuries of the brain and spinal cord and their coverings.* New York: Springer.

Key v. State, 480 So.2d 488 (Fla., 1983).

Kihlstrom, J. F. (1994). Hypnosis, delayed recall, and the principles of memory. *International Journal of Clinical and Experimental Hypnosis, 42,* 337–345.

Kihlstrom, J. F., & Harackiewicz, J. M. (1982). The earliest recollection: A new survey. *Journal of Personality, 50,* 134–138.

King, B. H., & Ford, C. V. (1988). Pseudologia fantastica. *Acta Psychiatrica Scandinavica, 77,* 1–6.

Kinnunen, T., Zamansky, H. S., & Block, M. L. (1994). Is the hypnotized subject lying? *Journal of Abnormal Psychology, 103,* 184–191.

Kirchner, W. K. (1961). "Real-life" faking on the Strong Vocational Interest Blank by sales applicants. *Journal of Applied Psychology, 45,* 273–276.

Kleinmuntz, B. (1989). Review of The Phase II Profile Integrity Status Inventory and Addendum. In J. C. Conoley & J. J. Kramer (Eds.), *The tenth mental measurements yearbook* (pp. 635–638). Lincoln, NE: Buros Institute of Mental Measurements.

Kleinmuntz, B. (1995). True lies: The dishonesty of honesty tests. *The Humanist, 56,* 4–8.

Kleinmuntz, B., & Szucko, J. J. (1984). A field study of the fallibility of polygraphic lie detection. *Nature, 308,* 449–450.

Kline, R. B., & Snyder, D. K. (1985). Replicated MMPI subtypes for alcoholic men and women: Relationship to self-reported drinking behaviors. *Journal of Consulting and Clinical Psychology, 53,* 70–79.

Klonoff, E. A., Youngner, S. J., Moore, D. J., & Hershey, L. A. (1983). Chronic factitious illness: A behavioral approach. *International Journal of Psychiatry in Medicine, 13,* 173–183.

Kluft, R. P. (1987). The simulation and dissimulation of multiple personality disorder. *American Journal of Clinical Hypnosis, 30,* 104–118.

Kolarsky, A., & Madlafousek, J. (1977). Variability of stimulus effect in the course of phallometric testing. *Archives of Sexual Behavior, 6,* 135–141.

Kolb, L. C. (1985). The place of narcosynthesis in the treatment of chronic and delayed stress reactions of war. In S. M. Sonnenberg, A. S. Blank, & J. A. Talbott (Eds.), *The trauma of war stress and recovery in Vietnam veterans* (pp. 211–226). Washington, DC: American Psychiatric Association Press.

Kopelman, M. D. (1987). Amnesia: Organic and psychogenic. *British Journal of Psychiatry, 150,* 428–442.

Kopelman, M. D., Christensen, H., Puffett, A., & Stanhope, N. (1994). The great escape: A neuropsychological study of psychogenic amnesia. *Neuropsychologia, 32,* 675–691.

Korsakoff, S. S. (1891). Erinnerungstäuschungen (Pseudoreminiscenzen) bei polyneuritischer Psychose [Delusions of memory (pseudoreminiscences) in polyneuritic psychosis]. *Allegemeine Zeitschrift für Psychiatrie, 47,* 390–410.

Koson, D., & Robey, A. (1973). Amnesia and competency to stand trial. *American Journal of Psychiatry, 130,* 588–592.

Koss, M. P., & Butcher, J. N. (1973). A comparison of patients' self-report with other sources of clinical information. *Journal of Research in Personality, 7,* 225–236.

Kraepelin, E. (1887). Ueber Erinnerungsfälschungen [On delusions of remembrance.] *Archiv für Psychiatrie und Nervenkrankheiten, 18,* 395–436.

Kraus, A. (1994). Phenomenology of the technical delusion in schizophrenia. *Journal of Phenomenological Psychology, 25,* 51–69.

Kraut, R. E., & Price, J. D. (1976). Machiavellianism in parents and their children. *Journal of Personality and Social Psychology, 33,* 782–786.

Kreiger, M. J., & Levin, S. M. (1976). Schizophrenic behavior as a function of role expectation. *Journal of Clinical Psychology, 32,* 463–467.

Kritchevsky, M. (1989). Transient global amnesia. In F. Boller & J. Grafman (Eds.), *Handbook of neuropsychology* (Vol. 3, pp. 167–182). Amsterdam: Elsevier.

Kroger, R. O., & Turnbell, W. (1975). Invalidity of validity scales: The case of the MMPI. *Journal of Consulting and Clinical Psychology, 43,* 48–55.

Kroger, W., & Douce, R. (1979). Hypnosis in criminal investigation. *International Journal of Clinical and Experimental Hypnosis, 27,* 358–374.

Kropp P. R. (1992). *Antisocial personality disorder and malingering.* Unpublished doctoral dissertation, Simon Fraser University, Burnaby, British Columbia, Canada.

Kropp, P. R. (1994). The relationship between psychopathy and malingering of mental illness. *Dissertation Abstracts International, 54-B,* 5945–5946.

Kropp, P. R., & Rogers, R. (1993). Understanding malingering: Motivation, method, and detection. In M. Lewis & C. Saarni (Eds.), *Lying and deception in everyday life* (pp. 201–216). New York: Guilford Press.

Kruesi, M. J., Dale, J., & Straus, S. E. (1989). Psychiatric diagnoses in patients who have chronic fatigue syndrome. *Journal of Clinical Psychiatry, 50,* 53–56.

Krupp, L. B., Mendelson, W. B., & Friedman, R. (1991). An overview of chronic fatigue syndrome. *Journal of Clinical Psychiatry, 52,* 403–410.

Kuplicki, F. P. (1988). Fifth, sixth, and fourteenth amendments—A constitutional paradigm for determining the admissibility of hypnotically refreshed testimony. *Journal of Criminal Law and Criminology, 78,* 853–876.

Kurtz, R., & Meyer, R. G. (1994, March). *Vulnerability of the MMPI-2, M Test, and SIRS to different strategies of malingering psychosis.* Paper presented at the meeting of the American Psychology–Law Society, Santa Fe, NM.

Kwentus, J. A. (1981). Interviewing with intravenous drugs. *Journal of Clinical Psychiatry, 42,* 432–436.

Lacey, J. H. (1993). Self-damaging and addictive behavior in bulimia nervosa. *British Journal of Psychiatry, 163,* 190–194.

Lachar, D., & Gdowski, C. L. (1979). Problem-behavior factor correlates of the Personality Inventory for Children. *Journal of Consulting and Clinical Psychology, 47,* 39–48.

Lachar, D., & Wrobel, T. A. (1979). Validating clinicians' hunches: Construction of a new MMPI critical item set. *Journal of Consulting and Clinical Psychology, 47,* 277–284.

Lacoursiere, R. B. (1993). Diverse motives for fictitious post-traumatic stress disorder. *Journal of Traumatic Stress, 6,* 141–149.

La Greca, A. M. (1983). Interviewing and behavioral observations. In C. E. Walker & M. C. Roberts (Eds.), *Handbook of clinical child psychology* (pp. 109–131). New York: Wiley.

La Greca, A. M. (1990). Issues and perspectives on the child assessment process. In A. M. La Greca (Ed.), *Through the eyes of the child: Obtaining self-reports from children and adolescents* (pp. 3–17). Boston: Allyn & Bacon.

Lalumière, M. L., & Quinsey, V. L. (1994). The discriminability of rapists from non-sex offenders using phallometric measures: A meta-analysis. *Criminal Justice and Behavior, 21,* 150–175.

Lamb, D. G., Berry, D. T. R., Wetter, M. W., & Baer, R. A. (1994). Effects of two types of information on malingering of closed head injury on the MMPI-2: An analog investigation. *Psychological Assessment, 6,* 8–13.

Lambert, C., & Rees, W. L. (1944). Intravenous barbiturates in the treatment of hysteria. *British Medical Journal, 2,* 70–73.

Landry v. Bill Garrett Chevrolet, Inc., 430 So.2d 1051 (La. Ct. App., 1983).

Lang, P. J. (1985). The cognitive psychophysiology of emotion: Fear and anxiety. In A. H. Tuma & J. Maser (Eds.), *Anxiety and the anxiety disorders* (pp. 131–170). Hillsdale, NJ: Erlbaum.

Langevin, R. (1988). Defensiveness in sex offenders. In R. Rogers (Ed.), *Clinical assessment of malingering and deception* (1st ed., pp. 269–290). New York: Guilford Press.

Langevin, R., Paitich, D., Russon, A., Handy, L., & Langevin, A. (1990). *Clarke Sex History Questionnaire for Males manual.* Etobicoke, Ontario: Juniper Press.

Langevin, R., Wright, P., & Handy, L. (1990). Use of the MMPI and its derived scales with sex offenders: II. Reliability and criterion validity. *Annals of Sex Research, 3,* 453–486.

Lanyon, R. I. (1993). Validity of MMPI Sex Offender scales with admitters and nonadmitters. *Psychological Assessment, 5,* 302–306.

Lanyon, R. I., Almer, E. R., & Curran, P. J. (1993). Use of biographical and case history data in the assessment of malingering during examination for disability. *Bulletin of the American Academy of Psychiatry and the Law, 21*(4), 495–503.

Lanyon, R. I., & Lutz, R. W. (1984). MMPI discrimination of defensiveness and nondefensive felony sex offenders. *Journal of Consulting and Clinical Psychology, 52,* 841–843.

Larkin, A. R. (1979) The form and content of schizophrenic hallucinations. *Psychiatry, 136,* 940–943.

Larrabee, G. J. (1992). Interpretive strategies for evaluation of neuropsychological data in legal settings. *Forensic Reports, 5,* 257–264.

Laughlin, H. P. (1970). *The ego and its defenses.* New York: Appleton-Century-Crofts.

Laurence, J. H., Nadon, R., Nogrady, H., & Perry, C. (1986). Duality, dissociation and memory creation in highly hypnotizable subjects. *International Journal of Clinical and Experimental Hypnosis, 34,* 295–310.

Laws, D. R., & Holmen, M. L. (1978). Sexual response faking by pedophiles. *Criminal Justice and Behavior, 5,* 343–356.

Layden, M. (1966). Symptoms separate hysteric, malingerer. *Psychiatric Progress, 1,* 7.

Lebowitz, M. R., & Blumenthal, S. A. (1993). The molar ratio of insulin to C-peptide. An aid to the diagnosis of hypoglycemia due to surreptitious (or inadvertent) insulin administration. *Archives of Internal Medicine, 153,* 650–655.

Lee, G. P., Loring, D. W., & Martin, R. C. (1992). Rey's 15-Item Visual Memory Test for the detection of malingering: Normative observations on patients with neuroogical disorders. *Psychological Assessment, 4,* 43–46.

Lees-Haley, P. R. (1991). Ego strength denial on the MMPI-2 as a clue to simulation of personal injury in vocational neuropsychological and emotional distress evaluations. *Perceptual and Motor Skills, 72,* 815–819.

Lees-Haley, P. R. (1992). Efficacy of MMPI-2 validity scales and MCMI-II modifier scales for detecting spurious PTSD claims: F, F–K, Fake Bad scale, Ego Strength, subtle–obvious subscales, DIS, and DEB. *Journal of Clinical Psychology, 48,* 681–688.

Lees-Haley, P. R., & Brown, R. S. (1992). Biases in perception and reporting following a perceived toxic exposure. *Perceptual and Motor Skills, 75,* 531–544.

Lees-Haley, P. R., & Dunn, J. T. (1994). The ability of naive subjects to report Symptoms of mild brain injury, post-traumatic stress disorder, major depression, and generalized anxiety disorder. *Journal of Clinical Psychology, 50,* 252–256.

Lees-Haley, P. R., English, L. T., & Glenn, W. J. (1991). A fake bad scale on the MMPI-2 for personal-injury claimants. *Psychological Reports, 68,* 203–210.

Lees-Haley, P. R., & Fox, D. D. (1990). MMPI subtle–obvious scales and malingering: Clinical versus simulated scores. *Psychological Reports, 66,* 907–911.

Lees-Haley, P. R., Smith, H. H., Williams, C. W., & Dunn, J. T. (1996). Forensic neuropsychological test usage: An empirical study. *Archives of Clinical Neuropsychology, 2*(1), 45–51.

Leitch, A. (1948, May 26). Notes on amnesia in crime for the general practitioner. *Medical Press,* 459–463.

Lennox, W. G. (1943). Amnesia, real and feigned. *American Journal of Psychiatry, 99,* 732–743.

Leung, A. (1992). Review of the Hogan Personnel Selection Series. In J. J. Kramer & J. C. Conoley (Eds.), *The eleventh mental measurements yearbook* (pp. 384–386). Lincoln, NE: Buros Institute of Mental Measurements.

Levin, H. S. (1989). Neurobehavioral outcome of mild to moderate head injury. In J. Hoff, T. Anderson, & T. Cole (Eds.), *Mild to moderate head injury* (pp. 153–185). Boston: Blackwell Scientific.

Levin, H. S. (1990). Predicting the neurobehavioral sequelae of closed head injury. In R. L. Wood (Ed.), *Neurobehavioral sequelae of traumatic brain injury* (pp. 89–109). New York: Taylor & Francis.

Levin, H. S., & Grossman, R. G. (1978). Behavioral sequelae of closed head injury. *Archives of Neurology, 35,* 720–727.

Levin, H. S., Lilly, M. A., Papanicolaou, A., & Eisenberg, H. M. (1992). Posttraumatic and retrograde amnesia after closed head injury. In L. R. Squire & N. Butters (Eds.), *Neuropsychology of memory* (2nd ed., pp. 290–308). New York: Guilford Press.

Levinson, M. R., Aldwin, C. M., Butcher, J. N., De Labry, L., Workman-Daniels, K., & Boxxe, R. (1990). The MAC scale in a normal population: The meaning of "false positives." *Journal of Studies on Alcohol, 51,* 457–462.

Lewinsohn, P. M. (1970). An empirical test of several popular notions about hallucinations in schizophrenic patients. In W. Keup (Ed.), *Origin and mechanisms of hallucinations* (pp. 401–403). New York: Plenum.

Lewis, M. (1993). The development of deception. In M. Lewis & C. Saarni (Eds.), *Lying and deception in everyday life* (pp. 90–105). New York: Guilford Press.

Lezak, M. D. (1983). *Neuropsychological assessment* (2nd ed.). New York: Oxford University Press.

Lezak, M. D. (1995). *Neuropsychological assessment* (3rd ed.). New York: Oxford University Press.

Libbin, A. E., Mendelsohn, S. R., & Duffy, D. P. (1988). Employee medical and honesty testing. *Personnel, 65,* 38–48.

Liberty, P. G., Jr., Lunneborg, C. E., & Atkinson, G. C. (1964). Perceptual defense, dissimulation, and response styles. *Journal of Consulting Psychology, 28,* 529–537.

Lidz, C. W., & Hoge, S. K. (Eds). (1993). Coercion in mental health care. *Behavioral Sciences and the Law, 11,* 237–345 (whole issue).

Lifton, P. D., & Nannis, E. D. (1986). Hogan Personality Inventory: Hogan Personnel Selection Series. In D. J. Keyser & R. C. Sweatland (Eds.), *Test critiques* (Vol. 6, pp. 216–225). Kansas City, MO: Test Corporation of America.

Lilienfeld, S. O., Alliger, G., & Mitchell, K. (1995). Why integrity testing remains controversial. *American Psychologist, 50,* 457–458.

Lilienfeld, S. O., Andrews, B. P., & Stone-Romero, E. F. (1994). The relations between a self-report honesty test and personality measures in prison and college samples. *Journal of Research in Personality, 28,* 154–169.

Linblad, A. D. (1991). *Detection of malingered mental illness with a forensic population: An analogue study.* Unpublished doctoral dissertation, University of Manitoba, Winnepeg.

Lindblad, A. D. (1994). Detection of malingered mental illness within a forensic population: An analogue study. *Dissertation Abstracts International, 54-B,* 4395.

Lindemann, E. (1932). Psychological changes in normal and abnormal individuals under the influence of sodium amytal. *American Journal of Psychiatry, 88,* 1083–1091.

Lindsay, D. S., & Johnson, M. K. (1987). Reality monitoring and suggestibility: Children's ability to discriminate among memories from different sources. In S. J. Ceci, M. P. Toglia, & D. F. Ross (Eds.), *Children's eyewitness testimony* (pp. 92–121). New York: Springer-Verlag.

Lindsay, D. S., & Poole D. A. (1995). Remembering childhood sexual abuse in therapy. *Journal of Psychiatry and Law, 23,* 461–476.

Link, B. G., & Stueve, C. A. (1994). Psychotic symptoms and the violent/illegal behavior of mental patients compared to community controls. In J. Monahan & H. Steadman (Eds.), *Violence and mental disorder: Developments in risk assessment.* Chicago: University of Chicago Press.

Links, P. S., Steiner, M., & Mitton, J. (1989). Characteristics of psychosis in borderline personality disorder. *Psychopathology, 22,* 188–193.

Lipman, F. D. (1962). Malingering in personal injury cases. *Temple Law Quarterly, 35,* 141–162.

Lipscomb, T. J., Bregman, N., & McCallister, H. A. (1984). A developmental inquiry into the effects of post-event information on eyewitness accounts. *Journal of Genetic Psychology, 146,* 551–556.

Lipton, J. P. (1977). On the psychology of eyewitness testimony. *Journal of Applied Psychology, 62,* 90–95.

Lishman, W. A. (1978). *Organic psychiatry.* Oxford: Blackwell Scientific Publications.

Littlepage, G., & Pineault, T. (1978). Verbal, facial, and paralinguistic cues to the detection of truth and lying. *Personality and Social Psychology Bulletin, 4,* 461–464.

Loftus, E. F. (1979). *Eyewitness testimony*. Cambridge, MA: Harvard University Press.

Loftus, E. F. (1993a). Desperately seeking memories of the first few years of childhood: The reality of early memories. *Journal of Experimental Psychology: General, 122,* 274–277.

Loftus, E. F. (1993b). The reality of repressed memories. *American Psychologist, 48,* 518–537.

Loftus, E. F. (1994). The repressed memory controversy. *American Psychologist, 49,* 443–444.

Loftus, E. F. (1995, October). *Memory distortion.* Lecture presented at the 26th annual meeting of the American Academy of Psychiatry and the Law, Seattle, WA.

Loftus, E. F., Donders, K., Hoffman, H. G., & Schooler, J. W. (1989). Creating memories that are quickly accessed and confidently held. *Memory and Cognition, 17,* 607–616.

Loftus, E. F., & Doyle, J. F. (1987). *Eyewitness testimony: Civil and criminal.* Norwell, MA: Kluwer Press.

Loftus, E. F., Garry, M., & Feldman, J. (1994). Forgetting sexual trauma: What does it mean when 38% forget? *Journal of Consulting and Clinical Psychology, 62,* 1182–1186.

Loftus, E. F., & Hoffman, H. G. (1989). Misinformation and memory: The creation of new memories. *Journal of Experimental Psychology: General, 118,* 100–104.

Loftus, E. F., & Ketcham, K. (1991). *Witness for the defense.* New York: St. Martin's Press.

Loftus, E. F., Miller, D. G., & Burns, H. J. (1978). Semantic integration of verbal information into visual memory. *Journal of Experimental Psychology: Human Learning and Memory, 4,* 19–31.

Loftus, E. F., & Palmer, J. C. (1974). Reconstruction of automobile destruction: An example of the interaction between language and memory. *Journal of Verbal Learning and Verbal Behavior, 13,* 585–589.

Loftus, E. F., & Zanni, G. (1975). Eyewitness testimony: The influence of wording of a question. *Bulletin of the Psychonomic Society, 5,* 86–88.

Logan, W. S., Reuterfors, D. L., Bohn, M. J., & Clark, C. L. (1984). The description and classification of presidential threateners. *Behavioral Sciences and the Law, 2,* 151–167.

Lorei, T. W. (1970). Staff ratings of the consequence of release from or retention in a psychiatric hospital. *Journal of Consulting and Clinical Psychology, 34,* 46–55.

Lorenz, W. F. (1932). Criminal confessions under narcosis. *Wisconsin Medical Journal, 31,* 245–250.

Lykken, D. T. (1981). *A tremor in the blood: Uses and abuses of the lie detector.* New York: McGraw-Hill.

Lynch, B. E., & Bradford, J. W. (1980). Amnesia: Its detection by psychophysiological measures. *Bulletin of the American Academy of Psychiatry and Law, 8,* 288–297.

Lynn, E. J., & Belza, M. (1984). Factitious posttraumatic stress disorder: The veteran who never got to Vietnam. *Hospital and Community Psychiatry, 35,* 697–701.

Lynn, S. J., Milano, M., & Weekes, J. R. (1991). Hypnosis and pseudomemories: The effects of prehypnotic expectancies. *Journal of Personality and Social Psychology 60,* 318–326.

Lynn, S. J., Rhue, J. W., Myers, B., & Weekes, R. (1994). Pseudomemory in hypnotized and simulating subjects. *International Journal of Clinical and Experimental Hypnosis, 42,* 118–129.

Lyon, L. S. (1985). Facilitating telephone number recall in a case of psychogenic amnesia. *Journal of Behavior Therapy and Experimental Psychiatry, 16,* 147–149.

Lyons, J. A., Caddell, J. M., Pittman, R. L., Rawls, R., & Perrin, S. (1994). The Potential for faking on the Mississippi Scale for Combat-Related PTSD. *Journal of Traumatic Stress, 7,* 441–445.

Maag, J. W., Irvin, D. M., Reid, R., & Vasa, S. F. (1994). Prevalence and predictors of substance abuse use: A comparison between adolescents with and without learning disabilities. *Journal of Learning Disabilities, 27,* 223–234.

MacAndrew, C. (1965). The differentiation of male alcoholic outpatients from nonalcoholic psychiatric outpatients by means of the MMPI. *Quarterly Studies of Alcohol, 47,* 161–166.

MacAndrew, C. (1986). Toward the psychometric detection of substance misuse in young men: The SAP scale. *Journal of Studies in Alcohol, 47,* 161–166.

MacDonald, J. M. (1976a). *Psychiatry and the criminal: A guide to psychiatric examinations for the criminal courts* (3rd ed.). Springfield, IL: Charles C Thomas.

MacDonald, J. M. (1976b). The simulation of mental disease. In J. M. MacDonald (Ed.), *Psychiatry and the criminal* (pp. 425–441). Springfield, IL: Charles C Thomas.

MacDonald, S., & Roman, P. M. (1994). *Drug testing in the workplace.* New York: Plenum

MacLeish, R. (1984, March). Gifted by nature, prodigies are still mysteries to Man. *Smithsonian,* pp. 71–79.

Maier, N. R. S., & Thurber, J. A. (1968). Accuracy of judgement of deception when an interviewer is watched, heard, and read. *Personnel Psychology, 21,* 23–30.

Makaremi, A. (1992). Birth order, neuroticism, and psychoticism among Iranian children. *Psychological Reports, 71,* 919–922.

Malmquist, C. P. (1986). Children who witness parental murder: Post-traumatic aspects. *Journal of the American Academy of Child Psychiatry, 25,* 320–325.

Maloney, M. P., Duvall, S. W., & Friesen, J. (1980). Evaluation of response consistency on the MMPI. *Psychological Reports, 46,* 295–298.

Maloney, M. T., Glasser, A., & Ward, M. P. (1980). *Malingering: An overview.* Unpublished manuscript.

Mansouri, L., & Dowell, D. A. (1989). Perceptions of stigma among the long-term mentally ill. *Psychosocial Rehabilitation Journal, 13,* 79–91.

Marceil, J. C. (1977). Implicit dimensions of idiography and nomothesis: A reformulation. *American Psychologist, 32,* 1046–1055.

Marcos, L. R., Goldberg, E., Feazell, D., & Wilner, M. (1977). The use of sodium amytal interviews in a short term community-orientated inpatient unit. *Diseases of the Nervous System, 38,* 283–286.

Marcum, J. M., Wright, K., & Bissell, W. G. (1986). Chance discovery of multiple personality disorder in a depressed patient by amobarbital interview. *Journal of Nervous and Mental Disease, 174,* 489–492.

Marks, P. A., Seeman, W., & Haller, D. L. (1974). *The actuarial use of the MMPI with adolescents and adults.* Baltimore: Williams & Wilkins.

Marquis, K. H., Marshall, J., & Oskamp, S. (1972). Testimony validity as a function of question form, atmosphere, and item difficulty. *Journal of Applied Social Psychology, 2,* 167–186.

Marriage, K., Govorchin, M., George, P., & Dilworth, C. (1988). Use of an amytal interview in the management of factitious deaf mutism. *Australian and New Zealand Journal of Psychiatry, 22,* 454–456.

Martin, M. J. (1970). Psychiatric aspects of patients with compensation problems. *Psychosomatics, 11,* 81–84.

Martin, R. D. (1974). Secondary gain, everybody's rationalization. *Journal of Occupational Medicine, 16,* 800–801.

Mash, E. J., & Terdal, L. G. (1988). Behavioral assessment of child and family disturbance. In E. J. Mash & L. G. Terdal (Eds.), *Behavioral assessment of childhood disorders* (2nd ed., pp. 3–65). New York: Guilford Press.

Matarazzo, J. D. (1990). Psychological assessment versus psychological testing. *American Psychologist, 45,* 999–1017.

Matthews, C. G. (1992). The neuropsychology of epilepsy: An overview. *Journal of Clinical and Experimental Neuropsychology, 14,* 133–144.

Maurice-Williams, R. S., & Marsh, H. (1985). Simulated paraplegia: An occasional problem for the neurosurgeon. *Journal of Neurology, Neurosurgery, and Psychiatry, 48,* 826–831.

Mayer, J., & Filstead, W. J. (1979). The Adolescent Alcohol Involvement Scale: An instrument for measuring adolescents' use and misuse of alcohol. *Journal of Studies on Alcohol, 40,* 291–300.

Mayfield, D., McLeod, G., & Hall, P. (1974). The CAGE questionnaire: Validation of a new alcoholism screening instrument. *American Journal of Psychiatry, 131,* 1121–1123.

Mayo, J. P., & Haggerty, J. J. (1984). Long-term psychotherapy of Munchausen syndrome. *American Journal of Psychotherapy, 38,* 571–578.

Mazmanian, D., Mendonca, J. D., Holden, R. R., & Dufton, B. (1987). Psychopathology and response styles in the SCL-90 responses of acutely distressed persons. *Journal of Psychopathology and Behavioral Assessment, 9,* 135–148.

McAllister, L. W. (1986). *A practical guide to CPI interpretation.* Palo Alto, CA: Consulting Psychologists Press.

McAllister, T. W. (1994). Mild traumatic brain injury and the postconcussive syndrome. In J. M. Silver, S. C. Yudofsky, & R. E. Hales (Eds.), *Neuropsychiatry of traumatic brain injury* (pp. 357–392). Washington, DC: American Psychiatric Association Press.

McAnulty, R. D., Adams, H. E., & Wright, L. W. (1994). Relationship between MMPI and penile plethysmograph in accused child molesters. *Journal of Sex Research, 31,* 179–184.

McCaffrey, R. J., & Lynch, J. K. (1992). A methodological review of "Method Skeptic" reports. *Neuropsychology Review, 3,* 193–214.

McCall, W. V., Shelp, F. E., & McDonald, W. M. (1992). Controlled investigation of the amobarbital interview for catatonic mutism. *American Journal of Psychiatry, 149,* 202–206.

McCann, T., & Sheehan, P. W. (1988). Hypnotically induced pseudomemories: Sampling their conditions among hypnotizable subjects. *Journal of Personality and Social Psychology, 54,* 339–346.

McCann, T., & Sheehan, P. W. (1989). Confident persistence in the face of disbelief: A response to commentaries. *British Journal of Experimental and Clinical Hypnosis, 6,* 66–70.

McCloskey, M., & Zaragosa, M. (1985). Misleading postevent information and memory for events: Arguments and evidence against memory impairment hypotheses. *Journal of Experimental Psychology: General, 114,* 1–16.

McClure, R. F. (1978). Admitting personal problems and outcomes in hospitalized psychiatric patients. *Journal of Clinical Psychology, 34,* 44–49.

McConkey, K. M., Labelle, L., Bibb, B. C., & Bryant R. A. (1990). Hypnosis and suggested pseudomemory: The relevance of test context. *Australian Journal of Psychology 42,* 197–205.

McConkey, K. M., Sheehan, P. W., & White, K. D. (1979). Comparison of the Creative Imagination Scale and the Harvard Group Scale of Hypnotic Susceptibility, Form A. *International Journal of Clinical and Experimental Hypnosis, 27,* 267–277.

McCrae, R. R., Costa, P. T., Jr., Dahlstrom, W. G., Barefoot, J. C., Siegler, I. C., & Williams, R. B., Jr. (1989). A caution on the use of the MMPI K-correction in research on psychosomatic medicine. *Psychosomatic Medicine, 51,* 58–65.

McCranie, E. J. (1980). Neurasthenic neurosis: Psychogenic weakness and fatigue. *Psychosomatics, 21,* 19–24.

McDaniel, J. S., Desoutter, L., Firestone, S., & McDonell, K. (1992). Factitious disorder resulting in bilateral mastectomies. *General Hospital Psychiatry, 14,* 355–356.

McDaniel, M. A., & Jones, J. W. (1986). A meta-analysis of the Employee Attitude Inventory theft scales. *Journal of Business and Psychology, 1,* 31–50.

McDaniel, M. A., & Jones, J. W. (1988). Predicting employee theft: A quantitative review of the vaildity of a standardized measure of dishonesty. *Journal of Business and Psychology, 2,* 327–345.

McDonald, A., Kline, S. A., & Billings, R. F. (1979). The limits of Munchausen's syndrome. *Canadian Journal of Psychiatry, 24,* 323–328.

McHugh, P. R. (1992, Autumn). Psychiatric misadventures. *American Scholar,* pp. 497–510.

McKinley, J. C., Hathaway, S. R., & Meehl, P. E. (1948). The MMPI: K scale. *Journal of Consulting Psychology, 12,* 20–31.

McLellan, A. T., Luborsky, L., Woody, G. E., & O'Brien, C. P. (1980). An improved diagnostic evaluation instrument for substance abuse patients: The Addiction Severity Index. *Journal of Nervous and Mental Disease, 168,* 26–33.

McMordie, W. R. (1988). Twenty-year follow-up of the prevailing opinion on the posttraumatic or postconcussional syndrome. *Clinical Neuropsychologist, 2,* 198–212.

McVaugh, W. H., & Grow, R. T. (1983). Detecting faking on the Personality Inventory for Children. *Journal of Clinical Psychology, 39,* 567–573.

Meadow, R. (1977). Munchausen syndrome by proxy: The hinterland of child abuse. *Lancet, 2,* 343–345.

Means, B., & Loftus, E. F. (1991). When personal history repeats itself: Decomposing memories for recurring events. *Applied Cognitive Psychology, 5,* 297–318.

Mednick, S., & Christiansen, K. (1977). *Biosocial bases of criminal behavior.* New York: Gardner Press.

Meehl, P. E., & Hathaway, S. R. (1946). The K factor as a suppressor variable in the MMPI. *Journal of Applied Psychology, 30,* 525–564.

Meehl, P. E., & Rosen, A. (1955). Antecedent probability and the efficiency of psychometric signs, patterns, or cutting scores. *Psychological Bulletin, 52,* 194–216.

Megargee, E. I. (1972). *The California Psychological Inventory handbook.* San Francisco: Jossey-Bass.

Meisner, S. (1988). Susceptibility of Rorschach distress correlates to malingering. *Journal of Personality Assessment, 52,* 564–571.

Mellor, S. (1986). Employee Attitude Inventory. In D. J. Keyser & R. C. Sweatland (Eds.), *Test critiques* (Vol. 8, pp. 173–181). Kansas City, MO: Test Corporation of America.

Meloy, J. R. (1988). *The psychopathic mind: Origins, dynamics, and treatment.* Northvale, NJ: Jason Aronson.

Meloy, J. R., & Gacano, C. B. (1995). Assessing the psychopathic personality. In J. N. Butcher (Ed.), *Clinical personality assessment* (pp. 410–422). New York: Oxford University Press.

Melton, R. (1984). Differential diagnosis: A commonsense guide to psychological assessment. *Vet Center Voice Newsletter, 5,* 1–12.

Mendelson, G. (1981). Persistent work disability following settlement of compensation claims. *Law Institute Journal (Melbourne), 55,* 342–345.

Mendelson, G. (1982). Not "cured by verdict." Effect of legal settlement on compensation claimants. *Medical Journal of Australia, 2,* 132–134.

Mendelson, G. (1984). Follow-up studies of personal injury litigants. *International Journal of Law and Psychiatry, 7,* 179–187.

Mendelson, G. (1985). Compensation neurosis. An invalid diagnosis. *Medical Journal of Australia, 142,* 561–564.

Menninger, K. A. (1934). Polysurgery and polysurgical addiction. *Psychoanalytic Quarterly, 3,* 173–199.

Menninger, K. A. (1935). Psychology of a certain type of malingerer. *Archives of Neurology and Psychiatry, 33,* 507–515.

Merback, K. (1984). The vet center dilemma: Post-traumatic stress disorder and personality disorders. *Vet Center Voice Newsletter, 5,* 6–7.

Merrin, E. L., Van Dyke, C., Cohen, S., & Tusel, D. J. (1986). Dual factitious disorder. *General Hospital Psychiatry, 8,* 246–250.

Merritt, K. A., Ornstein, P. A., & Spicker, B. (1994). Children's memory for a salient medical procedure: Implications for testimony. *Pediatrics, 94,* 17–23.

Merskey, H. (1994, December). *Repression, belief in the patient and other nostrums.* Paper presented at the Johns Hopkins/False Memory Syndrome Foundation Conference, Baltimore, MD.

Merskey, H., & Woodforde, J. M. (1972). Psychiatric sequelae of minor head injury. *Brain, 95,* 521–528.

Mesmer, F. A. (1948). *Mesmerism by Doctor Mesmer: Dissertation on the discovery of animal magnetism* (V. R. Myers, Trans.). London: Macdonald. (Original work published in 1779)

Meyer, P., & Davis, S. (1992). *The CPI applications guide: An essential tool for individual, group, and organizational development.* Palo Alto, CA: Consulting Psychologists Press.

Mieczkowski, T., Barzelay, D., Gropper, B., & Wish, E. (1991). Concordance of three measures of cocaine use in an arrestee population: Hair, urine, and self-report. *Journal of Psychoactive Drugs, 23,* 241–249.

Mieczkowski, T., Landress, H. J., Newel, R., & Coletti, S. D. (1993, January). Testing hair for illicit drug use. *National Institute of Justice: Research in Brief,* pp. 1–5.

Mikkelsen, E. J. (1985). Substance abuse in adolescents and children. In R. Michels, J. O. Cavenar, A. M. Cooper, S. B. Guze, L. L. Judd, G. L. Klerman, & A. J. Solnit (Eds.), *Psychiatry* (Vol. 2). Philadephia: J. B. Lippincott.

Mikkelsen, E. J., Gutheil, T. G., & Emens, M. (1992). False sexual-abuse allegations by children and adolescents: Contextual factors and clinical subtypes. *American Journal of Psychotherapy, 46,* 556–570.

Milanovich, J. R., Axelrod, B. N., & Millis, S. R. (1996). Validation of the Simulation Index-Revised with a mixed clinical population. *Archives of Clinical Neuropsychology, 11,* 50–53.

Miller, G. A. (1985). *The Substance Abuse Subtle Screening Inventory—Revised (SASSI-R) manual.* Bloomington, IN: SASSI Institute.

Miller, G. A. (1990). *The SASSI adolescent manual.* Bloomington, IN: SASSI Institute.

Miller, G. A. (1994). *The Substance Abuse Subtle Screening Inventory (SASSI) manual.* Bloomington, IN: SASSI Institute.

Miller, G. R., & Stiff, J. B. (1993). *Deceptive communication.* Newbury Park, CA: Sage.

Miller, H. (1961). Accident neurosis. *British Medical Journal, 1,* 919–925.

Miller, H. (1966). Mental sequelae of head injury. *Proceedings of the Royal Society of Medicine, 59,* 257–266.

Miller, H., & Cartlidge, N. (1972). Simulation and malingering after injuries to the brain and spinal cord. *Lancet, 1,* 580–585.

Miller, H. R., & Streiner, D. L. (1990). Using the Millon Clinical Multiaxial Inventory's Scale B and the MacAndrew Alcoholism Scale to identify alcoholics with concurrent psychiatric diagnoses. *Journal of Personality Assessment, 54,* 736–746.

Miller, L. J., O'Connor, E., & DiPasquale, T. (1993). Patients' attitudes toward hallucinations. *American Journal of Psychiatry, 150,* 584–588.

Miller, T. R., Bauchner, J. E., Hocking, J. E., Fontes, N. E., Kaminsky, A. P., & Brendt, D. R. (1981). How well can observers detect deceptive testimony? In B. D. Sales (Ed.), *Perspectives in law and psychology: Vol. 2. The trial process* (pp. 145–179). New York: Plenum.

Miller, W. R., Crawford, V. L., & Taylor, C. A. (1979). Significant others as corroborative sources for problem drinkers. *Addictive Behaviors, 4,* 67–70.

Miller, W. R., & Marlatt, G. A. (1984). *Manual for the Comprehensive Drinker Profile.* Odessa, FL: Psychological Assessment Resources.

Miller, W. R., & Marlatt, G. A. (1987). *Comprehensive Drinker Profile: Manual supplement.* Odessa, FL: Psychological Assessment Resources.

Millis, S. R. (1992). The Recognition Memory Test in the detection of malingered and exaggerated memory deficits. *Clinical Neuropsychologist, 6,* 405–413.

Millis, S. R. (1994). Assessment of motivation and memory with the Recognition Memory Test after financially compensable mild head injury. *Journal of Clinical Psychology, 50,* 601–605.

Millis, S. R., & Putnam, S. H. (1994). The recognition memory test in the assessment of memory impairment after financially compensable mild head injury: A replication. *Perceptual and Motor Skills, 79,* 384–386.

Millis, S. R., Putnam, S. H., Adams, K. M., & Ricker, J. H. (1995). The California Verbal-Learning Test in the detection of incomplete effort in neuropsychological evaluation. *Psychological Assessment, 7,* 463–471.

Millon, T. (1983). *Millon Clinical Multiaxial Inventory.* Minneapolis: National Computer Systems.

Millon, T. (1987). *Millon Clinical Multiaxial Inventory—II manual.* Minneapolis: Interpretive Scoring Systems.

Millon, T. (1994). *Millon Clinical Multiaxial Inventory—III manual.* Minneapolis: Interpretive Scoring Systems.

Mills, C. J., & Noyes, H. L. (1984). Patterns and correlates of initial and subsequent drug use among adolescents. *Journal of Consulting and Clinical Psychology, 52,* 231–243.

Milner, B. (1968). Disorders of memory after brain lesions in man: Preface: Material-specific and generalized memory loss. *Neuropsychologia, 6,* 175–179.

Milner, B. (1978). Clues to the cerebral organization of memory. In P. A. Buser & A. Rougeul-Buser (Eds.), *Cerebral correlates of conscious experience* (pp. 139–153). Amsterdam: Elsevier.

Mitchell, J., & Vierkant, A. D. (1991). Delusions and hallucinations of cocaine abusers and paranoid schizophrenics: A comparative study. *Journal of Psychology, 125,* 301–310.

Mittenberg, W., Azrin, R., Millsaps, C., & Heilbronner, R. (1993). Identification of malingered head injury on the Wechsler Memory Scale—Revised. *Psychological Assessment, 5,* 34–40.

Mittenberg, W., D'Attilio, J., Gage, R., & Bass, A. (1990, Februrary). *Malingered symptoms following mild head trauma: The post-concussion syndrome.* Paper presented at the 18th meeting of the International Neuropsychological Society, Orlando, FL.

Mittenberg, W., DiGiulio, D. V., Perrin, S., & Bass, A. E. (1989). Symptoms following mild head injury: Expectations as etiology. *Clinical Neuropsychologist, 3,* 297.

Mittman, B. L. (1983). Judges ability to diagnose schizophrenia on the Rorschach: The effect of malingering (Doctoral dissertation, California School of Professional Psychology). *Dissertation Abstracts International, 44,* 1248B.

Modell, J. G., Mountz, J. M., & Ford, C. V. (1992). Pathological lying associated with thalamic dysfunction demonstrated by [^{99m}Tc]HMPAO SPECT. *Journal of Neuropsychiatry, 4,* 442–446.

Modlin, H. (1960). *Neurosis and trauma, roundtable presentation.* Washington, DC: American Psychiatric Association Press.

Modlin, H. (1986). Compensation neurosis. *Bulletin of the American Academy of Psychiatry and the Law, 14,* 263–271.

Moeller, M. R., Fey, P., & Sachs, H. (1993) Hair analysis as evidence in forensic cases. *Forensic Sciences International, 63,* 43–53.

Monahan, J. (1980). *Who is the client? The ethics of psychological intervention in the criminal justice system.* Washington, DC: American Psychological Association Press.

Monteiro, K. P., MacDonald, H., & Hilgard, E. R. (1980). Imagery, absorption and hypnosis: A factoral study. *Journal of Mental Imagery, 4,* 63–81.

Moore, R. A. (1972). The diagnosis of alcoholism in a psychiatric hospital: A trial of the Michigan Alcoholism Screening Test (MAST). *American Journal of Psychiatry, 128,* 1565–1569.

Moore, R. D., Bone, L. R., Geller, G., Mamon, J. A., Stokes, E. J., & Levine, D. M. (1989). Prevalence, detection, and treatment of alcoholism in hospitalized patients. *Journal of the American Medical Association, 261,* 403–407.

Moore, R. H. (1984). The concurrent and construct validity of the MacAndrew Alcoholism Scale among at-risk adolescent males. *Journal of Clinical Psychology, 40,* 1264–1269.

Moreland, K. L. (1989). Review of the Phase II Profile Integrity Status Inventory and Addendum. In J. C. Conoley & J. J. Kramer (Eds.), *The tenth mental measurements yearbook* (pp. 638–640). Lincoln, NE: Buros Institute of Mental Measurements.

Morency, N. L., & Krauss, R. M. (1982). Children's nonverbal encoding and decoding of affect. In R. S. Feldman (Ed.), *Development of nonverbal behavior in children* (pp. 181–200). New York: Springer-Verlag.

Morey, L. C. (1991). *Personality Assessment Inventory professional manual.* Odessa, FL: Psychological Assessment Resources.

Morey, L. C. (1993, August). *Defensiveness and malingering indices for the PAI.* Paper presented at the 101st annual meeting of the American Psychological Association, Toronto.

Morgan, A. H., Johnson, D. L., & Hilgard, E. R. (1974). The stability of hypnotic susceptibility: A longitudinal study. *International Journal of Clinical and Experimental Hypnosis, 22,* 249–257.

Morgan J. P. (1984). Problems of mass urine screening for misused drugs. *Journal of Psychoactive Drugs, 16*(4), 305–317.

Moscovitch, M. (1984). The sufficient conditions for demonstrating preserved memory in amnesia: A task analysis. In L. R. Squire & N. Butters (Eds.), *Neuropsychology of memory* (1st ed.). New York: Guilford Press.

Moses, J. A., Golden, C. J., Wilkening, G. N., McKay, S. E., & Ariel, R. (1983). *Interpretation of the Luria–Nebraska neuropsychological battery* (Vol. 2). New York: Grune & Stratton.

Mott, R. H., Small, I. F., & Andersen, J. M. (1965). Comparative study of hallucinations. *Archives of General Psychiatry, 12,* 595–601.

Moulton, J. (1987, April). *Assessment of head injuries.* Presentation to American Academy of Psychiatry and the Law, Midwest Chapter, Cincinnati, OH.

Mouton, G. J., Peterson, S. A., Nicholson, R. A., & Bagby, R. M. (1995, August). *Detecting simulated malingering with the MMPI-2: Receiver operating characteristic analysis.* Paper presented at the annual convention of the American Psychological Association, New York, NY.

Mulhern, S. (1994). Satanism, ritual abuse, and multiple personality disorder: A sociohistorical perspective. *International Journal of Clinical and Experimental Hypnosis 42,* 265–288.

Mullen, P. E., Martin, J. L., Anderson, J. C., Romans, S. E., & Herbison, G. P. (1993). Childhood sexual abuse and mental health in adult life. *British Journal of Psychiatry, 163,* 721–732.

Murphy, J. M., Berwick, D. M., Weinstein, M. C., Borus, J. F., Budman, S. H., & Klerman, G. L. (1987). Performance of screening and diagnostic tests: Application of receiver operating characteristic analysis. *Archives of General Psychiatry, 44,* 550–555.

Murphy, K. R. (1993). *Honesty in the workplace.* Pacific Grove, CA: Brooks–Cole.

Murphy, W. D., & Peters, J. M. (1992). Profiling child sex abusers: Psychological considerations. *Criminal Justice and Behavior, 19,* 24–37.

Murrey, G. L., Cross, H. L., & Whipple, J. (1992). Hypnotically created pseudomemories: Further investigation into the "memory distortion or response bias" question. *Journal of Abnormal Psychology, 101,* 75–77.

Muscio, B. (1916). The influence of the form of a question. *British Journal of Psychology, 8,* 351–389.

Nadel, L., & Zola-Morgan, S. (1984). Infantile amnesia: A neurobiological perspective. In M. Moscovitch (Ed.), *Infant memory: Its relation to normal and pathological memory in humans and other animals* (pp. 145–172). New York: Plenum.

Nadelson, T. (1979). The Munchausen syndrome: Borderline character features. *General Hospital Psychiatry, 2,* 11–17.

Nakahara, Y., Shimamine, M., & Takahashi, K. (1992). Hair analysis for drugs of abuse: III. Movement and stability of methoxyphenamine (as a model compound of methamphetamine) along hair shaft with hair growth. *Journal of Analytic Toxicology, 16,* 253–257.

Naples, M., & Hackett, T. P. (1978). The amytal interview: History and current uses. *Psychosomatics, 19,* 98–105.

National Institute on Drug Abuse. (1991). *National household survey on drug abuse: Population estimates, 1990.* Rockville, MD: U.S. Department of Health and Human Services.

National Institute of Mental Health. (1991). *NIMH Diagnostic Interview for Children, Version 2.3.* Rockville, MD: Author.

Netter, B. E. C., & Viglione, D. J. (1994). An empirical study of malingering schizophrenia on the Rorschach. *Journal of Personality Assessment, 62,* 45–57.

Newcomb, M. D., & Bentler, P. M. (1989). Substance use and abuse among children and teenagers. *American Psychologist, 44,* 242–248.

Nichols, D. S., & Greene, R. L. (1991, March). *New measures for dissimulation on the MMPI/MMPI-2.* Paper presented at the 26th Annual Symposium on Recent Developments in the Use of the MMPI (MMPI-2/MMPI-A), St. Petersburg Beach, FL.

Nichols, D. S., Greene, R. L., & Schmolck, P. (1987). Criteria for assessing inconsistent patterns of item endorsement on the MMPI: Rationale, development, and empirical trials. *Journal of Clinical Psychology, 45,* 239–250.

Nichols, H. R., & Molinder, I. (1984). *Multiphasic Sex Inventory.* (Available from Nichols and Molinder, 437 Bowes Drive, Tacoma, WA 98466.)

Note. (1952). Hypnotism, suggestibility and the law. *Nebraska Law Review, 31,* 575–596.

Novack, D. H., Detering, B. J., Arnold, R., Forrow, L., Ladinsky, M., & Pezzullo, J. C. (1989). Physicians' attitudes toward using deception to resolve difficult ethical problems. *Journal of the American Medical Association, 261,* 2980–2985.

O'Bannon, R. M., Goldinger, L. A., & Appleby, G. S. (1989). *Honesty and integrity testing.* Atlanta, GA: Applied Information Resources.

O'Connor, M., Butters, N., Miliotis, P., Eslinger, P., & Cermak, L. S. (1992). The dissociation of anterograde and retrograde amnesia in a patients with herpes encephalitis. *Journal of Clinical and Experimental Neuropsychology, 14,* 159–178.

Oddy, M., Humphrey, M., & Uttley, D. (1978). Subjective impairment and social recovery after closed head injury. *Journal of Neurology, Neurosurgery, and Psychiatry, 41,* 611–616.

Ofshe, R. J. (1992). Inadvertent hypnosis during interrogation: False confession due to dissociative state; misidentified multiple personality and the satanic cult hypothesis. *International Journal of Clinical and Experimental Hypnosis, 40,* 125–156.

Ofshe, R. I., & Singer, M. T. (1994). Recovered-memory therapy and robust repression: Influence and pseudomemories. *International Journal of Clinical and Experimental Hypnosis, 42,* 391–410.

Ogloff, J. R. (1990). The admissibility of expert testimony regarding malingering and deception. *Behavioral Sciences and the Law, 8,* 27–43.

Ogloff, J. R. P., Wong, S., & Greenwood, A. (1990). Treating criminal psychopaths in a therapeutic community program. *Behavioral Sciences and the Law, 8,* 181–190.

Olkinuora, M. (1984). Psychogenic epidemics and work. *Scandanavian Journal of Work Environment and Health, 10,* 501–504.

O'Neill, B., Williams, A. F., & Dubowski, K. M. (1983). Variability in blood alcohol concentrations: Implications for estimating individual results. *Journal of Studies on Alcohol, 44*, 222–230.

Ones, D. S., Mount, M. K., Barrick, M. R., & Hunter, J. E. (1994a). Personality and job performance: A critique of the Tett, Jackson, and Rothstein (1991) meta-analysis. *Personnel Psychology, 47*, 147–156.

Ones, D. S., Schmidt, F. L., & Viswesvaran, C. (1994b, April). Examination of construct validity with linear composites and generalizability coefficient corrected correlations. In F. L. Schmidt (Chair), *What is new in construct-based research methodology?* Symposium conducted at the Annual Meeting of the Society for Industrial and Organizational Psychology, Nashville, TN.

Ones, D. S., Schmidt, F. L., & Viswesvaran, C. (1994c, April). Do broader personality variables predict job performance with higher validity. In R. Page (Chair), *Personality and job performance: Big Five versus specific traits.* Symposium conducted at the Annual Meeting of the Society for Industrial and Organizational Psychology, Nashville, TN.

Ones, D. S., Viswesvaran, C., & Schmidt, F. L. (1993). Comprehensive meta-analysis of integrity test validities: Findings and implications for personnel selection and theories of job performance. *Journal of Applied Psychology, 78*, 679–703.

Ones, D. S., Viswesvaran, C., & Schmidt, F. L. (1995). Integrity tests: Overlooked facts, resolved issues, and remaining questions. *American Psychologist, 50*, 456–457.

Orndoff v. Lockhart, 906 F.2d 1230 (8th Cir., 1990).

Orne, M. T. (1959). The nature of hypnosis: Artifact and essence. *Journal of Abnormal and Social Psychology, 58*, 277–299.

Orne, M. T. (1961). The potential uses of hypnosis in interrogation. In A. D. Biderman & H. Zimmer (Eds.), *The manipulation of human behavior* (pp. 169–215). New York: Wiley.

Orne, M. T. (1972). On the simulating subject as a quasi-control group in hypnosis research: What, why and how. In E. Fromm & R. E. Shor (Eds.), *Hypnosis: Research developments and perspectives* (pp. 399–443). Chicago: Aldine–Atherton.

Orne, M. T. (1979). The use and misuse of hypnosis in court. *International Journal of Clinical and Experimental Hypnosis, 27*, 311–341.

Orne, M. T. (1985, October). Forensic hypnosis. *Newsletter of the American Academy of Psychiatry and the Law, 10*, 4–5.

Orne, M. T., Dinges, D. F., & Orne, E. C. (1984). On the differential diagnosis of multiple personality in the forensic context. *International Journal of Clinical and Experimental Hypnosis, 32*, 118–169.

Orne, M. T., Hilgard, E. R., Spiegel, H., Spiegel, D., Crawford, H. J., Evans, F. J., Orne, E. C., & Frischholz, E. I. (1979). The relationship between the Hypnotic Induction Profile and the Stanford Hypnotic Susceptibility Scales, Forms A and C. *International Journal of Clinical and Experimental Hypnosis, 27*, 85–102.

Orne, M., Soskis, D., Dinges, D., Orne, E., & Tonry, M. (1989). *Hypnotically refreshed testimony: Enhanced memory or tampering with evidence?* Washington, DC: National Institute of Justice Issues and Practices in Criminal Justice.

Orr, S. P., Pitman, R. K., Lasko, N. B., & Herz, L. R. (1993). Psychophysiological assessment of post-traumatic stress disorder imagery in World War II and the Korean combat veterans. *Journal of Abnormal Psychology, 102*, 620–624.

Ossipov, V. P. (1944). Malingering: The simulation of psychosis. *Bulletin of the Menninger Clinic, 8*, 31–42.

Otto, R. K., & Hall, J. E. (1988). The utility of the Michigan Alcoholism Screening Test in the detection of alcoholics and problem drinkers. *Journal of Personality Assessment, 52*, 499–505.

Otto, R. K., Lang, A. R., Megargee, E. I., & Rosenblatt, A. I. (1988). Ability of alcoholics to escape detection by the MMPI. *Journal of Consulting and Clinical Psychology, 56,* 452–457.

Overholser, J. C. (1990). Differential diagnosis of malingering and factitious disorder with physical symptoms. *Behavioral Sciences and the Law, 8,* 55–65.

Pankratz, L. (1979). Procedures for the assessment and treatment of functional sensory deficits. *Journal of Consulting and Clinical Psychology, 47,* 409–410.

Pankratz, L. (1983). A new technique for the assessment and modification of feigned memory deficit. *Perceptual and Motor Skills, 57,* 367–372.

Pankratz, L. (1985, May). *The spectrum of factitious post-traumatic stress disorder.* Presentation to American Psychiatric Association, Dallas, TX.

Pankratz, L. (1988). Malingering on intellectual and neuropsychological measures. In R. Rogers (Ed.), *Clinical assessment of malingering and deception* (1st ed., pp. 169–192). New York: Guilford Press.

Pankratz, L., Binder, L. M., & Wilcox, L. (1987). Assessment of an exaggerated somatosensory deficit with Symptom Validity Assessment [Letter]. *Archives of Neurology, 44,* 798.

Pankratz, L., & Erickson, R. (1990). Two views of malingering. *Clinical Neuropsychologist, 4,* 379–389.

Pankratz, L., Fausti, S., & Peed, S. (1975). A forced-choice technique to evaluate deafness in the hysterical or malingering patient. *Journal of Consulting and Clinical Psychology, 43,* 421–422.

Pankratz, L., Hickam, D., & Toth, S. (1989). The identification and management of drug-seeking behavior in a medical center. *Drug and Alcohol Dependence, 24,* 115–118.

Pankratz, L., & Jackson, J. (1994). Habitually wandering patients. *New England Journal of Medicine, 331,* 1752–1755.

Parker, N. (1977). Accident litigants with neurotic symptoms. *Medical Journal of Australia, 2,* 318–322.

Parker, N. (1979). Malingering: A dangerous diagnosis. *Medical Journal of Australia, 1,* 568–569.

Parwatikar, S. D., Holcomb, W. R., & Menninger, K. A., II. (1985). The detection of malingered amnesia in accused murders. *Bulletin of the American Academy of Psychiatry and the Law, 13,* 97–103.

Patrick, C. J., & Iacono, W. G. (1986). The validity of lie detection with criminal psychopaths. *Psychophysiology, 23,* 452–453.

Patrick, C. J., & Iacono, W. G. (1991a). A comparison of field and laboratory polygraphs in the detection of deception. *Psychophysiology, 28,* 632–638.

Patrick, C. J., & Iacono, W. G. (1991b). Validity of the control question polygraph test: The problem of sampling bias. *Journal of Applied Psychology, 76,* 229–238.

Patterson, G. R. (1982). *Coercive family interactions.* Eugene, OR: Castalia Press.

Pearlson, G. D., Kreger, L., Rabins, R. V., Chase, G. A., Cohen, B., Wirth, J. B., Schlaepfer, T. B., & Tune, L. E. (1989). A chart review study of late-onset and early-onset schizophrenia. *American Journal of Psychiatry, 146,* 1568–1574.

Peck, C. J., Fordyce, W. E., & Black, R. G. (1978). The effect of the pendency of claims for compensation upon behavior indicative of pain. *Washington Law Review, 53,* 251–279.

Peck, R. E. (1960). Use of hydroxydione as a truth serum. *Journal of Neuropsychiatry, 1,* 163–166.

Pendergrast, M. (1995). *Victims of memory: Incest accusations and shattered lives.* Hinesburg, VT: Upper Access.

People v. Boudin, Ind. No. 81–285 (S.C.N.Y., Opinion filed March 11, 1983).

People v. Buono, No. 81–A354231 (Cal Super. Ct. November 18, 1983).

People v. Cornell, 338 P.2d 447 (1959).

People v. Ebanks, 49 P. 1049 (1897).

People v. Harper, 204. 250 N.E.2d 5 (1969).

People v. Hurd, Sup. Ct. N.J. Somerset Cty., April 2, 1980.

People v. Marsh, 338 P.2d 495 (1959).

People v. McBroom, 70 Cal. Rptr. 326 (1968).

People v. McNichol, 544, 244 P.2d 21 (1950).

People v. Milner, 753 P.2d 669 (Cal. 1988).

People v. Ritchie, No. C-36932 (Super. Ct. Orange Cty. Cal. April 7, 1977).

People v. Shirley, 31 Cal.3d 18 641 P.2d 775, 181 Cal. Rptr. 243 (1982).

People v. Thompson, C12495 (San Mateo Sup. Ct. 1983).

People v. Worthington, 38 P. 689 (1894).

Perconte, S. T., & Goreczny, A.J. (1990). Failure to detect fabricated posttraumatic stress disorder with the use of the MMPI in a clinical population. *American Journal of Psychiatry, 147*, 1057–1060.

Perry, G. G., & Kinder, B. N. (1990). The susceptibility of the Rorschach to malingering: A critical review. *Journal of Personality Assessment, 54*, 47–57.

Perry, G. G., & Kinder, B. N. (1992). Susceptibility of the Rorschach to malingering: A schizophrenia analogue. In C. D. Spielberger & J. Butcher (Eds.), *Advances in personality assessment* (Vol. 9, pp. 127 140). Hillsdale, NJ: Erlbaum.

Perry, J. C., & Cooper, S. H. (1985). Empirical studies of psychological defense mechanisms. In R. Michels, J. O. Cavenar, A. M. Cooper, S. B. Guze, L. L. Judd, G. L. Klerman, & A. J. Solnit (Eds.), *Psychiatry* (Vol. 1). Philadelphia: J. B. Lippincott.

Perry, J. C., & Jacobs, D. (1982). Overview: Clinical applications of the Amytal interview in psychiatric emergency settings. *American Journal of Psychiatry, 139*, 552–559.

Persinger, M. A. (1992). Neuropsychological profiles of adults who report "sudden remembering" of early childhood memories: Implications for claims of sex abuse and alien visitation/abduction experiences. *Perceptual and Motor Skills, 75*, 259–266.

Persinger, M. A. (1994). Elicitation of "childhood memories" in hypnosis-like settings is associated with complex partial epileptic-like signs for women but not for men: Implications for the false memory syndrome. *Perceptual and Motor Skills, 78*, 643–651.

Petersen, E., & Viglione, D. (1991). *The effect of psychological knowledge and specific role instruction of MMPI malingering.* Unpublished manuscript, California School of Professional Psychology, San Diego.

Peterson, G. W., Clark, D. A., & Bennet, B. (1989). The utility of MMPI subtle–obvious scales for detecting fake good and fake bad response sets. *Journal of Clinical Psychology, 45*, 575–582.

Pettigrew, C. G., Tuma, J. M., Pickering, J. W., & Whelton, J. (1983). Simulation of psychosis on a multiple-choice projective test. *Perceptual and Motor Skills, 57*, 463–469.

Petzel, T., Johnson, J., & McKillip, J. (1973). Response bias in drug surveys. *Journal of Consulting and Clinical Psychology, 40*, 427–439.

Pfohl, B., Blum, N., Zimmerman, M., & Stangl, D. (1989). *The Structured Interview for DSM-III Personality: SIDP-R.* Iowa City: University of Iowa.

Pfohl, B., Coryell, W., Zimmerman, M., & Stangl, D. (1986). DSM-III personality disorders: Diagnostic overlap and internal consistency of individual DSM-III criteria. *Comprehensive Psychiatry, 27*, 21–34.

Pfohl, B., Stangl, D., & Zimmerman, M. (1982). *The Structured Interview for DSM-III Personality Disorders (SIDP).* Iowa City: University of Iowa Press.

Phillips, M. R., Ward, N. G., & Ries, R. K. (1983). Factitious mourning: Painless patienthood. *American Journal of Psychiatry, 140*, 420–425.

Pillemer, D. B., & White, S. H. (1989). Childhood events recalled by children and adults. In H. W. Reese (Ed.), *Advances in child development and behavior* (Vol. 21, pp. 297–340). San Diego, CA: Academic Press.

Piper, A. (1993). "Truth serum" and "recovered memories" of sexual abuse: A review of the evidence. *Journal of Psychiatry and Law, 21,* 447–471.

Pitman, R. K., & Orr, S. P. (1993). Psychophysiologic testing for post-traumatic stress disorder: Forensic psychiatric application. *Bulletin of the American Academy of Psychiatry and Law, 21,* 37–52.

Pitman, R. K., Saunders, L. S., & Orr, S. P. (1994, April). Psychophysiologic testing for post-traumatic stress disorder, *Trial,* pp. 22–26.

Pitman, R. K., Sparr, L. F., Saunders, L. S., & McFarlane, A. (1996). Legal issues in posttraumatic stress disorder. In B. A. van der Kolk, A. C. McFarlane, & L. Weisaeth (Eds.), *Traumatic stress* (pp. 378–397). New York: Guilford Press.

Plum, F., & Posner, J. B. (1980). *The diagnosis of stupor and coma* (3rd ed.). Philadelphia: F. A. Davis Company.

Pollack, S. (1982). Dimensions of malingering. In B. H. Gross & L. E. Weinberger (Eds.), *New directions for mental health services: The mental health professional and the legal system* (pp. 63–75). San Francisco: Jossey-Bass.

Pope, H. G., & Hudson, J. I. (1995). Can memories of childhood sexual abuse be repressed? *Psychological Medicine, 25,* 121–126.

Pope, H. G., Jonas, J. M., & Jones, B. (1982). Factitious psychosis: Phenomenology, family history, and long-term outcome of nine patients. *American Journal of Psychiatry, 139,* 1480–1483.

Pope, K. S., Butcher, J. N., & Seelen, J. (1993). *The MMPI, MMPI-2 and MMPI-A in court: A practical guide for expert witnesses and attorneys.* Washington, DC: American Psychological Press.

Potter, B. A. & Orfali, J. S. (1990). *Drug testing at work: A guide for employers and employees.* Berkeley, CA: Ronin.

Powell, K. E. (1991). *The malingering of schizophrenia.* Unpublished doctoral dissertation, University of South Carolina.

Power, D. J. (1977). Memory, identification and crime. *Medicine, Science and the Law, 17,* 132–139.

Price, G. E., & Terhune, W. B. (1919). Feigned amnesia as a defense reaction. *Journal of the American Medical Association, 72,* 565–567.

Price, K. P. (1994). Posttraumatic stress disorder and concussion: Are they incompatible? *Defense Law Journal, 43,* 113–120.

Prigatano, G. P., & Amin, K. (1993). Digit memory test: Unequivocal cerebral dysfunction and suspected malingering. *Journal of Clinical and Experimental Neuropsychology, 15,* 537–546.

Prince, M. (1906). *The dissociation of a personality: A biographical study in abnormal personality.* New York: Longmans, Green.

Putnam, F. W., Guroff, J. J., Silberman, E. K., Barban, L., & Post, R. M. (1986). The clinical phenomenology of multiple personality disorder: Review of 100 recent cases. *Journal of Clinical Psychiatry, 47,* 285–293.

Putnam, W. H. (1979). Hypnosis and distortions in eyewitness memory. *International Journal of Clinical and Experimental Hypnosis, 27,* 437–448.

Pyle, C. H. (1985). Asking the wrong questions. *Society, 22,* 54–55.

Quaglino v. California, cert. denied, —U.S.—, 99 S. Ct. 212, *pet. rehearing denied,* —U.S.—, 99 S. Ct. 599 (1978).

Quay, H. C., & La Greca, A. M. (1986). Disorders of anxiety, withdrawal, and dysphoria. In H. C. Quay & J. S. Werry (Eds.), *Psychopathological Disorders of Childhood* (3rd ed., pp. 73–110). New York: Wiley.

Quinn, K. M. (1988). Children and deception. In R. Rogers (Ed.), *Clinical assessment of malingering and deception* (pp. 104–119). New York: Guilford Press.

Quinsey, V. L. (1984). Sexual aggression: Studies of offenders against women. In D. N. Weisstub (Ed.), *Law and mental health: International perspectives* (Vol. 1, pp. 84–122). New York: Pergamon Press.

Quinsey, V. L., Arnold, L. S., & Pruess, M. G. (1980). MMPI profiles of men referred for a pretrial psychiatric assessment as a function of response type. *Journal of Clinical Psychology, 36,* 410–417.

Quinsey, V. L., & Bergersen, S. G. (1976). Instructional control of penile circumference in assessments of sexual preference. *Behavior Therapy, 7,* 489–493.

Quinsey, V. L., & Chaplin, T. C. (1988). Preventing faking in phallometric assessment of sexual preference. In R. A. Prentky & V. L. Quinsey (Eds.), *Human sexual aggression: Current perspectives* (pp. 49–58). New York: New York Academy of Sciences.

Quinsey, V. L., & Laws, D. R. (1990). Validity of physiological measures of pedophilic sexual arousal in a sexual offender population: A critique of Hall, Proctor, and Nelson. *Journal of Consulting and Clinical Psychology, 58,* 886–888.

Rabinowitz, S., Mark, M., Modai, I., & Margalit, C. (1990). Malingering in the clinical setting: Practical suggestions for intervention. *Psychological Reports, 67,* 1315–1318.

Raskin, D. C. (1989). Polygraph techniques for the detection of deception. In D. C. Raskin (Ed.), *Psychological methods in criminal investigation and evidence* (pp. 247–296). New York: Springer.

Raskin, D. C., Honts, C. R., & Kircher, J. C. (1996). The scientific status of research on polygraph techniques: The case for polygraph tests. In D. L. Faigman (Ed.), *The West companion to scientific evidence.* Minneapolis: West Publishing.

Rathus, S. A., Fox, J. A., & Ortins, J. B. (1980). The MacAndrew scale as a measure of substance abuse and delinquency among adolescents. *Journal of Clinical Psychology, 36,* 579–583.

Rawling, P., & Brooks, N. (1990). Simulation index: A method for detecting factitious errors on the WAIS-R and WMS. *Neuropsychology, 4,* 234–238.

Ray, I. (1871). *Treatise on the medical jurisprudence of insanity.* Boston: Little, Brown.

Reales, J. M., & Ballesteros, S. (1994). SDT-SP, a program in Pascal for computing parameters and significance tests from several detection theory designs. *Behavior, Research Methods, Instruments, and Computers, 26,* 151–155.

Redlich, R. C., Ravitz, L. J., & Dession, G. H. (1951). Narcoanalysis and the truth. *American Journal of Psychiatry, 107,* 586–593.

Reich, P., & Gottfried, L. A. (1983). Factitious disorders in a teaching hospital. *Annals of Internal Medicine, 99,* 240–247.

Reid, W. H. (1978). *The psychopath: A comprehensive study of antisocial disorders and behaviors.* New York: Brunner/Mazel.

Reiser, M. (1986). Admission of hypnosis-induced recollections into evidence. *American Journal of Forensic Psychiatry, 7,* 31–40.

Resnick, P. J. (1984). The detection of malingered mental illness. *Behavioral Sciences and the Law, 2*(1), 20–38.

Resnick, P. J. (1987, October). *The detection of malingered mental illness.* Workshop presented at the American Academy of Psychiatry and Law, Ottawa, Canada.

Resnick, P. J. (1988). Malingered psychosis. In R. Rogers (Ed.), *Clinical assessment of malingering and deception* (1st ed., pp. 34–53). New York: Guilford Press.

Resnick, P. J. (1993). Defrocking the fraud: The detection of malingering. *Israel Journal of Psychiatry and Related Sciences, 30*(2), 93–101.

Retzlaff, P. D., & Gilbertini, M. (1994). Neuropsychometric issues. In R. D. Vanderploeg (Ed.), *Clinician's guide to neuropsychological assessment* (pp. 185–209). Hillsdale, NJ: Erlbaum.

Retzlaff, P. D., Sheehan, E. P., & Fiel, A. (1991). MCMI-II report style and bias: Profile and validity scale analysis. *Journal of Personality Assessment, 56,* 478–486.

Rey, A. (1964). *L'examen clinique en psychologie* [Clinical exam in psychology]. Paris: Presses Universitaires de France.

Reynolds, C. R., & Kamphaus, R. W. (1992). *Behavior assessment system for children.* Toronto: American Guidance Service, Inc.

Reynolds, W. M. (1993). Self-report methodology. In T. H. Ollendick & M. Herson (Eds.), *Handbook of child and adolescent assessment* (pp. 98–123). Boston: Allyn & Bacon.

Rice, M. E., Harris, G. T., & Quinsey, V. L. (1990). A follow-up of rapists in a maximum-security psychiatric facility. *Journal of Interpersonal Violence, 5,* 435–448.

Rickarby, G. A. (1979). Compensation-neurosis and the psycho-social requirements of the family. *British Journal of Medical Psychology, 52,* 333–338.

Rieke, M. L., & Guastello, S. J. (1995). Unresolved issues in honesty and integrity testing. *American Psychologist, 50,* 458–459.

Rigler, C. T. J. (1879). *Uber die Folgen der Verletzungen auf Eisenbahnen* [Concerning the consequences of injuries occurring on railroads]. Berlin: Reimer.

Rim, S. B., & Lowe, B. (1988). Family environments of underachieving gifted students. *Gifted Child Quarterly, 32,* 353–359.

Ripley, H. S., & Wolf, S. (1947). Intravenous use of sodium amytal in psychosomatic disorders. *Psychosomatic Medicine, 9,* 4–10.

Ritson, B., & Forrest, A. (1970). The simulation of psychosis: A contemporary presentation. *British Journal of Medical Psychology, 43,* 31–37.

Robins, L. N., Helzer, J. E., Cottler, L. B., & Goldring, E. (1989). *NIMH Diagnostic Interview Schedule, Version III—Revised.* St. Louis: Washington University School of Medicine.

Robins, L. N., Helzer, J. E., Cottler, L. B., Works, J., Goldring, E., McEvoy, L., & Stoltzman, R. (1985). *The DIS Version III-A training manual.* St. Louis: Washington University School of Medicine.

Robins, L. N., Helzer, J. E., Croughan, J. L., & Ratcliff, K. (1981). The NIMH Diagnostic Interview Schedule: Its history, characteristics, and validity. *Archives of General Psychiatry, 38,* 381–389.

Robitcher, J. B. (1980). *The powers of psychiatry.* Boston: Houghton Mifflin.

Rock v. Arkansas, 107 S. Ct. 2704 (1987).

Rockwell, R. B. (1994). One psychiatrist's view of satanic ritual abuse. *Journal of Psychohistory 21,* 443–460.

Roediger, H. L., III, & McDermott, K. B. (1995). Creating false memories: Remembering words not presented in lists. *Journal of Experimental Psychology: Learning, Memory, and Cognition, 21,* 803–814.

Rogers, R. (1984a). *Rogers criminal responsibility assessment scales (RCRAS) and tests manual.* Odessa, FL: Psychological Assessment Resources.

Rogers, R. (1984b). Towards an empirical model of malingering and deception. *Behavioral Sciences and the Law, 2,* 93–112.

Rogers, R. (1986). *Conducting insanity evaluations.* New York: Van Nostrand Reinhold.

Rogers, R. (1987). The assessment of malingering within a forensic context. In D. N. Weisstub (Ed.), *Law and psychiatry: International perspectives* (Vol. 3, pp. 209–237). New York: Plenum.

Rogers, R. (1988a). Researching dissimulation. In R. Rogers (Ed.), *Clinical assessment of malingering and deception* (1st ed., pp. 309–327). New York: Guilford Press.

Rogers, R. (1988b). Structured interviews and dissimulation. In R. Rogers (Ed.), *Clinical assessment of malingering and deception* (1st ed., pp. 250–268). New York: Guilford Press.

Rogers, R. (1990a). Development of a new classificatory model of malingering. *Bulletin of the American Academy of Psychiatry and Law, 18,* 323–333.

Rogers, R. (1990b). Models of feigned mental illness. *Professional Psychology, 21,* 182–188.

Rogers, R. (1992). *Structured Interview of Reported Systems.* Odessa, FL: Psychological Assessment Resources.

Rogers, R. (1994). Malingering. *Harvard Mental Health Letter, 10*(9), 3–5.

Rogers, R. (1995). *Diagnostic and structured interviewing: A handbook for psychologists.* Odessa, FL: Psychological Assessment Resources.

Rogers, R., Bagby, R. M., & Chakraborty, D. (1993). Feigning schizophrenic disorders on the MMPI-2: Detection of coached simulators. *Journal of Personality Assessment, 60,* 215–226.

Rogers, R., Bagby, R. M., & Dickens, S. E. (1992). *Structured Interview of Reported Symptoms (SIRS) and professional manual.* Odessa, FL: Psychological Assessment Resources.

Rogers, R., Bagby, R. M., & Gillis, J. R. (1992). Improvements in the M Test as a screening measure for malingering. *Bulletin of the American Academy of Psychiatry and the Law, 20*(1), 101–104.

Rogers, R., Bagby, R. M., & Prendergast, P. (1993). *Vulnerability of the Structured Interview of DSM-III-R (SCID) to dissimulation and distortion.* Unpublished manuscript.

Rogers, R., Bagby, R. M., & Rector, N. (1989). Diagnostic legitimacy of factitious disorder with psychological symptoms. *American Journal of Psychiatry, 146,* 1312–1314.

Rogers, R., Bagby, R. M., & Vincent, A. (1994). Factitious disorders with predominantly psychological signs and symptoms: A conundrum for forensic experts. *Journal of Psychiatry and Law, 22,* 91–106.

Rogers, R., Cashel, M. L., Johansen, J., Sewell, K. W., & Gonzalez, C. (in press). Evaluation of adolescent offenders with substance abuse: Validation of the SASSI with conduct-disordered youth. *Criminal Justice and Behavior.*

Rogers, R., & Cavanaugh, J. L., Jr. (1983). "Nothing but the truth": . . . A reexamination of malingering. *Journal of Law and Psychiatry, 11,* 443–460.

Rogers, R., Cruise, K., & Sewell, K. W. (1996). *Effects of instructional sets on feigned depression.* Manuscript in preparation.

Rogers, R., & Cunnien, A. J. (1986). Multiple SADS evaluation in the assessment of criminal defendants. *Journal of Forensic Sciences, 30,* 222–230.

Rogers, R., & Dickens, S. E. (1987). [Outpatients evaluations of mentally disordered offenders.] Unpublished raw data.

Rogers, R., & Dickey, R. (1991). Denial and mimimization among sex offenders: A review of competing models of deception. *Annals of Sex Research, 4,* 49–63.

Rogers, R., Dion, K. L., & Lynett, E. (1992). Diagnostic validity of antisocial personality disorder. *Law and Human Behavior, 16,* 677–689.

Rogers, R., Dolmetsch, R., & Cavanaugh, J. L., Jr. (1983). Identification of random responders on MMPI protocols. *Journal of Personality Assessment, 47,* 364–368.

Rogers, R., Duncan, J. C., Lynett, E., & Sewell, K. W. (1994). Prototypical analysis of antisocial personality disorder: DSM-IV and beyond. *Law and Human Behavior, 18,* 471–484.

Rogers, R., Gillis, J. R., & Bagby, R. M. (1990). The SIRS as a measure of malingering: A validational study with a correctional sample. *Behavioral Sciences and the Law, 8,* 85–92.

Rogers, R., Gillis, G. R., Dickens, S. E., & Bagby, R. M. (1989). *Standardized assessment of malingering: Validation of the SIRS.* Paper presented at the 97th meeting of the American Psychological Association, New Orleans, LA.

Rogers, R., Gillis, J. R., Dickens, S. E., & Bagby, R. M. (1991). Standardized assessment of malingering: Validation of the Structured Interview of Reported Symptoms. *Psychological Assessment, 4*, 89–96.

Rogers, R., Gillis, J. R., Turner, R. E., & Frise-Smith, T. (1990). The clinical presentation of command hallucinations. *American Journal of Psychiatry, 147*, 1304–1307.

Rogers, R., Harrell, E. H., & Liff, C. D. (1993). Feigning neuropsychological impairment: A critical review of methodological and clinical considerations. *Clinical Psychology Review, 13*, 255–274.

Rogers, R., Hinds, J. D., & Sewell, K. W. (1995, August). *Feigning psychopathology among adolescent offenders: Validation of the SIRS, MMPI-A, and SIMS.* Paper presented at the 103rd meeting of The American Psychological Association, New York, NY.

Rogers, R., Kropp, P. R., Bagby, R. M., & Dickens, S. E. (1992). Faking specific disorders: A study of the Structured Interview of Reported Symptoms (SIRS). *Journal of Clinical Psychology, 48*, 643–648.

Rogers, R., & McKee, G. R. (1995). *Use of the MMPI-2 in the assessment of criminal responsibility.* In Y. S. Ben-Porath, J. R. Graham, G. C. N. Hall, R. D. Hirschman, & M. S. Zaragoza (Eds.), *Forensic applications of the MMPI-2* (pp. 103–126). Thousand Oaks, CA: Sage.

Rogers, R., & Mitchell, C. N. (1991). *Mental health experts and the criminal courts: A handbook for lawyers and clinicians.* Toronto: Carswell.

Rogers, R., & Nussbaum, D. (1991). Interpreting response styles of inconsistent MMPI profiles. *Forensic Reports, 4*, 361–366.

Rogers, R., Ornduff, S. R., & Sewell, K. W. (1993). Feigning specific disorders: A study of the Personality Assessment Inventory (PAI). *Journal of Personality Assessment, 60*, 554–560.

Rogers, R., Salekin, R. T., Sewell, K. W., & Goldstein, A. (1996). *Prototypical analysis of malingering: A comparsion of forensic and nonforensic cases.* Manuscript in preparation.

Rogers, R., Salekin, R. T., Sewell, K. W., & Zaparnik, D. (1996). *Prototypical analysis of antisocial personality disorder with correctional samples..* Manuscript in preparation.

Rogers, R., Sewell, K. W., & Goldstein, A. (1994). Explanatory models of malingering: A prototypical analysis. *Law and Human Behavior, 18*, 543–552.

Rogers, R., Sewell, K. W., Morey, L. C., & Ustad, K. L. (1990). Detection of feigned mental disorders on the Personality Assessment Inventory: A discriminant analysis. *Journal of Personality Assessment, 67*, 629–639.

Rogers, R., Sewell, K. W., & Salekin, R. T. (1994). A meta-analysis of malingering on the MMPI-2. *Assessment, 1*, 227–237.

Rogers, R., Sewell, K. W., & Ustad, K. L. (1995). Feigning among chronic outpatients on the MMPI-2: A systematic examination of fake-bad indicators. *Assessment, 2*, 81–89.

Rogers, R., Thatcher, A., & Cavanaugh. J. L. (1984). Use of SADS diagnostic interview in evaluating legal insanity. *Journal of Clinical Psychology, 40*, 1537–1541.

Rogers, R., & Webster, C. D. (1989). Assessing treatability in mentally disordered offenders. *Law and Human Behavior, 13*, 19–29.

Rohsenow, D. J. (1982). The Alcohol Use Inventory as predictor of drinking by male heavy social drinkers. *Addictive Behaviors, 7*, 387–395.

Rosanoff, A. J. (1920). *Manual of psychiatry.* New York: Wiley.

Rose, F. E., Hall, S., & Szalda-Petree, D. (1995). Portland Digit Recognition Test—computerized: Measuring response latency improves the detection of malingering. *Clinical Neuropsychologist, 9*, 124–134.

Rosen, T. H. (1987). Identification of substance abusers in the workplace. *Public Personnel Management, 16*, 197–207.

Rosenberg, C. E. (1968). *The trial of the assassin Guiteau.* Chicago: University of Chicago Press.

Rosenberg, D. A. (1987). Web of deceit: A literature review of Munchausen syndrome by proxy. *Child Abuse and Neglect, 11,* 547–563.

Rosenberg, S. J., & Feldberg, T. M. (1944). Rorschach characteristics of a group of malingerers. *Rorschach Research Exchange, 8,* 141–158.

Rosenfeld, J. P., Angell, A., Johnson, M., & Qian, J. (1991). An ERP-based, control-question lie detector analog: Algorithms for discriminating effects within individuals' average waveforms. *Psychophysiology, 28,* 319–335.

Rosenfeld, J. P., Ellwanger, J., & Sweet, J. (1995). Detecting simulated amnesia with event-related brain potentials. *International Journal of Psychophysiology, 19,* 1–11.

Rosenfeld, J. P., Nasman, V. T., Whalen, R., Cantwell, B., & Mazzeri, L. (1987). Late vertex positivity in event-related potentials as a guilty knowledge indicator: A new method of lie detection. *International Journal of Neuroscience, 34,* 125–129.

Rosenfeld, J. P., Sweet, J. J., Chuang, J., Ellwanger, J., & Song, L. (in press). Detection of simulated malingering using forced choice recognition enhanced with event-related potential recording. *Clinical Neuropsychologist.*

Rosenhan, D. (1973). On being sane in insane places. *Science, 172,* 250–258.

Ross, H. E., Gavin, D. R., & Skinner, H. A. (1990). Diagnostic validity of the MAST and the alcohol dependence scale in the assessment of DSM-III alcohol disorders. *Journal of Studies on Alcohol, 51,* 506–513.

Ross, R. J., Ball, W. A., Sullivan, K. A., & Caroff, S. N. (1989). Sleep disturbance as the hallmark of posttraumatic stress disorder. *American Journal of Psychiatry, 146,* 697–707.

Rothke, S. E., Friedman, A. F., Dahlstrom, W. G., Greene, R. L., Arredondo, R., & Mann, A. W. (1994). MMPI-2 normative data for the *F–K* index: Implications for clinical, neuropsychological, and forensic practice. *Assessment, 1,* 1–15.

Rothman, A. L., & Weintraub, M. I. (1995). The sick building syndrome and mass hysteria. *Neurologic Clinics, 13,* 405–411.

Rounsaville, B. J. (1985). Epidemiology of drug use and abuse in adults. In R. Michels, J. O. Cavenar, A. M. Cooper, S. B. Guze, L. L. Judd, G. L. Klerman, & A. J. Solnit (Eds.), *Psychiatry* (Vol. 3). Philadelphia: J. B. Lippincott.

Rounsaville, B. J., Cacciola, J., Weissman, M. M., & Kleber, H. D. (1981). Diagnostic concordance in a follow-up study of opiate addicts. *Journal of Psychiatric Research, 16,* 191–201.

Rowan, C. (1982, June 21). *Cleveland Plain Dealer,* p. 10B.

Rubinsky, E. W., & Brandt, J. (1986). Amnesia and criminal law: A clinical overview. *Behavioral Sciences and the Law, 4,* 27–46.

Ruch, J. C., Morgan, A. H., & Hilgard, E. R. (1974). Measuring hypnotic responsiveness: A comparison of the Barber Suggestibility Scale and the Stanford Hypnotic Susceptibility Scale, Form A. *International Journal of Clinical and Experimental Hypnosis, 22,* 365–376.

Ruff, R. M., Wylie, T., & Tennant, W. (1993). Malingering and malinger-like aspects of mild closed head injury. *Journal of Head Trauma Rehabilitation, 8,* 60–73.

Rumans, L. W., & Vosti, K. L. (1978). Factitious and fraudulent fever. *American Journal of Medicine, 65,* 745–755.

Russell, W. R., & Nathan, P. W. (1946). Traumatic amnesia. *Brain, 69,* 280–300.

Rutherford, W. H., Merrett, J. D., & McDonald, J. R. (1977). Sequelae of concussion caused by minor head injuries. *Lancet, 1,* 1–4.

Rutter, M., Tizard, J., & Whitmore, K. (1970). *Education, health and behavior.* New York: Wiley.

Ryan, A. M., & Sackett, P. R. (1987). Pre-employment honesty testing: Fakability, reactions of test takers, and company image. *Journal of Business and Psychology, 1,* 248–256.

Sabin, J. E. (1994). Caring about patients and caring about money: The American Psychiatric Association code of ethics meets managed care. *Behavioral Sciences and the Law, 12,* 317–330.

Sabourin, S., Bourgeois, L., Gendreau, P., & Morval, M. (1989). Self-deception, impression management, and consumer satisfaction with mental health treatment. *Psychological Assessment: A Journal of Consulting and Clinical Psychology, 1,* 126–129.

Sabourin, S., Laferriere, N., Sicuro, F., Coallier, J. -C., Cournoyer, L. -G., & Gendreau, P. (1989). Social desirability, psychological distress, and consumer satisfaction with mental health treatment. *Journal of Counseling Psychology, 36,* 352–356.

Sachs, M. H., Carpenter, W. T., & Strauss, J. S. (1974). Recovery from delusions. *Archives of General Psychiatry, 30,* 117–120.

Sackett, P. R. (1994). Integrity testing for personnel selection. *Current Directions in Psychological Science, 3,* 73–76.

Sackett, P. R., Burris, L. R., & Callahan, C. (1989). Integrity testing for personnel selection: An update. *Personnel Psychology, 42,* 491–529.

Sackett, P. R., & Harris, M. M. (1984). Honesty testing for personnel selection: A review and critique. *Personnel Psychology, 37,* 221–246.

Sadoff, R. L. (1974). Evaluation of amnesia in criminal–legal situations. *Journal of Forensic Sciences, 19,* 98–101.

Sadoff, R. L. (1978). Personal injury and the psychiatrist. *Weekly Psychiatry Update Series* (Lesson 38). Princeton, NJ: Biomedia.

Sadow, L., & Suslick, A. (1961). Simulation of a previous psychotic state. *Archives of General Psychiatry, 4,* 452–458.

Salekin, R. T., Rogers, R., & Sewell, K. W. (in press). A review and meta-analysis of the Psychopathy Checklist and the Psychopathy Checklist—Revised: Predictive validity of dangerousness. *Clinical Psychology: Science and Practice.*

Sanders, S. (1986). The Perceptual Alteration Scale: A scale for measuring dissociation. *American Journal of Clinical Hypnosis, 29*(2), 95–102.

Sarbin, J. E. (1994). Caring about patients and caring about money: The American Psychiatric Association code of ethics meets managed care. *Behavioral Sciences and the Law, 12,* 315–330.

Sarbin, T. R., & Coe, W. C. (1972). *Hypnosis: A social psychological analysis of influence communication.* New York: Holt, Rinehart & Winston.

Sargant, W., & Slater, E. (1941). Amnesic syndromes in war. *Proceedings of the Royal Society of Medicine, 34,* 757–764.

Sauser, W. I. (1985). Review of London House Personnel Selection Inventory. In J. V. Mitchell, Jr. (Ed.), *The ninth mental measurements yearbook* (pp. 870–871). Lincoln, NE: Buros Institute of Mental Measurements.

Saywitz, K. J., Goodman, G. S., Nicholas, E., & Moan, S. F. (1991). Children's memories of a physical examination involving genital touch: Implications for reports of child sexual abuse. *Journal of Clinical and Consulting Psychology, 59,* 682–691.

Schacter, D. L. (1986). Feeling-of-knowing ratings distinguish between genuine and simulated forgetting. *Journal of Experimental Psychology: Learning, Memory, and Cognition, 12,* 30–41.

Schacter, D. L. (1987). Implicit memory: History and current status. *Journal of Experimental Psychology: Learning, Memory, and Cognition, 13,* 501–518.

Schacter, D. L., Harbluk, J. L., & McLachlan, D. R. (1984). Retrieval without recognition: An experimental analysis of source amnesia. *Journal of Verbal Learning and Verbal Behavior, 23,* 593–611.

Schacter, D. L., Wang, P. L., Tulving, E., & Freedman, M. (1982). Functional retrograde amnesia: A quantitative case study. *Neuropsychologia, 20,* 523–532.

Schafer, D. W., & Rubio, R. (1978). Hypnosis and the recall of witnesses. *International Journal of Clinical and Experimental Hypnosis, 26,* 81–91.

Schafer, E. (1986). *Workers' Compensation Workshop.* American Academy of Psychiatry and the Law Meeting, Philadelphia, PA.

Schlenger, W. E., & Kulka, R. A. (1987, August). *Performance on the Kean–Fairbank MMPI scale and other self-report measures in identifying post-traumatic stress disorder.* Paper presented at the annual meeting of the American Psychological Association, New York, NY.

Schmaling, K. B., DiClementi, J. D., Cullum, C. M., & Jones, J. F. (1994). Cognitive functioning in chronic fatigue syndrome and depression: A preliminary comparison. *Psychosomatic Medicine, 56,* 383–388.

Schneck, J. M. (1967). Hypnoanalytic study of a false confession. *International Journal of Clinical and Experimental Hypnosis, 15,* 11–18.

Schneck, J. M. (1970). Pseudo-malingering and Leonid Andreyev's *The Dilemma. Psychiatric Quarterly, 44,* 49–54.

Schooler, J. W., Clark, C. A., & Loftus, E. F. (1988). Knowing when memory is real. In M. Gruneberg, P. Morris, & R. Sykes (Eds.), *Practical aspects of memory: Current research and issues* (Vol. 1, pp. 83–88). New York: Wiley.

Schooler, J. W., Gerhard, D., & Loftus, E. F. (1986). Qualities of the unreal. *Journal of Experimental Psychology: Learning, Memory, and Cognition, 12,* 171–181.

Schreiber, F. R. (1973). *Sybil.* New York: Henry Regnery.

Schretlen, D. (1990). A limitation of using the Wiener and Harmon obvious and subtle scales to detect faking on the MMPI. *Journal of Clinical Psychology, 46,* 782–786.

Schretlen, D., & Arkowitz, H. (1990). A psychological test battery to detect prison inmates who fake insanity or mental retardation. *Behavioral Sciences and the Law, 8,* 75–84.

Schretlen, D., Brandt, J., Krafft, R. V., & Van Gorp, W. (1991). Some caveats in using the Rey 15-item memory test to detect malingered amnesia. *Psychological Assessment: A Journal of Consulting and Clinical Psychology, 3,* 667–672.

Schretlen, D., Neal, J., & Hochman, S. (1995). *Screening for malingered mental illness in a court clinic.* Manuscript submitted for publication.

Schretlen, D., Wilkins, S. S., Van Gorp, W. G., & Bobholz, J. H. (1992). Cross-validation of a psychological test battery to detect faked insanity. *Psychological Assessment, 4*(1), 77–83.

Schretlen, D. J. (1988). The use of psychological tests to identify malingered symptoms of mental disorder. *Clinical Psychology Review, 8,* 451–476.

Schwartz, L. A. (1946). Neurosis following head and brain injuries. *Harper Hospital Bulletin, 4,* 179–182.

Scoville, W. B., & Milner, B. (1957). Loss of recent memory after bilateral hippocampal lesions. *Journal of Neurology, Neurosurgery, and Psychiatry, 20,* 11–12.

Scriven, M. (1976). Maximizing the power of casual investigation: The modus operandi method. In G. V. Glass (Ed.), *Evaluation studies review annual* (Vol. 1, pp. 101–118). Beverly Hills, CA: Sage.

Scully, D. (1990). *Understanding sexual violence: A study of convicted rapists.* Boston: Unwin Hyman.

Seamons, D. T., Howell, R. J., Carlisle, A. L., & Roe, A. V. (1981). Rorschach simulation of mental illness and normality by psychotic and nonpsychotic legal offenders. *Journal of Personality Assessment, 45,* 130–135.

Sears, R. R. (1932). An experimental study of hypnotic anesthesia. *Journal of Experimental Psychology, 15,* 1–22.

Sechrest, L. (1963). Incremental validity: A recommendation. *Educational and Psychological Measurement, 23,* 153–158.

Seigel, R. K., & West, L. J. (Eds.). (1975). *Hallucinations: Behavior, experience and theory*. New York: Wiley.

Selzer, M. L. (1971). Michigan Alcoholism Screening Test: The quest for a new diagnostic instrument. *American Journal of Psychiatry, 127,* 1653–1658.

Sewell, K. W., & Rogers, R. (1994). Response consistency and the MMPI-2: Development of a simplified screening scale. *Assessment, 1,* 293–299.

Shalev, A. Y., Orr, S. P., & Pitman, R. K. (1993). Psychophysiologic assessment of traumatic imagery in Israeli civilian post-traumatic disorder patients. *American Journal of Psychiatry, 150,* 152–159.

Sheehan, P. W. (1971). A methodological analysis of the simulating technique. *International Journal of Clinical and Experimental Hypnosis, 19,* 83–99.

Sheehan, P. W., Green, V., & Truesdale, P. (1992). Influence of rapport on hypnotically induced pseudomemory. *Journal of Abnormal Psychology, 101,* 690–700.

Sheehan, P. W., & McConkey, K. M. (1979). Australian norms for the Harvard Group Scale of Hypnotic Susceptibility, Form A. *International Journal of Clinical and Experimental Hypnosis, 27,* 294–304.

Sheehan, P. W., Statham, D., & Jamieson, G. A. (1991). Pseudomemory effects over time in the hypnotic setting. *Journal of Abnormal Psychology, 100,* 39–44.

Sheehan, P. W., & Tilden, J. (1985). The consistency of occurrences of memory distortion following hypnotic induction. *International Journal of Clinical and Experimental Hypnosis, 34,* 122–137.

Shelp, F. E., & Perl, M. (1985). Denial in clinical medicine. *Archives of Internal Medicine, 145,* 697–699.

Sherman, M., Trief, P., & Strafkin, R. (1975). Impression management in the psychiatric interview: Quality, style and individual differences. *Journal of Consulting and Clinical Psychology, 43,* 867–871.

Shimamura, A. P., & Squire, L. R. (1986). Memory and metamemory: A study of the feeling-of-knowing phenomenon in amnesic patients. *Journal of Experimental Psychology: Learning, Memory, and Cognition, 12,* 452–460.

Shimamura, A. P., & Squire, L. R. (1987). A neuropsychological study of fact memory and source amnesia. *Journal of Experimental Psychology: Learning, Memory, and Cognition, 13,* 464–473.

Shoichet, R. P. (1978). Sodium amytal in the diagnosis of chronic pain. *Canadian Psychiatric Association Journal, 23,* 219–238.

Shor, R. E. (1959). Hypnosis and the concept of the generalized reality-orientation. *American Journal of Psychotherapy, 13,* 582–602.

Shor, R. E. (1962). Three dimensions of hypnotic depth. *International Journal of Clinical and Experimental Hypnosis, 10,* 23–38.

Shor, R. E., & Orne, E, C. (1962). *Harvard Group Scale of Hypnotic Susceptibility*. Palo Alto, CA: Consulting Psychologists Press.

Sierles, F. S. (1984). Correlates of malingering. *Behavioral Sciences and the Law, 2,* 113–118.

Sigal, M., Gelkopf, M., & Meadow, R. S. (1989). Munchausen by proxy syndrome: The triad of abuse, self-abuse, and deception. *Comprehensive Psychiatry, 30,* 527–533.

Silver, M., Sabini, J., & Miceli, M. (1989). On knowing self-deception. *Journal for the Theory of Social Behavior, 19,* 213–227.

Silverton, L., & Gruber, C. P. (in press). *The Malingering Probability Scale (MPS) manual*. Los Angeles: Western Psychological Services.

Simon, G. E., Katon, W. J., & Sparks, P. J. (1990). Allergic to life: Psychological factors in environmental illness. *American Journal of Psychiatry, 147,* 901–906.

Simon, W. T., & Schouten, P. G. (1992). Problems in sexual preference testing in child sexual abuse cases: A legal and community perspective. *Journal of Interpersonal Violence, 7*, 503–516.

Simpson, A. J., & Fritter, M. J. (1973). What is the best index of detectability? *Psychological Bulletin, 80*, 481–488.

Simpson, G. (1987). Accuracy and precision of breath-alcohol measurements for a random subject in the postabsorptive state. *Clinical Chemistry, 32*, 261–268.

Singer, H., & Krohn, W. (1924). *Insanity and the law*. Philadelphia: J. Blackiston's Son.

Sivec, H. J., Hilsenroth, M. J., & Lynn, S. J. (1995). Impact of simulating borderline personality disorder on the MMPI-2: A cost–benefits model employing base rates. *Journal of Personality Assessment, 64*, 295–311.

Sivec, H. J., Lynn, S. J., & Garske, J. P. (1994). The effect of somatoform disorder and paranoid psychotic disorder role-related dissimulations as a response set on the MMPI-2. *Assessment, 1*, 69–81.

Skinner, H. A. (1982). The Drug Abuse Screening Test. *Addictive Behaviors, 7*, 363–371.

Skodol, A. E. (1989). *Problems in differential diagnosis*. Washington, DC: American Psychiatric Association Press.

Slaby, A. E. (1994). *Handbook of psychiatric emergencies* (4th ed.). Norwalk, CT: Appleton & Lange.

Slick, D., Hopp, G., Strauss, E., Hunter, M., & Pinch, D. (1994). Detecting dissimulation: Profiles of simulated malingerers, traumatic brain-injury patients, and normal controls on a revised version of Hiscock and Hiscock's Forced-Choice Memory Test. *Journal of Clinical and Experimental Neuropsychology, 16*, 472–481.

Small, G. W., & Nicholi, A. M., Jr. (1982). Mass hysteria among school children. *Archives of General Psychiatry, 39*, 721–724.

Small, I. F., Small, J. G., & Andersen, J. M. (1966). Clinical characteristics of hallucinations of schizophrenia. *Diseases of the Nervous System, 27*, 349–353.

Smart, R. G., & Jarvis, G. K. (1981). Do self-report studies of drug use really give dependable results? *Canadian Journal of Criminology, 23*, 83–92.

Smith, B. H. (1967). A handbook of tests to unmask malingering. *Consultant, 7*, 41–47.

Smith, B. M., Hain, J. D., & Stevenson, I. (1970). Controlled interviews using drugs. *Archives of General Psychiatry, 22*, 2–10.

Smith, G. P. (1992). *Detection of malingering: A validation study of the SLAM Test*. Unpublished doctoral dissertation, University of Missouri–St. Louis. St. Louis, MO.

Smith, G. P., & Borum, R. (1992). Detection of malingering in a forensic sample: A study of the M Test. *Journal of Psychiatry and Law, 20*(4), 505–514.

Smith, G. P., Borum, R., & Schinka, J. A. (1993). Rule-Out and Rule-In scales for the M Test for Malingering: A cross-validation. *Bulletin of the American Academy of Psychiatry and the Law, 21*(1), 107–110.

Smith, G. P., & Burger, G. K. (in press). Detection of malingering: Validation of the SIMS. *Bulletin of the American Academy of Psychiatry and Law*.

Smith, M. L. (1989). Memory disorders associated with temporal-lobe lesions. In F. Boller & J. Grafman (Eds.), *Handbook of neuropsychology* (Vol. 3, pp. 91–106). Amsterdam: Elsevier.

Smith, S. S., & Newman, J. P. (1990). Alcohol and drug abuse-dependence disorders in psychopathic and nonpsychopathic criminal offenders. *Journal of Abnormal Psychology, 99*, 430–439.

Sneed, R. C., & Bell, R. F. (1976). The dauphin of Munchausen: Factitious passage of renal stones in a child. *Pediatrics, 58*, 127–129.

Snowdon, J., Solomons, R., & Druce, H. (1978). Feigned bereavement: Twelve cases. *British Journal of Psychiatry, 133*, 15–19.

Snyder, S. (1986). *Pseudologia fantastica* in the borderline patient. *American Journal of Psychiatry, 143,* 1287–1289.

Sobell, M. B., Sobell, L. C., & Vanderspek, R. (1979). Relationships among clinical judgment, self-report, and breath-analysis measurements of intoxication in alcoholics. *Journal of Consulting and Clinical Psychology, 47,* 204–206.

Sogi, C., Warthon, D., Mezzich, J. E., Valverde, J., Saavedra-Castillo, A., & Ahn, C. W. (1989). Comparative distributions of DSM-III diagnoses in North and South American clinical samples. *British Journal of Psychiatry, 154*(Suppl. 4), 91–95.

Soniat, T. L. (1960). The problem of "compensation" neurosis. *South Medical Journal, 53,* 365–368.

Spanos, N. P. (1986). Hypnotic behavior: A social-psychological interpretation of amnesia, analgesia, and "trance logic." *Behavioral and Brain Sciences, 9,* 449–467.

Spanos, N. P., & Barber, T. X. (1974). Toward a convergence in hypnotic research. *American Psychologist, 29,* 500–511.

Spanos, N. P., & Bures, E. (1993). Pseudomemory responding in hypnotic, task-motivated and simulating subjects: Memory distortion or reporting bias? *Imagination, Cognition and Personality, 13,* 303–310.

Spanos, N. P., Burgess, C. A., & Burgess, M. F. (1994). Past-life identities, UFO abductions, and satanic ritual abuse: The social construction of memories. *International Journal of Clinical and Experimental Hypnosis 42,* 433–446.

Spanos, N. P., deGroot, H. P., & Gwynn, M. I. (1987). Trance logic as incomplete responding. *Journal of Personality and Social Psychology 53,* 911–921.

Spanos, N. P., Gwynn, M. I., Comer, S. I., Baltruweit, W. J., & de Groh, M. (1989). Are hypnotically induced pseudomemories resistant to cross-examination? *Law and Human Behavior, 13,* 271–289.

Spanos, N. P., James, B., & deGroot, H. P. (1990). Detection of simulated hypnotic amnesia. *Journal of Abnormal Psychology, 99,* 179–182.

Spanos, N. P., & McLean, J. (1986). Hypnotically created pseudomemories: Memory distortion or response biases? *British Journal of Experimental and Clinical Hypnosis, 3,* 155–159.

Spanos, N. P., Radtke, H. L., Bertrand, L. D., Addie, D. L., & Drummond, J. (1982). Disorganized recall, hypnotic amnesia, and subjects' faking: More disconfirmatory evidence. *Psychological Reports, 50,* 383–389.

Sparr, L. F., & Atkinson, R. M. (1986). Post- traumatic stress disorder as an insanity defense: Medicolegal quicksand. *American Journal of Psychiatry, 143,* 608–613.

Sparr, L. F., & Pankratz, L. D. (1983). Factitious posttraumatic stress disorder. *American Journal of Psychiatry, 140,* 1016–1019.

Spector, R. S., & Foster, T. E. (1977). Admissibility of hypnotic statements: Is the law of evidence susceptible? *Ohio State Law Journal, 38,* 567–611.

Speedie, L., & Heilman, K. (1982). Amnesic disturbance following infarction of the left dorsomedial nucleus of the thalamus. *Neuropsychologia, 20,* 597–604.

Spiegel, D., & Fink, R. (1979). Hysterical psychosis and hypnotizability. *American Journal of Psychiatry, 136,* 777–781.

Spiegel, D., Detrick, D., & Frischholz, E. (1982). Hypnotizability and psychopathology. *American Journal of Psychiatry, 139,* 431–437.

Spiegel, D., & Spiegel, H. (1984). Uses of hypnosis in evaluating malingering and deception. *Behavioral Sciences and the Law, 2,* 51–65.

Spiegel, H., & Bridger, A. A. (1970). *Manual for hypnotic induction profile.* New York: Soni Medica.

Spiro, H. R. (1968). Chronic factitious illness: Munchausen's syndrome. *Archives of General Psychiatry, 18,* 569–579.

Spitzer, M. (1992). The phenomenology of delusions. *Psychiatric Annals, 22,* 252–259.

Spitzer, R. L. (1974). Critiques of Rosenhan. *Journal of Abnormal Psychology, 84,* 442–452.

Spitzer, R. L., & Endicott, J. (1978). *Schedule of Affective Disorders and Schizophrenia.* New York: Biometric Research.

Spitzer, R. L., Endicott, J., & Robbins, E. (1978). Research diagnostic criteria for the use in psychiatric research. *Archives of General Psychiatry, 35,* 773–782.

Spitzer, R. L., Williams, J. B. W., Gibbon, M., & First, M. B. (1990). *Structured Clinical Interview for DSM-III-R (SCID).* Washington, DC: American Psychiatric Association Press.

Spivak, H., Rodin, G., & Sutherland, A. (1994). The psychology of factitious disorders: A reconsideration. *Psychosomatics, 35,* 25–34.

Sprehe, D. J. (1984). Workers' compensation: A psychiatric follow-up study. *International Journal of Law and Psychiatry, 7,* 165–178.

Squire, L. R. (1994). Declarative and nondeclarative memory: Multiple brain systems supporting learning and memory. In D. L. Schacter & E. Tulving (Eds.), *Memory systems 1994* (pp. 203–231). Cambridge, MA: MIT Press.

Squire, L. R., & Moore, R. Y. (1979). Dorsal thalamic lesion in a noted case of chronic memory dysfunction. *Annals of Neurology, 6,* 503–506.

Squire, L. R., & Zola-Morgan, S. (1991). The medial temporal lobe memory system. *Science, 253,* 1380–1386.

Stafford v. Maynard, 848 F. Supp. 946 (W.D. Okla. 1994).

Stalnaker, J. M., & Riddle, E. E. (1932). The effect of hypnosis on long-delayed recall. *Journal of General Psychology, 6,* 429–440.

State ex rel. Collins v. Superior Court, 644 P.2d 1266 (1982), supplemental opinion filed May 4, 1982.

State ex rel. Sheppard v. Koblentz, 120 187 N.E.2d 40 (1962).

State v. Alley, 776 S.W.2d 506 (Tenn. 1989).

State v. Armstrong, 329 N.W.2d 386 (Wis. 1983).

State v. Bianchi, No. 79-10116 (Wash. Sup. Ct., October 19, 1979).

State v. Cheshier, 846 F. Supp. 654 (N.D.Ill. 1994).

State v. Hurd, 432 A.2d 86 (1981).

State v. Joly, 593 A.2d 96 (Conn., 1991).

State v. Mack, 292 N.W.2d 764 (1980).

State v. McClendon, 437 P.2d 421 (1948).

State v. McQueen, 244 S.E.2d 414 (1978).

State v. Papp, No. 78-02-00229 (C.P. Summit Co., Ohio, Lorain Cty. No. 16682, March 23, 1978); *cert. denied,* U.S. Sup. Ct. No. 79-5091 (Oct. 1, 1979).

Steblay, N. M., & Bothwell, R. K. (1994). Evidence for hypnotically refreshed testimony: The view from the laboratory. *Law and Human Behavior, 18,* 635–651.

Stein, L. A. R., Graham, J. R., & Williams, C. L. (1995). *Detecting fake-bad MMPI-A profiles.* Unpublished manuscript, Department of Psychology, Kent State University.

Stephens, R. C., Meiselas, H., & Brill, L. (1977). The uses of urinalysis in New York City drug treatment programs. *Drug Forum, 6*(2), 101–115.

Stermac, L. (1988). Projective testing and dissimulation. In R. Rogers (Ed.), *Clinical assessment of malingering and deception* (1st ed., pp. 159–168). New York: Guilford Press.

Stern, T. A. (1980). Munchausen's syndrome revisited. *Psychosomatics, 21,* 329–336.

Stevens, H. (1986). Is it organic or is it functional: Is it hysterial or malingering? *Psychiatric Clinics of North America, 9*, 241–254.

Stevenson, I., Buckman, J., Smith, B. M., & Hain, J. D. (1974). The use of drugs in psychiatric interviews: Some interpretations based on controlled experiments. *American Journal of Psychiatry, 131*, 707–710.

Stewart, M. A., & DeBlois, C. S. (1984). *Diagnostic criteria for aggressive conduct disorder.* Unpublished manuscript.

Stiebel, V. G., & Kirby, J. V. (1994). The amytal interview in the treatment of conversion disorder: Three case reports. *Military Medicine, 159*, 350–353.

Stipek, D. J. (1981). Children's perceptions of their own and their classmates' ability. *Journal of Educational Psychology, 73*, 404–410.

Stone, A. A. (1984). The ethics of forensic psychiatry: A view from the ivory tower. In A. Stone (Ed.), *Law, psychiatry and morality.* Washington, DC: American Psychiatric Association Press.

Stouthamer-Loeber, M. (1986). Lying as a problem in children. A review. *Clinical Psychology Review, 6*, 267–289.

Strauss, D. H., Spitzer, R. L., & Muskin, P. R. (1990). Maladaptive denial of physical illness: A proposal for DSM-IV. *American Journal of Psychiatry, 147*, 1168–1172.

Strauss, E., Spellacy, F., Hunter, M., & Berry, T. (1994). Assessing believable deficits on measures of attention and information processing capacity. *Archives of Clinical Neuropsychology, 9*, 483–490.

Stuss, D. T., & Guzman, D. A. (1988). Severe remote memory loss with minimal anterograde amnesia: A clinical note. *Brain and Cognition, 8*, 21–30.

Sundberg, N. D. (1992). Review of the Hogan Personnel Selection Series. In J. J. Kramer & J. C. Conoley (Eds.), *The eleventh mental measurements yearbook* (pp. 386–387). Lincoln, NE: Buros Institute of Mental Measurements.

Sutcliffe, J. P. (1958). *Hypnotic behaviour: Fantasy or simulation.* Unpublished doctoral dissertation, University of Sydney, Australia.

Sutherland, A. J., & Rodin, G. M. (1990). Factitious disorders in a general hospital setting: Clinical features and a review of the literature. *Psychosomatics, 31*, 392–399.

Svanum, S., & McGrew, J. (1995). Prospective screening of substance dependence: The advantages of directness. *Addictive Behaviors, 20*, 205–213.

Swanson, D. W. (1984). Chronic pain as a third pathologic emotion. *American Journal of Psychiatry, 141*, 210–214.

Swanson, J., Borum, R., Swartz, M., & Monahan, J. (1996). Psychotic symptoms and disorders and the risk of violent behavior in the community. *Criminal Behavior and Mental Health, 6*, 317–338.

Swartz, J. D. (1985). Review of Inwald Personality Inventory. In J. V. Mitchell, Jr. (Ed.), *The ninth mental measurements yearbook* (pp. 713–714). Lincoln, NE: Buros Institute of Mental Measurements.

Swenson, W. M., & Grimes, B. P. (1969). Characteristics of sex offenders admitted to a Minnesota state hospital for pre-sentence psychiatric investigation. *Psychiatric Quarterly Supplement, 34*, 110–123.

Swenson, W. M., & Morse, R. M. (1975). The use of Self-Administered Alcoholism Screening Test (SAAST) in a medical center. *Mayo Clinic Proceedings, 50*, 204–208.

Swets, J. A. (1973). The relative operating characteristic in psychology. *Science, 182*, 990–999.

Swets, J. A. (1988). Measuring the accuracy of diagnostic systems. *Science, 240*, 1285–1293.

Swigar, M. E., Clemow, L. P., Saidi, P., & Kim, H. C. (1990). "Superwarfarin" ingestion. A new problem in covert anticoagulant overdose. *General Hospital Psychiatry, 12*, 309–312.

Szasz, T. S. (1956). Malingering: "Diagnosis" or social condemnation? *AMA Archives of Neurology and Psychiatry, 76*, 432–443.

Tardi v. Henry, 571 N.E.2d 1020 (Ill. App. 1991).

Tarsh, M. J., & Royston, C. (1985). A follow-up study of accident neurosis. *British Journal of Psychiatry, 146*, 18–25.

Tarter, R. E., & Hegedus, A. M. (1991). The Drug Use Screening Inventory: 1st applications in evaluation and treatment of alcohol and other drug use. *Alcohol Health and Research World, 15*, 65–75.

Tarter, R. E., Laird, S. B., Kabene, M., Bukstein, O., & Kaminer, Y. (1990). Drug abuse severity in adolescents is associated with magnitude of deviation in temperament traits. *British Journal of Addictions, 85*, 1501–1504.

Taylor, S., & Hyler, S. E. (1993). Update on factitious disorders. *International Journal of Psychiatry in Medicine, 23*, 81–94.

Terr, L. C. (1991). Childhood traumas: An outline and overview. *American Journal of Psychiatry, 149*, 10–20.

Terr, L. C. (1994). *Unchained memories: True stories of traumatic memories, lost and found.* New York: Basic Books.

Tesser, A., & Paulhus, D. (1983). The definition of self: Private and public self-evaluation management strategies. *Journal of Personality and Social Psychology, 44*, 672–682.

Tett, R. P., Jackson, D. N., & Rothstein, M. (1991). Personality measures as predictors of job performance: A meta-analytic review. *Personnel Psychology, 44*, 703–742.

Thompson, G. N. (1965). Post-traumatic psychoneurosis—a statistical survey. *American Journal of Psychiatry, 121*, 1043–1048.

Thompson, J. S., Stuart, G. L., & Holden, C. E. (1992). Command hallucinations and legal insanity. *Forensic Reports, 5*, 29–43.

Thornton, G. C., III, & Gierasch, P. F., III. (1980). Fakability of an empirically derived selection instrument. *Journal of Personality Assessment, 44*, 48–51.

Timbrook, R. E., Graham, J. R., Keiller, S. W., & Watts, D. (1993). Comparison of the Wiener–Harmon subtle–obvious scales and the standard validity scales in detecting valid and invalid MMPI-2 profiles. *Psychological Assessment, 5*, 53–61.

Timmons, L. A., Lanyon, R. L., Almer, E. R., & Curran, P. J. (1993). Development and validation of sentence completion test indices of malingering during examination for disability. *American Journal of Forensic Psychology, 11*, 23–38.

Tisher, M., & Lang, M. (1983). The Children's Depression Scale: Review and further developments. In D. P. Cantwell & G. A. Carlson (Eds.), *Childhood depression* (pp. 181–203). New York: Spectrum.

Toth, E. L., & Baggaley, A. (1991). Coexistence of Munchausen's syndrome and multiple personality disorder: Detailed report of a case and theoretical discussion. *Psychiatry, 54*, 176–183.

Travin, S., & Protter, B. (1984). Malingering and malingering-like behavior: Some clinical and conceptual issues. *Psychiatric Quarterly, 56*, 189–197.

Trichter, J. G., McKinney, W. T., & Pena, M. (1995). DWI demonstrative evidence: Show and tell the easy way. *Voice, 24*(3), 34–47.

Trimble, M. R. (1981). *Post-traumatic neurosis from railway spine to the whiplash.* New York: Wiley.

Trueblood, W. (1994). Qualitative and quantitative characteristics of malingered and other invalid WAIS-R and clinical memory data. *Journal of Clinical and Experimental Neuropsychology, 16*, 597–607.

Trueblood, W., & Binder, L. M. (1995, October). *Psychologists' accuracy in identifying neuro-*

psychological test protocols of clinical malingerers. Paper presented at the National Academy of Neuropsychology, San Francisco.

Trueblood, W., & Schmidt, M. (1993). Malingering and other validity considerations in the neuropsychological evaluation of mild head injury. *Journal of Clinical and Experimental Neuropsychology, 15,* 578–590.

Udolf, R. (1983). *Forensic hypnosis: Psychological and legal aspects.* New York: Lexington Books.

Underwood, B. J. (1965). False recognition produced by implicit verbal responses. *Journal of Experimental Psychology, 70,* 122–129.

United States Congressional Office of Technology Assessment. (1990). *The use of integrity tests for pre-employment screening* (Report No. OTA-SET-442). Washington, DC: U.S. Government Printing Office.

United States ex rel. Parson v. Anderson, 354 F.Supp. 1060 (D.Del. 1972), *affirmed,* 481 F.2d 94 (3d Cir.) (en banc), *cert. denied,* 414 U.S. 1072 (1973).

United States v. Adams, United States v. Pinkerton, 581 F.2d 193 (9th Cir.), *cert. denied,* 439 U.S. 1006 (1978).

United States v. Andrews, General Court-Martial No. 75-14 (N.F. Jud. Cir. Navy, Marine Corps Judiciary, Phila., Pa., Oct. 6, 1976).

United States v. Borum, 464 F.2d 896 (10th Cir., 1972).

United States v. Gatto, 924 F.2d 491 (3rd Cir., 1991).

United States v. Miller, 411 F.2d 825 (1969).

United States v. Stevens, 461 F.2d 317, (7th Cir.) *cert.denied,* 409 U.S. 948 (1972).

United States v. Todd, 964 F.2d 925 (9th Cir., 1992).

Usher, J. A., & Neisser, U. (1993). Childhood amnesia and the beginnings of memory for four early life events. *Journal of Experimental Psychology: General, 122,* 155–165.

Ustad, K. L. (1996). *Assessment of malingering on the SADS in a jail referral sample.* Unpublished doctoral dissertation, University of North Texas, Denton.

Ustad, K. L., & Rogers, R. (1996). Malingering and deception: Conceptual and clinical issues in forensic practice. In L. B. Schlesinger (Ed.), *Explorations in criminal psychopathology: Clinical syndromes with forensic implications* (pp. 300–319). Springfield, IL: Charles C Thomas.

van der Kolk, B., Blitz, R., Burr, W., Sherry, S., & Hartmann, E. (1984). Nightmares and trauma: A comparison of nightmares after combat with lifelong nightmares in veterans. *American Journal of Psychiatry, 141,* 187–190.

Viglione, D. J. (1990). Severe disturbance or trauma-induced adaptive reaction: A Rorschach child study. *Journal of Personality Assessment, 55,* 280–295.

Viglione, D. J., Fals-Stewart, W., & Moxham, E. (1995). Maximizing internal and external validity in MMPI malingering research: A study of a military population. *Journal of Personality Assessment, 65,* 502–513.

Viglione, D. J., & Landis, P. (1994, March). *The development of an objective test for malingering.* Paper presented at the biennial meeting of the American Psychology–Law Society, Santa Fe, NM.

Viglione, D. J., & Landis, P. (1995). *The inventory of problems.* Unpublished manuscript. California School of Professional Psychology, San Diego.

Wachspress, M., Berenberg, A. N., & Jacobson, A. (1953). Simulation of psychosis. *Psychiatric Quarterly, 27,* 463–473.

Wakefield, H., & Underwager, R. (1992). Recovered memories of alleged sexual abuse: Lawsuits against parents. *Behavioral Sciences and the Law, 10,* 483–507.

Walker, J. I. (1981). Vietnam combat veterans with legal difficulties: A psychiatric problem? *American Journal of Psychiatry, 138,* 1384–1385.

Wallach, J. (1994). Laboratory diagnosis of factitious disorders. *Archives of Internal Medicine, 154,* 1690–1696.

Waller, N. D. (1992). Review of the Inwald Personality Inventory. In J. J. Kramer & J. C. Conoley (Eds.), *The eleventh mental measurements yearbook* (pp. 418–419). Lincoln, NE: Buros Institute of Mental Measurements.

Walters, G. D. (1988). Assessing dissimulation and denial on the MMPI in a sample of maximum security, male inmates. *Journal of Personality Assessment, 52,* 465–474.

Walters, G. D., White, T. W., & Greene, R. L. (1988). Use of the MMPI to identify malingering and exaggeration of psychiatric symptomatology in male prison inmates. *Journal of Consulting and Clinical Psychology, 56,* 111–117.

Wanberg, K. W., Horn, J. L., & Foster, F. M. (1977). A differential assessment model for alcoholism: The scales of the Alcohol Use Inventory. *Journal of Studies on Alcohol, 38,* 512–543.

Wanberg, K., Lewis, R. A., & Foster, F. M. (1978). Alcoholism and ethnicitiy: A comparative study of alcohol use patterns across ethnic groups. *International Journal of the Addictions, 13,* 1245–1262.

Ward, L. C. (1986). MMPI item subtlety research: Current issues and directions. *Journal of Personality Assessment, 50,* 73–79.

Ward, L. C., & Rothaus, P. (1991). The measurement of denial and rationalization in male alcoholics. *Journal of Clinical Psychology, 47,* 465–468.

Ward, N. G., Rowlett, D. B., & Burke, P. (1978). Sodium amylobarbitone in the differential diagnosis of confusion. *American Journal of Psychiatry, 135,* 75–78.

Ward, R., Hudson, S. M., & Marshall, W. L. (1995). Cognitive distortions and affective deficits in sex offenders. *Sexual Abuse: A Journal of Research and Treatment, 7,* 67–83.

Warrington, E. K. (1984). *Recognition Memory Test: Manual.* Berkshire, UK: NFER-Nelson.

Washington v. Texas, 388 U.S. 14 (1967).

Wasyliw, O. E., Grossman, L. S., & Haywood, T. W. (1994). Denial of hostility and psychopathology in the evaluation of child molestation. *Journal of Personality Assessment, 63,* 185–190.

Wasyliw, O. E., Grossman, L. S., Haywood, T. W., & Cavanaugh, J. L. (1988). The detection of malingering in criminal forensic groups: MMPI validity scales. *Journal of Personality Assessment, 52,* 321–333.

Watkins, J. G. (1984). The Bianchi (L.A. Hillside Strangler) case: Sociopath or multiple personality? *International Journal of Clinical and Experimental Hypnosis, 32,* 67–101.

Wechsler, D. (1987). *Wechsler Memory Scale—Revised manual.* San Antonio, TX: Psychological Corporation.

Weed, N. C., Ben-Porath, Y. S., & Butcher, J. N. (1990). Failure of Wiener and Harmon MMPI subtle scales as personality descriptors and as validity indicators. *Psychological Assessment, 2,* 281–285.

Weed, N. C., Butcher, J. N., McKenna, T., & Ben-Porath, Y. S. (1992). New measures for assessing alcohol and drug abuse with the MMPI-2: The APS and AAS. *Journal of Personality Assessment, 58,* 389–404.

Weekes, J. R., Lynn, S. J., Green, J. P., & Brentar, J. T. (1992). Pseudomemory in hypnotized and task-motivated subjects. *Journal of Abnormal Psychology, 101,* 356–360.

Weighill, V. E. (1983). Compensation neurosis: A review of the literature. *Journal of Psychosomatic Research, 27,* 97–104.

Weingardt, K. R., Loftus, E. F., & Lindsay, D. S. (1995). Misinformation revisited: New evidence on the suggestibility of memory. *Memory and Cognition, 23,* 72–82.

Weinstein, E. A., Kahn, R. L., Sugarman, L. A., & Linn, L. (1953). The diagnostic use of amobarbital sodium ("amytal sodium") in brain disease. *American Journal of Psychiatry, 109,* 789–794.

Weinstein, E. A., Kahn, R. L., Sugarman, L. A., & Malitz, S. (1954). Serial administration of "amytal test" for brain disease. *Archives of Neurology and Psychiatry, 71,* 217–226.

Weissman, H. N. (1990). Distortions and deceptions in self-presentation: Effects of protracted litigation in personal injury cases. *Behavioral Sciences and the Law, 8,* 67–74.

Weitzenhoffer, A. M., & Hilgard, E. R. (1959). *Stanford Hypnotic Susceptibility Scales, Forms A and B.* Palo Alto, CA: Consulting Psychologists Press.

Weitzenhoffer, A. M., & Hilgard, E. R. (1962). *Stanford Hypnotic Susceptibility Scale, Form C.* Palo Alto, CA: Consulting Psychologists Press.

Weitzenhoffer, A. M., & Hilgard, E. R. (1963). *The Stanford Profile Scales of Hypnotic Suseptibility: Forms I and II.* Palo Alto, CA: Consulting Psychologists Press.

Weitzenhoffer, A. M., & Sjoberg, B. M., Jr. (1961). Suggestibility with and without "induction of hypnosis." *Journal of Nervous and Mental Disease, 132,* 204–220.

Wells, G. L. (1978). Applied eyewitness-testimony research: System variables and estimator variables. *Journal of Personality and Social Psychology, 36,* 1546–1557.

Wertham, F. (1949). *The show of violence.* Garden City, NY: Doubleday.

Wessely, S. (1990). Old wine in new bottles: Neurasthenia and "ME." *Psychological Medicine, 20,* 35–53.

Wessely, S., Buchanan, A., Reed, A., Cutting, J., Everitt, B., Garety, P., & Taylor, P. J. (1993). Acting on delusions: I. Prevalence. *British Journal of Psychiatry, 163,* 69–76.

Wessinger, C., & Wodarski, J. S. (1994). Accuracy of national surveys of drug use: A comparison with local studies. *Journal of Alcohol and Drug Education, 39,* 62–73.

Weston, W. A. (1996). Pseudologia fantastica and pathological lying. In L. B. Schlesinger (Ed.), *Explorations in criminal psychopathology: Clinical syndromes with forensic implications* (pp. 98–115). Springfield, IL: Charles C Thomas.

Wetter, M. W., Baer, R. A., Berry, D. T. R., & Reynolds, S. K. (1994). The effect of symptom information on faking on the MMPI-2. *Assessment, 1,* 199–207.

Wetter, M. W., Baer, R. A., Berry, D. T. R., Robinson, L. H., & Sumpter, J. (1993). MMPI-2 profiles of motivated fakers given specific symptom information: A comparison to matched patients. *Psychological Assessment, 5,* 317–323.

Wetter, M. W., Baer, R. A., Berry, D. T. R., Smith, G. T., & Larsen, L. H. (1992). Sensitivity of MMPI-2 validity scales to random responding and malingering. *Psychological Assessment, 4,* 369–374.

Wetzler, S., & Marlowe, D. (1990). "Faking bad" on the MMPI, MMPI-2, and Millon-II. *Psychological Reports, 67,* 1117–1118.

Wheeler, K. G. (1985). Review of the Stanton Survey and the Stanton Survey Phase II. In J. V. Mitchell, Jr. (Ed.), *The ninth mental measurements yearbook* (pp. 1472–1473). Lincoln, NE: Buros Institute of Mental Measurements.

Whipple, G. M. (1918). The obtaining of information: Psychology of observation and report. *Psychological Bulletin, 15,* 217–248.

White, H. R., & Labouvie, E. W. (1989). Towards the assessment of adolescent problem drinking. *Journal of Studies on Alcohol, 50,* 30–37.

White, M. M. (1930). The physical and mental traits of individuals susceptible to hypnosis. *Journal of Abnormal and Social Psychology, 25,* 293–298.

White, R. W. (1941). A preface to the theory of hypnotism. *Journal of Abnormal and Social Psychology, 36,* 477–505.

White v. Leyoub, 25 F.3d 245 (8th Cir., 1994).

Wickens, D. D. (1970). Encoding categories of words: An empirical approach to meaning. *Psychological Review, 77,* 1–15.

Wiener, D. W. (1948). Subtle and obvious keys for the Minnesota Multiphasic Personality Inventory. *Journal of Consulting Psychology, 12,* 164–170.

Wierzbicki, M. (1993). Use of MCMI subtle and obvious subscales to detect faking. *Journal of Clinical Psychology, 49,* 809–814.

Wierzbicki, M., & Daleiden, E. L. (1993). The differential responding of college students to subtle and obvious MCMI subscales. *Journal of Clinical Psychology, 49,* 204–208.

Wierzbicki, M., & Howard, B. J. (1992). The differential responding of male prisoners to subtle and obvious MCMI subscales. *Journal of Personality Assessment, 58,* 115–126.

Wiggins, E. C., & Brandt, J. (1988). The detection of simulated amnesia. *Law and Human Behavior, 12,* 57–78.

Wiggins, J. S. (1959). Interrelationships among MMPI measures of dissimulation under standard and social desirability instructions. *Journal of Consulting Psychology, 23,* 419–427.

Wiggins, S. L., Lombard, E. A., Brennan, M. J., & Heckel, R. V. (1964). Awareness of events in a case of amnesia. *Archives of General Psychiatry, 11,* 67–70.

Wilcox, R., & Krasnoff, A. (1967). Influence of test-taking attitudes on personality inventory scores. *Journal of Consulting Psychology, 31,* 188–194.

Wilhelm, K. L., Franzen, M. D., Grinvalds, V. M., & Dews, S. M. (1991, November). *Do people given knowledge and offered money fake better?* Paper presented at the Annual Conference of the National Academy of Neuropsychology, Dallas.

Williams, J. B. W., Gibbon, M., First, M. B., Spitzer, R. L., Davies, M., Borus, J., Howes, M. J., Kane, J., Pope, H. G., Jr., Rounsaville, B., & Wittchen, H. U. (1992). The structured clinical interview for DSM-III-R (SCID): II. Multisite test–retest reliability. *Archives of General Psychiatry, 49,* 630–636.

Williams, L. M. (1994). Recall of childhood trauma: A prospective study of women's memories of child sexual abuse. *Journal of Consulting and Clinical Psychology, 62,* 1167–1176.

Willis, C. G. (1986a). Reid Report/Reid Survey. In D. J. Keyser & R. C. Sweatland (Eds.), *Test critiques* (Vol. 2, pp. 631–636). Kansas City, MO: Test Corporation of America.

Willis, C. G. (1986b). Stanton Survey. In D. J. Keyser & R. C. Sweatland (Eds.), *Test critiques* (Vol. 5, pp. 451–457). Kansas City, MO: Test Corporation of America.

Wilson, J. P. (1981). *Cognitive control mechanisms in stress response syndromes and their relation to different forms of the disorder.* Unpublished manuscript, Cleveland State University.

Wilson, J. P., & Zigelbaum, S. D. (1983). The Vietnam veteran on trial: The relation of posttraumatic stress disorder to criminal behavior. *Behavioral Sciences and the Law, 1,* 69–83.

Wilson, L., Greene, E., & Loftus, E. R. (1985). Beliefs about forensic hypnosis. *International Journal of Clinical and Experimental Hypnosis, 33,* 110–121.

Wilson v. United States, 391 F.2d 460 (D.C. Cir., 1968).

Wimmer, H., Gruber, S., & Perner, J. (1984). Young children's conception of lying: Lexical realism-moral subjectivism. *Journal of Experimental Child Psychology, 37,* 1–30.

Winters, K. C. (1992). Development of an adolescent alcohol and other drug abuse screening scale: Personal Experience Screening Questionnaire. *Addictive Behaviors, 17,* 479–490.

Winters, K. C., & Henly, G. A. (1989). *The Personal Experience Inventory (PEI) test and manual.* Los Angeles: Western Psychological Services.

Winters, K. C., Stinchfield, R. D., & Henly, G. A. (1993). Further validation of new scales measuring adolescent alcohol and other drug abuse. *Journal of Studies on Alcohol, 54,* 534–541.

Winters, K. C., Stinchfield, R. D., Henly, G. A., & Schwartz, R. H. (1991). Validity of adolescent self-report of alcohol and other drug involvement. *International Journal of the Addictions, 25,* 1379–1395.

Wirt, R. D., Lacher, D., Klinedinst, J., & Seat, P. D. (1984). *Multidimensional description of child personality: A manual of the Personality Inventory for Children* (rev. ed.). Los Angeles: Western Psychological Services.

Wolf, A. W., Schubert, D. S. P., Patterson, M., Grande, T., & Pendleton, L. (1990). The use of the MacAndrew Alcoholism Scale in detecting substance abuse and antisocial personality. *Journal of Personality Assessment, 54,* 747–755.

Wong, C. K. (1990). Too shameful to remember: A 17-year-old Chinese boy with psychogenic amnesia. *Australian and New Zealand Journal of Psychiatry, 24,* 570–574.

Wood, G. C., Bentall, R. P., Gopfert, M., & Edwards, R. H. (1991). A comparative psychiatric assessment of patients with chronic fatigue syndrome and muscle disease. *Psychological Medicine, 21,* 619–628.

Woodruff, R. (1966). The diagnostic use of the amylobarbital interview among patients with psychotic illness. *British Journal of Psychiatry, 112,* 727–732.

Woolley, R. M., & Hakstian, A. R. (1992). An examination of the construct validity of personality-based and overt measures of integrity. *Educational and Psychological Measurement, 52,* 475–489.

Wooten, A. J. (1984). Effectiveness of the K correction in the detection of psychopathology and its impact on profile height and configuration among young adult men. *Journal of Consulting and Clinical Psychology, 52,* 468–473.

Worthington, D. L., & Schlottmann, R. S. (1986). The predictive validity of subtle and obvious empirically derived psychological test items under faking conditions. *Journal of Personality Assessment, 50,* 171–181.

Worthington, T. S. (1979). The use in court of hypnotically enhanced testimony. *International Journal of Clinical and Experimental Hypnosis, 27,* 402–416.

Woychyshyn, C. A., McElheran, W. G., & Romney, D. M. (1992). MMPI validity measures: A comparative study of original with alternative indices. *Journal of Personality Assessment, 58,* 138–148.

Wrightson, P., & Gronwall, D. (1980). Time off work and symptoms after minor head injury. *Injury, 12,* 445–454.

Wrightson, P., & Gronwall, D. (1981). Time off work and symptoms after minor head injury. *British Journal of Accident Surgery, 12,* 445–454.

Wrobel, T. A., & Lachar, D. (1982). Validity of the Wiener subtle and obvious scales for the MMPI: Another example of the importance of inventory-item content. *Journal of Consulting and Clinical Psychology, 50,* 469–470.

Wydra, A., Marshall, W. L., Earls, C. M., & Barbaree, H. E. (1983). Identification of cues and control of sexual arousal by rapists. *Behaviour Research and Therapy, 21,* 469–476.

Yapko, M. D. (1994). Suggestibility and repressed memories of abuse: A survey of psychotherapists' beliefs. *American Journal of Clinical Hypnosis, 36,* 163–171.

Yochelson, S., & Samenow, S. (1976). *The criminal personality: Vol. 1. A profile for change.* New York: Jason Aronson.

Yochelson, S., & Samenow, S. (1977). *The criminal personality: Vol. 2. The change process.* New York: Jason Aronson.

Yoneda, Y., Yamadori, A., Mori, E., & Yamashita, H. (1992). Isolated prolonged retrograde amnesia. *European Neurology, 32,* 340–342.

Yonge, G. D. (1966). Certain consequences of applying the K factor to MMPI scores. *Educational and Psychological Measurement, 26,* 887–893.

Young, J. (1972). The fakability of the Thematic Apperception Test under conditions of instruction to fake and test clues: Arnold's story sequence analysis scoring for achievement motivation. *Dissertation Abstracts International, 33,* 3379-A.

Youngjohn, J. R. (1991). Malingering of neuropsychological impairment: An assessment strategy. *A Journal for the Expert Witness, the Trial Attorney, the Trial Judge, 4,* 29–32.

Youngjohn, J. R., Burrows, L., & Erdal, K. (1995). Brain damage or compensation neurosis? The controversial post-concussion syndrome. *Clinical Neuropsychologist, 9,* 112–123.

Yudofsky, S. (1985). Malingering. In H. Kaplan & B. Sadock (Eds.), *Comprehensive textbook of psychiatry* (4th ed., pp. 1862–1865). Baltimore: Williams & Wilkins.

Zahner, G. E. P. (1991). The feasibility of conducting structured diagnostic interviews with preadolescents: A community field trial of the DISC. *Journal of American Academy of Child and Adolescent Psychiatry, 30,* 659–668.

Zelig, M., & Beidleman, W. B. (1981). The investigative use of hypnosis: A word of caution. *International Journal of Law and Psychiatry, 4,* 433–444.

Zellmann, H. E. (1979). Iatrogenic and factitious thyroidal disease. *Medical Clinics of North America, 63,* 329–335.

Zielinski, J. J. (1994). Malingering and defensiveness in the neuropsychological assessment of mild traumatic brain injury. *Clinical Psychology: Science and Practice, 1,* 169–184.

Zimmerman, B. J. (1970). The relationship between teacher, class behavior and student school anxiety levels. *Psychological in the Schools, 7,* 89–93.

Zimmerman, M., & Coryell, W. (1989). DSM-III personality disorder diagnoses in a nonpatient sample: Demographic correlates and comorbidity. *Archives of General Psychiatry, 46,* 682–689.

Zitman, F. G., Linssen, A. C., & Van, H. R. (1992). Chronic pain beyond patienthood. *Journal of Nervous and Mental Disease, 180,* 97–100.

Zitter, J. M. (1994). Sufficiency of evidence that witness in criminal case was hypnotized, for purposes of determining admissibility of testimony given under hypnosis or of hypnotically enhanced testimony. *American Law Reports, 16,* 841–854.

Author Index

Abbey, S. E., 40, *427*
Abel, G. G., 337, 340, 345, 347, 417, *427*
Abeles, M., 87, *427*
Abrams, S., 261, *427*
Achenbach, T. M., 155, 160, *427*
Adams, H. E., 344, *463*
Adams, J. J., *432*
Adams, K. M., 231, *466*
Adams, P. A., 52, 53, *455*
Adatto, C. P., 242, 247, *428*
Addie, D. L., 286, *482*
Adelman, R. M., 250, *428*
Aduan, R. P., 26, *428*
Ahn, C. W., *482*
Albert, M. S., *436*
Albert, S., 212, 213, 220, 221, *428*
Alderman v. Zant, 296, *428*
Alderson, P., 50, *447*
Aldwin, C. M., *460*
Alexander, M. P., 224, *428*
Allan, C. A., 35, *428*
Allen, J. J., 263, 264, *428*
Allen, V. L., 154, *428*
Alliger, G., 276, *460*
Alliger, G. M., 277, 278, *428*
Allison, R. B., 300, *428*
Almer, E. R., 217, 362, 367, *458, 485*
Alperin, J. J., 411, *428*
Alpert, M., 54, 60, 211, 220, 221, *428, 431*
Altarriba, J., 2, *428*

Altshuler, L. L., 56, *428*
American Medical Association, *428*
American Medical Association Council on Scientific Affairs, 292, *428*
American Psychiatric Association, 7, 11, 24, 25, 27, 33, 36, 48, 54, 56, 68, 69, 70, 75, 86, 123, 130, 131, 132*n*, 137, 142, 275, 416, *428, 429*
American Psychological Association, 265, 279, *429*
Amin, K., 229, *472*
Amos, N. L., 332, *430*
Anastasi, A., 281*n*, *429*
Andersen, J. M., 50, *467, 481*
Anderson, E. W., 49, 59, *429*
Anderson, J. C., 40, *467*
Anderson, W. P., 346, *429*
Andrews, B., 235, *435*
Andrews, B. P., 267, *460*
Andreyev, L., 48, *429*
Angell, A., 90, 263, *477*
Annon, J. S., 342, *429*
Annotation, 250, *429*
Antin, S. P., 86, *446*
Appleby, G. S., 253, *468*
Arbisi, P. A., 177, 205, *429*
Archer, R. A., 118, *446*
Archer, R. P., 119, 411, *428, 436, 454*
Ariel, R., 412, *467*
Arkes, H. R., 155, *444*

Arkowitz, H., 358, 359, *479*

Arnett, P. A., 230, *429*

Arnold, D., 277, *454*

Arnold, D. W., 280, *429*

Arnold, L. S., 346, *473*

Arnold, R., *468*

Arona, G. W., 207, *430*

Arons, H., 288, *429*

Arredondo, R., 118, *448, 477*

Asher, R., 26, 30, 33, 407, *429*

Ashlock, L., 146, 147, 149, *429*

Assad, G., 53, *429*

Association for Personnel Test Publishers, 280, *429*

Atkins, E. L., 246, *429*

Atkinson, G. C., *460*

Atkinson, M. L., 154, *428*

Atkinson, R. M., 146, 147, 148, 150, *429, 482*

Aubrey, J. B., 137, *429*

Aubuchon, I. N., 143, *439*

Audubon, J. J., 423, *429*

Auerbach, A. H., 224, *429*

Auffrey, J. J., 328, *450*

Austin, J. S., 185, 190, 197, *429*

Averbach, A., 135, *429*

Axelrod, B. N., 231, *465*

Ayres, S. Y., 192, *441*

Azrin, R., 94, 231, *466*

Babor, T. F., 113, *430*

Bachman, J. G., 109, *430*

Baddeley, A. D., 93, *430*

Baer, J. D., 124, *430*

Baer, R. A., 2, 4, 14, 177, 178, 180, 184, 185, 186, 187, 194, 196, 199, 200, 216, 217, 325, 351, 377, 380, 383, 402, 416, 423, *430, 432, 433, 458, 488*

Bagby, R. M., 14, 18, 19n, 24, 25, 27, 34, 43, 49, 71, 73, 74, 98, 153, 185, 186, 187, 188, 193, 194, 195, 197, 199, 201, 301, 320, 321, 322, 323, 324, 325, 351, 353, 354, 355, 357, 368, 369, 402, 404, 419, 421, *430, 446, 467, 475, 476*

Baggaley, A., 29, *485*

Baile, W. F., 32, *430*

Bailey, S. L., 109, *430*

Baker, G. A., 90, 96, *430*

Baker, J. N., 305, *430*

Baker, W. J., 94, 226, *448*

Baldesserini, R. J., 207, *430*

Ball, W. A., 145, *477*

Balla, J. I., 140, *430*

Ballesteros, S., 426, *473*

Ballinger, B. R., 126, *430*

Baltruweit, W. J., 293, *482*

Bandura, A., 158, *430*

Barban, L., 28, *472*

Barbaree, H. E., 332, 334, 341, 347, *430, 442, 490*

Barber, T. X., 282, 283, 284, 285, 286, *431, 482*

Barefoot, J. C., *463*

Barghout, N. K., 97, *453*

Barkemeyer, C. A., 361, 367, *431, 436*

Barley, W. D., 201, *441*

Barlow, D. H., 2, 340, 347, *427, 431*

Barnard, G. W., 16, 354, 355, 357, 416, *450*

Barnier, A. L., 293, *431*

Baro, W. Z., 143, *431*

Barr, M. A., 53, *455*

Barrett, K. C., 160, *438*

Barrick, M. R., 267, 274, 275, *431, 469*

Barry, H., Jr., 283, *431*

Barth, J. T., 136, *431*

Bartlett, F. C., 103, 287, *431*

Barzelay, D., 125, *465*

Bash, I. Y., 60, 211, 220, 221, *431*

Bass, A., 137, *466*

Bass, A. E., 137, *466*

Bass, E., 39, 292, *431*

Bateman, D., 86, *455*

Bauchner, J. E., *465*

Bauer, W., 249, *454*

Baumgartner, W. A., 124, 125, *430, 431*

Beaber, R. J., 323, 352, 353, 354, 355, 356, 357, 419, *431*

Beachum v. Tansy, 296, *431*

Beck, J., 54, *431*

Becker, J. V., 337, 343, *427, 432*

Beetar, J. T., 231, *432*

Behar, L., 70, *432*

Beidleman, W. B., 242, *491*
Bejerot, N., 34, *432*
Bell, I. R., 41, *432*
Bell, R. F., 31, *481*
Belli, R. F., 104, *432*
Belza, M., 28, 146, 147, 148, 461
Ben-Porath, Y. S., 118, 177, 187, 192, 205, 402, *429, 432, 436, 487*
Ben-Shakar, G., 254, 255, 257, *432*
Bennet, B., 195, *471*
Bennett, W. S., 72, 385, *451*
Bentall, R. P., 41, *490*
Bentler, P. M., 108, *468*
Benton, A. L., 209, 210, 219, *432*
Berenberg, A. N., 59, 209, 408, *486*
Bergersen, S. G., 347, *473*
Bergmann, T. J., 279, *432*
Berman, E., 134, *432*
Bernard, L. C., 91, 93, 94, 95, 99, 230, 403, *432*
Bernardin, H. J., 120, *439*
Bernardin, K., 120, *439*
Berney, T. P., 48, *432*
Bernheim, H. M., 283, *432*
Berrios, G. E., 52, *432*
Berry, D. T. R., 2, 4, 5, 14, 177, 178, 180, 184, 185, 186, 187, 194, 196, 216, 217, 325, 351, 377, 380, 383, 387, 402, 416, 423, *430, 432, 433, 458, 488*
Berry, T., 231, *484*
Bertrand, L. D., 286, *482*
Berwick, D. M., *467*
Betts, G. L., 265, *433*
Betts, T., 31, *433*
Bibb, B. C., 293, *463*
Bickart, W. T., 404, *433*
Billick, S. B., 250, *443*
Billings, R. F., 244, 246, *464*
Binder, L. M., 91, 94, 95, 136, 137, 223, 224, 226, 227, 228, 229, 230, 232, 236, 396, *433, 470, 485*
Binder, R. L., 37, *433*
Binet, A., 287, *433*
Bishop, E. R., 27, 47, *433*
Biskup v. McCaughtry, 296, *433*
Bissell, W. G., 244, *462*
Bitzer, R., 147, *433*

Bjork, R., 89, *434*
Black, R. G., 140, *470*
Blahd, W. H., 124, 125, *430, 431*
Blanchard, E. B., 143, 340, 347, *427, 434*
Blanchard, R., 333, 342, 344, *434, 445*
Blitz, R., 145, *486*
Block, M. L., 286, *456*
Bloom, P. B., 292, *434*
Blum, N., 320, *471*
Blumenthal, S. A., 32, *459*
Boake, C., 93, *447*
Boat, B. W., 29, 334, *443*
Bobholz, J. H., 231, 358, *479*
Boden, S., 31, *433*
Boffeli, T. J., 244, *434*
Bohn, M. J., 397, *461*
Bohn, R. W., 239, *434*
Bohnen, N., 137, *434*
Boisvenu, G. A., 258, *453*
Boll, T. J., *431*
Bolton, B., 266, *434*
Bone, L. R., *467*
Bongartz, W., 284, *434*
Borden, J. W., *432*
Borg, S., 396, *434*
Borum, R., 55, 353, 354, 355, 357, 368, 419, *481, 484*
Borus, J., *487*
Borus, J. F., *467, 489*
Bothwell, R. K., 295, *483*
Bouchard-Voelk, B., 116, *448*
Boudewyns, P. A., 149, *453*
Bourdeau, D., 10, *438*
Bourgeois, L., 4, 305, *478*
Bourget, D., 336, 338, *434*
Bowman, E. S., 32, *434*
Boxxe, R., *460*
Bradford, J. M. W., 336, 338, *434*
Bradford, J. W., 90, 286, 287, 297, *434*, 461
Bradley, M. T., 98, *434*
Bradley v. Preston, 297, *434*
Braginsky, B. M., 8, 47, 305, 332, *434*
Braginsky, D. D., 8, 47, 305, 332, *434*
Brahams, D., 243, *434*
Brand, L., 140, *441*
Brandt, J., 85, 91, 92, 93, 95, 96, 97, 99, 100, 137, 376, *435, 477, 479, 489*

Brantley, P. J., 361, *436*
Braverman, M., 134, 135, 145, 152, *435*
Bregman, N., 105, *460*
Brems, C., 192, *435*
Brena, S. F., 41, *437*
Brendt, D. R., *465*
Brenman, M., 283, *446*
Brenna, D. C., 110, 111, 121, *449*
Brennan, M. J., 90, *489*
Brentar, J., *448*
Brentar, J. T., 293, *487*
Breslau, N., 148, 155, *435*
Breuer, J., 285, *435*
Brewin, E., 235, *435*
Bridger, A. A., 284, *482*
Brill, L., *483*
Brittain, R. P., 62, *435*
Brockting, W. O., 330, *441*
Brodsky, S. L., 266, *435*
Brooks, N., 231, *473*
Brown, J. P., 27, *436*
Brown, N., *452*
Brown, R. S., 77, 235, *441, 448, 459*
Browner, W. S., 356, *435*
Brozovich, R., 219, *435*
Bruck, M., 105, *437*
Bruhn, A. R., 231, *435*
Brunetti, D. G., 192, *452*
Brus, I., *452*
Bryan, W., 288, *435*
Bryant R. A., 293, *463*
Bryer, J. B., 119, *435*
Buchanan, A., *488*
Buck, O. D., 29, *435*
Buckhout, R., 146, *435*
Buckman, J., 240, *435, 484*
Budman, S. H., *467*
Buis, T., 185, 188, 193, 194, 197, 199, *430*
Bukalew, L. W., 250, *435*
Bukstein, O., 115, 117, *455, 485*
Buller, D. B., 17, *435*
Bulman, R. J., *435*
Buongiorno, G., 227, *449*
Bures, E., 288, 293, *482*
Burger, G. K., *481*
Burger, T. L., *432*
Burgess, C. A., 294, *482*

Burgess, M. F., 294, *482*
Burgoon, J. K., 17, *435*
Burgoon, M., 17, *436*
Burke, P., 245, *487*
Burns, H. J., 104, *461*
Burr, W., 145, *486*
Burris, L. R., 266, *478*
Burrows, E. H., 87, *455*
Burrows, L., 227, *490*
Bursten, B., 30, *436*
Bussey, K., 155, 156, *436*
Bustamante, J. P., 48, *436*
Butcher, J. N., 77, 118, 157, 169, 172, 173, 176, 177, 181, 185, 186, 186n, 188, 188n, 189, 189n, 192, 196, 197, 198, 198n, 199, 199n, 200, 200n, 203, 203n, 204n, 205, *436, 448, 457, 460, 472, 487*
Butters, N., 86, *436, 468*

Cacciola, J., 116, *477*
Caddell, J. M., 143, *455, 461*
Caine, E. D., 86, *436*
Caldwell, A. B., 188, *436*
Callahan, C., 266, *478*
Callister, M., 17, *436*
Callon, E. B., 361, 362, 367, *431, 436*
Calverly, D. S., *431*
Camara, W. J., 276, *436*
Campbell, D. T., 89, 407, *436, 438*
Canter, A., 41, *453*
Cantwell, B., 90, *477*
Cantwell, H. B., 29, *436*
Caradoc-Davies, G., 27, *436*
Carlin, A. S., 174, 377, *436*
Carlisle, A. L., 211, 364, *479*
Carlson, B. W., *448*
Carlson, R. J., *436*
Carney, M. W., 27, *436*
Caroff, S. N., 145, *477*
Carp, A. L., 210, 216, 220, *436*
Carpenter, W. T., 55, *478*
Carsky, M., 4, 12, *437*
Carter, J. E., 421, *437*
Carter, M., 92, 97, 100, 407, *445*
Cartlidge, N., 58, 133, 134, 224, 244, *465*

Cash, W. S., 106, *437*
Cashel, M. L., 122, 202, 410, 423, *437, 475*
Casper, R. C., 239, 244, *441*
Cattell, R. B., 273, 335, *437*
Cavanaugh, J. L., Jr., 2, 12, 65, 72, 146, 174, 309, 329, 336, 337, 338, 388, *449, 451, 475, 476, 487*
Ceci, A., 154, *437*
Ceci, S. J., 105, *437*
Cercy, S. P., 85, 93, 96, 100, *437*
Cermak, L. S., 86, *468*
Chakraborty, D., 49, 186, 187, 188, 193, 194, 369, 402, *475*
Chan, S., 343, *445*
Chance, J., 118, 196, *438*
Chandler, M., 155, *437*
Chaney, H. S., 139, *437*
Chang, S. S., 239, 244, *441*
Chaplin, T. C., 332, 341, *437, 473*
Chapman, L. J., 215, *442*
Chapman, S. L., 41, *437*
Charcot, J. M., 283, *437*
Chase, G. A., *470*
Chaves, J. F., 282, *431*
Chittum, R., 93, *437*
Choca, J. P., 170, *437*
Christensen, H., 88, 245, *457*
Christiansen, K., 69, *464*
Chuang, J., 90, *477*
Clark, C., 68, 180, *433*
Clark, C. A., 104, *479*
Clark, C. D., *432*
Clark, C. L., 397, *461*
Clark, D. A., 195, *471*
Clark v. State, 295, *437*
Clarke-Stewart, A., 154, *447*
Cleckley, H., 9, 10, 69, 70, *437*
Clemow, L. P., 32, *484*
Clevenger, S. V., 130, *437*
Clopton, J. R., 117, *437*
Cluff, L., 41, *453*
Coallier, J. -C., *478*
Coates, G. D., 411, *428*
Coe, W. C., 282, 283, 284, 286, 288, *437, 456, 478*
Cofer, C. N., 118, 196, 199, *438*

Cogburn, R-. A. K., 75, 82, *437*
Cohen, B., *470*
Cohen, J. B., 213, *438*
Cohen, N. J., *438*
Cohen, S., 32, 123, *438, 464*
Cohn, C. K., 139, *437*
Colbus, D., 155, *455*
Colby, F., 171, *438*
Cole, E. S., 138, 159, 160, *438*
Cole, P. M., 159, *438*
Coletti, S. D., 124, *465*
Collie, J., 132, *438*
Collinson, G. D., 62, *438*
Comer, S. I., 293, *482*
Commonwealth ex rel. Cummins v. Price, 297, *438*
Connell, D. K., 322, 325, 404, *433, 438*
Connolly, D. A., 97, *453*
Connor, E. J., 396, *434*
Cook, T. D., 89, 407, *438*
Coons, P. M., 28, 34, 294, *438*
Cooper, S. H., 9, *471*
Corcoran, K., 2, *438*
Cornelius, J. R., 54, *438*
Cornelius, M. D., *438*
Cornell, D. G., 50, 71, 304, 361, *438*
Cornell v. Sup. Ct., 298, *438*
Corradi, R. B., 37, *438*
Coryell, W., 77, 320, *471, 491*
Costa, P. T., Jr., 273, 276, *438, 463*
Cottfield, K. E., 250, *435*
Cotterill, J. A., 32, *438*
Cottler, L. B., 319, *474*
Coulthard, R., 343, *445*
Cournoyer, L. -G., *478*
Cox, B., 334, *450*
Cox, B. J., 10, *438*
Cox, D. N., 75, *450*
Coyne, J. C., 160, *438*
Craig, J. R., 266, *439*
Craig, R. J., 119, *439*
Cramer, B., 30, *439*
Crawford, H. J., *469*
Crawford, V. L., 117, 319, *465*
Crockett v. Haithwaite et al., 298, *439*
Croft, R. D., 36, *439*
Cronbach, L. J., 209, 210, 221, 281n, *439*

Cross, H. L., 294, *467*
Croughan, J. L., 77, *474*
Crowley, M. E., *439*
Crowne, D. P., 12, *439*
Cruise, K., 399, *475*
Cullum, C. M., 41, *479*
Cummings, J. L., 54, 56, 57, *428, 439*
Cummings, S. R., 356, *435*
Cunnien, A. J., 23, 30, 77, 308, *439, 475*
Cunningham-Rathner, J., 337, 417, *427*
Cunningham-Rundles, C., *452*
Curran, P. J., 217, 362, 367, *458, 485*
Curran, W. J., 250, *439*
Cutting, J., *488*

Dacey, C. M., 118, *449*
Dahlstrom, L. E., 169, 187, 346, *439*
Dahlstrom, W. G., 77, 169, 174, 182, 187,
    192, 346, *436, 439, 463, 477*
Dahmus, S., 120, *439*
Daldin, 162
Dale, D. C., 26, *428*
Dale, J., 40, *457*
Dale, P. S., 105, *439*
Daleiden, E. L., 195, *489*
Dalton, J. E., 143, 149, 385, *439*
Damasio, A. R., 87, *439*
Damasio, H., 87, *439*
Daniel, A. E., 57, *439*
Danielson, K. D., 263, *428*
Dannenbaum, S. E., 192, *440*
Darton, N., 105, *440*
D'Attilio, J., 137, *466*
Daubert v. Merrell Dow Pharmaceuticals, 252,
    440
Davidson, H., 91, *440*
Davidson, H. A., 56, 57, 58, 133, 135, 139,
    145, 407, *440*
Davidson, J., 141, *440*
Davies, M., *489*
Davis, G. C., 148, *435*
Davis, H. D., 118, *448*
Davis, H. G., *448*
Davis, J. M., 239, 240, 243, 244, 249, *441*
Davis, J. W., 31, *440*
Davis, L., 39, 292, *431*
Davis, L. W., 283, *440*

Davis, S., 170, *465*
Davis, T., 414, *440*
Davis v. State, 297, *440*
Davison, G. C., 407, *440*
Deale, S., 146, 147, *429*
DeBlois, C. S., 70, *484*
de Groh, M., 293, *482*
deGroot, H. P., 286, *440, 482*
De Labry, L., *460*
Delis, D. C., 95, *440*
Dell, P. F., 28, *440*
Denker, P. G., 224, *440*
Denney, R. L., 92, 97, 100, *440*
Department of Health and Human Services,
    136, *440*
DePaulo, B. M., 226, 414, *440*
De Puysegur, A. M., 283, *440*
Desoutter, L., 32, *463*
Dession, G. H., 57, 143, 243, *473*
Detering, B. J., *468*
Detrick, D., 289, *482*
Deutsch, H., 38, *440*
de Wit, H., 111, *440*
Dews, S. M., 403, *489*
Diamond, B., 66, *441*
Diamond, B. L., 67, 292, 295, *440*
Dicken, C. F., 305, *441*
Dickens, S. E., 14, 18, 19*n*, 49, 71, 73, 74,
    98, 301, 320, 321, 322, 323, 324, 325,
    351, 392, 404, *475, 476*
Dickey, R., 7, 10, 328, 329, 330, 331, 332,
    339, 340, 341, *475*
DiClementi, J. D., 41, *479*
DiGiulio, D. V., 137, *466*
Dignan, M. A., 119, *435*
Dikmen, S. S., 232, *441*
Dilloff, N. J., 295, *441*
Dilworth, C., 246, *462*
Dinges, D. F., 289, 300, *469*
Dinning, W. D., 178, *443*
Dion, K. L., 70, 77, *475*
DiPasquale, T., 53, *465*
Direnfeld, D. M., 10, *438*
Dobbs, A. R., 137, *429*
Dolmetsch, R., 174, *475*
Donaldson, W., 426, *441*
Donchin, E., 90, 263, 264, *444*
Donders, K., 104, *461*

Doren, D. M., 69, *441*
Douce, R., 288, *457*
Douglas, C. J., 42, *441*
Dowell, D. A., 2, *462*
Downing, J., 134, *441*
Doyle, J. F., 292, *461*
Druce, H., 28, *481*
Drummond, J., 286, *482*
Druss, R. G., 42, *441*
DuAlba, L., 422, *441*
Dubinsky, S., 191, *441*
Dubois, R. E., *452*
Dubowski, K. M., 123, *469*
Duckworth, J., 194, 201, 424, *441*, 449
Duffy, D. P., 23, 253, *460*
Duffy, J. B., 159, *441*
Duffy, T. P., *441*
Dufton, B., 12, *463*
Dukes, W. F., 407, *441*
Duncan, J., 51, 309, 311n, 312n, 314n, 315n, 317n, 318n, *441*
Duncan, J. C., 5, 70, 77, *475*
Dunn, J. T., 58, 233, *441, 459*
Dush, D. M., 192, 193, *441*
Duvall, S. W., 178, *462*
Dworkin, R. H., 140, *441*
Dwyer, S. M., 330, *441*
Dysken, M. W., 239, 240, 243, 244, 249, *441*

Earhart v. State, 298, *441*
Earl, J., 249, *454*
Earls, C. M., 347, *490*
Earls, F., 141, *441*
Early, E., 148, *442*
East, N. W., 56, 57, 58, 66, 146, *442*
Easton, K., 210, 219, *442*
Eber, H. W., 335, *437*
Eccles, A., 341, *442*
Eckblad, M., 215, *442*
Eckenhoff, M. F., 105, *442*
Edelbrock, C. S., 160, *427*
Edwards, R. H., 41, *490*
Egan, K., 41, *455*
Eisendrath, S. J., 25, 26, 31, *442*
Eissler, K. R., 48, 68, *442*
Ekman, P., 18, 226, *442*

Elaad, E., 255, *442*
Ellinwood, E. N., Jr., 54, *442*
Ellison, D., 87, *455*
Ellwanger, J., 90, *477*
Emens, M., 29, 334, *465*
Emerson, J., 235, *442*
Emmons, J., 91, *451*
Endicott, J., 18, 77, 116, 307, *442, 481, 483*
Enelow, A. J., 135, *442*
Engel, G. L., 139, *442*
English, L. T., 177, 206, *441, 459*
Eno, T. D., 352, *449*
Erdal, K., 227, *490*
Erdelyt, M. H., 292, *442*
Erdman, H. P., 319, *442*
Erickson, M. H., 285, 289, *443*
Erickson, R., 236, *470*
Erickson, W. D., 346, *443*
Eron, L. D., 218, *455*
Eslinger, P., 86, *468*
Esveldt-Dawson, K., 155, *455*
Evans, F. I., 284, *443*
Evans, F. J., *469*
Evans, I. M., 158, *443*
Evans, J., 86, *443*
Evans, R. G., 178, *443*
Everitt, B., *488*
Everson, M. D., 29, 334, *443*
Exner, J. E., 211, 213, 214, 216, 220, 221, *443*
Eysenck, H. J., 407, *443*

Fabian, C. A., 250, *443*
Fabrega, H., *438*
Fairbank, J. A., 142, 148, 149, 186, *443, 456*
Fallon, J. H., 149, *453*
Falloon, I., 53, *443*
Fals-Stewart, W., 201, 416, *443, 486*
False Memory Syndrome Foundation, 39, *443*
Fantoni-Salvador, P., 119, *443*
Farina, A., 218, *450*
Farwell, L. A., 90, 263, 264, *444*
Fauci, A. S., 26, *428*
Faust, D., 155, 157, 226, *444*

Fausti, S., 91, 228, 407, *470*
Fauteck, P. K., 375, *444*
Feazell, D., 241, *462*
Feigenbaum, K., 210, 219, *442*
Fekken, G. C., 178, 266, *444*
Feldberg, T. M., 209, 219, *477*
Feldman, J., 106, *461*
Feldman, M. D., 26, 27, 31, 33, 35, 36, *444*
Feldman, M. J., 210, 219, *444*
Feldman, R., 156, *444*
Fenichel, O., 25, 34, 37, 42, *444*
Ferguson, L. R., 70, *444*
Feucht, T. E., 125, *444*
Fey, P., 129, *466*
Fiel, A., 201, *474*
Filstead, W. J., 115, *463*
Fine, E. W., 123, *454*
Fink, P., 41, *444*
Fink, R., 27, *482*
Finkelstein, S., 207, *430*
Firestone, S., 32, *463*
First, M. B., 116, 320, *483, 489*
Fleming, I., 98, *434*
Fleming, J. A., 258, *453*
Flewelling, R. L., 109, *430*
Flynn, M., 104, *448*
Folks, D. G., 48, *444*
Folstein, M. F., 50, *444*
Folstein, S. E., 50, *444*
Fombonne, E., 421, *444*
Fontana, A. F., 305, *444*
Fontes, N. E., *465*
Ford, C. V., 26, 31, 33, 35, 36, 38, 48, 77, *436, 444, 456, 466*
Fordyce, W. E., 41, 140, *444, 470*
Forrest, A., 27, 59, 408, *474*
Forrow, L., *468*
Fosberg, I. A., 208, 209, 210, 216, *445*
Foster, F. M., 120, 122, *453, 487*
Foster, H. G., 231, 376, 381, *445*
Foster, T. E., 295, *482*
Fowler, W., 91, *432*
Fox, D. D., 192, 193, *445, 459*
Fox, H., 213, *455*
Fox, H. M., 212, *428*
Fox, J. A., 118, *473*
Frame, C. L., 52, *455*

Francis, L. J., 159, *445*
Frank, L. K., 209, *445*
Frankel, F. H., 39, 282, *445*
Franzen, M. D., 92, 184, 185, 230, 403, *445, 454, 489*
Frederick, R. I., 92, 97, 100, 228, 231, 376, 381, 407, 421, *445*
Freedman, M., 87, *478*
Freeman, A. M., 48, *444*
French, N. H., 155, *455*
Freud, S., 285, *435*
Freund, K., 333, 341, 343, 344, 347, *445*
Friedlander, J. W., 283, *445*
Friedman, A. F., *477*
Friedman, M. J., 146, *445*
Friedman, R., 40, *457*
Friesen, J., 178, *462*
Friesen, W. V., 226, *442*
Frischholz, E. I., 289, *469, 482*
Frise-Smith, T., 52, *476*
Fritter, M. J., 426, *481*
Fritz, A. S., 155, *437*
Fritz, G. K., 153, *445*
Frosch, W., 52, *451*
Frueh, B. C., 143, 149, 215, 220, 221, *445*
Frumkin, L. R., 32, *445*
Fuchs, D., 158, *445*
Furedy, J. J., 254, 255, 257, *432*

Gacano, C. B., 74, 76, *446, 464*
Gade, A., 86, *446*
Gage, R., 137, *466*
Gallucci, N. T., 178, *446*
Gamble, D. J., 191, *441*
Ganellen, R. J., 215, 216, 217, 416, *446*
Ganguli, H. C., 266, *446*
Ganter, A. B., 118, *446*
Gantz, N. M., *452*
Garety, P., *488*
Garfield, P., 145, *446*
Garfinkel, P. E., 40, *427*
Garry, M., 106, 293, *446, 461*
Garske, J. P., 186, *481*
Garte, S. H., 143, *439*
Gaston, L., 4, *446*
Gauthier, R., 334, *450*
Gavin, D. R., 114, 116, *446, 477*

Gdowski, C. L., 162, *458*
Gelkopf, M., 36, *480*
Geller, G., *467*
Gelles, R. J., 425, *446*
Gendreau, P., 4, 305, *478*
George, P., 246, *462*
Gerardi, R. J., 143, *434*
Gerhard, D., 104, *479*
Gershberg, M. R., 30, *439*
Gerson, A., 193, *445*
Gerson, M. J., 88, 247, *446*
Gianetti, R., 319, *454*
Gibbon, M., 116, 320, *483, 489*
Gibson, G. S., 108, *446*
Gierasch, P. F., 10, *485*
Gilbertini, M., 356, *474*
Gill, M. M., 283, *446*
Gillespie, C. F., 345, *427*
Gillespie, R., 221, *443*
Gillis, G. R., 71, *475*
Gillis, J. R., 34, 52, 73, 195, 353, 354, 355, 357, 368, 419, *430, 446, 475, 476*
Ginton, A., 255, *442*
Giordani, B., *431*
Giulianao, A. J. O., 229, *449*
Giuliano, A. J., 91, *449*
Glass, L. B., 284, *431*
Glasser, A., 134, *462*
Glenn, W. J., 177, 206, *459*
Glisky, E. L., 104, *446*
Goebel, R. A., 225, *446*
Gola, T., 94, 226, *448*
Goldberg, E., 86, 241, *446, 462*
Goldberg, J., 195, *430*
Goldberg, J. D., 91, *446*
Goldberg, L. R., 265, 267, 269, 270, 272, 273, 277, 278, 280, *446*
Golden, C. J., 412, *467*
Goldinger, L. A., 253, *468*
Goldring, E., 319, *442, 474*
Goldstein, A., 4, 6, 61, 68, 72, 78, 356, 385, 416, 424, *476*
Goldstein, F. C., 93, 96, *447*
Golechha, G. R., 249, *447*
Gonzalez, C., 122, 423, *474*
Goodman, G. S., 105, 154, *447, 478*
Goodnow, J. J., 160, *447*
Goodwin, D. W., 50, 51, 52, 53, *447*

Goodwin, J., 29, 30, *447*
Gopfert, M., 41, *490*
Gorden, P., 32, *449*
Goreczny, A. J., 149, *471*
Gorman, W. F., 33, 136, 244, 287, *447*
Gothard, S., 73, 323, 324, 325, 326, 405, *447*
Gotlib, I., 235, *435*
Gottesman, I. I., 118, *447*
Gottfried, L. A., 26, 235, *473*
Gough, H. G., 72, 75, 170, 182, 185, 186n, 188n, 189n, 190, 195, 203n, 204n, 205, 206, 265, 267, 268, 273, 275, *447*
Gouvier, W. D., 324, *451*
Govorchin, M., 246, *462*
Graber, R. A., 117, *447*
Graf, P., 96, *447*
Graff-Radford, N. R., 87, *439*
Graham, J. R., 77, 118, 157, 169, 174, 185, 190, 192, 198, 199, 207, 365, *436, 446, 448, 483, 485*
Graham, N., 124, *448*
Graley, J., 210, 219, *444*
Grande, T., 118, *490*
Grant, B. F., 77, 116, *450*
Grayson, D. A., 421, *448*
Grayson, H. M., 188, *448*
Green, J. P., 288, 293, *448, 487*
Green, V., 293, *480*
Greene, E., 104, 295, *448, 489*
Greene, R., 377, *430*
Greene, R. L., 4, 19n, 118, 119, 142, 169, 171, 173, 174, 176, 177, 182, 184, 185, 186, 189, 191, 192, 194, 198, 198n, 199n, 199, 200, 200n, 203n, 204, 204n, 206, 207, 233, 303, 424, *448, 468, 477, 487*
Greenfield, D., 48, 157, *448*
Greenfield v. Commonwealth, 296, *448*
Greenwald, J., 319, *448*
Greenwood, A., 332, *468*
Greiffenstein, M. F., 94, 95, 98, 226, 227, *448*
Greist, J. H., *442*
Grenier, J. R., 265, *446*
Griffin, M. L., 116, *448*
Griffith, J. L., 36, *448*

Grillo, J., 77, *448*

Grimes, B. P., 346, *484*

Grinvalds, V. M., 403, *489*

Gripshover, D. L., 118, *449*

Gronwall, D., 224, *490*

Gronwall, D. M. A., 136, 231, *449*

Gropper, B., 125, *465*

Grossman, L. S., 10, 72, 215, 329, 331, 336, 337, 338, 416, *446, 449, 451, 487*

Grossman, R. G., 232, *459*

Grow, R., 162, 163, 352, *449*

Grow, R. T., *464*

Gruber, C. P., 362, 368, 423, *480*

Gruber, S., 156, *489*

Grubin, D. H., 329, 334, *456*

Grunberger, G., 32, *449*

Guastello, S. J., 268, 269, 270, 277, *449, 474*

Guberman, A., 31, *449*

Gudjonsson, G. H., 87, 231, 331, 376, *449*

Guilmette, T. J., 91, 155, 226, 227, 228, 230, *444, 449*

Guion, R. M., 265, *446*

Guroff, J. J., 28, *472*

Gutheil, T. G., 29, 334, *465*

Guthmann, D. R., 110, 111, 121, *449*

Guttmacher, M. S., 69, 76, *449*

Guze, S. B., 244, *434*

Guzman, D. A., 88, *484*

Gwynn, M. I., 286, 293, *440, 482*

Hackett, T. P., 239, *468*

Haggerty, J. J., 31, *463*

Hain, J. D., 240, 247, 249, *435, 449, 481, 484*

Haines, M. E., 230, *449*

Hakstian, A. R., 267, 273, 274, 276, *450, 490*

Hala, S., 155, *437*

Hale, D. B., 324, *451*

Hale, G., 194, 424, *449*

Hall, C. G. N., 341, 346, *450*

Hall, G. C., 340, *450*

Hall, G. C. N., *449*

Hall, H. V., 63, 65, *450*

Hall, J. E., 114, *469*

Hall, P., 115, *463*

Hall, S., 90, 229, 376, *476*

Halleck, S., 67, *450*

Halleck, S. L., 2, *450*

Haller, D. L., 194, 387, *462*

Hamburger, M., *442*

Hamilton, J. D., 28, 148, *450*

Hamilton, J. E., 130, *450*

Hammeke, T. A., 230, *429*

Hammond, J. A., 185, *454*

Hamsher, J. H., 218, *450*

Han, K., 197, 198n, 200n, 200, 203n, 204n, 205, *436*

Handlin, D. S., 140, *441*

Handy, L., 334, 336, 338, *458*

Hankins, G. C., 16, 354, 355, 356, 357, 358, 359, 416, *450*

Hanley, J. R., 90, *430*

Hanson, R. K., 334, *450*

Happel, R. M., 328, *450*

Harackiewicz, J. M., 105, *456*

Haraszti, J. S., 240, 244, 249, *441*

Harbluk, J. L., 104, *478*

Harding v. State, 295, *450*

Hardy, D. W., 10, 329, *451*

Hare, R. D., 10, 69, 70, 75, 76, 276, *450*

Harford, R. J., 124, *450*

Harmand, J., 146, *429*

Harpur, T. J., 276, *450*

Harrell, A. V., 115, *450*

Harrell, E. H., 4, 90, 134, 225, 228, 230, 324, 375, 376, 403, 418, *476*

Harris, G. T., 331, 332, *437, 474*

Harris, M. J., 2, 54, *431, 433*

Harris, M. M., 268, 269, 278, *478*

Harris, W. G., 14, 177, 184, 194, 216, 270, 277, 351, 380, 416, *423, 450, 454*

Harrison, W. R., 149, *453*

Hart, K., 155, 226, *444*

Hart, K. J., 91, 229, *449*

Hart, S. D., 75, *450*

Harter, S., 57, *450*

Hartmann, E., 145, *486*

Hartshorne, H., 170, 266, *450*

Harvey, M. R., 105, *452*

Hasher, L., 96, *451*

Hasin, D. S., 77, 116, *451*

Haskett, J., 360, 368, *451*

Hathaway, S. R., 72, 170, 171, 335, 384, 411, *451, 464*

Hawk, G. L., 50, 71, 304, 361, *438*

Hawkins, K. A., 233, *451*

Hay G. G., 27, 47, 48, 49, 408, *451*

Hayes, J. S., 324, *451*

Hays, J. R., 91, *451*

Hays, R. D., 4, 12, *451*

Haywood, T. W., 10, 72, 215, 329, 330, 331, 335, 336, 337, 338, 416, *446, 451, 487*

Heaton, R. K., 134, 225, 226, 232, 385, *451*

Heckel, R. V., 90, *489*

Hegedus, A. M., 115, *485*

Heilbronner, R., 94, 231, *466*

Heilbrun, K., 72, 385, *451*

Heilman, K., 86, *482*

Heins v. Commonwealth of Pennsylvania, 279, *451*

Hellerstein, D., 52, *451*

Helzer, J. E., 77, 319, *442, 474*

Henderson, J., 134, *451*

Henderson, R. G., 146, 147, *429*

Henly, G. A., 10, 110, 120, *451, 489*

Herbison, G. P., 40, *467*

Herman, J. L., 105, *452*

Herman, M., 241, 242, 247, *452*

Hershey, L. A., 31, *457*

Herz, L. R., 144, *469*

Herzberg, J. H., 26, *428*

Hewitt, P. L., 174, 377, *436*

Hickam, D., 235, *470*

Hilgard, E. R., 283, 284, 287, 288, 293, *452, 466, 469, 477, 488*

Hill, V. A., 124, 125, *430, 431*

Hilsabeck, R., 77, *448*

Hilsenroth, M. J., 186, *481*

Hinds, J. D., 164, 166n, 324, 365, *476*

Hinojosa, L., 72

Hinton, J. W., 342, *452*

Hintzman, D. L., 104, *452*

Hirschel, J. D., 125, *452*

Hirschman, R., 340, *450*

Hiscock, C. K., 91, 227, 228, *452*

Hiscock, M., 91, 227, 228, *452*

Hochman, S., 353, 354, 355, 357, 359, *479*

Hocking, J. E., *465*

Hodes, R. L., 258, *452*

Hodges, J. R., 86, *443*

Hoffman, H. G., 104, *461*

Hoffman, R. E., *451*

Hofling, C. K., 133, 139, 143, *452*

Hoge, S. K., 2, *460*

Holcomb, W. R., 297, *470*

Holden, C. E., 52, *485*

Holden, R. R., 12, 178, 181, *444, 452, 463*

Hollender, M. H., 35, 77, *444*

Hollrah, J. L., 192, *452*

Holmen, M. L., 347, *459*

Holmes, D. S., 218, *452*

Holmes, G. P., 40, 41, *452*

Holt, A. R., 27, 47, *433*

Honts, C. R., 256, 258, *452, 473*

Hopp, G., 230, *481*

Horn, J. L., 120, 122, *453, 487*

Horsley, J. S., 239, *453*

Horton, K. D., 97, *453*

Horvath, F., 260, 261, *453*

Hough, L. M., 266, *453*

House v. State, 296, *453*

Houston, W., 94, 230, *432*

Howard, A., 250, *428*

Howard, B. J., 195, *489*

Howell, C. T., 155, *427*

Howell, R. J., 211, 364, *479*

Howes, M. J., *489*

Howieson, D., 94, 230, *433*

Huba, G. J., 174, *453*

Huddleston, J. H., 139, *453*

Hudson, J. I., 39, *472*

Hudson, S. M., 331, *487*

Hughes, J. E. O., 86, *446*

Humphrey, M., 224, *468*

Hunsaker, F. G., 18, *436*

Hunt, W. A., 209, 219, *453*

Hunter, J. A., 343, *432*

Hunter, J. E., 270, 275, *453, 469*

Hunter, M., 230, 231, *481, 484*

Hurt, S. W., 4, *437*

Hurwitz, T. A., 243, *453*

Husband, R. W., 283, *440*

Husted, J. J., *442*

Hyer, L., 149, *453*

Hyler, S. E., 23, 26, 30, *453, 485*

Iacono, W. G., 252, 253, 254, 255, 256, 257, 258, 259, 260, 261, 262, 263, 264, 268, 400, *428, 453, 469, 470*
Illgen, E. J., 279, *432*
Imboden, J. B., 41, *453*
Inbau, F. E., 59, *453*
Irvin, D. M., 115, *461*
Iverson, G. L., 92, 99, 184, 185, 190, 225, 230, 235, *445, 453*

Jackson, D. N., 114, 192, 267, *453, 454, 485*
Jackson, H. F., 90, *430*
Jackson, J., 235, *470*
Jacobs, D., 239, *471*
Jacobson, A., 59, 209, 408, *486*
Jacobson, S. A., 224, *454*
Jaffe, L. T., 119, *454*
Jalazo, J., 123, *454*
James, B., 286, *482*
Jamieson, G. A., 293, *480*
Jane, J. A., *431*
Janet, P., 283, *454*
Janowsky, J. S., 104, *454*
Jarvis, G. K., 111, *481*
Jauch, T. E., 249, *454*
Jayaprakash, N. P., 249, *447*
Jellinek, E. M., 34, *454*
Jervis, M., 36, *439*
Johansen, J., 122, 423, *475*
Johanson, C. E., 111, *440*
Johnson, D. L., 284, *467*
Johnson, J., 110, 319, *471*
Johnson, J. A., 266, *454*
Johnson, J. H., 420, *454*
Johnson, M., 90, 263, *477*
Johnson, M. E., 192, *435*
Johnson, M. K., 105, *460*
Johnson, M. M., 90, *454*
Johnston, J. D., 228, *445*
Jolles, J., 137, *434, 453*
Jonas, J. M., 24, 26, 28, 34, 43, 48, 139, 408, *454, 472*
Jones, A. B., 59, 134, *454*
Jones, B., 26, 48, 408, *472*
Jones, G. N., 361, *436*
Jones, J. F., 41, 43, *452, 479*

Jones, J. W., 270, 277, *454, 463*
Joos, S., 235, *442*
Jourard, S. M., 12, *454*
Judson, A. J., 118, 196, *438*
Jung, K. G., 141, *441*
Junginger, J., 52, 53, *454, 455*
Jungman, N., 255, *442*
Juni, S., 266, *455*
Jureidini, J., 36, *455*

Kabene, M., 115, *485*
Kaemmer, B., 77, 169, *436*
Kahn, M. W., 212, 213, 220, *428, 455*
Kahn, R. L., 244, *487*
Kalas, R., *455*
Kalemba, V., 185, 188, 193, 194, 197, 199, *430*
Kalman, G., 143, *455*
Kaminer, Y., 115, 117, *455, 485*
Kaminsky, A. P., *465*
Kamphaus, R. W., 163, *474*
Kanas, N., 53, *455*
Kane, J., *489*
Kanin, E. J., 33, *455*
Kanovitz, J., 292, 299, *455*
Kanzer, M., 87, 287, *455*
Kaplan, E., 95, *440*
Kaplan, H. I., 249, *455*
Kaplan, J. E., *452*
Kaplan, M. F., 218, *455*
Kaplan, M. S., 343, *432*
Kapur, B., 123, 124, *455*
Kapur, N., 86, 87, *455*
Karlstrom, E., 345, *427*
Karson, S., 170, 182, *455*
Kasper, M. E., 52, 53, *455*
Katon, W., 41, *455*
Katon, W. J., 41, *480*
Kazdin, A. E., 155, *455*
Keane, T. M., 142, 143, 144, 148, 149, 186, *443, 455, 456*
Keiller, S. W., 192, *485*
Keiser, H. R., 32, *456*
Keiser, L., 134, 135, *456*
Kelly, J., 72, 385, *451*
Kelly, K., 16, 108, 125, *456*
Kelly, M. P., 229, 230, *433*

Kelly, R., 136, 140, 224, *456*
Kenna, J. C., 49, *429*
Kennedy, B. P., 120, *456*
Kennedy, F., 139, *456*
Kennedy, H. G., 329, 334, *456*
Kennedy, J., 286, 288, *456*
Kennedy, P., 86, *455*
Keschner, M., 287, *456*
Ketcham, K., 104, *461*
Key v. State, 295, *456*
Kihlstrom, J. F., 105, 292, *456*
Kim, H. C., 32, *484*
Kimmance, S., 90, *430*
Kinder, B. N., 143, 149, 208, 214, 215, 219, 220, 221, *445, 471*
King, B. H., 35, 38, 77, *444, 456*
Kinnunen, T., 286, 288, *456*
Kirby, J. V., 243, *484*
Kircher, J. C., 256, 258, *452, 473*
Kirchner, W. K., 305, *456*
Kirwin, B. R., 423, *429*
Kleber, H. D., 116, 124, *450, 477*
Klein, E. B., 305, *444*
Klein, M. H., *442*
Kleinmuntz, B., 261, 266, 276, 277, 278, *456*
Klerman, G. L., *467*
Kline, R. B., 122, *456*
Kline, S. A., 244, 246, *464*
Klinedinst, J., 162, *489*
Klingler, D. E., 319, 420, *454*
Klonoff, E. A., 31, *457*
Kluft, R. P., 28, 34, 54, 55, 58, *457*
Koenigsberg, H. W., 52, *451*
Kolarsky, A., 342, *456*
Kolb, L., 144, *455*
Kolb, L. C., 143, 243, *434, 456*
Komaroff, A. L., *452*
Kooser, J. A., 240, 244, 249, *441*
Kopelman, M. D., 88, 89, 97, 98, 100, 245, *457*
Korsakoff, S. S., 103, *457*
Koson, D., 298, *457*
Koss, M. P., 185, 186n, 188, 188n, 189, 189n, 196, 203n, 204n, *457*
Kraepelin, E., 103, *457*
Krafft, R. V., 91, *479*
Kramer, J. H., 95, *440*

Krasnoff, A., 8, 332, *489*
Kraus, A., 55, *457*
Krauss, R. M., 154, 156, *467*
Kraut, R. E., 160, *457*
Kravitz, H. M., 331, 336, 337, *451*
Kreger, L., *470*
Kreiger, M. J., 218, *457*
Kritchevsky, M., 86, *457*
Kroger, R. O., 378, *457*
Kroger, W., 288, *457*
Krohn, W., 58, *481*
Kroner, D. G., 181, *452*
Kropp, P. R., 8, 14, 74, 75, 157, 322, 404, 405, *456, 457, 476*
Kruesi, M. J., 40, *457*
Krupp, L. B., 40, *457*
Kubie, L. S., 289, *443*
Kuehn, C. V., 32, *430*
Kulka, R. A., 142, *479*
Kunce, J. T., 346, *429*
Kuncel, R., 119, *439*
Kuplicki, F. P., 297, *457*
Kurtz, R., 323, *458*
Kurzhals, R., *448*
Kwentus, J. A., 239, 244, 249, *458*

Labelle, L., 293, *463*
Labouvie, E. W., 114, *488*
Lacey, J. H., 35, *458*
Lachar, D., 162, 185, 186n, 188, 188n, 189, 189n, 192, 196, 203n, 204n, *458, 489, 490*
Lacoursiere, R. B., 28, *458*
Ladinsky, M., *468*
Laferriere, N., 4, 305, *478*
La Greca, A. M., 154, 159, 161, 162, *458, 472*
Laird, S. B., 115, *485*
Lalumiére, M. L., 340, *458*
Lamb, D. G., 186, 187, 402, *433, 458*
Lambert, C., 242, 245, 247, *458*
Landis, E. E., 396, *434*
Landis, P., 366, *486*
Landress, H. J., 124, *465*
Landry v. Bill Garrett Chevrolet, Inc., 298, *458*
Lang, A. R., 114, 118, *470*

Lang, M., 155, *485*
Lang, P. J., 143, *458*
Langevin, A., *458*
Langevin, R., 328, 329, 333, 334, 336, 338, *458*
Lanier, K., 414, *440*
Lankshear, D. W., 159, *445*
Lanyon, R. I., 192, 336, 339, 347, 362, *440, 458*
Lanyon, R. L., 217, 367, *485*
Larkin, A. R., 53, *458*
Larrabee, G. J., 224, *458*
Larsen, L., *433*
Larsen, L. H., 178, 180, *488*
Lasko, N. B., 144, *469*
Lassen, G., 91, 376, *435*
Lassiter, G. D., 226, 414, *440*
Latham, L., *448*
Laughlin, H. P., 9, *459*
Laurence, J. H., 293, *459*
Lawry, S. S., 345, *427*
Laws, D. R., 341, 347, *459, 473*
Lawson, K. A., 91, *451*
Layden, M., 145, *459*
Lazarus, A. A., 407, *440*
Lebowitz, M. R., 32, *459*
Lee, G. P., 230, *459*
Lees–Haley, P. R., 58, 71, 77, 177, 192, 193, 206, 233, 235, 422, *441, 445, 448, 459*
Lehman, R. A. W., 134, 225, 385, *451*
Leichtman, M. D., 105, *437*
Leininger, B. E., 91, *449*
Leitch, A., 297, *459*
Lender, J., 360, 368, *451*
Lennox, W. G., 287, *459*
Lester, B. M., 70, *444*
Leung, A., 266, *459*
Levin, H. S., 93, 137, 225, 226, 232, *447, 459*
Levin, S. M., 218, *457*
Levine, D. M., *467*
Levine, L., 305, *444*
Levinson, M. R., 118, *460*
Levitou, L. C., 407, *438*
Lewinsohn, P. M., 50, *460*
Lewis, R. A., 122, *487*
Lewis, E., 305, *444*

Lewis, M., 156, *460*
Lezak, M. D., 91, 230, *460*
Libbin, A. E., 253, *460*
Liberty, P. G., Jr., *460*
Lidz, C. W., 2, *460*
Liff, C. D., 4, 90, 134, 225, 228, 230, 324, 375, 376, 403, 418, *476*
Lifton, P. D., 266, *460*
Lilienfeld, S. O., 267, 274, 276, 278, *428, 460*
Lilly, M. A., *459*
Linblad, A. D., 8, 75, 321, 323, *460*
Lindemann, E., 239, *460*
Lindsay, D. S., 104, 105, 292, *460, 487*
Link, B. G., 55, *460*
Links, P. S., 27, *460*
Linn, L., 244, *487*
Linssen, A. C., 42, *491*
Lipman, F. D., 135, 138, *460*
Lipscomb, T. J., 105, *460*
Lipton, J. P., 287, *460*
Lishman, W. A., 136, *460*
Littlepage, G., 412, *460*
Llewellyn, J., 59, 134, *454*
Loch, J., 249, *454*
Loftus, E. F., 4, 39, 103, 104, 105, 106, 146, 287, 288, 292, 293, 294, *437, 439, 446, 448, 452, 461, 464, 479, 487*
Loftus, E. R., 295, *489*
Logan, W. S., 397, *461*
Lombard, E. A., 90, *489*
Lorei, T. W., 4, 388, *461*
Lorenz, W. F., 239, *461*
Loring, D. W., 230, *459*
Lowe, B., 158, *474*
Luborsky, L., 117, *464*
Lunneborg, C. E., *460*
Lutz, R. W., 336, 339, 347, *458*
Luxenberg, M. G., 346, *443*
Lykken, D. T., 253, 254, 257, 258, 260, 262, *453, 461*
Lynch, B. E., 90, *461*
Lynch, J. K., 155, *463*
Lynett, E., 5, 70, 77, *475*
Lynn, E. J., 28, 146, 147, 148, *461*
Lynn, S. J., 186, 288, 293, 294, *448, 461, 481, 487*

Lyon, L. S., 88, *461*
Lyons, J. A., 143, 149, *461*

Maag, J. W., 115, *461*
MacAndrew, C., 117, 118, *461*
Macciocchi, S. N., *431*
MacDonald, H., 284, *466*
MacDonald, J. M., 59, 60, 112, 241, 242, 247, *462*
MacDonald, P., 98, *434*
MacDonald, S., 124, *462*
Machamer, J. E., 232, *441*
MacKinnon, D. W., 283, *431*
MacLeish, R., 158, *462*
Madlafousek, J., 342, *457*
Maier, N. R. S., 412, *462*
Maiuro, R. D., 346, *449*
Makaremi, A., 160, *462*
Malitz, S., 244, *487*
Malloy, P. R., 142, *456*
Malmquist, C. P., 105, 106, *462*
Maloney, M. P., 178, *462*
Maloney, M. T., 134, *462*
Mamon, J. A., *467*
Mandel, A., 91, *440*
Mandler, G., 96, *447*
Manley, S., 108, *446*
Mann, A. W., *477*
Mansouri, L., 2, *462*
Marceil, J. C., 407, *462*
Marcos, L. R., 241, *462*
Marcum, J. M., 244, *462*
Margalit, C., 388, *473*
Mark, M., 388, *473*
Marks, P. A., 194, 387, *462*
Marlatt, G. A., 111, 113, 116, 319, *430, 465, 466*
Marlowe, D., 12, 73, *439, 488*
Marquis, K. H., 287, *462*
Marriage, K., 246, *462*
Marsh, H., 245, *462*
Marshall, J., 287, *462*
Marshall, W. L., 331, 341, 347, *442, 487, 490*
Marston, A., 323, 352, 355, 357, 419, *431*
Martin, J. L., 40, *467*
Martin, M. J., 138, *462*

Martin, P. P., 159, *441*
Martin, R. C., 230, *459*
Martin, R. D., 37, *462*
Martines, K. A., 119, *435*
Mash, E. J., 158, 159, *462*
Matarazzo, J. D., 224, 225, *462*
Matthews, C. G., 251, *462*
Mattis, S., 86, *446*
Maurice-Williams, R. S., 245, *462*
Mavissakalian, M., 347, *427*
May, M. A., 170, 266, *450*
Mayer, J., 115, *463*
Mayfield, D., 115, *463*
Mayo, J. P., 31, *463*
Mazmanian, D., 12, *463*
Mazzeri, L., 90, *477*
McAllister, L. W., 170, 182, *463*
McAllister, T. W., 137, *463*
McAnulty, R. D., 344, *463*
McCaffrey, R. J., 148, 149, 155, 186, *443, 463*
McCall, W. V., 240, 244, *463*
McCallister, H. A., 105, *460*
McCann, T., 293, 294, *463*
McCarthy, B. R., 125, *452*
McCloskey, M., 104, *463*
McClure, R. F., 42, *463*
McConaughy, S. H., 155, *427*
McConkey, K. M., 284, 293, *431, 463, 480*
McCracken, L. M., 92, 184, 230, *445, 453*
McCrae, R. R., 171, 273, 276, 411, *438, 463*
McCranie, E. J., 40, *463*
McDaniel, J. S., 32, *463*
McDaniel, M. A., 270, *463*
McDermott, K. B., 104 *474*
McDonald, A., 244, 246, *464*
McDonald, J. R., 136, *477*
McDonald, W. M., 240, *463*
McDonell, K., 32, *463*
McElheran, W. G., 185, *490*
McEvoy, L., *474*
McFarlane, A., 142, *472*
McGrath, M. J., 94, *432*
McGrew, J., 121, *484*
McHugh, P. R., 50, 103, *444, 464*
McKay, S. E., 412, *467*

McKee, G. R., 10, 73, 325, *476*
McKenna, T., 118, *487*
McKillip, J., 110, *471*
McKinley, J. C., 72, 335, 411, *451, 464*
McKinney, W. T., 123, *485*
McLachlan, D. R., 104, *478*
McLean, J., 293, *482*
McLellan, A. T., 117, *464*
McLellan, D. L., 87, *455*
McLeod, G., 115, *463*
McMordie, W. R., 224, 233, *464*
McNiel, D. E., 37, *433*
McVaugh, W., 162, 163, 352, *449*
McVaugh, W. H., *464*
Meadow, R., 36, *464*
Meadow, R. S., 36, *480*
Means, B., 106, *464*
Mednick, S., 69, *464*
Meehl, P. E., 170, 171, 259, 281n, 384, 411, *439, 464*
Megargee, E. I., 114, 118, 182, 195, *464, 470*
Meiselas, H., *483*
Meisner, S., 213, 219, 220, *464*
Mellor, S., *464*
Meloy, J. R., 68, 69, 70, 73, 74, 76, *446, 447, 464*
Melton, R., 150, 151, *464*
Mendelsohn, S. R., 253, *460*
Mendelson, G., 6, 37, 131n, 140, 141, *464*
Mendelson, W. B., 40, *457*
Mendonca, J. D., 12, *463*
Menninger, K. A., 30, 33, 297, *464, 470*
Merback, K., 150, *464*
Merrett, J. D., 136, *477*
Merrin, E. L., 32, *464*
Merritt, K. A., 105, *465*
Merskey, H., 224, 292, *465*
Mesmer, F. A., 283, *465*
Meyer, P., 170, *465*
Meyer, R. G., 323, 404, *433, 458*
Mezzich, J., *438*
Mezzich, J. E., *482*
Miceli, M., 153, *480*
Michel, D., 146, *429*
Michelli, J., 323, 352, 355, 357, 419, *431*
Mieczkowski, T., 124, 125, *465*
Mikkelsen, E. J., 29, 111, 123, 334, *465*

Milano, M., 294, *461*
Milanovich, J. R., 231, *465*
Miliotis, P., 86, *436, 468*
Miller, A. R., 91, *446*
Miller, B. L., 54, *439*
Miller, D., 41, *455*
Miller, D. G., 104, *461*
Miller, G. A., 111, 120, 121, *465*
Miller, G. R., 154, *465*
Miller, H., 6, 7, 37, 58, 133, 134, 140, 223, 224, 244, *465*
Miller, H. R., 118, 119, *465*
Miller, J. P., *442*
Miller, L. J., 53, *465*
Miller, T. R., 412, *465*
Miller, W. R., 111, 116, 117, 319, *447, 466*
Millis, S. R., 95, 99, 227, 230, 231, *466*
Millon, T., 73, 77, 119, 170, 195, 201, *466*
Mills, C. J., 108, *466*
Mills, M. J., 56, 323, 352, 355, 357, 419, *428, 431*
Millsaps, C., 94, 231, *466*
Milner, B., 86, 93, 105, *466, 479*
Minami, M., 120, *456*
Miner, M. H., 330, *441*
Mirin, S. M., 116, *448*
Misra, S. L., 249, *447*
Mitchell, C. N., 109, 112, *476*
Mitchell, J., 53, 54, *466*
Mitchell, K., 277, *460*
Mitchell, K. E., 278, *428*
Mittenberg, W., 94, 99, 137, 231, *466*
Mittman, B. L., 214, *466*
Mitton, J., 27, *460*
Moan, S. F., 105, *478*
Modai, I., 388, *473*
Modell, J. G., 38, *466*
Modlin, H., 38, 139, 141, *466*
Moeller, M. R., 129, *466*
Molinder, I., 335, *468*
Monahan, J., 2, 55, *466, 484*
Monroe, K., 180, *433*
Monteiro, K. P., 284, *466*
Moore, D. J., 31, *457*
Moore, R. A., 114, *467*
Moore, R. D., 112, 126, *467*
Moore, R. H., 118, *467*
Moore, R. T., 94, 230, *433*

Moore, R. Y., 86, *483*
Moraitis, S., 140, *430*
Moreland, K. L., 266, *467*
Morency, N. L., 154, 156, *467*
Morey, L. C., 170, 173, 195, 201, 202, 323, 382, 423, *467, 476*
Morgan, A. H., 284, *467, 477*
Morgan, J. P., 124, *467*
Mori, E., 87, *490*
Morse, R. M., 114, *484*
Mortensen, E. L., 86, *446*
Morval, M., 4, 305, *478*
Moscovitch, M., 96, *467*
Moses, J. A., 412, *467*
Moss, A. J., 106, *437*
Mott, R. H., 50, 51, 52, 54, *467*
Moulton, J., 136, *467*
Mount, M. K., 267, 274, 275, *431, 469*
Mountz, J. M., 38, *466*
Mouton, G. J., 421, *467*
Moxham, E., 416, *486*
Mudrak, P., *450*
Mulhern, S., 294, *467*
Mullen, P. E., 40, *467*
Mundt, D. H., Jr., 279, *432*
Murphy, J. M., *467*
Murphy, K. R., 264, 268, 278, *467*
Murphy, W. D., 333, 346, 347, *467*
Murray, H. A., 283, *431*
Murrey, G. L., 294, *467*
Muscio, B., 287, *467*
Muskin, P. R., 42, *484*
Myer, J., *438*
Myers, B., 162, 288, *461*

Nadel, L., 105, *468*
Nadelson, T., 26, 31, 33, 43, *468*
Nadon, R., 293, *459*
Nakahara, Y., 125, *468*
Nannis, E. D., 266, *460*
Nantau, K., 91, *440*
Naples, M., 239, *468*
Nasman, V. T., 90, *477*
Nathan, P. W., 88, *477*
Nation, P. C., 192, *441*
National Institute on Drug Abuse, 108, *468*
National Institute of Mental Health, *468*

Natoli, L., 94, 230, *432*
Neal, J., 353, 354, 355, 357, 359, *479*
Neisser, U., 106, *486*
Nelson, G. M., 341, *450*
Nelson, R. O., 158, *443*
Netter, B. E. C., 215, 220, *468*
Newcomb, M. D., 108, *468*
Newel, R., 124, *465*
Newman, J. P., 276, *481*
Newman, T. B., 356, *435*
Nicholas, D., 194, 424, *449*
Nicholas, E., 105, *478*
Nicholi, A. M., Jr., 235, *481*
Nichols, D. S., 174, 198n, 199, 199n, 200, 203n, 204n, 206, 377, *430, 468*
Nichols, H. R., 335, *468*
Nicholson, R. A., 421, *467*
Nogrady, H., 293, *459*
Norris, M. P., 230, *449*
Novack, D. H., 23, *468*
Noyes, H. L., 108, *466*
Nussbaum, D., 365, 384, *476*

O'Bannon, R. M., 253, 266, 267, 268, 269, 278, 279, 280, *468*
O'Brien, C. P., 117, *464*
O'Connor, E., 53, *465*
O'Connor, M., 86, *468*
O'Dell, J. W., 170, 182, *455*
O'Malley, P. M., 109, *430*
O'Neill, B., 123, *469*
O'Neill, M. T., 342, *452*
O'Sullivan, M., 226, *442*
Ober, B. A., 95, *440*
Oddy, M., 224, *468*
Ofshe, R. I., 103, 292, *468*
Ofshe, R. J., 39, *468*
Ogloff, J. R., 24, 34, 332, *468*
Olkinuora, M., 235, *468*
Olson, R. E., 119, *439*
Ones, D. S., 267, 268, 270, 272, 273, 274, 275, 276, 277, 279, 280, *469*
Orenczuk, S., 91, *440*
Orfali, J. S., 124, *472*
Orleans, J. F., *451*
Orndoff v. Lockhart, 296, *468*
Ornduff, S. R., 14, 195, *476*

Orne, E, C., 284, 289, 300, *469, 480*
Orne, M., 289, *469*
Orne, M. T., 242, 284, 286, 288, 291, 295, 296, 300, *469*
Ornstein, P. A., 105, *465*
Orr, S. P., 143, 144, *469, 472, 480*
Ortins, J. B., 118, *473*
Osborn, C. A., 345, *427*
Oskamp, S., 287, *462*
Ossipov, V. P., 59, 407, *469*
Otto, R. K., 114, 118, *470*
Overholser, J. C., 25, *470*

Pahwa, S., *452*
Paitich, D., *458*
Pallmeyer, T. P., 143, *434*
Palmer, J. C., 104, 287, *461*
Pankratz, L., 27, 91, 147, 150, 223, 225, 228, 235, 236, 396, 407, *433, 442, 470*
Pankratz, L. D., 148, *482*
Papanicolaou, A., *459*
Parker, N., 133, 140, *470*
Partyka, L. B., 70, *444*
Parwatikar, S. D., 297, *470*
Patrick, C. J., 252, 253, 255, 256, 257, 259, 260, 261, 263, 268, 276, 400, *453, 470*
Patterson, G. R., 70, *470*
Patterson, M., 118, *490*
Paulhus, D., 12, *485*
Pearlson, G. D., *470*
Pearson, P. R., 159, *445*
Peck, C. J., 140, *470*
Peck, R. E., 249, *470*
Peed, S., 91, 228, 407, *470*
Pena, M., 123, *485*
Pendergrast, M., 243, *470*
Pendleton, L., 118, *490*
People v. Boudin, Ind., 295, *471*
People v. Buono, 300, *471*
People v. Cornell, 298, *471*
People v. Ebanks, 295, *471*
People v. Harper, 295, *471*
People v. Hurd, 296, *471*
People v. Marsh, 298, *471*
People v. McBroom, 298, *471*

People v. McNichol, 298, *471*
People v. Milner, 297, *471*
People v. Ritchie, 298, *471*
People v. Shirley, 296, *471*
People v. Thompson, 297, *471*
People v. Worthington, 298, *471*
Perconte, S. T., 149, *471*
Perl, M., 42, *480*
Perner, J., 156, *489*
Perrin, S., 137, 143, *461, 466*
Perry, C., 293, *459*
Perry, G. F., 224, *440*
Perry, G. G., 208, 214, 219, 220, 221, *471*
Perry, J. C., 9, 239, 245, *471*
Persinger, M. A., 39, *471*
Peters, J. M., 333, 346, 347, *467*
Petersen, E., 194, *471*
Peterson, G. W., 195, *471*
Peterson, J. M., 41, *432*
Peterson, S. A., 421, *467*
Pettigrew, C. G., 211, 220, 374, *471*
Petzel, T., 110, *471*
Pezzullo, J. C., *468*
Pfohl, B., 77, 320, *471*
Phillips, M. R., 28, *471*
Pickering, J. W., 211, 375, *471*
Pierri, J., 111, *440*
Pillemer, D. B., 105, *472*
Pinch, D., 230, *481*
Pineault, T., 412, *460*
Piper, A., 242, 243, *472*
Pitman, R. K., 142, 143, 144, *469, 472, 480*
Pittman, R. L., 143, *461*
Platt, M., 192, *441*
Plum, F., 244, 245, *472*
Plummer, B., 117, *455*
Pollack, S., 133, *472*
Polster, M. R., 104, *446*
Poole D. A., 292, *460*
Pope, H. G., 24, 26, 27, 28, 34, 39, 43, 48, 49, 139, 157, 408, *454, 472, 489*
Pope, K. S., *472*
Posner, J. B., 244, 245, *472*
Post, R. M., 28, *472*
Potter, B. A., 124, *472*
Powel, J., 92, 228, 407, *445*
Powell, K. E., 50, 54, 60, 145, *472*

Power, D. J., 286, 287, *472*
Prendergast, P., 320, *475*
Prescott, C. A., 118, *447*
Preston, D. L., 332, *430*
Price, G. E., 287, *472*
Price, J. D., 160, *457*
Price, J. R., 77, *448*
Price, K. P., 137, *472*
Prigatano, G. P., 229, *472*
Prince, M., 285, *472*
Proctor, W. C., 341, *450*
Proctor, W. D., 347, *449*
Protter, B., 33, 46, 47, 63, 68, *485*
Pruess, M. G., 346, *473*
Puffett, A., 88, 245, *457*
Purtilo, D. T., *452*
Putnam, F. W., 28, *472*
Putnam, S. H., 95, 227, 230, *466*
Putnam, W. H., 242, 288, *472*
Pyle, C. H., 254, *472*

Qian, J., 90, 263, *477*
Quaglino v. California, 295, *472*
Quay, H. C., 154, *472*
Quinlan, D. M., *451*
Quinn, K. M., 64, 154, 156, 157, *473*
Quinsey, V. L., 331, 340, 341, 346, 347, *458, 473, 474*

Rabinowitz, S., 388, *473*
Rabins, R. V., *470*
Racansky, I. G., 342, *434*
Rachal, J. V., 109, *430*
Rada, R. T., 29, *447*
Radtke, H. L., 286, *482*
Radtke, R. C., 93, *437*
Rakfeldt, J., *451*
Rakic, P., 105, *442*
Raskin, D. C., 255, 256, 258, 260, 261, *452, 473*
Ratcliff, K., 77, *474*
Rathbun, L., 105, *439*
Rathus, S. A., 118, *473*
Ravitz, L. J., 57, 143, 243, *473*
Rawling, P., 231, *473*
Rawls, R., 143, *461*

Ray, I., 59, *473*
Reales, J. M., 426, *473*
Rector, N., 25, *475*
Redlich, R. C., 57, 143, 243, *473*
Reed, A., *488*
Reed, M. R., 231, *435*
Rees, W. L., 242, 245, 247, *458*
Reich, P., 26, 235, *473*
Reich, W., 141, *441*
Reid, J. E., 59, *453*
Reid, R., 115, *461*
Reid, W. H., 74, *473*
Reiser, M., 288, *473*
Resnick, P. J., 27, 57, 62, 74, 130, 351, 360, 361, 364, 401, *439, 473*
Retzlaff, P. D., 201, 356, *474*
Reuterfors, D. L., 397, *461*
Rey, A., 91, 93, 376, *474*
Reynolds, C. R., 163, *474*
Reynolds, S. K., 186, 402, *488*
Reynolds, W. M., 154, *474*
Rhode, R., 213, *455*
Rhue, J. W., 288, *461*
Rice, M. E., 331, 332, *437, 474*
Richlin, D. M., 140, *441*
Rickarby, G. A., 139, *474*
Ricker, J. H., 231, *466*
Riddle, E. E., 288, *483*
Rieke, M. L., 268, 269, 270, 277, *449, 474*
Rienzo, D., 343, *445*
Ries, R. K., 28, *471*
Rigler, C. T. J., 139, *474*
Rim, S. B., 158, *474*
Rimel, R., *431*
Ring, K., 8, 332, *434*
Ripley, H. S., 242, 247, 288, *474*
Ritson, B., 27, 59, 408, *474*
Robbins, E., 307, *483*
Robbins, L., 16, 354, 355, 357, 416, *450*
Roberts, A. H., 41, *444*
Robey, A., 298, *457*
Robins, L. N., 77, 116, 319, *442, 474*
Robinson, B., 185, 330, *441*
Robinson, L. H., 185, *488*
Robitcher, J. B., 2, *474*
Rock v. Arkansas, 296, *474*
Rockwell, R. B., 294, *474*
Rodgers, A., 155, *455*

Rodin, G., 26, *483, 484*
Rodin, G. M., *483*
Roe, A. V., 211, 364, *479*
Roediger, H. L., 104, *474*
Rogers, M. L., 191, *441*
Rogers, R., 2, 4, 5, 7, 8, 9, 10, 11, 12, 13, 14, 14*n*, 16, 18, 19*n*, 24, 25, 26, 27, 34, 43, 46, 47, 48, 49, 52, 53, 61, 65, 68, 69, 70, 71, 72, 73, 74, 75, 77, 78, 79, 82, 84, 90, 98, 108, 109, 112, 116, 117, 119, 122, 125, 134, 146, 154, 157, 164, 165, 166*n*, 174, 177, 181, 184, 185, 186, 187, 188, 191, 193, 194, 195, 197, 199, 202, 225, 226, 228, 230, 239, 242, 247, 301, 303, 306, 307, 308, 309, 310, 311*n*, 312*n*, 314*n*, 315*n*, 317*n*, 318*n*, 319, 320, 321, 322, 323, 324, 325, 327, 328, 329, 330, 331, 332, 339, 340, 341, 350, 351, 353, 354, 355, 356, 357, 364, 365, 368, 369, 373, 374, 375, 376, 379, 380, 382, 383, 384, 385, 388, 392, 394, 398, 399, 401, 402, 403, 404, 409, 410, 411, 413, 416, 417, 418, 419, 423, 424, 425, *430, 437, 441, 443, 446, 455, 456, 457, 474, 475, 476, 478, 480, 486*
Rohling, M. L., 224, *433*
Rohsenow, D. J., 122, *476*
Roman, P. M., 124, *462*
Romans, S. E., 40, *467*
Romney, D. M., 185, *490*
Rosanoff, A. J., 138, 139, *476*
Rose, F. E., 90, 98, 229, 376, *476*
Rosen, A., 259, *464*
Rosen, T. H., 108, *476*
Rosenberg, C. E., 63, *477*
Rosenberg, D. A., 36, *477*
Rosenberg, S. J., 209, 219, *477*
Rosenblatt, A. I., 114, 118, *470*
Rosenblum, M. L., 143, *439*
Rosenfeld, J. P., 90, 263, *454, 477*
Rosenhan, D., 49, 59, 302, 401, 414, *477*
Rosenthal, R., 50, *447*
Roske, A., 76, *446*
Ross, B. L., 232, *441*
Ross, D., 154, *437*
Ross, H. E., 114, 116, *446, 477*

Ross, R. J., 145, *477*
Rothaus, P., 34, *487*
Rothke, S. E., 190, *477*
Rothman, A. L., 235, *477*
Rothstein, M., 267, *485*
Rouleau, J. L., 417, *427*
Rounsaville, B. J., 108, 116, *477, 489*
Routhieaux, B. C., 104, *446*
Rowan, C., 63, *477*
Rowlett, D. B., 245, *487*
Royston, C., 140, *485*
Rubinsky, E., 91, 376, *435*
Rubinsky, E. W., 85, *477*
Rubio, R., 287, 288, *479*
Ruch, J. C., 284, *477*
Ruff, R. M., 235, *477*
Rule, B. G., 137, *429*
Rumans, L. W., 32, *477*
Russell, J. L., 27, *444*
Russell, W. R., 88, *477*
Russon, A., *458*
Rutherford, W. H., 136, *477*
Rutter, M., 70, *477*
Ryan, A. M., 277, *477*

Saavedra-Castillo, A., *482*
Sabin, J. E., 2, *478*
Sabini, J., 153, *480*
Sabourin, S., 4, 305, *446, 478*
Sachs, H., 129, *466*
Sachs, M. H., 55, *478*
Sackett, P. R., 265, 266, 267, 268, 269, 270, 272, 277, 278, *477, 478*
Sadock, B. J., 249, *455*
Sadoff, R. L., 145, 287, *478*
Sadow, L., 408, *478*
Sahd, D., 29, *447*
Saidi, P., 32, *484*
Salekin, R. T., 4, 6, 14, 69, 71, 184, 303, 324, 328, 380, 383, 385, 423, *475, 478*
Samenow, S., 70, *489*
Sanders, S., 363, *478*
Santiago-Rivera, A. L., 2, *428*
Sarbin, J. E., *478*
Sarbin, T. R., 282, 283, *445, 478*

Sarfaty, S. D., 228, *445*
Sargant, W., 88, *478*
Satow, Y., 319, *448*
Saunders, L. S., 142, 143, *472*
Sauser, W. I., 266, *478*
Sax, D. S., *436*
Saywitz, K. J., 105, *478*
Schacter, D. L., 87, 88, 96, 97, 98, 104, *478, 479*
Schafer, D. W., 287, 288, *479*
Schafer, E., 135, 142, *479*
Schefflen, N. A., 224, *429*
Schilder, P., 87, *427*
Schinka, J. A., 354, 355, 357, *481*
Schlaepfer, T. B., *470*
Schlenger, W. E., 142, *479*
Schlottmann, R. S., 185, 192, *452, 490*
Schmaling, K. B., 41, *479*
Schmeidler, D., 284, *443*
Schmidt, F. L., 267, 268, 270, 272, 273, 275, 277, *453, 469*
Schmidt, M., 95, 99, *486*
Schmolck, P., 174, *468*
Schneck, J. M., 48, 289, *479*
Schneider, D. L., 276, *436*
Scholz, C. K., 224, *429*
Schonberger, L. B., *452*
Schooler, J. W., 104, *461, 479*
Schooley, R. T., *452*
Schouten, P. G., 340, *481*
Schreiber, F. R., 285, *479*
Schretlen, D., 91, 183, 184, 192, 231, 353, 354, 355, 356, 357, 358, 359, 368, 369, *479*
Schretlen, D. J., 85, 208, 232, 351, *479*
Schubert, D. S. P., 118, *489*
Schwartz, G. E., 41, *432*
Schwartz, L., 230, *429*
Schwartz, L. A., 146, *479*
Schwartz, R. H., 110, *489*
Scott, A. B., 192, *452*
Scott, R. L., 422, *441*
Scoville, W. B., 105, *479*
Scriven, M., 407, *479*
Scully, D., 334, *479*
Seamons, D. T., 211, 216, 219, 220, 364, *479*
Sears, R. R., 285, *479*

Seat, P. D., 162, *489*
Sechrest, L., 396, *479*
Sechrest, L. B., 265, *446*
Seelen, J., 157, *472*
Seely, R. K., 346, *443*
Seeman, W., 194, 387, *462*
Seifer, R., 117, *455*
Seigel, R. K., 50, *480*
Selzer, M. A., 4, *437*
Selzer, M. L., 112, 113, *480*
Serin, R. C., 332, *430*
Sethi, I. C., 249, *447*
Seto, M. C., 332, *430*
Sewell, K. W., 4, 5, 6, 14, 61, 68, 69, 70, 71, 72, 77, 78, 122, 164, 166*n*, 174, 177, 184, 185, 195, 202, 206, 303, 324, 328, 356, 365, 380, 382, 383, 385, 399, 416, 423, 424, *437, 475, 476, 478, 480*
Shackleton, H., 231, 376, *449*
Shadish, W. R., 407, *438*
Shalev, A. Y., 144, *480*
Shanley, L. A., 170, *437*
Shapiro, B., 53, *429*
Shavzin, A. R., 210, 216, 220, *436*
Sheehan, E. P., 201, *474*
Sheehan, P. W., 284, 286, 293, 294, *463, 480*
Shelp, F. E., 42, 240, *463, 480*
Shepherd, J. B., *450*
Sheppard, K., 76, *446*
Sherman, J., 216, *443*
Sherman, M., 50, 60, 73, 302, 305, *447, 480*
Sherry, S., 145, *486*
Shimamine, M., 125, *468*
Shimamura, A. P., 97, 104, *454, 480*
Shoichet, R. P., 243, 244, 245, *480*
Shondrick, D. D., 340, *450*
Shor, R. E., 283, 284, *480*
Sicuro, F., *478*
Siegler, I. C., *463*
Sierles, F. S., 33, 76, *480*
Sigal, M., 36, *480*
Silberman, E. K., 28, *472*
Silver, M., 153, *480*
Silverman, R., 32, *449*
Silvers, K. N., 54, *428*

Silverton, L., 368, 423, *480*
Simon, G. E., 41, *480*
Simon, W. T., 340, *481*
Simons, L. E., 192, *441*
Simpson, A. J., 426, *481*
Simpson, E., 126, *430*
Simpson, G., 123, *481*
Singer, H., 58, *481*
Singer, M. T., 103, 292, *468*
Sivec, H. J., 186, *481*
Sjoberg, B. M., Jr., 286, *488*
Skare, S. S., *442*
Skinner, H. A., 112, 114, 116, *446, 477, 481*
Skodol, A. E., 8, *481*
Slaby, A. E., *481*
Slade, P., 90, *430*
Slater, E., 88, *478*
Sledge, W. H., *451*
Slick, D., 230, *481*
Slovik, L. S., 36, *448*
Small, G. W., 31, 235, *440, 481*
Small, I. F., 50, 51, 52, *467, 481*
Small, J. G., 50, *481*
Smart, R. G., 111, *481*
Smith, B. H., 138, *481*
Smith, B. M., 240, 247, 249, *435, 449, 481, 484*
Smith, B. N., 140, *456*
Smith, E., 141, *441*
Smith, G. P., 351, 353, 354, 355, 357, 364, 368, 419, *481*
Smith, G. T., 178, *488*
Smith, H. H., 134, 225, 233, 385, *451, 459*
Smith, M. L., 86, *481*
Smith, M. P., 87, *455*
Smith, S., 235, *442*
Smith, S. A., 97, *453*
Smith, S. M., 286, 287, 297, *434*
Smith, S. S., 276, *481*
Sneed, R. C., 31, *481*
Snowdon, J., 28, *481*
Snyder, D. K., 122, *456*
Snyder, S., 35, *482*
Sobell, L. C., 123, 126, *482*
Sobell, M. B., 123, 126, *482*
Sogi, C., 26, *482*
Solomons, R., 28, *481*

Song, L., 90, 477
Soniat, T. L., 139, *482*
Soskis, D., 289, *469*
Spanos, N. P., 282, 284, 286, 288, 293, 294, *431, 482*
Sparadeo, F. R., 227, *449*
Sparks, P. J., 41, *480*
Sparr, L. F., 27, 142, 146, 147, 148, *429, 472, 482*
Spector, R. S., 295, *482*
Speedie, L., 86, *482*
Spellacy, F., 231, *484*
Speth, E., 76, *446*
Spicker, B., 105, *465*
Spiegel, D., 27, 289, 296, *468, 482*
Spiegel, H., 284, 296, *469, 482*
Spirito, A., 153, *445*
Spiro, H. R., 25, 30, *483*
Spitzer, M., 55, *483*
Spitzer, R. L., 18, 42, 77, 116, 307, 320, 401, *442, 481, 484, 489*
Spivak, H., 26, *483*
Sprehe, D. J., 37, *483*
Squire, L. R., 86, 96, 97, 104, 105, *447, 454, 480, 483*
Stafford v. Maynard, 296, *483*
Stalnaker, J. M., 288, *483*
Stangl, D., 77, 320, *471*
Stanhope, N., 88, 245, *457*
Stanley, J. C., 407, *436*
Starkey, T. W., 146, *429*
State ex rel. Collins v. Superior Court,, 296, *483*
State ex rel. Sheppard v. Koblentz,, 298, *483*
State v. Alley, 297, *483*
State v. Armstrong, 296, *483*
State v. Bianchi, 300, *483*
State v. Hurd, 296, *483*
State v. Joly, 299, *483*
State v. Mack, 296, *483*
State v. McClendon, 297, *483*
State v. McQueen, 295, *483*
State v. Papp, 298, *483*
Statham, D., 293, *480*
Steblay, N. M., 295, *483*
Steer, R. A., 123, *454*
Steffy, R. A., 334, *450*
Stein, L. A. R., 157, 164, *483*

Stein, R. M., 343, *432*
Steinberg, J., 243, *441*
Steiner, B. W., 342, *434*
Steiner, M., 27, *460*
Stephens, R. C., 125, *444, 483*
Stephens, R. S., 113, *430*
Stermac, L., 208, 211, *483*
Stern, M., 30, *439*
Stern, T. A., 407, *483*
Sternbach, R. A., 41, *444*
Stevens, H., 243, 244, 245, *484*
Stevenson, I., 240, 247, *435, 449, 481, 484*
Stewart, M. A., 70, *484*
Stewart, M. J., 126, *430*
Stiebel, V. G., 243, *484*
Stiff, J. B., 154, *465*
Stinchfield, R. D., 110, 120, *489*
Stipek, D. J., 157, *484*
Stokes, E. J., *466, 467*
Stoltzman, R., *474*
Stone, A. A., 63, *484*
Stone, J. I., 226, 414, *440*
Stone, T., 33, *444*
Stone-Romero, E. F., 267, *460*
Stouthamer-Loeber, M., 70, 154, 159, *484*
Straker, D., 32, *430*
Straus, S. E., 40, *452, 457*
Strauss, D. H., 42, *484*
Strauss, E., 230, 231, *481, 484*
Strauss, J. S., 55, *478*
Streiner, D. L., 118, 119, *465*
Stuart, G. L., 52, *485*
Stueve, C. A., 55, *460*
Stuss, D. T., 88, *484*
Suffield, B., 91, *440*
Sugarman, L. A., 244, *487*
Sullivan, K. A., 145, *477*
Sumpter, J., 185, *488*
Sundberg, N. D., 266, *484*
Suslick, A., 408, *478*
Sussman, N., 30, *453*
Sutcliffe, J. P., 286, *484*
Sutherland, A., 26, *484*
Sutherland, A. J., *484*
Svanum, S., 121, *484*
Swanson, D. W., 41, *484*
Swanson, J., 55, *484*

Swartz, J. D., 266, *484*
Swartz, M., 55, *483*
Sweet, J., *476*
Sweet, J. J., 90, *477*
Swenson, W. M., 114, 346, *484*
Swets, J. A., 420, *484*
Swigar, M. E., 32, *484*
Swinson, R. P., 10, *438*
Szalda-Petree, D., 90, 229, 376, *476*
Szasz, T. S., 25, 33, *485*
Szucko, J. J., 261, *456*

Takahashi, K., 125, *468*
Talbot, R., 53, *443*
Tardi v. Henry, 298, *485*
Tarsh, M. J., 140, *485*
Tarter, R. E., 115, 117, *455, 485*
Tatsuoka, M. M., 335, *437*
Taylor, C. A., 117, 319, *465*
Taylor, K. L., 143, *455*
Taylor, P. J., 87, *449, 488*
Taylor, S., 23, 26, 32, *449, 488*
Tellegen, A., 77, 169, 172, *436*
Temkin, N. R., 232, *441*
Tennant, W., 235, *477*
Terdal, L. G., 158, 159, *462*
Terhune, W. B., 287, *472*
Terkelson, K., 4, *437*
Terr, L. C., 243, 292, *4853*
Tesser, A., 12, *485*
Tett, R. P., 267, 274, 275, *485*
Thacker, S. R., *432*
Thatcher, A., 65, 309, *476*
Thelen, M., 158, *445*
Thomas, R. G., 144, *456*
Thompson, G. N., 140, *485*
Thompson, J. S., 52, 66, *485*
Thompson, L. L., 236, *433*
Thornton, G. C., 10, *485*
Thurber, J. A., 412, *462*
Tilden, J., 286, *480*
Timbrook, R. E., 185, 192, *448, 485*
Timmons, L. A., 217, 367, *485*
Tisher, M., 155, *485*
Tizard, J., 70, *477*
Toglia, M., 154, *437*
Tom, A., 143, *439*

Toner, B. B., 195, *430*
Tonry, M., 289, *469*
Tosato, G., *452*
Toth, E. L., 29, *485*
Toth, S., 235, *470*
Travin, S., 33, 46, 47, 63, 68, *485*
Trethowan, W. H., 49, *429*
Trichter, J. G., 123, *485*
Trief, P., 50, 302, *480*
Trimble, M. R., 37, 130, 134, 135, 136,
    138, 139, 140, *433, 485*
Trueblood, W., 95, 99, 226, 229, 232, *485,*
    486
Truesdale, P., 293, *480*
Tulving, E., 87, *478*
Tuma, J. M., 211, 375, *471*
Tune, L. E., *470*
Turnbell, W., 378, *457*
Turner, R. E., 52, *476*
Tusel, D. J., 32, *465*
Twijnstra, A., 137, *434*

Udolf, R., 292, *486*
Uhlenhuth, E. H., 111, *440*
Ulrich, R. F., *438*
Underwager, R., 4, 39, 294, *486*
Underwood, B. J., 104, *486*
Unis, A. S., 155, *455*
United States Congressional Office of
    Technology Assessment, 264, 265,
    266, 268, 270, 272, 277, 278, 279,
    280, *489*
United States ex rel. Parson v. Anderson, 297,
    486
United States v. Adams, 296, *486*
United States v. Andrews, 296, *486*
United States v. Borum, 297, *486*
United States v. Gatto, 296, *486*
United States v. Miller, 295, *486*
United States v. Stevens, 295, *486*
United States v. Todd, 298, *486*
Usher, J. A., 106, *486*
Ustad, K. L., 5, 185, 195, 309, 310, 311*n*,
    312*n*, 314*n*, 315*n*, 317*n*, 318*n*, *323,* 382,
    423, *476, 486*
Uttley, D., 224, *468*

Valverde, J., *482*
Van, H. R., 42, *491*
Van Denburg, E. J., 170, *437*
van der Kolk, B., 145, *486*
Vanderspek, R., 123, *482*
Van Dyke, C., 32, *464*
Van Gorp, W. G., 91, 231, 358, *479*
Vannucci, C., 140, *441*
Vasa, S. F., 115, *461*
Victoroff, J. I., 32, *445*
Victoroff, V. M., 88, 247, *446*
Vierkant, A. D., 53, 54, *466*
Viglione, D., 194, *471*
Viglione, D. J., 73, 215, 220, 221, 366,
    416, *447, 468, 486*
Villanueva, M. R., 94, 230, *433*
Vincent, A., 24, 27, 43, *475*
Vincent, K. R., 139, *437*
Viswesvaran, C., 267, 268, 272, 273, 275,
    277, *469*
Vitaliano, P. P., 347, *449*
Vogt, A. T., 134, 225, 385, *451*
Vosti, K. L., 32, *477*

Wachspress, M., 59, 209, 219, 408, *486*
Wagner, E., 117, *455*
Wakefield, H., 4, 39, 294, *486*
Walbek, N. H., 346, *443*
Walker, J., 146, *429*
Walker, J. I., 150, *486*
Walker, M. L., 125, *444*
Wallach, J., 32, *486*
Waller, N. D., 266, *487*
Walters, G. D., 8, 185, 332, *487*
Wanberg, K. W., 120, 122, *453, 487*
Wang, P. L., 87, *478*
Ward, L. C., 34, 191, *487*
Ward, M. P., 134, *462*
Ward, N. G., 28, 245, *471, 487*
Ward, R., 331, *487*
Ware, J. E., Jr., 4, 12, *451*
Warrington, E. K., 93, 95, *430, 487*
Warthon, D., *482*
Washington v. Texas, 297, *487*
Wasyliw, O. E., 72, 215, 331, 336, 337,
    416, *446, 449, 451, 487*

Watkins, J. G., 300, *487*
Watson, R. J., 341, 343, *445*
Watts, D., 185, 192, *448, 485*
Webster, C. D., 388, *476*
Webster, S., 342, *452*
Wechsler, D., 94, *487*
Weed, N. C., 118, 192, *448, 487*
Weekes, J. R., 293, 294, *448, 461, 487*
Weekes, R., 288, *461*
Weighill, V. E., 140, *487*
Weihofen, H., 69, 76, *449*
Weinberg, D., 119, *439*
Weiner, J. L., 32, 184, *449*
Weingardt, K. R., 104, *487*
Weinstein, E. A., 244, 245, *487*
Weinstein, M. C., *467*
Weintraub, M. I., 235, *477*
Weiss, R. D., 116, *448*
Weissman, H. N., 37, *488*
Weissman, M. M., 116, *477*
Weitzenhoffer, A. M., 283, 284, 286, *488*
Wells, G. L., 287, *488*
Welsh, G. S., 169, 187, 346, *439*
Wertham, F., 48, *488*
Wessely, S., 40, 55, *488*
Wessinger, C., *488*
West, L. J., 50, *480*
Weston, W. A., *488*
Wetter, M. W., 4, 178, 180, 181, 185, 186, 187, 194, 196, 217, 325, 377, 383, 402, *430, 432, 433, 458, 488*
Wetzler, S., 73, *488*
Whalen, R., 90, *477*
Wheeler, K. G., 266, *488*
Whelihan, W., 227, 230, *449*
Whelton, J., 211, 375, *471*
Whipple, G. M., 287, *488*
Whipple, J., 294, *467*
White, A. J., 72, 385, *451*
White, H. R., 114, *488*
White, J., 156, *444*
White, K. D., 284, *463*
White, M. M., 283, *488*
White, R. W., 283, *488*
White, S. H., 105, *472*
White, T. W., 185, *487*
White v. Leyoub, 296, *488*

Whitmore, K., 70, *477*
Wickens, D. D., 96, *488*
Widiger, T. A., 187, *433*
Wiener, D. W., 72, 186n, 189n, 191, 192, 193, 196, 197, 199, *488*
Wierzbicki, M., 195, *489*
Wiggins, E. C., 92, 93, 95, 96, 97, 99, 100, *489*
Wiggins, J. S., 196, 197, 198n, 199, 200n, 200, 203n, 204n, 207, *489*
Wiggins, S. L., 90, *489*
Wijnen, G., 137, *434*
Wilcox, L., 228, *470*
Wilcox, R., 8, 332, *489*
Wilhelm, K. L., 403, *489*
Wilkening, G. N., 412, *467*
Wilkins, S. S., 231, 358, *479*
Wilkinson, L., 421, *437*
Williams, A. F., 123, *469*
Williams, C. L., 157, 169, 198, 199, *436, 483*
Williams, C. W., 233, *441, 459*
Williams, J. B. W., 116, 320, *483, 489*
Williams, J. M., 231, *432*
Williams, L. M., 4, 39, 106, *489*
Williams, R. B., Jr., *463*
Williams, S. G., 139, *437*
Williams, T., 319, *454*
Williams, T. A., 420, *454*
Willis, C. G., 266, *489*
Willis, S. C., 91, 94, 226, 228, 232, 266, *433*
Wilner, M., 241, *462*
Wilson, B., 86, *443*
Wilson, H., 116, *448*
Wilson, J. P., 146, 147 *489*
Wilson, L., 295, *489*
Wilson, S. C., 284, *431*
Wilson v. United States, 297, *489*
Wimmer, H., 156, *489*
Wing, H., 265, *446*
Winn, H. R., 232, *441*
Winograd, M., 33, *447*
Winslade, W. J., 2, *438*
Winters, K. C., 10, 110, 111, 115, 120, *451, 489*
Wirt, R. D., 162, *489*
Wirth, J. B., 47, *470*
Wirtz, P. W., 115, *450*

Wish, E., 125, 465
Wish, E. D., 124, 448
Wittchen, H. U., 489
Wodarski, J. S., 488
Wolf, A. W., 118, 490
Wolf, S., 242, 247, 288, 474
Wolff, S. M., 26, 428
Wong, C. K., 87, 88, 490
Wong, S., 332, 468
Wood, G. C., 41, 490
Woodforde, J. M., 224, 465
Woodruff, R., 244, 490
Woody, G. E., 117, 464
Woolley, R. M., 267, 273, 274, 276, 490
Wooten, A. J., 171, 490
Workman-Daniels, K., 460
Works, J., 474
Worthington, D. L., 185, 490
Worthington, T. S., 295, 490
Wortman, C. B., 435
Woszcyna, C., 334, 450
Woychyshyn, C. A., 185, 190, 490
Wraight, E. P., 86, 443
Wright, K., 244, 462
Wright, L. W., 344, 463
Wright, P., 334, 336, 338, 458
Wrightson, P., 136, 224, 231, 449, 490
Wrobel, T. A., 185, 186n, 188, 188n, 189,
    189n, 192, 196, 203n, 204n, 458, 490
Wydra, A., 347, 490
Wylie, T., 235, 477
Wynkoop, T. F., 92, 97, 100, 440

Yamadori, A., 87, 490
Yamashita, H., 87, 490
Yapko, M. D., 294, 490
Yeung, A., 153, 445
Yochelson, S., 70, 490
Yoneda, Y., 87, 490
Yonge, G. D., 411, 490
Young, A., 86, 455
Young, J., 218, 490
Youngjohn, J. R., 134, 227, 490
Youngner, S. J., 31, 457
Yudofsky, S., 71, 76, 491

Zacks, R. T., 96, 451
Zahn-Waxler, C., 160, 438
Zahner, G. E. P., 320, 491
Zamansky, H. S., 286, 456
Zanni, G., 104, 287, 461
Zaparnik, D., 71, 475
Zaragosa, M., 104, 463
Zegans, L. S., 452
Zelig, M., 242, 491
Zellmann, H. E., 32, 491
Zielinski, J. J., 230, 491
Zigelbaum, S. D., 146, 489
Zimmerman, B. J., 159, 491
Zimmerman, M., 77, 320, 471, 491
Zimostrad, S., 194, 424, 449
Zitman, F. G., 42, 491
Zitter, J. M., 299, 491
Zola-Morgan, S., 105, 468, 483

Subject Index

Note. Italicized page numbers refer to tables and figures.

Amnesia
  dissociative amnesia, 80, 85, 87–89
  malingered amnesia, 81, 82, 89–99, 137,
    338
  organic amnesia, 86, 87
Amobarbital. *See* Drug-assisted interviews
Antisocial personality disorder (APD), 7,
    68–84, 150, 275
Assumptions of patients' veracity, 1, 2, 4,
    69, 411
Auditory Verbal Learning Test (AVLT), 93,
    95, 227, *376*

Bender–Gestalt, 231, 358
Breathalyzer, 111, 123, 126

California Psychological Inventory. *See* CPI
Case study. *See* research methods
Chronic fatigue syndrome, 40, 41
Clinical decision models, 19, 44, *45, 46,*
    61, *62,* 102, *103, 128,* 129, *146,*
    235, 247, *248, 317,* 325, *326,* 348,
    349, 350, 382

Coached malingering or dissimulation, 141,
    186, 187, 212, 214, 243, 379, *380,*
    381, 383
Common symptoms. *See* Interview-
    detection strategies for defensiveness
Compensation neurosis, 6, 37, 38, 130,
    140, 141
Control Question Test. *See* Polygraph
Conversion disorder, 33, 57, 130, 138, 139,
    140
CPI, 181, 182, 195, 196, 273, 276, *375, 381*

Deception. *See also* Polygraph, 12, 15, 23, 24
  in children, 153–166
  in sexual abuse allegations, 29, 40, 242,
    243, 291–293, 299
Defensiveness. *See also* Sex offenders, 4, 9–
    10, 11, 12, 13, 66, 67, 306, 307,
    376, 377, 382, 390, 391, 394, *395,*
    410–412
Defensive symptoms. *See* Interview—
    detection strategies for defensiveness
Degree of certainty, 14, 393
Denial, 42, 109, *110*

Detection apprehension, 154
Detection strategies—neuropsychological
   floor effect, 90
   symptom validity testing, 91
Dissimulation
   associated with disorders
      eating disorders, 35
      personality disorders, 35, 150
      PTSD, 130–152, 304
      substance abuse, 34, 35
   confrontation of, 142, 390–392
   detection, 19 379, *380, 381*
   treatment, 6, 13, 387, 388, 424, 425
Drug-assisted interviews
   amphetamines, 240, 249
   barbiturates, 57, 143, 239–251
   droperidol, 249
   hydroxydione, 240, 249
   ketamine, 249, 251
   usefulness, *380*
DSM-IV classification—limitations, 25, 26,
   42, 43, 44, 75, 77, 78, 385, 416, 417

Electromyelogram (EMG), 143,144
Explanatory models of malingering and
   defensiveness, 5–10
   adaptational, 5, 8, 11, 69, 74, 78, 332,
      337, 424
   criminological, 5, 7, 9, 10, 34, 78, 331,
      332
   pathogenic, 5, 6, 9, 68, 78, 330, 331
   socioevaluative, 332, 333

Factitious disorders, 24–33, 43–45
   factitious bereavement, 28
   factitious child abuse, 29, 36
   factitious dissociative identity disorder,
      28, 29
   factitious posttraumatic stress disorder,
      27, 28
   factitious psychosis, 27, 49, 408
   Munchausen syndrome, 30, 31, 407
   physical factitious behavior, 29–32
   pseudodementia, 30, 49
Factitious disorders by proxy, 29, 36, 37, 44

Factitious posttraumatic stress disorder, 27,
   28
False memory syndrome, 24, 36, 39, 40,
   103, 107
Forced-choice testing. *See also* Symptom
   validity testing, 228–230
Forensic issues
   admissibility of drug-assisted interviews,
      250
   admissibility of hypnosis, 295–300
   admissibility of polygraph, 252, 253, 265
   child custody, 385, *386*
   competence to stand trial, 48, 64–65,
      297, 323
   insanity, 48, 61–67, 147, 298, *386,* 400
   legal status of integrity testing, 280
   personal injury, 134, 135, 139, 367, *386,*
      394

Ganser syndrome, 50
Guilty Knowledge Test. *See* Polygraph

Hair analysis, 16, 125, 126, 128, *377,* 417,
   425
Hybrid responding, 11, 393, 394
Hypnosis, 282–300, *380, 382*
   historical truth, 285, 292
   narrative truth, 285, 292, 300
Hypnotic susceptibility scales
   Barber Suggestibility Scale, 284
   Harvard Hypnotic Suggestibility Scale,
      284
   Hypnotic Induction Profile, 284
   Stanford Hypnotic Suggestibility Scale,
      284

Impression management, 12
Integrity testing, 264–281, *380, 382*
   Biographical Case History (BCH), 265
   Employment Attitude Inventory, 270
   Employment Productivity Index, 266
   Inwald Personality Inventory, 266, 273
   PDI Employment Inventory, 273
   Personnel Reaction Blank (PRB),
      265–268, 273, 275

Personnel Selection Inventory, 266, 267, 270, 273
Phase II Profile, 266, 267
Prospective Employee Potential Inventory, 266, 273
Reid Report, 265–268, 270, 273, 274
Stanton Survey, 266, 267, 270
Intelligence tests. *See* Neuropsychological and intelligence tests
Interpretability of dissimulated protocols, *380, 381,* 384
Interview—detection strategies for defensiveness
common symptoms, 316, *317*
overview, 305
symptom underendorsement, 318, 319
Interview—detection strategies for malingering
blatant symptoms (BL), 303, *322,* 323
contradictory symptoms, 310, *311, 322*
improbable symptoms (IA), 304, *322*
indiscriminant symptom endorsement (*also called* selectivity of symptoms or SEL), 303, 313, *315, 322,* 375
rare symptoms (RS), 303, 310, *311, 322, 375*
reported versus observed symptoms (RO), 321, *322*
symptom combinations (SC), 310, *312, 322, 375*
symptom severity (SEV), 313, *314, 322, 375*
Intricate strategies, 403
Investigative hypnosis, 288, 296
Irrelevant responding, 5, 11, 363, 369, 377, 378, 391, 397

Malingered delusions, 55, 56, *62,* 81
Malingered hallucinations, 48, 50–55, *51,* 61, *62,* 79–83, 304
Malingered mutism, 56, 57
Malingering and dissimulation
gradations, 13, 14, 394, *395*
interviewing, 58, 59, 60, 63, 64, 142, 148

motivation. *See also* Explanatory models, 9, 33, 48, 60, 134, 135, 147, 157, 225, 226, 301, 302, 422
prevalence, 4, 5, 47, 71, 72, 73, 134, 146, 147, 422
MCMI (Millon Clinical Multiaxial Inventory), 73, 77, 84, 119, 120, 182, 195, 196, 304, *375, 378, 381*
Memories, early, 105–106
Millon Clinical Multiaxial Inventory. *See* MCMI
Minnesota Multiphasic Personality Inventory. *See* MMPI
Mississippi Scale—PTSD, 142, 149
MMPI (Minnesota Multiphasic Personality Inventory; *also includes* MMPI-2)
defensiveness, 4, 14, 170, 183–193, 196–201, *203, 204,* 217, 218, 302, 317, 318, 334, 335, *336,* 337–339, 344, 346, 347, 350, *381,* 385, 387, 411, 422
malingering, 49, 72, 73, 77, *83,* 84, 171, 183–195, *203, 204,* 216, 233, 302–304, 322, 324, 327, 351, 358, 360, 361, 364, 365, 367, 368, 377, 380 *381,* 383, 392, 393, 411, 420
normative data, 169, *173, 174, 175, 176, 179, 188, 189, 203, 204,* 383
PTSD, 142, 149, 422
response consistency, 4, 5, 170, 174–181, *378, 381,* 384
substance abuse, 117–119
MMPI-A, 163, 164–166, 365, 411
MSI (Multiphasic Sexual Inventory), 335, *336,* 337
M Test, 352–359, *369, 370,* 419
Munchausen syndrome, 30, 31, 407
by proxy. *See* Factitious disorder by proxy

Narcoanalysis. *See* Drug-assisted interviews
Neurodiagnostic tests
CT scans, 136, 245
EEG, 90, 245, 251
MRI scans, 136, 245

Neuropsychological assessment—detection
    strategies
  atypical performance, 231, 232
  floor effect, *376*
  inconsistencies, 232–234, *376*
  increased latency, *376*
  magnitude of error, *376, 383*
  performance curve, 231, *376, 383*
  qualitative differences, 231
Neuropsychological deficits in learning
  feeling-of-knowing, 97, 98, 100
  implicit memory, 96, 97, 100
  proactive interference (PI), 95, 96,
    100
Neuropsychological measures of
    malingering
  Auditory Verbal Learning Test (AVLT),
    93, 95, 227, *376*
  Hiscock test, 229
  Personal History Interview (PHI), 93,
    376
  Portland Digit Recognition Test
    (PDRT), 94, 98, 227–229, *376*
  Recall–Recognition test, 91, 92, 99,
    230
  Recognition Memory Test (RMT), 95,
    227, 230
  Rey-15 (Rey 15-Item Memory Test),
    91, 230, *376*
  serial positioning, 93
  symptom validity testing (SVT). *See also*
    Forced-choice testing, 91–93, 99,
    100, 286, 375, 376, 392, 393, 396,
    407
  TONI-modified, 231, 381
Neuropsychological and intelligence tests
    (standard)
  Bender–Gestalt, 231, 358
  Luria–Nebraska, 412
  Weschler Adult Intelligence Scale-
    Revised (WAIS-R), 136, 225, 231,
    325, 375
  Weschler Intelligence Scale for Children,
    382
  Weschler Memory Scale—Revised, 383
  Weschler Memory Test, 94, 101, 231,
    376

PAI (Personality Assessment Inventory),
    173, 182, 195, 196, 197, 323, *375,
    378, 381,* 410
Pain disorders, 41, 42, 243
Paralinguistic cues, 306
PCL (Psychopathy Checklist), 70, 75, 76,
    276, 332, 333
Penile plethysmography (PPG, *also termed*
    phallometric), 332, 334, 340–347,
    350, *377, 380,* 384, 409, 414, 417,
    418
Personal History Questionnaire, 93
Personality Assessment Inventory. *See* PAI
Phallometry. *See* Penile plethysmography
Polygraph, 16, 90, 252–264, *380,* 382, 383,
    414, *415,* 417
  Control Question Test, 253, 255–264,
    380, 383
  Directed lie test, 256
  Guilty Knowledge Test, 254, 255,
    262–264, *380,* 384
  relevant/irrelevant screening, 253, 254
Portland Digit Recognition Test (PDRT),
    94, 98, 227–229, *376*
Posttraumatic stress disorders, 130–152
Postconcussion syndrome, 136–138
Pseudodementia. *See* Factitious disorders
Pseudologia fantastica, 24, 30, 38, 39, *44*
Pseudomemories, 85, 102–107, 242,
    287, 293, 294
Pseudopsychosis. *See* Factitious disorders
Pseudoseizures, 31, 32
Psychogenic amnesia. *See* Amnesia,
    dissociative
Psychological testing—children
  Behavior Assessment System for Children
    (BASC), 163
  MMPI-A, 163, 164–166, 365, 411
  Personality Inventory for Children (PIC),
    162, 163
Psychological testing-personality measures.
    See also Neuropsychological and
    intelligence tests
  CPI, 181, 182, 195, 196, 273, 276, *375,
    381*
  Group Personality Projective Test, 219,
    220

Holtzman Inkblot Technique,
218–220
MCMI. *See* MCMI
MMPI. *See* MMPI
NEO Personality Inventory, 273,
276
Personality Assessment Inventory (PAI),
173, 182, 195, 196, 197, 323, *375,
378, 381,* 410
Psychopathy Checklist (PCL), 70, 75, 76,
276, 332, 333
Rorschach, 149, 208–217, 219–222, 374,
375, 381
Sentence Completion Tasks (SCT), 217,
218, 220
Sixteen Personality Factor Questionnaire
(16PF), 182, 183, 197, 273, 335,
364
TAT, 218, 220
Psychopathy Checklist. *See* PCL
Psychophysiological research. *See* Research
methods

Random responding. *See* Irrelevant
responding
Recall–Recognition test, 91, 92, 99,
230
Recognition Memory Test (RMT), 95,
227, 230
Recovered memories. *See also*
Memories, early, 103, 107,
291–294, 298
Relevant/irrelevant screening. *See*
Polygraph
Research components. *See also* Research
designs
coaching. *See also* Coached malingering
or dissimulation, 402, 403, *412*
debriefing, 405, *406*
incentives, *227,* 400, 403–405, *406,
412, 413,* 419
instructions, 399–401, 403, *406*
preparation, 401–402, *406*
Research designs
differential prevalence, 17,
418–420

known groups comparison, 16, 225, 226,
303, 322, 324, 353, 359, 362, 368,
370, 374, *377, 378,* 414, 415–419,
425
simulation design, 15, 16, 89, *113,* 225,
303, 322, 324, 353, 363, 368, 374,
377, 378, 409–411, *412,* 414, 418,
419, 425
Research methods
case study, 17, 407–409, 418, 425
psychophysiological, 16, *113,* 414, 415
social-psychological, 15, 412–414
Rey-15 (Rey 15-Item Memory Test), 91,
230, *376*
Rorschach, 149, 208–217, 219–222, 374,
375, 381

SADS (Schedule of Affective Disorders and
Schizophrenia), 65, 77, 116, 306–
319, 327, 374, *375, 380,* 384, 409
SASSI (Substance Abuse Subtle Screening
Inventory), 111, 121, 122, 423, 425
Screening measures for malingering
Inventory of Problems (IOP), 366, 367,
370
Malingering Detection Scale (MDS),
361, 362, *369, 370*
Malingering Probability Scale (MPS),
362–364, *369, 370,* 423
Malingering Scale (MS), 352, 364, *369,
370*
M Test, 352–359, *369, 370,* 419
Screening Inventory of Malingered
Symptomatology (SIMS), 364–366,
369, 370, 425
Sentence Completion Test (SCT), 367,
368, *370*
Tehachapi Malingering Scale (TMS),
360, 362, *369, 370*
Secondary gain, 25, 26, 287
Self-disclosure, 10, 12
Sex offenders
Abel Screen, 345, 346
explanatory models, 330–333, 337
Multiphasic Sexual Inventory (MSI), 335,
336, 337

Sex offenders (*continued*)
  penile plethysmography (PPG, *also termed*
      phallometric), 332, 334, 340–347,
      350, *377, 380,* 384, 409, 414, 417,
      418
  typology of defensiveness and admission,
      328–330, 334
Sexual abuse allegations, 29, 40, 242, 243,
      291–293, 297
Simulation design. *See* Research designs
Simulation–malingering paradox, 12, 16
SIRS (Structured Interview of Reported
      Symptoms), 49, 71, 73, 74, 75,
      82, *83,* 84, 98, 164–166, 301,
      303, 304, 320–327, *349,* 350,
      351, 374, *375, 380,* 382–384,
      392, 393, 405, 425
Social desirability, 4, 12, 196, *198–200,*
      319, 377, 410
Sixteen Personality Factor Questionnaire
      (16PF), 182, 183, 197, 273, 335,
      364
Social psychological research. *See* Research
      methods
Sociopathy. *See* Antisocial personality
      disorder
Sodium amytal. *See* Drug-assisted
      interviews
Statistical applications
  latent trait analysis, 421
  Receiver Operating Characteristic
      (ROC) analysis, 420, 421
  taxonmetric analysis, 421
Structured Clinical Interview for
      DSM-III-R Disorders
      (SCID), 116, 320, 409
Structured Interview of Reported
      Symptoms. *See* SIRS
Structured interviews,
  DIS, 319, 320
  DISC, 320
  PHI, 93, *376*
  PCL, 70, 75, 76, 276, 332, 333
  SADS. *See* SADS
  SCID, 116, 320, 409
  SIDP, 320, 409
  SIRS. *See* SIRS

Substance abuse and deception, 34, 35,
      108–129
  blood alcohol concentrations (BAC),
      111, 112
  external validity, *113*
  prevalence, 108, 109–111
Substance abuse—laboratory measures,
      123–125
  Breathalyzer, 111, 123, 126
  hair analysis, 16, 125, 126, 128, *377,*
      417, 425
  urinalysis, 124, 125, 128
Substance abuse measures and deception
  Adolescent Drinking Inventory (ADI),
      115
  Adolescent Alcohol Involvement Scale
      (AAIS), 115
  Alcohol Use Inventory (AUI),
      122,
  CAGE, 115
  Client Substance Index (CSI), 110,
  Comprehensive Drinker Profile, 111,
      116, 117, 319
  Drug Abuse Screening Test (DAST),
      112, 114,
  Drug Use Screening Inventory (DUSI),
      115, 116
  Michigan Alcohol Screening Test
      (MAST), 112–114
  Personal Experience Inventory (PEI),
      115, 120, 121
  Rutgers Alcohol Problem Index (RAPI),
      114, 115
  Self-Administered Alcoholism Screening
      Test (SAAST), 114
  Substance Abuse Subtle Screening
      Inventory (SASSI), 111, 121,
      122, 423, 425
Substance abuse scales on standard
      inventories
  MCMI, 119, 120
  MMPI, 117–119
Substance abuse—specific response styles
  denial, 109, *110,* 380
  disacknowledgment, 109, *110*
  exaggeration, 109, *110*
  misappraisal, 109, *110*

Susceptibility of measures to malingering, 379, *380, 381*
Symptom underendorsement. *See* Interview—detection strategies for defensiveness
Symptom validity testing (SVT) *See also* Forced-choice testing, 91–93, 99, 100, 286, 375, 376, 392, 393, 396, 407
Synthesis of clinical data, 392–396

Threshold models, 19, 43, *44,* 61, *62, 83, 102, 127, 128, 144, 166, 222, 233,* 234, 245–247, 291, *316,* 325, *326,* 348, 351, 368, 369, 382

Traumatic neurosis. *See also* Compensation neurosis
Treatment considerations, 6, 13, 386, 387, 388

Unreliability, 11, 12, 394
Urinalysis, 124, 125, 128

Vorbeireden, 49

Woozle effect, 42